Readings in Social Problems:
Contemporary Perspectives

Harper & Row's
CONTEMPORARY PERSPECTIVES READER SERIES
Phillip Whitten, Series Editor

Readings in Social Problems: Contemporary Perspectives

1977-1978 edition

edited by
Peter Wickman
State University of New York at Potsdam

Harper & Row, Publishers

New York   Hagerstown   San Francisco   London

Sponsoring Editor: Dale Tharp
Project Editor: Lois Lombardo
Production Supervisor: Stefania J. Taflinska
Printer and Binder: The Murray Printing Company
Cover: "Street for Survivor," © Hundertwasser, Vienna.

**Readings in Social Problems:
Contemporary Perspectives**

Library of Congress Cataloging in Publication Data
Main entry under title:

Readings in social problems.

  (Harper & Row's contemporary perspectives
reader series)
   1. United States—Social conditions—Addresses,
essays, lectures.   I. Wickman, Peter M.
HN59.R3   1977   309.1′73′092   76–30917
ISBN: 0–06–047053–4

ACKNOWLEDGMENTS

1. Prolog: Social Problems Awareness Test by Peter M. Wickman

I. SOCIOLOGICAL PERSPECTIVES
2. SOCIAL PROBLEMS AND DEVIANCE: SOME PARALLEL ISSUES by John I. Kitsuse and Malcolm Spector'' is reprinted by permission from the journal of SOCIAL PROBLEMS and the Society for the Study of Social Problems and the authors.
3. THE CONCEPT OF SOCIAL PROBLEMS: VOX POPULI AND SOCIOLOGICAL ANALYSIS by Jerome G. Manis is reprinted by permission from the JOURNAL OF SOCIAL PROBLEMS and the Society for the Study of Social Problems and the author.

II. PERSPECTIVES ON PROBLEMS OF PERVASIVE SOCIAL CHANGE
4. CITIES IN TROUBLE by Peter Wilshire and Rosemary Righter. Copyright © 1975 by Times Newspapers Limited. Reprinted by permission of Quadrangle/The New York Times Book Company. From *The Exploding Cities* by Peter Wilshire and Rosemary Righter, as appeared in ATLAS WORLD PRESS REVIEW, December 1975.
Photograph by Diego Goldberg, Camera Press London.
5. DEATH WARRANT FOR THE CITIES: THE NATIONAL URBAN POLICY by David M. Muchnick is reprinted with permission from DISSENT and the author.
6. THE DECLINE OF URBAN SERVICES: WHO NEEDS PEOPLE? by Carol Brown is reprinted with permission from the author.
7. THE HUMAN PROSPECT: A QUESTION OF SURVIVAL by Eduard Pestel is reprinted with permission from the author; translated from L'Express, Paris, in ATLAS WORLD PRESS REVIEW, February 1975. Photograph by Ray Ellis, Photo Researchers, Inc., New York.
8. NUCLEAR ENERGY: A PROBLEM, NOT AN ANSWER by Mike Edelhart is reprinted with permission from THE NATION. Editorial cartoon by Pat Oliphant, Copyright, Washington Star. Reprinted with permission, Los Angeles Times Syndicate.
9. THE ENERGY CRISIS—ALL OF A PIECE by Barry Commoner is reprinted from THE CENTER MAGAZINE, a publication of the Center for the Study of Democratic Institutions, Santa Barbara, California, and by permission of the author.
10. THE INTELLECTUAL IN VIDEOLAND by Douglass Cater is reprinted with permission from SATURDAY REVIEW. Photographs from THE BETTMAN ARCHIVE and the Bettmann/Springer Film Archive.
11. COMPUTERIZED INFORMATION AND EFFECTIVE PROTECTION OF INDIVIDUAL RIGHTS by Marguerite Guzman Bouvard and Jacques Bouvard is reprinted by permission of Transaction, Inc. from SOCIETY Volume 12 # 6. Copyright © 1975 by Transaction, Inc.
12. WHO ARE THE REAL PEOPLE? by James S. Kunen. Copyright © 1976 by James S. Kunen. Reprinted by permission of The Sterling Lord Agency, Inc.

III. PERSPECTIVES ON PROBLEMS OF STRUCTURAL INEQUALITY
13. BLAMING THE VICTIM: IDEOLOGY SERVES THE ESTABLISHMENT by William Ryan is condensed by permission of Pantheon Books, a Division of Random House, Inc. from BLAMING THE VICTIM, by William Ryan. Copyright © 1971 by William Ryan.
14. THE POSITIVE FUNCTIONS OF POVERTY by Herbert Gans copyright ©. Reprinted from MORE EQUALITY by Herbert Gans, by permission of Pantheon Books, a Division of Random House, Inc.
15. SURPLUS PEOPLE: THEIR LOST FAITH IN SELF AND THE SYSTEM by D. D. Braginsky and B. M. Braginsky is reprinted by permission of PSYCHOLOGY TODAY Magazine. Copyright © 1975 Ziff-Davis Publishing Company.
16. MAKING IT IN AMERICA: ETHNIC GROUPS AND SOCIAL STATUS by Andrew M. Greeley is reprinted by permission from SOCIAL POLICY published by Social Policy Corporation, New York 10010. Copyright © 1973 by Social Policy Corporation.
Photograph by George W. Gardner, Hillsdale, New York.
17. THE BLACK FAMILY: A PROUD REAPPRAISAL by Hamilton Bims is reprinted by permission of EBONY Magazine, Copyright © 1974 by Johnson Publishing Company, Inc. Photograph from Stock, Boston, Inc.
18. THE INDIAN MOVEMENT: OUT OF A WOUNDED PAST by Vine Deloria Jr. Copyright © Vine Deloria Jr. reprinted from RAMPARTS Magazine.
19. HOW NURSERY SCHOOLS TEACH GIRLS TO SHUT UP by Lisa A. Serbin and K. Daniel O'Leary is reprinted by permission of PSYCHOLOGY TODAY Magazine. Copyright © 1975, Ziff-Davis Publishing Company.
20. SEX DISCRIMINATION AND EMPLOYMENT PRACTICES: AN EXPERIMENT WITH UNCONVENTIONAL JOB INQUIRIES by Richard M. Levinson is reprinted by permission from the JOURNAL OF SOCIAL PROBLEMS and the Society for the Study of Social Problems and the author.
21. IF WE'RE SO SMART, WHY AREN'T WE RICH? by Gloria Steinen. Copyright © 1973 MS Magazine Corp. Reprinted with permission.

IV. PERSPECTIVES ON CHANGING INSTITUTIONS
22. THE FAMILY OUT OF FAVOR by Michael Novak. Copyright © 1976 by HARPER'S Magazine. Reprinted from the April 1976 issue by special permission. Artwork by Evelyn Taylor, New York.
23. THE AMERICAN WAY OF MATING, MARRIAGE SI, CHILDREN ONLY MAYBE by Angus Campbell, is reprinted by permission of PSYCHOLOGY TODAY Magazine. Copyright © 1975 Ziff-Davis Publishing Company.
24. THE AMERICAN FAMILY: AN EMBATTLED INSTITUTION by Robert S. Pickett. This article first appeared in THE HUMANIST, May/June 1975 and is reprinted by permission.
25. DEPRIVING THE BEST AND THE BRIGHTEST by Jack Fincher. Adaptation reproduced from HUMAN INTELLI-

V. PERSPECTIVES ON DEVIANCE AND SOCIAL CONTROL

VI. PERSPECTIVES ON SOCIAL POLICY

CONTENTS

PREFACE

My primary purpose in compiling this reader is to make available to college students engaged in the study of social problems readings that will assist them in their critiques of some of the major social issues of contemporary society. The articles are organized into a framework influenced by a simplified rendition of the conflict perspective that is explicated in Part I. I find this perspective useful in the analysis of social problems in that it helps avoid the conventional view that such issues can be studied independently of the social structure and core values of society. We also eschew the conservative, optimistic (liberal) idea which promotes the image of our society as a self-adjusting system within which problems are resolved by correcting major institutions or by adjusting individuals to the needs of society.

This reader is, in a sense, a byproduct of a course in the Problems of Contemporary Society, which I developed and teach at the State University of New York College at Potsdam. For this course I draw on perspectives, ideas, and materials from a wide variety of sources to complement traditional text materials. Articles from Harper's, the New York Times Magazine, Society, and Psychology Today are less prone to use "socspeak" and thus are frequently both more interesting and comprehensible than journal articles to those undergraduates who are not sociology majors. Most of the articles selected for this book are of that genre. They may be more often descriptive than quantitative, but they provide interior views of the pathos of "private troubles" which converge into "public issues."

It is our assumption that as the student pursues the study of social problems, he or she will learn to develop information and resources relevant to the total social environment. The student will then be confronted with conflicts and even irreconcilable contradictions that exist in contemporary society.

These articles have been selected, not because they exemplify the conflict perspective, for that might distort the original intentions of the authors, but because they present historical and cross-cultural critiques that reveal the interrelatedness of social issues. They also tend to promote a utopian view—that is, that human beings can, through individual and collective effort, shape the future.

The reader is divided into six sections—five of which identify major problem areas inherent in the social structure of our industrialized urbanized society. The introductory section provides a sociological perspective for social problems which makes explicit my assumptions vis-à-vis the conflict perspective and emphasizes the cumulative, unfinished nature of statements about social reality as opposed to the revelationary and even ideological conventional mechanistic approach.

Our first series of problems in Part II deal with three problematic issues that have great consequence for all contemporary societies: urban and environmental crises and the alienating effects of mass society. Part III seeks to demystify the social issues of inequality—that is, racism and sexism. The problematic relations of individuals and groups relative to changing institutions are described in Part IV. Part V deals with the issue of conformity, and the focus is on the social control of criminal and noncriminal deviance. The final part raises the issue of alternative social policies requisite to provide for a more human society.

Basically, the book is intended as a complement to the typical textbook in social problems. It can also be used as a core reader for such a course. The contemporary emphasis will be maintained through revisions every two years.

This book has been made possible by over fifty authors who allowed us to use their articles. A special note of appreciation is due Carol Brown, Joseph Cocozza, Henry Steadman, and Gilbert Geis, who provided the three original articles. Although the final selection of readings was made by me, I received valuable suggestions from colleagues, and also from students in my social problems classes. I owe a special debt to Phillip Whitten, series editor, who kept us on track and on schedule, and without whose assistance this book would not have become a reality. Clare King also rendered valuable clerical and editorial assistance, as did Leslie Palmer, who also handled with admirable efficiency the task of securing permissions.

P. W.

Social Problems Awareness Test

(Pre-Test Form)

This Social Problems Awareness Test has been used for several years by the editor of this book to stimulate class participation during the initial meeting of his classes. The statements are written to create interest and focus on salient social issues. It is important that you respond to each question on the SPAT in terms of your present knowledge. Indicate in the appropriate space provided on the answer sheet, whether you completely agree, tend to agree, tend to disagree, or completely disagree, with each statement.

1 The existence of a given social problem and its resolution can be decided upon objectively, i.e., without reference to the values and interests of the various groups concerned.

_____Completely Agree   _____Tend to Agree
_____Tend to Disagree   _____Completely Disagree

2 Fornication, adultery, cohabitation, as well as homosexual relations between consenting adult partners are all violations of the criminal codes in most of our states.

_____Completely Agree   _____Tend to Agree
_____Tend to Disagree   _____Completely Disagree

3 Since the United States occupies a continent rich in natural resources we have no population problem of any significance.

_____Completely Agree   _____Tend to Agree
_____Tend to Disagree   _____Completely Disagree

4 During the first sixteen years of his/her life, the typical child now spends at least as much time watching television as in school.

_____Completely Agree   _____Tend to Agree
_____Tend to Disagree   _____Completely Disagree

5 Through a national urban policy which provides public housing for lower income groups, it now appears that urban decay will disappear by the end of the decade.

_____Completely Agree   _____Tend to Agree
_____Tend to Disagree   _____Completely Disagree

6 Although the "Green Revolution" increased food production in developing countries it did not provide a long-term solution to the international food problem.

_____Completely Agree   _____Tend to Agree
_____Tend to Disagree   _____Completely Disagree

7 Some surveys indicate that heavy TV viewers are more apt than others to be politically active and vote more frequently.

_____Completely Agree   _____Tend to Agree
_____Tend to Disagree   _____Completely Disagree

8 Large corporations, with their emphasis on profits, require irrational practices, such as planned obsolescence and wasteful consumption.

_____Completely Agree   _____Tend to Agree
_____Tend to Disagree   _____Completely Disagree

9 The "multi-problem" poor suffer from the impoverishment of the "culture of poverty" and a "deviant" value system; thus, they unwittingly cause their own troubles.

_____Completely Agree   _____Tend to Agree
_____Tend to Disagree   _____Completely Disagree

10 Although there are differences in IQ scores between races, these are not as great as the differences in IQ scores found within given racial groupings.

_____Completely Agree   _____Tend to Agree
_____Tend to Disagree   _____Completely Disagree

11 Native Americans (American Indians) in our society have not borne the brunt of institutional racism to the extent that Blacks and Chicanos have.

_____Completely Agree   _____Tend to Agree
_____Tend to Disagree   _____Completely Disagree

12 The higher the occupational status of the worker, the higher will be his/her job satisfaction.

_____Completely Agree   _____Tend to Agree
_____Tend to Disagree   _____Completely Disagree

13 In general there is an inverse correlation between socioeconomic status and involvement in voluntary organizations and political involvement.

_____Completely Agree   _____Tend to Agree
_____Tend to Disagree   _____Completely Disagree

14 If gambling and other victimless crimes were de-criminalized, our criminal justice system would operate more efficiently.

_____Completely Agree   _____Tend to Agree
_____Tend to Disagree   _____Completely Disagree

15 The social consequences of death and dying fall with equal severity on all socioeconomic groups in society.

_____Completely Agree   _____Tend to Agree
_____Tend to Disagree   _____Completely Disagree

16 Since untreated mental patients have nearly the same rate of recovery as those committed to mental hospitals, it is questionable that institutionalization of the mentally ill is effective.

_____Completely Agree   _____Tend to Agree
_____Tend to Disagree   _____Completely Disagree

17 Psychiatrists now know how to identify and treat potentially dangerous and aggressive individuals.

_____Completely Agree   _____Tend to Agree
_____Tend to Disagree   _____Completely Disagree

18 The direct and indirect cost of alcoholism and alcoholics is much greater than that of drug addiction.

_____Completely Agree   _____Tend to Agree
_____Tend to Disagree   _____Completely Disagree

19 Since homosexual acts between consenting adults are no longer illegal in some states homosexuals are seldom stigmatized.

_____Completely Agree   _____Tend to Agree
_____Tend to Disagree   _____Completely Disagree

20 White collar criminals are underrepresented in terms of arrests and severity of prison sentences compared with other types of criminals.

_____Completely Agree   _____Tend to Agree
_____Tend to Disagree   _____Completely Disagree

21 There is conclusive evidence that marijuana use leads to the use of heroin and other "hard" drugs.

_____Completely Agree   _____Tend to Agree
_____Tend to Disagree   _____Completely Disagree

22 There is more crime in the sunny and warm states of the West and South than in any other part of the country.

_____Completely Agree   _____Tend to Agree
_____Tend to Disagree   _____Completely Disagree

23 Our free public education system provides an equal "ladder" of opportunity and success for all youths.

_____Completely Agree   _____Tend to Agree
_____Tend to Disagree   _____Completely Disagree

24 The family's child rearing function has been largely replaced by alternative public and private agencies.

_____Completely Agree   _____Tend to Agree
_____Tend to Disagree   _____Completely Disagree

25 Medicare programs provide complete health care for the aged.

_____Completely Agree   _____Tend to Agree
_____Tend to Disagree   _____Completely Disagree

I. Sociological Perspectives

Sociologists are in general agreement as to what constitutes the field of study termed *social problems*—the unit of study is society and existing current social ills. However sociologists do not always agree as to the theoretical orientation or perspectives which may help explain how problems came about and which may influence their conclusions relative to appropriate social policy on reform efforts. This field of study, then, is fraught with conflict and controversy, in academic circles as well as in the marketplace. Consequently, it is incumbent upon the editor of a book of readings in social problems to make explicit his or her underlying value assumptions and beliefs concerning social reality. For one's perspective is doubtless reflected in the problem areas set forth, and certainly on the materials selected to provide the reader with a basis for the analysis of such issues.

Before we further attempt to identify our perspective we will briefly suggest a definition of the term *social problems*. Whether we are lay persons or sociologists we are concerned with problematic events which occur in our everyday world, unless of course we are totally lacking in social awareness. So, when our attention is attracted to an event or situation which contradicts our perception of what society is, or ought to be, and we ask, in effect, "why does this situation exist?; what can be done to correct it?" we are making a statement about a social problem. Such statements need not, and indeed should not be couched in incomprehensible jargon to be meaningful statements about reality. A more specific definition was proposed by the sociologist Arnold Rose some years ago, and the readings encompassed in this book reflect this definition explicitly or implicitly. Rose (1964) defined a social problem as:

> . . . a situation affecting a significant number of people that is believed by them and/or by a significant number of others in the society to be a source of difficulty or unhappiness, and one that is capable of amelioration. Thus a social problem consists of both an objective situation and a subjective interpretation.

Rose suggested, in this same essay, that there are essentially two perspectives commonly implicit in the definition and analysis of the causation of social problems. The two articles from *Social Problems* included in this section each deal separately with one of these perspectives. They have been included in this section, not as a gesture of "objectivity," but because they illustrate the "unfinished" nature of statements dealing with social reality. We recognize the hazards of oversimplification which a summary of these perspectives involves, but in order to make our orientation explicit and to provide a useful backdrop for these readings, we will attempt it.

The first major perspective is the *order* or *consensus* theory, often called the "social disorganization" theory. From this perspective society is seen as a relatively stable organization which is greater than the "units" that comprise it, and is based on a consensus of values. The individual is seen as a result of the socialization process; if problems exist, they are due to social disorganization which results in *anomie,* which makes it difficult for an individual to learn the rules. Consequently, problems can be resolved through more effective social control efforts to correct the situation or bring the individual into "adjustment" with society.

The contrasting *conflict* perspective sees society as subject to change, and it manifests dissensus and conflict between opposing power groups. The needs of the individual and human groups are paramount and society is seen as an extension of the individual. The self is seen as choosing courses of action and members of society are "history-makers." However, as C. Wright Mills (1959:181) suggests, "If men do not make history, they tend increasingly to become . . . the mere objects of history-making." Conflict theory asserts that social problems are built into the nature and structure of society and that they are in part problems of alienation—that is, they result from the thwarting of individual and group potential. This latter perspective is frequently seen as radical although its proponents rely on Max Weber as well as Karl Marx.

As the two readings in this section cogently demonstrate, there are unfinished elements in each of these major perspectives. These articles will provide alternative viewpoints *vis à vis* social problems and lend insights into some of the theoretical controversies within, as well as between, the two major perspectives.

The readings contained in this book have been selected in part because they illustrate the conflict perspective. The framework within which these selections are organized has also been informed by that perspective, at least to the extent that this schema emphasizes institutional analysis and societal reaction to nonconformity. The articles have been taken from books, magazines, and journals. They have been written by journalists, novelists, and playwrights, as well as social scientists. The main sections include perspectives on social change, social inequality, institutions in transition, deviance and social control, and social policy.

References

1. C. Wright Mills, *The Sociological Imagination.* New York: Oxford University Press, 1959.
2. Arnold M. Rose, "Social Problems," in J. Gould and W. L. Kolb, *A Dictionary of the Social Sciences.* New York: The United Nations Education, Scientific and Cultural Organization, 1964.

Social Problems And Deviance:
Some Parallel Issues

JOHN I. KITSUSE
University of California
Santa Cruz

MALCOLM SPECTOR
Institut de Criminologie
Université de Paris, II

This paper explores parallel developments in labeling theory and in the value-conflict approach to social problems. Similarities in their critiques of functionalism and etiological theory as well as their emphasis on the definitional process are noted. In addition, the failure of both formulations to develop the distinctiveness of their common insight is examined. An analysis of this failure is presented.

Two traditions of writing have attempted to make the field of social problems theoretically respectable. One is a tradition of functionalist textbooks, most recently restated by Merton and Nisbet (1971). The other is a tradition of dissent from the functionalist view, frequently referred to as the value-conflict school (Fuller, 1937, 1939; Fuller and Myers, 1941a; Waller, 1936; Lemert, 1951a; Becker, 1966; Blumer, 1971). Neither of these attempts has produced a full-fledged sociology of social problems (Kitsuse and Spector, 1973). The dominant tradition has used a functionalist theory to identify the subject matter of study —i.e., dysfunctional conditions, role conflicts, violations of norms or values (deviant behavior)—and then attempted to identify the causes of these conditions. This approach has not created a distinctive field but simply assimilated social problems into functional analysis, emphasizing dysfunctions and disorganization.

The value-conflict school contains the seeds of a distinctive approach with its emphasis on the process by which definitions and categories of social problems are constructed. To date, however, it has failed to generate a research tradition or to translate its

critique of functionalist formulations into a positive approach to theory and research. We believe the direction suggested by Waller and Fuller and Myers was much more profoundly innovative than they themselves realized. They did not follow their own bold and provocative beginning to its logical conclusion. Recent developments in sociological theory make the implications of their writings easier to recognize. Perhaps the most important of these developments is the emergence of the labeling theory of deviance and the criticism and controversy that has come to surround it. Labeling theory mirrors many of the developments of the value-conflict school: The substantive nature of its innovation, its relation to traditional etiological approaches, and we believe, its inability to pursue its own internal logic. Analyzed together, labeling theory and the value-conflict writings show striking parallels, in their common ambitions, as well as shortcomings.

In particular, we note three striking similarities in the two theoretical perspectives. (1) Social problems and deviance are conceived as products of social processes in which members of a group, community, or society perceive, interpret, evaluate, and treat behaviors,

persons and conditions as problems. (2) They shift attention from the behaviors and conditions of those who are commonly thought to constitute the problem to the members of society who conceive those behaviors and conditions as problems. (3) Such a focus demands a theory and method to document and account for the symbolic processes through which the meanings of such behaviors and conditions are generated and institutionalized. In the first part of our paper, we shall document parallels in the two perspectives.

Both labeling theory and the value-conflict school have been plagued by ambiguities and seemingly illogical elements. These two theories have sometimes abandoned their stated intention to address the definitional process and subtly returned their attention to more traditional concerns. In the second part we describe these failures to follow the logic of the definitional perspective, noting again remarkable parallel developments.

In the final section we attempt to explain the difficulties of remaining faithful to the kind of argument that the value-conflict and labeling theorists set out to make. Neither approach recognizes that the enterprise of sociology must itself be conceived as part of the data for the study of social problems and deviance, i.e., that sociologists are participants in the definitional process. Consequently, their role is not that of objective observer but that of society members. As participants in the definitional process they are subject to the pressures exerted on participants to be relevant, to address practical policy questions, and accept institutional arrangements and their positivist underpinnings. By failing to place themselves within the framework of analysis, the sociologist of social problems fails to achieve the distance needed to focus on the definitional process, rather than unknowingly participate in it.

NEW PERSPECTIVE ON DEVIANCE AND SOCIAL PROBLEMS

Both the value-conflict and labeling formulations developed as reactions and correctives to the prevailing views of the sociological specialty then known as Social Pathology. Frank (1925) noted the ethnocentrism implicit in the study of social problems, and he employed the perspective of "the man from Mars" to describe the particular value system within which conditions, such as slums and illegitimacy were viewed and sustained as social problems. Ten years later, Willard Waller (1936) formalized Frank's remarks in a vigorous criticism of the sociologist's failure "to achieve a scientifically defensible treatment of social problems." (1936:922) He charged that social scientists, in dealing with the "objective side of social problems" ignored the fact that "there can be no social problem without a value-judgment." As a consequence, he said their analyses were marred by logical difficulties, rendering them "useless because they have dealt only with the objective side of social problems and failed to include the attitude which constituted them problems." (1936:922)

Waller, in turn, laid the theoretical ground for Fuller and Myers to assert that "*Social problems are what people think they are,* and if conditions are not defined as social problems by the people involved in them, they are not problems to those people, although they may be problems to outsiders or to scientists. . . ." (1941a:320). The writers argued that social conditions do not in themselves constitute prob-

lems; rather, their problematic character is a consequence of the values and attitudes that inform judgments of those conditions as undesirable, immoral, harmful, or disruptive. This view implies that the distinctive subject matter of the sociology of social problems is the value-judgmental process, rather than the putative conditions about which judgments are made.

The new perspective on deviance called labeling theory is most clearly traced to an early statement by Lemert (1951b) in which he emphasized the process of societal reaction as the basis for the definition and differentiation of deviance. Becker (1963) gave new impetus to this conception of deviance in *Outsiders* which contains the definition "The deviant is one to whom that label has successfully been applied; deviant behavior is behavior that people so label" (1963:9). Both Lemert and Becker rejected the etiological concerns of existing theories of deviance and proposed that attention shift from the behaviors of the presumed deviants to those who perceive and define them as deviant. The logic of this shift contained the implication that "the essential feature of a deviant or deviant act is *external* to the actor and the act" (Gibbs, 1966:11). The point is crucial for the value-conflict theory of social problems as well: "Social problem" is not a quality that inheres in social conditions; rather, it is an emergent product of definitional processes in which people perceive, define, and assert conditions to be social problems. The central theoretical question, then, is not how the conditions are generated by the social structure, but how conditions come to be perceived and defined as social problems, how members generate definitions and constructions of conditions. The thrust of these formulations, is toward a set of questions and concerns that the conventional approaches to deviance and social problems left unstated, ignored, or took for granted.

SOME STRATEGIC AMBIGUITIES

The value-conflict and labeling theorists share a fundamental perspective and present striking parallels in the logical structure of their formulations. We have presented what we consider the distinctive and core elements of the perspectives. Their vulnerability to criticism is a consequence of ambigui-

ties in the statement of central issues in those formulations. These ambiguities reflect a failure to press the distinctive implications of the two perspectives to their logical conclusions. The literature of both formulations has been clouded by a confusion that is rooted in these ambiguities. While both value-conflict and labeling perspectives were shaped by an explicit criticism and rejection of previous formulations, both failed to shed the burdens of the conventional concerns and conceptions that were the targets of their criticisms.

The labeling formulation. The shift in focus from the presumed deviants and their deviant acts to the definitional activities of others was blurred in the early statements of Lemert and Becker. In preparing the ground for his theory of sociopathic behavior, Lemert set forth a set of postulates in which he posited modalities of behavior and deviations from those modalities (1951b:22). He further posited societal reactions to such deviations, i.e., that such deviations are defined and treated as deviant by members of the society. Having posited deviations from the modalities of behavior as the bases for societal reactions, Lemert was committed to the theoretical position that these reactions were reactions to *empirically observable behaviors.*

This commitment, reflected in Lemert's discussion of the social and cultural sources of deviation and differentiation, is commonly unrecognized either by critics or those who support his work. Lemert moves from (1) a statistical conception of deviation ("deviations from modalities") to (2) a conception of normative deviation ("differentiation which can be related to modal structures and values") to (3) a "narrower sociological viewpoint" in which "deviations are not significant until they are organized subjectively and transformed into active roles and become the social criteria for assigning status" (1951b:75). This last conception is the basis for Lemert's oft-cited distinction between primary and secondary deviation, a distinction that provides the basis for his social psychological theory of sociopathic deviation.

The societal reaction perspective as originally articulated contains a theoretical compromise. It presupposed an objective act observable and definable by the sociologist by statistical standards of normality and by normative standards posited as an essential feature of social systems. Societal reactions were conceived as reactions to acts that violate social norms presumably extant in the society. Norms, then, provide the sociologist with a vantage point to define, observe and classify behaviors as deviant.

Becker (1963:20) provided for an objectively observable basis for the classification of behavior in his typology of deviant behavior. The two axes of this typology reveal his attempt to represent both the perspective of members ("perceived as deviant/not perceived as deviant") and that of the independent observer ("rule-breaking/ obedient behavior"). Like Lemert, Becker focused on the object being defined, i.e., the behavior of the individual, as the stimulus for the application of labels. Four of the five empirical chapters of *Outsiders* report not how groups produce deviance by creating rules and applying them to others, but rather how persons create deviance by participating in the kinds of actions that will be offensive to others. Similarly, while Lemert has insisted that sociologists study secondary deviation, much of his own work (on check forgers and paranoia, for example) deals with primary deviation. These remnants of the traditional approach— the concept of rule-violating behavior, the distinction between primary and secondary deviation, and an empirical focus on deviants—have invited the interpretation, both by proponents and opponents, that labeling theory is an etiological theory that attempts to explain, not deviant acts, but deviant identities, behavior systems, life styles, and subcultures.

The value-conflict formulation. The early value-conflict theorists were as radical in their emphasis on the definitional process as were the labeling theorists. Waller boldly asserted that "Value judgments are the formal causes of social problems just as the law is the formal cause of crime" (1936:925). These theorists appeared to prepare the ground for a sociology of social problems with a distinctive focus on the definitional process. In elaborating their formulation, however, Fuller and Myers proposed a typology of social conditions, rather

than a typology of definitions of conditions. Their three-fold classification of problems as physical, ameliorative and moral distinguishes various causes of the condition, rather than causes of the definition of the condition. Fuller and Myers first consider how earthquakes and hurricanes are defined as physical problems.[1] They discuss the commonsense causes that are part of how the condition is defined by people. However, they soon abandon what the members believe the causes of the condition to be—i.e., how those members define the condition—and proceed to discuss the "real man-made" causes of which members may or may not be aware. As Fuller and Myers move to consider ameliorative and moral problems as well as physical problems, they insist even more strongly that the causes of the condition are "man-made." For example: "Value schemes prohibiting the frank discussion of sexuality are the cause of venereal disease and illegitimacy" (1941a:29). Here Fuller and Myers have abandoned the study of social definitions and returned to the study of objective conditions. When they claim that values inhibit solutions to social problems they duplicate the social disorganization formulation they had attempted to discard.

THE "BALANCED" APPROACH

It is likely that Waller and Fuller and Myers simply did not see the full implications of their own statements. From the vantage point of more than three decades of certain theoretical developments in sociology—symbolic interactionism, phenomenological sociology, ethnomethodology, as well as la-

---

[1] The crucial passage is the following: "We find no public forums debating the question of what to do about preventing earthquakes and hurricanes; the causation is thought of as non-human, resting in natural forces outside the control of man . . . If we may anticipate the time when scientists tell us how to prevent earthquakes, control hurricanes and make rain for drought stricken areas, we can imagine some element of the population who will oppose the application of scientific techniques on the grounds that they are too costly and threaten budget balancing or that they interfere with nature or God's will or for some other reason . . . At this point . . . we do have a man-made problem since the will of certain groups is a causal element in the occurrence of the condition itself." (Fuller and Myers, 1941a:28-29)

beling theory, all emphasizing the socially constructed character of social reality—the distinctiveness of the early statements is more readily seen. Others who were proponents of these views may have seen the implications, but rejected them as too radical, or too far removed from application to solutions to social problems.

Labeling and value-conflict theorists have been sensitive to the charge of subjectivism from their critics. They argued for a balanced approach that acknowledged the importance of objective, as well as the subjective aspects of deviance and social problems. Lemert balanced the concept of social differentiation with that of secondary deviation, complementing societal reaction processes with a concern for the development of sociopathic behavior. This view is also expressed by those who complain that some versions of labeling theory are increasingly one-sided, treating the reactors and definers much less sympathetically than the deviants whom they attempt to control (Bordua, 1967).

Writers on social problems have been sensitive about the subjectivism of their approach. They compromised their view by insisting the sociologist study the definitions of conditions *as well as* the objective conditions themselves. For all their balance, their timidity was well-founded—the leading functionalist social problem text characterizes their approach as "heedless subjectivism" (Merton and Nisbet, 1971:806). Sensitivity to this issue is reflected in the most recent statement of the value-conflict approach by Howard S. Becker (1966) who updates the Fuller and Myers attempt to provide a balanced view:

> In short, as Fuller and Myers argued, no objective condition is necessarily a social problem. Social problems are what people say they are. But where does that leave the role of objective conditions? The question has two parts: Can people define any condition that exists as a social problem, and can people define a condition that does *not* exist—an illusion— as a social problem? (5)

Becker points out that people *can* define "nonexistent" conditions as social problems—witches, flying saucers —and then says:

> If any set of objective conditions, even nonexistent ones, can be defined as a social problem, it is clear that the conditions themselves do not either produce

the problem or constitute a necessary component of it. Why must we include them in our conception of social problems? We include them because *the definitions of most social problems refer to an area of social life that objectively and verifiably exists.* Most citizens and almost all social scientists in modern society feel the need to buttress their assertions about the existence of a social problem by referring to facts, and they are aware that arguments which can be shown to have no factual foundation can be disposed of easily by opponents. (6, emphasis added.)

Even as Becker moves theoretically toward the assertion that objective conditions are neither necessary nor sufficient for the development of social problems, he tacitly retracts the assertion by conceptually making provision for such conditions. He provides explicitly for objective conditions on the basis of his "in most cases." A major consequence of this phrase is that the study of social problems is seemingly able then to move on to the business at hand—those "most of the cases." The balanced view suggests that definitions of social problems may be understood as reactions to conditions. "Competent" socialized members of society do not see and complain about conditions that do not exist. Therefore, the existence of the objective condition itself helps explain the societal reaction to it. This reduces the definition from a social construction of reality, an accomplishment of members of the society, to a mere mechanical reaction to exterior forces. The integrity of the definitional process is sacrificed for the balanced view.

INTERPRETATION

We have analyzed similar problems of logical development in two related bodies of writings. Why should it be so difficult to develop this form of sociological argument? We shall suggest that several kinds of memberships deflect attention away from the traditional questions toward traditional positivist concerns. Three kinds of memberships will be discussed: the sociologist as member of society; as member of a profession; and as occupant of active roles in the definitional process itself.

Sociologists as Members of Society. Sociologists who study their own society are, of course, also members of it. As members they have their own views of what social conditions exist and which ones are problems. We do

not deny the possibility that sociologists may, on the basis of their own values and moral judgments identify and define certain conditions as social problems. But this practice must be clearly separated from a *theoretical* mandate to do so.

In recognition of this membership based source of definitions, sociologists have two methodological options. One is to suspend their own definitions as external to the phenomena under investigation and attend solely to the definitions of members. No question would ever arise concerning divergences between the sociologists' and the members' definitions or perspective. The second option is that sociologists treat their own definitional activity as part of the phenomenon. This behavior might lead sociologists to examine the grounds on which they define a given condition as a problem. On what grounds do conditions command their attention? What common sense constructions do they use to attribute meanings? Both options suggest a kind of reflexive examination usually absent from writings on social problems. Unfortunately, neither is easily translated into a set of procedures guaranteeing that attitudes, values and opinions sociologists hold by virtue of their membership in society (or a sector or class of a society) will not influence their professional thinking or research.

Sociologists as members of a profession. A second type of pressure away from analysis of definitional questions stems from the fact that sociology competes with a variety of other disciplines and professions. Students of the professions (Hughes, 1971; Freidson, 1970, 1971) tend to view such conflicts between disciplines, not as questions of truth, but as fundamentally political programs to gain custody of some problem condition or population and the lucrative treatment apparatus associated with it. For example, when psychiatrists clashed with clinical psychologists over the medical nature of mental disturbances (Goode, 1960), more was at stake than simply an abstract theory of mental illness. There were underlying issues concerning who may dispense what kind of therapy to whom at what price. Clinical psychologists were trying to invade the lucrative treatment business, and psychiatrists were trying to stop

such encroachment and preserve their monopoly over the treatment of mental illness.

These battles appear as scientific debates between proponents of rival theories, research findings, causal explanations and interpretations. Analyses of such controversies are themselves data for the sociology of social problems. Given such a view of professional and inter-disciplinary competition, is there less reason to suspect that the activities of sociologists are expressions of hidden agendas and interests than those of psychiatrists or clinical psychologists? After all, if as Fuller and Myers argue, the *real* causes of venereal disease are social, does this not suggest that sociologists should run the venereal disease bureaucracy? Should not the research grants and training programs go to departments of sociology? Perhaps those who staff these programs and bureaucracies should be required to complete an approved course of study in sociology?

We need not impute venality or Machiavellian motives to Fuller and Myers. On the other hand, it would be naive and ethnocentric to believe their statements (and those of many other sociologists) have no consequences or implications for professional sociology. We do not mean to imply that sociologists should not engage in research to document social conditions, as they conceive them. There certainly are antecedents to every condition, and sociologists manage to identify a number of them. We merely make the point that various groups find it to their advantage to promote and call attention to some antecedents of a condition and to ignore or dismiss others as of minor significance. One component of *the definition of a social problem* is that groups lobby for their own type of causal analysis of the condition in question. The logic of the value-conflict approach would insist that when any person, profession, or organization presses for public recognition of their theory or explanation of some condition, they cease to analyze the social problem and become part of it. Willard Waller (1936) recognized this problem thirty-five years ago and recommended:

When our attitude toward a phenomenon is involved in our concept of it, logical difficulties arise which can only be avoided by shifting to an inclusive point of view which enables us to study both the thing and our attitude toward it. (922)

Sociologists have sometimes been aware of this dilemma but their response has been to shift to an inclusive point of view that defines their own role, not as one category of member among many, but rather as scientists, laboring on behalf of society, protecting society, trying to improve society, providing expertise to determine the most effective policy (Merton and Nisbet, 1971). They invariably fail to consider the sociologist as an interested party to social problems definitions— as empire builders, academic entrepreneurs, lobbyists and expert consultants. In short, they fail to subject their own activities to the kind of political analysis they would apply to all other categories of participants in the definitional process.

When the sociologist has a different view of the world from some other group or organization, such differences are not treated as member-member conflicts, but rather, for example, as manifest versus latent problems. The technical quality of the language shields the sociologist from serious scrutiny. This tactic is not confined to the functionalist theorists from whom it certainly might be expected. Fuller and Myers, and Waller do not hesitate to treat the causes claimed by others as part of the definition while viewing their own causal statements as part of the analysis. Similarly, in his section "What Can Social Science Contribute?" Becker (1966:23-28) casts the sociologist in the helping role of expert, supplying knowledge, falsifying incorrect assumptions and otherwise assisting in developing rational, informed policies. More recently, Manis (1974) in a statement that is critical of Merton's concept of latent social problems, himself invokes the mantle of science to exempt his own definitions as data for an understanding of how social problems emerge and develop in society.

The logic of the value-conflict approach, then, pursued to its logical conclusion requires that sociologists, when they participate in the politics of defining social problems, be viewed as member-participants and that they be denied the special status of those who stand outside the process as objective observers or scientists. *Whether the so-ciologist will be treated as a scientist by other participants in the process is a problematic, empirical question.*

We shall illustrate this problem with two schematic but not so hypothetical situations:

Case One: The president of a university, trained as a psychologist, publicly states that women will continue to occupy inferior positions within university faculties in terms of rank, salary, and tenure because they lack the required skills and motivations to succeed due to early childhood training. These patterns of differential achievement by sex are observable from the age of two on, and no amount of ideological rhetoric can get around this matter of fact.

Case Two: In a debate on a bill to legalize sexual acts between consenting adults of the same sex, a member of parliament says he will vote against the bill because he fears for the safety of his young children.

Confronted with these statements the sociologist is likely to ask whether or not the assertions made are factually true and if the inferences based on them are logically warranted. Addressing the statements in this way, the sociologist may find it difficult to remain aloof and uninvolved. With reference to Case One, sociologists might argue that discrimination on tenure committees, rather than early socialization, explains observed differences in the position of women faculty members. In Case Two, they might refute the stereotype that most homosexuals are also child molesters. By responding in such ways to the assertions of community members about social conditions, sociologists are no longer analysts of social problems but participants in the process of definition that should be the subject matter of their study.

The hypothetical cases above pose quite different questions for the value-conflict approach to social problems, questions that do not address the truth of the assertions made by the participants. Quite apart fom the truth of the statements of the university president or member of parliament, can such assertions about the status of women and homosexuals be sustained politically? Can the speakers "get away" with them? Who are the audiences for such statements and how will they respond? How strongly will these spokesmen defend their views? Whom would they cite or consult to document their assertions? If sociologists and psychologists are consulted and thus enter the controversy, what is the relative prestige of these two disciplines should they disagree? Who would have standing to refute their testimony or resolve their disagreement? All of these questions, suggested by the value-conflict approach, are quite apart from and unrelated to the truth of the assertions in question.

Sociologists as experts. A third type of pressure stems from the participation of sociologists as experts in the policymaking process. To enter the arena is to become subject to the pressures that may soon lead to the abandonment of definitional questions in favor of the applied, practical, policy-oriented issues that are adjudicated there. For example, a sociologist may have researched the history of how marijuana came to be defined as an illegal drug. When called to testify as an expert, he or she is asked whether marijuana is *in fact* harmful to those who use it. If she or he is unwilling to address that issue, the expert status, whether coveted or not, will be short-lived. A partisan personal view of the matter may lead one to respond to the question and claim expertise where in fact the sociologist has none. Knowledge of the criminalization of marijuana use provides no basis for testifying as to its harmfulness. Similarly, an "expert" on social definitions of homosexuality, testifying to a parliamentary committee, is not asked how the phenomenon is defined but whether or not homosexuals are also *in fact* dangerous child molesters. The very phrasing of the question as well as the responses of the "sociologist-expert" are data for the study of social problems.

Three kinds of pressures have been outlined that tend to deflect the attention of labeling and social problems theorists away from their chosen subject matter. As members of society they fail to examine their own interpretive activities. As members of an aspiring profession in a competitive organizational environment, vested interests make them compete in traditionally defined arenas. Finally, as individual experts they are expected to address the practical policy questions and thus accept their underlying positivistic assumptions.

CONCLUSION

A sociology of social problems must take the members' perspective as the starting point, focusing in particular on definitional and claims-making activities as the primary subject matter. If we pursue this conception of the field, we arrive at "macro-sociological" concerns from a different direction from the functionalist route. Rather than investigating how institutional arrangements produce certain social conditions, we examine how individuals and groups become engaged in collective activities organized and directed toward establishing institutional arrangements, recognizing putative conditions as problems, and attempting to relieve, ameliorate, and eliminate them.

We propose that the central interest of sociologists of social problems and deviance is the interaction between claims-making groups and others about the definition of social conditions and what should be done about them. What is in contention throughout the social problems producing process (as in the deviant producing process) are the definitions of reality that groups and organizations assert, sponsor, impose, reject or subvert. The initial definition of social reality may undergo modification and changes, such that the condition asserted to be the problem at one point in time turns out to be a different and apparently unrelated condition at another point.

The task of a theory of social problems and deviance, would be to provide a description and explanation of the definitional process in which morally objectionable conditions or behaviors are asserted to exist, and the collective activities that become organized around *those assertions*. It would seek to explain how those definitions and assertions come to be made, the processes by which they are acted upon by institutions, and how those institutional responses do or do not produce socially legitimated categories of social problems and deviance.

If the subject matter is definitions of social problems and deviance, then *it is definitions that are socially processed*. In this sense, we can say that definitions have careers, one aspect of which is their institutionalization as official categories. In like manner, we would say the central subject matter of the sociology of deviance is the processing of the definitions of deviance which may result in the development of informally recognized and enforced categories, as well as the establishment of official categories and populations of deviants. The theoretical problem is to account for how categories of social problems and deviance are produced and how methods of social control and treatment are institutionally established.

REFERENCES

Becker, Howard S.
1963 Outsiders: Studies in the Sociology of Deviance. New York: Free Press.
1966 "Introduction." In Social Problems: A Modern Approach. New York: John Wiley.

Blumer, Herbert
1971 "Social problems as collective behavior." Social Problems 18 (Winter): 298-306.

Bordua, David
1967 "Recent trends: deviant behavior and social control." Annals of the American Academy of Political and Social Science 369 (January): 140-163.

Frank, Lawrence K.
1925 "Social problems." American Journal of Sociology 30 (January): 462-473.

Freidson, Eliot
1970 The Profession of Medicine. New York: Dodd, Mead.

1971 Professional Dominance. New York: Atherton.

Fuller, Richard C.
1937 "Sociological theory and social problems." Social Forces 4 (May): 496-502.
1939 "Social problems." In R. E. Park (ed.), An Outline of the Principles of Sociology. New York: Barnes and Nobles.

Fuller, Richard C., and Richard Myers
1941a "Some aspects of a theory of social problems." American Sociological Review 6 (February): 24-32.
1941b "The natural history of a social problem." American Sociological Review 6 (June): 320-328.

Gibbs, Jack
1966 "Conceptions of deviant behavior: the old and the new." Pacific Sociological Review 9 (Spring): 9-14.

Goode, William J.
1960 "Encroachment, charlatanism, and the emerging profession: psychology, sociology, and medicine." American Sociological Review 25 (December): 902-914.

Hughes, Everett C.
1971 The Sociological Eye, Book 2. Chicago: Aldine-Atherton.

Kitsuse, John I., and Malcolm Spector
1973 "Toward a sociology of social problems: social conditions, value-judgments and social problems." Social Problems 20 (Spring): 407-419.

Lemert, Edwin M.
1951a "Is there a natural history of social problems?" American Sociological Review 16 (April): 217-223.
1951b Social Pathology. New York: McGraw-Hill.

Manis, Jerome
1974 "The concept of social problems vox populi and sociological analysis." Social Problems 21 (Winter): 305-315.

Merton, Robert K., and Robert Nisbet
1971 Contemporary Social Problems, 3rd ed. New York: Harcourt, Brace and World.

Waller, Willard
1936 "Social Problems and the Mores." American Sociological Review 1 (December): 922-932.

The Concept Of Social Problems:
Vox Populi And Sociological Analysis*

JEROME G. MANIS
Western Michigan University

To many sociologists, social problems are conditions considered to be undesirable by many people. While the concept relies upon public judgments, exponents of the definition claim to be value-free. This questionable position is maintained in Merton's distinction between manifest and latent problems. The categories indicate the existence of unrecognized social problems while retaining the public's value perspective. Unlike functional analysis, which distinguishes between objective conditions and subjective interpretations, the manifest-latent social problems categories are limited to the latter. Current usage ignores the possibility that some perceived social problems may be trivial or spurious. Applying the scientific values and norms of sociology offers a possible alternative. The values of modern science may provide useful criteria for redefining the concept of social problems.

The aim of this analysis is to assess the concept of social problems as it is currently defined and applied by contemporary sociology. My thesis is that, in attempting to achieve a value-free conception of social problems, sociologists have adopted definitions which are based upon popular values, beliefs, and biases. While seeking to avoid middle-class moral ideologies (Mills, 1943), sociologists have come to conceive of social problems in the imagery of popular majorities. In doing so, values are not eliminated. They are only exchanged.

The common feature of current definitions of social problems is acceptance of "the voice of the people." A recent dictionary of sociology defines social problems as, "any undesirable condition or situation that is judged by an influential number of persons within a community to be intolerable and to require group action toward constructive reform" (Theodorson and Theodorson, 1969:392). One widely used text explicitly specifies that "no condition, no

matter how dramatic or shocking to someone else is a social problem *unless* and *until* the values of a considerable number of people define it as a problem" (Horton and Leslie, 1970:5).

With few exceptions, social problems textbooks rely on such definitions. Yet, in their choice of specific social problems, they do not provide evidence for the congruence of their chosen topics with popular norms and values. Rather than relying upon public opinion surveys or other justifications for their chosen topics, social problems appear to be selected by some unknown set of criteria. The consequence is an academic literature consisting of a congeries of scattered categories difficult to relate to theory, method, or social significance.

As Reissman has noted: "Sociologists have not been as successful as Carson or Nader in calling attention to social problems. What they have developed to a fine art is an ability to react quickly as soon as a social problem reaches the first stage of identification" (1972:7). The dependence upon public awareness of problems has directed sociological inquiry toward a concern with social issues and prevented sociology from identifying emergent and critical social problems. The neglect of poverty by

sociologists in recent decades is a case in point.

Equally critical is the danger that sociology may focus its attention upon trivial, surface, or spurious topics. The voice of the people can guide sociology toward a greater awareness of public troubles, but may also misdirect sociology toward a concern for public phobias and fantasies.

BATHTUBS, INDIANS, AND MARIHUANA

The fusion of social problems with public issues may be clarified by considering some topics which appear to fit current definitions of social problems. If a social problem is "an alleged situation which is incompatible with the values of significant numbers of people" (Rubington and Weinberg, 1971:5-6), then sociologists would probably agree that bathtubs were an American social problem just over a century ago. According to W. I. Thomas (1937:728), "In the 1840's the newspapers in the United States attacked the introduction of bathtubs as extravagant and undemocratic. Doctors denounced them as dangerous to health, and the government was called upon to restrict or suppress them. In 1843 Vir-

* I would like to express my appreciation to R. Greg Emerton, Paul B. Horton, Charles B. Keely, Bernard N. Meltzer, Stanley S. Robin, Morton O. Wagenfeld, and Lewis Walker for their helpful suggestions.

11

ginia put a tax of $30 a year on bath-tubs and in 1845 a Boston municipal ordinance made bathing unlawful except on medical advice."

If bathtubs were social problems, should sociologists study the causes and the effects of possessing or using bathtubs in the 1840's? Or is the proper focus of study the norms or values concerning bathtubs? Or is it the controversy over bathtubs which should be the subject of research and theory?

We may note that during the late 1830's and early 1840's, the Cherokee and Seminole Indians were dispossessed from their lands and driven westward on their tragic "trail of tears." Some Americans, such as Emerson, were opposed to this policy; the majority appeared to favor it. From the standpoint of American public opinion, the Indian was *the* social problem. Their expulsion and near-extermination was an attempt at a "final solution" of the Indian problem.

A more contemporary illustration of the shortcomings of current definitions of social problems are popular attitudes toward marihuana. Public opinion, particularly among those over thirty, appears to be strongly opposed to the legalization of marihuana. Long term prison sentences for possession of marihuana have been approved in many states. Yet consumption of alcohol and of cigarettes is acceptable, though the former has produced millions of problem drinkers and the latter is empirically and officially "dangerous to your health."

From the standpoint of popular values, the use of alcohol and of cigarettes is not a social problem, though some of their consequences are conceived so. The use of marihuana as well as its presumed (and unknown) consequences must be conceived as social problems on the basis of standard sociological definitions. Defining social problems in terms of public norms and values is a dubious procedure for a "neutral" sociology.

The reliance by sociologists on the "voice of the people" for their definition of social problems is a modern equivalent of an ancient aphorism. The Roman belief that "the voice of the people is the voice of God" is paralleled by the sociologists' acceptance of public opinion as the ultimate arbiter of social problems.

Discussing the concept of Vox Populi, George Boas (1969:4) has pointed out that: "the people who use the proverb assume that in case of popular desires, desire creates goodness. The People are assumed to have an infallible source of knowledge, knowledge that is self-substantiated, requiring no analysis or criticism. The proverb is in this respect related to one of the many forms of cultural primitivism, the form that maintains that nature is better than art, that instinct is better than learning, that feelings are wiser than learning, that feelings are wiser than reason, that the 'heart' is sounder than the 'mind.' "

Accepting the public's views of social problems assumes that the public knows best what society's problems *really* are. While social problems textbooks appear to make this assumption, they often note that public opinion is influenced by political leaders, pressure groups, advertising, and the mass media of communication. These influences upon the public's conceptions of undesirable social conditions suggest that the "voice of the people" may be, at times, only the echo of a society's opinion makers.

MANIFEST AND LATENT SOCIAL PROBLEMS

The empirical utility of current definitions of social problems must depend upon the quality of public opinion. If the public is fully aware of its problems, the task of the sociologist in identifying these social problems would not be very difficult. Survey researchers using national samples could provide standardized procedures for determining societal problems. The research questions could then be focused wholly on causation and consequences.

If, however, the public's awareness of its problems is not clearly articulated, the task of the sociologist is more troublesome. How does the sociologist deal with unformed attitudes, ambivalent feelings, etc.? Merton has sought to resolve this difficulty through the dichotomy of manifest versus latent social problems.

"Apart from manifest social problems—those objective social conditions identified by problem-definers as at odds with social values—are latent social problems, conditions that are also at odds with values current in the society but are not generally recognized as being so. The sociologist does not impose his values upon others when he undertakes to supply knowledge about latent social problems" (Merton, 1971: 806).

To Merton, the ultimate criteria of social problems are popular values. His categories distinguish between recognized and unrecognized conditions contrary to social values. The sociologist remains neutral by specifying the society's values and ferreting out the actions or emergent conditions at variance with those values. When the people sleep or their voice is silent, the sociologist becomes the spokesman of the popular will.

Merton's claim that "the sociologist does not impose his values upon others when he undertakes to supply knowledge about social problems" is correct only in the sense that his personal values may conflict with social values. Whose side is he on—the silent or the vocal majority of the group? In a racist society, the unrecognized actions of the equalitarians are a latent social problem. When the war-lovers are in the saddle, the hidden peace-seekers are a latent social problem.

Where social values are congruent with the personal or scientifically derived beliefs of the sociologist, the issue may appear irrelevant. To Myrdal (1944), the American dilemma was the contradiction between democratic values imbedded in the American Creed and the ongoing practices of racial discrimination. The personal values of most sociologists appear to be in accord with the value-premise of the Myrdal volume: equality is the value; discrimination is the problem (Lipset and Ladd, 1972:71). No textbook on social problems takes the opposite position.

For the purposes here, let us consider that opposite condition. Many American blacks contend that America is a racist society, that the American Creed is a pious fiction, that prejudice is a deeply rooted, dominant, and widespread attitude of most Americans. Consider the possibility that they are correct. Racial prejudice and discrimination would then be defined as social values. A manifest social problem is the harmful myth of the American Creed. A latent social problem is the emerging values which contend that discrimination is inhuman or immoral.

In order to remain neutral in studying social problems, the sociologist may not question the values of the group. A traditionally functionalist assumption sustains this posture. If social values are consequences of societal needs, then social conditions at variance with social values would endanger the survival of the group. By seeking out the hidden shoals, the trained eyes of the sociologist can sound the alarm —a latent social problem dead ahead.

Merton (1967:84) has pointed out the fallacy of Malinowski's postulate "that all standardized social or cultural forms have positive functions." He also emphasized the importance of social dysfunctions, as well as of functional alternatives, to societal values and practices. By this logic, a widely accepted social value may be functional or dysfunctional. Further, some values or practices inimical to the larger or more widespread social values may also be functional or dysfunctional. Finally, we conclude that a social problem—manifest or latent— may be functional or may be dysfunctional for the society or its sub-units.

Our reasoning has led us to a cul-de-sac. Merton's version of functional analysis may convince us that a certain widely held value is seriously harmful to group survival, i.e., dysfunctional. Social problems analysis accepts the value as a criterion for defining the opposite, functional, and unrecognized value as a latent social problem. The latent social problem is a functional necessity for group survival. The solution of the problem could seriously harm the society.

What are our options? We can accept both perspectives and view any objections to the logical outcome as mere semantic hang-ups. We can reject one or both types of analysis. Or, and this is obviously more difficult, we may attempt to reconcile the two perspectives by assessing the basic sources of the apparent anomaly of functionally necessary major social problems.

Spurious and Genuine Social Problems

The preceding section has been focused on the distinction between publicly recognized and unrecognized problems. My concern at this point is with trivial versus important, imaginary and real, spurious and genuine social problems. If the public is strongly opposed to bathtubs, Indians, marihuana, busing, subversives, or

witches, must the sociologist choose these topics as the substantively appropriate domain of social problems? Is the sociologist who joins the search for witches, their causes, and consequences, a neutral observer or a participant in witch-hunting?

The key question is, are some "social problems" no more than popular myths and prejudices? The response hinges upon the sociological controversy over value-free versus value-committed analyses. Why should the norms and values of a popular majority be considered a more neutral basis of sociological concepts and perspectives than the values or judgments of a professional sociologist? Does a sociological education or the sociological imagination provide no basis for assessing traditional or transient value-judgments of popular majorities?

To rank sociological knowledge and judgments over public knowledge and judgments does not imply that the former is always superior to the latter. We need only concede that the latter may be based, at times, upon erroneous information or emotional fears. We need only contend that, at such times, perceived social problems may be illusions or insignificant.

Examining Merton's (1967:105) paradigm for functional analysis offers some basis for clarification. The distinction between manifest and latent social problems was derived, obviously, from his previously reported distinction between manifest and latent functions. His interpretation of the former is both phenomenological (focusing upon public cognitions and purposes) and behavioral (stressing effects or consequents). "*Manifest functions* are those objective consequences contributing to the adjustment or adaptation of the system which are intended and recognized by participants in the system; *latent functions,* correlatively, being those which are neither intended nor recognized." The latter statement specifically excludes subjective meanings, leaving only the objective consequences for sociological analysis of latent functions.

Like other sociologists, Merton has deleted the objective criteria from his definitions of both manifest and latent social problems. These definitions, focusing on subjective purposes, are a nearly complete reversal of his objective definitions of manifest and latent

functions. The turnabout would be more complete if we note an inconsistency in his paradigm.

The major categories of the latent-manifest paradigm differentiate: "2. Concepts of subjective dispositions (motives, purposes). . . . 3. Concepts of objective consequences (functions, dysfunctions)." These opposing concepts are presented to overcome "the tendency to confuse the subjective category of *motive* with the objective category of *function*" (Merton, 1967: 105). However, in defining manifest and latent *social problems,* Merton has limited both to the subjective category of "recognition."

From the functionalist perspective, objective conditions are the basis of social functions and dysfunctions. From the social problems perspective, subjective social values are used to assess objective social conditions. A comparison of Merton's definitions may be useful at this point.

Manifest functions those objective consequences contributing to the adjustment or adaptation of the system which are intended and recognized by the participants in the system	*Manifest social problems* those objective social conditions identified by problem-definers as at odds with social values
Latent functions those (objective consequences contributing to the adjustment or adaptation of the system) which are neither intended nor recognized	*Latent social problems* conditions that are also at odds with values but are not generally recognized as being so

Thus, Merton's social problems analysis takes subjective values (recognized or unrecognized) as its premise, while his functional analysis is founded on the objective conditions relevant to societal survival. Values are the starting point of social problems analysis; the concept of values is not mentioned in Merton's (1967:106) three page paradigm. In the latter, he points out that "embedded in every functional analysis is some conception, tacit or expressed, of functional requirements (needs, prerequisites) of the system under observation."

A critical shortcoming of functional analysis has been the inability of its proponents to specify these societal requirements. Some critics have argued that its equilibrium orientation entails a status quo or conservative position. In attempting to avoid this possible bias, Merton has called attention to the divergent interests and needs of diverse social sub-units. What is good for General Motors may be costly or harmful to the worker or the consumer.

It is, perhaps, for these reasons that the social problems perspective has ignored the functionalist issue of societal requirements, needs, pre-requisites, or their objective mechanisms. Instead, its emphasis is placed wholly on social values. Current definitions of social problems do not provide any basis for determining whether popular beliefs and values are relevant or irrelevant to societal, sub-group, or individual well-being. By accepting subjective values as the criterion for social problems, objective consequences are ignored and public preferences are given a seemingly scientific rationale. At the same time, the sociologist is said to be neutral and value-free.

If we accept Merton's distinction between recognized and unrecognized social problems, we concede the fallibility of public opinion. Presumably, the sociologist can identify and designate unrecognized social conditions contrary to accepted social values as latent social problems. Is that critique the boundary of sociological inquiry? Must the sociologist accept every social value as an implicit criterion of group or societal well-being?

Some recent social problems textbooks would appear to answer these questions in the negative. ". . . the greatest difficulty with the sociological treatment of social problems has been the tendency to equate social problems with a failure to adhere to social norms themselves . . . the sociologist often fails to examine the extent to which the norms themselves and their attendant behavior—that is to say, the existing social order—might constitute the most important social problem of all" (Sykes, 1971:8).

Viewed thusly, a perceived social problem—identified as such by the public—could be misleading and spurious. However, Sykes' (1971:9-10) criterion for such an assessment, "what is considered the statisfactory and unsatisfactory organization of society," is not spelled out. What is satisfactory and what is not depends upon the views and the values of the specifier. If the public's judgments are questioned, whose values will take their place?

In their textbook on social problems, Perrucci and Pilisuk (1971:xviii) present the issue in blunt terms: "The definition of a social problem reflects the norms and values of the definer." Opposing current usage in sociology, they adopt specifically value-oriented criteria for social problems: intrinsic worth of the individual, the value of life, freedom, etc. On the basis of these values, they attempt to differentiate between "central" and "peripheral" social problems. Their choice of values is avowedly personal, moral, and extra-scientific.

Since social problems analysis, like social deviance, social pathology, social disorganization, and dysfunctionalism rely on evaluative interpretation, it may suffice for some sociologists to propose their own personal judgments as against those of the public. Others, perhaps most, would consider such a position as unscientific and untenable. One hazardous option appears open—to seek for social values in the assumptions and norms of the discipline of sociology.

SCIENCE, VALUES, AND SOCIAL PROBLEMS

The title for this section is intended to be suggestive rather than definitive or conclusive. My aim is *not* to propose precise, scientifically derived value-criteria but rather to propose their *consideration* as potential alternatives to current sociological usage. An attempt to formulate a scientific rationale for society's values may appear as an impossible dream. Still, for many sociologists, the goal of a value-free sociology seems to be a modern parallel to the search for the philosopher's stone —turning the dross of values into the gold of facts.

The value-free sociologist contends that science can only tell us "what is" not "what should be." According to Friedrichs (1970:80), it was Max Weber who helped in translating "the articles of faith of 19th century science into the scriptures of the mid-20th century sociologist." During the 19th century, scientists "investigating the structure of the universe imagined themselves as the equivalent of the early explorers and map makers" (Conant, 1952:93).

That older image of science is being replaced. As Conant points out, modern science not only observes but also creates and invents. The scientist has become a producer of new phenomena,

such as penicillin, nylon, nuclear fission, and "smart" missiles. Scientific knowledge includes what "shall be" as well as "what is."

To Conant (1952:97), "however, in view of the revolution in physics, anyone who now asserts that science is an exploration of the universe must be prepared to shoulder a heavy burden of proof. To my mind, the analogy between the map maker and the scientist is false. A scientific theory is not even the first approximation to a map; it is not a creed; it is a policy—an economical and fruitful guide to action by scientific investigators."

Viewing science as a set of policies has transformed 20th century physics, chemistry, and biology. The alteration is not a novel intrusion of values into a previously neutral set of disciplines. Science is a social institution with its own set of norms and values. The emerging sociology of science, however, has been limited largely to imaginative constructions of traditional scientific values.

Kaplan (1964:857) has indicated that ". . . the [scientific] values posited by Merton and Barber and Parsons have been fully accepted as those which prevail today, without any empirical verification or theoretical analysis." Those values are said to include the desirability of knowledge, freedom of inquiry, responsibility for accuracy, and dissemination of theories and research findings. More recently, some scientists have become concerned with the social consequences of proposed scientific studies, including the rights, dignity, and safety of the individual, the survival of human society, and the protection of the environment.

These concerns have emerged as a consequence of modern science's capabilities for transforming the empirical world. Knowledge in the natural sciences is not limited to natural phenomena but includes science-made phenomena. What the scientist chooses to seek out or to create can alter substantially the conditions of human life. Such actions are not mere neutral observations but involve value-choices. The necessity for making such choices is a growing dilemma for all of the sciences.

Currently, science represents only a small though rapidly increasing and influential segment of modern society. Like other social groups, scientists are guided in their behavior by norms and values. Unlike other groups, scientists are restricted by traditional norms against "imposing" their values upon their society. Yet, as scientific activity has shifted from observation to innovation, this norm of neutrality is violated intentionally or unintentionally. To describe the behavior of the oncologist or the nuclear physicist as neutral and value-free is inaccurate and misleading.

The actions and consequences of the sociological enterprise are especially value-laden. The selection of topics, the choice of perspectives, the definition of concepts, the designation of populations, the specification of research techniques, and the interpretation and implications of findings involve norms and values. Survey researchers are guided by the norms and values of costs, speed, and ease of data-processing as much or more than by the norms of truth and accuracy. Criminologists operate within the framework of popular values, power structures, and judicial interpretations. Functionalist and conflict theories in sociology produce divergent data, interpretations, and conclusions concerning the same phenomena.

The value-free perspective has aided in the development of sociology by illuminating certain professional biases, by encouraging objectivity, by stimulating methodology, and by raising the stature of the discipline. It has also sustained popular values and the status quo. Most serious is its implication of the sociological equality of every social norm and value.

In Strauss' (1963:425, 431) view, "Weber's thesis necessarily leads to nihilism or to the view that every preference, however evil, base, or insane, has to be judged before the tribunal of reason to be as legitimate as any other preference. . . . Many social scientists of our time seem to regard nihilism as a minor inconvenience which wise men would bear with equanimity, since it is the price one has to pay for obtaining that highest good, a truly scientific social science." If the norms of science are changing, that price may turn out to be not only excessive but unnecessary.

Like other dichotomies, the value-free and value-oriented perspectives in sociology, at best, are ideal-types. Many proponents of the former do not deny the existence of the scientific values of truth, accuracy, replication, and com-munication. Many critics neither reject those values nor espouse an uncritical acceptance of individual preferences. The major difficulty with the position of these critics is their diversity and the resulting lack of agreement on the other values involved in the scientific ethos.

My purpose in this discussion is not aimed at a revision of the value premises of modern science. To Kuhn (1970:92-110), new paradigms in science emerge out of the shortcomings of "normal science." As the natural sciences have shifted from neutral observation to creative innovation, their activities are altering the basic norms and values of science far more than could exhortation or pleading.

It is my contention that the emerging values of modern science do not sustain the traditional conception of value-free sociology. Social problems analysis, I believe, exemplifies the shortcomings of the supposedly neutral perspective. Defining social problems in terms of public values is neither value-free nor scientifically justifiable.

TOWARD REDEFINING SOCIAL PROBLEMS

Instead of retaining a given society's values as the criteria for social problems, our definition should be transcultural and comparative. Using American values as a basis for specifying American social problems is ethnocentric as well as relativistic. A broader time-frame, historical as well as comparative, is needed to move beyond culture-bound norms and values.

Historical and anthropological knowledge can be supplemented by the findings of biology and the other sciences. The incest taboo, for example, comes close to being a cultural universal. It appears to be highly functional for sex-role relationships and for social solidarity. It is also consonant with the findings of modern genetics. The practice of incest is contrary to most societies' norms; it also appears to be biologically dangerous for the individual.

A heuristic definition of social problems may begin with the values of a given group. It need not be restricted to those values. With that premise in mind, we may examine the values of the scientific community as one possible frame of reference. In the absence of empirical evidence concerning those values, my assessment should be con-sidered as a set of hypotheses. My purpose is to apply those values as possible criteria for a revised definition of social problems.

Among the broad and basic values which I believe characterize modern science are: 1) individual and group survival which includes life and health; 2) the desirability of knowledge, accurate and truthful; 3) the freedom to dissent, to hold opposing ideas, theories, and values; 4) the sharing of knowledge with others; 5) responsibility for actions harmful to the well-being of humanity. The listing, is neither exhaustive nor definitive but rather illustrative and, hopefully, useful.

Scientists strongly advocate the use of objectivity and the right to hold dissenting views for members of their discipline. Many would agree that societies, such as Nazi Germany, which reject these values are detrimental to the scientific enterprise. Is the scientist who espouses these values for human societies behaving unscientifically? Does the scientist who advocates responsibility for the scientific community and for society at large do damage to the scientific ethos?

My thesis has been that changes in the scientific activity from a somewhat passive observation to a more active innovation have altered the scientific value-structure. These changes not only permit but increasingly require the wider dissemination of scientific values. The altered role of science is especially pertinent to the activities of the sociologist, particularly in the analysis of social problems.

The values of science, supplementing its theories and research findings, offer a possible avenue for revising the sociologist's definitions of social problems. Such a procedure does not deny the utility of public conceptions of what is socially harmful or undesirable. Common sense knowledge derived from the experience of every day living is a necessary component of sociological inquiry (Manis, 1972). It is not sufficient for sociological analysis. Sociological knowledge, guided by contemporary scientific norms and values, is required.

The congruence of these presumed values of science with those of other groups and societies is an empirical research question. Their congruence with functionalist interpretations of objective group and intergroup requirements is another area of inquiry. Their utility for specifying the well-being of a group or society may constitute a basis for redefining the concept of social problems.

Using the framework of scientific values, however they may be conceived and specified, the following definitions of social problems are proposed.

> Social problems are those social conditions identified by scientific inquiry and values as detrimental to the well-being of human societies.
>
> Perceived social problems are those social conditions which are identified by groups or individuals as contrary to their group or personal values.
>
> Spurious social problems are those perceived social problems which are not contrary to personal or group values or are not detrimental to the well-being of human societies.

These definitions are proposed in order to stimulate sociological discussion and analysis. They are intended as vehicles for shifting sociological inquiry from its uncritical acceptance of societal values in defining social problems. As wholly tentative formulations, they require thorough assessment and, perhaps, extensive modification. Viewed thusly, they may facilitate the application of sociological knowledge and the sociological imagination to the analysis and the solution of social problems.

REFERENCES

Boas, George
1969 Vox Populi: Essays in the History of an Idea. Baltimore: Johns Hopkins Press.

Conant, James B.
1953 Modern Science and Modern Man. Garden City, New Jersey: Doubleday Anchor Books.

Freidrichs, Robert W.
1970 A Sociology of Sociology. New York: Free Press.

Horton, Paul B., and Gerald R. Leslie
1970 The Sociology of Social Problems. New York: Appleton-Century-Crofts.

Kaplan, Norman
1964 "Sociology of Science." Pp. 852-881 in Robert E. L. Faris (ed.), Handbook of Modern Sociology. Chicago: Rand McNally.

Kuhn, Thomas S.
1970 The Structure of Scientific Revolutions. International Encyclopedia of Unified Science, Vol. II, No. 2. Chicago: University of Chicago Press.

Lipset, Seymour Martin, and Everett Carl Ladd, Jr.
1972 "The politics of American sociologists." American Journal of Sociology 78(July): 67-104.

Manis, Jerome G.
1972 "Common sense sociology and analytic sociology." Sociological Focus 5(spring): 1-15.

Merton, Robert K.
1967 On Theoretical Sociology. New York: Free Press.
1971 "Social problems and sociological theory." Pp. 793-845 in Robert K. Merton and Robert Nisbet (eds.), Contemporary Social Problems. New York: Harcourt, Brace, Jovanovich.

Mills, C. Wright
1943 "The professional ideology of social pathologists." American Journal of Sociology 49(September): 165-80.

Myrdal, Gunnar
1944 An American Dilemma. New York: Harper.

Perrucci, Robert, and Marc Pilisuk
1971 The Triple Revolution Emerging. Boston: Little, Brown

Reissman, Leonard
1972 "The solution cycle of social problems." American Sociologist 7(February): 7-9.

Rubington, Earl, and Martin S. Weinberg
1971 The Study of Social Problems. New York: Oxford University Press.

Strauss, Leo
1963 "Natural right and the distinction between facts and values." Pp. 419-457 in Maurice Natanson (ed.), Philosophy of the Social Sciences: A Reader. New York: Random House.

Sykes, Gresham M.
1971 Social Problems in America. Glenview, Illinois: Scott, Foresman and Company.

Theodorson, George A., and Achilles G. Theodorson
1969 A Modern Dictionary of Sociology. New York: Thomas Y. Crowell.

Thomas, W. I.
1937 Primitive Behavior. New York: McGraw-Hill.

II. Perspectives on Problems of Pervasive Social Change

An understanding of social change is crucial to an understanding of social problems, for change is a fundamental characteristic of modern society. We developed our ideas, even myths, of the inevitability of progress from the attempts of the *philosophes* to explain the far-reaching social changes of the eighteenth-century. Yet change and growth are usually seen as a "mixed blessing." For change also creates stress and strain not only upon the social structure but upon the human organism as well. It makes us nervous! So although change is commonplace in western society it is still problematic, for it invariably creates fundamental changes in our basic social arrangements.

Social change as a persistent modification in the social structure is exemplified in the modern city, which has resulted from several centuries of accelerating socio-economic changes and technological developments. The growth of cities and their attendant urban problems is a worldwide phenomenon, as Wilsher and Righter point out in "Cities in Trouble." By 1985, one person in six will live in urban centers. Urban problems are not new, for since the turn of the century Americans have been aware of overcrowded slums, racial segregation, substandard housing, polluted air, transportation problems, corrupt politics and related problems in our cities.

However, continuing population shifts since World War II have resulted in the migration of southern rural blacks to cities in the South as well as the North. This migration was accompanied by the exodus of many white urban residents to the surrounding suburbs over the past three decades. These shifts in population were concomitants of technological changes in agriculture and an increasing reliance on the automobile for transportation plus a housing policy favorable to the middle classes.

By 1970 not only were seventy percent of our population living in only 267 metropolitan areas, but a majority of these people dwelt in the suburban fringe. As the more affluent middle class moved to the suburbs, the cities were forced to tax those who remained still more heavily. Business and industry also moved to the suburbs adding to the social and economic dislocation. Thus, the central cities of our urban regions became dependent on federal monies and deficit fiscal policies in order to maintain the level of services required. And they were overextended and vulnerable when the economic recession of the 1970's struck. Imaginative national, as well as regional planning is necessary to deal with the crises in the cities. Yet the absence of such policies, and the diminished political salience of the cities is highlighted in the manner in which New York City's fiscal crisis became a "political football," on the state as well as on the national level. David Muchnick argues for a national accountability for urban problems in "Death Warrant for the Cities." Carol Brown critiques the business interests' neoconservative views as she points out in "City Services: Who Needs People?" that human services are now seen as "too expensive" by banks and business enterprises who no longer need the city residents or services cities provide. Urban problems, then, must be redefined in human and social terms, not merely fiscal terms.

Our urbanized, industrialized society's growing reliance on technology has not only made ever increasing demands on natural resources but has contributed to the myth that somehow we can and should master nature. Consciousness of ecological problems and recognition that we live in a universe of finite resources, fortunately, have begun to dismantle such myths. As early as 1798, the Reverend Thomas Malthus was questioning the norm "be fruitful and multiply," and by now we are quite accustomed to phrases such as, "the earth's population will double in the next thirty years." The dimensions of ecological issues, as consequences of our continuing emphasis on growth were diagnosed in the reports issued by the Club of Rome. As the article by Pestel *et al.* points out, the industrialized societies consume a disproportionate amount of the finite supply of raw materials. The United States, for instance, with 6 percent of the world's population uses over one third of the world's energy. Barry Commoner stresses the interrelatedness denoted by the phrase "ecological problems," for the energy crisis has had world-wide consequences. Yet, as the third article indicates, reliance on nuclear energy may result in numerous problems, both anticipated and unanticipated, rather than in solutions.

The extension of technology into the field of electronics has made mass communications and mass society feasible. The amount of communication taking place has increased, but it is an impersonal-one-way flow of ideas and images. Children spend more time in front of the "boob tube" than in school, and the "family hour" is a type of program not a family gathering. We sell politicians the way we sell soap and object to the first but not the latter, for, after all, television commercials gross over $4 billion a year. Another change making mass society more of a reality is the exponential expansion of computer data banks. This control of information and communication contributes to the feeling of uneasiness and alienation or powerlessness in society.

CITIES IN TROUBLE

THE URBAN EXPLOSION

The harsh consequences of a worldwide migration from the land

PETER WILSHER, ROSEMARY RIGHTER

Peter Wilsher and Rosemary Righter, both staff members of the "Sunday Times" of London, are co-authors of the book "The Exploding Cities," based on a World Population Year conference at Oxford co-sponsored by the UN Fund for Population Activities and the "Sunday Times." These excerpts from the book appear by permission of the publishers, André Deutsch, Ltd., in England and Quadrangle in the U.S.

•

Plato laid down the ideal size for a community of citizens as 5,040—the number who could comfortably gather into the Athens marketplace. Shortly afterward Aristotle said that men came to the city to live but that they stayed to live the good life. In the past fifteen years some 577 million extra citizens have been born or have moved into those communal aggregations of 100,000 or more people which are now designated by the word "city." In the next twenty-five years, saving pestilence, famine, or thermonuclear war, they will be joined by a further 1.4 billion—more than half the world's population at the beginning of the

1960s. How will they live, these almost unimaginable hordes, and in what sense is it possible to hope that more than an infinitesimal, privileged fraction will succeed in living anything resembling "the good life"?

Under UN demographic definitions, big cities start at 500,000; million-cities, as their name suggests, are in the seven-figure class; multi-million cities weigh in at 2.5 million; and super-conurbations, like Tokyo-Yokohama and Greater New York, range from 12.5 million upward.

New categories, however, may soon be required. By 1985, the present trends suggest, there may be three or four countries with metropolitan areas containing over 25 million, and possibly one (Calcutta? São Paulo? Mexico City?) with over 50 million. And the mathematical extrapolation suggests there could even be one monster of 100 million or more by the end of the century.

Today it is in the cities which already have over a million inhabitants that the incipient city explosion is taking place. As recently as 1950 only seventy-five places would have been on this list. But in 1975 there are 191 entries, with new

names like Curtiba in Brazil and Lyallpur, West Pakistan, joining such slower-developing but longer-established cities as Vancouver, Damascus, and Odessa. A decade further on, in 1985, the rollcall will have stretched to 273, with Siberia's Krasnoyarsk and Madagascar's Tananarive coming in alongside Cuglin, Aleppo, and Kabul. More than 800 million people will then be living in a sprawling urban nightmare—one in six of the human race.

By then it is likely that Mexico City, São Paulo, Los Angeles, and Shanghai (despite China's much-trumpeted efforts at decentralization) will have joined New York and Tokyo in the super-conurbation class—with Peking, London, Bombay, Calcutta, Osaka-Kobe, Seoul, Buenos Aires, West Germany's Rhine-Ruhr complex, Paris, Rio de Janeiro, and Cairo-Giza, each with well over 10 million, coming up fast. This group, aggregating some 262 million people, will outstrip the world's whole major-city population of ten years ago.

Three separate though interrelated demographic phenomena are turning the screws on the world's major cities: the very rapid growth in population overall; the accelerating switch everywhere from rural to urban lifestyles; and the apparently universal tendency for this change to concentrate on the largest available settlements. The consequences are urban poverty amid affluence, the breakdown in public services, the inner-city decay, and the cultural deprivation of sprawling low-income suburbs. These symptoms of disorder affront traditional Western pride in its great cities. Planners, politicians, and economists acknowledge the crisis in the cities of the rich but tend to find it absurd and even immoral that we do not find and implement solutions.

Prof. William Robson points out in *Great Cities of the World* that only five or six metropolitan regions have seriously tried to set up governmental schemes capable of meeting their "present and future needs in regard to organization, services, finance, coordination, planning; or democratic control, and even in these exceptional areas the measures taken are barely adequate."

This failure is particularly serious in the cities of the developed world, with their complex economic interrelations and their social and cultural patina. The city's resources and mechanisms for control are being stretched by the growth of the suburbs, the outward reach of the metropolis, and the dimming of the distinction between urban and rural. But how are we to resolve the question of city government?

The megaregion, which nowadays includes not only the metropolis and its ring of outer suburbs but an amorphous and extensive extra-urban commuting area, puts immense strain not just on the services but on the identity of the city. Planning battles rage between the advocates of centralized control and integrated metropolitan government and "regionalists" who argue for decentralization and the encouragement of local initiative. The chaotic overlapping of rival administrative territories remains the daily reality. And underlying these arguments is the urgency of creating or preserving that most elusive element, the quality of human interchange.

The problem is worldwide. São Paulo and Calcutta are growing faster than the great cities of the West. In the U.S. and Japan the number of million-cities has more than doubled since 1950.

Western societies are attuned to "problem-solving." They expect answers: the bigger the question the more all-embracing must be the solu-

São Paulo—"A monster of 100 million by the end of the century?"

Diego Goldberg/Photo Trends

tion. They are societies geared to accelerating change. They recognize that the cities will require more complex mechanisms to guide them and expect that these will be forthcoming. But there is also an awareness that the great cities have not adjusted to a fundamental shift of function: the displacement of diminishing manufacturing capacity by the service industries. Neither planners nor economists have successfully mounted that particular tiger.

Certain problems are common to most cities—migration, the cost of services and the maintenance of "minimum standards" (whatever each country may hold them to be), the outmoded structures of governmental machinery, crises in law and order, education and social mobility. In the rich cities their very affluence requires more regulatory techniques, in line with their greater amenities. Higher standards mean more ambitious public planning. Yet never has there been sharper concern

about "alienation," about the individual's inability to influence decisions which affect his daily life. This is fundamentally a political question; and it goes to the heart of the metropolitan crisis.

Recently Simon Jenkins, a British journalist specializing in planning problems, said that London had faced all the problems of the exploding cities of the developing world: faced them and largely overcome them in the last century. "I know," he said, "that when foreigners visit London they are infuriated by the smugness with which Londoners present the city to other people, taking them round all their successes. The fact of the matter is . . . London has managed to solve many of its problems. . . . Two aspects are of interest, the first being the importance of public sanitation policies. . . . The second is the importance of public finance—getting the balance of taxation right between town and country and between different portions of the town.

. . . And linked to this is the importance of the structure of local goverment."

Undoubtedly London has a good record on all three points. Yet recently the Government raised in Pariiament the question of organizing a conference to look into London's urban problems and an urban commission was proposed "to study how stress, poverty, and racial tension in inner city areas should be tackled." These trouble spots do not invalidate Jenkins's optimism. London, carefully regulated within its two-tier structure and thirty-two boroughs, is by most standards remarkably free of friction. Yet the breakdown in essential services is no chimera.

Many of the problems with which city governments must theoretically deal do not come under their sole aegis. In very few is there working machinery to deal with questions that spill over local borders: in New York about three million enter the city each day to work; Tokyo jams in 1.3 million and hopes soon to rival New York. In neither is there a unified regional transit system. In Tokyo the situation is absurd. Commuters struggle into the city via one of nine privately owned railway systems (three belonging to department stores), seven privately owned bus companies, or the single publicly owned subway system, which hires retired wrestlers as "pushers" to ensure maximum utilization at rush hours.

The inner city rarely has adequate powers to deal with pollution, solid waste disposal, or its public housing programs. Tokyo's population has increased since the War from 3.5 million to nearly 12 million. Less than 40 per cent of its most highly developed section has sewerage facilities. And, although Tokyo now builds 120,000 dwelling units a year (double New York's average), the housing shortage is estimated at well over half a million. Whole families are crowded into rooms of forty square feet. The astonishing fact about Tokyo is that it remains an exceptionally law-abiding city in which the major outbursts of violence are from students.

The extent to which modern metropolitan life must be organized in terms of communal goods—sewerage, education, public transport, health service—has politicized the government of cities and diminished the importance of individual goods. The development of the public sector is more overwhelming in the affluent societies, if only because they demand more communally purchased ingredients for the "good life." Because the individual cannot apply to these the same yardsticks of satisfaction and relative cost that he can use for his personal economic choices he increasingly feels alienated from decisions that intimately affect his daily well-being. The "they" of the industrial era were a simple object of hostility, the "bosses." In the technological age the individual feels disquieting uncertainty as to who is taking which of the multiple decisions in the ever-growing public field, and as to the criteria "they" adopt.

The most acute challenge, if the cities are to be humane communities, is to strike a balance between the "human angularities" of the people who live in them and the planned environment; to encourage the private voice within the context of public commitment.

5

David M. Muchnick

Death Warrant for the Cities?

The National Urban Policy

Running against New York has emerged as a Ford administration campaign strategy, symbolizing middle-American contempt for the Eastern Establishment and spendthrift politicians, as well as central cities, blacks, and welfare recipients. The presidential demand for and surveillance of municipal belt-tightening appeal to conservative budget-balancers and corporate borrowers. Federal support for southern and southwestern urbanization suits the Republican "southern strategy" and regional banks. These policies, together, have imposed a heavy share of the burden for the recession, uncertain recovery, and restructuring of American life-styles and expectations on northern and eastern central-city residents and workers. And now they threaten to sever traditional Democratic party loyalties. The new breed of fiscally conservative Democratic governors and mayors, who are dependent on Washington and private banks for financing, have been forced to levy new taxes, cut popular services, and break the municipal labor unions. New York's unions are expected to make up their city's budget shortage by accepting massive layoffs and a wage freeze, by investing their pension funds in risky bond issues, and by renegotiating their pension benefits. In 1976, there may be sufficient disenchantment with *all* politicians for many traditional and young Democrats to stay home in November and deny their party's presidential candidate many habitual votes. Shades of 1968!

Presidential politics are a necessary but insufficient explanation of the city's plight. As a matter of policy, long before Jerry Ford's presidential fate depended on it, the White House decided that America's immediate future no longer resides in her older central cities in the North and the East.

This policy not only reveals the transparency of the Administration's hardening-softening line on New York's fiscal crisis; it also dispels the major anomaly in current political posturing—the presidential golf partner of U.S. industries and multinational corporations campaigning as prairie populist, defending America's working people against the "large investors and big banks" who "bankrolled New York City's policies for so long."

What this policy is, however, has never been "perfectly clear." Law and order, the new federalism, benign neglect and impoundments have been misinterpreted by liberal critics as the absence of domestic vision. Economic and diplomatic crisis-management has seemed to preoccupy Washington. Nor is there a strong personality with whom to identify a coherent program—there is no domestic Kissinger. Instead, responsibility has rested with dispersed and unglamorous operatives, primarily in the Office of Management and Budget (OMB) and the Domestic Council. Many White House outsiders, special interests, congressional staff, and local officials still doubt the existence of a national urban policy. So far, because of this uncertainty and the narrow, partisan explanations of what happened in New York, the opposition has failed to seriously confront the Administration.

Three programs reveal the contours of executive thinking and the new limits of American democracy: community development, housing assistance, and welfare reform.

These three programs, involving upward of $50 billion annually in federal outlays and income tax subsidies, embody a centrally determined, not-so-neglectful national urban policy. This policy limits federal investment in metropolitan social needs, shifts development priorities in favor of growing cities and suburbs (especially in the South and Southwest), and hampers the emergence of a political coalition able to challenge these decisions with alternative national goals. The Administration's stand on New York City's financial catastrophe not only follows this policy but strengthens it.

The Community Development Revenue Sharing program is a keystone of the Administration's national urban policy and new federalism. It was introduced by President Nixon in March 1973 and signed into law by President Ford only 13 days after he assumed office. It provides relatively unrestricted grants for the development of public facilities to states and so-called metropolitan cities—to each central city, each suburban city of more than 50,000 people, and to about 70 urban counties in the country's 243 metropolitan areas. As a result, a city's planning and development process has gained almost complete administrative discretion and nearly total freedom from federal red tape and supervision. Said President Nixon (in a radio message on March 4, 1973), ''The time has come to reject the patronizing notion that federal planners, peering over the point of a pencil in Washington, can guide your lives better than you can.'' Presidential rhetoric is deceptive.

The Office of Management and Budget (OMB) and the Department of Housing and Urban Development (HUD) never surrendered power to dictate the amount and regional allocation of federal investment in local communities. Their determination of the program's $2.3 billion first-year level ignored not only inflation and the advice of the U.S. Conference of Mayors but also a grass-roots survey of over 200 communities that estimated a national need for $5.5 billion in fiscal 1974 alone.

OMB and HUD have shifted federal capital away from the redevelopment of older, eastern and northern industrial central cities in favor of the development of growing, prosperous suburbs and cities, especially in the South and the Southwest.

Excepting New York and Chicago (which, because of their sheer size, will fare better financially than they have in the past), the next 17 biggest central cities in the North and the East eventually will lose an estimated $168 million yearly, compared to their combined average yearly receipts between 1968 and 1972 under previous programs. From a five-year average of $378 million, their funding will be sliced almost in half, to $210 million yearly in fiscal 1980. Philadelphia, Detroit, Baltimore, Washington, D.C., Boston, and Cincinnati will lose over $97 million annually among them. By contrast, Houston, Dallas, Memphis, New Orleans, Phoenix, Jacksonville, Fort Worth, Miami, El Paso, and Birmingham together will gain over $71 million annually. Although ten other large southern and southwestern cities will suffer a 32 percent cut by fiscal 1980, these cities will enjoy a 140 percent increase, and the total grants for these 20 cities will rise to $211 million.

To finish the illustration, Massachusetts' 14 central cities will lose $46 million annually by fiscal 1980, while aid for its suburbs and rural areas will increase by $15 million and $1 million respectively—a net annual statewide loss of $30 million. Alabama's 18 central cities will gain $5.4 million annually, while funding for its suburbs and rural areas will increase by $23 million and $6 million respectively—a net annual statewide increase of $34 million. Nationwide, central cities will lose $276 million annually by 1980, while federal investment in suburbs and rural areas will increase by $757 million and $291 million respectively.[1]

---

[1]Fiscal 1980 estimates use the $3 billion appropriation projected by the U.S. House of Representatives, Committee on Banking and Currency, *Directory of Recipients: Housing and Community Development Act of 1974*, 93rd Congress, 2nd session (Washington, D.C.: Government Printing Office, September 1974).

This regional distribution occurs because all metropolitan cities are "entitled" for the first time to funds as a matter of right. A technical mechanism was needed to provide an automatic basis for dividing the national pie. Population, poverty, and overcrowded housing are three relevant census characteristics of all of these localities and so provide the national data base for the allocation formula. The older central cities dispute the validity of these factors as measures of local needs. They prefer more direct indicators, such as the age or deterioration of an area's physical housing stock or a community's past redevelopment efforts. Local officials of these older central cities argue that the consequences of universal entitlement on the basis of population result in the loss of dollars by cities with declining populations, in the provision of scarce funds to wealthy communities with no poor and no overcrowding, and in the financial, administrative, and political reinforcement of those suburbs that deny residential and occupational opportunities to lower-income workers, poor people, and minorities. Both the Nixon and the Ford administrations have rejected these objections as matters of national development planning, rationalized budget procedure, and local self-determination.

The limit on metropolitan investment and the shift in regional priorities express the fear of a capital shortage and the decision to invest federal money where it will be "profitable" in the future. That is, scarce public capital should subsidize private economic and demographic growth in a mutually supportive way rather than be wasted in decaying centers already abandoned by business and the middle class. As early as 1972, former HUD Secretary Romney warned the annual convention of the nation's Mortgage Bankers Association that "America faces investment decisions more critical—more consequential—than at any previous time in our history. They will have a direct impact on money and credit for housing and community development." In addition to capital for energy and environmental needs and economic expansion, he advised

population migration, despite decreasing population growth, is forcing major new investment in housing, retailing, superhighways, water and waste disposal systems, hospitals, schools and all the rest of the community physical structure—but now in more dispersed geographical areas—a dispersal that raises the per capita cost of facilities.

Among the trends, Romney noted, were not only the apparent stabilization of growth, and possible decline, in the New York, Chicago, and Los Angeles/Long Beach metropolitan areas, but also interregional migrations from north to south, from east to west; from hinterland to coastline; from smaller metropolitan areas to those between 1 million and 2 million —the "dynamic growth centers of the next several decades."

> One thing is clear [he cautioned], these population shifts stimulate and also force major new investment in growing areas—and endanger previous investments in declining areas. ... We must avoid at all costs 100 billion dollar public and private investment mistakes. For we cannot afford gigantic waste in any area. The pressure and demands on our economy in the next decade will not permit such a luxury.

At the national level, universal entitlement according to an objective formula rationalizes previous federal funding practices. It weakens the power of senior congresspeople to influence commitments to particular localities. It automatically provides funds to many cities that for political, ideological, or other reasons stayed away from the earlier grant programs, and it reduces the significance of "grantsmanship" by enterprising municipalities. The Domestic Council argues that none of these factors is reasonably related to a distribution on the basis of need, and that their control is necessary to avoid waste and fiscal irresponsibility. One consequence is the reduction suffered by most northern and eastern central cities.

Another effect is more curious—the increased aid anticipated by New York City under this particular program, from $101 million the first year to $157 million by fiscal year 1978. Previously, the city had been "underfunded" relative to any measure of need because of longstanding congressional and executive hostility to meeting what are thought to be the city's unique problems. New York appears to place unlimited demands on the Treasury, and mid-American congresspeople and executive decision-makers are unwilling to tax their constituents or distort their priorities to pay for the city's troubles. Universal allocation by formula recognizes New York's needs somewhat less arbitrarily and constrains the provincial hostility a bit by providing funds to all localities. The city remains starkly underfunded, however, relative to its own determination of needs—an estimated $240 million for community development in the first year alone. As recent events testify, the antagonism persists whenever the city's needs are made to appear special.

At the metropolitan level, fiscal rationalization has had to be imposed because of the failure of the reform movements for metropolitan government and planning. Metropolitan agencies were to have coordinated community development activities of central cities and suburbs, ending the inflationary pressures of waste, duplication, and unnecessary spending. But traditions of localism proved too strong, and the Administration's fiscal planners had to act. Their technique is straightforward. After OMB determines the national funding level, the community-development allocation formula makes its first apportionment to each census-defined metropolitan area. Only then are the central city and each suburb alloted their shares from the metropolitan pot to use as they see fit. From a federal budget perspective, the simple step of allocating the first sum to the statistical metropolitan area transcends local boundaries and rationalizes the *aggregate* level of spending in each metropolis.

Because the community development program implements a national development policy and rationalizes the fiscal planning process, the details of local administration are essentially irrelevant to Washington. Therefore, they can be delegated to municipalities under the rhetoric of returning power to local communities. As Ford's Deputy OMB Director Paul

O'Neill put it, "[ours is] a national perspective of what the Federal role is, what is happening in the country, what the other levels of government are doing, what the private institutions are doing and where our legislative thrust should be."[2]

Housing is the second element of the national urban policy. In January 1973, the White House unilaterally suspended the country's four subsidized housing programs. The *Washington Post* subsequently revealed government memos indicating the cut-off was for fiscal, not programmatic reasons. "We had to save a half-billion dollars," said Nixon HUD Secretary and Ford OMB Director James Lynn.[3] Concerned about the federal deficit's inflationary consequences, the budget planners slashed the $500 million programs as part of a $10 billion domestic cut in fiscal year 1974, and, as O'Neill later testified, to avoid being locked into a 40-year obligation for over $17 billion.[4]

Nine months later, President Nixon outlined the Administration's thinking on housing—continued support for private homeownership, termination of production subsidies for low- and moderate-income housing, and initiation of housing allowances, starting first with the elderly poor. He proposed an interim subsidized construction program (now known as Section 8) to be terminated on December 31, 1975, after which direct-cash assistance would become the nation's *exclusive* assistance policy. (In the 1974 Housing and Community Development Act, Congress refused to ratify the cessation, insisting first on a feasibility report on allowances *early in 1976*. The "interim" program is in effect, and local communities fear to protest the switch to allow-

[2]Quoted in John Herbers, "The Other Presidency," *New York Times Magazine*, March 3, 1974, p. 36.
[3]Susanna McBee, "Subsidized Housing Frozen Before Justification by H.U.D.," *Washington Post*, Sunday, December 3, 1973, p. 1.
[4]U.S. Senate, Committee on Government Operations, *Hearings on the Nomination of Paul O'Neill*, November 20, 1974, p. 66.

ances too strongly lest their applications for subsidies be adversely affected.)

The support for homeownership follows the historic thrust of U.S. housing policy—accounting for about $10.2 billion of the almost $15.3 billion in direct expenditures and tax revenues foregone by the federal government for housing in 1972—but now it takes on an additional dimension. This policy will underwrite the residential and industrial development of the rapidly urbanizing South and Southwest. In the 70s, 17 southern and southwestern cities are projected to grow by more than a third, and most smaller southern cities by nearly 20 percent. (Only four northern and eastern metropolitan areas are expected to increase by a third).[5] In 1972, two out of every three new private homes in the country were built in the South and West, and the South and Southwest accounted for more than 50 percent of all federally insured mortgages on new dwellings. The southern and southwestern real estate industry's contribution to the GNP reached more than $41.6 billion in 1971, providing nearly 2 million jobs in the nonagricultural sector.[6]

In the North and the East, this policy will continue to provide subsidies for suburban homeowners and secure transfers of ownership in the existing stock of private homes. More than nine out of ten federally insured mortgages in the northeast in 1972 covered such transactions, compared to 75 percent nationally. In that year, New England, New York, New Jersey, and Pennsylvania accounted for only 5 percent of the FHA-insured new homes. Only on the fringes of metropolitan areas are new federally insured units likely to be built. Elsewhere in the metropolis, the higher costs of land, construction, and financing have pushed prices of new single-family dwellings to the limits of federal insurance

ceilings, and, more important, beyond the financial reach of more than four out of five American families.

Consequently, access to established communities will be crucial, and competition for reasonably priced housing in better neighborhoods should intensify. Because of higher costs, pressures for new apartment complexes and lower-quality homes on less land should continue. Resistance can be expected not only from homeowners in wealthy suburbs but also from moderate-income groups who, feeling trapped in their present neighborhoods, will seek to protect themselves from encroachment by lower-class and minority people.

In its shift to housing allowances, the Administration provides support for the strategy of residential exclusion. The termination of production subsidies eliminates the most direct method for supplying low- and moderate-income housing in the better parts of the metropolis. It also circumvents the legal requirements that federally subsidized developments be located on sites fostering integration. No longer should residents of exclusively white or wealthy communities have to fear federal housing programs—notwithstanding HUD claims that allowances will achieve its "first" urban policy goal, "a fairer and more even distribution across the metropolitan area of the central city's basic social and economic problem ... the artificial concentrations in the city's core of low-income populations."[7]

Allowances represent a significant technical innovation. Instead of subsidizing new production, Washington would add to its system of "invisible" supports for the residential market an income supplement for low-income elderly households, enabling them to pay the costs demanded by the private sector. The change appeals to conservatives because, in the words of HUD Deputy Assistant Secretary William Lilley, III,

We have accepted Banfield's counsel to let nature take its course. We have accepted the ulti-

---

[5]Joint Center for Urban Studies of the Massachusetts Institute of Technology and Harvard University, *America's Housing Needs: 1970 to 1980*, pp. 3–6 ff. and Exhibit 3–1.

[6]Norman B. Ture, Inc., *Real Estate in the U.S. Economy*, report for the National Realty Committee, Inc., tables XVII, XX, XXV, XXVIII.

[7]William Lilley III, H.U.D. Deputy Assistant Secretary for Policy Development, "Toward a Rational Housing Policy," speech delivered at the 1973 Congress of Cities, San Juan, Puerto Rico, December 3, 1973.

mate futility of state-administered allocation decisions ... in favor of a strategy that emphasizes *free choice* and promises to achieve the goal of a decent home in a suitable living environment for all, not by crashing through the barriers that stand in the way but by subverting them through the *essentially peaceful* bargaining of the market-place.[8]

This technique receives support from many housing experts who stress the need for the maintenance of existing housing—not for new construction—in older cities with decreasing population and increasing abandonment.

The Administration's version most likely will curtail its residential investment in declining areas, maintain residential segregation, and provide a strategic link with national welfare reform. For fiscal reasons, HUD and OMB apparently are planning a low-cost program that will provide a small allowance payment to a limited class of eligibles, the elderly poor. The Nixon administration criticized the budgetary impact of the production subsidy programs whose annual costs reached slightly over $2 billion in 1973. By contrast, housing experts estimate costs between $5 and $10 billion for alternative allowance programs covering all families with incomes below $5,000, $7,000, or $10,000. Restricting the plan to the elderly with incomes below $7,500 (not just the elderly poor) would still require an estimated $3.7 billion to $4.8 billion.[9]

Since the White House has little enthusiasm for spending a lot of money, and since most of the country does not need the deep subsidies that New York and a few other big cities do, the eventual program is unlikely to provide payments high enough to increase the supply of low- and moderate-income housing in high-cost metropolitan areas. Rehabilitation and better maintenance are also unlikely because individual allowance recipients will have little bargaining power, especially in tight rental markets. Rather, there will be more dollars chasing existing low-rent units and, therefore, an increase in rents. Whether this rise will at least stem abandonment in the short term is problematic; but collective pressures for tenants' unions, rent control, code enforcement, building maintenance, and the legalization of rent strikes seem necessary to do much more.

The priority on the elderly poor will promote neither residential improvements nor mobility. The elderly poor are probably the least mobile group in the metropolis for numerous reasons unaffected by rent supplements. Many of them live in fear or passivity and may be unable to bargain with their landlords for repairs. Or, in this inflationary period, they may be forced to neglect their desires for home improvements and have to use their increased buying power for food and other essentials. A substantial increase in the number of eligibles and the amount of payments is unlikely. Not only the budget but politics too would work against it.

Were the allowance program extended for all the poor, opposition would come from the approximately 11 million families, above the poverty line but below the income level necessary to purchase a new home, who would be omitted from the Administration's housing policy. If the extension were large enough to permit all the poor residential mobility, the impact would fall on this group, especially those somewhat above the allowance eligibility level, e.g., with incomes between $5,000 and $10,000.[10] Since the allowance recipients could only afford their housing, since the competition would raise costs, and since they have lost the chance for homeownership to inflation, they will be forced to protect their homes from potential competition by ''mobile'' allowance recipients. One tack would be to limit the program. The Administration would be sensitive to this pressure—judging from then HUD

[8]*Ibid.*, (italics in original).

[9]See, e.g., General Accounting Office, *Observations on Housing Allowances and the Experimental Allowances Program* (Document B-171630, March 28, 1974, Washington, D.C.); Henry Aaron, *Shelter and Subsidies* (Washington, D.C.: Brookings Institute, 1972), pp. 168–70.

[10]See Ira Lowry, ''Housing Assistance for Low-Income Families: A Fresh Approach,'' in U.S. House of Representatives, Committee on Banking and Currency, *Papers Submitted to Subcommittee on Housing Panels on Housing Production, Housing Demand, and Developing a Suitable Living Environment*, 92nd Congress, First session (Washington, D.C.: Government Printing Office, 1971).

Secretary (now OMB Director) Lynn's 1974 refusal to reactivate the subsidized home-ownership program because middle-income groups would not look favorably on subsidies to modest-income homebuyers when they could not get mortgage money and housing.[11]

Should the political and budgetary constraints fail, there could be a final irony—further metropolitan segregation. Allowances would enable many white recipients to flee the stable, integrated central city neighborhoods in which they are now "trapped" by low incomes. But these allowances would not necessarily foster black migration into white communities. Providing blacks with equal residential purchasing power is itself insufficient to achieve integration.[12] For allowances to do so would require the uncustomarily strict enforcement of open housing laws; and this, as a matter of state and local politics, is improbable.

Since allowances provide neither residential investment nor mobility, what do they offer the elderly poor? The answer is income maintenance. In New York, for example, only 6 percent of the city's more than 2 million rental units are occupied by potential allowance recipients, and therefore the impact on the housing stock would be marginal. But, in human terms, 132,000 elderly poor households—more than a third of the city's impoverished renters—would receive aid. According to economist George Sternlieb, the city's elderly have "largely been dependent upon the protection of the old rent control law and their relative immobility to keep down housing costs."[13] Yet, in 1970, more than two out of every five of the city's elderly paid over 25 percent of their incomes for rent; fewer than three out of ten paid less than 20 percent. Therefore, the elderly poor will probably not move even with allowances, and the payments

should provide some relief for those most oppressed by rising housing costs. Nor is this scenario unique to cities with rent control. In most areas, continued occupancy of their present dwellings may be the elderly poor's best protection against inflation. Adding the social reasons for the elderly's stability suggests that income maintenance will be the human contribution of housing allowances.

It is not surprising, therefore, that the allowance strategy provides an important link to national income maintenance; the coordination of these programs would lessen objections to welfare reform. Conservatives opposed the Nixon-Moynihan Family Assistance Plan (FAP), warning that

> a uniform minimum national income guarantee that might do relatively minor harm in California or the northeast would be so high compared with prevailing incomes in the deep south as to tempt a third or more of the population to quit their jobs and climb aboard the welfare wagon. ... A uniform minimum welfare handout, in a nation with divergencies of up to 138 percent in median family incomes among the states, would create far more serious problems than any it might solve.[14]

One suggested compromise was a federal minimum that took into account regional variations in the cost of living. Housing allowances could effect this compromise because, on a regional basis, the cost of housing varies most of all of life's necessities and provides an index for differential payments. Tying a variable housing allowance to a relatively low national minimum income could provide the necessary device for conciliation.

Overcoming southern conservative opposition is critical since it is the legacy of the "old," rural, agricultural South. National income maintenance, by contrast, represents the future of the "new," urban, industrial South and Southwest. The federal government and national corporations now have made the decision in favor of urban industrialism and its ancillary investments in human resources and

---

[11] *Housing Affairs Letter*, May 17, 1974, p. 2.

[12] See, e.g., U.S. Commission on Civil Rights, *Homeownership for Lower Income Families* (Washington: Government Printing Office, 1971).

[13] George Sternlieb, *Housing and People in New York City* (City of New York Housing and Development Administration, Department of Rent and Housing Maintenance, January, 1973), p. 209–10.

[14] Henry Hazlitt, "Compounding the Welfare Mess," *National Review*, February 24, 1970, p. 205.

lessen the pulling power of higher urban wages by subsidizing life in more "comfortable" rural areas. (Consequently, its underwriting of rural wages would stabilize the agricultural labor force for agribusiness.) On the other hand, these rural male migrants would probably lack the qualifications to obtain better jobs since they are working at the peak of their capabilities. Their alternative would be welfare. Without the proposed reforms, this could require a man to desert his family and lead, according to the Moynihan perspective, to family breakdown and the ancillary social problems that would plague the new cities.

In the North and East, the federal assumption of state welfare costs up to the national payment level would relieve some pressure from state and local treasuries. Also, it is argued, the migration of poor people from regions with archaic welfare systems might abate, and reverse migration might even begin. Poor whites and blacks might leave the slums and ghettos of the industrial cities for the more pleasant environment, albeit lesser benefits, of southern and southwestern states. This argument, however, is probably rhetoric. Its premise—that the poor migrate in search of welfare—is disputed as a "welfare myth."

Nonetheless, for poor people in the North and the East the reforms are of dubious benefit since state welfare levels usually exceed the proposed federal standard; indeed, many may even have to bear the cost of developing a new system. According to an Institute for Research on Poverty comment on a HEW study paper,

> The Administration is not likely to propose, nor is Congress likely to pass, a program that leaves no beneficiary less well off. What is more likely is that a new universal program would provide more generous benefits to many of the poor, particularly the working poor, than they are now receiving, but less generous benefits than they are now receiving to other poor groups, particularly aid to families with dependent children beneficiaries in the high-benefit states.[19]

A housing allowance tied to the high living costs in these areas would be a useful supplement to limit the political opposition and human suffering induced by an inadequate income maintenance plan.

In sum, reflecting fears of inflation and a capital shortage, the national urban policy underinvests in the country's metropolitan development and redirects its limited investment priorities in favor of suburban, southern, and southwestern growth. The President's position on New York's financial dilemma extends this policy.

New York's fiscal crisis has given the White House the opportunity to force a reduction in the spending and capital investment of state and local governments and a curtailment of the "diseased" borrowing practices that sent the nationwide state and local debt over $200 billion in 1975 and threaten to drain off scarce capital in the near future. The President's preference for bankruptcy and a subsequent emergency loan to the city—the "Drop Dead" message to New York and "every other city that follows the tragic example of our largest city"—left the municipal bond market uptight, uncertain, and closed to all but the most prosperous or fiscally conservative cities. Given the federally reinforced strictures on the public fisc, higher interest rates, and marketing difficulties, most cities face hard decisions on critical services and projects; northern and eastern central cities with declining populations and economies, the hardest.

In New York, according to the President, the Administration's "firm" position hastened the state and city action that default and bankruptcy would otherwise have necessitated: raising additional revenues from taxes and pension-fund loans, restructuring the city's short-term debt, refinancing the city's pension plans, and cutting hundreds of millions more from state and city budgets. After these "concrete actions" were taken, the President softened only on the timing of federal aid, offering $2.3 billion in short-term, seasonal loans under "stringent conditions" and Treasury Secretary Simon's continuing surveillance in order to

[19]I. Garfinkel, "Toward an Effective Income Support System: An Overview Paper," in Barth, *et al.*, *Toward an Effective Income Support System*: *Problems*, *Prospects and Choices*, H. E. W. staff paper (Madison: Institute for Research on Poverty, 1974), p. 162.

avert default and maintain essential services during the next two-and-a-half years. The basic objectives had been accomplished.

The foundations of the national urban policy and the White House's tightfistedness on New York rest not on a particular presidential incumbency but on an increasingly unquestioned, neoconservative vision of America's future and the role its leaders should play in planning the nation's future. Amid the growing concern about a "debt economy" and a capital shortage, Treasury Secretary Simon has emerged, according to *Business Week*, as "Washington's No. 1 Capital Gap Crusader," and the capital demands of private economic expansion, independent energy production, and military modernization have downgraded the priority on metropolitan development and social needs. Moreover, within the new limits on metropolitan investment, the Administrations' support for urban, industrial growth in the South and Southwest has wide backing among economists, corporate interests, Cabinet departments, and the Presidential Commission on Population Growth. Arguably, it will alleviate the pressures of migration on northern ghettos, provide urban and rural southerners with opportunities for a decent income in a pleasant environment, and avoid the uncontrolled and wasteful growth characteristic of the northern metropolis. (Whether it can be achieved is another question.) Therefore, given the dictates of national economic, political, and social realities, the declining northern and eastern central cities must accept their fate, reduce their standards of living, lower their "swollen expectations"—as *Time* labeled New York's—and live within their newly "shrunken means." They are not to question the national and international forces that have shrunk their means; they are but to do *and* die.

Underlying this new urban realism, furthermore, is a particular conception of the past decade's urban crisis. Ignoring the widening inequalities between central city and suburban life, the Nixon and Ford administrations declared the 1960s urban crisis over because the explosive features of that period had disap-

peared. The perspective is Edward Banfield's.[20]

Most of the "problems" that are generally supposed to constitute "the urban crisis" could not conceivably lead to disaster [Banfield wrote in 1968]. They are—some of them—important in the sense that a bad cold is important, but they are not serious in the sense a cancer is serious. They have to do with comfort, convenience, amenity and business advantage, all of which are important, but they do not affect either the essential welfare of individuals or what may be called the good health of the society. ... One problem that is both serious and unique to the large cities is the existence of huge enclosures of people (many, but not all of them, Negro) of low skill, low income, and low status. ... [T]he existence of huge enclaves of people who are in some degree alienated from it constitutes a kind of hazard not only to the present peace and safety but also to the long-run health of the society. ... Unlike those who live on farms and in small towns, disaffected people who live in huge enclaves may develop a collective consciousness and sense of identity. ... In the shortrun, however, they represent a threat to peace and order. ... This political danger in the presence of great concentrations of people who feel little attachment to the society has long been regarded by some as *the* serious problems of the cities—the one problem that might conceivably produce a disaster that would destroy the quality of the society.[21]

If it contains this political danger, the national urban policy need not pay the price for *all* cities to be comfortable, convenient, amenable, and economically advantageous. If it arrests the cancer, it need not treat the fatal complications of pneumonia.

Finally, the national urban policy enacts the administrative structure that enables the White House to fulfill its world role and frees the president for the personal triumphs of international diplomacy. As Melvin Laird and Daniel Patrick Moynihan once argued,

---

[20] In his 1973 speech, Lilley named Banfield, Moynihan, and Jay Forrester as setting the "intellectual framework which, necessarily, must define the present discussion of future policy options."

[21] E. Banfield, *The Unheavenly City* (1968), pp. 6; 12–13.

The biggest problem of running the nation from Washington is that the real business of Washington in our age is pretty much to run the world. An American national government in this age will always give priority to foreign affairs. A system has to be developed, therefore, under which domestic programs go forward regardless of what international crisis is preoccupying Washington at the moment.[22]

Within the budget priorities of this global mission, new federalism's techniques of revenue sharing and income supplements delegate administrative discretion and market choices to state and local governments and individuals, freeing the federal executive from the time, cost, and political conflicts of domestic details. They do not resolve the social, economic, and political conflicts of metropolitan development; but they seek to insulate Washington from direct involvement. Following new federalism's decentralist rationale, therefore, President Ford and Secretary Simon repeatedly labeled New York's and any city's financial distress a local responsibility, avoiding any direct national accountability until, interestingly enough, a short time after West European leaders expressed their fears of the international effects of default.

Whether or not new federalism's administrative delegation will revive democratic participation in local development conflicts remains to be seen in most cities. But its response to the fiscal crisis has hastened the death of political democracy in New York, and, nationwide, it has not increased the public's right to participate in national decision-making. For, cloaked in the ideology of restoring power to local communities and freedom of choice to individuals, new federalism rationalizes and legitimizes the centralized political power and economic planning that produced the national urban policy and the fiscal quarantine on New York City. New federalism is Tenth Amendment federalism turned upside down: all effective power not specifically delegated to states and localities is reserved by Washington.

<hr>

[22]M. Laird, "The Case for Revenue Sharing," in Laird, *Republican Papers*, pp. 63, 73; quoted in D. P. Moynihan, *The Politics of a Guaranteed Income*, p. 207.

What then is necessary for change? Once upon a time, municipal default and bankruptcy appeared to be the ultimate mayoral weapon to force Washington to provide more aid to the cities, assuming major banks and private investors pressed for protection of their holdings. But the White House's reaction to New York indicates otherwise, using default to extend the national urban policy. As vital as its predefault loans and the liberals' predefault loan guarantees are for the uninterrupted provision of essential services and the ongoing administration of New York city and state governments, their enactment would not change it. Even the loan guarantees were conditioned on state tax increases, local budget cuts, restructuring of the city's debt, and renegotiation of municipal employees' wages and pensions—all under the monitoring of a nonelected board of federal officials. No proposal challenged federal disinvestment from the central cities. No proposal would soothe the municipal bond market sufficiently to empower political democracy in New York and other troubled cities to challenge the national political and economic forces of decline.

Central city riots may break out again, but, as with bankruptcy, the White House can accommodate them. Rioting would not only generate coercive measures but could also push enactment of national income maintenance (albeit after the election). Nevertheless, although nationalization of welfare would anger old-line political conservatives and ease an estimated $700 million annual burden on New York City, it is a part and not a reversal of the national urban policy. Following the Administration's view of the urban cancer, national income maintenance is more than humanitarian. Its political objective is civil order in the cities. Not only would it defuse the rural poor's migration to the hard-pressed cities; it also maintains a monetary pacifier for the "critical mass" of poor people already there. It would directly attack the locus and political danger of the urban cancer—the hearts and minds of the city poor.

At a minimum, all Americans, regardless of

race, class, region, urban, suburban, or rural residence, share a common interest in a stronger federal investment in the quality of domestic social life, public and private. To realize this requires a united national polity able to press Washington for the curtailment of unnecessary military spending, an end to favoritism for irresponsible private capital accumulation, and the elimination of budget ceilings dictated by the economy's inflationary potential and the government's inequitable tax structure rather than by human needs and public choices.

Nonetheless, the national urban policy divides the country. It not only channels capital into the South and Southwest where recently attained urban affluence and lingering conservatism make demand for reform least likely, but Washington's paramount concern for strong armed forces supports the South's military heritage and its economy's continuing reliance on defense installations. It must seem too good to be true that all this can be accomplished under a new governmental structure that appears consistent with states' rights and eliminates the Great Society's links between Washington and local black, poor, and liberal activists.

In northern and eastern states, this policy reinforces metropolitan segregation and political divisions. It accepts racial and economic inequalities as natural, inevitable, and just, and it gives local governments, with whose boundaries these differences often coincide, a principal role in their defense. It provides financial support, administrative discretion, and political legitimacy to present municipal structure and practice, enabling many localities to continue their denials of equal residential, educational, and occupational opportunities by invoking the heretofore neutral value of localism. In the process, the American democratic ideal of an integrated national community of equally participant individuals is abandoned.

Struggling among themselves to protect their communities, to obtain better homes, or to slice meager local and household pies, middle-class, working-class, and poor families continue to define each other as enemies. Suburbanites fear integrationists. Middle- and working-class taxpayers fear the poor's economic and residential threat. The poor feel the others as the albatross upon their necks. And the President's condemnation of New York's local politicans as solely responsible for the city's fiscal catastrophe polarizes these suspicions and divides communities from one another. Thus the power of a potential domestic coalition is turned inward upon itself.

The national urban policy not only sets priorities for urban development and *dis*development; it also restricts unified, effective public participation in national choice-making. Ironically, perhaps, two conservative Republican presidents have brought the United States to the point where national planning is an emergent institutional reality. Their concern for world affairs is intimately connected with the structure of domestic planning. Regardless of its local consequences, new federalism has turned American democracy into a national technocracy free to plan and manage its domestic and foreign objectives from a global perspective without effective popular participation. Or—to draw on President Nixon's characterization of the American people as children in need of a strong father—under the new federalism, Washington's technocratic patriarch retains the power over critical national choices and leaves America's children to play, more or less democratically, with an allowance of local toys. If the patriarch decides that any city has overspent its allowance, its spanking will be severe, its democratic privileges will be suspended and its allowance will be "seasonally administered" and terminable at will. As Secretary Simon told the Senate Banking Committee, he should be put in charge of any New York aid "to determine that the city was irrevocably and unalterably on the path to fiscal responsibility. Such aid should be so punitive in its terms and so painful that no other city not facing absolute disaster would think of applying for help."

6

The Decline
of Urban Services:
Who Needs People?

by Carol A. Brown, Ph.D.

Cities are places where people live and work. They are massive concentrations of population which resulted from industrialization and which concentrated economic activities in factories, stores, and offices. The particular form of industrialization reflected in American cities is capitalism. Capitalism depends on profit, and decisions of these businesses are based on expectations of enhancing profit-making. In the abstract sense, then, people in the capitalist system may be seen as a means of making profits. Concentrations of people in cities are a means to an end—for if business and industry are to make profits, they need workers and consumers. They also need people to maintain and reproduce the workers and consumers if they are going to continue creating profits. In Marxist terms, the reproduction of capital requires the reproduction of labor. From this political economy point of view, the costs of wages, taxes, city services, and even those vaguely defined phenomena, "social problems," are part of the necessary costs of doing business.

The people who live in cities do not see themselves as "costs" but as "benefits." For people do not consider themselves to be a means to an end, but to be an end in themselves. To the average middle- and working-class Americans, cities are places to live in, to make their lives better. One thing that improves people's lives is jobs that give them the wages to buy goods and services; another is city services, including housing, parks, playgrounds, theatres, and stores, as well as the traditional services such as police, fire, sanitation, education, and public health services. These public services are part of the high standard of living that Americans boast of and desire. If cities fail to make people's lives better, the people may move, they may rebel, or they may just suffer. Each of these responses to the "urban crisis" has been evident in recent history.

Today urban public services are being cut back drastically from the high point of the 1960s, which itself was inadequate. To understand why urban services have borne the brunt of the accountants' knives we have to examine more fully the role of services in urban life.

Past and Present

Extensive public services are a twentieth-century phenomenon associated with welfare capitalism. Under the more overtly exploitative individualized capitalism of the nineteenth century, employers provided wages and the rest was up to the family. "The family" in this case really meant "the woman," who out of her husband's wage was expected to provide food, children, health care, sanitation, education, happiness, etc. Unpaid except for a share of her husband's earnings, her job was to maintain and reproduce the labor force that in a real sense, enabled capitalism to make profits.* These aspects of women's work has been the most altered by the development of urban services.

As cities increased in size and density and industry required better trained and more disciplined workers, the family was not able to provide the quantity and quality of production services required. It became cheaper and more efficient to provide these services in an organized structure either through the auspices of the city government or in nonprofit organizations. The savings due to specialization of labor and capital intensity are great, and the control of both the workers and the products becomes more effective than when each family provides services for itself. The maintenance and reproduction of the labor force moved out of the home and into the public domain, and became more subjected to public scrutiny and control.

Some services are provided out of tax funds, some are provided by private businesses at a profit. For instance, we do not think of restaurants and supermarkets as public services, but to generations of women who lived out the cliché "slaving over a hot kitchen stove," this development was an enormous improvement in their standard of living.

The sex segregation of work typical of the family has been carried over to the public domain. Even as in

---

* Not all family work was women's work. To this day men are expected to protect the family and take out the garbage— the same police, fire, and sanitation work that men do on a city-wide level.

the family, most of this work is done by women. The only highly male groups are police, fire, sanitation, and management. Hospitals, schools, welfare departments, children's services, even restaurants and department stores are all staffed with women. The women are doing at low pay essentially the same work they would have done at home without pay. Women work at low pay not out of preference, but because these are the jobs available. For many women, working for wages providing public services is a considerable improvement over working without pay to provide private services.

The creation of public services does not always take place at the initiative of city officials. Concentrations of people in a city means a concentration of "people-power." This "people-power" has enabled the lower and middle-income public to demand and obtain a higher standard of living through political organization, and direct action such as strikes and street agitation. The power of people has been such that urban dwellers have been able to increase the quantity of resources, money, and services going to them rather than to the private corporations or the privately wealthy. The hostility to "cities" that is voiced both by the elite and by rural dwellers is often envy and resentment by both ends of the sociopolitical spectrum "against the middle."

City workers have formed powerful trade unions (sometimes called "benevolent societies" where unionism is outlawed) which have become successful on behalf of their membership and often on behalf of the city as a whole.* Although there have been highly publicized examples of city employees and the public at odds—for example, school board control and police review boards—service workers' unions on the whole favor public demands for more services, as such increases will provide more jobs for their members. In many cities unions have raised the wages of service workers to as high as, and sometimes higher than the wages of production workers in private industry. Strong unions have always been seen as a threat to employers, who prefer full power over workers, especially the power to set wage rates. As we shall see, the current urban crisis has been used to decrease the power of municipal unions.

Crisis

The current crisis of the cities can be seen as a conflict between the citizens of the city and the economic system. The demand being heard from the more affluent beneficiaries of the capitalist system is that city budgets must be cut because services are too expensive; for to the profit-making economy such services are only a means to an end. Thus the purpose of spending money on services is to produce workers who will produce profits.* For if workers are too expensive (that is, they are receiving too many goods and services), profits are

reduced. Moreover if large sums of money are expended to sustain people who are not even workers, there will be no profits at all.

To the citizens of the cities however, these services are part of their standard of living. They expect these services, and do not want to see their standard of living decline.

In the current recession, capitalism no longer needs to spend money on people because it already has more people than it needs. Neither the quantity nor quality of potential workers being maintained is needed, for the unemployment rate is high. There are not enough jobs, nationwide, for the workers there are, while the labor force, augmented by an influx of women and minorities, continues to grow. Thus, many of the services that are oriented to enabling workers to maintain their jobs, such as day-care centers for working mothers, are dispensable.

The quality of workers is both too high and too low. Many young people have received college or graduate school education and now expect the jobs and wages commensurate with their status. But many employers prefer lower status, less costly workers. A solution to this dilemma is to decrease public support of schools and colleges so that potential workers will not gain such high status.

The other end of the status ladder is filled with the welfare population. Over the past century the capitalist system has been willing to maintain a welfare population so as to maintain and reproduce a set of low-skilled and low-wage workers who are marginally or only occassionally employed. As technology takes over, this *lumpenproletariat* is no longer needed, and those who see welfare as a waste of money are carrying the day.

There is also the question of salaries to the people delivering the services. In only some cases is there opposition to the service itself—for example, the belief that day-care centers are destroying the family or that welfare encourages laziness. In most cases the objection is not to the service but to the cost, and most of the cost of city services is in the salaries of the municipal workers. Various solutions are proposed: lower the wages of everyone; fire part of the work force; or break the power that municipal unions have to defend the standard of living of their members. Many cities have fired some of their workers and hired them back at lower wages on federal Comprehensive Employment Training Act [CETA] funds. Others simply fire the workers, impose wage freezes, or offer payless paydays.

Unions, of course, fight such plans, and city administrations oppose the unions; however, city administrations are themselves often on the receiving end of pressure from higher up. Some of the conflict in New York City has been the demand of the banks and federal officials that union power be destroyed, partly because service workers are making too much money in the eyes of the powerful elites, and also because any well-

---

* Municipal unions have been able to organize successfully for the same reasons production unions have been able to organize successfully—a large concentration of workers sharing the same employer and the same conditions of labor, under circumstances of easy communication.

---

* Piven and Cloward point out with respect to welfare, in particular, historically this service has been provided to keep the poor from disrupting the system and has been withdrawn to discipline the labor force into working harder.

organized public is a threat to established economic power. For those who gain power can demand a larger share of the pie, and capitalism prefers cheaper labor that does not talk back. Although the unions ostensibly are fighting their employer, City Hall, in the current crisis the indirect relation of municipal unions to the private business community has become more clear as banks and unions publicly confront each other. The New York City municipal unions held one of their largest demonstrations not in front of City Hall but in front of the banks' headquarters.

Conflict

On the political scene then, the result is a continuing conflict between the political powers and the economic powers. Since the only power people have is the political system, people pressure their representatives to keep services high. This pressure has been applied through demonstrations, labor walkouts, letter-writing, and even bomb threats. The elected and appointed city officials are the focus of such pressure, since these officials are beholden to local citizens.

However, cities do not have control over their economies. The economy of a city is controlled by private enterprise. For the power of capitalism is economic, and in the current crisis, the role of economic institutions is becoming more obvious. Banks and bondholders are, for the first time, seen as prime actors on the public urban stage. Often the particular crisis is precipitated by a bond sale or a bank warning. Representatives of major corporations in a given city frequently become members of formal or informal committees to advise or decide on urban futures. Many cities have the equivalent of New York's Emergency Finance Control Board and Municipal Assistance Corporation (Big Mac); both are made up of business interests.

Lack of local control can also be seen in the political struggles between city, state, and federal governments. Local politicians need the residents' votes, and often are reluctant to hurt their population by cutting services. State and national politicians are less dependent on such local support and, despite campaign reform laws, are still dependent for their political futures on corporate and business interests. State and federal decisions to refuse to help the cities, or to invoke a high price for cooperation, can be seen as the attempt of powerful national groups to bring the local people back into line.

When cities attempt to fight back directly, by asserting control over their economy, the city's dependence on capitalism becomes more apparent. Capital locates where it can make the best profit, and if permanent urban dwellers have become too powerful and therefore too prosperous, capital is free to flow to areas where people have less power and labor is cheaper. As corporations move out, the people who work for them may move or are abandoned. Abandonment is more likely, and the threat to move is a powerful lever that corporations hold over the cities they live in. Since we are a capitalist system, the capitalists ultimately have the power to control events, and the people's representa-

tives will often back down from their support of business taxes, pollution controls, etc., rather than lose the companies on which the city's economy depends.

Over the past quarter century corporations have often moved from the urban north to the rural south; multinational corporations have moved many factories to the Third World where wages may be a tenth of American wages (the standard of living is also a tenth and services are almost nonexistent). A third move to obtain less powerful workers who have no choice but to accept low wages is to the suburbs, where supposedly privileged suburban women lack needed employment. Many urban corporations have moved to the suburbs of cities in order to take advantage of this cheap labor.

Many northern city dwellers have attempted to maintain their standard of living by moving out of the big cities, where problems are apparent, to the suburbs or to southern cities that appear to have fewer problems. The movers tend to be affluent citizens who do not need public services and can afford private services. However, as they have attempted to escape these problems they have found that the problems move with them —higher school taxes, air pollution, racial tensions, and a higher welfare bill are only a few of the costs that the population exodus to the suburbs or the south brings with it.*

Effects

As services get cut, the standard of living goes down. The entire city suffers from the loss of some of the services, such as parks, clean streets, safe sidewalks. Some of the losses, such as public summer concerts, museums, and libraries, may affect the middle and upper income groups more than the poor. But generally, removal of services affects the poor most. Fire protection is an example: Although everyone has less fire protection, it is the poorer people's housing that is oldest, most dry, most poorly wired, and most likely to burn. Richer people do not need as much protection and therefore do not suffer as much from its removal.

Poorer people are more dependent on publicly provided services, for the poorer, dependent population suffers the brunt of the cuts—welfare mothers, the chronically ill, and low-wage working women needing day care for their children are examples. The more affluent can buy services in the open market when public services are withdrawn, or have depended all along on bought services and do not feel the loss. High-wage families often use private babysitters instead of day-care centers, or send their chronically ill parents to private nursing homes.

Women tend to suffer the consequences of loss of services more than men, and many of the publicly provided services directly affect women's work. Child care services relieve the mother of child care labor; hospitals and nursing homes relieve women of nursing labor; police protection enables women to have the same

---

* Ironically, as people move away, the older areas get better. The northeastern cities now have lower crime rates than the southwestern cities. New England, the region of earliest urbanization and industrialization, is becoming a winter and summer vacation area.

freedom from attack that men enjoy. Better sanitation means less sickness in the family. Prepared foods and clean air mean less housework. As each such service is withdrawn, the burden for women increases. Minority women, having on the whole less money and security than white women, are more likely to bear the greater burden.

The whole city suffers from having a less affluent population and an increased welfare burden. Particular people, especially minorities, suffer from losing the jobs they previously held. First, the "essential" services of police, fire, and sanitation, which tend to be white male's work, are less often cut than the "nonessential" human services which employ large numbers of women and/or minority workers. Second, within each service area women and minorities tend to be the last hired and therefore the first fired, despite attempts to balance out seniority with affirmative action.*

Since these workers no longer have money; they can no longer support themselves and often they and their families must apply for welfare. The recession has virtually wiped out the relative gains made by minority families in the more prosperous Sixties, and in particular female-headed families have been hurt.

As women lose their jobs in disproportionate numbers, they lose the economic power they have fought for over recent years. If men keep jobs and women lose them, the male sex as a whole ends up with more economic power than the female sex as a whole; within marriages, unemployed wives become more dependent on the economic power of their employed husbands. When married men lose jobs, the effect is often a breakup of the family, leaving the women with all the responsibility and no money. Cases of men brutalizing women and children in frustration, as well as child abuse by mothers, tend to rise in times of high unemployment.

The loss of jobs and services interact to produce a double loss. For example, if schools go on shorter schedules and after-school services are abolished, teachers and school aides lose their jobs and mothers lose the child-care services. Many mothers who have jobs providing services for other people now have to stop working in order to take care of their own children, and other people no longer have the services provided by these mothers. Because the teachers, school aides, and mothers no longer have jobs, they can no longer afford to buy or subsidize other services, which may lead to other service workers losing both jobs and services. Thus the standard of living declines.

If services are not provided, families either must do without them or must provide them within the family. It is usually the wife/mother who has to provide them without pay. It is much harder work for one person to try to do everything than for a large organization to

work with a division of labor and a fair amount of capital equipment. So the married mother has to work harder, for no pay yet with greater dependence on her husband, who in turn may be working harder for less on his job. The husbandless mother who could be self-supporting, with the assistance of public and private services, now may work harder in return only for a welfare check. The families have less money and fewer, less efficient services.

Conclusion

Cities are centers of profit-making in a capitalist economy. People concentrate in cities in order to obtain jobs on which they are dependent for survival. Although to the population, public services are part of a decent standard of living, to capitalistic enterprises these services are a means to an end—the maintenance and reproduction of the labor force for the purpose of producing profits. However, the concentration of people-power in cities has enabled the population to obtain many services and has enabled service workers to obtain decent paying jobs, thus raising the urban standard of living. Women and minorities have benefitted most from this development.

The desire of the affluent in the recession of the late 1970s to cut services and destroy the organized power of municipal unions has been an attempt to cut the costs of labor and to reestablish the power of capitalism. The groups that always suffered the most under capitalism—minorities and women—are now bearing the brunt of the service cuts.

The power of capitalism to shape the nation is seen in the threats, by bondholding banks to create bankruptcy, by the federal government to withdraw support for needed services, by industry which controls the precious resource of jobs to move out of the city or even out of the country.

Whether the cities will survive depends on policy decisions made at the highest levels. The federal government must decide whether to decrease the military budget and increase money for services; whether to implement a national welfare policy instead of requiring local and state governments to pay those costs. Industries must decide whether to make use of the advantages of already built cities or to escape established costs by building new cities which, although initially advantageous (and profitable to the builders), will bring with them similar costs. City governments have to decide whether to fight the cuts or knuckle under; whether to join together with other cities in a united front or to compete with other cities for the favors of industry. Organized groups of minority workers, women, and the working class in general also must decide whether to cooperate with each other, or to cooperate with City Hall and its backers against each other.

It appears at present that the decisions are going against cities and services. The question continues to be: should the citizens of the United States and their cities exist for the benefit of the economic system, or should the economic system exist for the benefit of the American people and their cities?

---

* The New York City Commission on Human Rights, having studied city layoffs, concluded: "It is difficult to believe that the remainder of the city's three-year austerity program, if it is to involve still more layoffs, can avoid virtually wiping out the city's minority workforce and crippling female representation as well."

THE HUMAN PROSPECT

A QUESTION OF SURVIVAL

The Club of Rome's somber warning: time is running out

Two of the most provocative documents on the future have been the Club of Rome studies "The Limits to Growth" (1972) and "Mankind at the Turning Point," released last October. The latter report was directed by Eduard Pestel, professor of engineering at Hanover University in Germany, and Mihajlo Mesarovic, professor and director of the Systems Research Center at Case Western Reserve University in Cleveland, with major research assistance from systems engineering consultant Jean Mermet of Grenoble and agriculture specialist Maurice Guernier of Paris. The study as summarized by the French newsmagazine "L'Express" is excerpted below.

•

The course which the world is presently following leads straight to catastrophe. Accordingly we must question all the premises long accepted as axiomatic and change course. There is, for example, the matter of growth, which we often hear blamed for current evils. Some people deduce in consequence that growth must either be stopped or slowed down. Others, however, contend that only by maintaining growth will our problems be solved.

The question is badly put. Before determining whether growth must be stopped, we must define the concept precisely. There are in Nature two types of growth. One is the indiscriminate growth through which cells reproduce by splitting into two, then into four, in a geometric progression, the multiples invariably being exact replicas of the original. This is a purely quantitative process. However, there is also organic growth, a process whereby the cells of an organism are specialized according to the laws of harmonious development. Brain cells, for instance, differ from liver cells. Evolution

also changes organs: some develop, others atrophy.

Today when we refer to growth we are generally implying the first definition. Yet if we ruled out the second we would have to stop all growth immediately because at the rate of 5 per cent per year, by the end of the next century, the world economy would be 500 times its present size. Long before this the earth's natural resources would be exhausted. Obviously this type of growth cannot continue indefinitely. There is also the fact that it is inequitably distributed around the globe, proliferating like a cancer in the industrialized world, while underdevelopment condemns millions elsewhere to famine and poverty. In other words, growth per se is not the root of the current crisis but rather its anarchic nature. The solution is

Unlike Nature, which provides laws to govern organic growth, we have no scheme for the harmonious development of the world. Yet mankind's salvation depends on adopting such a plan at once. This is not a matter of drawing up a worldwide economic program but rather of finding a pattern of development which respects the regional diversity of the planet, a global system of interdependent components each of which would contribute economic, cultural, and natural resources. And the pluralistic character of the earth must not only be considered but preserved at all costs.

How can we turn from anarchic to organic growth? History, alas, teaches us that we cannot rely too much on the wisdom of nations. Necessity alone, such as the crises of the present and the future, will dictate the law. To be sure, there have been crises since the beginning of time and man has always been able to surmount them. Then why worry now? Because it is plain that the crises of our age will not automatically end. And we are running out of time. Decisions made in today's

Tanzania—"in the face of galloping demography . . . limited resources."

complex world will produce results only twenty years hence because, for example, it takes five to ten years to build an electric power plant. Unless action is taken at once, by the year 2000 Southeast Asia will have a 30 per cent food deficit —which will be 100 per cent twenty-five years later. Then it will be irretrievable In other words, if we start at once we would have no more than fifty years to implement a system of organic growth. After that it will be too late.

The 150 nations which make up the world community can no longer resolve their individual problems alone; they depend on one another. The decision of an official at one end of the planet could precipitate disaster at the other end. In demography, sociology, economics, science, agriculture, even religion, problems can no longer be solved separately. It is not enough merely to increase agricultural production to overcome food shortages without considering the supply of fertilizers, methods of land cultivation, soil fertility, demography, meteorology, even education. As another example, medicine has made such strides that millions of human lives can be saved. But the result is a population explosion that looms as a new threat to life. Cynics among us have calculated that each child saved today will condemn another three children to death by hunger by the end of the century. Must we let today's child die because of this? Of course not.

One of the world's most grievous problems currently is the gap between industrialized and poor nations. All human societies in history have known one type of inequality or another but sooner or later it had to be eliminated. If this did not happen societies disintegrated. The same will be true of our world.

We do not, of course, know whether the planet's raw material resources will be sufficient to satisfy a world economy which will have grown by 500 per cent. Southeast Asia alone under the study's hypotheses would require five times the energy used by Western Europe in 1970. Should the underdeveloped countries begin to consume oil at the same rate as the industrialized nations, world oil resources would be exhausted at the very latest by 1985. All this underscores the urgency of a working global plan for saving and distributing equitably the planet's natural resources.

The survival of the human race is at stake, with world population increasing at an incredible rate. By the middle of the next century world population growth each year will be equivalent to the total of the first 1,500 years AD. For the poor regions of the world such figures are hair-raising. Even if we assume that we are able over the next fifty years to stabilize the world population, by then the population density per square kilometer will have increased by four in the U.S. and by 140 in Southeast Asia. What can we do?

FIRST SCENARIO: We do nothing. By the year 2000 the poor regions alone will have a population exceeding the present world total. Calcutta will have 60 million inhabitants.

SECOND SCENARIO: Starting in 1975 steps are taken to stabilize the world birth rate within thirty-five years. Even then population of the poor regions will not stop growing until seventy-five years later. And the level of population will be double that of today.

THIRD AND FOURTH SCENARIOS: We wait ten or twenty years before taking action. The ten-year wait will find the poor regions with 3 billion inhabitants instead of 1.7 billion. If we wait twenty years, there will be 10 billion. At present the available labor force in Southeast Asia increases by 350,000 each week. By the end of the century the figure will rise to 750,000. This means that every year an additional 40 million persons will seek employment. In another ten years the figure will rise to a million a week.

To meet the demands made on a vastly increased population India would have to build 1,000 schools, 1,000 hospitals, and 10,000 housing units a day for the next twenty years. These cold figures do not begin to convey the hidden suffering beneath them. For example, in Southeast Asia, if effective birth control measures are postponed for five years and the region must rely solely on its own resources, by the year 2025 an additional 170 million children will die. On the other hand, if action is taken in 1975, the lives of 500 million children between the ages of one and fifteen will be saved within the next fifty years. In the event that we elect to do nothing, Nature will obviously take charge. But at what cost? The death of millions is a statistic; the death of each individual—a tragedy.

"Interests of the producing and consuming countries will coalesce . . ."

In the face of galloping demography, the world has only limited natural resources. Following a long period of plenty, we have entered an age of scarcity that pits the producing against the consuming nations. How can we resolve this problem? On a strictly economic plane, the conflict could be settled through the price mechanism—that is, by finding the "optimal price" advantageous to both producers and consumers. In the case of oil, for example, there is reason to believe, contrary to most expectations, that a certain price increase would, in the long run, prove more advantageous to all concerned than the stabilization of the present prices. Here are the alternatives:

FIRST SCENARIO: Oil prices are kept low, possibly at the 1970 level. Under these circumstances, industrialized countries have no incentive to save oil or to create new sources of energy. By the year 2000 the existing world oil reserves will be exhausted. The resulting drop in the gross national product, unemployment, and the related social tensions would become intolerable. The producing countries of the Middle East, too, will fare poorly; their chief source of income will be exhausted and, as a result, their development will be blocked.

SECOND SCENARIO: Oil prices reach their optimal level. The producing nations will double their income when the increase reaches 50 per cent of the 1974 price. Then they will begin to lower prices, since otherwise the consuming countries will practice austerity or seek other sources of energy. Thus the optimal price for the producers will be fixed at 50 per cent of the existing increase. No more.

What happens if oil prices rise by 3 per cent per year until they reach the optimum? Thanks to the considerable revenues accrued by the Middle East, its regional income within fifty years will be five times the amount of the first scenario. And the developed countries, too, will fare better, for their

collective income also will go up. Despite a slowdown in growth after the year 2000 there will be no more problems of recession or breakdown.

The conclusion is that, contrary to appearances, the interests of the producing and the consuming nations will, in the long run, coalesce. Should either attempt to outsmart the other everybody would lose. The same is true of all natural resources: foods, fertilizers, raw materials. Each has an optimal price advantageous to all. To avert crises agreement is needed among all the nations of the globe, under which optimal prices would be set, adopted, and maintained. But unfortunately when a crisis becomes acute, competition leads to a contest of strength, and the mechanism of prices is no longer enough to restore the balance, since each of the two camps embarks on political or economic countermeasures, or even the use of force.

Of all natural resources food is the most precious. In this area the crisis is not of tomorrow; it is already here. According to UNESCO, 400 to 500 million children suffer from malnutrition. Ten years ago emergency food reserves amounted to eighty days of consumption. Today they have been reduced to thirty days. In more than half of the world the protein content of the food consumed is about two-thirds of normal needs. Clearly the situation is catastrophic, as attested by the current famine in Asia and Africa. All the indications are that it will soon become apocalyptic.

Some optimists contend that all the crises of the present age are strictly technical and that "Technology" with a capital "T," like a fairy with a magic wand, will perform a new miracle. In the realm of energy they claim the atom can supplant oil. In this view, within twenty-five years the atom could satisfy one-third of the energy needs of the industrialized world, equivalent to the current total. While we wait for nuclear energy, oil will be used only for transportation, and additional sources of natural gas, coal, and bituminous schists will be tapped. In fifty years, they say, nuclear energy will meet all our needs.

Where would these assumptions take us in 100 years, when the world population will have quadrupled? To satisfy the demand, 3,000 "nuclear parks"—each equipped with eight reactors—would be needed. This would require in turn the construction worldwide of four automatic reactors per week for a century, starting today. The lifespan of reactors is estimated to be thirty years; hence, to ensure replacements, two a day would have to be built. Today it takes seven to eight years to construct a far simpler reactor; $2 trillion per year would be needed to finance this project (the present world product totals $3.4 trillion); to feed these reactors, we need 15 million kilos of plutonium-239 per year.

Although with proper precautions plutonium does not present radioactive danger, inhalation of ten micrograms of it (ten one-millionths of a gram) is enough to produce lung cancer. A plutonium ball the size of a grapefruit contains enough poison to annihilate the population of the planet. Furthermore, plutonium's radioactivity lasts 25,000 years. And we would have to produce and transport 15 million kilos every year! Truly, betting on the atom is like signing a Faustian contract with the Devil, a contract even more absurd since the atom is not our only option and since we are bound to realize that the nuclear prescription is impossible to fill after we have missed the chance to study other alternatives. Among these are:

—SHORT-RANGE SOLUTION: The producing countries guarantee sufficient oil supplies to ensure the socioeconomic stability of the industrialized world until 1985. In exchange, the latter guarantees the producing nations permanent participation in the exploitation of the new energy sources that will eventually supersede oil.

—MIDDLE-RANGE SOLUTION: Between 1985 and the year 2000 coal, natural gas, and bituminous schists will provide the supplementary energy needed for the transition from oil to the energy type that will replace it. Despite its limitations and inconvenience, coal could ensure the transition. It would be employed as heating fuel, thus freeing oil quantities for nobler pursuits, such as the production of fertilizers, synthetic fibers, proteins, etc.

—LONG-RANGE SOLUTION: Starting in the year 2000, solar energy will replace oil. Solar energy is cleaner, less dangerous, and far less costly than nuclear energy. If present oil producers become associated with this project they would be assured new revenues when their oil resources are exhausted. The construction of solar-energy plants would con-

"Crises lead to war and war today means nuclear conflagration."

Marino/Excelsior/Mexico City

stitute the most ambitious project of all time. For this purpose 1 per cent of the globe's surface would have to be covered. The cost would be between $20 trillion and $50 trillion. Scientifically the solar solution is realistic. Only technical problems remain to be resolved. And if the various governments allocate to it as much in credits as for nuclear, space, and supersonic aviation development it could be implemented fast. But for the time being no such investment is being made, perhaps because it has no military use.

Above all a change in attitude of the developed nations is essential. They must realize that wasting energy is like taking bread out of a child's mouth; that their world is overdeveloped; that growth in only one part of the globe to the detriment of the others jeopardizes the social, moral, economic, scientific, and political growth of mankind as a whole. For the first time in human history nations are asked not

to do what they are capable of doing—to curb economic and technological progress, or at least to share their good fortune with the disinherited of this earth—in their own interest.

The current crisis raises issues not concerning our political, economic, and social system but concerning man himself, his attitude to Nature, his way of life. There is a limit to how much man can tamper with Nature, as exemplified by the waste of water. The increase in the amount of irrigated land has resulted in an evaporation rate of approximately 400 gallons per person per day, a figure which will multiply as more and more land is exploited in order to feed the world population. Within fifty years it may be necessary to obtain half of the amount of water required for irrigation by desalinating ocean water (since well and river waters will no longer suffice). And such a project will require five to ten times the world's total energy consumption today.

Man, too, has limitations within himself. The artificial world which he is creating could very well cloud his reason, eclipse his intelligence, and blur his conception of himself and the world—indeed, disturb his very soul. Human institutions have limitations. Yet the population growth and further technological advances require increasingly larger and more complex organization. We are already beginning to witness deterioration in services, despite enormous and burdensome expenditures. The transportation and postal services are daily examples of this phenomenon.

A regrouping of the regions of the world is necessary in order to achieve some equilibrium. What possible equilibrium could there be today betwen the U.S. and Dahomey? Rather than trying to beat the industrialized world at its own game, the poor regions must forge their own methods of development. Universalism must under no circumstances end up in uniformity. Not one world, one government, one language but—on the contrary—diversity is the key to adaptation, which in turn is the key to survival. An "instrument" of world planning must be forged to enforce, test, and evaluate the necessary measures. This agency must be trusted and understood not only by all governments but by the people themselves because sacrifices will inevitably be demanded of all in the immediate present in order to save the future.

The only alternative to this solution is divisiveness, conflict, hatred, and nuclear annihilation. In sum, the report concludes:
— The current crises are not temporary, but mark a turning point in the evolution of the world.
— The solutions can only be global.
— Cooperation will prove more advantageous than confrontation.

Only a global plan for balanced organic growth can avert universal catastrophe. This would require the establishment of an international system, within which the necessary decisions would be made collectively so that the crises threatening the world might be dealt with now. Action must be taken immediately lest the crises turn into catastrophe by the end of the century. Crises lead to war, and war today means nuclear conflagration which, in turn, spells collective suicide.

The governments and international organizations of today are obsessed with military alliances and bloc politics, not realizing that in the event of a nuclear war these would prove useless. The only way of escaping nuclear destruction is to try to meet together the greatest challenge which has ever confronted mankind.

8

NUCLEAR ENERGY

A PROBLEM, NOT AN ANSWER

MIKE EDELHART

In the public statements of the nuclear establishment the numbers are solid, the cost projections firm, the growth curves lofty, the fuel predictions bountiful. Unfortunately, when one leaves the aseptic world of statistical studies, a gap develops between the impression of a smoothly running technology—the clean, cheap, virtually inexhaustible peaceful atom—and the actuality of a badly confused, uncertain development.

Numerous factors that are coming to bear on nuclear power plants in the field have been skipped, ignored, forgotten, misinterpreted, or baldly excluded from the reports which have served as stepping stones into the Atomic Age. Nuclear proponents haven't lied to sustain the momentum of atomic power. Instead, they've followed the more elusive course of wrapping selected, educated opinions in the cloth of fact. To be fair, the anti-atomic plant forces have used the same tactic. On balance, however, the opponents come out ahead, if only because the official position assumes "fail-safe": the nothing-can-possibly-go-wrong factor. And no one can deny that, on the job, much *has* gone wrong with power plants.

In the area of safety in particular, a startling difference can be noted between the theoretical performance of power plants and their actual record in the field. The following set of circumstances, for example, has only a one-in-a-trillion chance of happening, according to one interpretation of the AEC's Rasmussen study of potential nuclear power plant accidents:

An atomic plant worker, checking with a lighted candle for air leaks in cable couplings around the reactor core, accidently sets the cable sealant afire. Flames race along cable coverings, swiftly disabling power, telephone signal, coaxial, control, thermocouple and special control lines. A guard, alerted to the blaze, fails to dial either of two emergency numbers prescribed for the situation; instead,

Oliphant, Denver Post

he dials an unrelated employee, who then has to inform plant controllers.

Seven of eleven critical pressure relief systems fail. The control board begins to signal false information. Two systems for pumping vital water around the reactor core remain in operation; one of these fails. The coolant level drops from 16 feet to a mere 4 feet from the top of the fuel. A fire-fighting spray system can't be opened because nobody has the right kind of screwdriver. The facility must be shut down by hand, and the fire continues to burn for seven hours.

Despite the almost impossible odds, this fire actually occurred on March 22, 1975, at TVA's Brown's Ferry nuclear power unit. The Nuclear Regulatory Commission called it the second worst disaster in the eighteen-year history of nuclear power, following the partial core melt-down of the Enrico Fermi experimental breeder plant in Detroit in 1966.

That kind of event makes the safety figures which purport to apply to it look ridiculous. Obviously, the Brown's Ferry crisis developed in ways that had virtually nothing to

Mike Edelhart is a free-lance writer living in Flat Rock, N.C.

do with the mathematical prediction of its impossibility. Somewhere along the chain from theory to design to production to construction to operation, variables had crept into the mix and stirred things up unexpectedly.

What kind of factors might these be? The insurance pool which underwrites Brown's Ferry recently stated that the fire stemmed from poor design and maintenance which, if continued, would result in "a loss beyond imagination." A spokesman also reportedly said that five of the twenty-three plants covered by the consortium contain similar errors. Such design problems at Brown's Ferry included cables which ran under the control room floor, and which filled the command center with heat and smoke during the fire. The AEC and nuclear contractors also missed similar potential hazards in earlier units. In November 1972, for instance, an anonymous letter awoke the AEC for the first time to the danger of permitting main steam pipes to pass directly beneath the control rooms of some models.

Another example from TVA's atomic program shows how amazingly far design blunders of even the grossest nature can proceed without being spotted. Reactor cores sit inside huge concrete cylinders, balanced on concrete pads. The pads for TVA's Sequoyah facility were in the wrong places. This was discovered only after the containers had been completely finished and the cores had been lowered into them by a giant crane. The reactor cores had to be laboriously pulled out again, and millions of dollars and months of redundant work went into tearing down and rebuilding the concrete jackets.

A TVA mechanical engineer said of the incident: "This was a major design error. It cost a lot of money. If we can have something this big go wrong and nobody notices it until it is too late, it seems inevitable to me that some time we will have an error in the design of safety-related equipment."

After the plans are drawn, other bugs can enter the system in the form of unregulated changes made during construction, often on the sole authority of field personnel. A nuclear civil engineer explained:

> For one reason or another, 10 per cent of the things we design up here don't work out in the field. So, the construction people do what we call "field routing." They change the location of pipes and conduits and other things. This means that as much as 10 per cent of the details in the plant don't come from the original design at all but from a construction man's head. I've never heard of information being routed back to us after these changes for us to evaluate their safety and efficiency. The designs are great on paper, but the design and the plant are two different things.

However, the biggest factor in the margin of safety isn't the machine but the men who run it. The Alabama fire was caused by human misjudgment, and it was kept from galloping forward into catastrophe by human capability. While official studies deal almost entirely with the fallibility of the mechanical components of nuclear plants, the reaction of the operators more than anything else spells the difference between disaster and anticlimax.

All of this is not to say that power plants are unsafe. It does, however, argue strongly that reactors can't be fail-safe, and that statistics and industry statements which imply that they are go beyond logical justification. Con-

versely, some anti-nuclear groups have stated flatly that atomic units *are not* safe. They have no more basis for making that claim than the industry does for saying they are foolproof. In short, one can say only that the interior of atomic plants in performance is an unknown quantity.

Consistent overestimation of and fudging with safety predictions cause damage primarily because the public gets shortchanged. Once, when she was head of the AEC, Dixy Lee Ray said that the chances of a major nuclear accident were less than one in a billion. A statement like that sounds good but means little. Wittingly or not, such assertions prevent the public from gaining an accurate view of the situation. Even Norman Rasmussen, the man who devised the system upon which almost all nuclear power safety figures now used are based, recently said, "Nuclear power plants have not performed with the degree of reliability we would expect from machines built with the care and attention to safety and reliability that we have so often claimed."

As the Environmental Protection Agency wrote, in an unusual attack on the work of another federal bureau (specifically lambasting the AEC report on emergency core cooling systems): "Unamplified, it includes an inappropriately supported statement regarding class 9 accidents (the largest nuclear mishaps), therefore depriving the public of a quantified prospective on the risks being taken relative to this category." In nonbureaucratese, that means the public could be getting a trick cigar.

However, plant safety is not the only important issue. Here is a review of some other notable areas where development of the atom for energy has fallen short of expectations; they will probably become steadily more important to the continuing debate.

Evacuation. In theory, areas around nuclear power plants have effective mobilization plans for their populations in case of a major accident. In practice, such has not often been the case. At Brown's Ferry, the Civil Defense coordinator for Limestone County—the man responsible for removing the people potentially threatened—told the Nuclear Regulatory Commission (NRC): "I heard about the fire at Brown's Ferry on the morning of March 24, 1975 [two days after the fact]. No one in the Civil Defense system notified me or attempted to do so." The county sheriff heard about the blaze "after it was over."

The town of Waterford, Conn. has had similar experiences. In two separate cases, radioactive waste water was inadvertently spilled at the Millpoint power plant, near Waterford. In both instances, local officials were among the last to hear about the accidents, and generally not from plant sources. While these two leaks posed no significant danger to the community, they convinced local office-holders that existing channels of communication weren't working.

As with most phases of the nuclear discussion, there is a distance here between expectations and what has happened in the field. The Rasmussen study estimated that 90 per cent of the population contiguous to a nuclear power plant could be evacuated within eight hours. E. Erie Jones, director of Illinois' Office of Civil Preparedness, on the other hand, has stated a fairly typical pragmatic position: "We think we have a good first draft for the Zion [a major power plant site] area. But to tell you we have an acceptable plan for all the nukes in this state would be a blatant lie. Even the Zion plan isn't acceptable until it's been exercised with a drill."

Seismic Faults. In California, as you might expect, but in Eastern states as well, several power plants have been found to lie on or uncomfortably close to seismic fault lines. In at least one case, the power company definitely knew the instability was there before it began construction, and hid that information from the NRC. The commission assumes that a utility has satisfied itself that no dangerous geological formations lie near a proposed site before it applies to build a power plant there. In addition, the NRC is supposed to review the company's findings to make sure the proposed location is stable. In several cases, though, power companies have failed to find faults that were dangerously close to favored lots. And the NRC does not make its own geological study but works with the information the utilities furnish.

In California, evidence of a fault was found only 2 miles from Pacific Gas & Electric's Diablo complex. Prior to that discovery, plant designers had been convinced that the nearest crack was 20 miles away. Asked at the time if the newly discovered instability could jeopardize the unit, an AEC official admitted: "It's possible. . . ."

Back East, a fault was found to run directly beneath Virginia Electric Power Company's North Anna facility. While Virginia hasn't been geologically active in any serious way for some time, the power plant fault troubled scientists who knew of it. As J.F. Devine, a U.S. Geological Survey staffer told *The Washington Post*: "No one would be worried about earthquake possibilities if we weren't talking about a nuclear power plant . . . but we are talking about a nuclear power plant."

The company had studiously removed any hint of the fault from its application with NRC, going so far as to delete Neuschel's lineament, a principal geologic feature, from maps submitted to the commission. An environmental group jumped on the issue, and Virginia Electric ended up paying a $60,000 fine for "material false statements" before the licensing body. The NRC refused, however, to restrict construction over the fault, judging it to be inactive.

In a similar case, Dr. David M. Stewart, a geologist at the University of North Carolina, has claimed that the next big earthquake along the Eastern seaboard will probably be centered at the site of a Carolina Power and Light unit near Southport, N.C. He cites new evidence to indicate that within the foreseeable future eastern North Carolina will be the epicenter of a potentially catastrophic quake. CP&L contends that its preconstruction land surveys showed scant evidence of seismic activity, but Stewart and his supporters reply that the area's earthquake tendency was discovered with techniques developed since the plant was finished. The NRC, at the scientists' urging, has ordered CP&L to look further into the possibility that its plant may lie on a dangerous spot.

Money. Much of the impetus for nuclear plants has arisen from soaring projections of America's future electrical needs. In the recent past, when these tremendous increases were linked with then-current plant construction costs, uranium prices and efficiency estimates, atomic plants looked quite the handsome investment.

Over the past year, American electrical usage has risen only 1.7 per cent. Companies which had based their nuclear plans on much greater increases, find themselves saddled with expensive plans to produce electricity their customers may not need, or at least won't need as soon as expected. As a result, according to an industry-related journal, *Engineering News Record*, 24,000 megawatts of atomic power orders were canceled between March 1974 and March 1975.

An example of the current economic squeeze comes from Middle South Utilities of Louisiana. Floyd Lewis, the holding company's president, explained its problems: "Our decision to cancel two nuclear units and defer construction on another was simply a question of our ability to finance them and the pattern of use of electricity in recent months by our customers. . . . Our peak load this year was three-tenths of a per cent below that of 1974, and came in April instead of August for the first time in twenty years."

Duke Power, of the Southeastern states, has revised its estimate of electrical demand over the next fifteen years downward by 1.5 million kilowatts, and has postponed for two years ground breaking on two important nuclear installations. The Tucson Gas and Electric Company, as a third example, has sold its percentage of Arizona's atomic power development to South California Edison for $7 million, citing lowered use projections as the reason.

Diminished use curves wouldn't have such industry-wide effect if they weren't linked to staggering, inflationary cost overruns in plant construction. Middle South's plants were figured to cost $1.3 billion in 1973; in 1975, the price had leaped to $2.3 billion. A few years ago, the Midland power complex in Michigan was expected to open in 1974 at a cost of only $349 million. By the summer of 1974, the price had nearly tripled, to $940 million and the unit's start-up date had been pushed back to 1980. Then, on April 15, the estimated cost jumped again, to $1.4 billion, and completion was kicked back yet another year. Over this course, Midland went from being one of the cheapest light-water reactors ever conceived, to being one of the most expensive—all before it had ever been built.

In addition to inflation, the ultimate operating costs of nuclear facilities have been bedeviled by an elusive figure called a "capacity factor." This percentage compares the amount of power a plant could theoretically produce with the amount it actually does produce. At present, no one can be absolutely certain what the true capacities of nuclear plants will be. Several estimates have been made, but few of the nuclear units have been in operation long enough to verify their performance. As might be expected, though, friends and foes of the plants are far apart on this question. David Comey, a highly effective anti-nuclear researcher, has produced a factor of 50.4 per cent of the possible power, based on intensive computer evaluations. Sacramento Municipal Power, on the other hand, assumed a capacity figure of 80 per cent for its proposed Rancho Seco installation. Coal plants average in the 60s and 70s. The capacity factor is crucial in determining the eventual cost to consumers of electricity from any facility. A hard and fast average is necessary to determine if nuclear plants are actually cost effective with coal-fired and other types.

Uranium Problems. The current dreary economic picture and uncertain cost status of atomic plants will surely be made even worse in the next few months by the development of an even bigger drawback: Uranium, the lifeblood of nuclear reactors, is getting both unmanageably expensive and increasingly hard to find. This new problem was the principal reason for the recent scuttling of South Carolina Electric and Gas Co.'s V.C. Sumner plant, Unit 2. The utility announced that it just couldn't find an "acceptable" supplier of uranium ore.

The seriousness of the uranium situation was pointed up in September when Westinghouse, manufacturer of about 40 per cent of the world's nuclear plants and the largest single supplier of uranium, announced that it was going to limit fuel shipments to customers, and cut off service altogether after 1978. The company took this action in direct defiance of contracts it had signed with reactor firms over the past ten years. Westinghouse defended its action by claiming that a little-noted section of the Uniform Commercial Code allowed it to abrogate contractual agreements for the company's general health. While the legality of the argument has yet to be tested—angry power companies are lining up, suits in hand—there is no doubt that Westinghouse's uranium program has been bleeding the company white.

It got into the uranium business in the first place as a way to sweeten power plant deals. Customers who invested in a reactor were assured of an adequate supply of fuel at cheap, stable prices until 1992. But the price of uranium has more than quadrupled, from $6 to about $26 per pound. So Westinghouse has been losing its shirt selling the stuff at unnaturally low prices. Now, it has decided to provide only 18.75 per cent of ordered amounts until 1978, after which it will close out its uranium business. Irwin Stelzer, a utility consultant, remarked that the Westinghouse cutback "puts the whole nuclear program up for grabs."

It looks as if the grabbing will get increasingly frantic in the years ahead. Nuclear expert Ralph Lapp has pointed out in *Fortune* that, whereas the United States will need four to eight times the current known reserves over the next twenty-five years, to carry out the nuclear power program now projected, no new major American uranium producing areas have been identified in seventeen years. Such an irrefutable shortfall, many in the industry feel, will lead to an eventual requirement for significant uranium imports to meet national demand. Uranium *is* found widely across the globe. However, if America were forced to use foreign supplies of uranium, much as it now draws on Middle Eastern stores of oil, the country would be subject to the same kind of cartel economics that drove it to nuclear power in the first place. Already, a group of uranium producers calling itself the Uranium Producers Forum, has held meetings and adopted a strikingly noncompetitive pricing structure.

The one alternative to boxing ourselves into an atomic corner, hardly better than the petroleum fix we're now in, is the liquid metal fast breeder reactor, which produces more nuclear fuel than it consumes. But the breeder has been attacked by environmentalists, who think it too dangerous, and by scientists, who fear the ramifications of an economy based on the unmatchably toxic substance, plutonium. The government has de-emphasized breeders because of the controversy, and the odds of America

having a breeder capability of any size within fifteen years are slim and getting slimmer.

One of the strongest original arguments for atomic power was that, in spite of the high construction costs, uranium fuel was so cheap that it kept overall investment on a par with other energy systems. However true that was when first proposed, it no longer has any touch with reality. If atomic plants are to be cost effective in the immediate future, it must be on the basis of using a hard-to-get, dearly priced fuel. Few people think nuclear facilities *could* favorably compete under such circumstances.

World Safety. The expansion of atomic energy throughout the world—in addition to increasing pressure on limited supplies of uranium—may involve serious dangers for international stability. A study recently published in *Harvard Magazine* concluded that nuclear war will almost certainly erupt before 1999, but that the antagonists, initially at least, won't be the United States and Russia but two smaller countries with recently acquired nuclear capabilities. However, if small, unstable nations obtain nuclear weapons, it can only be because current members of the nuclear community gave them the raw materials. Obviously, no reasonable state would give away A-bombs, but many countries are currently involved in the worldwide dissemination of nuclear power facilities. The United States is giving power plants to Egypt; West Germany is selling them to Brazil; France is reportedly even considering the sale of a nuclear waste-recycling plant to South Korea.

In at least one case, that of India, nuclear material provided for peaceful development was used to produce an atomic blast. Yet the U.S. Government insists that power plants are an effective and safe tool of foreign policy, a token we can bestow upon governments we deem solid and reasonable. It emphasizes that bomb uranium and power-plant uranium are far removed from each other, and that very few nations have the capability to "enrich" uranium to bomb purity. The process is so expensive and complex, and requires such enormous amounts of raw ore, that only countries with huge military needs and budgets have been able to develop it. That would be fine if the situation were static, but it is not. In fact, the expense and intricacy of nuclear separation may already be an obsolete assumption. Earlier this year, teams in Russia and the United States independently discovered relatively simple, cheap ways to enrich uranium with lasers.

With this development, the nuclear situation reaches perhaps its bleakest impasse, where it becomes impossible, given the world's current state, to find a clear demarcation between the peaceful atom and its warlike twin. Power plants aren't innately harmful devices, but when a connection develops, no matter how tenuous, between them and bombs, their loudly proclaimed purity is sadly besmirched.

Ralph Lapp, who believes in the development of nuclear power, unwittingly pointed up the basic paradox of the atomic question when he wrote: "It is probably no exaggeration to state that the economic vitality of the nation in the year 2000 will hinge on how well it solves its nuclear power problems." Nuclear problems? Atomic power was supposed to *solve* the problems we face today with fossil fuels. We have ended up, it seems, playing an energy Zen game—solving a puzzle with another puzzle, even more confusing than the original.

9

The Energy Crisis–All of a Piece

We live in a time of unending crises. A series of grave, seemingly intractable problems clamor for attention: degradation of the environment; the rapid growth of world population; the food crisis; the energy crisis — rapidly mounting calamities that may merge into a worldwide economic collapse. And, overshadowing all, war and the threat of war.

As each crisis rises to the top of the public agenda, we try to respond: the environmental crisis is met by pollution controls; population growth by attempts to control fertility; the energy crisis by efforts to control demand and to develop new supplies; the economic crisis by proposals to control consumption, wages, and prices; the threat of war is met by a patchwork of negotiations.

But each effort to solve one crisis seems to founder on conflict with another: pollution controls are blamed for the shortage of energy; population control conflicts with the need for economic development; energy conservation leads to unemployment; proposals to feed the hungry of the world are condemned as inflationary; in the growing economic panic we hear cries against almost any effort to alleviate all the rest; and already there are those who seek to end all these problems by incinerating them in the flames of war.

All this seems to be a dismal confirmation that the world is staggering toward catastrophe. But the very links that make up this web of crises are themselves a source of optimism, a clue to what needs to be done. The close connections among them suggest that all these problems are symptoms of some common fault that lies deep within the design of modern society. The energy crisis is so closely linked to this pivotal defect as to offer the hope that it can become a guiding thread which, once seized, can lead us out of the labyrinth. In this sense, the energy crisis signalizes a great watershed in the history of human society. What we do in response to it will determine, I believe, for the United States and for every nation in the world, whether our future continues the progress toward humanism and democracy, or ends in catastrophe and oppression.

❦

When engineers want to understand the strength of a new material they stress it to the breaking point and analyze how it responds. The energy crisis is a kind of "engineering test" of the United States' economic system, and it has revealed a number of deep-seated faults.

Although energy is useless until it produces goods or services, and although nearly all the energy that we use is derived from limited, nonrenewable sources which will eventually run out (all of which pollute the environment), we have perversely reduced the efficiency with which fuels are converted into goods and services. In the last thirty years, in agriculture, industry, and transportation, those productive processes that use energy least efficiently and stress the environment most heavily are growing most rapidly, driving their energetically efficient competitors off the market.

In agriculture the older, energy-sparing methods of maintaining fertility by crop rotation and manuring have been displaced by the intensive use of nitrogen fertilizers synthesized from natural gas. In the same way, synthetic fibers, plastics, and detergents made from petroleum have captured most of the markets once held by wood, cotton, wool, and soap — all made from energy-sparing and renewable resources. In transportation, railroads — by far the most energetically efficient means of moving people and freight — are crumbling, their traffic increasingly taken over by passenger cars, trucks, and airplanes that use far more fuel per passenger- or ton-mile.

Naturally, such energy-wasting enterprises are threatened when the price of energy increases — the only real outcome of the illusory 1973 fuel shortage. If they were not so serious, some of these economic consequences could only be regarded as absurd. When the multi-billion-dollar petrochemical industry cheerfully bid up the price of propane — an essential starting material in plastics production — farmers had trouble finding the propane they needed to dry their grain, and then had to pay triple its former price. In order to sustain the surfeit of plastic trivia that gluts the modern market, food production was threatened. When, in response to urgent appeals, householders reduced their demand for electricity, the power companies asked for rate increases to make up for the lost business. Automobile manufacturers, having scornfully rejected environmentalists' appeals to produce smaller, more fuel-efficient vehicles, have lost about half their sales, throwing one hundred thousand auto workers out of work.

The deepest fault that is revealed by the impact of the energy crisis on the United States' economic system is not that we are running out of energy or of environmental quality — but of capital. As oil wells have gone deeper, petroleum refineries have become more complex; power plants have given up the reliability of coal- or oil-fired burners for the elaborate,

THE POLITICAL LUXURIES

...to survive the environmental crisis, the people of industrialized nations will [not] need to give up their "affluent" way of life. . . . This "affluence," as judged by conventional measures — such as G.N.P., power consumption, and production of metals — is itself an illusion. . . .

There are, however, certain luxuries which the environmental crisis and the approaching bankruptcy that it signifies will, I believe, force us to give up. These are the *political* luxuries which have so

shaky technology of the nuclear reactor, and the capital cost of producing a unit of energy has sharply increased. The projected production of total United States energy is expected to rise from about 57,000 trillion Btu in 1971 to about 92,000 trillion Btu in 1985 (an increase of about sixty per cent) and requiring that annual capital expenditures for energy rise from about $26.5 billion to $158 billion over that period — an increase of about 390 per cent. This trend, coupled with the growing inefficiency in the use of energy, means that, if we follow the present course, energy production will consume an increasing fraction of the total capital available for investment in new enterprises including factories, homes, schools, and hospitals.

One projection, based on present maximum estimates of energy demand, indicates that energy production could consume as much as eighty per cent of all available capital in 1985. This is, of course, an absurdly unrealistic situation in which the energy industry would, in effect, be devouring its own customers. Thus, the compounded effects of a trend toward enterprises that inefficiently convert energy into goods and services and power plants that inefficiently convert capital into energy production threaten to overrun the economic system's capacity to produce its most essential factor — capital. This may well explain why, according to a recent New York Stock Exchange report, we are likely to be $650 billion short in needed capital in the next decade. The economic effects of the increasingly large proportion of available capital that would need to be tied up in this vast enterprise would be broadly felt by society. For example, according to the recent New York Stock Exchange report, in order to assure the availability of capital, the following changes are called for:

long been enjoyed by those who can benefit from them: the luxury of allowing the wealth of the nation to serve preferentially the interests of so few of its citizens; of failing fully to inform citizens of what they need to know in order to exercise their right of political governance; of condemning as anathema any suggestion which reexamines basic economic values; of burying the issues revealed by logic in a morass of self-serving propaganda.

BARRY COMMONER
(From The Closing Circle, *Bantam Books)*

"... corporate tax rates should be adjusted to permit increased accumulation of funds ... tax exemption for reasonable amounts of capital gains ... excessive regulation and restrictive controls (especially in the utilities industry) should be relaxed ... environmental standards should be modified, with target dates deferred."

The report acknowledges that federal tax revenues will be reduced, but proposes to match this deficit with a reduction in federal expenditures.

୬

What has gone wrong? Why has the postwar transformation of agriculture, industry, and transportation set the United States on the suicidal course of consuming, ever more wastefully, capital goods and nonrenewable sources of energy, and destroying the very environment in which we must live?

The basic reason is one that every businessman well understands. It paid. Soap companies significantly increased their profit per pound of cleaner sold when they switched from soap to detergents; truck lines are more profitable than railroads; synthetic plastics and fabrics are more profitable than leather, cotton, wool, or wood; nitrogen fertilizer is the corn farmer's most profit-yielding input; power companies claim that capital-intensive nuclear plants improve their rate of return; and as Henry Ford II has said, "minicars make miniprofits."

All this is the natural outcome of the terms that govern the entry of new enterprises in the United States' economic system. Regardless of the initial motivation for a new productive enterprise — the entry of nuclear plants into the power market, of synthetics into the fabric market, of detergents into the cleaner market, or of trucks into the freight market — it will succeed relative to the older competitor only if it is capable of yielding a greater return on the investment. At times, this advantage may be expressed as a lower price for the new goods, an advantage that is likely to drive the competing ones off the market. At other times, the advantage may be translated into higher profits, enabling the new enterprise to expand faster than the older one, with the same end result.

Some economists believe that private enterprise can adapt to the rising price of energy by turning to energetically efficient productive technologies in order to save costs. Where this can be accomplished by reducing the waste of energy within a given enterprise it may well succeed. But in other cases — for example, the petrochemical industry — the intensive use of energy is built into the very design of the enterprise in order to eliminate human labor, thereby raising labor productivity and the resultant profits. In these cases improved energetic efficiency can be achieved only by rolling back the rapid growth of such inherently inefficient industries — but, for that very reason, these are precisely the industries that are most profitable. Any attempt to reduce their level of activity would necessarily encroach on the profit yielded by the economic system as a whole.

Another possible adaptation is to pass the extra cost of measures that conserve energy and reduce environmental stress along to the consumer. Thus the energy dependence of agriculture could be reduced by cutting back on the rate of application of nitrogen fertilizer, with the inevitable result that the price of food would rise. This would place an extra burden on the poor, which, in turn, might be rectified *if* the principles of private enterprise could accommodate measures that would remedy the growing gap between the rich and the poor. Once more, this is a challenge to the basic design of the economic system.

In a sense there is nothing new here, only the recognition that in the United States' economic system, decisions about what to produce and how to produce it are governed most powerfully by the expectation of enhanced profit. What *is* new and profoundly unsettling is that the thousands of separate entrepreneurial decisions that have been made during the last thirty years in the United States regarding new productive enterprises have, with such alarming uniformity, favored those which are less efficient energetically and more damaging to the environment than their alternatives. This is a serious challenge to the fundamental precept of private enterprise — that decisions made on the basis of the producer's economic self-interest are also the best way to meet social needs. That is why the environmental crisis, the energy crisis, and the multitude of social problems to which they are linked suggest — certainly as an urgently-to-be-discussed hypothesis — that the operative fault, and therefore the locus of the remedy, lies in the design of our profit-oriented economic system.

Comparable claims of service to the public welfare are, of course, made by the Soviet and other socialist economic systems, and insofar as such systems are based on social rather than private decisions regarding the design of the productive system, these claims may, at least in principle, be justified. However, when we look at the recent practice of the Soviet Union and certain other socialist countries we see a strange tendency to acquire from the United States and other industrialized capitalist countries, precisely the productive technology that has driven these countries down the path of wasteful consumption of energy and capital. After all, when Fiat automobiles are produced in Moscow they can be expected to use as much gasoline and emit as much pollution as they do in Rome. And when the petrochemical complexes that are so largely responsible for the wasteful, environmentally destructive use of energy in the United States are imported by Russia, Poland, and even China, they will certainly impose these same pernicious hazards in their new locations.

We are all aware, of course, that neither capitalist nor socialist societies will lightly tolerate inquiries that question the basic roots of their economic systems. The environmental crisis, the energy crisis, and all the difficult, interwoven social issues to which they are linked is an urgent signal that it is time to give up this taboo. Surely, those who are convinced that private enterprise is in fact the most effective way to live in harmony with our resources and the natural world now have an unparalleled opportunity to make their case and to convince a troubled citizenry that there are ways, within the context of that system, to right its grave faults. And for those who see in the present situation opportunities to support socially oriented ways to organize our productive and economic enterprise, there is an equally important challenge to prove their case.

❧

If we pay heed to the basic facts about the production and use of energy, we can begin to find a rational way out of this tragic and absurd state of affairs.

To begin with, we now know that we can readily squeeze out of the productive process much of the wasted energy that has been devoted, not to the improvement of human welfare, but to the replacement of worthwhile and meaningful labor by the cheaper and more tractable alternative of energy. A number of studies have shown that in the United States the nation's energy budget could be reduced by about a third in this way with no significant reduction in the standard of living. Every unit of energy thus saved is reduced in its environmental impact to zero and relieves the pressure for hasty adventures into dubious and dangerous power technologies such as the breeder and fusion reactors.

In their place we can turn to solar energy, which has none of the faults that promise to cripple the present energy system. Unlike oil, gas, coal, or uranium, solar energy is renewable and virtually free of untoward environmental effects. Unlike the non-renewable sources, which become more difficult and costly to acquire as the rate of their use increases, the use of solar energy is readily extendable at no loss in efficiency. The capture of one sunbeam, after all, in no way hinders the capture of the next one. Only solar energy can avoid the capital crunch which promises to paralyze the further development of the present energy system. Finally, solar energy is uniquely adaptable to different scales of economic organization. A conventional power plant now typically requires an investment approaching one billion dollars. In contrast, many solar collectors can be constructed in a range of sizes suitable for everything from a single household to an entire city.

The myth that solar energy is impractical, or too expensive, or in the realm of future technology is easily dispelled by a series of recent analyses done for the National Science Foundation. For example, a project, based on installing readily constructed solar-heat systems in the nation's housing, could readily reduce the United States' energy budget by twelve to fifteen per cent, at a cost that could be recovered in the form of fuel savings in ten to twelve years.

Thus, we are at a crossroads. Along one path lies the continued consumption of fossil fuels by productive enterprises that waste energy for the sake of extracting maximum profits out of labor; the continued pollution of the environment; an escalating scramble for oil, which, as it diminishes in amount, will inevitably become an irresistible lure to military adventures. Along this path lies the increasing expansion of the size of power units, even beyond the present billion-dollar size, so that the chief prerequisite to power production will become a huge accumulation of wealth. In a country such as the United States, this will mean that our energy system will fall increasingly under the domination of a few huge, wealthy corporations. In the world at large it will favor the rich and the powerful nations as against the small, poor nations that are struggling to develop.

Finally, along this road as the fossil fuels are exhausted and nuclear reactors begin to dominate the energy system, creating a plutonium economy that ties power production directly to the violence of nuclear weapons, the threat of terroristic thefts — whether real, or not — can be used as a pretext to establish a system of military "protection." Already a recent report to the Atomic Energy Commission calls for elaborate military protection of power plants, together with domestic espionage and all the other trappings of fascism — all in the name of enabling the operation of a nuclear energy system.

The other path relies on energy conservation and the sun. Full use of existing methods of capturing solar energy for heating and cooling could remove fifteen to twenty per cent of the need for fossil fuels. By this means, together with feasible measures to conserve energy at no expense to the resulting goods and services, within perhaps the next decade about one-half of the present demand for energy from conventional sources could be deleted from the national energy budget — a step that with sensible planning could readily permit us to phase out the operation of most of the existing nuclear reactors.

Meanwhile, with a research and development effort that would be quite modest relative to the expenditures that have been devoted to the development of nuclear power, the technology for the economic production of solar cells for the production of electricity could be reduced to practicality. (According to a recent government report such a program could, by 1990, establish economical solar-powered electric stations for cities of one hundred thousand.) Given the wide flexibility of solar power units with respect to size, they could then be adapted to enterprises of any size and degree of centralization that seem socially desirable. Such changes could take place in small, graded steps, avoiding the huge accumulation of capital necessary to create conventional power stations. In this way a nation's power system could be made to serve its own particular needs, reversing a situation now frequently encountered in which the huge size and centralized location of power sources often dictates what can be produced. Energy can then more readily serve social needs, rather than create them.

And finally, through the wide use of solar energy and other alternative sources such as geothermal energy, the energy system can be separated from nuclear weaponry and freed from the dead hand of military control.

Consider, now, the implications of these alternatives for international relations. If the industrial countries follow the conventional path, they will have little to offer in the way of useful energy technology to the developing nations, which lack capital, are rich in natural materials and labor, and are usually favored by intense sunlight. In contrast, if the industrialized countries were to develop new productive technologies that emphasized the use of natural materials — synthesized from solar energy through photosynthesis — rather than synthetic ones, and techniques for solar power, they could provide real help in the struggle of the poor countries to develop their economies. This is the kind of help that would enable developing countries to increase both agricultural and industrial production, and to raise living standards to the levels that encourage the motivation for self-limitation of fertility.

If we take this path we can begin to find also new ways to harmonize the needs of industrialized and developing nations and to end the growing trend toward the creation of opposing camps of nations that produce and use natural resources. For example, if for the sake of environmental and energetic sanity, the industrialized countries were to cut back on the production of synthetic substitutes for natural materials such as cotton, their needs could be met, in part, by goods produced from such natural products in developing countries. Thus, Malaysia, for example, may wish to supply the industrialized nations not with natural rubber, but with tires; India may wish to supply not cotton, but finished fabrics and even clothes; West Africa may wish to supply the world not with palm oil, but with soap.

Perhaps the most immediate threat that has been generated by the energy crisis is the growing menace of a catastrophic worldwide economic collapse. International trade and monetary relations have already felt its heavy force, and the impact of the sharply rising price of energy has begun to disrupt industrial and agricultural production in both the rich nations and the developing ones. Here, too, a rational approach to the production and use of energy is a key to restoring the stability of world economic relations, without which no nation can hope to serve the needs of its own people.

If for the sake of the world's ecological survival we undertake the massive reconstruction of the economies of both the industrialized and developing nations, clearly we are faced, as well, with equally sweeping political changes. Thus, it is inconceivable that the United States could find the huge capital resources for the needed reconstruction of industry and agriculture along ecologically sound lines unless we give up not only capital-intensive forms of energy production but also our preoccupation with large-scale military activities.

But such a course would not only erode the economic motivations for war, it would also give us good grounds for ridding the world — at last — of the most dangerous means of modern war, nuclear weapons. This new course could halt the spread of nuclear reactors and, with it, the proliferation of nuclear weapons; and it encourages the existing nuclear powers to eliminate their own stocks of these insanely suicidal weapons.

~ع~

All this is described neither as a blueprint of the future nor as a panacea for the ills of the world. I am aware that, stated in these simplistic terms, this picture does not take into account the numerous difficult obstacles that lie along the path to environmental and energetic sanity and peace. Rather, these views are put forward as a kind of exercise that is designed only to demonstrate the crucial role — for good or evil — that energy plays in determining our future. It shows, I believe, that we cannot hope to develop, either in an industrialized country such as the United States, or in the world as a whole, a

rational system of production or an economic and social organization that fosters democracy and peace unless we do understand that the irrational production and use of energy is a fatal obstacle to this goal.

The energy crisis has become the world's most dangerous political issue as it wrenches back into open view the brutality of national competition for survival, the basic faults in existing economic systems, and the tragic absurdity of war. The crisis forces us to make long-avoided choices. If ecological sanity demands the sharp curtailment of power consumption and the production of synthetics and built-in obsolescence, where in society will the necessary controls be localized? If nations must on ecological grounds become more dependent on each other's indigenous goods, how can we avoid the ancient evils of international exploitation?

The lesson of the energy crisis is this: to survive on the earth, which is our habitat, we must live in keeping with its ecological imperatives. And if we are to take this course of ecological wisdom we must accept, at last, the wisdom of placing our faith not in production for private gain, but for public good; not in the exploitation of one people by another, but in the equality of all peoples; not in arms which devastate the land and the people and threaten world catastrophe, but in the desire which is shared everywhere in the world — for harmony with the environment, and for peace among the peoples who live in it.

Mr. Commoner is the director of the Center for the Biology of Natural Systems at Washington University in St. Louis and chairman of the Scientists' Institute for Public Information.

THE INTELLECTUAL IN VIDEOLAND

With 25 years of commercial television under his belt, the bewildered TV viewer now confronts yet another, more radical communications revolution.

by Douglass Cater

On a hot summer night in 1968 I was sitting in my Washington home, watching TV coverage of the disastrous Democratic convention in Chicago. Suddenly, all hell broke loose where the Wisconsin delegation was seated. TV cameras quickly zoomed in, of course, and reporters rushed to the area with walkie-talkies.

The whole nationwide TV audience thus knew in an instant what the uproar was all about. But Speaker Carl Albert, who was presiding over the convention, didn't have a clue, and he was the one who had to decide what to do about it. There, in microcosm, one saw how our leadership can be hustled by the formidable communications system of television.

No doubt about it, television is a looming presence in American life, even though most of us hardly know what to make of the medium. It arrived so swiftly and so totally: in January 1949 only 2.3 percent of American homes had the box with the cathode-ray tube. Five years later television had penetrated more than half of our homes. Today, 97 percent of them have one or more sets—a distribution roughly matching that of indoor plumbing. With American TV approaching its quarter-century anniversary as a household phenomenon, one

Douglass Cater, author and political correspondent, is currently director of the Aspen Institute's Program on Communications and Society.

might think we would by now have devoted serious attention to the effects of this medium on our culture, our society, our lives. Certainly, we might expect at this point to be trying to anticipate the consequences of the even more enveloping telecommunications environment that lies ahead. Yet, as the prescient Mr. Marconi predicted a long time ago, telecommunications has become part of the "almost unnoticed working equipment of civilization."

Why unnoticed? What has prevented thinking people from applying their critical faculties to this medium, which reaches greater masses than do all the other mass media combined (the number of sets in U.S. homes is nearly double the total daily circulation of newspapers)? Why haven't more of our talented scholars been attracted to the study of this new environment? Why do the media themselves devote so little attention to serious television analysis and criticism? Why have our foundations provided only very limited resources for the study of communications, which is as fundamental to society as education, health, and the physical environment?

I WOULD SUGGEST three reasons for these failures. In the first place, scientific evidence suggests that thinking people—at least those over 25—are left-brained in development. That is, they rely mainly on the left hemisphere, which controls sequential, analytical tasks based on the use of propositional thought. But TV,

we are informed, appeals mainly to the *right* hemisphere of the brain, which controls appositional—that is, non-sequential, non-analytic—thought.

Scientists and theologians alike have pondered how the two halves of the brain relate—whether they ignore, inhibit, cooperate, or compete with each other, or simply take turns at the control center. Whole cultures seem to show a preference for one or the other mode of thought, and thinking people of the Western world up until now have plighted their troth with propositional thought. After five centuries of slowly acquired sophistication in distinguishing the truth from the trickery transmitted by Mr. Gutenberg's invention, we now find ourselves having to master the non-linear logic created by a steady bombardment of sights and sounds on our senses. The thinking person is therefore apt to be somewhat bewildered by the telly and to regard it in the same way that a backsliding prohibitionist regards hard liquor—as something to be indulged in with a sense of guilt.

According to *Television and the Public,* Robert T. Bower's analysis of viewing habits, the "educated viewer" has learned to live with ambivalence: although he may be scornful of commercial TV fare, "he watches the set (by his own admission) as much as others during the evening and weekend hours; . . . even when he had a clear choice between an information program and some standard entertainment fare, he was just

51

as apt as others to choose the latter."

The peculiar structure of the American television industry is a second reason why the thinking person refuses to think seriously about the medium. The broadcast industry is based on a marketplace unlike any other in our private enterprise economy. Broadcasting offers its product "free" to the consumer and depends on advertising to supply, by the latest count, gross annual revenues of $4.5 billion. As a result, commercial TV's prime allegiance is to the merchant, not to the viewer. To attract the advertising dollar, the programmer seeks to capture the dominant portion of the viewers and to hold them unblinking for the longest period of time. Everything else is subordinated to this dogged pursuit of mankind in the mass. A program attracting many millions of viewers is deemed a failure and discarded if it happens to be scheduled opposite a program attracting even more millions.

Within this iron regime of dollars and ratings, a few ghettos of do-goodism exist. Network news and documentaries, as well as occasional dramas of exceptional quality, reveal an upward striving in television (some cynics dismiss this as tithing to the federal regulators). But these programs fare poorly in the competition for television's most precious commodity —time. A former network news chief has remarked of TV management, "They don't mind how much money and talent we devote to producing documentaries so long as we don't ask for prime-time evening hours to show them." Even the daylight hours have to be tightly rationed when the real-life marathon melodramas of Washington start competing with the soap operas of Hollywood.

Thinking people do not know how to cope with a system whose economic laws, they are led to believe, are immutable. Any suggestions they may have for the betterment of TV are characterized as naive, elitist, and offensive to the First Amendment. The proper posture is to sit back and be thankful when broadcast officialdom chooses to violate its own laws and reveal fleetingly what a fantastic instrument of communication television can be.

A third reason why thinking people have difficulty coming to grips with television is that they have yet to develop satisfactory ways to gauge the effects of this environmental phenomenon. Consider, as an example, the Surgeon General's inquiry into the effect of televised violence on the behavior of children. Conducted over a period of three years, at a cost of $1.8 million, and based on 23 separate laboratory and field studies, this probe was the most far-reaching to date into the social consequences of television. In its final report, the Surgeon General's committee could acknowledge only "preliminary and tentative" evidence of a causal relationship between TV violence and aggression in children.

As members of an industry dedicated to the proposition that 30-second commercials can change a viewer's buying behavior, producers would be foolish to ignore this warning about the not-so-subliminal effects of its program content. But these studies, mostly gauging immediate response to brief TV exposure, could not adequately measure the impact of the total phenomenon—the experience of the child who spends as many as six hours a day, year in and year out, before the set. This cumulative effect is what makes watching television different from reading books or going to the movies.

How to measure the longer-term, less flamboyant effects of the environment created by television? In 1938 E. B. White witnessed a TV demonstration and wrote, "A door closing, heard over the air, a face contorted, seen in a panel of light, these will emerge as the real and the true. And when we bang the door of our own cell or look into another's face, the impression will be of mere artifice."

Now, a third of a century later, comes Tony Schwartz to carry the speculation further in his book *The Responsive Chord*. Mr. Schwartz's insights have peculiar power, because he created the ill-famed political commercial for the 1964 campaign, which showed a child innocently picking daisy petals, one after another, as a countdown for a hydrogen bomb blast. Though there was no mention of the Presidential candidate at whom the message was aimed, the effect of the commercial was so unnerving that its sponsors withdrew it after a single showing. Schwartz appears to know whereof he theorizes.

Gutenberg man, he writes, lived by a communication system requiring the laborious coding of thought into words and then the equally laborious decoding by the receiver—similar to the loading, shipping, and unloading of a railway freight car. Electronic man dispenses with this by communicating experience without the need of symbolic transformations. What the viewer's brain gets is a mosaic of myriad dots of light and vibrations of sound that are stored and recalled at high speed. Amid this electronic bombardment, Schwartz speculates, a barrier has been crossed akin to the supersonic sound barrier—or, in his image, the 90-mile-an-hour barrier beyond which a motorcycle racer must turn *in to* rather than *out with* a skid: ". . . In communicating at electronic speed, we no longer direct information into an audience but try to evoke stored information out of it in a patterned way."

The function of the electronic communicator, according to Schwartz, "is to achieve a state of resonance with the person receiving visual and auditory stimuli." The Gutenberg communicator —for the past 500 years patiently transmitting experience line by line, usually left to right, down the printed page—is no longer relevant. TV man has become conditioned to a total communication environment, to constant stimuli which he shares with everyone else in society and to which he is conditioned to respond instantly. Schwartz believes that the totality and instantaneousness of television, more than its program content, contributes to violence in society.

His premises lead him to the shattering conclusion that "truth is a print ethic, not a standard for ethical behavior in electronic communication." We must now be concerned not with Gutenberg-based concepts of truth, but with the *effects* of electronic communication: "A whole new set of questions must be asked, and a whole new theory of communications must be formulated."

Without going all the way with Schwartz, we clearly need to examine the effects of TV more diligently. What, for example, is television doing to the institutions and forms and rituals of our democracy? Politicians are still struggling to learn the grammar of TV communication and to master its body English, which is so different from that of the stump speech. TV has markedly influenced the winnowing process by which some politicians are sorted out as prospects for higher office from those who are not. TV has contributed to the abbreviation of the political dialogue and even changed the ground rules by which candidates map their campaign itineraries.

TV has encouraged the now widespread illusion that by using the medium we can create a Greek marketplace of direct democracy. When citizens can see and hear what they believe to be the actuality, why should they rely on inter-mediating institutions to make the de-cisions for them? When political leaders can directly reach their constituents without the help of a political party, why should they not opt for "the people's" mandate rather than "the party's"? Re-cent Presidents and Presidential candi-dates have been notably affected by this line of reasoning. It exposes an ancient vulnerability of our Republic, in which too much political lip service is paid to the notion that public opinion should rule everything.

How can democracy be strengthened within the environment of television? Why, in an age of abundant communi-cation, has there been a continuing de-cline in voter participation? Prof. Mi-chael Robinson, a political scientist, has cited surveys indicating that heavy TV viewers are more apt than light viewers to be turned off by politics. He specu-lates that the more dependent someone becomes on TV as his principal source of information, the more likely he is to feel that he cannot understand or affect the political process. TV, unlike news-papers, reaches many who are not inter-ested in public affairs, and these "inad-vertent" audiences, in Robinson's view, are frequently confused and alienated by what they see. Such a proposition runs directly counter to the usual re-formist instinct to prescribe more pro-gramming to overcome voter apathy. Professor Robinson's speculations need to be probed more deeply.

What will be the future? George Or-well had a vision of a time—now less than a decade away—when the commu-nications environment would be em-ployed for the enslavement, rather than the enlightenment, of mankind. Orwell called his system "Big Brother." For the present, anyway, we can conceive of a less ominous communications future with MOTHER, which is the acronym for "Multiple Output Telecommunica-tion Home End Resources."

What will be the technical character-istics of MOTHER? First, she will offer infinitely more channels—via microwave, satellite, cable, laser beam—than the present broadcast spectrum provides. There will also be greater capacity crammed within each channel—more information "bits" per gigahertz—so that one can simultaneously watch a program and receive a newspaper print-out on the same channel.

Bettmann

"The Gutenberg communicator—for the past 500 years patiently transmitting experience line by line, usually left to right, down the printed page—is no longer relevant. TV man has become conditioned to a total communication environment, to constant stim-uli which he shares with everyone else in society."

A life-sized MOTHER, the images on her screens giving the illusion of three-dimensionality, will be able to *narrow-cast* to neighborhoods or other focused constituencies. MOTHER will be "inter-active," permitting us to talk back to our television set by means of a digital de-vice on the console. Recording and re-play equipment, which is already being marketed, will liberate us from the tyr-anny of the broadcast schedule, and computer hookup and stop-frame con-trol will bring the Library of Congress and other Gutenberg treasuries into our living room.

Finally, via the satellite, MOTHER will offer worldwide programming in what the communications experts art-fully call "real time" (even if real time means that Muhammad Ali must fight at 4:00 A.M. in Zaire in order to suit the prime-time needs of New Yorkers). Al-though MOTHER will be able to beam broadcasts from the People's Republic of China directly to a household in the

United States and vice versa, she may face political barriers.

Until recently, prophets foresaw that the cable and other technological ad-vances would transform television from a wholesale to a retail enterprise, directly offering the consumer a genuine diver-sity of choice. The "television of abun-dance" would bring not just greater vari-ety of programs but also new concepts of programming—continuing education, health delivery, community services. Television would become a participatory instrument of communication rather than a one-way flow.

TODAY, THESE VISIONS are not so bright. Some critics now glumly predict that the new technology will suffer the fate of the supersonic transport. Others expect that the technology will be developed, but that it will serve strictly commercial, rather than social, purposes. Computer may be talking to computer by cable and satellite, but householders will still watch "I Love Lucy" on their TV sets.

My own expectation is that the next decade or two will radically alter America's communications. The important issue is whether the change will be for better or for worse. If it is to be for better, we must give more critical attention to TV than we have given in the past. Too much critical time has been wasted worrying about the worst of television. More attention should be paid to the best, not simply laudatory attention but a systematic examination of style and technique and message. Criticism should also extend its reach beyond the intellectual elite into elementary and secondary schools, where children can be stimulated to think about the medium that so dominates their waking hours. We must endeavor to raise the viewers' capacity to distinguish truth from sophistry or at least their awareness, in Tony Schwartz's vocabulary, of the "resonance" being evoked from them.

We should have more widespread analysis and debate on the potential for new media and for new forms within the media. Could an electronic box office for pay programming repeal the iron laws governing "free" commercial television? How do we move beyond the limits of present broadcasting toward broader social purposes for television? In an era when lifelong learning has become essential for the prevention of human obsolescence, television surely has a role to play. And television might regularly deliver some types of health service now that the doctor is seldom making house calls. Health and education are gargantuan national enterprises, which cost upward of $200 billion annually. Yet only paltry sums are being invested for research and demonstration to develop TV's capacity to enrich and extend these vital fields of social service.

Finally, we must move beyond our preoccupation with the production and transmission processes in media communication. An equally important question is, What gets through? The editors of *Scientific American* report that man's visual system has more than a million channels, capable of transmitting instantly 10 million bits of information to the brain. Yet the brain has the capacity for receiving only 27 bits of information per second. These are the raw statistics of communication within the human anatomy. They lead Sir John Eccles, the Nobel Prize–winning physiologist, to believe that the most important frontier of brain research involves the study of inhibition—our capacity to censor stimuli in order to prevent overload. Sir John makes the comparison: "It's like sculpture. What you cut away from the block of stone produces the statue."

Our journalists, both on TV and in print, pledge fealty to the proposition that society thrives by the communication of great gobs of unvarnished truth. Our law courts make us swear to tell "the truth, the whole truth, and nothing but the truth." Yet we only dimly understand how, in an all-enveloping informational environment, man chisels his little statues of perceived reality. As we approach a time when communication threatens to fission like the atom, we need to delve more deeply into these mysteries.

Looking far ahead, Robert Jastrow, director of the Goddard Institute of Space Studies, foresees a fifth communications revolution even more radical than the previous four revolutions of speech, writing, printing, and radio. "In the long term," Jastrow predicts, "the new satellites will provide a nervous system for mankind, knitting the members of our species into a global society." He compares this breakthrough with that change in the history of life several billion years ago when multicellular animals evolved out of more primitive organisms.

Before such an awesome prospect, thinking people may feel overwhelmed. Or else, we can screw up our courage, ask the fundamental questions, and make the critical choices necessary for the shaping of our destiny.

by Marguerite Guzman Bouvard *and* Jacques Bouvard

Computerized Information and Effective Protection of Individual Rights

When the founding fathers assembled to draft the Constitution of the United States, they did not anticipate the need to establish privacy as an inalienable right. However, because of the need to reinterpret democratic values in changing social contexts, the state of California amended its constitution in 1972 in order to list privacy as a fundamental right.

Privacy is not an abstract concept. It has meaning only in relation to a national culture, a particular political system and a specific period of time. It has become an issue in modern democratic societies which are characterized by large-scale, sophisticated bureaucratic structures and advanced technology in communications and information systems.

Technological development has been permitted to evolve without regard for its impact on our democratic political system. Twenty years ago, information about individuals was stored on paper in file cabinets. Information-sharing between federal agencies and/or private concerns was both expensive and time-consuming and hence limited. Today, thanks to advances in computer technology, public and private institutions collect, maintain and exchange vast quantities of personal information concerning the American people. Federal data banks in particular contain all sorts of personal data, sometimes of a most unexpected nature. The air force lists religious affiliations in one of its personnel files and the Department of Agriculture keeps a file on children of migrant workers.

Growth of behavioral research has encouraged data collection and storage in a variety of institutional settings: government agencies, such as the Department of Health, Education and Welfare (HEW), bureaus and centers within schools and universities, hospitals and private businesses. Continuing advances in computer technology make it increasingly possible to maintain extensive records of historical data on millions of people. Once captured and entered into a computerized data bank, this personal data can be retained forever. At a moment's notice, it can be retrieved and flashed across a city or around the world to a police cruiser, a credit officer or a prospective employer via worldwide networks of telecommunications.

Data Profile

The real impact of the computer goes far beyond these efficient archival and broadcasting capabilities. It lies in the computer's ability to transform a mass of raw data into

> Information about a person is an extension of selfhood, for him to communicate or withhold as he sees fit.

meaningful and usable information. Advances in data management technology provide the means for organizing data banks so that each item of data can be cross-indexed with other relevant elements to form a context of interpretation. Random facts about an individual may appear meaningless or innocuous when considered in isolation. When aggregated and interrelated with other facts, they form a composite "data profile" from which one can draw conclusions and make decisions.

Unless this profile is reasonably complete and properly balanced, it may project a distorted picture of reality and lead to false conclusions and unfair decisions, which may have a devastating impact upon a person's life. *The New York Times* has reported the case of a person who became the object of mail surveillance by the Federal Bureau of Investigation (FBI) after she was found to have corresponded with the American Socialist party. In the context of the radical unrest of the sixties, this was sufficient ground for the government to suspect this person of subversive activities and treat her as a potential threat to the internal security of the United States. Different conclusions might have been drawn if it had been known that the suspect was a 14-year-old high school student researching the Socialist movement for a term paper.

Personal data within a file has a market value. It can be bought, sold, stolen or traded for other data. Police, license bureaus, credit reporting agencies, housing agencies, educational insitutions and welfare agencies routinely exchange data with one another, although the concerned individuals are usually unaware of it. More than 60 percent of the federal data banks surveyed by Senator Sam Ervin's Committee on the Judiciary were found to engage in various data exchange programs. In many cases, exchanges between agencies, such as the Central Intelligence Agency (CIA), Internal Revenue Service (IRS) and the FBI, are performed without adequate audit trail procedures so that the original source of the data and the circumstances under which it was gathered cannot be traced.

Some data interchanges among agencies are clearly deceptive. The IRS and the Selective Service System share personal data with other agencies despite pledges of confidentiality on the forms used to collect the data. This is all the more serious in that individuals refusing to disclose this information are subject to criminal penalties.

Confidentiality

Standards of confidentiality vary among federal agencies and the information passed from one agency to another is likely to be handled in different ways. The Census Bureau is unique among federal agencies in maintaining strict confidentiality rules. While some agencies have been successful in establishing specific guidelines for maintaining confidentiality of information within their own operations, they have found it difficult to generalize these rules to their exchange of data with other agencies. The transfer of data between federal, state and local governments constitutes an even greater threat to the individual than the exchange of information between federal agencies. Local information handlers are more numerous and more apt to be insensitive to privacy concerns.

A major factor of the privacy problem is the absence of legislation and organizational rules ensuring privacy, confidentiality and due process to the subjects of computerized information. Data banks have been established at all levels of government, business and the military services without any real knowledge or concern for their potential impact over individual rights.

A survey of federal data banks conducted by the Senate Judiciary Committee listed 858 data banks operated by fifty-four executive branch agencies that contain over one billion pieces of personal data about Americans. Only 10 percent of these data banks have been specifically authorized by law, and more than 40 percent do not inform individuals that records are being kept on them. The existence of secret data banks, surreptitiously collecting data about innocent Americans, is not science fiction, but contemporary reality. Americans now face a double challenge: to develop a public awareness of the privacy problem and to establish appropriate procedures to regulate the use and dissemination of computer stored information.

The spectacular advances in computer technology of the last twenty years have not ended. Within the next ten years, computer data processing price/performance is expected to improve by nearly tenfold over present levels. Industry experts also anticipate storage capacities to increase dramatically, by a factor of 100 or more, while storage costs will drop about 100 times below current figures. By 1985, on-line data banks, with capacities of ten to fifty trillion characters and retrieval time of a fraction of a second, will be in operation.

The privacy issue is all the more urgent because of the widespread use of information systems to administer services which many Americans consider essential to their well-being. Along with the values of a democratic system, Americans have constantly rising expectations in terms of medical services, health insurance, credit, family assistance and education. Those in search of jobs, credit, housing, welfare and other services must disclose extensive information of a private nature in order to obtain these benefits. This information further accumulates into the files maintained by various private and public institutions. Postponing attention to this problem may lead Americans to believe that an encroachment into their personal privacy is the price they have to pay to enjoy these services.

An even bigger challenge lies ahead with the proposed national health insurance program, which many people believe will be enacted within the next few years. Sensitive information involved in the patient-doctor relationship will be entered into computerized data banks. The prospect of this information becoming available, at the push of a button, to any terminal user connected with a data bank, unknown to the patient, is a frightening thought.

Most Americans support the concept of a privacy with a sense that it is somehow related to other values, such as individual freedom or the pursuit of happiness. So important is the value of privacy that one can use it to distinguish between different types of political systems. In authoritarian systems, such as the Soviet Union, privacy is enjoyed by the Politburo, the highest organ of the Communist party and the source of all policy in that society. On the other hand, the Soviet citizenry is subjected to thorough surveillance. In liberal democratic societies, individuals enjoy privacy in order to pursue their happiness and interest groups enjoy privacy in order to form public consensus, resolve conflicts and promote the expression of independent ideas. The partial autonomy of individual, family, religious and corporate groups in a liberal society prevents total politicizing of life.

Value Conflict

Every democratic society develops particular privacy balances between the need of governmental agencies for privacy and the need of the free press and interest groups for knowledge of government operations. At any time in an open society, there are conflicts between values, such as national security (which requires a certain amount of secrecy), freedom of the press, the right to know and the right to privacy. Compromises between these conflicts of interest vary according to time and place. However, fundamental values of individual and group autonomy cannot be compromised without transforming the entire political system.

Privacy is the guarantor of individual moral autonomy, a basic value in a democratic system of government. Privacy can be defined as the right to control one's information system and one's physical being. The latter right has been traditionally conceived in American society as the right to be secured against unauthorized entries and seizures. Both rights are closely related to the principle of respect for persons. Both must be reinterpreted in the light of changing technological and social contexts. Typical of this kind of reinterpretation is the study conducted by the Hastings Insti-

tute concerning nonvoluntary use of psychoactive drugs and behavior modification programs for incarcerated people. To what extent do these programs constitute an intrusion into the personal privacy of inmates? Should inmates be given the right to refuse participation in these programs?

Privacy is violated whenever a person's moral autonomy or self-image are impinged upon, even without affecting his conduct. Altering an individual's self-perception against his will offends human dignity. If we are able to regulate a person's conduct or keep it under surveillance (as in the system of dispensing welfare), we are, in fact, curtailing his responsibility as a moral agent making free choices. This limits the options open to persons regarding their relationship with others, their physical mobility and their own self-perception.

Unless data is complete and balanced, it may project a distorted picture of reality.

Privacy, the control of one's own person and of the extension of one's person in the form of information, is at the basis of man's claim for human dignity. Information about a person is an extension of selfhood, for him to communicate or withhold as he sees fit. Even when an individual divulges personal information to receive certain benefits, such as credit or insurance or to win a lawsuit, he has a continuing interest in retaining control over that information beyond the original disclosure, and especially the right to decide whether this information should be communicated to third parties.

The notion of self is associated with a person's recorded history of his individual and social activities. Information pertaining to these activities should be distinguished by degree of sensitivity and treated accordingly. A student's course selection or grade records are administrative in nature, while his request for contraceptives or psychological counseling from a university health service should be considered sensitive and should be disclosed only to those with a legitimate need to know.

Recognizing this distinction is extremely important and must keep pace with the growing trend toward integrating information systems. Unless such precautions are taken, a student's records, including such sensitive information, may be routinely passed on to prospective employers and become part of his employee record. It is in such cases that the combination of information from various files will present an inroad into personal privacy. To lose control over one's record of activities or traits is to lose control over one's self. On the other hand, the notion of consent is made possible by the control of one's information. If the facts about a person are freely disclosed with the knowledge and consent that they may be shared with others, there has been no violation of privacy.

A person's control over personal information and access to

and dissemination of that information are at the heart of individual autonomy. The relationship of individual autonomy to the functioning of an open society requires renewed attention and emphasis at all levels of civic education. Too often, because the values of privacy are not clearly defined and are not sufficiently stressed, the young adult concludes that institutional efficiency and society's "right to know" are more important than his right to make decisions.

Individuals vs. Institutions

The privacy issue involves other concerns often emotionally associated with, but not actually included in the concept of privacy. People may feel threatened by the very existence of massive and efficient information systems even though their privacy has not actually been invaded. They are often concerned about the endless search for personal data by social scientists, market researchers, opinion pollsters and the institutions that use this data. When the institutions seeking information also control funds, the threat appears much greater.

A recent incident involving HEW illustrates this concern. HEW requested the New York City Board of Education to disclose personal information on its students for the purpose of developing a new data bank. The data bank was to identify the racial and ethnic background of pupils, their language background and their ability to speak English. When the school board insisted that it would supply such information only anonymously or statistically in order to preserve the privacy of the pupils, HEW threatened to withhold millions in federal funds.

Although people may charge institutions that operate information systems with invasion of privacy, their real complaint is often about institutional power and its linkage to possession of information. An issue frequently associated with privacy is the relationship of the individual to any large institution operating a data bank. A student who recently completed an independent study on privacy and banking complained that while banking institutions are able to acquire a great deal of information about their customers, the reverse is not true.

Another element in the privacy issue is the right to be presumed innocent until proven guilty. An article in *The New York Times Magazine* by Aryeh Neir, executive director of the American Civil Liberties Union (ACLU), documents the inability of a would-be cab driver to find a job because of an arrest record. The record contained no information regarding disposition of the case, which was later dismissed. It followed that person whenever he moved and prevented him from finding employment.

While arrest records are frequently incomplete and inaccurate, the individuals concerned have no access to them and no way to correct them or to know that potential employers have access to them. There are no criminal or civil sanctions against misuse of records and no clear set of standards in any state as to which jobs should require review of criminal arrest

records. In cases of incomplete or inaccurate records, the burden of proof often rests with the injured party, rather than with the managers of a data system, who should shoulder the burden.

Legislation ensuring persons' access to files containing information about them is sorely lacking.

Trust is at the foundation of cooperative attitudes toward government agencies and institutions in the American political system. If people feel that the information they divulge to the census, for driver's registration or for immigration and naturalization will not be treated confidentially or will be sold on the marketplace as a trivial commodity, they may become alienated from the goals and operations of institutions which are supposed to serve them and which rely upon their support.

These concerns focus on the place of the individual in a technological society and reveal, not that too much power is held by too few, but that so little is held by so many. In the relationship between individuals and organizations, the scales are balanced in favor of the latter. A Canadian task force on "Privacy and Computers" stated that the information process is one way in which institutions learn more about individuals, but individuals learn no more about institutions or even what institutions learn about them.

Concern for privacy is caught up in the more general debate regarding the effect of technology on society. Some contemporary thinkers share a pessimistic view of this relationship and conclude that what is technically feasible is allowed to occur without regard for the consequences. Hannah Arendt, Herbert Marcuse and Lewis Mumford share this attitude. At the other end of the spectrum are those who argue with Alvin Toffler that technology has allowed the individual a greater range of choice than he has ever enjoyed before, one that may even be bewilderingly broad. They argue further that problems resulting from modern technology can be solved by the use of more technology. The privacy issue, however, will suffer from being embroiled in this debate. Since technology is here to stay, the privacy discussion should not focus on its desirability, but rather on finding ways to protect humanistic values and goals.

Guidelines for Protection

Regulation of the use of digitally stored information is in its early stages. However, general guidelines for protecting privacy can be articulated for handling personal data at various stages of gathering and dissemination.

Data-gathering practices are related to the problem of privacy insofar as they involve acquiring personal information from individuals, their neighbors or associates. The information gathered may be derogatory, inaccurate or clearly irrelevant to the purposes of the data bank. In the absence of guidelines, the individual concerned has no right of redress. The law of defamation does not prevent derogatory information from being collected or disseminated, provided the information is true. Harmful information can be so labeled only in the context of particular uses. Information regarding a person's drinking habits or marital status, while not harmful in itself, may prevent that person from acquiring a job when passed on to a prospective employer.

Most data banks operate without guidelines regarding types of information to be collected in order to fulfill the objectives of the data bank, and without provisions for insuring either the currency, completeness or accuracy of the information. In the absence of clear definitions of relevant information, there is little to prevent private organizations or government agencies from gathering more information than necessary. Some critics have charged the Census Bureau with securing information of more interest to marketing and manufacturing concerns than to the bureau itself; others have charged credit bureaus with maintaining incomplete information.

In addition to establishing standards of relevance, there is a real need to clearly define areas which may not be the subject of inquiry and to enforce these limitations. Any kind of information which could serve as a source of prejudice against individuals, such as race, religion or marital status, should not be gathered. The incident in which the New York City Board of Education resisted HEW's request for sensitive information about pupils is a clear case in point. Given the ease and speed with which information passes from one organization to another, it could become the basis for unjust discrimination.

There should also be an enforceable code of conduct for those who collect information. Often, investigators are sent out in the field without guidelines on how to conduct themselves or on how to insure confidentiality of the data they gather. Nor are there any rules regarding permissible sources of information. Investigators all too frequently rely upon hearsay and gossip in order to supply their needs. Recent legislation in the Canadian provinces of Quebec, Manitoba and Saskatchewan has provided guidelines for credit reporting agencies regarding permissible contents of personal reports, disclosure of information to subjects and methods of collecting information.

Once a data file is established, its contents should be subject to periodic review for insuring currency, completeness and accuracy of information. Legislation ensuring persons access to files containing information about them is sorely lacking. The Fair Credit Reporting Act of 1972 allows an individual to discuss the contents of his file when denied credit, but he may not personally review the file or clarify certain details by inserting his own account in the record. In the field of public education, there have been many cases in which parents were forbidden access to the educational records of their children by school officials and also cases in which a child's school records were given out to persons and groups outside the school without the knowledge or consent of the child or his parents. Legislation enacted in August, 1974, is intended to correct this situation.

Currently, there are no provisions for expunging obsolete or correcting incomplete information on criminal records. In the absence of regulations regarding the use, completeness and accuracy of records, the individual must rely upon expensive and lengthy litigation to obtain relief. While free access of individuals to records maintained on them is an important step in the verification process, the burden of responsibility for accuracy and completeness should rest entirely with the user of information systems.

Before the right of access to files containing personal information can be secured, individuals must gain the right to be informed of the existence of any file containing information about them. Even when people are aware that information is being held in a particular institution, the transfer and sharing of data among agencies is usually accomplished on a discretionary basis and out of public view. Individuals who divulge personal information in order to obtain a benefit or fulfill a requirement may not discover that this information has been used by third parties in a wholly different context.

At the federal level, data dissemination is partially encouraged by pressures from the House Ways and Means Committee and the Senate Finance Committee calling on federal agencies, such as HEW, to make more productive use of their data. The massive FEDNET system, which was proposed by the General Services Administration in order to provide efficient and economical computer services, is a case in point. Privacy should not be sacrificed for the sake of government efficiency any more than other basic freedoms. Alan Westin suggests developing the right of waiver and consent through legislation, the requirement that personal information be passed along only when the individual concerned consents to the transfer.

These considerations point to the pressing need for a flow of information from the user to the subject of data banks. The individual American needs to be informed of the existence of data banks which contain personal information on him and of the extent of data dissemination. Above all, he needs the opportunity to exercise his informed consent. Equally important is the need for the managers of data systems to accept and enforce guidelines regarding data-gathering practices as well as data maintenance, dissemination and usage. The data gathered by the user should be strictly relevant to a clearly articulated purpose and checked for accuracy. The sources of information should be reliable and made known to the data subject.

Guidelines for data maintenance should include appropriate procedures to insure accuracy, completeness and currency of files. These should provide for periodic purging of obsolete information and the opportunity of the file subject to review and correct his record. In the absence of statutory regulation of data dissemination, the "need to know" of government agencies, credit bureaus and employers should be carefully examined and balanced with the right of the individual to monitor the flow of his personal records.

Legislation for Privacy

Perhaps because of Watergate, the 93rd Congress has been called the "Privacy Congress." Although the Senate Subcommittee on Constitutional Rights, under the Committee on the Judiciary, and the House Special Subcommittee on the Invasion of Privacy have been investigating the problem of information systems and privacy for almost a decade, it was not until 1974 that legislation was passed which embodies some general guidelines for protecting privacy.

A continuing national concern with privacy must be sustained if technology is not to outstrip our capacity to regulate it.

The executive has also become concerned with the privacy implications of its massive automated files. In 1973, a report entitled "Records, Computers and the Rights of Citizens" was published by the Advisory Committee on Personal Data Systems established by Elliott Richardson when he was secretary of HEW. The report suggests the enactment of a Code of Fair Information Practices for all automated personal data systems. Among the principles included in the code were the right of Americans to know about records held on them and to be involved in insuring the accuracy and currency of these records.

In February, 1974, a Domestic Council Committee on the Right of Privacy was created by the President. The mission of the council is to study some of the more pressing privacy problems associated with automated files and to request ways of handling them. Among its action items for 1975 are a review of the growing use of the Social Security number as a universal single identifier and of policy regarding dissemination and use of federal mailing lists.

While these general guidelines for privacy rights may seem praiseworthy, any legislation which seeks to make them operative will have to be passed in a context of opposing interests. The August, 1974, law governing access to educational records is a case in point. The Family Educational Rights and Privacy section of the Elementary and Secondary School Act prohibits federal funds to any educational institution that has the policy of denying or which effectively prevents parents of students from inspecting and reviewing any and all official records, files and data directly related to their children. It also restricts release of file documents to third parties without the consent of parent or student.

The months of hearings which preceded enactment of this law gave evidence of considerable controversy. Once the law was passed, many universities proceeded to remove letters of recommendation from files which would be open to their subjects. For these institutions, the principle of confidentiality of letters of recommendation is more important than the right of students to see their records.

Another bill passed in 1974 is intended to insure that some privacy protection principles be observed in federal data systems. According to this legislation, data files will be listed annually by type and general content in the *Federal Register* and also published in an annual data bank directory available to the public. Citizens will be allowed to examine and correct their records, and agencies must insure the accuracy and currency of the data each time it is used or disseminated. This legislation does not apply to law enforcement records and some military and civil service commission records.

Three significant privacy areas are still not covered by legislation: criminal justice records, data banks maintained by the private sector and state and local government responsibility for taxes and welfare records. Senators Sam Ervin and Roman Hruska introduced two criminal justice bills in 1974. They contained provisions for sealing an individual's record seven years after a felony has been committed and five years after the commission of a misdemeanor if there had been no conviction during those years, if no prosecution was pending and if the person was not a fugitive. The Hruska bill prohibited disclosure of arrest records to other agencies without a disposition of the case. Both bills were opposed by the Justice Department and the FBI and were eventually defeated. Presumably, incomplete arrest records will continue to hinder some Americans as they seek jobs, housing or credit.

Despite this promising start in assuring citizen rights and despite a varied group of interests supporting vigorous legislation from the leaders of the computer industry and society of computer professionals, civil libertarians and constitutional conservatives, much remains to be done. A continuing national concern with privacy must be sustained if technology is not to outstrip our capacity to regulate it with timeliness.

12

Who are the real people?

By James S. Kunen

Ronald Reagan says, in his campaign speech, that he opposes school busing but favors "periodically busing some of the bureaucrats in Washington out into the country to meet the real people."

Does Ron mean that bureaucrats do not exist, that they are a myth? He can't mean that; if they don't exist, how could they be bused? Ron must mean that bureaucrats lead irrelevant existences, deserve no attention, and thus in a figurative or *metaphorical* sense are not "real people."

Who are the real people? This has always been a matter of speculation, because up to now there has never been devised a dependable reality test. But today, we have an unprecedented opportunity to study real people, because they are cropping up in droves in television advertisements, which is odd because advertising is the business of unreality, of creating illusion, of making products appear to be what they are not. An automobile becomes the love of your life. Detergent becomes fairy dust which secures a husband's love and stills a mother-in-law's acid tongue. An insurance man becomes an angel of the Lord who bestows everlasting life.

Into this melange of images strides a dowdy housewife, looking a little embarrassed to be on the wrong side of the TV screen, like Alice through the looking glass, out of this world. What we have here is the breach, at last, of that thin but heretofore impenetrable glass wall between the world of the real people and the world of the personalities, a barrier up to now crossed only by calamities and campaign stops.

Here, at her own sink, stands Mrs. Rita Medina, of El Cerrito, California, proudly telling us that 20 Mule Power tub and tile cleaner "just cleans better. That's it." But *is* that it? Who is this Rita Medina, anyway? How much does she know about cleaning? Above all, what is she doing on my TV?

Selling.

It seems we've been flimflammed a little too often by beautiful actresses. What parts us most promptly from our money these days is people like ourselves, people we can trust. They are such effective salespeople that last year, according to the Screen Actors Guild, 6,000 acting jobs in commercials went to non-professionals, or "real people," a term the Guild does not approve of.

Generally, the real people are found by the sponsor's market researchers, who survey people at shopping centers, or by random phone calls, then go back to those who had something good to say and have them re-say it for the cameras. The Federal Trade Commission requires that the real person sign an affidavit that she is speaking her own words and means them. The real people are paid the same wages as a S.A.G. union member—$300 to $400 for a typical ad.

If a real person's endorsement is a tempting carrot to the consumer, a real person's humiliation is a potent stick. The typical humiliation ad is filmed by a hidden camera. The hidden camera itself teaches the viewer an important lesson—you never know when you're being watched. The housewife is urged by an interviewer (who is an actor) to test *her* product against the sponsor's product.

A Mrs. Garnett tests Comet against *her* cleanser on a sink that has tough food stains, pot marks and cooking grease. The Comet works fine. "How did your cleanser do?" the interviewer asks. "Oh well, it can't—it didn't compare with Comet," she admits. "In what respect?" he presses. "In—in saving time, for one thing," says Mrs. Garnett, haltingly. "So what do you think now?" Mrs. Garnett's voice quavers under the weight of a dawning realization: "Maybe—maybe I've been spending 20 years cleaning more than I should have."

From humiliation flows penitence and conversion. The chastened housewife resolves always to buy the sponsor's product in the future. And she no doubt brings the sponsor more joy than all the housewives who never strayed.

But do real people really attach so much importance to cleansers?

Mrs. Rita Medina was so pleased with 20 Mule Power tub and tile cleaner that she wrote a letter to the manufacturer, an inspired move on her part since it led to a role in an ad, which earned her enough money to buy a dishwasher. "I enjoy cleaning," Mrs. Medina told me with a chuckle.

A common motif in ads has one neighbor telling another of the latest technological developments in the laundry room. Does Mrs. Medina actually discuss cleaning with her neighbors?

"Oh yes," she laughed. "Especially when you have a stubborn problem. Of course, there are some people that you wouldn't discuss cleaning problems with."

Eureka! Here is the test of who is a real person and who is not: Would you discuss cleaning problems with him? Mrs. Medina didn't elaborate, but I suspect that she wouldn't discuss cleaning problems with bureaucrats. *Or* Ronald Reagan.

III. Perspectives on Problems of Structural Inequality

American myths and traditions, replete with references to equality and freedom, obscure the reality of social inequality in the present as well as the past. The American Revolution was essentially a middle-class political movement, yet during the Colonial epoch there was a segment of the population on the bottom of the social ladder, as well as others who did not belong to the appropriate religion, who were excluded from participation in decisions. The Constitution was written by the propertied class and its suspicion of the urban masses is well documented in the *Federalist Papers*. Yet Americans both professed and practiced equality, a fact noted by de Tocqueville and other European obeservers of the American scene in the early nineteenth century. However, it took nearly a century for the freed slaves to overcome the political disability of the "grandfather clauses" and *Plessey v. Ferguson* (1896).

Some gains were made in the area of sexual inequality when the Nineteenth Amendment, guaranteeing women the right to vote, was passed in 1920, but the Equal Rights Amendment, written to broaden these guarantees, has yet to be ratified. Women make up over half of the population, and they now comprise about 40 percent of the work force. And although an increasing number of women have college degrees, women college graduates still earn about $5,000 a year less than men with comparable education.

Those sociologists who share the *order* perspective are inclined to view the American stratification system as an "open" one in which the economic pyramid is becoming less unequal. The *conflict* perspective, however, contends that the unequal distribution of wealth in America is continuing. For although our expanding economy—until "stagflation" hit in the seventies— has extended the number of people in the middle income stratum, the top 5 percent still earn about 20 percent of total income whereas the bottom 20 percent earn 5 percent. Even before the recent recession there were over 25 million people below the poverty line, many of whom were underemployed. Even with the well publicized "War on Poverty" in the sixties, which was more a skirmish than a war, we were spending far less per capita for welfare than many of the other Western nations. Our emphasis on the American Dream and the work ethic has buttressed what Robert Heilbroner has termed a policy of "benign neglect" of the poor (1970). Our failure to recognize inequality obscures the true nature of poverty.

By relating poverty to the larger issue of inequality we confront the myth of equality. For as Ryan, in his essay "Blaming the Victim" informs us, our ideology distorts reality and we blame the poor for being poor. Such myths die hard, as Michael Harrington discovered when writing his book *The Other America,* which was influential in stimulating the so-called "War on Poverty." He writes that even though he had data which proved there were 50 million poor in America he had difficulty believing his own figures (1962). So if we can cast aside the myths of the "undeserving," "disreputable," and "culturally deprived" poor, which are the result of distortions which lead to "blaming the victim," we will be in a position to view poverty as serving a necessary "function" in our affluent social structure. Herbert Gans sums up this and other functions of poverty in our society in "The Positive Functions of Poverty." For those who would avoid "methodological purism" this is an excellent example of the *order* perspective used in a radical critique. The article "Surplus People" informs us of another way the unemployed, the "new poor," are "functional" to the political economy of our system during an economic recession.

Two of the most crucial issues of inequality which we must face up to as we move into our nation's third century are *racism* and *sexism*. Our historical treatment of blacks and native Americans has been buttressed by a heritage of racial superiority, or racism. During the recession of 1975–76, the unemployment rate among young urban blacks was over four times that of the national rate of 7.5 percent. Policy makers could find many ways of blaming the victims: they were unskilled, school dropouts, etc. And in the 1960s, then Assistant Secretary of Labor Daniel P. Moynihan blamed the "black family" and its "matrifocal" orientation as a rationale for a policy of "benign neglect" of the urban poor. However, the black family described by Bims has definite strengths.

The "melting pot" seems to have worked for the Europeans and their descendants, for they "made it." Greely describes their achievements. But, as Deloria suggests, native Americans have not gotten their foot on the "ladder of success" yet, and selling trinkets to tourists is hardly a start.

Sexism is more than economic inequality, and the conditioning of nursery school children to accept their ascribed status is documented by Serbin and O'Leary. Gloria Steinem neatly turns some clichés and stereotypes into cogent arguments for advancing economic and social equality for women as well as blacks. Levinson's experiment demonstrates how sexual discrimination functions for males as well as females. What would be the consequences for the liberation of men, as well as women, if social inequality between races and sexes were to be eliminated?

References

Michael Harrington, *The Other America*. Baltimore: Penguin Books, 1962, p. 2.
Robert L. Heilbroner, "Benign Neglect in the United States." *Transaction,* Vol. 7, October 1970, pp. 15–22.

Blaming the Victim: Ideology Serves the Establishment

by William Ryan

Twenty years ago, Zero Mostel used to do a sketch in which he impersonated a Dixiecrat Senator conducting an investigation of the origins of World War II. At the climax of the sketch, the Senator boomed out, in an excruciating mixture of triumph and suspicion, "What was Pearl Harbor *doing* in the Pacific?" This is an extreme example of Blaming the Victim.

Twenty years ago, we could laugh at Zero Mostel's caricature. In recent years, however, the same process has been going on every day in the arena of social problems, public health, anti-poverty programs, and social welfare. A philosopher might analyze this process and prove that, technically, it is comic. But it is hardly ever funny.

Consider some victims. One is the miseducated child in the slum school. He is blamed for his own miseducation. He is said to contain within himself the causes of his inability to read and write well. The shorthand phrase is "cultural deprivation," which, to those in the know, conveys what they allege to be inside information: that the poor child carries a scanty pack of cultural baggage as he enters school. He doesn't know about books and magazines and newspapers, they say. (No books in the home: the mother fails to subscribe to *Reader's Digest*.) They say that if he talks at all—an unlikely event since slum parents don't talk to their children—he certainly doesn't talk correctly. (Lower-class dialect spoken here, or even—God forbid!—Southern Negro [*Ici on parle nigra*].) If you can manage to get him to sit in a chair, they say, he squirms and looks out the window. (Impulse-ridden, these kids, motoric rather than verbal.) In a word he is "disadvantaged" and "socially deprived," they say, and this, of course, accounts for his failure (*his* failure, they say) to learn much in school.

Note the similarity to the logic of Zero Mostel's Dixiecrat Senator. What is the culturally deprived child *doing* in the school? What is wrong with the victim? In pursuing this logic, no one remembers to ask questions about the collapsing buildings and torn textbooks, the frightened, insensitive teachers, the six additional desks in the room, the blustering, frightened principals, the relentless segregation, the callous administrator, the irrelevant curriculum, the bigoted or cowardly members of the school board, the insulting history book, the stingy taxpayers, the fairy-tale readers, or the self-serving faculty of the local teachers' college. We are encouraged to confine our attention to the child and to dwell on all his alleged defects. Cultural deprivation becomes an omnibus explanation for the educational disaster area known as the inner-city school. This is Blaming the Victim.

Pointing to the supposedly deviant Negro family as the "fundamental weakness of the Negro community" is another way to blame the victim. Like "cultural deprivation," "Negro family" has become a shorthand phrase with stereotyped connotations of matriarchy, fatherlessness, and pervasive illegitimacy. Growing up in the "crumbling" Negro family is supposed to account for most of the racial evils in America. Insiders have the word, of course, and know that this phrase is supposed to evoke images of growing up with a long-absent or never-present father (replaced from time to time perhaps by a series of transient lovers) and with bossy women ruling the roost, so that the children are irreparably damaged. This refers particularly to the poor, bewildered male children, whose psyches are fatally wounded and who are never, alas, to learn the trick of becoming upright, downright, forthright all-American boys. Is it any wonder the Negroes cannot achieve equality? From such families! And, again, by focusing our attention on the Negro family as the apparent *cause* of racial inequality our eye is diverted. Racism, discrimination, segregation, and the powerlessness of the ghetto are subtly, but thoroughly, downgraded in importance.

The generic process of Blaming the Victim is applied to almost every American problem. The miserable health care of the poor is explained away on the grounds that the victim has poor motivation and lacks health information. The problems of slum housing are traced to the characteristics of tenants who are labeled as "Southern rural migrants" not yet "acculturated" to life in the big city. The "multiproblem" poor, it is claimed, suffer the psychological effects of impoverishment, the "culture of poverty," and the deviant value system of the lower classes; consequently, though unwittingly, they cause their own troubles. From such a viewpoint, the obvious fact that poverty is primarily an absence of money is easily overlooked or set aside.

The growing number of families receiving welfare are fallaciously linked together with the increased number of illegitimate children as twin results of promiscuity and sexual abandon among members of the lower orders. Every important social problem—crime, mental illness, civil disorder, unemployment—has been analyzed within the framework of the victim-blaming ideology.

I have been listening to the victim-blamers and pondering their thought processes for a number of years. That process is often very subtle. Victim-blaming is cloaked in kindness and concern, and bears all the trappings and statistical furbelows of scientism; it is obscured by a perfumed haze of humanitarianism. In observing the process of Blaming the Victim, one tends to be confused and disoriented because those who practice this art display a deep concern for the victims that is quite genuine. In this way, the new ideology is very different from the open prejudice and reactionary tactics of the old days. Its adherents include sympathetic social scientists with social consciences in good working order, and liberal politicians with a genuine commitment to reform. They are very careful to dissociate themselves from vulgar Calvinism or crude racism; they indignantly condemn any notions of innate wickedness or genetic defect. "The Negro is *not born* inferior," they shout apoplectically. "Force of circumstance," they explain in reasonable tones, "has *made* him inferior." And they dismiss with selfrighteous contempt any claims that the poor man in America is plainly unworthy or shiftless or enamored of idleness. No, they say, he is "caught in the cycle of poverty." He is trained to be poor by his culture and his family life, endowed by his environment (perhaps by his ignorant mother's outdated style of toilet training) with those unfortunately unpleasant characteristics that make him ineligible for a passport into the affluent society.

Blaming the Victim is, of course, quite different from old fashioned conservative ideologies. The latter simply dismissed victims as inferior, genetically defective, or morally unfit; the emphasis is on the intrinsic, even hereditary, defect. The former shifts its emphasis to the environmental causation. The old-fashioned conservative could hold firmly to the belief that the oppressed and the victimized were born that way—"that way" being defective or inadequate in character or ability. The new ideology attributes defect and inadequacy to the malignant nature of poverty, injustice, slum life, and racial difficulties. The stigma that marks the victim and accounts for his victimization is an acquired stigma, a stigma of social, rather than genetic, origin. But the stigma, the defect, the fatal difference—though derived in the past from environmental forces—is still located *within* the victim, inside his skin. With such an elegant formulation, the humanitarian can have it both ways. He can, all at the same time, concentrate his charitable interest on the defects of the victim, condemn the vague social and environmental stresses that produced the defect (some time ago), and ignore the continuing effect of victimizing social forces (right now). It is a brilliant ideology for justifying a perverse form of social action designed to change, not society, as one might expect, but rather society's victim.

As a result, there is a terrifying sameness in the programs that arise from this kind of analysis. In education, we have programs of "compensatory education" to build up the skills and attitudes of the ghetto child, rather than structural changes in the schools. In race relations, we have social engineers who think up ways of "strengthening" the Negro family, rather than methods of eradicating racism. In health care, we develop new programs to provide health information (to correct the supposed ignorance of the poor) and to reach out and discover cases of untreated illness and disability (to compensate for their supposed unwillingness to seek treatment). Meanwhile, the gross inequities of our medical care delivery systems are left completely unchanged. As we might expect, the logical outcome of analyzing social problems in terms of the deficiencies of the victim is the development of programs aimed at correcting those deficiencies. The formula for action becomes extraordinarily simple: change the victim.

All of this happens so smoothly that it seems downright rational. First, identify a social problem. Second, study those affected by the problem and discover in what ways they are different from the rest of us as a consequence of deprivation and injustice. Third, define the differences as the cause of the social problem itself. Finally, of course, assign a government bureaucrat to invent a humanitarian action program to correct the differences.

Blaming the Victim is an ideological process, which is to say that it is a set of ideas and concepts deriving from systematically motivated, but *unintended,* distortions of reality. In the sense that Karl Mannheim[1] used the term, an ideology develops from the "collective unconscious" of a group or class and is rooted in a class-based interest in maintaining the *status quo* (as contrasted with what he calls a *utopia,* a set of ideas rooted in a class-based interest in *changing* the *status quo*). An ideology, then, has several components: First, there is the belief system itself, the way of looking at the world, the set of ideas and concepts. Second, there is the systematic distortion of reality reflected in those ideas. Third is the condition that the distortion must not be a conscious, intentional process. Finally, though they are not intentional, the ideas must serve a specific function: maintaining the *status quo* in the interest of a

[1] Karl Mannheim, *Ideology and Utopia,* trans. Louis Wirth and Edward Shils. (New York: Harcourt, Brace & World, Inc., A Harvest Book, 1936). First published in German in 1929.

specific group. Blaming the Victim fits this definition on all counts. Most particularly, it is important to realize that Blaming the Victim is not a process of *intentional* distortion although it does serve the class interests of those who practice it. And it has a rich ancestry in American thought about social problems and how to deal with them.

Thinking about social problems is especially susceptible to ideological influences since, as John Seeley has pointed out,[2] defining a social problem is not so simple. "What is a social problem?" may seem an ingenuous question until one turns to confront its opposite: "What human problem is *not* a social problem?" Since any problem in which people are involved is social, why do we reserve the label for some problems in which people are involved and withhhold it from others? To use Seeley's example, why is crime called a social problem when university administration is not? The phenomena we look at are bounded by the act of definition. They become social problems only by being so considered. In Seeley's words, "*naming* it as a problem, after naming it as a *problem.*"

We must particularly ask, "To whom are social problems a problem?" And usually, if truth were to be told, we would have to admit that we mean they are a problem to those of us who are outside the boundaries of what we have defined as the problem. Negroes are a problem to racist whites, welfare is a problem to stingy taxpayers, delinquency is a problem to nervous property owners.

Now, if this is the quality of our assumptions about social problems, we are led unerringly to certain beliefs about the causes of these problems. We cannot comfortably believe that *we* are the cause of that which is problematic to us; therefore, we are almost compelled to believe that *they*—the problematic ones—are the cause and this immediately prompts us to search for deviance. Identification of the deviance as the cause of the problem is a simple step that ordinarily does not even require evidence.

This has been the dominant style in American social welfare and health activities, then: to treat what we call social problems, such as poverty, disease, and mental illness, in terms of the individual deviance of the special, unusual groups of persons who had those problems. There has also been a competing style, however—much less common, not at all congruent with the prevalent ideology, but continually developing parallel to the dominant style.

Adherents of this approach tended to search for defects in the community and the environment rather than in the individual; to emphasize predictability and usualness rather than random deviance; they tried to think about preventing rather than merely repairing or treating—to see social problems, in a word, as social. In the field of disease, this approach was termed public health, and its practitioners sought the cause of disease in such things as the water supply, the sewage system, the density and quality of housing conditions. They set out to prevent disease, not in individuals, but in the total population, through improved sanitation, inoculation against communicable disease, and the policing of housing conditions. In the field of income maintenance, this secondary style of solving social problems focused on poverty as a predictable event, on the regularities of income deficiency. And it concentrated on the development of standard, generalized programs affecting total groups. Rather than trying to fit the aged worker ending his career into some kind of category of special cases, it assumed all sixty-five-year-old men should expect to retire from the world of work and have the security of an old age pension, to be arranged through public social activity.

These two approaches to the solution of social problems have existed side by side, the former always dominant, but the latter gradually expanding, slowly becoming more and more prevalent.

Elsewhere[3] I have proposed the dimension of *exceptionalism-universalism* as the ideological underpinning for these two contrasting approaches to the analysis and solution of social problems. The *exceptionalist* viewpoint is reflected in arrangements that are private, voluntary, remedial, special, local, and exclusive. Such arrangements imply that problems occur to specially-defined categories of persons in an unpredictable manner. The problems are unusual, even unique, they are exceptions to the rule, they occur as a result of individual defect, accident, or unfortunate circumstance and must be remedied by means that are particular and, as it were, tailored to the individual case.

The universalistic viewpoint, on the other hand, is reflected in arrangements that are public, legislated, promotive or preventive, general, national, and inclusive. Inherent in such a viewpoint is the idea that social problems are a function of the social arrangements of the community or the society and that, since these social arrangements are quite imperfect and inequitable, such problems are both predictable and, more important, preventable through public action. They are not unique to the individual, and the fact that they encompass individual persons does not imply that those persons are themselves defective or abnormal.

The danger in the exceptionalistic viewpoint is in its impact on social policy when it becomes the dominant component in social analysis. Blaming the Victim occurs exclusively within an exceptionalistic framework, and it consists of applying exceptionalistic explanations to universalistic problems. This represents an illogical departure from fact, a method, in Mannheim's words, of systematically distorting reality, of developing an ideology.

[2] John Seeley, "The Problem of Social Problems," *Indian Sociological Bulletin,* II, No. 3 (April 1965). Reprinted as Chapter Ten in *The Americanization of the Unconscious* (New York: International Science Press, 1967), pp. 142–48.

[3] William Ryan, "Community Care in Historical Perspective: Implications for Mental Health Services and Professionals," *Canada's Mental Health,* supplement No. 60, March–April, 1969. This formulation draws on, and is developed from the *residual-institutional* dimension outlined in H. L. Wilensky and C. N. Lebeaux, *Industrial Society and Social Welfare* (paperback ed.; New York: The Free Press, 1965). Originally published by Russell Sage Foundation, 1958.

Blaming the Victim can take its place in a long series of American ideologies that have rationalized cruelty and injustice.

Slavery, for example, was justified—even praised —on the basis of a complex ideology that showed quite conclusively how useful slavery was to society and how uplifting it was for the slaves.[4] Eminent physicians could be relied upon to provide the biological justification for slavery since after all, they said, the slaves were a separate species—as, for example, cattle are a separate species. No one in his right mind would dream of freeing the cows and fighting to abolish the ownership of cattle. In the view of the average American of 1825, it was important to preserve slavery, not simply because it was in accord with his own group interests (he was not fully aware of that), but because reason and logic showed clearly to the reasonable and intelligent man that slavery was good. In order to persuade a good and moral man to *do* evil, then, it is not necessary first to persuade him to *become* evil. It is only necessary to teach him that he is doing good. No one, in the words of a legendary newspaperman, thinks of himself as a son of a bitch.

In late-nineteenth-century America there flowered another ideology of injustice that seemed rational and just to the decent, progressive person. But Richard Hofstadter's analysis of the phenomenon of Social Darwinism[5] shows clearly its functional role in the preservation of the *status quo*. One can scarcely imagine a better fit than the one between this ideology and the purposes and actions of the robber barons, who descended like piranha fish on the America of this era and picked its bones clean. Their extraordinarily unethical operations netted them not only hundreds of millions of dollars but also, perversely, the adoration of the nation. Behavior that would be, in any more rational land (including today's America), more than enough to have landed them all in jail, was praised as the very model of a captain of modern industry. And the philosophy that justified their thievery was such that John D. Rockefeller could actually stand up and preach it in church. Listen as he speaks in, of all places, Sunday school:

The growth of a large business is merely a survival of the fittest. . . . The American Beauty rose can be produced in the splendor and fragrance which bring cheer to its beholder only by sacrificing the early buds which grow up around it. This is not an evil tendency in business. It is merely the workingout of a law of nature and a law of God.[6]

This was the core of the gospel, adapted analogically from Darwin's writings on evolution. Herbert Spencer and, later, William Graham Sumner and other beginners in the social sciences considered Darwin's work to be directly applicable to social processes: ultimately as a guarantee that life was progressing toward perfection but, in the short run, as a justification for an absolutely uncontrolled laissez-faire economic system. The central concepts of "survival of the fittest," "natural selection," and "gradualism" were exalted in Rockefeller's preaching to the status of laws of God and Nature. Not only did this ideology justify the criminal rapacity of those who rose to the top of the industrial heap, defining them automatically as naturally superior (this was bad enough), but at the same time it also required that those at the bottom of the heap be labeled as patently *unfit*—a label based solely on their position in society. According to the law of natural selection, they should be, in Spencer's judgment, eliminated. "The whole effort of nature is to get rid of such, to clear the world of them and make room for better."

For a generation, Social Darwinism was the orthodox doctrine in the social sciences, such as they were at that time. Opponents of this ideology were shut out of respectable intellectual life. The philosophy that enabled John D. Rockefeller to justify himself self-righteously in front of a class of Sunday school children was not the product of an academic quack or a marginal crackpot philosopher. It came directly from the lectures and books of leading intellectual figures of the time, occupants of professional chairs at Harvard and Yale. Such is the power of an ideology that so neatly fits the needs of the dominant interests of society.

If one is to think about ideologies in America in 1970, one must be prepared to consider the possibility that a body of ideas that might seem almost self-evident is, in fact, highly distorted and highly selective; one must allow that the inclusion of a specific formulation in every freshman sociology text does not guarantee that the particular formulation represents abstract Truth rather than group interest. It is important not to delude ourselves into thinking that ideological monstrosities were constructed by monsters. They were not; they are not. They are developed through a process that shows every sign of being valid scholarship, complete with tables of numbers, copious footnotes, and scientific terminology. Ideologies are quite often academically and socially respectable and in many instances hold positions of exclusive validity, so that disagreement is considered unrespectable or radical and risks being labeled as irresponsible, unenlightened, or trashy.

Blaming the Victim holds such a position. It is central in the mainstream of contemporary American social thought, and its ideas pervade our most crucial assumptions so thoroughly that they are hardly noticed. Moreover, the fruits of this ideology appear to be fraught with altruism and humanitarianism, so it is hard to believe that it has principally functioned to block social change.

---

[4] For a good review of this general ideology, see I. A. Newby, *Jim Crow's Defense* (Baton Rouge: Louisiana State University Press, 1965).

[5] Richard Hofstadter, *Social Darwinism in American Thought* (revised ed.; Boston: Beacon Press, 1955).

[6] William J. Ghent, *Our Benevolent Feudalism* (New York: The Macmillan Co., 1902), p. 29.

14

The Positive Functions of Poverty

by Herbert J. Gans

Columbia University and Center for Policy Research

Mertonian functional analysis is applied to explain the persistence of poverty, and fifteen functions which poverty and the poor perform for the rest of American soicety, particularly the affluent, are identified and described. Functional alternatives which would substitute for these functions and make poverty unnecessary are suggested, but the most important alternatives are themselves dysfunctional for the affluent, since they require some redistribution of income and power. A functional analysis of poverty thus comes to many of the same conclusions as radical sociological analysis, demonstrating anew Merton's assertion that functionalism need not be conservative in ideological outlook or implication.

I

Over 20 years ago, Merton (1949, p. 71), analyzing the persistence of the urban political machine, wrote that because "we should ordinarily . . . expect persistent social patterns and social structures to perform positive functions which are at the time not adequately fulfilled by other existing patterns and structures . . . perhaps this publicly maligned organization is, under present conditions, satisfying basic latent functions." He pointed out how the machine provided central authority to get things done when a decentralized local government could not act, humanized the services of the impersonal bureaucracy for fearful citizens, offered concrete help (rather than law or justice) to the poor, and otherwise performed services needed or demanded by many people but considered unconventional or even illegal by formal public agencies.

This paper is not concerned with the political machine, however, but with poverty, a social phenomenon which is as maligned as and far more persistent than

the machine. Consequently, there may be some merit in applying functional analysis to poverty, to ask whether it too has positive functions that explain its persistence. Since functional analysis has itself taken on a maligned status among some American sociologists, a secondary purpose of this paper is to ask whether it is still a useful approach.[2]

II

Merton (1949, p. 50) defined functions as "those observed consequences which make for the adaptation or adjustment of a given system; and dysfunctions, those observed consequences which lessen the adaptation or adjustment of the system." This definition does not specify the nature or scope of the system, but elsewhere in his classic paper "Manifest and Latent Functions," Merton indicated that social system was not a synonym for society, and that systems vary in size, requiring a functional analysis "to consider a *range* of units for which the item (or social phenomenon H.G.) has designated consequences: individuals in diverse statuses, subgroups, the larger social system and cultural systems" (1949, p. 51).

In discussing the functions of poverty, I shall identify functions for *groups* and *aggregates*; specifically, interest groups, socioeconomic classes, and other population aggregates, for example, those with shared values or similar statuses. This definitional approach is based on the assumption that almost every social system—and of course every society—is composed of groups or aggregates with different interests and values, so that, as Merton put it (1949, p. 51), "items may be functional for some individuals and subgroups and dysfunctional for others." Indeed, frequently one group's functions are another group's dysfunctions.[3] For example, the

[1] Earlier versions of this paper were presented at a Vassar College conference on the war on poverty in 1964, at the 7th World Congress of Sociology in 1971, and in *Social Problems* (July–August 1971) 20–24. The present paper will appear in a forthcoming book on poverty and stratification, edited by S. M. Lipset and S. M. Miller, for the American Academy of Arts and Sciences. I am indebted to Peter Marris, Robert K. Merton and S. M. Miller for helpful comments on earlier drafts of this paper.

[2] The paper also has the latent function, as S. M. Miller has suggested, of contributing to the long debate over the functional analysis of social stratification presented by Davis and Moore (1945).

[3] Probably one of the few instances in which a phenomenon has the same function for two groups with different interests is when the survival of the system in which both participate is at stake. Thus, a wage increase can be functional for labor and dysfunctional for management (and consumers), but if the wage increase endangers the firm's survival, it is dysfunctional for labor as well. This assumes, however, that the firm's survival is valued by the workers, which may not always be the case, for example, when jobs are available elsewhere.

political machine analyzed by Merton was functional for the working class and business interests of the city but dysfunctional for many middle class and reform interests. Consequently, functions are defined as those observed consequences which are positive *as judged by the values of the group under analysis*; dysfunctions, as those which are negative by these values.[4] Because functions benefit the group in question and dysfunctions hurt it, I shall also describe functions and dysfunctions in the language of economic planning and systems analysis as benefits and costs.[5]

Identifying functions and dysfunctions for groups and aggregates rather than systems reduces the possibility that what is functional for one group in a multi-group system will be seen as being functional for the whole system, making it more difficult, for example, to suggest that a given phenomenon is functional for a corporation or political regime when it may in fact only be functional for their officers or leaders. Also, this approach precludes reaching a priori conclusions about two other important empirical questions raised by Merton (1949, pp. 32–36), whether any phenomenon is ever functional or dysfunctional for an entire society, and, if functional, whether it is therefore indispensable to that society.

In a modern heterogeneous society, few phenomena are functional or dysfunctional for the society as a whole, and most result in benefits to some groups and costs to others. Given the level of differentiation in modern society, I am even skeptical whether one can empirically identify a social system called society. Society exists, of course, but it is closer to being a very large aggregate, and when sociologists talk about society as a system, they often really mean the nation, a system which, among other things, sets up boundaries and other distinguishing characteristics between societal aggregates.

I would also argue that no social phenomenon is indispensable; it may be too powerful or too highly valued to be eliminated, but in most instances, one can suggest what Merton calls "functional alternatives" or equivalents for social phenomena, that is, other social

patterns or policies which achieve the same functions but avoid the dysfunctions.

III

The conventional view of American poverty is so dedicated to identifying the dysfunctions of poverty, both for the poor and the nation, that at first glance it seems inconceivable to suggest that poverty could be functional for anyone. Of course, the slum lord and the loan shark are widely known to profit from the existence of poverty; but they are popularly viewed as evil men, and their activities are, at least in part, dysfunctional for the poor. However, what is less often recognized, at least in the conventional wisdom, is that poverty also makes possible the existence or expansion of "respectable" professions and occupations, for example, penology, criminology, social work, and public health. More recently, the poor have provided jobs for professional and paraprofessional "poverty warriors," as well as journalists and social scientists, this author included, who have supplied the information demanded when public curiosity about the poor developed in the 1960s.

Clearly, then, poverty and the poor may well serve a number of functions for many nonpoor groups in American society, and I shall describe 15 sets of such functions—economic, social, cultural, and political—that seem to me most significant.

First, the existence of poverty makes sure that "dirty work" is done. Every economy has such work: physically dirty or dangerous, temporary, dead-end and underpaid, undignified, and menial jobs. These jobs can be filled by paying higher wages than for "clean" work, or by requiring people who have no other choice to do the dirty work and at low wages. In America, poverty functions to provide a low-wage labor pool that is willing—or, rather, unable to be unwilling—to perform dirty work at low cost. Indeed, this function is so important that in some Southern states, welfare payments have been cut off during the summer months when the poor are needed to work in the fields. Moreover, the debate about welfare—and about proposed substitutes such as the negative income tax and the Family Assistance Plan—has emphasized the impact of income grants on work incentive, with opponents often arguing that such grants would reduce the incentive of—actually, the pressure on—the poor to carry out the needed dirty work if the wages therefore are no larger than the income grant. Furthermore, many economic activities which involve dirty work depend heavily on the poor; restaurants, hospitals, parts of the garment industry, and industrial agriculture, among others, could not persist in their present form without their dependence on the substandard wages which they pay to their employees.

Second, the poor subsidize, directly and indirectly, many activities that benefit the affluent.[6] For one thing, they have long supported both the consumption and in-

---

[4] Merton (1949, p. 50) originally described functions and dysfunctions in terms of encouraging or hindering adaptation or adjustment to a system, although subsequently he has written that "dysfunction refers to the particular inadequacies of a particular part of the system for a designated requirement" 1961, p. 732). Since adaptation and adjustment to a system can have conservative ideological implications, Merton's later formulation and my own definitional approach make it easier to use functional analysis as an ideologically neutral or at least ideologically variable method, insofar as the reesarcher can decide for himself whether he supports the values of the group under analysis.

[5] It should be noted, however, that there are no absolute benefits and costs just as there are no absolute functions and dysfunctions; not only are one group's benefits often another group's costs, but every group defines benefits by its own manifest and latent values, and a social scientist or planner who has determined that certain phenomena provide beneficial consequences for a group may find that the group thinks otherwise. For example, during the 1960s, advocates of racial integration discovered that a significant portion of the black community no longer considered it a benefit but saw it rather as a policy to assimilate blacks into white society and to decimate the political power of the black community.

[6] Of course, the poor do not actually subsidize the affluent. Rather, by being forced to work for low wages, they enable the affluent to use the money saved in this fashion for other purposes. The concept of subsidy used here thus assumes belief in a "just wage."

vestment activities of the private economy by virtue of the low wages which they receive. This was openly recognized at the beginning of the Industrial Revolution, when a French writer quoted by T. H. Marshall (forthcoming, p. 7) pointed out that "to assure and maintain the prosperities of our industries, it is necessary that the workers should never acquire wealth." Examples of this kind of subsidization abound even today; for example, domestics subsidize the upper middle and upper classes, making life easier for their employers and freeing affluent women for a variety of professional, cultural, civic, or social activities. In addition, as Barry Schwartz pointed out (personal communication), the low income of the poor enables the rich to divert a higher proportion of their income to savings and investment, and thus to fuel economic growth. This, in turn, can produce higher incomes for everybody, including the poor, although it does not necessarily improve the position of the poor in the socioeconomic hierarchy, since the benefits of economic growth are also distributed unequally.

At the same time, the poor subsidize the governmental economy. Because local property and sales taxes and the ungraduated income taxes levied by many states are regressive, the poor pay a higher percentage of their income in taxes than the rest of the population, thus subsidizing the many state and local governmental programs that serve more affluent taxpayers.[7] In addition, the poor support medical innovation as patients in teaching and research hospitals, and as guinea pigs in medical experiments, subsidizing the more affluent patients who alone can afford these innovations once they are incorporated into medical practice.

Third, poverty creates jobs for a number of occupations and professions which serve the poor, or shield the rest of the population from them. As already noted, penology would be miniscule without the poor, as would the police, since the poor provide the majority of their "clients." Other activities which flourish because of the existence of poverty are the numbers game, the sale of heroin and cheap wines and liquors, pentecostal ministers, faith healers, prostitutes, pawn shops, and the peacetime army, which recruits its enlisted men mainly from among the poor.

Fourth, the poor buy goods which others do not want and thus prolong their economic usefulness, such as day-old bread, friut and vegetables which would otherwise have to be thrown out, second-hand clothes, and deteriorating automobiles and buildings. They also provide incomes for doctors, lawyers, teachers, and others who are too old, poorly trained, or incompetent to attract more affluent clients.

In addition, the poor perform a number of social and cultural functions:

Fifth, the poor can be identified and punished as alleged or real deviants in order to uphold the legitimacy of dominant norms (Macarov 1970, pp. 31–33). The defenders of the desirability of hard work, thrift,

honesty, and monogamy need people who can be accused of being lazy, spendthrift, dishonest, and promiscuous to justify these norms; and as Erikson (1964) and others following Durkheim have pointed out, the norms themselves are best legitimated by discovering violations.

Whether the poor actually violate these norms more than affluent people is still open to question. The working poor work harder and longer than high-status jobholders, and poor housewives must do more housework to keep their slum apartments clean than their middle-class peers in standard housing. The proportion of cheaters among welfare recipients is quite low and considerably lower than among income taxpayers.[8] Violent crime is higher among the poor, but the affluent commit a variety of white-collar crimes, and several studies of self-reported delinquency have concluded that middle-class youngsters are sometimes as delinquent as the poor. However, the poor are more likely to be caught when participating in deviant acts and, once caught, to be punished more often than middle-class transgressors. Moreover, they lack the political and cultural power to correct the stereotypes that affluent people hold of them, and thus continue to be thought of as lazy, spendthrift, etc., whatever the empirical evidence, by those who need living proof that deviance does not pay.[9] The actually or allegedly deviant poor have traditionally been described as undeserving and, in more recent terminology, culturally deprived or pathological.

Sixth, another group of poor, described as deserving because they are disabled or suffering from bad luck, provide the rest of the population with different emotional satisfactions; they evoke compassion, pity, and charity, thus allowing those who help them to feel that they are altruistic, moral, and practicing the Judeo-Christian ethic. The deserving poor also enable others to feel fortunate for being spared the deprivations that come with poverty.[10]

Seventh, as a converse of the fifth function described previously, the poor offer affluent people vicarious participation in the uninhibited sexual, alcoholic, and narcotic behavior in which many poor people are alleged to indulge, and which, being freed from the constraints of affluence and respectability, they are often thought to enjoy more than the middle classes. One of the popular beliefs about welfare recipients is that many are on a permanent sex-filled vacation. Although it may be true that the poor are more given to unin-

[7] Pochman (1969) and Herriott and Miller (1971) found that the poor pay a higher proportion of their income in taxes than any other part of the population: 50% among people earning $2,000 or less according to the latter study.

[8] Most official investigations of welfare cheating have concluded that less than 5 percent of recipients are on the rolls illegally, while it has been estimated that about a third of the population cheats in filing income tax returns.

[9] Although this paper deals with the functions of poverty for other groups, poverty has often been described as a motivating or character-building device for the poor themselves; and economic conservatives have argued that by generating the incentive to work, poverty encourages the poor to escape poverty. For an argument that work incentive is more enhanced by income than lack of it, see Gans (1971, p. 96).

[10] One psychiatrist (Chernus 1967) has even proposed the fantastic hypothesis that the rich and the poor are engaged in a sadomasochistic relationship, the latter being supported financially by the former so that they can gratify their sadistic needs.

hibited behavior, studies by Rainwater (1970) and other observers of the lower class indicate that such behavior is as often motivated by despair as by lack of inhibition, and that it results less in pleasure than in a compulsive escape from grim reality. However, whether the poor actually have more sex and enjoy it more than affluent people is irrelevant; as long as the latter believe it to be so, they can share it vicariously and perhaps enviously when instances are reported in fictional, journalistic, or sociological and anthropological formats.

Eighth, poverty helps to guarantee the status of those who are not poor. In a stratified society, where social mobility is an especially important goal and class boundaries are fuzzy, people need to know quite urgently where they stand. As a result, the poor function as a reliable and relatively permanent measuring rod for status comparison, particularly for the working class, which must find and maintain status distinctions between itself and the poor, much as the aristocracy must find ways of distinguishing itself from the *nouveau riche.*

Ninth, the poor also assist in the upward mobility of the nonpoor, for, as Goode has pointed out (1967, p. 5), "the privileged . . . try systematically to prevent the talent of the less privileged from being recognized or developed." By being denied educational opportunities or being stereotyped as stupid or unteachable, the poor thus enable others to obtain the better jobs. Also, an unknown number of people have moved themselves or their children up in the socioeconomic hierarchy through the incomes earned from the provision of goods and services in the slums: by becoming policemen and teachers, owning "Mom and Pop" stores, or working in the various rackets that flourish in the slums.

In fact, members of almost every immigrant group have financed their upward mobility by providing retail goods and services, housing, entertainment, gambling, narcotics, etc., to later arrivals in America (or in the city), most recently to blacks, Mexicans, and Puerto Ricans. Other Americans, of both European and native origin, have financed their entry into the upper middle and upper classes by owning or managing the illegal institutions that serve the poor, as well as the legal but not respectable ones, such as slum housing.

Tenth, just as the poor contribute to the economic viability of a number of businesses and professions (see function 3 above), they also add to the social viability of noneconomic groups. For one thing, they help to keep the aristocracy busy, thus justifying its continued existence. "Society" uses the poor as clients of settlements houses and charity benefits; indeed, it must have the poor to practice its public-mindedness so as to demonstrate its superiority over the *nouveaux riches* who devote themselves to conspicuous consumption. The poor play a similar function for philanthropic enterprises at other levels of the socioeconomic hierarchy, including the mass of middle-class civic organizations and women's clubs engaged in volunteer work and fundraising in almost every American community. Doing good among the poor has traditionally helped the church to find a method of expressing religious sentiments in action; in recent years, militant church activity among

and for the poor has enabled the church to hold on to its more liberal and radical members who might otherwise have dropped out of organized religion altogether.

Eleventh, the poor perform several cultural functions. They have played an unsung role in the creation of "civilization," having supplied the construction labor for many of the monuments which are often identified as the noblest expressions and examples of civilization, for example, the Egyptian pyramids, Greek temples, and medieval churches.[11] Moreover, they have helped to create a goodly share of the surplus capital that funds the artists and intellectuals who make culture, and particularly "high" culture, possible in the first place.

Twelfth, the "low" culture created for or by the poor is often adopted by the more affluent. The rich collect artifacts from extinct folk cultures (although not only from the poor ones), and almost all Americans listen to the jazz, blues, spirituals, and country music which originated among the Southern poor—as well as rock, which was derived from similar sources. The protest of the poor sometimes becomes literature; in 1970, for example, poetry written by ghetto children became popular in sophisticated literary circles. The poor also serve as culture heroes and literary subjects, particularly, of course, for the Left, but the hobo, cowboy, hipster, and the mythical prostitute with a heart of gold have performed this function for a variety of groups.

Finally, the poor carry out a number of important political functions:

Thirteenth, the poor serve as symbolic constituencies and opponents for several political groups. For example, parts of the revolutionary Left could not exist without the poor, particularly now that the working class can no longer be perceived as the vanguard of the revolution. Conversely, political groups of conservative bent need the "welfare chiselers" and others who "live off the taxpayer's hard-earned money" in order to justify their demands for reductions in welfare payments and tax relief. Moreover, the role of the poor in upholding dominant norms (see function 5 above) also has a significant political function. An economy based on the ideology of laissez faire requires a deprived population which is allegedly unwilling to work; not only does the alleged moral inferiority of the poor reduce the moral pressure on the present political economy to eliminate poverty, but redistributive alternatives can be made to look quite unattractive if those who will benefit from them most can be described as lazy, spendthrift, dishonest, and promiscuous. Thus, conservatives and classical liberals would find it difficult to justify many of their political beliefs without the poor; but then so would modern liberals and socialists who seek to eliminate poverty.

Fourteenth, the poor, being powerless, can be made to absorb the economic and political costs of change and growth in American society. During the 19th century, they did the backbreaking work that built the cities;

---

[11] Although this is not a contemporary function of poverty in America, it should be noted that today these monuments serve to attract and gratify American tourists.

today, they are pushed out of their neighborhoods to make room for "progress." Urban renewal projects to hold middle-class taxpayers and stores in the city and expressways to enable suburbanites to commute downtown have typically been located in poor neighborhoods, since no other group will allow itself to be displaced. For much of the same reason, urban universities, hospitals, and civic centers also expand into land occupied by the poor. The major costs of the industrialization of agriculture in America have been borne by the poor, who are pushed off the land without recompense, just as in earlier centuries in Europe, they bore the brunt of the transformation of agrarian societies into industrial ones. The poor have also paid a large share of the human cost of the growth of American power overseas, for they have provided many of the foot soldiers for Vietnam and other wars.

Fifteenth, the poor have played an important role in shaping the American political process; because they vote and participate less than other groups, the political system has often been free to ignore them. This has not only made American politics more centrist than would otherwise be the case, but it has also added to the stability of the political process. If the 15% of the population below the federal "poverty line" participated fully in the political process, they would almost certainly demand better jobs and higher incomes, which would require income redistribution and would thus generate further political conflict between the haves and the have-nots. Moreover, when the poor do participate, they often provide the Democrats with a captive constituency, for they can rarely support Republicans, lack parties of their own, and thus have no other place to go politically. This, in turn, has enabled the Democrats to count on the votes of the poor, allowing the party to be more responsive to voters who might otherwise switch to the Republicans, in recent years, for example, the white working class.

IV

I have described fifteen of the more important functions which the poor carry out in American society, enough to support the functionalist thesis that poverty survives in part because it is useful to a number of groups in society. This analysis is not intended to suggest that because it is functional, poverty *should* persist, or that it *must* persist. Whether it should persist is a normative question; whether it must, an analytic and empirical one, but the answer to both depends in part on whether the dysfunctions of poverty outweigh the functions. Obviously, poverty has many dysfunctions, mainly for the poor themselves but also for the more affluent. For example, their social order is upset by the pathology, crime, political protest, and disruption emanating from the poor, and the income of the affluent is affected by the taxes that must be levied to protect their social order. Whether the dysfunctions outweigh the functions is a question that clearly deserves study.

It is, however, possible to suggest alternatives for many of the functions of the poor. Thus, society's dirty work (function 1) could be done without poverty, some by automating it, the rest by paying the workers who do it decent wages, which would help considerably to cleanse that kind of work. Nor is it necessary for the poor to subsidize the activities they support through their low-wage jobs (function 2), for, like dirty work, many of these activities are essential enough to persist even if wages were raised. In both instances, however, costs would be driven up, resulting in higher prices to the customers and clients of dirty work and subsidized activity, with obvious dysfunctional consequences for more affluent people.

Alternative roles for the professionals who flourish because of the poor (function 3) are easy to suggest. Social workers could counsel the affluent, as most prefer to do anyway, and the police could devote themselves to traffic and organized crime. Fewer penologists would be employable, however, and pentecostal religion would probably not survive without the poor. Nor would parts of the second- and third-hand market (function 4), although even affluent people sometimes buy used goods. Other roles would have to be found for badly trained or incompetent professionals now relegated to serving the poor, and someone else would have to pay their salaries.

Alternatives for the deviance-connected social functions (functions 5–7) can be found more easily and cheaply than for the economic functions. Other groups are already available to serve as deviants to uphold traditional morality, for example, entertainers, hippies, and most recently, adolescents in general. These same groups are also available as alleged or real orgiasts to provide vicarious participation in sexual fantasies. The blind and disabled function as objects of pity and charity, and the poor may therefore not even be needed for functions 5–7.

The status and mobility functions of the poor (functions 8 and 9) are far more difficult to substitute, however. In a hierarchial society, some people must be defined as inferior to everyone else with respect to a variety of attributes, and the poor perform this function more adequately than others. They could, however, perform it without being as poverty-stricken as they are, and one can conceive of a stratification system in which the people below the federal "poverty line" would receive 75% of the median income rather than 40% or less, as is now the case—even though they would still be last in the pecking order.[12] Needless to say, such a reduction of economic inequality would also require income redistribution. Given the opposition to income redistribution among more affluent people, however, it seems unlikely that the status functions of poverty can be replaced, and they—together with the economic functions of the poor, which are equally expensive to replace—may turn out to be the major obstacles to the elimination of poverty.

The role of the poor in the upward mobility of other groups could be maintained without their being

---

[12] In 1971, the median family income in the United States was about $10,000, and the federal poverty line for a family of four was set at just about $4,000. Of course, most of the poor were earning less than 40% of the median, and about a third of them, less than 20% of the median.

so low in income. However, if their incomes were raised above subsistence levels, they would begin to generate capital so that their own entrepreneurs could supply them with goods and services, thus competing with and perhaps rejecting "outside" suppliers. Indeed, this is already happening in a number of ghettoes, where blacks are replacing white storeowners.

Similarly, if the poor were more affluent, they would make less willing clients for upper- and middle-class philanthropic and religious groups (function 10), although as long as they are economically and otherwise unequal, this function need not disappear altogether. Moreover, some would still use the settlement houses and other philanthropic institutions to pursue individual upward mobility, as they do now.

The cultural functions (11 and 12) may not need to be replaced. In America, the labor unions have rarely allowed the poor to help build cultural monuments anyway, and there is sufficient surplus capital from other sources to subsidize the unprofitable components of high culture. Similarly, other deviant groups are available to innovate in popular culture and supply new culture heroes, for example, the hippies and members of other counter-cultures.

Some of the political functions of the poor would, however, be as difficult to replace as their economic and status functions. Although the poor could probably continue to serve as symbolic constituencies and opponents (function 13) if their incomes were raised while they remained unequal in other respects, increases in income are generally accompanied by increases in power as well. Consequently, once they were no longer so poor, people would be likely to resist paying the costs of growth and change (function 14); and it is difficult to find alternative groups who can be displaced for urban renewal and technological "progress." Of course, it is possible to design city-rebuilding and highway projects which properly reimburse the displaced people, but such projects would then become considerably more expensive, thus raising the price for those now benefiting from urban renewal and expressways. Alternatively, many might never be built, thus reducing the comfort and convenience of those beneficaries. Similarly, if the poor were subjected to less economic pressure, they would probably be less willing to serve in the army, except at considerably higher pay, in which case war would become yet more costly and thus less popular politically. Alternatively, more servicemen would have to be recruited from the middle and upper classes, but in that case war would also become less popular.

The political stabilizing and "centering" role of the poor (function 15) probably cannot be substituted for at all, since no other groups is willing to be disenfranchised or likely enough to remain apathetic so as to reduce the fragility of the political system. Moreover, if the poor were given higher incomes, they would probably become more active politically, thus adding their demands for more to those of other groups already putting pressure on the political allocators of resources. The poor might continue to remain loyal to the Democratic party, but like other moderate-income voters, they could also be attracted to the Republicans or to third parties. While improving the economic status of the presently poor would not necessarily drive the political system far to the left, it would enlarge the constituencies now demanding higher wages and more public funds. It is of course possible to add new powerless groups who do not vote or otherwise participate to the political mix and can thus serve as "ballast" in the polity, for example, by encouraging the import of new poor immigrants from Europe and elsewhere, except that the labor unions are probably strong enough to veto such a policy.

In sum, then, several of the most important functions of the poor cannot be replaced with alternatives, while some could be replaced, but almost always only at higher costs to other people, particularly more affluent ones. Consequently *a functional analysis must conclude that poverty persists not only because it satisfies a number of functions but also because many of the functional alternatives to poverty would be quite dysfunctional for the more affluent members of society.*[13]

V

I noted earlier that functional analysis had itself become a maligned phenomenon and that a secondary purpose of this paper was to demonstrate its continued usefulness. One reason for its presently low status is political; insofar as an analysis of functions, particularly latent functions, seems to justify what ought to be condemned, it appears to lend itself to the support of conservative ideological positions, although it can also have radical implications when it subverts the conventional wisdom. Still, as Merton has pointed out (1949, p. 43; 1961, pp. 736–37), functional analysis per se is ideologically neutral, and "like other forms of sociological analysis, it can be infused with any of a wide range of sociological values" (1949, p. 40). This infusion depends, of course, on the purposes—and even the functions—of the functional analysis, for as Wirth (1936, p. xvii) suggested long ago, "every assertion of a 'fact' about the social world touches the interests of some individual or group," and even if functional analyses are conceived and conducted in a neutral manner, they are rarely interpreted in an ideological vacuum.

In one sense, my analysis is, however, neutral; if one makes no judgment as to whether poverty ought to be eliminated—and if one can subsequently avoid being accused of acquiescing in poverty—then the analysis suggests only that poverty exists because it is useful to many groups in society.[14] If one favors the elimination of poverty, however, then the analysis can have a variety of political implications, *depending in part on how completely it is carried out.*

---

[13] Or as Stein (1971, p. 171) puts it: "If the non-poor make the rules . . . antipoverty efforts will only be made up to the point where the needs of the non-poor are satisfied, rather than the needs of the poor."

[14] Of course, even in this case the analysis need not be purely neutral, but can be put to important policy uses, for example, by indicating more effectively than moral attacks on poverty the exact nature of the obstacles that must be overcome if poverty is to be eliminated. See also Merton (1961, pp. 709–12).

If functional analysis only identifies the functions of social phenomena without mentioning their dysfunctions, then it may, intentionally or otherwise, agree with or support holders of conservative values. Thus, to say that the poor perform many functions for the rich might be interpreted or used to justify poverty, just as Davis and Moore's argument (1945) that social stratification is functional because it provides society with highly trained professionals could be taken to justify inequality.

Actually, the Davis and Moore analysis was conservative because it was incomplete; it did not identify the dysfunctions of inequality and failed to suggest functional alternatives, as Tumin (1953) and Schwartz (1955) have pointed out.[15] Once a functional analysis is made more complete by the addition of functional alternatives, however, it can take on a liberal and reform cast, because the alternatives often provide ameliorative policies that do not require any drastic change in the existing social order.

Even so, to make functional analysis complete requires yet another step, an examination of the functional alternatives themselves. My analysis suggests that the alternatives for poverty are themselves dysfunctional for the affluent population, and it ultimately comes to a conclusion which is not very different from that of radical sociologists. To wit: *that social phenomena which are functional for affluent groups and dysfunctional for poor ones persist; that when the elimination of such phenomena through functional alternatives generates dysfunctions for the affluent, they will continue to persist; and that phenomena like poverty can be eliminated only when they either become sufficiently dysfunctional for the affluent or when the poor can obtain enough power to change the system of social stratification.*[16]

---

[15] Functional analysis can, of course, be conservative in value or have conservative implications for a number of other reasons, principally in its overt or covert comparison of the advantages of functions and disadvantages of dysfunctions, or in its attitudes toward the groups that are benefiting and paying the costs. Thus, a conservatively inclined policy researcher could conclude that the dysfunctions of poverty far outnumber the functions, but still decide that the needs of the poor are simply not as important or worthy as those of other groups, or of the country as a whole.

[16] On the possibility of radical functional analysis, see Merton (1949, pp. 40–43) and Gouldner (1970, p. 443). One difference between my analysis and the prevailing radical view is that most of the functions I have described are latent, whereas many radicals treat them as manifest: recognized and intended by an unjust economic system to oppress the poor. Practically speaking, however, this difference may be unimportant, for if unintended and unrecognized functions were recognized, many affluent people might then decide that they ought to be intended as well, so as to forestall a more expensive antipoverty effort that might be dysfunctional for the affluent.

References

Chernus, J. 1967. "Cities: A Study in Sadomasochism." *Medical Opinion and Review* (May), pp. 104–9.

Davis, K., and W. E. Moore. 1945. "Some Principles of Stratification." *American Sociological Review* 10 (April): 242–49.

Erikson, K. T. 1964. "Notes on the Sociology of Deviance." In *The Other Side,* edited by Howard S. Becker. New York: Free Press.

Gans, H. J. 1971. "Three Ways to Solve the Welfare Problem." *New York Times Magazine,* March 7, pp. 26–27, 94–100.

Goode, W. J. 1967. "The Protection of the Inept." *American Sociological Review* 32 (February): 5–19.

Gouldner, A. 1970. *The Coming Crisis of Western Sociology.* New York: Basic.

Herriot, A., and H. P. Miller, 1971. "Who Paid the Taxes in 1968." Paper prepared for the National Industrial Conference Board.

Macarov, D. 1970. *Incentives to Work.* San Francisco: Jossey-Bass.

Marshall, T. H. Forthcoming. "Poverty and Inequality." Paper prepared for the American Academy of Arts and Sciences volume on poverty and stratification.

Merton, R. K. 1949. "Manifest and Latent Functions." In *Social Theory and Social Structure.* Glencoe, Ill.: Free Press.

———. 1961. "Social Problems and Sociological Theory." In *Contemporary Social Problems,* edited by R. K. Merton and R. Nisbet. New York: Harcourt Brace.

Pechman, J. A. 1969. "The Rich, the Poor, and the Taxes They Pay." *Public Interest,* no. 17 (Fall), pp. 21–43.

Rainwater, L. 1970. *Behind Ghetto Walls.* Chicago: Aldine.

Schwartz, R. 1955. "Functional Alternatives to Inequality." *American Sociological Review* 20 (August): 424–30.

Stein, B. 1971. *On Relief.* New York: Basic.

Tumin, M. B. 1953. "Some Principles of Stratification: A Critical Analysis." *American Sociological Review* 18 (August): 387–93.

Wirth, L. 1936. "Preface." In *Ideology and Utopia,* by Karl Mannheim. New York: Harcourt Brace.

15

SURPLUS PEOPLE: THEIR LOST FAITH IN SELF AND SYSTEM

Jobless men feel small, and talk the language of insignificance. Even if a new job patches up self-esteem, they still hurt from a gut-level cynicism about society.

by D. D. Braginsky and B. M. Braginsky

The Higher They Are, The Harder They Fall.

HE IS 52, FATHER OF TWO, and the unemployment checks are running out. He did not miss a day unless sick in 15 years on the last job. When he lost it, he sent out 235 résumés seeking another chance to do what he's good at: technical-engineering writing. On our psychological tests, his self-esteem is now low, his alienation index very high.

But he maintains a strict schedule on his job hunts, and stays in writing trim by unpaid work, such as a novel about an executive who suddenly finds himself moved out of the mainstream and into the backwater of surplus people. When we asked precisely where the pain is, he told us without whining:

I thought my conscientiousness and diligence would pay off. Hard work, you know, the old go go go. Nothing could be more erroneous. The ones that were brown-nosing the boss, that went to his house and painted it, that mowed his lawn, that washed his cars, that took him to the ball game, drove him to the A & P, bought groceries for him, maybe babysat for his children, washed out his swimming pool, took care of his winter cabin—painted it, refurnished it—with their own materials, mind you. They're still doing it. With half the education I had, half the perseverance, half the talent, they are still here.

The hardest part for me to swallow is my pride and have some blue-collar worker say, right to your face, "With all your education now, Bob, how far did it get you?" Do you believe I have friends that work overtime now, running a lathe, working on machines?

You have no friends when you're unemployed. They think it's a disease that is contagious and might jump on them. I've found open resentments, like, "I'm glad it happened to you and not me, brother." Without my writing I would be out. I would be with the rest of the boys in a tavern drinking and drowning my troubles. If a man is gainfully employed, and then you take away his employment, he's like a tool and just what happens to an idle tool. It's like being in a prison. If a man is going to contribute to society, he has to be gainfully employed.

Let's face it, on $76.00 a week what can you do? Certain department stores don't give a damn whether you're broke or dishonored or disbarred. They want their check, no questions asked. I had a few thousand in the bank. I made a point to pay all my bills to get some of these people out of my hair. I wouldn't do another penny's worth of business with these people if you paid me.

I don't know what I'll do when the checks stop. I've

The fate of the Jews of Nazi Germany is perhaps the purest and most grotesque example of a population that became surplus.

never been on relief before. I've never had food stamps or collected welfare. I used to have my opinions about that. Anyone who didn't work, who was unfortunate—but now I've learned so much compassion. I've made friends, actually, from going to the unemployment office.

The higher one's status and the more sudden one's fall, the greater the impact. Several researchers have provided inferential evidence of the social transformation that follows. After the Depression, E. Wight Bakke described the struggles of laid-off workers to readjust to their friends, families, religious organizations, and political groups. In 1963, Jacqueline D. Goodchilds and Ewart E. Smith found that higher-status men suffer more as unemployment runs longer, growing more defensive, conformist and self-critical, and less humorous, while lower-status men adapt and go the other way. Other studies show the extra agony of the older worker, and the rising bitterness of those who have served in a company for many years. However, M. Harvey Brenner finds in recent work that the economically insecure undergo greater psychological risk in recessions, and more often end up in mental hospitals (see page 74).

Our study of the unemployed grew out of years of research among old people, the retarded, women, students, and the inmates of mental institutions [see PT articles: "Mental Hospitals as Resorts," March 1973, "Society's Hansels and Gretels," March 1974, and "High Priests of the Middle Class," December 1973]. We found that powerful authorities, especially our fellow psychologists, often serve as judges who define people in each of these groups as virtually expendable. The destructive effects came through clearly in lowered self-esteem and heightened alienation from social institutions. These results led us toward a sociopsychological model of surplus populations.

Surplus status is not a function of low social and economic class. It may be purely accidental, as in the case of the physically disabled. It may also be self-initiated, as in the cases of upper-middle-class students who drop out and live in communes. It may be natural, as in the cases of children and old people. Children, of course, outgrow their relative uselessness; old people rarely do. Finally, there are the unemployed, who become surplus as a result of unexpected social forces. The fate of the Jews of Nazi Germany is perhaps the purest and most grotesque example of a population that became surplus as a result of unexpected social forces.

A Permanent Scar. Regardless of how a person becomes surplus, he or she is socially transformed. Lifestyle, expectations, goals, roles and appearance all change, and the higher one's status to begin with, the greater the impact of the social transformation. The trauma leaves a permanent scar, our research shows, long after the victim moves out of surplus status and back into the social mainstream.

We expected that the shift from steady work to unemployment would lead to an equally dramatic shift in a person's views of himself and of society. Obviously, someone who loses a job is likely to feel more or less unhappy. But we are concerned with more fundamental changes in perceptions and behavior. "I'm Suzy homemaker now," said a once-proud male, and conventional executives came to think like student radicals.

In one study, we interviewed 46 jobless men whom we had recruited through an advertisement in a big-city Sunday newspaper. For purposes of comparison we also questioned 53 employed men of similar backgrounds. The unemployed group ranged in age from 23 to 59. Nearly half of them had graduated from college, and many of them had held managerial or engineering positions. About 80 percent, moreover, were experiencing their first unemployment after 20 years of steady work.

The World of the Unemployed. We gave each man a questionnaire designed to gauge three different values: society's judgment of him, his judgment of himself, and his judgment of others. We hoped, in this way, to penetrate beyond the familiar statistics and demographics of unemployment and learn something about the world of the unemployed man himself.

Most of these jobless men felt unwanted by society. More than two thirds agreed with such propositions as: "Society is callous when it deals with you on a personal level," "Society doesn't value you unless you can do something for it," and "Society judges your worth by the product of your labors."

In contrast to their feelings about society's callousness and indifference, these educated, middle-class men felt they had done socially worthwhile work and would love to do the same again someday. Moreover, although they had been out of work for an average of six months, nearly all of them agreed with the following, rather optimistic statements: "Every individual contributes in one way or another to society," and "All people are valuable."

Nevertheless, these jobless men felt small and spoke the language of insignificance. Unlike movie stars, say, and others whom they heard about in the media every day, they were utterly unknown. The kinds of things they did from day to day, whether painting a house or waiting in line at the employment office, were the kinds of things ordinary and unglamorous people did—obscure people caught up in the dreariness of life.

"A small part of society" . . . "a statistic" . . . "they don't know me" . . . "part of the census" . . . "society is four billion people and the individual is one." These are the typical reflections of the unemployed.

The Insolence of Office. Many of the jobless, apparently, had experienced the dehumanization, insolence and degradation of bureaucratic offices since losing their jobs. Because the support systems are designed for the chronically helpless, they felt further demeaned. For example: "If I go down to the employment office and I'm

They were being discarded, they believed, by the institutions in which they had placed their trust.

talking to the girl there, she'll ask me straightforward questions...Whatever I say, she puts down. It doesn't really matter to her. She's callous."

Another man tells it this way: *Going down to sign for your checks—God, I hope I won't have to do it again. They treat you as if you were a nobody. Get in line! Do this! I'm there to get it over with and they dilly-dally. She says, "Well, you'll have to wait."*

Some unemployed men believe that their society turns away from productive citizens who need a helping hand, while it gives lavish aid and comfort to nonproductive citizens and to unfriendly nations. A 44-year-old engineer with three children at home told us bitterly:

I never got any help from society ... What I have gotten I had to do on my own. I had to go to school. Nobody gave me anything. Nowadays society is going a little too far, like welfare, for example—all this nonsense on illegitimate children and all ... I can't get any aid at all. Maybe it's because of my education. What I had saved is gone now. I saved the money for the children, for their college education. That went because of the unemployment.

The man's beliefs are changing deeply:

The purpose of going to school to get a degree was that you would have some kind of security. You would have a job, be able to raise a family the way you chose to ... As far as welfare is concerned, forget it. They are not about to lift a little finger to help me. Now I have some pride, and I'm not going to go crawling on my hands and knees. I'll go dig ditches first. I told the girl at welfare—she was going to get married— "I suggest you don't get married." She says, "Why?" "Because if you're in need of any help and you are not married and have children, welfare will give you anything and everything." If I leave my wife tomorrow they'll come in and take over payments of the house and all and help my wife. The welfare system certainly has to be changed.

The Pain of Private Problems. Shifts in

emotional and personal life are as dramatic as in opinions—only more painful. Here are some typical comments on the private problems of those who have become surplus people as a result of losing their jobs:

I don't know what I'm going to do. I am right now in a position where I can't even sleep at night trying to figure out where I could go to work ... My wife is forced to work. I don't know how else to survive.

Unemployment—it causes an abnormal amount of tension within a family.

It makes me very mad, really. I am so depressed. I am actually depressed because I feel, well, I've wasted my time by going to school ... I really can't understand it.

These men, who previously maintained and lived by traditional social values, felt suddenly confused, disillusioned and betrayed. They believed they were being discarded by the very social institutions in which they had once placed their trust.

We asked each man to describe how he spent a typical day. Most of them dedicated at least part of their waking hours to the search for work—reading the want ads, mailing off résumés, applying in person for jobs. Many also reported sleeping late and watching a lot of TV.

Too Ashamed for Company. A few felt good enough to spend their new leisure time socializing with friends and relatives, but most of the unemployed men we talked with felt too ashamed for company. They got the impression that their friends avoided them. So they stayed at home, more or less hidden from the world, and they comforted themselves with solitary pleasures like reading and walking. Often, too, they felt that their new roles were less masculine than they had been.

The transformation from mainstream man to surplus man, from jobholder to a number at the employment office, affects nearly every aspect of life. The shifts and changes are obvious when we compare unemployed men to men with jobs.

Whereas half the unemployed men felt

they were doing nothing socially useful, only about 20 percent of the control group, men with jobs, took this self-critical view. Nearly three quarters of the unemployed men considered society "callous." Only half the men with jobs felt this way.

Interestingly enough, the employed and unemployed groups held *identical* views on the standards by which society evaluates its members. The unemployed man's status thus struck him as especially intolerable. The men we interviewed had developed highly specialized abilities over the years, and believed that society should judge everybody according to the products of their labor, and that special worth is a function of special skills. Their scarce skills and high salaries were two reasons why they lost their jobs. The men understood this irony perfectly, and it made their futures look even bleaker.

A Permanent Cynicism. Three months after the first interviews, our unemployed group reported some good news and some bad news. The good news: 65 percent had found jobs. The bad news: half of those who had found jobs considered their new occupations inferior to their old ones. Those who were reemployed felt somewhat more useful, as we anticipated, and more valuable to society; their cynicism toward society, however, was not only still prominent but had actually increased.

Thus it appears that the social transformation is not only sudden and total, but its impact can lead to lasting changes in one's conception of society, self, friendships, ethics, family, and even in one's experience of everyday life. Via a vicious circle, these changes may increase the difficulty of getting a new job. They also intensify the crisis at home. Among those still unemployed three months after the first interview, fully 64 percent believed that they could be replaced in their families. "The only thing that is required," one said, "is that there is enough money coming in and that they (whoever) appreciate the family. Generally, anybody can replace anybody else in those terms."

Their scarce skills and high salaries were two reasons why they lost their jobs. The men understood this irony perfectly.

In further experiments with the surplus model, we found that unemployed men, mainly middle-managers, engineers and skilled semiprofessionals, increased their sense of impotence as they continued in the jobless state. Those who got new jobs regained some of their self-esteem, but it never reached the level of the control group who were never laid off.

Our research suggests that any modern society, whatever its ideology, must be concerned about economic change that assigns proud people to the surplus category. The reemployment and support systems seem, without intending it, to increase the damage rather than restore willing workers to productive roles. We find ourselves concerned even that the publication of these data may add to the woes of the diligent unemployed, either by confirming their despair or by rousing

suspicion on the part of those who might offer jobs.

This danger is quite real, but so is the evidence that once a man understands that he is not alone in his agony, he can better grasp the remedy. Whatever the destructive effects of surplus status, there remains the life-long pursuit of work and respect for work, and with it the tenacious sense of the future. The technical writer quoted at the opening of this article expressed this deeper sense in his first talk with us. "It's been a harrowing situation and some day I will look back at it and tell my wife, 'My God, how did we ever get through this?'"

The questions that disturb us are what scars are left from this "harrowing" experience and on whom. Disruptions in lifestyles, changes in political beliefs, lower personal worth, and lack of confi-

dence in the social order are among the many lasting wounds. This damage is not only inflicted on the unemployed man, but also on his family, neighbors, co-workers, and ultimately on all of us. We who witness his degradation are forced to raise questions similar to the ones the unemployed man raises: How much are we really valued? How much faith should we have in our social institutions? What are valid political beliefs?

The impact of unemployment upon our society is incalculable. The very ideals, beliefs and values that made this country a viable and strong democracy are being threatened. Unless we understand in human terms the meaning of being surplus, we are not meeting the threat.

16

ANDREW M. GREELEY

Making It in America: Ethnic Groups and Social Status

If the Republican party is ever to become the "New Majority"—which the dreams of Kevin Philips and Richard Nixon suggest that it might—it will have to capture the "Catholic ethnics." For this group seems to be the most vulnerable component of the old New Deal coalition; indeed, it is a component that many of the theorists of the "New Politics" were willing to write off in 1972 on the grounds that the "minorities" and the "young" would more than compensate for the loss of the ethnic hardhats.

Just as Jean Westwood quickly closed down the "ethnic" desk at Democratic headquarters when she ushered the New Politics into the now safely debugged Watergate headquarters, the Republicans went out of their way to cultivate the "nationalities" operations in their campaign. Mr. Nixon had been very attentive to the "nationality" leadership during his first three years in office, even after Kevin Philips, routed by the California German-Americans and decamped from the Justice Department, set himself up as an entrepreneur in the knowledge industry. Nor is there any reason to doubt that in 1974 and 1976 the "blue-collar ethnics" are going to be a favorite target for Republican bush-beaters and a group to be treated with tender loving care by those trying to put back together the battered Democratic coalition.

But both those New Politics Democrats who wrote off the ethnics in favor of Gloria Steinem and Jesse Jackson and the Republican theorists of the New Majority shared a common assumption about the ethnics—that they were blue-collar workers caught in a bind between high taxes and inflation and deeply resentful of the attention and assistance being given the Blacks. Kevin Philips might not have used the work "racist" but he shared with his left-liberal foes the assumption that the ethnics were both blue-collar and racist.

Occasionally I would try to persuade a colleague that there were ethnics who were not blue-collar workers. Indeed, I had worked for a whole decade in a neighborhood of well-educated Irish Catholics who were not all firemen or policemen or bailiffs in Mr. Daley's court system. The response was skeptical: "You mean they have money like the Kennedys?" It was inconceivable that there could be a massive Irish upper-middle class somewhere, existing between police sergeants and Cape Cod millionaires. Nor did it seem believable that there could be Polish Ph.Ds, Italian city planners, Lithuanian television writers, and Slovak philosophers. The ethnics were blue-collar workers, and that was that. Research efforts, summarized briefly in the accompanying tables, are an attempt to explore, if not to explode, the myth of the blue-collar ethnic.

ETHNIC GROUP STATUS

Even though the data referred to in this article are inadequate when compared with the decennial United States Census or even the monthly *Current Population Surveys*, they are the best available on the subject of American ethnic groups. Indeed, they are almost the only ones available. Census materials are not of much value in estimating the demographic distributions of American religio-ethnic groups, because the U.S. Census cannot ask questions about religion and religion is an essential part of ethnic self-definition for some groups. As far as we know, the analysis that the National Opinion Research Center (NORC) has undertaken, which is based on a composite of seven NORC samples and a composite of twenty samples from the Survey Research Center (SRC) at the University of Michigan, is the only attempt in recent years to go beyond guessing about the demography of American ethnic groups.

ANDREW M. GREELEY is Director of the Center for the Study of American Pluralism at the National Opinion Research Center. The material on which this article is based has been extracted from NORC research monograph "The Demography of Religio-ethnic Identification."

Two-fifths of the American population are white-collar workers.[1] Jews and British-Americans are the most likely to be white-collar workers, followed by Irish and German Catholics and Scandinavian Protestants. Italian Catholics are on the national average and Polish Catholics only five percentage points behind it. The Irish are just behind the Jews in mean years of education, and Italian, Polish, and Slavic Catholics are only a fraction of a year beneath the American mean. Finally, the Irish are second only to the Jews in annual family income, and the Italians, Poles, and Slavs are all above the national average. In short, in terms of education, income, and occupational prestige, two of the Catholic ethnic groups,—the Irish and the German—are substantially above the national mean, the Italians are about on the national mean, and the Poles and the Slavs just slightly beneath it. The adjective "blue-collar" is no more appropriate before the descriptive noun "ethnic" than it is before "American." The ethnics are no more "blue-collar" than anyone else.

With the exception of the French, the Catholics are predominantly metropolitan dwellers, with the Italian and the Spanish-speaking the most likely (44 and 45 percent respectively) to be in the great cities of over two million population. (Presumably, the Italians are especially likely to be found in New York and the Spanish-speaking in Los Angeles.) The most rural Gentile ethnic group is the French Catholic (32 percent), followed by the Irish Protestant (29 percent), the "Other Protestant" (28 percent), and the German Protestant (25 percent). The Jews, of course, are the least rural of all—in fact, none of the 240 Jews in the NORC composite sample reported rural residence. The Spanish-speaking Catholics, the Italian Catholics, Polish Catholics, and Irish Catholics also report less than 5 percent of their population to have rural residence.

The Jews, those with no religion, and "other religion" are the most likely to have attended graduate school; but among the Gentiles, the Irish Catholics are both the most likely to have attended graduate school (3 percent) and the most likely to have gone to college at all (40 percent as opposed to 37 percent for the British Protestants). Among the English-speaking white Gentiles, the Polish are the least likely to have gone to college (15 percent), followed by the Slavic group (16 percent) and the Italians (17 percent). The eastern and southern European Catholics, in other words, have not yet caught up to the national average in college attendance, though their German coreligionists are slightly ahead of the national average and their Irish coreligionists are substantially above the national average.

On the other hand, the Italians have reached the national average in the percentage of those who have become managers or owners, or professional or technical workers (26 percent). However, the Poles and the other eastern European Catholics are still substantially beneath that average (17 and 19 percent respectively). The Jewish groups, as one might expect, are the most likely to be found in these two categories, and the Blacks and the Spanish-speaking the least likely. Among English-speaking white Gentiles, British Protestants have a minuscule advantage over Irish Catholics in the proportion in these two top categories (36.5 percent as against 36.2 percent). It is interesting to note that the occupational distribution of the Irish Protestants is virtually the same as the national average. The Germans and the Scandinavians are the most likely to be farmers; the Italians, Spanish-speaking, Blacks, and Orientals most likely to be service workers; the Poles and the Slavs the most likely to be skilled or craft workers; the Spanish-speaking, Blacks, and French the most likely to be operatives or unskilled factory workers (though the Poles are also disproportionately represented in this group).

"Kevin Philips might not have used the word "racist" but he shared with his left-liberal foes the assumption that the ethnics were both blue-collar and racist."

---

1 In the American Pluralism program at the National Opinion Research Center we use "ethnicity" in the broad sense of the word, including differences of race, religion, language, and national origin. However, in this article the principal focus will be on diversity based on religion and national origin. Data will be presented about "Spanish-speaking" and "Black" for the sake of completeness of our tables. Because there is census data of much higher quality than ours on Black and Spanish-speaking Americans, I shall refrain from detailed commentary on the demography of those collectivities. I wish to emphasize that this decision is based on the limited nature of our data, not on any lack of interest in or concern for the so-called nonwhite ethnics.

Jews, Orientals, and those with no religion are the most likely to be earning more than $15,000 a year. Among white Gentiles the Irish Catholics and the German Catholics (16 percent and 12 percent respectively) are the most likely to be in the $15,000-plus category, with the British Protestants (11 percent) right behind them. The Blacks and the Spanish-speaking are most likely to be under $4,000 a year in income (with 48 percent of the Blacks in this category). Among the white English-speaking groups, 30 percent of the Irish Protestants earn less than $4,000, as do approximately one-fifth of the Italian, Polish, Slavic, and French Catholics.

In summary, then, American society has bestowed economic, occupational, and educational success on its Jewish, British-Protestant, and Irish-Catholic populations. German and Scandinavian groups have done moderately well. The southern and eastern European Catholic groups have done less well, and the Blacks and the Spanish-speaking, quite badly. Surprisingly, the Irish Protestants are on most measures in last place among the white English-speaking groups, in part, perhaps, because of their heavy concentration in the South and in rural areas. It is the purpose of this article to report these phenomena; data are not available in this analysis to sort out the social, cultural, psychological, historical, and racial discrimination factors that may be responsible for these differences. We can, however, in a crude sort of way take into account differences of region and city size as they affect education and income.

Education

Based on the national average of 10.9 years of education, we note that the Jews, the British Protestants, and the Irish Catholics have the greatest educational advantage, while the Blacks and the Spanish-speaking have the greatest educational disadvantage. The two German groups and the Scandinavian Protestants are virtually at the educational mean. Among English-speaking white Gentile groups, the Poles are almost a year beneath the national average, and the Slavs and the French Catholics are almost a half-year beneath the national average. But the performance of the southern and eastern European Catholics may be even worse than may appear, because these groups excluding the French) tend to be concentrated in large cities and in the North where there is more opportunity for education and educational achievement is higher. Hence let us see how these groups do in a situation in which geographic and metropolitan distribution are held constant.

Standardizing for region and size of place does not affect the mean scores of the British, German, and Scandinavian Protestant groups very much. However, the deviation from the educational mean of the Irish and Other Protestants is eliminated in the former case and substantially reduced in the latter. The lower educational scores of these two groups, in other words, result from their rural and southern locations.

On the other hand, the low scores of the Italian, Polish, Slavic,

French, and Spanish-speaking Catholics grow even lower when region and city size are held constant. If the southern and eastern European Catholics are compared with those who live in the same size places and the same regions, they are at even more of an educational disadvantage. The Poles, for example, have a minus deviation of 1.1 years of school—the same as the Blacks.

The high scores of the Irish Catholics and the Jews are diminished somewhat by standardizing for region and size of place, but the educational success of these two groups cannot be explained merely by their nonsouthern and metropolitan locations.

Income

Surprisingly, the educational disadvantage of the eastern and southern European Catholics is not translated into income disadvantage. While the Jews, the Irish Catholics, and the German Catholics have the highest gross incomes, the Italian, Polish, and French Catholics are all above the national average. The Irish Protestants are substantially ($566) beneath the national average, and the Other Protestants are somewhat ($313) beneath the national average. Indeed, Polish and Italian Catholics have higher annual incomes than do any of the Protestant groups, with the exception of the British Protestants. The incomes of the Black and Spanish-speaking groups are deplorably beneath the national average.

When education, region, and city size are all held constant, Irish, German, Italian, and Polish Catholics all have higher net incomes than do any of the Protestant groups under these circumstances (such for the Protestant ethic!). Further, even when we asked what the difference in educational attainment would be if all ethnic groups had the same regional and metropolitan distributions, the income disadvantage for Spanish-speaking Catholics was cut in half and for Blacks it was reduced from $2,163 to $1,437. But here again the phenomenon of the Irish Protestants continues to be surprising. In fact, they make on the average $500 less than the national average, and the standardization only slightly reduces that deficit. There is every reason to assume that the Blacks and the Spanish-speaking have been the objects of discrimination, but one wonders whether there has been any discrimination against Irish Protestants.[2] Equally surprising is the finding that both in the real world and the world created by standardization techniques the southern and eastern European Catholic groups earn more money than the national average and in many cases more than their native-born American counterparts.

One is led to wonder whether the surprising income levels of the Catholic ethnics may be the result of an acculturation process by which the children and grandchildren of these immi-

---

2   I am reminded of Arnold Toynbee's essay on the success of the Protestant ethic among Scotch Presbyterians who migrated to Ulster and its failure among the Ulster Presbyterians who migrated to the United States.

"The English-Protestant Americans, then, are substantially ahead of the national average for their age group during the 1950s, and remain ahead in the 1960s. . . ."

grants have not only achieved some sort of rough parity in American society but have actually managed to fight their way to the middle of the pack, if not to the top of the heap as the Irish Catholics have nearly done.

Intergenerational Mobility

Since the SRC data include both the 1950s and the 1960s, they enable us to explore from a different perspective the question of the recent economic history of cohort religio-ethnic groups. We assume that those who were in their twenties during the 1950s are a representative sample of those born between 1931 and 1940, and those who were in their thirties in the 1960s are a representative sample of that same group ten years later. Thus by looking at those who were in their twenties in the 1950s and in their thirties in the 1960s, we are able to see how a specific segment of the population changed its income over the course of a decade. The technique of cohort analysis is elementary and used often. But even though we are dealing with a sample of 15,000 respondents, our analysis has a basic weakness: the cross-tabulation by age, decade, and ethnic group leaves us with rather small numbers of respondents for each ethnic cohort. Thus the most we can say is that we are dealing with very tentative and speculative data.

The figures in Table I, A-K represent deviations in income from a cohort mean which is shown below.[3] Thus to say that the English Protestants in Cohort I (between twenty and thirty years old during the 1960s) have a score of -16 is to say that they earned $16 less than the mean for their cohort during that de-

---

[3] *Mean Income in Dollars for Age Cohorts in the 1950s and 1960s (SRC Composite Sample)*

	1950s	1960s	Change
Cohort I (Born 1941–1950; in its twenties during the 1960s.)		$7,723	
Cohort II (Born 1931–1940; in its twenties during the 1950s and its thirties during the 1960s.)	$4,837	9,345	$4,508
Cohort III (Born 1921–1930; in its thirties during the 1950s and its forties during the 1960s.)	5,633	9,459	3,826
Cohort IV (Born 1911–1920; in its forties during the 1950s and its fifties during the 1960s.)	5,888	8,136	2,248
Cohort V (Born 1901–1910; in its fifties during the 1950s and its sixties during the 1960s.)	5,222	5,478	256

cade. The mean for Cohort I during the 1960s (see footnote 3) is $7,723, which makes the mean for English Protestants $7,707. By looking down the columns in each panel of Table I, one can see the income differences among various age groups in the specific ethnic groups during each of the decades. Thus during the 1950s, English Protestants in their twenties made $631 more than the average of all Americans at the same age level. Those in their thirties made $1,997 more than their age-level average, those in their forties made $1,781 more, and those in their fifties made $1,060 more than their age-level average. Similarly, as one looks down the second column (1960s), one can see that except for the English Protestants in their twenties, each age level among the English-Protestant ethnic collectivity made more than the mean for the national cohort at that age level.

If one looks at the rows in the table, one can see how a specific age cohort improved its relative position in the decade between the 1950s and 1960s. Thus those English Protestants (Table IA) who were born between 1931 and 1940 made $631 more than the national cohort mean in the 1950s and $1,360 more than the national cohort mean in the 1960s. They not only improved their absolute level of income—as did every ethnic group—but also improved their relative position. They were even more ahead of the mean for their age peers in the 1960s than they were in the 1950s.

The English-Protestant Americans, then, are substantially ahead of the national average for their age group during the 1950s, and remain ahead in the 1960s except in Cohort I where they fall slightly beneath the national average for those who were in their twenties during that decade. It may well be that the reason for the $16 deficit in Cohort I during the 1960s is that a substantial segment of the English-American population was still in college or graduate school while in their twenties. However, it is also worth noting that in Cohorts III and IV the relative advantage of English-Protestant Americans over the national mean diminishes considerably.

A very different picture is presented by the Irish Protestants (Table IB). While they are above their respective cohort averages in three of the four levels in the 1950s, they are below the national average in three of the five levels in the 1960s; and in all four cases they experience a negative change in deviation from the mean in the two decades. It is true that the Irish Protestants in their twenties during the 1960s are substantially above the national mean for that cohort. However, it should be noted that their predecessors, who were in their twenties during the previous decade, slipped badly ($1,569) in the 1960 decade. This

"If there are any ethnic groups, then, that have suffered in the last two decades, they are the older groups, those who have been here since the beginning of the Republic."

Table I　*Income Deviation in Dollars of Ethnic Groups in the 1950s and the 1960s by Cohort (SRC Composite Sample)*

	1950s	1960s	Net Change in Deviation from Cohort Mean		1950s	1960s	Net Change in Deviation from Cohort Mean
A. English Protestants				**H. Polish Catholics**			
Cohort I	$	$− 16 (193)	$	Cohort I	$	$− 345 (24)	$
Cohort II	+ 631 (51)	+1,360 (168)	+ 729	Cohort II	+ 706 (19)	+ 446 (15)	− 260
Cohort III	+1,997 (106)	+ 748 (217)	−1,252	Cohort III	− 226 (28)	− 245 (33)	+ 20
Cohort IV	+1,781 (138)	+1,443 (193)	− 338	Cohort IV	− 517 (35)	− 429 (20)	+ 88
Cohort V	+1,060 (139)	+1,384 (155)	+ 324	Cohort V	−1,745 (13)	− 342 (13)	+1,403
B. Irish Protestants				**I. Italian Catholics**			
Cohort I	$	$+2,260 (99)	$	Cohort I	$	$+1,036 (46)	$
Cohort II	+1,326 (39)	− 243 (65)	−1,569	Cohort II	− 338 (36)	+ 426 (46)	+ 764
Cohort III	+ 741 (51)	+ 127 (79)	− 614	Cohort III	+ 102 (61)	+ 256 (48)	+ 154
Cohort IV	− 67 (39)	− 957 (79)	− 890	Cohort IV	− 152 (50)	+1,073 (37)	+1,225
Cohort V	+ 699 (32)	− 101 (67)	− 800	Cohort V	+ 595 (26)	+2,437 (21)	+1,842
C. Scandinavian Protestants				**J. Jews**			
Cohort I	$	$+ 663 (46)	$	Cohort I	$	$+2,804 (40)	$
Cohort II	+ 548 (38)	+2,160 (65)	+1,612	Cohort II	+2,444 (24)	+2,382 (41)	− 72
Cohort III	+ 748 (34)	+ 670 (53)	− 78	Cohort III	+1,681 (42)	+3,769 (37)	+2,088
Cohort IV	+1,054 (43)	+2,859 (37)	+1,779	Cohort IV	+2,265 (51)	+2,910 (26)	+ 645
Cohort V	+ 37 (49)	+ 329 (33)	+ 292	Cohort V	+1,522 (40)	+1,358 (22)	− 164
D. German Protestants				**K. Blacks**			
Cohort I	$	$+ 75 (200)	$	Cohort I	$	$−2,258 (148)	$
Cohort II	+ 308 (93)	+ 977 (152)	+ 699	Cohort II	−1,495 (192)	−3,613 (148)	−2,118
Cohort III	+ 530 (113)	+ 629 (156)	+ 99	Cohort III	−2,556 (148)	−4,198 (121)	−3,826
Cohort IV	+ 449 (128)	+ 683 (143)	+ 234	Cohort IV	−2,923 (119)	−5,291 (106)	−2,998
Cohort V	+ 380 (85)	− 144 (83)	− 524	Cohort V	−2,712 (77)	−2,633 (69)	− 79
E. Other Protestants ("American")							
Cohort I	$	$− 134 (325)	$				
Cohort II	− 155 (475)	− 874 (287)	− 719				
Cohort III	− 28 (606)	−1,093 (305)	−1,125				
Cohort IV	− 195 (457)	−1,311 (263)	−1,506				
Cohort V	− 456 (339)	−1,111 (186)	− 655				
F. Irish Catholics							
Cohort I	$	$+1,148 (50)	$				
Cohort II	+ 928 (24)	+1,006 (44)	+ 78				
Cohort III	+1,821 (49)	+1,046 (51)	− 775				
Cohort IV	+ 274 (40)	+ 680 (34)	+ 406				
Cohort V	+ 288 (30)	+2,349 (34)	+2,061				
G. German Catholics							
Cohort I	$	$+ 296 (52)	$				
Cohort II	+ 750 (27)	− 172 (46)	− 922				
Cohort III	+ 640 (49)	+2,145 (49)	+1,501				
Cohort IV	+ 122 (32)	+ 990 (30)	+ 968				
Cohort V	+ 140 (20)	− 139 (30)	− 273				

KEY:

Cohort I　Born 1941–1950; in its twenties during the 1960s.

Cohort II　Born 1931–1940; in its twenties during the 1950s and its thirties during the 1960s.

Cohort III　Born 1921–1930; in its thirties during the 1950s and its forties during the 1960s.

Cohort IV　Born 1911–1920; in its forties during the 1950s and its fifties during the 1960s.

Cohort V　Born 1901–1910; in its fifties during the 1950s and its sixties during the 1960s.

NOTE: Numbers in parentheses are respondents.

suggests that the income advantage of the Irish Protestants in their twenties in both decades may be the result of the fact that they began their occupational lives early, so that in their twenties they earned more than their age peers of other groups who may still have been in college. However, by the time they reached their thirties, this initial advantage was canceled out by the college education of other groups. Thus while English-Protestant Americans display a picture of maintaining economic superiority, though perhaps with some erosion, Irish Protestants present one of a rapid erosion of economic superiority. The SRC data, then, like the NORC data, indicate that the Irish Protestants—an ethnic group that seems to lack consciousness, organization, and visibility—are downwardly mobile.

Just the opposite is true of the Scandinavian Protestants (Table IC). In all cohorts in both decades the Scandinavians are higher than their cohort mean, and in three of the four cohorts they improved their relative position in the decade of the 1960s. Twenty years ago Scandinavians were already above the national income average, and in the course of the two decades they improved their position even more. The most notable improvements are among those who were in their twenties in the

1950s and those who were in their forties in the same decade. Cohort III of the Scandinavian Protestants did not improve that much, possibly (and this is extremely speculative) because they were born or spent their childhood years during the worst years of the Great Depression.

Another group that has made the most of the last two decades is the German Protestants (Table ID). They are above the national average at all age cohorts in the 1950s and at four of the five age cohorts in the 1960s. Only in Cohort V during the 1960s does one German age group fall beneath the national mean. The $520 loss in relative position among German Protestants in their sixties during the 1960s may possibly be the result of the fact that this group is heavily composed of farmers, and a deterioration of farm income among people in their sixties may be more serious than among other groups in the population. The relative improvement in the economic condition of German Protestants is not as strong as that among Scandinavian Protestants. Nonetheless, the former group continues to improve its relative position in the decade between 1960 and 1970 vis-à-vis the rest of American society.

But the Other Protestants (for the most part, those who re-

sponded that they were "American" to the SRC ethnic question) are the major losers among the white groups. All four age cohorts of Other Protestants are beneath their respective means in the 1950s and even further beneath those means in the 1960s. In two of the cohorts (III and IV) they suffer a loss in relative position of more than $1,000. Granted that the Other Protestants tend to be rural and farm people, Table IE establishes that not only does a population segment concentrated in rural areas earn less than more urban population segments but also that its relative position is deteriorating. In each age cohort in the 1960s, income is even further from the cohort mean than it was in the 1950s. Neither the Irish Protestants nor the Other Protestants are ethnic groups in the sense that the Polish or the Italian Catholics are. Neither of the two Protestant groups have much self-conscious ethnic identity nor are they so identified by the rest of American society. It just so happens that they include the element in the white American population that is not keeping pace with the general increase in income level. Precisely be-

decline beneath the cohort mean at the level of Cohort V (those who were in their fifties in the 1950s and in their sixties in the 1960s). In addition, German Catholics suffer a decline in Cohort II (those who passed from their twenties to their thirties during the last two decades). NORC data for the same age cohort do not indicate the same phenomenon. German Catholics improved their relative position in American society during the 1950s and 1960s but not as much as the Irish Catholics did.

The Polish-Catholic performance (Table IH) indicates a slow upward movement of that population, however, the number of respondents are sufficiently low that judgments should be made cautiously. The three oldest age cohorts of Poles were beneath the national mean for those age cohorts in both the 1950s and the 1960s, although they improved their relative position somewhat during the two decades. Cohort II was the first Polish cohort to be above the national mean, but its relative advantage slipped somewhat between the 1950s and the 1960s. Polish Catholics, then, seem to be improving their relative position in

> **" . . .the upward mobility system, which worked extremely well for the Jews, the Irish, and the Italians, reasonably well for the Germans, and has at least begun to work for the Poles, has not yet worked at all for the Blacks."**

cause they do not identify themselves as a group and are not so identified by others, their deteriorating position is not obvious to the rest of society and perhaps not even obvious to many of them.

Irish Catholics, on the other hand, are the most successful of the white immigrant groups. In all age cohorts in both the 1950s and 1960s, the Irish Catholics are very substantially ahead of the national average in their respective age cohorts (see Table IF). Indeed, in five cases they are more than $1,000 ahead and in one case, more than $2,000. Furthermore, the Irish who were under thirty in the 1960s are $1,000 ahead of the cohort mean for that group, indicating that the movement upward of Irish Catholics continues unabated. In only one age cohort (III) was there a decline in relative advantage of the 1960s over the 1950s. Interestingly, it is this same Cohort III in which a $1,252 decline in deviation from the mean was also recorded among the English-Protestant Americans. We may speculate, just as we did in reporting on this phenomenon for the Scandinavians, that the Great Depression may have had some impact on this cohort's capacity to take advantage of the opportunities of the last twenty years. Let it be noted, however, that Cohort III is well above the national average for that cohort during the 1960s for both the English-Protestant and Irish-Catholic groups. It is not as far above as one might have expected based on their performance in the 1950s.

German Catholics (Table IG) like German Protestants suffer a

American society, but much more slowly than the earlier Catholic immigrant groups.

The Italian Catholics (Table II) are doing much better than the Poles. They are substantially above the mean for their respective age levels, and all of them improved their relative position notably since the 1950s. The Italians are in fact the only group to have improved their position in all four age cohorts between the two decades. Only the Jews have scored a greater increase in income between the 1950s and the 1960s. Thus, while the evidence about the upward mobility of Polish-Americans is unclear, there is no doubt at all that the Italians are moving very rapidly into the upper-middle class of American society.

The Jews (Table IJ) are already solidly in the upper-middle class. At all but the oldest age cohort, the relative Jewish advantage over the cohort income mean in both the 1950s and the 1960s is in excess of $2,000, and while Jews in Cohort II slipped a little ($72) in their relative advantage over the cohort mean between the 1950s and 1960s, they are still almost $2,400 ahead of the average for their age level in the 1960s. Finally, Jews in their twenties in the 1960s have the greatest advantage ($2,437) over their age peers of any ethnic group. It is twice that of their nearest competitor, the Irish Catholics.

The last panel (Table IK) is extremely depressing. While much better evidence can be made for the case with data more reliable than ours, and while perhaps in the late 1960s and early 1970s there has been some change, still one is forced to conclude that in the two decades between 1950 and 1970, the upward mobility system, which worked extremely well for the Jews, the Irish, and the Italians, reasonably well for the Germans, and has at least begun to work for the Poles, has not yet worked at all for the Blacks. Whether it may have begun working since 1965 is beyond the scope of this presentation.

CONCLUSION

To return to our initial question of whether the ethnics are "blue-collar" or not, the evidence in the NORC and SRC composite samples on which this presentation is based leaves little doubt that the Irish Catholics, Germans, Scandinavians, and Italians have moved rapidly into the upper-middle class of American society during the last two decades. Furthermore, despite fears that these groups would become alienated, there is no evidence that between 1950 and the late 1960s any of them suffered appreciable decline in their relative incomes. Whatever the inflationary income squeeze of the 1960s may have been, it does not seem to have affected these ethnic groups disproportionately. The English Protestants have managed to hold their own in American society, although they seem to have been displaced as the second richest group by the Irish Catholics. The Polish-Catholic situation is uncertain. While there is some evidence that the Poles are leaving their blue-collar status behind and are moving upward relatively as well as absolutely, the speed of their movement seems to be considerably less than that of the Italians, who entered American society at approximately the same time. The mobility system did not work at all for the Blacks between the 1950s and the 1960s. It seems to work to the disadvantage of the Irish Protestants and Other Protestants or "Americans," who have slipped even further beneath the cohort means despite an income increase in absolute terms. If there are any ethnic groups, then, that have suffered in the last two decades, they are the older groups, those who have been here since the beginning of the Republic.

Let us observe in conclusion that while the data presented in this article represent the best information we have on the demography of American religio-ethnic groups, they are still extremely tentative. Even in dealing with samples of more than 10,000 respondents, one ends up with very small subsamples of American religio-ethnic groups. Therefore, while we can be quite confident of the general picture of upward mobility of American ethnic groups, we must exercise considerable reservations about the details of such a picture.

Regarding the assumption shared by liberals and conservatives alike that ethnics are predominantly blue-collar workers, the data presented here suggest that both are wrong in their assumption. Only the Poles are still disproportionately blue-collar and are not moving rapidly out of that status. Yet the Polish vote for Democratic candidates has been over 70 percent since 1952 and it is very likely that of all American groups only

the Blacks were more inclined to support McGovern in 1972. One could argue that as new members of the middle class, the ethnics are most likely to be the victims of "status anxiety" and hence most likely to react unfavorably to those beneath them on the status ladder. But while the Catholic proportion voting Democratic in 1972 declined some 12 percentage points (from 60 to 48 percent), Catholics were still more likely to vote for McGovern than the national average. Over 50 percent of both Poles and Irish voted for McGovern. In other words, for all his "ethnic" activity, Mr. Nixon was not able to make any greater inroads on them than on the whole American population. On the contrary, there is every reason to think that in congressional voting in 1972, the ethnics were as Democratic as they ever were—which is very Democratic indeed.

In the era between 1950 and 1970, then, the Catholic ethnic groups, with the possibe exception of the Poles, moved from the lower-middle class and working class into the upper-middle class. Not all of their members, of course, enrolled in the white-collar world, but they were as likely to be in that world—and in most cases, more likely—than the American average. Those critics who label ethnics as hard-hats and racists will concede, if pressed, that they have made dramatic social progress since the end of World War II. But the critics will add that the ethnics show singular unconcern about the lack of success of other Americans. They will assert that the Catholic ethnics, once the backbone of the liberal coalition, have slipped away from that coalition because their upward mobility has made them conservative. The ethnic, it seems, can't win. But it may well be that the most fascinating political phenomenon of the 1970s is that the white-collar ethnics are remaining Democrats. Dogmatic ideology should not be permitted to obscure the possibilities for building a social-change coalition in which the ethnics would be a prime component. There is substantial evidence that during the past two decades the ethnics have turned to the left, not to the right. But that is another story and perhaps another article.

---

1 In the American Pluralism program at the National Opinion Research Center we use "ethnicity" in the broad sense of the word, including differences of race, religion, language, and national origin. However, in this article the principal focus will be on diversity based on religion and national origin. Data will be presented about "Spanish-speaking" and "Black" for the sake of completeness of our tables. Because there is census data of much higher quality than ours on Black and Spanish-speaking Americans, I shall refrain from detailed commentary on the demography of those collectivities. I wish to emphasize that this decision is based on the limited nature of our data, not on any lack of interest in or concern for the so-called nonwhite ethnics.

2 I am reminded of Arnold Toynbee's essay on the success of the Protestant ethic among Scotch Presbyterians who migrated to Ulster and its failure among the Ulster Presbyterians who migrated to the United States.

17

By HAMILTON BIMS

The Black Family: A Proud Reappraisal

WHEN Bea took sick, hard times beset the Williamson family. Bea had been more than just a housewife and a mother: she was the one individual on whom others had depended. When Yvonne came home after breaking with her husband, it was Bea who had taken on the couple's three children—who had brought them up proper, had taught them to "behave." Often it was she who made the everyday decisions, since Eddie, her husband, was seldom around the house because of a job he had taken driving cabs after work. In family disagreements, her decision was law. Bea had been the hub, the center of the household. In the family itself, and among its relatives around the town, it was Bea—called Big Mama—to whom all the others looked.

Yet family matters did not disintegrate entirely because of Bea's sudden illness. Some cousin or other, neglecting children of her own, began dropping by the house to keep a finger on things, often staying on to cook and to assist with the housework. Medical bills began to pile up rapidly, but each fortnight or so, as regularly as you please, money would arrive from some distant

New scholarly study takes positive approach to an often misinterpreted social unit

location—Cleveland, Chicago, New York City—where a member of the family, or one of its derivatives, might be living. The amounts were never much—but they could always be relied upon.

Then Bea passed away. Not once did it occur to any member of the family to have her burial in Michigan, where she had lived for two decades. Instead, it was felt that sheer decency would require that her body go "home," where her ancestors were all buried. Home for the family was rural Alabama where young Bea and Eddie had met and been married, where their children had been born, and where occasionally they returned, whether summers or for Christmas, to visit with the clan and to decide on family business.

Bea's funeral was an exceedingly large one. The family converged from every corner of the country, and a distant cousin took leave from the Army to fly in from Europe to be present at the graveside. The family's patriarch—an octogenarian—was assisted to the church by deferential grandchildren; and the overall crowd may have numbered in the scores, including cousins, uncles, nephews and grandchildren, and even in-laws and god-parents.

The events that you have read are just a hypothetical case, conceived to include many of the characteristic patterns of what often is described as the "black extended family," a new subject of analysis, and of increasing respect. In a new study of this unit, based largely upon studies in Holmes County, Miss., and in Chicago's black ghetto, an investigatory team from the University of Illinois has taken a fresh new look at this often misinterpreted entity.

The study, which was prepared for the recent International Congress of Anthropological and Ethnological Sciences in Chicago, makes the following observations:

• The traditional black family is not structurally derived from white family patterns and thus is subject to "correction." Rather, says the study, it is a unique cultural form enjoying its own inherent resources.

• Such a family is comprised of several individual households, but its channels of authority transcend the units which comprise it. Its structure, in fact, is "multi-household."

• In periods of crisis, and at ceremonial times, such a family is most visible, providing needed emotional and economic support to its constituent members.

• Such a family may perform many vital social functions, including education of its young and the adjudication of the family's internal conflicts.

• Though some of its features are explained "situationally" (they are adaptive responses to certain pressures of the moment), and through borrowing, the underlying structure of the black extended family is ultimately traceable to Africa, where such patterns often dominate.

Dr. Demitri B. Shimkin, one of the study's three co-authors, and a professor of anthropology at the Illinois campus, has elaborated on the findings. "Much of this report can be taken as a response to the Moynihan Report," he emphasizes strongly. "Daniel Moynihan has depicted black families as a sort of defective variant of a dominant white model; and I'm sorry to say that this view of black life has deeply affected much of governmental attitude—toward welfare reform, as a particular example. This is all the more serious in that his methodology is faulty. What disturbed me most is his curious confusion of family with household. That a child, for example, is living with his grandparents does not mean that that child is abandoned by his 'family.' It means no such thing. But that's the sort of risk that a researcher runs when approaching such a problem from our census statistics, which assume there's an ideal family in this country. There is no such thing as *the* American family structure. Families are quite variable. Indeed, extended families are probably the rule around the world."

D R. SHIMKIN and his collaborators—Gloria J. Louie and Dennis A. Frate—have based their study, *The Black Extended Family:*

a Basic Rural Institution and a Mechanism of Urban Adaptation, on an increasing new body of material being amassed among Holmes County blacks and their relatives in other areas. Of particular interest are two representative families—called the "Bidwells" and the "Mitchells" for the purposes of the study—whom Miss Louie studied closely over several months' time, both locally and in Chicago, a principal migratory beacon. The Bidwells are described as an "upward-mobile" family with noticeable strivings toward stable employment, better education, home ownership and other mainstream goals. The Mitchells, by contrast, are considerably less goal-directed, totally without property and generally poorer in a material sense.

Miss Louie has identified 101 Bidwells (actually, the family and its allies, including those with other surnames)—some 93 of whom interact periodically—whether in the county itself, in Jackson, Chicago, Detroit, New York or St. Louis; and "the aggregate picture of a stable, hardworking and hopeful group is profoundly different from the stereotype of black family life available from the literature." The Bidwells are typical of the stronger Holmes Countians, but even representative families departed noticeably, it was found, from the predominant image which is encountered in the literature.

The authors have been cautious about generalizing the findings, but the Bidwell example—and that of Holmes Countians generally—may represent families, of comparable economic level, throughout rural black life.

The Holmes County families are described essentially as follows:

> Critical is the presence of a group of sociological adults, male and female, who are siblings or siblings-in-law, and who are the centers of economic activity, decision-making, and care for children and dependents. Also important is a relatively permanent local base, where many members live, own homes and perhaps farmland, participate in a common church, and are buried in its cemetery . . . Sometimes there is a joint economic enterprise, such as a café. In other cases the pooling of labor and the exchange of goods are elaborately developed as systems of obligations and equities, guided by joint decision-making. There is much reciprocal visiting and communication; the reassembly of dispersed extended families at the funerals of adults, including the burial in Holmes County of those dying in other cities, is particularly important.
>
> Members . . . recognize obligations for mutual aid in job-hunting, housing, and the care of children and the ailing. Often, a particular member of the family is recognized as its senior spokesman; thus, in 1967, the basic decisions to engage in community health research and health-care effort were formally and publicly affirmed by the spokesmen of all the major extended families. Formal meetings of the adult members of an entire extended family also are not uncommon. Among some families an annual meeting has been the custom. These . . . aid in the internal settlement of family quarrels, and in the formation and conduct of common family positions in relation to white people, county politics, and other black families. . . .

Additional features, among families of the county, include work cooperation, co-residence privileges, child fosterage, care in old age, rental of land on nominal terms, gifts and inheritance, education of the young, family adjudication of legal squabbles within the group, and related patterns. (But, interestingly enough, not the dominance of the female. This pattern, which has widely been imputed to black families, is not encountered in Holmes County.)

Certain rural white groups exhibit similar sorts of patterns, particularly in the South and the Appalachian region; and Mexican-Americans and many European immigrants preserve similar such groupings prior to ultimate acculturation. But Shimkin, in remarking on the findings of the study, feels the Holmes County patterns are quite special in many ways, and are not paralleled in other groups. "Certain patterns of adoption are distinctively black patterns," he insists, "differing markedly from those of white families of similar circumstances. And then there is the problem of preferred cousin marriage. Appalachian families are endogamous units—marriages are allowed *within* the larger family group, and may even be encouraged such as in the case of second cousins. The attitude of blacks differs sharply on this point. The extended black family is an exogamous unit, as are most corporately structured kin groups."

Another feature of such families—found noticeably among the Bidwells—is their ability to adapt to varying economic challenges, while preserving their integrity. As implied in the title, the extended black family is a rural institution, but "such families have shown that they have been functionally effective under varying circumstances, ranging from systematic migration and upward mobility to local survival on a bare subsistence level."

During the early 1940s, a period of accelerated exodus of blacks from the county, many Bidwell households were established in other cities—principally in Jackson, in Chicago and in Detroit—and the pattern has continued until comparatively recent times. Yet the structure of this family has been altered quite little, despite the divergencies of residence, of income and of life style. The structure has adjusted to the conditions as encountered.

The authors discovered another characteristic pattern—a unique system of values among the Holmes County families. Illegitimacy, for a family, is no lingering embarrassment, and nearly 23 percent of the black mothers are unmarried; and the "distinctions between . . . legal marriage, consensual marriage and liaisons are . . . not sharp cleavages between moral and immoral domains." Nor is divorce a truly catastrophic event. Much more important is one's deportment toward a "blood" kin—and ruptures in relations between a father and a son, or even a brother and a sister, are tragedies to be avoided. Moreover, while blacks in the county observed statuses, of a sort, with certain of the families judged "stronger" than others, in surprisingly few cases are such distinctions a reflection of educational, occupational or income differences. "Rather," says the study, "strong [for such families] is a subtle concept. It expresses a common striving for moral rightness, mutual concern, and economic betterment ('improvement') . . . despite the inevitable adversities, the surface compromises, the humiliations, and the periodic human failings . . . Its foundation is . . . explicitly Old Testament; middle-aged men particularly regard Moses as the ultimate role model."

The great Mitchell family exhibited similar sorts of features, although the members of this group were generally poorer and less educated than were the highly mobile Bidwells. Yet differences did exist, which have been interpreted economically.

Numbering 91 members (in 14 households), almost all of whom are still residents of the county, the Mitchells are said to have the dubious distinction of occupying "one of the lower socio-economic positions in this impoverished county." Yet its very poverty has assured for this family a very strong, complex and adaptable corporate structure, even by Holmes County standards.

"To compensate for their lack of economic resources," says the study, "the Mitchells have structured a complex set of economic interrelationships stressing cooperation and sharing"; for indeed "it is doubtful whether any single household . . . could, as a separate economic unit, continuously produce a standard of living comparable with that resulting from cooperation."

An example of the Mitchell family's corporate organization is the tendency toward fosterage, whether of children or of adults—a clearly economic adjustment. The two phenomena are quite different. Child fosterage "involves the transferring of children from one household to another and occurs under a variety of circumstances," varying from overcrowding to recurrent maltreatment to economic hardship to the proximity of schools. Adult fosterage, by contrast, is structurally very different and would seem to "center on the need for additional labor" within a household.

Among the Mitchells, in recent times, one example of child fosterage, and four cases of adult fosterage, have been observed and documented.

Such patterns, it is obvious, are economically explainable, and particularly those patterns relating to fundamental subsistence. Yet it is interesting, indeed, that the expressions that they assume should find recurring parallel in many black African cultures that contributed importantly to the trans-Atlantic slave trade.

THE report calls attention to the Ewe of Ghana as a particular example of such parallels in Africa. Yet another example, not discussed in the study, are the six million Yoruba of southwest Nigeria, whose culture and society are based essentially upon kin groups—the membership in which, for any given individual, may condition much of any individual's behavior.

The fundamental unit of Yoruba society is the *idile*, or lineage or family organization whose influence is felt in every facet of local life, whether political, economic, religious or emotional. The form has survived severe changes in Yoruba tribal life. There are *idiles* today which number 500 persons, a great number of whom may interact upon occasion. Members are those persons who can trace their descent to a common male progenitor (called an *orisun*) of generations back, and a common religion and other ritual activities have preserved their identities over centuries at a time. Such families are headed by a *bale*—or patriarch—often the eldest living male.

There are indeed certain resemblances of form between the Yoruba *idile* and the Holmes County black groups (though readers should know that any structural resemblances do not necessarily imply any isolated connection). The most striking resemblance is the *power* of the two, or the degree that the groups can make themselves felt in a member's interaction with the society as a whole. The politics of Yorubaland are structured around kin groups, and who will be mayor or the commissioner of streets may well be dependent upon the power of one's *idile*. Royal succession was decided in such a way, with *obas* (or kings) historically being chosen from the powerful *bales* of the tribe's major lineages. Among Holmes County blacks the pattern is quite similar with status being conferred upon families, as such, rather than directly on individuals.

It is basically the same in the area of economic life. Yoruba lineages are often special interest groups, monopolizing the commerce of some service or good and transmitting such advantages to the younger of the group. In Holmes County, again, it is the family, as such, that "is the functioning economic unit in the county." Indeed "in many black families, economic survival is tied to household cooperation and joint economic pursuits."

Legal disputes are often settled within *idiles*, which historically, at least, possessed the powers of a judiciary. That pattern is discerned among the Holmes County groups—in the settlement, for example, of conflicting property claims. The Yoruba religion is basically homage to an ancestor, and favor is sought through the entreaty of such a person. Among the Holmes County families, the report makes clear, the kin groups are established "by links to an honored ancestor or other relative, male or female . . . [And] in general, most adults know their own and each other's ancestry, bilaterally, for three or four generations past."

Even residence patterns are broadly similar between the groups. Members of *idiles* often establish their own communities, and whole areas of a city may be associated with a kin group. Historically they resided in multi-unit compounds with each household's apartment facing a promenade, or court, where all the members interacted. A parallel pattern has been recorded in Holmes County, where a single family may often dominate a community, with the local Baptist church the common point of interaction.

Such comparisons could go on. But it appears to be obvious that much of the black family's structure—whatever may have been its many situational contributants, or the extent of its borrowing—is at least to some extent an inheritance from West Africa: an inheritance which has survived many centuries of alienation.

The study concludes with an appeal for new thinking—both political and academic. For the authors have concluded what many blacks already know—that black cultures are "entities [unto themselves] with historical traditions and functional integrity; the old, inherently derogatory concepts of simple borrowing from white culture, or overwhelming situational determinations, whether by slavery or poverty, need to be buried once and for all . . ." Moreover, while whites may feel keenly that "marital instabilities and the acceptance of human frailties are signs of black failure . . . black folk feel as keenly that the inadequacies of white care for 'father and mother, brother and sister,' white favoritism among children, and white indifference to the needs of distant kin are even more profound weaknesses."

The study notes, as well, that the "extreme and supposedly

pathological changes [in black families], such as are suggested by Moynihan and others, appear to be localized and temporary catastrophes, or else pragmatic, nominal adjustments to the demands of welfare law."

Shimkin believes that the findings of the study "are only the first several pages of a large book that needs writing." For while black society has not suffered for white interpreters, earlier studies were focused largely upon race relations, or on the view of black life in terms of socio-economic patterning, in the way that whites are often approached.

"As more urbanized blacks ascend the ladder of success," remarks Shimkin, "the tendency will of course be toward a more viable nuclear household. That appears to be a concomitant of much of modern urban life and is probably inevitable. But younger blacks, in particular, should always remember that what they are leaving is not something to be ashamed of. It is not something that is reflective of some deficiency in their culture. And it should not be disparaged.

"Beyond that message, what our report has tried to say is that American family law, and much of white American attitudes, should respect the integrity of the black extended family—and of black social values—and not assume that such a family is defective in some manner."

18

The Indian Movement:

Out of a Wounded Past

by Vine Deloria, Jr.

Indians burst dramatically upon the domestic scene with the invasion of Alcatraz; the rapid-fire sequence of protests and occupations which followed seemed to carry the movement along to an inevitable confrontation at Wounded Knee. It seems difficult to remember that Alcatraz was half a decade ago, while even Wounded Knee, in retrospect, seems like one of the last battles of the 19th century Indian wars. The pace has cooled rapidly since the occupation of Wounded Knee: primarily because many of the activists have been tied down by trials arising from the occupation, but also, perhaps, because of the dilemma of how Wounded Knee can be surpassed using the protest technique.

The contemporary Indian movement was, and continues to be, so many things, that it is difficult to understand what happened, what it meant, and where things are today. Indians seemed to be a natural protest group in the late Sixties: when protest movements began forcing a review of America's historical blunders, no group seemed to have a greater claim to redress than did Indians. If Americans were seeking a domestic focus for their Vietnam frustrations they could hardly have chosen better than the Indians, victims of such 19th century massacres as Wounded Knee and Sand Creek—startling parallels with My Lai. When Dee Brown's classic history of the dispossession of Indians, *Bury My Heart At Wounded Knee,* hit the best seller lists, it was apparent that Indians had a temporary blank check to air their grievances.

With the historic mistreatment of Indians fresh in their minds Americans turned to their evening television programs to discover that if anything conditions had become worse for most of America's indigenous population. Suddenly Indians were fashionable, Southwestern Indian jewelry began to sell like hotcakes, and a benign form of radical chic arrived in Indian country. Protests veered from the intention of reclaiming lost lands to dramatizing conditions and symbolizing the discriminatory relationship which had grown up between white society—as exemplified by the Bureau of Indian Affairs—and the descendants of the Indian warriors of old, who had figured in so much of American history.

In reviewing the events of the last half decade we can take any number of viewpoints as we try to understand how deep and how broad the contemporary Indian protest

has been. By drawing the analysis as sharply as possible we can perhaps try to establish where the movement is today and project where it might go in the future. But the very process of analysis creates a kind of dissension, since arriving at an accounting involves a determination of wins and losses, while the very essence of a movement is to maintain the semblance of unified momentum in the face of reality.

Perhaps the first phenomenon that we can identify, then, is the very clever response of the federal establishment in warding off the Indian movement from the outset. Unlike the civil rights movement, which generated a certain resistance among federal officials until it proved its moral force and general popularity among private groups such as churches and labor unions, Indians were always fairly popular; federal officials had for years shunted Indians aside by maintaining publicly that they were doing everything possible to help while privately continuing to hamstring the tribes.

The Bureau of Indian Affairs, Justice Department, and other federal agencies seemed to have planned their strategy long before Indians began to protest. When the cry for self-determination by Indians became loudest, federal bureaucrats were already manipulating Indian politics to get their favorite people installed in key leadership roles. Advisory committees were used to set tribe against tribe, area against area, urban Indian against reservation Indian, and non-federal against federal Indians, so that the movement probably had little or no chance of escaping cooptation by the federal government.

Cooptation worked because the movement began on the assumption that there was a federal policy, or at least that there was someone at the controls in Washington, and that protests would effect change by placing pressures against the formal government structures. It seems, however—again looking at events in retrospect—that there really never was a federal policy for dealing with Indian problems. Indian problems and policies were in fact the province of numerous and nameless bureaucrats, none of whom had any desire to do more than keep the natives quiet, or at least to keep them off the front pages.

Indians hit the governmental structures like divers hitting a pool of marshmallows, and in spite of the best efforts of everyone, the marshmallow worked. No matter what proposals Indians put forth for reform, the government found a way to blunt them—by half-heartedly carrying out Indian demands or by making it appear that reforms would be forthcoming pending a reorganization of the Bureau of Indian Affairs. In the past five years we have had three commissioners, all Indians, who have pledged reform and reorganization as a means of fulfilling Indian demands. But in fact policy-makers higher up the ladder have never really wanted change and the bureaucracy has moved into the vacuum, thwarting even the feeble reformist efforts of the latest commissioners.

There are certainly many places, events, and policies of the last few years where Indians could probably have done much better than they did. But over the long term the staying power of an entrenched bureaucracy is so much greater than the stamina of an outside movement that it probably wouldn't have made much difference if we had won some more battles in different areas. The fundamental problem of Indians, understanding and dealing with the federal bureaucracy, has not been solved.

[A SENSE OF IMPENDING DOOM]

Yet paradoxically, Indians in the last decade would seem to have had more success than the environmentalists, the civil rights movement, consumer activists and other citizen constituency groups. Applying strict standards of judgment to the Indian movement, judging accomplishments on the basis of fundamental laws controlling Indian life either passed or blocked—until recently the standard by which many people evaluated Indian affairs—we can state that Indians in recent years have had fairly good success, at least until 1974. In the last five years the Taos Pueblo had its Sacred Blue Lake restored to it. The claims of the Alaska Natives, pending over a century, were finally resolved. Disputed lands taken by other government agencies in the early part of the century, such as those at Yakima and Warm Springs, have been returned. The Menominee tribe, which had been terminated from federal supervision, was restored to full federal services in 1973.

In the courts Indians have had a number of unexpected successes. The fishing rights struggle in the Pacific Northwest, which featured seemingly endless litigation and protest, resulted in a landmark decision in *United States* v. *Washington* (1973) in which the treaty fishing rights were upheld. Several very important income and sales tax cases were won and Indians held their own in the very important field of water rights. Cases on affirmative action in employing Indians were decided favorably (although the Bureau of Indian Affairs has been working hard to negate the effect).

To be sure, the record of legal victories won by the Indian movement, both in litigation and legislation, is very impressive, and when one considers the complexity of the field the success of Indians seems to be little short of miraculous. No corresponding five years in American history has seen so many Indian legal victories in so many fields. In remembering some of the hesitation and reluctance of Indians to fight some of these battles, or recalling how few people really worked to resolve the issues, the result does seem incredible. I can remember when the movement to restore the Menominees consisted of one or two people meeting to make plans and rally support.

Yet as the movement approaches its crest, one still feels a sense of impending doom because of the long-term nature of Indian problems with the federal bureaucracy. No satisfactory definition of either individual Indian rights or the rights and status of tribal governments has been worked out during these years and in these two areas there is a great need for new concepts. On the issue of how much self-government a tribe may exercise, neither thinking nor legal concepts have progressed since the introduction of the Indian Reorganization Act of 1934—outside of various undependable policy changes by the different administrations. Reform of tribal governments is a very touchy area. The situation on the reservations is neither as bad as the activists would have it nor as good as the incumbent tribal chairmen would see it, while the competency of the various tribal governments varies from one reservation to another. What many Indian people have refused to consider is the history of the different tribes and reservations; many tribal governments today are hampered more than they realize by events and policies of the past.

So while short-term victories have been impressive, many of them have been built upon the intensity of the white man's guilt and not on the permanent improvement of the legal status of Indians. Today tribal governments have a great deal of freedom because of the discretionary use of federal rules and regulations and not because of any fundamental change in their legal rights. The peril of this situation becomes clear when Indians try to consolidate their gains now that the feeling of white guilt has begun to wane, and the mass of white citizens finds other causes to champion. Things that seemed reasonable and just when events were moving at a fever pitch are suddenly neither new or reasonable when the emotion dies.

Moving from the legal field to the area of raised public consciousness, an avowed goal of the activists early in the movement, one could say that Indians achieved and perhaps even surpassed their wildest dreams. A substantial number of people have become aware of modern Indians and of that number perhaps a majority of sympathizers have learned a great deal about Indian history and about American history from the Indian side. If the moral arguments of American history had to be made, and they did, we could not have chosen a more eloquent historian than Dee Brown, whose chronology of the Indian wars shattered traditional views of manifest destiny and seemed to neutralize any discussion of the inevitability of American standards of historical morality. Coming at a time when the contemporary generation of whites was questioning the foundation of America's view of itself, the Indian movement forced the issue of what America had really been and who, in view of the disclosures of history, contemporary Americans really were.

[STALLED IN ITS OWN RHETORIC]

It is precisely at this point that the Indian movement seems to have stalled in its own rhetoric. Profound and sometimes heated discussion has been rocking Indian country concerning the Indian identity. Activist groups seem to maintain a strong sentiment that a return to traditions is imperative, and raise a broad range of questions about how Indians can really return to the old ways or stabilize Indian communities by evoking virtues of former days. The most devastating accusation against anti-Indian Senators and Congressmen has been that they are trying to extinguish Indian culture, and few people in Congress have ever wished to face this kind of attack while trying to reorganize the legal status of Indians. The cultural argument has thus been the most potent counterattack for trying to prevent the federal government from abandoning or "terminating" the special position of Indians.

Yet it must be apparent to everyone, and particularly to Indians, that times have indeed changed, and with that change have come irreversible shifts in cultural outlook. Today we make pottery, carve wood, and carry on many crafts traditions for the tourist trade. We do not use very many of those products ourselves. We have telephones, go to college, buy cars, and have jobs, and do a great many things that were simply absent in the old culture. In many ways Indians participate in the contemporary technical culture as much as other Americans. But very few Indians have come to realize how drastically this change affects the responsibility of their community as a whole to participate in the formation of a new American identity.

Time and life-styles have changed very rapidly in recent years and the Indian life-style—predominantly rural and perhaps even similar to contemporary folklife-style—is not as exotic as Indians would like to think. While we have been attacking Anglo-Saxon culture as represented by the older generation of white Americans, the immediate past generation of whites has created a new life-style which is quite compatible with many ideas and customs once advocated by Indians alone. Thus as we have worked to sensitize white America a part of it has made a quantum jump toward our original cultural position.

What may be the tragedy of contemporary Indian existence is the seemingly continual failure of Indians to recognize the change in America's post-Vietnam identity. If Indians are to survive the rapid cultural change that the rest of society is making, the Indian community will simply have to allow some of its members to develop their talents and contacts with the rest of American society. Today there is a feeling of betrayal and jealousy among Indians whenever another Indian attempts to relate to contemporary developments. Individual Indians attempting to succeed at any field unrelated to the general conception of Indian life—be it folksinging, small business, scholarship, or professional careers—come under tremendous pressure from other Indians and are the object of undeserved ridicule and suspicion. They face accusation of trying to be "better" or "smarter" than other Indians.

The result of this in-group attitude is that an increasing number of younger and educated Indians are becoming discontented at being unable to use their minds and talents in developing their careers as individuals. An unarticulated restlessness exists in Indian country: talented Indians, afraid of social pressure, do not contribute their best efforts toward either the solution of Indian problems or the leading of all Americans to understand the great similarity of Indian dreams and the dreams and goals of other citizens.

[A TRAGIC CONCLUSION]

The problems of joining in the formation of a real American identity are apparent in the field of Indian education. The new momentum in Indian education began in 1960, as Indians cast off the old stereotype of the "savage" who was "good with his hands." Indian education has made great progress in nearly every field. Indians now control nearly 90 school boards ranging from primary schools up through community colleges and the Navajos in particular have telescoped a century of educational progress into a mere 15 years, creating their own community college and numerous Navajo-controlled local educational institutions.

No one knows the exact numbers but reasonable estimates would place nearly 25,000 Indians in college or post-high school educational courses—an astounding figure given that as late as 1960 there were probably not more than 2,000 Indians in higher education. Today there are probably that many Indians in graduate courses, a substantial number of them in law school and medical school. Considering that there are only about 800,000 Indians in the country and over half of them are under 18 years of age the educational phenomenon and its ensuing problems become even more intense.

Where are all the educated Indians going to go? A traditional complaint has pointed to the lack of Indians in the Bureau of Indian Affairs. At the current rate of educational expansion, the bureau could soon be manned totally by Indians, with a continuing supply of educated Indians still to be placed. For some time government jobs have been considered stepping stones to other employment; and new organizations in the private sector have provided jobs for a substantial number of educated Indians. But as the economy declines, unemployment may cause considerable disruption in the Indian community.

Still, the current success of Indians in the field of education has been indisputable, and much of it was directly related in one way or another to the activist ideologies. The invaders of Alcatraz were college students and many of the proposals of the recent protests originated in the generation of Indians now in college. Yet the very success of Indians has created some severe problems which even participation in the movement as an activist cannot solve. Never has a minority group had to absorb so many educated members in such a short time as have Indians in this past decade. Much of the apparent confusion among Indians today is simply the process of adjusting to this massive change while trying to cope with political and social problems of long-standing duration.

Despite their successes, and the buoyant optimism of many Indians about the future of the movement, prospects for the future are bleak, and a great many Indians denounce the visionaries of that future as disloyal to the community. Yet it does not take a prophet to project the extent of the crisis which Indians face. Looming on the horizon are two world problems—famine and energy—which may combine to crush the best efforts of Indians to continue moving forward.

The guilt which white Americans have lavished on Indians in recent years is rapidly being transferred to world famine. And the need for energy, when it really comes, will demand that the government find a way to confiscate energy resources on Indian reservations. Guilt vanishes fast in a chilly office building in an energy-sparse urban society. Both of these crises are moving into center stage much faster than affluent whites can comprehend and while Indians are at least aware of the energy crunch very few are able to comprehend how the sight of starving millions on evening television will affect the attitude of American society towards its own poor and hungry.

Perhaps the movement could be saved or could cushion the shock which it must face if Indians could understand their role on the world scene. Continued isolation on cultural grounds and withdrawing from participation in domestic movements will simply result in making the vanishing American vanish once again. The Indian experience of oppression, concentrated in the past, but still present on many reservations and among urban Indians, is simply not as devastating as what the world will probably soon experience.

At present Indians show no sense of understanding the crises that are galloping onto the American foreign and domestic scene. Instead of reconciling old differences, forgiving ideological heresies, or seeking out new allies on the domestic scene, many Indian leaders seem to want to remain aloof from current problems and continue to recite the sins of the white man and the non-Indian activities of the current crop of activists. Unless the movement forgives itself for being too successful and concentrates on the consolidation of a new and better definition of America's responsibility to American Indians, the movement may well degenerate into a fratricidal struggle for declining federal dollars and public attention—a tragic conclusion to a struggle that has come so far in such a short time.

Vine Deloria, Jr., a Standing Rock Sioux, was born in Martin, South Dakota, a border town on the Pine Ridge Indian Reservation. Formerly Executive Director of the National Congress of American Indians, he is the author of Custer Died for Your Sins *(Delacorte).*

Sugar'n'Spice and Everything Nice

HOW NURSERY SCHOOLS TEACH GIRLS TO SHUT UP

Nursery-school teachers are much more likely
to react to a boy's behavior, bad or good, than to a girl's.
By rewarding boys for aggression and girls for passivity,
they mold behavior that will cause both sexes pain later.

by Lisa A. Serbin and K. Daniel O'Leary

As NURSERY-SCHOOL CHILDREN busily mold clay, their teachers are molding behavior. Unwittingly, teachers foster an environment where children learn that boys are aggressive and able to solve problems, while girls are submissive and passive. The clay impressions are transient, but the behavioral ones last into adulthood and present us with people of both sexes who have developed only parts of their psychological and intellectual capabilities.

There has been constant conjecture about when and how sex-role stereotypes develop. We looked into 15 preschool classrooms and found that teachers act and react in quite different ways to boys and to girls. They subtly encourage the very behavioral patterns that will later become painful for children of both sexes.

John was a five-year-old bully. When someone didn't follow his directions or give him the toy he wanted, John lost his temper. He pushed, shoved, shouted, and threw things. When we first watched John in his classroom, he was playing peacefully with another boy at building a Tinker-Toy tower.

Then John asked the other child for a piece of material the boy was using. When he was refused, John began to tear the tower apart. The other boy protested, and John raised his hand threateningly. The other children across the room instantly sang out in chorus: "Teacher, John's hitting!" Mrs. Jones looked over and ordered John to stop. She strode across the room, pulled John away, and spent the next two minutes telling him why he shouldn't hit people. Five minutes later, John was hitting another classmate.

This brief scene shows how a teacher can reinforce exactly the behavior that's causing a problem. For John, as for many children, being disruptive is an effective means of getting a far larger dose of attention than good behavior can bring. Children get attention for good behavior about as often as Congressmen get mail in praise of their activities, so it's not surprising that most children (and some Congressmen) become adept at attracting attention by bad-boy tactics.

Our classroom observations showed that disruption is far more likely to get attention for a John than it is for a Jane. Teachers responded over three times as often to males as to females who hit or broke things, and the boys usually got a loud public reprimand. When teachers did respond to girls, they most often delivered a brief, soft rebuke that others couldn't hear.

How to Cure a Bully. Bullies like John are made, not born. We taught his teacher how to get rid of the problem very simply: we explained that she was to ignore his aggressive acts, except to prevent the victim from being harmed. We suggested that instead she concentrate on the child John was attacking, by saying something warm like, "I am very sorry you got hurt. Let me get a nice game for you to play with." When children learn that they will be ignored for their misbehavior, they stop it almost immediately. John ceased bullying.

Teachers were not usually aware that they reacted differently to aggression from boys and girls. One teacher suggested that the behavior of boys is harder to ignore because "boys hit harder." If teachers really do perceive hitting by boys as potentially more dangerous to other children, it's easy to understand why they're reluctant to ignore the act, but it's ironic that their attention aggravates the problem.

In contrast to the aggression and disruptive behavior typical of boys, girls usually rely on dependency or withdrawal to get adult attention. Feminists have strongly criticized television, educational media and the schools for training girls to be passive and dependent. Television usually depicts women in subservient roles, and the very books from which a child learns to read show girls as unaggressive and dependent. Our observations confirm that these same stereotypes are being encouraged in the classroom. So children of either sex simply use the sex-typed tactic that fits adult prejudice.

We found that teachers were more likely to react to girls when they were within arm's reach, either literally or figuratively clinging to the teachers' skirts (all the teachers we observed were women). Sheila, for example, was so frequently underfoot that Mrs. Cox constantly stumbled over her. Sheila was a bright, attractive child who asked many interesting questions, but she refused to play with the other children. Except for her extreme dependency, Sheila's development was normal for her age.

In an attempt to deal with the problem and give her more self-confidence, Mrs. Cox talked with Sheila frequently, and often touched her affectionately. When she saw Sheila playing alone, Mrs. Cox would go over and encourage her to join the other youngsters. Despite considerable effort, this attention produced no change in Sheila's behavior.

The school director then asked Mrs. Cox to look at or speak to Sheila only when she was with other children. For several days, Sheila clung even more tenaciously to her teacher's skirt, but after a week she ventured out to join the other children. Two weeks later, her extreme dependency had vanished.

Girls Learn to Cling. The pattern of teachers giving attention to nearby, dependent girls repeated itself time and time again. When boys were near, the teacher would praise them and then give them directions to do things on their own. By contrast, she would praise and assist the girls but *not* send them off to work by themselves.

In our study, we sent trained observers into 15 classrooms to record behavior by using a well-defined set of criteria. We identified 13 specific types of teacher response to seven categories of the children's behavior. An observer watched for any of the 91 possible interactions during a 20-second period,

It's Tough to Nip Sexism in the Bud

The opponents of sexism have assumed, not illogically, that making people aware of their prejudices will cure them. Now an elaborate social-psychological study of schoolchildren cautions that teaching sexual equality is neither easy nor predictable. On this subject, girls learn their lessons more readily than boys.

Harvard psychologist Marcia Guttentag and a research team set up an ambitious program they thought would nip sexism in the bud. They developed a six-week curriculum in three large, ethnically diverse school districts in the Boston area, working with over 1,000 children in three age groups: kindergarten (age five), fifth grade (10), and ninth grade (14). The children read stories, saw films, acted out plays, and worked on special projects, all designed to raise their young consciousnesses.

The new curriculum concentrated on three types of stereotypes—work, family, and personality—and aimed to make the children more flexible in their assumptions about the sexes. Women, they learned, can do any job men do, and men can have fun doing things around the house with their families. Both sexes, they learned, should share desirable personality traits—men can be sensitive and warm and women assertive and competent.

Guttentag trained the teachers with behavior-modification techniques, so that they would not act according to the unconscious bias that O'Leary and Serbin found. And, recognizing the power of the peer group at any age, she talked to the kids about how friends influence their ideas and actions.

The researchers knew from tests they gave before the program began that by age five, most of the children were ripe old sexists. The majority were thoroughly convinced by television and their playmates that boys are strong and fine and can do all sorts of interesting jobs, but that girls are weak and silly and best kept at home. Children of all social classes and economic backgrounds held these stereotypes, and it didn't matter whether their mothers worked outside the home or not.

The children in every grade thought they knew exactly which jobs were for men and which for women; the boys had the more restricted opinion of what jobs were open to women. Everyone thought they knew which personality traits were "masculine" and which "feminine." But, like adults, they weren't as quick to apply these stereotypes to themselves. When they described their own personalities, both sexes picked admirable qualities that they would otherwise associate with either males or females, e.g., strong, obedient, good-looking. Finally, like adults, the kids were more likely to view the opposite sex in stereotypic terms than their own.

The efforts to broaden the children's views of sex roles did not work quite as the researchers had planned. To their surprise, fifth-grade boys with working mothers, and ninth-grade boys with working and nonworking mothers, became notably more stereotyped in their views of women and more rigid and outspoken about "woman's place" after the six-week program. It didn't matter whether their mothers were waitresses or doctors; peer-group pressures at school outweighed the example the boys got at home. The boys' ambivalence about sex-role equality was often reflected in projective tests. For instance, one 10-year-old began a story about a picture of a female mechanic working on a car:

". . . She fixes the car good and she's been asking for a raise for a long time. Since she did a good job . . . he is going to give her a big raise. She thought that was great. When he gave her an extra bonus, she got to go home and cook a meal because her father was at work where he was a chef in a pizza place."

But then his uncertainties about working women took over:

"But when she went home, the boss found a mistake. There was a hole in a gasoline part and it cost him a whole lot of money. But he decided that he wouldn't take off the raise because she did a good job on all the other parts. When he shut the trunk the whole car fell apart. And then he got ferocious and called her up and said, 'You are fired.' The end."

If many of the boys remained traditional, many of the girls turned into fledgling feminists as a result of the new curriculum. From five to 14, they were consistently more ready than the boys to accept the ideas that women can enter a wide variety of jobs, and combine work and family. The ninth-grade girls were the most responsive to the intervention program, and showed the greatest attitude change; their self-esteem increased and they no longer felt that personal attractiveness was the sole route to success. Their male peers, by contrast, expressed their traditional opinions more freely. In only one ninth-grade class, taught by a strong and enthusiastic teacher, did boys join girls in shifting to more egalitarian views.

Guttentag's work reminds us that lessons about liberation are not enough to change attitudes and behavior. School programs do some good, and some teachers do even better. Indeed, the teachers' enthusiasm and extensive use of the curriculum materials were strongly related to the children's new attitudes. But kids pick up what they see around them far more than what adults tell them. What kids see is that men have more power, and that you can have things your way with power. They see men in a greater variety of jobs, and they see that mom is the main person who takes care of them. Those observations don't make them sexist, simply realistic. To change the observations, we would have to change the reality.

So I think it was unduly hopeful of the researchers to expect that six weeks' exposure to a vision of sex-role equality would outweigh the immediate benefits of the familiar division of labor. It's tough to persuade boys to give up the comforts of having mom at home to gain something so abstract as a flexible personality. Few children and not many adults are willing to let go of what they know for an uncertain, if well-intentioned, promise.

The researchers are optimistic about their work, concluding that school programs can be effective in shaping sex-role attitudes. To them, the glass is half full. What concerns me about the results of the study is that it increased the distance between the boys and the girls; the girls became less stereotyped about sex roles but the boys held tenaciously to the traditional views. This line of male resistance and misunderstanding is exactly what many adults who believe in sexual equality are facing. The glass is still half empty.—Carol Tavris

The full account of Guttentag's work will soon be available in *Undoing Sex Stereotypes* (McGraw-Hill).

then recorded results for 10 seconds. We did the classroom studies in half-hour units. Where we report differences in the teachers' reactions to boys and girls, statistical tests have shown that the differences we observed were far greater than what would be expected by chance alone.

Teachers, we found, actually teach boys more than they teach girls. Many studies show that there are sex differences in important cognitive skills. Boys, on the average, tend to have better analytic problem-solving abilities, to be better at spatial reasoning and to have higher mathematical abilities than girls. Girls, on the other hand, have better reading and other verbal skills [see "What We Know and Don't Know About Sex Differences," *pt*, December 1974].

These academic abilities may be nurtured, or nullified, by the classroom guardians. Parents make a major contribution to the shaping of social behavior, and there's evidence that they act differently toward boys and girls as early as the first few months of life. Fathers and mothers both turn boy infants out toward the world and push them; little girls more often get hugged up close, face to face. Children learn their academic skills, however, largely in the classroom, where boys learn to do one thing and girls learn to do another.

All 15 of the teachers gave more attention to boys who kept their noses to the academic grindstone. They got both physical and verbal rewards. Boys also received more directions from the teacher, and were twice as likely as the girls to get individual instructions on how to do things. Whether the directions were delivered by word or by demonstration, they made the boys much more capable of fending for themselves.

Boys Learn to Do. In one classroom, the children were making party baskets. When the time came to staple the paper handles in place, the teacher worked with each child individually. She showed the boys how to use the stapler by holding the handle in place while the child stapled it. On the girls' turns, however, if the child didn't spontaneously staple the handle herself, the teacher took the basket, stapled it, and handed it back.

On another occasion, a teacher was showing a small group of three-year-olds how the same quantity of water can be poured to fill several different containers of varying heights and widths.

Three children, Michael, Patty and Daniel, sat nearby, obviously fascinated by the activity, which demonstrates the "conversation" concept that marks a major milestone in a child's development.

The teacher let Michael try to pour the water himself, explaining how water can change shape without changing amount. Patty asked if she could try and was told to wait her turn. The teacher gave Daniel a chance to pour the water, and then put the materials away! Despite another request, Patty never got her turn. She never received the individual instruction the boys got in manipulating the materials.

There is ample evidence, from other studies, of the clear relationship between problem-solving ability and the amount of instruction and direction a child receives. So the superiority of boys over girls in spatial and analytic reasoning is at least partially a result of the way each sex learns to manipulate the environment—learning that begins in nursery school with boys who staple and pour, and girls who must sit passively by and watch.

It could be argued, of course, that boys require more instruction than girls, either because they are less well coordinated or because girls are more likely to acquire skills by watching others and therefore do not need as much individual instruction. Even if this is the case, however, boys and girls are still receiving a strikingly different amount of a type of adult attention that is important in the development of problem-solving ability. Boys are shown how lawn mowers and erector sets work, and they wind up with better spatial and analytic skills. Girls are encouraged to stay by their mothers and teachers, where they talk and read. It's the girls who rate higher in verbal and reading ability.

We found one exception to the general pattern. When the class engaged in an explicitly feminine, sex-typed activity such as cooking, the teachers did tend to pay more attention to the girls. Even so, they still offered brief conversation, praise and assistance, while the boys got detailed instructions.

Malignant Neglect. With this sole exception, then, we found that in nursery-school classrooms teachers are much less likely to react to a girl's behavior, whether appropriate or not, than to a boy's. The girls' actions have considerably less effect on their environment, at least in terms of adult reaction, than do the actions of boys. Coupled with portrayals of the ineffectual female on television and in books, benign neglect in the classroom rapidly becomes malignant.

The cure, of course, does not lie in reversing the situation so that boys become dependent and girls disruptive. Nor does it lie entirely with teachers, who are only one link in an important chain of events. Children of both sexes should learn to be neither too disruptive nor too dependent, and teachers need to be aware of how they can either perpetuate or prevent these qualities, depending on their actions.

We feel that the differential treatment of boys and girls limits the freedom of both sexes to develop psychologically and intellectually. Later psychological problems, as well as differences in academic and on-the-job achievements, may be the price we all pay for preschool inequities. We agree with Sandra Bem [see "Androgyny Vs. the Tight Little Lives of Fluffy Women and Chesty Men," *pt*, September] that people need access to the entire spectrum of human behavior in order to cope with the complexity of our current world. That access can be guaranteed to the molders of clay only by the molders of children.

20

Sex Discrimination And Employment Practices: An Experiment With Unconventional Job Inquiries

RICHARD M. LEVINSON*

Emory University

Males and females made job inquiries in response to 256 different classified advertisements. Clearcut discrimination was found in over one-third of the telephoned inquiries. Discrimination occurred in a greater proportion of male than female inquiries about sex-inappropriate jobs. Explanation was grounded in the degree of deviance attributed to male and female sex-inappropriate callers, the nature of "male" and "female" occupations, and employer's fear of being thought to discriminate against women.

People have fixed ideas about whether a job should be done by a man or a woman, but their reasons are as arbitrary as a Frenchman's attempt to explain what's so feminine about *la table* (Bird, 1971:68).

INTRODUCTION

Although women have become increasingly involved in the labor force, their collective failure to achieve the occupational success of men is well documented (e.g., Rossi, 1965; U.S. Department of Labor, 1969; Epstein, 1971:6-11). Particularly accountable for this discrepancy is a pattern of job segregation—remarkably stable since 1900 (Gross, 1968; Wilensky, 1968; Oppenheimer, 1970)—by which women are disproportionately employed in low status—low income occupations (Gross, 1968; Knudsen, 1969; Oppenheimer, 1970; Kreps, 1971; Martin and Posten, 1972) or in lower, subordinate positions within occupational categories (Kosa and Coker, 1965; Lopate, 1968; Gross, 1968; Epstein, 1970; Martin and Posten, 1972; Grimm and Stern, 1974). Additional explanations have been offered for the differential occupational distribution of women. Among them are sex role socializa-

tion (Maccoby, 1963; Davis, 1965:46-48; Simpson and Simpson, 1969:202-205; Pavalko, 1971:58-61) conflicting demands of marital and parental roles (Rossi, 1965; Garland, 1970; Kreps, 1971: 18-32); extensions of cultural norms asserting that women are best suited for socioemotional or subordinate roles (Parsons, 1942; Simpson and Simpson, 1969; Coser and Rokoff, 1971; Prather, 1971); psychological states of self-prejudice or lowered self-esteem (Goldberg, 1968; Horner, 1970); the sex-typing of occupations, themselves, which reinforces these processes by linking occupational roles and sex roles (Epstein, 1970); and, of course, acts of discrimination (e.g., Levitin et al., 1971; Bass et al., 1971; Bollough and Bollough, 1975).

Sex segregation in occupations remains despite legislation such as Title VII of the 1964 Civil Rights Act forbidding discrimination by sex and the efforts of agencies such as the Equal Employment Opportunities Commission to enforce it. In 1968 the Commission ruled to forbid sex discrimination in help-wanted advertisements and outlawed sex-segregated classified advertisements. Nevertheless the advertisements, themselves, often make it clear what sex is desired. Some occupations such as waitress, maid, hostess or maintenance man are obviously identified by sex.

Many others describe desired personnel in terms suggestive of a preferred sex. Consider some examples from the two major Atlanta, Georgia, newspapers in Spring, 1974.

SUPER JOB FOR SUPER GAL—Need ambitious person for Gen. ofc. duties and tel. sales.

RECEPTIONIST—Pretty downtown office interviewing Mon.-Wed. for front desk position. Type 45 wpm and Ans. busy phones. Wear your prettiest outfit and come in today.

SALESMAN—2 clean cut men to train as—salesmen for Ga.'s oldest . . .

PEST CONTROL—servicemen, drivers license necessary, unusually good opportunity for right men, will train.

AUTO SALES MGR.—A nice, sober and honest man with ability and drive.

OFFICE CLERK—3 girl office. Excellent benefits.

This paper deals with the extent of sex discrimination during job inquiries. It examines discriminatory acts at a very early stage in occupational recruitment which, by restricting access to certain positions, contributes to job segregation by sex.

METHODOLOGICAL PROCEDURES

Working in teams of one male and one female, undergraduate sociology students selected several classified advertisements from two major Atlanta newspapers during Spring, 1974. Jobs were defined as "male" or "female" on the basis of their present sex composition (Op-

* Some fifty Emory University undergraduates were involved in the experimental procedures and collectively share the paper's authorship. Comments on an earlier draft by Donna Brogan, Gwen Kennedy Neville, Jean Rogers, Larry Rogers and two anonymous reviewers were most appreciated.

penheimer, 1970:66-67; Kreps, 1971:34-35).[1]

responses to different sex callers could be attributed to the voice-indicated sex of each person making the inquiry. Should one sex be treated distinctively more favorably than the other, one might reasonably assert this to be an incident of sex discrimination.

These procedures investigate only a small element of sex discrimination in employment. Employers may appear quite negative over the phone yet behave very differently when confronted in person by a sex-inappropriate applicant (e.g., see LaPiere, 1934; Deutscher, 1973). Conversely, employers who are particularly sensitive to charges of sex discrimination might resist openly refusing a caller simply on the basis of sex but discriminate in a more subtle fashion later on in the hiring process.

After all calls were completed, information contained on standardized forms used by students (job,

In each team, one partner made an inquiry to a "sex-inappropriate" (SI) job followed approximately one-half hour later by a call from the other partner to the same number, a "sex-appropriate" situation (SA).

[1] Although either sex could have performed tasks required by the 256 listed jobs, Merton notes that "occupations can be described as 'sex typed' when a very large majority of those in them are of one sex and when there is an associated normative expectation that this is as it should be." (Epstein, 1970).
Very few advertisements included specific requests for male or female (such as those already noted in the text) although some may imply sex by job title, e.g., waitress, office girl, etc., or salesman, waiter, etc.
The following types of jobs were used: "*Male*" *Jobs*—security guards, officers (17); garage workers and attendants, auto mechanics (18); automobile sales (13); other sales—sporting goods, large appliances, etc. (10); truck, bus drivers (13) manager, manager trainee in large business corporation (15); manager, manager trainee in small business (restaurant, food, liquor, gas station, etc.) (12); skilled workers, servicemen (19); janitors, yardmen, maintenance, warehouse workers (29); "*Female*" *Jobs*—receptionist (15); waitress, hostess (12); maid, housekeeper (11); secretary, office worker, etc. (53); cosmetic, fashion sales (8); other (tupperware sales, dental assistants, day care workers, nurse's aides, etc.) (11). Due to the nature of jobs available through newspaper classified advertisements, few inquiries were made for jobs requiring advanced degrees, professional training and accorded the highest prestige and income in this society.

For example, the female would first call to inquire about an auto sales position (SI). This would be followed by a call from the male (SA). The procedure would be reversed in the case of a "female" job. Students were instructed to be polite, use nearly identical words and mannerisms in their inquiries and record in as much detail as possible the responses received from the employer to each call. In most situations the following dialogue was used:

"I would like to inquire about your advertisement in the newspaper for a _____." or "I am interested in applying for a job as _____." "How/where can I apply?"

Again, each partner was careful to match the other in further inquiries and responses to the employer's questions. In conclusion, students thanked the employers and said they would "think it over." Thus, each call was a controlled experiment providing the employer with nearly identical inquiries from persons matched on qualifications and differing only in sex.[2] Variations in caller's sex and caller-employer dialog) was coded. "Clearcut" discrimination was recorded in cases where employers clearly restricted or eliminated chances for employment due to sex. Cases where employers said one sex was unsuited for the job, when employers told an SI caller the job was filled but the SA caller it was still open, when the SI caller was deemed unqualified but the SA person with identical characteristics found qualified, were coded as "clearcut" instances. Cases were coded as "ambiguous" when males and females were accorded different responses but given no

[2] In some cases, more than one set of calls were made to the same employer. They were counted only once in data analysis. Remarkably, in each case of overlapping calls the same employer response was independently found. This serves as a strong indication of reliability.

impression that one would be excluded because of sex. Expressions of surprise or dismay, questions why a person of that sex would seek such a job, differences in the amount and nature of information offered, encouragement or discouragement differentially offered were coded in the "ambiguous" category. With similar responses to each caller, the classification of "none" was used. Finally, when information did not permit a coding decision to be made, it was classified as "not discernible."[3]

FINDINGS

Table 1 reveals that a substantial amount of sex discrimination was detected in job inquiries. Some 35% of the calls produced instances of clear-cut discrimination. Fewer (27%) showed "ambiguous" responses while less than one-third (31%) treated both callers similarly.

[3] The information forms were independently coded by the author and an assistant using the four discrimination categories. Over 90% agreement was reached. Those for which there was no agreement were placed in the "Not Discernible" category.
One issue in coding employer reactions involved the classification of responses to persons applying for positions in which sex might have some relevance for performance. For example, a male could adequately perform the tasks of a cocktail waitress but the management might prefer an attractive female to lure a businessman clientele. Is refusal to hire males for such jobs discriminatory? The 1965 EEOC guidelines for employers took a narrow view of "bonafide sex qualifications." Preference for sex could not be given simply to please customers, co-workers or clients or on the basis of generalizations about the ability of women or men in general. (Bird, 1969:13). Using EEOC guidelines, all such refusals by sex were classified as "discriminatory". It should be noted that such jobs comprised a small part of the total sample.
Finally, because our sample was restricted to the Atlanta, Georgia metropolitan area, generalizability of the findings is limited. However, as a cosmopolitan and rapidly growing city in the otherwise traditional Southeast, Atlanta may be quite similar to other regional urban settings on dimensions likely to influence these findings.

TABLE 1
SEX DISCRIMINATION IN JOB INQUIRIES

	Discrimination			
	Clear-Cut	Ambiguous	None	Not Discern
(N)	(90)	(70)	(80)	(16)
%	35.2	27.3	31.2	6.3

While we have no comparative data for other times or places, it appears that a large number of employers in the sample area practice discrimination by sex.

Clear-Cut Discrimination

Clear-cut cases of discrimination took place in a variety of ways. In a few cases the "sex-inappropriate" caller was told that the person responsible for hiring was not present or out or town while the "sex appropriate" caller was told by the individual answering the phone to come in for an interview or to make application. A variation on this strategy found employers telling SI callers they were "too busy" to deal with them at the time and asking them to call back on "a better day" (with a very receptive response to SA callers). Another method of handling SI callers was to discuss their qualifications and declare them unqualified for the job while accepting the sex-appropriate caller with identical qualifications. A female caller for a restaurant management training program was told that two years of college with no other management position was insufficient. A male who gave identical information was scheduled for an interview with the firm. A male caller for a secretarial position answered inquiries with an impressive list of skills including a college degree, shorthand and typing skills and previous experience but was turned down since the employer declared they were looking for someone more "career oriented." The female was invited to fill out an application without hesitation or further inquiry. A male caller for a receptionist job was told prior experience in credit checking was required for the job while the female (who also said she had no experience in credit checking) was told to come in anyway for an interview.

In some cases, employers assumed the sex-inappropriate person to be unqualified simply because of their sex and expressed this in the conversation before hanging up. A male inquiring about a "teacher-nurse-worker" position in a day care operation was told, "Well this is with one-year-old children and I doubt that you would want to work with them." A woman calling for a

"mechanics" job was told "I really don't think a woman can handle this sort of thing." A female inquiring about a shipping-receiving job met the response, "Honey, I'm sorry but we need a man to do that. All our employees are men and you'd need to unload heavy equipment . . . I'd like to help you but we really need someone pretty strong." In each case SA callers were encouraged to apply. One final example involves a female calling about a management trainee position for a tire corporation. She was told, "It's not for women. It requires lifting of 100 pound tires. I'm sorry—with the new laws I couldn't put that in (the advertisement)." The male was given a job description that involved no lifting and told explicitly that it involved "no heavy work." But even if it did, the male would probably have been assumed capable.

A blunt response that sex disqualified the caller (without any explanation) was another common occurrence. For example, women calling about jobs as liquor store manager, maintenance man and fuel attendant were told, "the job's for a man," "we are only interested in men" and "honey, we don't use girls as fuel attendants," respectively. Males calling for "female" jobs met similar responses. For a dental assistant inquiry one was told, "we are just looking for a girl" and for nurse's aid position, "Uh . . . we do not hire males . . . only females." One male was told "we would like to have female applicants only . . . we try to hire only women", when he inquired about hangers, packers and markers positions. In response to an inquiry about a medical secretary-receptionist, a male caller learned "I'm sure the doctors would rather have a woman . . . I'm afraid you're wasting your time because the doctors were quite specific about getting a woman" and a call about a receptionist typist job was answered, "Well, sir, I'm not sure how to put this but we're really looking for a nice young lady to fill the position and you don't really meet this criterion."

Another group of employers told SI callers they were not suitable for the position but suggested an alternative job. The male caller for a clerk-typist opening was told he should instead apply for the (more

prestigeful and lucrative) job as claims adjuster, "a position for men." Similarly, a male caller for a "shampoo help" advertisement was told he could be a hairstylist but "we don't hire men as shampoo help." A female inquiring about a janitorial position was told that it was filled (it was not according to a later SA inquiry) but she could have a job as a maid (for a lower wage). The female who asked about a job servicing vending machines was informed the company needed a "hostess" (at a lower salary). A final example involves a woman calling for a restaurant manager position. After indicating she had a variety of work experiences and would be a business school graduate, the caller was told she would be better suited now for positions as "hostess, cashier or waitress." The male caller was encouraged to interview for the manager position.

The most devious instances of clearcut discrimination occurred when the sex-inappropriate caller was told the job was filled while the following SA caller was led to believe it was still open. This happened for such jobs as medical receptionist, waitress, typist, nurses' aid, auto sales, store manager, truck driver. Thus, a variety of strategies were involved in clearly discriminatory employment actions against both sexes.

Ambiguous Discrimination

Another set of responses were labelled "ambiguous" cases of discrimination. Some of these involved responses stemming from the surprise of finding a person of that sex interested in the advertised job but in no instance did the employer eliminate the SI caller from consideration. For example, females heard the following comments not made to males applying for the same jobs:

(pest control serviceman)
"Do you want the job as secretary?" ("No, the pest control serviceman job.") "Well, er . . . oh maybe . . . I guess you can come in and apply."
(production manager—carpets)
"You *are* a female? And you're interested in this job?" ("Yes") . . . "You can come down and we'll see if this job is suitable for you. If not we can put you in the direction of where your interests lie."

Males were met with similar kinds of responses to SI calls not found in the female SA follow-up call.

(secretary)
"Are you inquiring for yourself?" ("Yes")
"Well . . . I'm very surprised you're interested in this job . . . and you type pretty good, do you. Well . . . if you really are interested I guess you can come on down for an interview . . ."

(drapery seamstress)
"It's hard to believe a guy is really qualified for this work."

A large number of callers found employers trying to discourage them from pursuing "sex-inappropriate" jobs. But males and females found a different set of tactics applied in these "ambiguous" cases. Typically, males were told jobs were either too simple, dull or low-paying. On the other hand, women were told jobs were too difficult, had "long or night hours," or required too much physical strength. While males were greeted with an encouraging reply for the following jobs females heard the following:

(laborer-lawn sprinkler installation)
"Is this for *you*?" . . . well, it's mighty hard work, out in the sun digging very deep ditches and the sprinkler systems are very complex . . . it's mighty hard . . . and long, long hours too."

(gas station attendant)
"It's pretty dirty work. Are you sure you wouldn't want to work somewhere else? The pay is minimum wage and you might have to work late shifts."

Similarly, male callers were discouraged as illustrated by the following:

(clerk-typist)
"I'm suprised you're interested in this. You realize it's general office work and typing—nothing very exciting."

(typist)
"It's only a part-time job without much security to it. We send typists to other offices with no guarantee of work all the time."

Comparison of Discrimination Towards Male and Female

Responses to inquiries were compared for overall "male" and "female" jobs in Table 2. In this study clear-cut discrimination against males was much more common than that against females. Forty-four percent of the males as compared with only 28% of the females faced job discrimination. Using a chi square test, the differences were significant at the .01 level of probability.

TABLE 2
PROPORTION OF INQUIRIES INTO "MALE" AND "FEMALE" JOBS WITH DISCRIMINATORY RESPONSES—COMPARISON OF TOTALS

	Discrimination				
	Clear-Cut	Ambiguous	None	Not Discern	Total
Female inquiries for "Male" Jobs	28%	31.5%	37%	3.5%	100% (N = 146)
Male inquiries for "Female" Jobs	44%	22%	24%	10%	100% (N = 110)

These data were dichotomized into a 2 × 2 table contrasting clear cut by other categories. $X^2 = 7.45$, significant, $P < .01$.

DISCUSSION

Long ago, Hughes (1945) called attention to a process whereby certain combinations of status-determining characteristics (such as sex) came to be associated with a particular position. This results in the expectation that all incumbents of that position possess such auxiliary characteristics. Bird has noted how capriciously such labels become applied by commenting that women are felt to be good for factory work on electronic circuits for the same reason men are said to be well suited for neurosurgery— finger dexterity and a steady hand (Bird, 1971:69). In this study, sex-typed jobs were approached by persons without those auxiliary characteristics. Their violation of social norms, i.e., deviance, was sometimes negatively sanctioned by comments expressing surprise or derogation and/or discriminatory acts of exclusion.

But this does not explain the greater discrimination against male than female sex-inappropriate callers. Perhaps sex is a more *salient* characteristic of "female" than "male" positions, i.e., more essential for the performance of functions required by "female" than "male" jobs included in this study. Although Epstein (1969; 1970) documents how gender sometimes interferes with female performance in professions of the male establishment, sex may be even more important for jobs associated with women, e.g., receptionist, secretary, fashion sales,—at least for the men doing the hiring. A secretary may be expected not only to type but to "decorate the office." As one male applicant for a receptionist's position was told by the (male) employer:

"Well you see in our office there are many important customers coming into the office and it just doesn't look right having a man behind the reception desk . . . it seems out of place . . . and it's liable to hurt the business. It shouldn't be that way, but you know how it is . . . And also, speaking for the guys around here, I think the day would be a lot more pleasant with a pretty face around."

Similarly, it might be felt that a woman in sales who displays her products well (cometics, fashions) will be a more effective employee than a male. Thus, one explanation for the differential discrimination may be the feeling of (male) employers that being a female is more central to filling the needs of female sex-typed jobs than being male is for male sex-typed positions.

Another possible explanation for the differential discrimination might be related to aspects of personal character attributed to the caller by the employer. The male SI caller may be seen as more deviant or abnormal than a female SI caller. Observers of sex role socialization (e.g., Lynn, 1961; Mussen, 1969) have noted that boys experience greater stigma and/or anxiety for acting like a girl ("sissy") than girls experience for acting like boys ("tomboys"). This may be the result of an indentification process (Lynn, 1961) or because male roles and traits are more culturally valued (Mussen, 1969; Broverman et. al., 1970). As with stereotypic male characteristics, for women to seek more highly desired and prestigeful male jobs may be perceived as rational, understandable and sometimes admirable. However, the male seeking a less valued "female" position is likely except, perhaps, in times of limited employment opportunities (Grimm and Stern, 1974:693), to be seen as peculiar and, hence, an undesirable employee. Interestingly, several male SI callers were questioned about their "masculinity" (e.g., "Are you a queer?") while no female SI callers reported such comments.

Finally, many employers were probably made sensitive to the legal consequences of discrimination against women through publicity of recent law suits, the activism of women's rights organizations and government warnings. To date, men have rarely made use of the law to gain access to female sex typed positions. Of twelve SI callers reporting an employer actually mentioning he could not legally discriminate simply because of sex, ten (83%) were females inquiring about "male" jobs.

(auto sales)
"Well, I can't turn you down because you're a girl. But really, I think you're barking up the wrong tree."

(manager)
"Don't tell me *you* want this job?" ("Are only men eligible for the job?") "No, it would be discriminatory if we did that."

While there is evidence for the operation of each of these processes, the degree to which each accounts for our findings cannot be determined by these data.

Although the findings reported here indicate women may find it easier gaining access to traditionally male fields than *vice versa,* others have argued just the opposite. Gross (1968) and Wilensky (1968) have speculated that traditionally female occupations have been more open to men than male occupations to women and Gross (1968) has offered data to substantiate that most male fields have remained more segregated than most female fields. Apparently, the increased demand for labor in traditional female areas has not only absorbed growing numbers of women, but attracted some men as well, mostly at higher, supervisory positions (Grimm and Stern, 1974).

Several considerations may resolve the seemingly contradictory findings. First, our sample of occupations culled from classified advertisements are primarily non-professional, low-prestige positions. Occupations investigated by Grimm and Stern (1974) were semi-professions (social work, teaching,

librarianship, nursing) with some prestige, job security, a modest but adequate income and opportunity for advancement. It is easy to understand why males might be attracted to such occupations, especially when they serve at the highest levels. By contrast, female occupations in this study are primarily "dead end" positions without opportunity for mobility. (Eighty-three percent were classified as either secretary, receptionist, waitress or maid.) While higher-status female semi-professions may even actively recruit males to "upgrade the profession" (Wilensky, 1964; Gross, 1968:51), there is no such self-conscious professionalization among female occupations in this study. Other reports of increasing integration of women's fields may be responding to changes occurring primarily among the higher prestige occupations or use categories so broad that they are unable to detect patterns of segregation in categories used in this study. As Gross (1968:207) cautions, "the finer the distinctions, the more segregation one will catch."

Our findings, in contrast with others, may also be a function of time. Several employers seemed very aware of the legal problems involved with discrimination against women. This study may have tapped a change taking place in which, as a result of increased feminist activism, employers are today much more hesitant to discriminate against women than men. Of course, employers might just be more cautious against overt refusals over the phone. Discrimination may occur later, in a more subtle fashion, yielding much less access to females than is indicated by this study.

It is therefore, unclear from the accumulating data how job opportunities for men and women will change in the future. If aggressive action on behalf of women is maintained, there may be some influx of women into jobs at all prestige levels formerly held by men. Combined with a tighter job market, men might increasingly seek employment in formerly women's fields at all levels of prestige and begin to use the statutes to their own advantage if access is denied. If previous patterns continue (Grimm

and Stern, 1974), those integrated occupations may become internally segregated and stratified by sex with males continuing their domination.

SUMMARY

Males and females made job inquiries in response to 256 different classified advertisements. Clearcut discrimination was found in over one-third of the telephoned inquiries. Discrimination occurred in a greater proportion of cases in which males applied for sex-inappropriate jobs than when females applied for sex-inappropriate jobs. The study documents a continuing sex discrimination and sex segregation in contemporary employment practices.

REFERENCES

Bass, Bernard M., Judith Krusell and Ralph A. Alexander
1971   "Male managers' attitudes toward working women," American Behavioral Scientist 15 (November/December): 221-236.
Bird, Carolyn
1971   Born Female: The High Cost of Keeping Women Down. New York: David McKay.
Bullough, Bonnie and Vern L. Bullough
1975   "Sex discrimination in health care," Nursing Outlook 23 (January): 40-45.
Broverman, I., D. M. Broverman, F. E. Clarkson, and S. R. Vogel
1970   "Sex role stereotypes and clinical judgments of mental health." Journal of Consulting and Clinical Psychology 34:1-7.
Coser, Rose L. and Gerald Rokoff
1971   "Women in the occupational world: social disruption and conflict." Social Problems 18 (Spring): 535-554.
Davis, James A.
1965   Undergraduate Career Decision. Chicago: Aldine.
Deutscher, Irwin
1973   What we say/What we do: Sentiments and Acts. Scott, Foresman: Glenview, ILL.
Epstein, Cynthia Fuchs
1969   "Women lawyers and their profession: inconsistency of social controls and their consequences for professional performance." Pp. 669-684 in Athena Theodore (ed.), The Professional Woman. Cambridge, Mass.: Schenkman.
1970   "Encountering the male establishment: sex-status limits on women's careers in the professions." American Journal of Sociology 75 (May): 965-991.

1971 Woman's Place. Berkeley, California: University of California Press.

Garland, T. Neal
1970 "The better half? The male in the dual profession family." Pp. 199-215 in Constantina Safilios-Rothschild (ed.), Toward A Sociology of Women. Lexington, Mass.: Xerox College Publishing.

Goldberg, Philip
1968 "Are women prejudiced against women?" Transaction 5 (April): 28-30.

Grimm, James W. and Robert N. Stern
1974 "Sex roles and internal labor market structures: the 'female' semi-professions," Social Problems 21 (June): 690-705.

Gross, Edward
1968 "Plus ca change. . . ? the sexual structure of occupations over time." Social Problems 16 (Fall): 198-208.

Horner, Matina
1970 "Femininity and successful achievement: a basic inconsistency." Pp. 45-74 in Judith M. Bardwick et al., Feminine Personality and Conflict. Belmont, California: Brooks/Cole.

Hughes, Everett Cherrington
1945 "Dilemmas and contradictions of status." American Journal of Sociology 50 (March): 353-359.

Knudsen, Dean D.
1969 "The declining status of women: popular myths and the failure of functionalist thought." Social Forces 48 (December): 183-193.

Kosa, John and Robert Cocker, Jr.
1965 "The female physician in public health: conflict and reconciliation of the sex and professional roles". Sociology and Social Research 49 (April): 294-305.

21

BY GLORIA STEINEM

IF WE'RE SO SMART, WHY AREN'T WE RICH?

There are all those familiar questions. Why are there no great women composers? inventors? painters? Or, a more sophisticated version: isn't it really mothers who train children into sex role stereotypes? Or, sillier but more humiliating since it implies we can't achieve greatness even on our own turf: why are most of the great couturiers men? and the great chefs?

Women may never grow used to those challenges, but we have finally begun to recognize them for what they are: subtler versions of the old vaudeville taunt, "If you're so smart, why aren't you rich?"

In recent years, we've learned some of the answers. Thanks to women's history courses, we now know more about the brave exceptions who *did* compose, invent, or paint; and we can document the power of cultural conditioning, of

the sexual caste system that continues to limit most women. Even more important, the Black Movement and other struggles for social justice have helped all of us to realize that the existing distribution of power is not "natural"; that poverty is no proof of unwillingness to work, and wealth is no measure of human value.

There is finally some understanding, therefore, of the real reasons why women of all races are still only 7 percent of the physicians in this country, but 99 percent of registered nurses; of why we are 4 percent of lawyers, but 97 percent of household workers. There is even a weakening of the notion that Amer-

ican women are better off relative to their men than are the women of other industrialized countries. (It's a truism, for instance, that Scandinavian countries are considerably more democratic toward their female citizens than we are, and that women are a far greater percentage of the physicians and other professionals in the Soviet Union than is true here—though all these European societies are still quite patriarchal.)

Gradually, painfully, we have learned that we are indeed one of the most race-conscious countries in the world; that we used our nonwhite population to build our agricultural and industrial wealth, and developed a complex of racist myths to make such inhuman use seem natural. Now we are learning that women have also been used as a source of unpaid or underpaid labor—whether in offices or factories or in our own kitchens. We are learning that women of all races have suffered not only as cheap labor, but in their role as a means of production; as the producers of workers and soldiers that this expanding country demanded in abnormally large supply. (Early American life was so hard and contraceptive information so suppressed that, until the early part of this century, it was common for a man to survive one or several wives. As a heritage of slavery, black women were even more likely to be thought of as breeders and lowly workers.) Sexist myths were elaborated to justify and enshrine this economic use of women: child-centered lives and unrewarded work became our "natural" domain.

We are just beginning to see racism and sexism as the twin problems of caste. One is more physically cruel and less intimate than the other, but both perpetuate themselves through myths—often the very same myths—of innate inferiority. Both are more ruthless than class, for they can never be changed or escaped. And both have an economic motive: the creation of a cheap labor force that is visibly marked for the job.

But women, black and brown as well as white, suffer from a dimension of economic prejudice that minority men do not; one that prolongs the problem by the very effective device of denying that any problem exists. We are perceived as *already powerful*—at least in relation to men of our own group, and often to society at large.

So, while most people now understand the discrimination that prevented women and minority men from becoming great painters or inventors, there is still the conviction that women exercise some great behind-the-scenes power.

We are said to be domineering or castrating (even if it is only retribution for our limited lives); to be matriarchs; to have more economic power than our counterpart men. We are even supposed to control the economy.

All the stereotypes come to mind: there is the pampered housewife, sitting at home in wall-to-wall comfort while her unfortunate husband works long hours to keep her that way. There are the lazy women getting a free ride on alimony because they were once married, or on welfare because they have children. There are those great figures of American mythology, the rich widows who are supposed to control most of the stock, and travel Europe on the life insurance of some overworked spouse. According to Patrick Moynihan, an experienced creator of socialized myth, there are the black women matriarchs who seized power because they could get jobs when black men could

---

Struggles for social justice helped us see that the existing distribution of power is not "natural"; that poverty is no proof of laziness, wealth no measure of human value

---

not. Still dominant, they are now supposed to get better-paying jobs because white America finds them less threatening; just another way of emasculating black men. There are the Puerto Rican and Chicana women who may not be so far ahead in jobs or education but are still said to rule their families and communities with an iron hand. Supposedly, even Native American women are leaving their Indian traditions, and catching this American disease called the Dominating Woman.

And, according to stereotype, it's getting worse. Women are being hired not because they're qualified, but because the employer has a quota to fill. Therefore, women's incomes are shooting up; especially unfortunate since women work for pin money, not because they need

to, and are taking jobs away from men. As for black or other minority women, they are widening the gap between themselves and their men: employers hire more minority females than minority males in order to fill two quotas for the price of one.

So goes the Popular Wisdom. It's very convincing. We ourselves often find ourselves believing it about women as a group, even though we personally have had no such experience. As a result, we take sex discrimination less seriously than we would if the very same discrimination were based on race; and we comfort ourselves for the conspicuous absence of women artists, executives, political leaders; and even chefs with the knowledge that, in some basic if rather underhanded way, we really *are* in control of the economy. Backseat drivers, yes, but drivers nonetheless. It must be true. Isn't that what everybody says?

Looking beyond the stereotype to women's real economic situation isn't easy. As with public opinion polls and other national measures, women as a category are not always broken out of economic statistics. Neither are minority groups; and minority women are the least likely of all to be paid separate attention. But here are some pertinent facts, all collected from the sources listed at the end of this article. There are many surprises, but also confirmations of what our personal experience has told us—even if the economic mythology about women has not.

To take the areas of greatest resentment first, what about unearned wealth and nonsalaried income? These are, after all, areas in which women are supposed to be living off the fat of the land.

The Great Alimony Myth. Perhaps it's the news stories about big Hollywood divorce settlements, or perhaps it's just public complaint by the few middle-class men who really do pay unfair alimony. Whatever the reason, the stereotype is very far from the fact. According to judges quoted in a 1965 study by the American Bar Association (the only nationwide report available), temporary alimony is awarded in fewer than 10 percent of all divorces, and serves largely to give the wife enough time to find a job. According to one judge quoted in the study, permanent alimony is awarded in less than 2 percent of divorces; usually when the wife is too old or ill to be employable. As for child support, the average payment is less than half the amount necessary to support a child.

Then there is the problem of collecting. Though nearly all states hold men criminally liable if they do not support their wives and children, most require that families be in "destitute or necessitous circumstances" before action is taken. Many women find they cannot afford the court costs and lawyers' fees, or that the ex-husbands simply move away and cannot be found. Though there are no reliable studies on the collection of alimony, the Citizens' Advisory Council on the Status of Women quotes a 1955 study as the only available one on the collection of child support. According to those findings, only 38 percent of fathers were in full compliance with the support order a year after the divorce; 20 percent were in partial compliance (which meant they had made at least one payment); and 42 percent had made no payment at all. Ten years after the divorce, only 13 percent of the fathers were making all payments and 79 percent were making no payments at all.

The Advisory Council notes rather drily that "mistaken ideas about a husband's responsibility for support of wife and children, which have been reinforced by opponents of the Equal Rights Amendment, are a great disservice. . . . Many young women, relying on the belief that marriage means financial security, do not prepare themselves vocationally."

Stocks. Perhaps this is the source of the notion that we control the economy: women *did* once constitute slightly more than half of all stockholders, and are still a big 49.9 percent. But here is the catch. They

are far more likely to have small holdings. For instance, women own only 42 percent of the dollar value and 38 percent of the total shares. Furthermore, the stock may belong to the woman in name only. Her husband may want to limit his liability in business investments, for example, or to leave the stock without inheritance tax to her and the children should he die, or be able to say for business or political reasons that the stock belongs not to him but to his wife. (Stock that is in women's names during or after the life of the husband is very often a necessary saving for the support of children.) And, no matter why the stock is attributed to her, it's rare that the woman actually controls it.

---

*The economic element
of the matriarchal myth
about black women
is not so much
the real power held
by black women
as black men's lack
of power
relative to white men*

A New York Stock Exchange study shows, for instance, that 75 percent of all securities transactions are carried out by men.

For whatever reason, very few women have the assets, expertise, or control to get rich in the stock market. In fact, female stockholders are poorer and far more likely to have clerical or sales jobs than are male stockholders.

Pensions, life insurance, and real estate. Pensions are based on salaries. Since women make only 59 percent of what men do, they're bound to feel the pinch at retirement time, too; supposing, that is, that they have not left dreary, futureless jobs too soon to be eligible.

(Because money is set aside for pension funds in companies where there is little incentive for women to stay the requisite years, their contributions often end up subsidizing the pensions of men.) Furthermore, pension or retirement plans rarely give the same benefits to families of women as they do to families of men. Accrued benefits may be lost entirely if the woman takes time out when her children are young; and plans often force women to retire earlier—in spite of their longer life expectancy. Finally, the companies with the greatest number of women workers are the least likely to have decent pension plans at all.

Now we come to life insurance. Yes, two-thirds of all beneficiaries *are* women (supposing that the policy hasn't either lapsed or been borrowed against before the holder's death). But the benefits are often low; far less, for instance, than a housewife might have saved had she been paid the estimated worth of her work in the home: currently, about $9,000 a year. And the benefits are frequently spent less for the wife's welfare than for the children's.

Insurance policies taken out on the lives of women constitute only 14 percent of all life insurance. The average size of ordinary policies purchased for men in 1971 was $17,810; for women, it was $6,580.

Real estate has to be included, too, in assessing women's wealth. The Internal Revenue Service hasn't released new figures since 1962, and the IRS only reported this kind of property wealth for individuals with estates worth more than $60,000. In that group, however, there were 2,194,000 men who held $118.3 billion in real estate among them; plus 1,250,000 women who held $69.7 billion. Of course, questions of control and who benefits have to be asked here, just as they do when assessing women's real degree of economic power in the stock market.

So how true is the stereotype of pampered and powerful women of large incomes? One good overall measure is this: if you look at all the people in this country who have incomes of $10,000 a year or more from whatever sources (jobs, alimony, stock dividends, real estate rental, insurance, pensions, gifts; everything), you find that less than 9 percent of them are women. And that includes all the divorcées and rich widows.

Welfare Cadillacs. Somewhere, there must be people who prefer welfare to a decently paid job, just as somewhere, there must be women awash in alimony. No stereotype can be wrong all the time. But it's difficult to figure out why anybody would opt for the humiliation and Kafka-esque red tape of a welfare existence if a good job, child care, and independence were real alternatives. It's especially hard to believe that a woman would have a child or children just to become eligible for welfare when the average monthly payment, in all but four states, is well below the poverty level; that is, below $331 per month for a family of four as of July, 1971. Furthermore, the typical increment per child is only $35 a month; barely enough for the most basic needs.

Several years ago, for instance, the National Welfare Rights Organization figured out that the money available for food from a welfare check, even in New York City, was 66 cents per person per day. They asked a group of Congresspeople and reporters to go on this welfare diet for one week.

It was hardly a fair test: the experimenters started out in good health, with access to warm clothes, telephones, transportation, and decent housing; all conditions that welfare clients don't usually enjoy. After a few days, the individuals or families were amazed at the effort required to shop; to go from store to store, figuring to the last penny. They were also slightly hungry, yet gaining weight because starchy, filling foods were all they could afford. By week's end, they were obsessed with food, could not concentrate on their jobs, and found that privation had begun to affect their personal

lives in strange ways. A Congressman's wife reported privately that her young son had stolen some food saved for the final day, and she herself had been frightened by the rage that she felt.

It could be an instructive exercise for anyone who hasn't experienced welfare: find out what the daily food budget would be for an individual or family on welfare in your area, and live on that budget for one week. The stereotype of the lazy, lackadaisical welfare mother is unlikely to survive.

Salaried work is an area in which more facts are known, and the Popular Wisdom may be less distant from the truth. It's probably not surprising, for instance, that women workers earn less than $3 for every $5 earned by men. Or that the sex-based differential survives, even where women are not confined to the lower-paying professions. (The 1970 median yearly salaries of women in scientific fields, for instance, were from $1,700 to $5,100 less than those earned by men with similar training and positions.)

But there is still a lot of mythology surrounding relative earning power.

Salaries: male and female, black and white. In 1970, the median incomes for full-time, year-round work went like this:

white men $9,373
minority men $6,598
white women $5,490
minority women $4,674

These figures, showing that women of all races earn less than men of all races, go against our ingrained beliefs about relative earning power. Race does, however, become the dominant factor going *down* the economic scale, though sex continues as a major influence: 35.5 percent of all black females lived beneath the poverty line in 1971 as opposed to 28.9 percent of black males; but 11.2 percent of white females were below that line, and only 8.5 percent of white males. Sex becomes more of a factor going *up* the income brackets, though race continues as a major influence: in

1971, 46.8 percent of fully employed white males and 17.4 percent of minority males earned over $10,000; while just 8.7 percent of white females and 6.5 percent of black females reached those heights.

Furthermore, education doesn't have as crucial an effect on those trends as we might think. Women with one to three years of college had lower incomes in 1971 than men who had gone to school for only eight years.

It's clear by any measure that black women, with the double stigma of sex and race, come out on the bottom. The fact that they could get jobs (though poorly paid ones, often domestic work) when black men could get none has obscured the economic truth that now, they have the highest unemployment rate of all adults, and the least access to upper income jobs.

Perhaps the economic element of the matriarchal myth is not so much the real power held by black women, as black men's lack of power relative to white men; a fact that has brought black men and black women into economically closer relationship than their white counterparts. In 1970, for instance, the median income of black women was 70 percent that of black men, as opposed to white women whose median income was 59 percent that received by their male counterparts.

Comparing the earning power of all women and minority men is important. It helps define the real dimensions of sexism to note, for instance, that a black woman with a college degree working full time makes less than a black man with an eighth-grade education. Or to explain that a white college-educated woman with a full-time job makes less than a minority workingman with a high school education. But such comparisons are dangerous if they imply that the only element of suffering is economic, or that minority men are somehow better off than we had thought.

There can be no illusion about the real effect of racial caste. For instance, families headed by black males in which the wife does not work had a median income of $6,024 in 1971; whereas families with white male heads and nonworking wives had a median income of $9,357. Clearly, some white women are able to benefit economically from being attached to white men. The lesson of all male-female comparisons is only that sexism runs from top to bottom of society, and penalizes the minority community by keeping half its number doubly oppressed.

But if we have any doubts about who is really benefiting from this double system of caste, we have only to look at the upper levels. Of all the jobs that pay $15,000 a year or more, for instance, 94 percent are held by white males—leaving a big 6 percent to all women and minority men combined.

Real progress will come only when we stop comparing second-class groups with each other, and direct all our energies toward fundamental change; toward the people who are really in power.

Families, poverty, and why women work. After the economic lessons of the Depression and World War II, the Economic Act of 1946 set forth the goal of "maximum employment"; a phrase officially interpreted as the "employment of those who want to work, without regard to whether their employment is, by some definition, necessary. This goal applies equally to men and to women." Nonetheless, the 38 percent of the work force that is female continues to be challenged on whether or not there is a "need to work," a question that is rarely put to the 62 percent of the work force that is male. (It's statistically possible that the number of men with enough assets to exist for the rest of their lives without working might equal the number of women who have a chance of being supported until death by a husband. If one group is resented in the labor force, why not the other?) Of course, the truth is that most of the

40 percent of all women who work do so for the same reason as their male counterparts: they desperately need the money. In fact, more women than men may be working out of that motive, since the jobs open to women are far less likely to offer a sense of accomplishment, respect in society, or other rewards.

Of the women in the work force in March, 1972, 20.5 million were single, widowed, divorced, separated, or married to a man who made less than $7,000 a year. Furthermore, 68 percent of all black wives under 35 work outside the home, as do 56 percent of all young white wives. The idea that two can live as cheaply as one is a myth. So is the notion that a man can (or should) be required to support an entire family.

The idea that women don't *need* to work is the most dangerous of the ways in which women are perceived as being unserious or somehow already powerful. It obscures women's real condition, and the degree to which sex discrimination is a cause of our basic social ills.

Why else are 38.4 percent of all female-headed families condemned to poverty, compared to only 8.3 percent of those headed by men? Why else do female-headed families make up more than 90 percent of those on welfare? Why are women over 65 the poorest group in the country? Or why is the percentage of female unemployed so much greater than even the terrible, punishing percentage of minority men?

Unless we learn to hire individuals by ability, not sex, we will condemn women to a half-life of powerlessness—and also condemn the children and others who are dependent on them. We can't begin to solve the riddle of poverty until we take seriously the ways in which it is perpetuated by caste.

Is women's economic plight getting better? Not in a mass way at all. In fact, the differential between male and female pay has been getting steadily bigger, not smaller;

the unemployment rate for women is up about 40 percent in four years; easier divorce laws, though a basic step forward, still have left many women with no job training and few alternatives; child care becomes more expensive and less adequate each year; older women on fixed incomes are suffering from spiraling prices; and the number of women and dependent children on welfare has gone up by nearly five million since 1968. All the recent trends of inflation combined with increased unemployment have hit women very hard.

But there are signs of hope. Job actions and back-pay suits have been successful enough to frighten big companies into at least taking a serious look at their employment policies. So have actions on promotion and hiring, though, at higher levels, we are only approaching tokenism. According to the 1970 census, women have begun to break out of traditionally female occupations, and into formerly male preserves; even into some of the blue-collar jobs. Altogether, women accounted for two-thirds of the employment increase in the 1960s.

But only constant effort, and unified action can begin to lighten women's economic burden. The changes to come must be basic: even equal pay for the women already in the work force would necessitate a major redistribution of wealth.

It will be a long road. The first step is believing in ourselves; understanding that we are indeed smart, even if we aren't rich. And the second is giving up the myths of power, so that we can see our economic plight as it really is.

Gloria Steinem has been a free-lance writer all her professional life, because "even though the money was poor, it's easier for women to get work where there's no conventional structure." "Ms." Magazine is her first full-time, salaried job.

IV. Perspectives on Changing Institutions

Social institutions reflect changes, conflicts, and strains present in the larger society. Thus, rather than to "view with alarm" changes in basic institutions and attribute social problems to their malfunction, we should be asking what conflicts in the larger social system contribute or lead to such institutional change and/or failure.

In pre-industrial societies the family was the basic institution, and it encompassed most socialization functions. In our industrial epoch many of these functions have been taken over by organizations outside the family, such as the school. However the family still is expected to carry out the primary aspects of socialization. And it has become a sociological cliche to refer to the "companionship" family as the basic type. This new family form, if indeed it is new, reflects both the strains and instability of the larger social structure and those which seem to result from the high expectations for personal fulfillment that society continues to place upon it. The divorce rate is at a new high—about one for every three marriages; remarriage rates have decreased and there is a corresponding increase in the number of female-headed families. The family is changing in other ways as well. The birth rate has declined steadily, and although the two-child family is favored by younger marriage partners, an increasing number of marriages are childless. Michael Novak has this latter trend in mind when he poses the question, "Why is it a political act to "have children?" He equates the reluctance to have and rear children with the immaturity of the marriage partners. Angus Campbell's report of research on the American family supports Novak's, but he takes a different and less moralistic tack. He reports that "child-free" marriages are seen as fulfilling in an increasing number of families. The evidence says more about the socioeconomic pressures on potential parents than about their maturity. Pickett calls for a family arrangement he terms the "actualized" family, which he sees as the means of fulfilling "The Promise of American Life." Can the family as described in these articles fulfill such expectations?

Americans often express great faith in their educational institutions. Yet prior to the twentieth century, high school and college were reserved mainly for the middle and upper classes. Now the ratio of youths in high school is reversed (from about 4 percent in 1890 to 94 percent in 1970). Even with this increased emphasis (and literally billions of dollars being expended) on public education, schools do not seem to be providing the kind of educational preparation required by our complex society. Several states, among them Missouri and New York, plan to make ninth grade reading and mathematical achievement levels mandatory for high school diplomas. What does this say about the failure of our schools? Schools have been the focus of the struggle for social equality since *Brown* v. *Topeka Board of Education* in 1954. However, resistance in the South has spawned hundreds of all-white private schools, whereas, in northern cities such as Boston, opposition to busing has resulted in open conflict replete with demonstrations and riots.

In expecting our schools to provide ladders of social mobility considerable emphasis has been placed on compensatory education for the "disadvantaged." Yet the schools themselves may well be the agents of deprivation, as described in Jack Fincher's article. What might be the consequences if Aviation High were to become the model for educating blue collar youths? In addition to preparing the young for a narrow vocation, wouldn't such schools also be strengthening the existing class structure? Does the new emphasis on career-oriented education portend a more rigid, stratified, class-bound society, as Fred Hechinger contends? Can our schools be reorganized to serve democratic ends without basic changes taking place in the larger social structure?

The work scene in the late 1970s shows a greater proportion of workers in service industries than in production. This series of articles on work hardly supports the often made observation that the work ethic has been replaced by the "leisure" ethic. Wage earners still perform menial, back-breaking work, even in highly automated industries. The articles included under this topic provide an interior view of the worker, which is crucial to an understanding of problems such as alienation. Ed Sadlowski's struggle with union bosses, as well as management, illustrates alienating forces in the world of work. The description of young workers in the steel mills underscores this alienation. The reader should ponder whether moving up the occupational scale, as described in the Earlner article, is as fulfilling as it seems from the bottom of the ladder.

Theoretically, political institutions exist to serve the people, at least in a democratic society. Yet the immense concentration of political power and the interlocking relationships between political and economic power centers in the Corporate State do not lead to democratic decision making. Can we resolve this issue by getting rid of "big government"? Starr argues that a strong government may be necessary to counterbalance other centers of power. The close tie between defense industries and big government is shown in the defense budget of $114.9 billion for fiscal 1976–77, a 12 percent increase from the previous year. While most of this goes to industries, a sizable amount goes for intelligence activities, i.e., spying. And far too much of this effort is directed against our own citizens, according to Rosenberg's article. The final article describes the difficulty of regulating the multinational corporations. A number of these are tied into the government through the sale of foreign military supplies. What effect does the will of the people have when confronted with such a concentration of power?

THE FAMILY OUT OF FAVOR

The courage to marry and raise children presupposes a willingness
(presently unfashionable) to grow up

by Michael Novak

RECENTLY A FRIEND OF MINE told me the following anecdote. At lunch in a restaurant, he had mentioned that he and his wife intended to have a second child soon. His listener registered the words, stood, and reached out his hand with unmistakable fervor: "You are making a political statement. Congratulations!"

We live in lucky times. So many, so varied, and so aggressive are the antifamily sentiments in our society that brave souls may now have (for the first time in centuries) the pleasure of discovering for themselves the importance of the family. Choosing to have a family used to be uninteresting. It is, today, an act of intelligence and courage. To love family life, to see in family life the most potent moral, intellectual, and political cell in the body politic is to be marked today as a heretic.

Orthodoxy is usually enforced by an economic system. Our own system. postindustrial capitalism, plays an ambivalent role with respect to the family. On the one hand, capitalism demands hard work, competition, sacrifice, saving, and rational decision-making. On the other, it stresses liberty and encourages hedonism.

Now the great corporations (as well as the universities, the political professions, the foundations, the great newspapers and publishing empires, and the film industry) diminish the moral and economic importance of the family. They demand travel and frequent change of residence. Teasing the heart with glittering entertainment and gratifying the demands of ambition, they dissolve attachments and loyalties. Husbands and wives live in isolation from each other. Children of the upwardly mobile are almost as abandoned, emotionally, as the children of the ghetto. The lives of husbands, wives, and children do not mesh, are not engaged, seem merely thrown together. There is enough money. There is too much emotional space. It is easier to leave town than to pretend that one's lives truly matter to each other. (I remember the tenth anniversary party of a foreign office of a major newsmagazine; none of its members was married to his spouse of ten years before.) At an advanced stage capitalism imparts enormous centrifugal forces to the souls of those who have most internalized its values; and these forces shear marriages and families apart.

To insist, in the face of such forces, that marriage and family still express our highest moral ideals, is to awaken hostility and opposition.

117

For many, marriage has been a bitter disappointment. They long to be free of it and also of the guilt they feel, a residual guilt which they have put to sleep and do not want awakened. They loathe marriage. They celebrate its demise. Each sign of weakness in the institution exonerates them of personal failure.

Urban industrial life is not designed to assist families. Expressways divide neighborhoods and parishes. Small family bakeries, cheese shops, and candy stores are boarded up. Social engineers plan for sewers, power lines, access roads, but not for the cultural ecology which allows families of different histories and structures to flower and prosper. The workplace is not designed with family needs in mind; neither are working hours.

Yet, clearly, the family is the seedbed of economic skills, money habits, attitudes toward work, and the arts of financial independence. The family is a stronger agency of educational success than the school. The family is a stronger teacher of the religious imagination than the church. Political and social planning in a wise social order begin with the axiom *What strengthens the family strengthens society*. Highly paid, mobile, and restless professionals may disdain the family (having been nurtured by its strengths), but those whom other agencies desert have only one institution in which to find essential nourishment.

The role of a father, a mother, and of children with respect to them, is the absolutely critical center of social force. Even when poverty and disorientation strike, as over the generations they so often do, it is family strength that most defends individuals against alienation, lassitude, or despair. The world around the family is fundamentally unjust. The state and its agents, and the economic system and its agencies, are never fully to be trusted. One could not trust them in Eastern Europe, in Sicily, or in Ireland—and one cannot trust them here. One unforgettable law has been learned painfully through all the oppressions, disasters, and injustices of the last thousand years: *if things go well with the family, life is worth living; when the family falters, life falls apart.*

Unfashionable families

THESE WORDS, I KNOW, go against the conventional grain. In America, we seem to look to the state for every form of social assistance. Immigrant Jews and Catholics have for fifty years supported progressive legislation in favor of

Evelyn Taylor

federal social programs: for minimum wage, Social Security, Medicare, civil rights. Yet dignity, for most immigrant peoples, resides first of all in family strength. Along with Southern blacks, Appalachians, Latins, and Indians, most immigrants to America are family people. Indeed, virtually all Americans, outside our professional classes, are family people.

There are, perhaps, radical psychological differences between people who center human life in atomic individuals—in "Do your thing," or "Live your own life," et cetera—and people who center human life in their families. There may be in this world two kinds of people: "individual people" and "family people." Our intellectual class, it seems, celebrates the former constantly, denigrates the latter.

Understandably, to have become a professional means, often enough, to have broken free from the family of one's birth. (How many wounds suffered there!) To have become successful, often enough, leads to the hubris of thinking one can live, now, in paradise, emotionally unfettered, free as the will to power is free.

There are many different traditions, styles, patterns, and emotional laws in different ethnic and regional cultures in America. The Jewish family is not quite like the Italian family; the families of the Scotch-Irish of Appalachia have emotional ties different from those of families from Eastern Europe. The communal families of the South Slavs are not like those of the Japanese. There is not *one* family pattern in America; there are many. All are alike in this, however: they provide such civilization as exists in these United States with its fundamental infusion of nurture, grace, and hope, and they suffer under the attacks of both the media and the economic system. Half the families of the nation have an annual income under $12,500; 90 percent have an income under $22,000. How can a family earning, say, $11,000 a year (too much for scholarship assistance) send three children to college? or care for its elderly?

As for the media, outrageous myths blow breezily about. Everyone says that divorces are multiplying. They are. But the figures hide as much as they reveal. Some 66 percent of all husbands and wives stick together until death do them part. In addition, the death that "parts" a marriage comes far later now than it did in any previous era. Faithful spouses stay together for a longer span of years than ever. For centuries, the average age of death was, for a female, say, thirty-two, and, for a male, thirty-eight. That so many modern marriages carry a far longer span of years with a certain grace is an unprecedented tribute to the institution.

Finally, aggressive sentiments against marriage are usually expressed today in the name of "freedom," "openness," "play," or "serious commitment to a career." Marriage is pictured as a form of imprisonment, oppression, boredom, and chafing hindrance. Not all these accusations are wrong; but the superstition surrounding them is. Marriage *is* an assault upon the lonely, atomic ego. Marriage *is* a threat to the solitary individual. Marriage does impose grueling, humbling, baffling, and frustrating responsibilities. Yet if one supposes that precisely such things are the preconditions for all true liberation, marriage is not the enemy of moral development in adults. Quite the opposite.

In our society, of course, there is no need to become an adult. One may remain—one is exhorted daily to remain—a child forever. It is difficult to have acquired a good education, a professional job, and a good salary, without meeting within one's circle of associates not a few adult children. In medieval paintings, children look like miniature adults. In tableaux from life today, adults appear as wrinkled adolescents.

The solitary self

BEFORE ONE CAN SPEAK intelligently of marriage, one must discuss the superstition that blocks our vision. We lack the courage nowadays to live by creeds, or to state our doctrines clearly (even to ourselves). Our highest moral principle is flexibility. Guided by sentiments we are embarrassed to put into words, we support them not by argument but by their trendiness.

The central idea of our foggy way of life, however, seems unambiguous enough. It is that life is solitary and brief, and that its aim is self-fulfillment. Next come beliefs in establishing the imperium of the self. Total mastery over one's surroundings, control over the disposition of one's time—these are necessary conditions for self-fulfillment. ("Stand not in my way.") Autonomy we understand to mean protection of our inner kingdom—protection around the self from intrusions of chance, irrationality, necessity, and other persons. ("My self, my castle.") In such a vision of the self, marriage is merely an alliance. It entails as minimal an abridgment of inner privacy as one partner or the other may allow. Children are not a welcome responsibility, for to have children is, plainly, to cease being a child oneself.

For the modern temper, great dreads here arise. Sanity, we think, consists in centering upon the only self one has. Surrender self-control, surrender happiness. And so we keep the other out. We then maintain our belief in our unselfishness by laboring for "humanity"—for women, the oppressed, the Third World, or some other needy group. The solitary self needs distant collectivities to witness to its altruism. It has a passionate need to love humankind. It cannot give itself to a spouse or children.

There is another secret to this aggressive sentiment, dominated as it is by the image of enlightenment. Ask, "Enlightenment from what?" and the family appears: carrier of tradition, habit, prejudice, confinement, darkness. In this view, the seeds of reaction and repression, implanted by the family of one's birth, are ready to sprout as soon as one sets up a family of one's own.

The great escape

THEORIES OF LIBERATION, of course, deserve to be studied in the light of flesh, absurdity, and tragedy. There is a pervasive tendency in Western thought, possibly the most profound cultural undercurrent in 3,000 years (compared to it, C. S. Lewis said, the Reformation was a ripple on the ocean), in which liberation is imagined as a breaking of the bonds of finiteness. Salvation comes as liberty of spirit. "Don't fence me in!" The Fall results from commitments that "tie one down," that are not subject to one's own controlling will. One tries to live as angels once were believed to live—soaring, free, unencumbered.

The jading of everyday, the routines of weekdays and weekends, the endless round of humble constraints, are, in this view, the enemies of human liberty.

In democratic and pragmatic societies, the dream of the solitary spirit often transfers itself into a moral assault upon institutions, traditions, loyalties, conventions. The truly moral person is a "free thinker" who treats every stage of life as a cocoon from which a lovely moth struggles to escape the habits of a caterpillar. This fuzzy sentiment names each successive breakaway "growth" and "development." It describes the cumulative process as "liberation."

There is, of course, a rival moral tradition. I do not mean the conventional variant, which holds that fidelity to institutions, laws, conventions, and loyalties is sufficient. The more compelling alternative—call it "realist"—differs from the romantic undercurrent by associating liberation with the concrete toils of involvement with family and/or familial communities. The romantic undercurrent takes as the unit of analysis the atomic individual. The realist alternative takes as the unit of analysis the family. To put it mythologically, "individual people" seek happiness through concentration upon themselves, although perhaps for the sake of service to others. Most television cops, detectives, cowboys, and doctors are of this tribe.

The "family people" define themselves through belonging to others: spouse, children, parents, siblings, nieces, cousins, and the rest. For the family people, to be human is to be, so to speak, molecular. I am not solely I. I am husband, father, son, brother, uncle, cousin; I am a family network. Not solitary. On television, both *All in the Family* and *Good Times* have as a premise the molecular identity of each character. The dramatic unit is the family.

There is, beyond the simplicities of half-hour television, a gritty realism in family life. Outside the family, we choose our own friends, like-minded folk whose intellectual and cultural passions resemble ours. Inside the family, however, divergent passions, intellections, and frustrations slam and batter us. Families today bring together professions, occupations, social classes, and sometimes regional, ethnic, or religious differences. Family life may remain in the United States the last stronghold of genuine cosmopolitanism and harsh, truthful differences.

So much of modern life may be conceived as an effort to make ourselves pure spirits. Our meals are as rationalized and unsensual as mind can make them. We write and speak about sexual activity as though its most crucial element were fantasy. We describe sex as though it were a stage performance, in which the rest of life is as little as possible involved. In the modern era, the abstract has grown in power. Flesh, humble and humbling, has come to be despised.

So it is no surprise that in our age many resistant sentiments should war against marriage and family. Marriage and family are tribute paid to earth, to the tides, cycles, and needs of the body and of bodily persons; to the angularity and difficulties of the individual psyche; to the dirty diapers, dirty dishes, and endless noise and confusion of the household. It is the entire symbolic function of marriage and family to remind us that we come from dust and will return to dust, that we are part of the net of earth and sky, inspirited animals at play for our brief moment on this planet, keeping alive our race. The point of marriage and family is to make us realistic. For it is one of the secrets of the human spirit that we long *not* to be of earth, not to be bound by death, routine, and the drag of our bodies. We long to be other than we are.

A generation ago, the "escape from freedom" was described in terms almost the reverse of those required today. In those days, as writers like Erich Fromm rightly worried, many persons were afraid of risks and responsibilities; many sought shelter in various fixed arrangements: in collectivism, in religion, in family. But dangers to freedom change with the generations. In our own time, the flight most loved is flight from flesh. The restraints

Fromm worried about have proven, under the pressures of suburbs, automobiles, jet planes, television, and corporate mobility, all too fragile. Today the atomic individual is as free as a bird. The threat to human liberation today is that the flesh, the embodied psyche, earthy roots, bodily loyalties, will be dismissed with contempt.

THE CONSEQUENCE OF THIS freedom is likely to be self-destruction. Whoever nourishes spirit alone must end by the ultimate denial of the flesh. A flaming burst of destruction and death is the image that fascinates us (as in *The Towering Inferno*), that most expresses our drift of soul. For fear of the flesh is fear of death. A love for the concrete and humble gestures of the flesh meant, even in the concentration camps, spiritual survival.

A return to the true conditions of our own humanity will entail a return, on the part at least of a dedicated few, to the disciplines and terrors of marriage and family. Many will resist these disciplines mightily. (Not all, of course, are called to marriage. The single life can have its own disciplines, and celibacy its own terrors. What counts is the governing cultural model. The commitment of "the family people" to the demands of our humanity provide a context within which singleness and even celibacy have a stabilizing strength; and the freedom and dedication of the single, in turn, nourish the family.)

People say of marriage that it is boring, when what they mean is that it terrifies them: too many and too deep are its searing revelations, its angers, its rages, its hates, and its loves. They say of marriage that it is deadening, when what they mean is that it drives us beyond adolescent fantasies and romantic dreams. They say of children that they are piranhas, eels, brats, snots, when what they mean is that the importance of parents with respect to the future of their children is now known with greater clarity and exactitude than ever before.

Marriage, like every other serious use of one's freedom, is an enormous risk, and one's likelihood of failure is rather high. No tame project, marriage. The raising of children, now that so few die in childbirth or infancy, and now that fate takes so little responsibility out of the hands of affluent and well-educated parents, brings each of us breathtaking vistas of our inadequacy. Fear of freedom—more exactly, fear of taking the consequences—adds enormously to the tide of evasion. The armies of the night find eager recruits.

It is almost impossible to write honestly of marriage and family. Who would like the whole world to know the secret failures known to one's spouse and one's children? We already hate ourselves too much. Given our affluence and our education, we are without excuses. We are obliged by our own vague sentiments of progress and enlightenment to be better spouses, better parents, than our ancestors—than our own parents, or theirs. Suppose we are not? We know we are not. Having contempt for ourselves, we want desperately to blame the institution which places our inadequacy in the brilliant glare of interrogation.

Still, just as marrying and having children have today the force of public political and moral statements, it is necessary to take one's private stand. Being married and having children has impressed on my mind certain lessons, for whose learning I cannot help being grateful. Most are lessons of difficulty and duress. Most of what I am forced to learn about myself is not pleasant.

The quantity of sheer impenetrable selfishness in the human breast (in *my* breast) is a never-failing source of wonderment. I do not want to be disturbed, challenged, troubled. Huge regions of myself belong only to me. Getting used to thinking of life as bicentered, even multicentered, is a struggle of which I had no suspicion when I lived alone. Seeing myself through the unblinking eyes of an intimate, intelligent other, an honest spouse, is humiliating beyond anticipation. Maintaining a familial steadiness whatever the state of my own emotions is a standard by which I stand daily condemned. A rational man, acting as I act? Trying to act fairly to children, each of whom is temperamentally different from myself and from each other, each of whom is at a different stage of perception and aspiration, is far more baffling than anything Harvard prepared me for. (Oh, for the unselfconscious box on the ears used so freely by my ancestors!)

My dignity as a human being depends perhaps more on what sort of husband and parent I am, than on any professional work I am called upon to do. My bonds to them hold me back (and my wife even more) from many sorts of opportunities. And yet these do not feel like bonds. They are, I know, my liberation. They force me to be a different sort of human being, in a way in which I want and need to be forced.

Nothing, in any case, is more poignant and private than one's sense of failing as a father. When my own sense of identity was that of a son, I expected great perfection from my father. Now that I am a father, I have undergone a psychic shift. Blame upon institutions, upon authorities, upon those who carry responsibilities, now seems to me so cheap. Those who fail in their responsibilities have a new claim upon my sympathies. I know the taste of uncertainty. To be a father rather than a son is to learn the inevitability of failure.

Family politics

IT WOULD BE A LIE, however, to write only of the difficulties of marriage and family, and not of the beauty. The joys are known. The more a man and a woman are in love, the more they imitate the life of husband and wife; long, sweet affairs are the tribute romances pay to matrimony. Quiet pleasures and perceptions flow: the movement of new life within a woman's belly; the total dependence of life upon the generosity and wisdom of its parents; the sense that these poor muscles, nerves, and cells of one's own flesh have recreated a message to the future, carried in relays generation after generation, carried since the dim beginnings. There may not be a "great chain of being." But parents do forge a link in the humble chain of human beings, encircling heirs to ancestors. To hold a new child in one's hands, only ounces heavy, and to feel its helplessness, is to know responsibilities sweet and awesome, to walk within a circle of magic as primitive as humans knew in caves.

But it is not the private pleasures of family life that most need emphasis today. Those who love family life do not begrudge the price paid for their adulthood. What needs elucidation is the political significance of the family. A people whose marriages and families are weak can have no solid institutions.

In intellectual terms, no theme is so neglected in American life and thought. The definition of issues given both by our conservatives and by our liberals is magnetized by two poles only: "the state" and "the individual." Both leave the family out. Emphasis on the family appears to conservatives a constraint upon the state, and to liberals a constraint upon the individual. Our remarkable humanitarianism holds that attention to family weaknesses will stigmatize those who suffer. No concept in the heavens of theory is as ill-starred. Turning toward the family, our minds freeze in their turning.

The time to break taboos in our minds must surely come. Every avenue of research today leads to the family. Do we study educational achievement? nutrition? the development of stable and creative personalities? resistance to delinquency and violence? favorable economic attitudes and skills? unemployment? sex-role identification? political affiliation? intellectual and artistic aspiration? religious seriousness? relations to authority and to dissent? In all these instances, family life is fundamental. A nation's social policies, taken as a whole, are most ac-curately and profoundly to be engaged by their impact upon the families that make up that nation.

There are three critical points in American political life today at which a more profound consideration of the politics of the family is closer to the essence than in any previous era: among white ethnics (some 70 million); among blacks (some 22 million); and among upper-class "opinion leaders" of all races (perhaps 10 million).

The meaning of Left and Right has, in recent years, come to be defined according to the tastes, interests, and prejudices of the upper 10 percent of the American population, that (roughly) 10 percent that has a four-year college education, an annual income over $20,000; and professional standing, so as to be paid monthly (not weekly), to possess travel privileges and expense accounts, and a considerable degree of control over the conditions of their work. Thus, Left and Right are now defined by culture rather than by economics, by attitudinal issues salient to those whose economic needs are well beyond the level of survival. The governing language of upper-class attitudes, therefore, distorts the true political struggle. The competition between the left and right wings of the upper 10 percent is interesting and important. It hardly begins to touch the restlessness of the bottom 90 percent.

In this context, the true political leanings and energies of "the white ethnics" are consistently misperceived. Richard Hamilton, in *Restraining Myths*, for instance, describes related gross distortions in the conventional wisdom. Suffice it to say that white ethnic voters, traditionally more Democratic than the national average and now more independent, are economic progressives. But in matters touching the family, they are fiercely traditional. The bulwark of conservatism in America is the white Anglo-Saxon Protestant—68 percent for Nixon in 1972; 16 percent for Wallace in 1968 (compared to 7.7 percent of the Catholic vote). Slavic-Americans gave George McGovern 53 percent of their vote in 1972 (down from 80 percent for Lyndon Johnson, and 65 percent for Hubert Humphrey). The white ethnics are becoming increasingly impatient with both Republicans (their traditional opponents) and Democrats (their former allies). Neglect of the politics of the family is the central issue. It is on this issue that "a new majority" will—or will not—be built.

For a thousand years, the family was the one institution the peoples of Eastern and Southern Europe, the Irish, and others could trust. The family constitutes their political, economic, and educational strength. The public schools of the United States failing them, they reached into their families and created an astonishingly successful system of parochial schools. Hardly literate, poor, and diffident peoples, they achieved something of an educational miracle. Economically, the Jews, the Greeks, the Lebanese established one another in as many small businesses as they could open. The Italians, the Poles, the Slovaks, the Croatians gave each other economic help amounting to two or three thousands of dollars a year per family. Cousin Joe did the electrical work; Pete fixed cars; Emil helped paint the house; aunts and uncles and grandparents canned foods, minded the children; fathers in their spare time built playrooms, boats, and other luxuries in the basements of row houses.

The family network was also a political force in precinct, ward, or district. People of the upper classes could pass on to their children advantages of inheritance, admission to exclusive schools, and high-level contacts. Children of the immigrants also made their families the primary networks of economic and political strength. Kinship is a primary reality in many unions and in all urban political "machines." Mothers and fathers instructed their children simultaneously, "Don't trust anybody," and "The family will never let you down."

In contemporary conditions, of course, these old family methods and styles have atrophied. There is no way of going back to the past. (Not everything about the past, in any case, was attractive.) Education media help children to become sophisticated about everything but the essentials: love, fidelity, childrearing, mutual help, care for parents and the elderly. Almost everything about mobile, impersonal, distancing life in the United States—tax policies, real-estate policies, the demands of the corporations, and even the demands of modern political forms—makes it difficult for families that feel ancient moral obligations to care for their aged, their mentally disturbed, their retarded, their needy.

I T IS DIFFICULT to believe that the state is a better instrument for satisfying such human needs than the family. If parents do not keep after the children to do their schoolwork, can the large, consolidated school educate? Some have great faith in state services: in orphanages, child-care centers, schools, job-training programs, and nursing homes. Some want the state to become one large centralized family. Such faith taxes credulity. Much of the popular resistance to federal child care arises from distrust of social workers and childhood engineers who would be agents of state power. Families need help in child care, but many distrust the state and the social-work establishment.

Almost everything about both "liberal" and "conservative" economic thought neglects, ignores, or injures family networks. It is not benign neglect. Millions of dollars are spent on the creation of a larger and larger state apparatus. Resources are systematically taken from the family. Is this an accident? One by one, all centers of resistance to the state are being crushed, including the strongest, family. The trend does not augur well for our liberties.

An economic order that would make the family the basic unit of social policy would touch every citizen at the nerve center of daily life. No known form of social organization weds affect to efficiency in so powerful a way. The family is the primary teacher of moral development. In the struggles and conflicts of marital life, husbands and wives learn the realism and adult practicalities of love. Through the love, stability, discipline, and laughter of parents and siblings, children learn that reality accepts them, welcomes them, invites their willingness to take risks. The family nourishes "basic trust." From this spring creativity, psychic energy, social dynamism. If infants are injured here, not all the institutions of society can put them back together. Familial arts that took generations to acquire can be lost in a single generation, can disappear for centuries. If the quality of family life deteriorates, there is no "quality of life." Again, emphasis on family life is politically important because it can unite people of diverse religious, ethnic, regional, and racial traditions. Families differ in their structures, needs, and traditional inclinations; but they share many basic economic and political necessities.

A politics based on the social unit of the family would have a revolutionary impact on the sterile debate between Democrats and Republicans, and between libertarians and socialists. To strengthen the family through legislative reform is, indeed, a social intervention, but one which creates a counterpoise to the state. It is the forgotten lever of social change.

In particular, a fresh approach here promises unparalleled gains for blacks. "The repair of the black condition in America disproportionately depends upon the succor of strong families," Eleanor Holmes Norton told the Urban League in Atlanta last year. "We must make marriage and family life unabashedly a tool for improving all our lives." The stunting of black progress in America, she held, was done most effectively through tearing asunder the black family both in slavery and by discrimination. No institution, she observed, had so nourished blacks in the darkness of slavery; none had helped them to joy, laughter, and affirmation through the bitter days, as had the family. No institution is so beloved in black consciousness. None is more at the heart of social hope. "Were it not for law-enforced slavery and discrimination," she said, "our families would have thrived like most others and our time in America would have waxed into prosperity as for all other immigrant groups." She told the assembly, in sorrow, that the percentage of black households headed by women increased to 35 percent in 1975. (By the age of sixteen, two-thirds of all black children have spent some years without a father. In 1973 46 percent of all black children were born outside of wedlock.) The psychological and economic penalties, she argued, are immense. She called for a resurgence of the love and loyalty that had carried blacks in America through the centuries.

Such a call instantly makes possible alliance between the white and black working class. The families of both are in trouble; the difference in degree does not remove the similarity in root and remedy. Our media exalt the flashy, the hedonistic, the individualistic; they dwell upon the destructive orbits of the doomed: James Bond and Patty Hearst. Destruction, hustling, and defiance—one side of the Black Panthers—is picked up; the feeding of children and the nourishing of families receives no public praise. Love between a husband and wife, discipline in children, virtues of work, effort, risk, and application—these now visibly embarrass, as pornography once did. Yet these are the substance of working-class morality. They are the base of all advantage.

A choice for survival

W HY DOES THE PREFERRED liberal solution for the sufferings of blacks look to every avenue of approach—school buses, affirmative action, welfare—except the family? Could it be that the family is too truly at the center, and is the one thing that liberals themselves cannot supply? That the family is the one social standing place for independence?

Economic and educational disciplines are learned only in the home and, if not there, hardly at all. Discipline in black families has been traditionally severe, very like that in white working-class families. Survival has depended on family discipline. Working-class people, white and black, cannot count on having their way; most of the time they have to be docile, agreeable, and efficient. Otherwise, they are fired. They cannot quit their jobs too often; otherwise their employment record shows instability. Blacks as well as whites survive by such rules, as long as authority in the home is strong. From here, some find the base for their mobility, up and out. Without a guiding hand, however, the temptations to work a little, quit, enjoy oneself, then work a little, are too much encouraged by one's peers on the street. *Either* the

home, *or* the street: This is the moral choice. Liberals too seldom think about the economic values of strong family life; they neglect their own source of strength, and legislate for others what would never have worked for themselves.

Consider the figures for unemployment for teen-agers. The figure frequently given for blacks in New York is 40 percent. The huge number of female-run households among blacks correlates with the unemployment rates. The rough discipline of Slavic, Italian, and Irish fathers regarding the employment of their sons is an economic advantage. One of the requirements for obtaining and holding a job, especially at the unskilled level, where jobs abound, is a willingness to accept patriarchal discipline. Many young black males find such disciplines both unfamiliar and intolerable. Many will not take available jobs; many others quit.

Consider, as well, the educational preparation of black children as they leave their homes, before they enter school. Among successful blacks, patterns are like those among whites. Parents watch over their children. Books and papers are available in the home. Where the parents take education seriously, there is high probability that children will. Where the parents do not, schools cannot reasonably be expected to reach the psyches of the young. Why, then, do we habitually try to help schools, but not families? For both blacks and whites of the working class and all the more for the still more needy "underclass," the provision of books and newspapers to the home, and sessions to assist parents in teaching their children, might be more profitable than efforts in the school.

In a word, a politics aimed at strengthening families, white and black, would be a politics of unity rather than of division. It would also have higher prospect of success. The chief obstacle in its execution is the mysterious contempt liberals unthinkingly manifest toward their own greatest source of advantage.

As Jean-Paul Sartre has taught us, it is bad faith to plead "to each his own," to permit intellectual laissez-faire. Actions speak louder than shrugs of the shoulder. To marry, to have children, is to make a political statement hostile to what passes as "liberation" today. It is a statement of flesh, intelligence, and courage. It draws its strength from nature, from tradition, and from the future. Apart from millions of decisions by couples of realistic love, to bring forth children they will nourish, teach, and launch against the void, the human race has no future—no wisdom, no advance, no community, no grace.

Only the emptiness of solitary space, the dance of death.

It is the destiny of flesh and blood to be familial.

23

The American Way of Mating
MARRIAGE SÍ, CHILDREN ONLY MAYBE

A survey of 2,164 adults shows:

- Marrieds Are Happier Than Singles
- The Patter of Little Feet Makes the Temples Pound
- Women Get Along Without Men Better Than Men Get Along Without Women
- After Marriage Women Report Less Stress and Men Report More
- Couples Snuggle Comfortably in the Empty Nest

by Angus Campbell

"AND SO THEY MARRIED, and lived happily ever after." This classic fairy-tale ending, which has raised the eyebrows and occasionally the hackles of many adult readers, may not be as far off the mark as skeptics suppose. We find that married Americans are far happier and more satisfied with their lives than singles are, in spite of national mumblings and grumblings about the tired institution of matrimony.

However, most marriages are followed by children, and having children, it turns out, is a mixed experience. The patter of little feet aggravates as well as delights. The positive effect of marriage and the stress-producing impact of children on the quality of life in America are two striking results from our recent national survey. Philip Converse,

Deanna Glad

William Rodgers, and I studied a random sample of 2,164 adults in order to get a sense of how people feel subjectively about the quality of their lives, and how their feelings change with experiences over the life cycle. Previous quality-of-life studies have concentrated on objective indicators—the money a person earns, health statistics, education, the amount of pollution one has to endure, and so on. We were less interested in how people's lives look from the outside than in how they *feel* to those who are living them.

We asked our interviewees, first, to give us a judgment of their satisfaction with their lives in general. Then we tapped more emotional dimensions, to find out whether they were in high spirits, jolly and optimistic, or discouraged, lonely, or bored. We gave them eight pairs of adjectives (such as "interesting/boring") and asked them to check, on each pair, the point that best represented their current mood about their lives. And finally, as a third measure of the emotional quality of life, we developed a scale of six questions that probed their feelings of pressure or stress.

Overall, men and women evaluate their lives in very similar terms; we did not find, as some might have expected, that more women than men are unhappy or dissatisfied. On the contrary, Americans of both sexes seem to be a contented crowd, in spite of their various problems. Fewer than 10 percent described their lives in sour terms—boring, miserable, lonely, empty, useless—and far more than half think their lives are worthwhile, full, hopeful, interesting, and other happy positives. They admit to some stress—about one fourth feel rushed all the time and often worry about bills—but overall they are stubbornly cheerful. (See chart, page 40.)

Dissatisfactions and sex differences show up, however, when we compare people at nine various phases of the life cycle. Six of these categories represent the typical life-patterns, from young adulthood before marriage, through marriage and parenthood, to the death of one's spouse. The last three categories cover people who diverge from the typical pattern: the four percent who never marry, the five percent who are married but never have children, and the 10 percent who, at any moment in time, are divorced.

"The world has grown suspicious of anything that looks like a happy married life," wrote Oscar Wilde, but if marriages aren't happy today, at least married people are. All of the married groups—men and women, over 30 and under, with children and without—reported higher feelings of satisfaction and general good feelings about their lives than all of the unmarried groups—the single, divorced, or widowed. (Remember, though, that I am talking about group averages—there are plenty of miserable married people and satisfied singles.) The link between marriage and satisfaction is striking and consistent, whichever the cause or effect: marriage may make people happy, or perhaps happy people are more likely to marry.

Good feelings about the emotional quality of one's life, oddly enough, are not necessarily related to the absence of stress. A person who feels many pressures may be less satisfied with his or her life overall; but a person under little stress is not automatically more satisfied with life. Widowed men and women, whose feelings about their lives are generally depressed, nonetheless report the lowest amount of stress and pressure. And married couples with small children, who are happier than singles, report the greatest amount of stress.

Carefree Spinsters, Anxious Bachelors. Unmarried women are healthier, physically and psychologically, than married women, according to many studies; but they aren't happier. Apparently most young women in America still believe that marriage is essential for fulfillment, for they consider their lives less worthwhile without it.

For women, age 30 is still the Great Divide. Most under 30 will eventually marry; those over 30 are much less likely to. Whether she doesn't marry by choice or circumstance, the older single woman is not as negative in her feelings about life and does not feel nearly as much stress as her younger counterpart. Perhaps this is because the longer a woman remains single, the more she likes it, or at least adjusts to it; and because she is more likely to hold a satisfying, better-paying job, and to have a well-defined career.

Women get along without men better than men get along without women, contrary to what John Wayne and Sam Peckinpah would have us believe. Single women of all ages are happier and more satisfied with their lives than single men. So much for the stereotype of the carefree bachelor and the anxious spinster; the truth is that there are more carefree spinsters and anxious bachelors.

Euphoric Brides, Nervous Grooms. The best of all possible worlds, for most Americans, is to be newly married and not have children. If single people in their 20s feel that something is lacking in their lives, married couples of that age are the happiest of all groups—especially young wives, who are more satisfied than anyone else, anywhere, any age. They are positively euphoric; they are the most likely group to enjoy doing housework, which single women consider drudgery. It appears that marriage is still considered a woman's greatest achievement, and when she marries, the sigh of relief is almost audible.

Young men get happier with their lives when they marry too—though they don't reach the glowing level of their wives—but the two sexes' feelings of pressure change in opposite ways. The women report much *less* stress after marriage than before, but their husbands now feel *more* stress. This cannot be explained by any storybook scenario that pictures the carefree young wife spending her day getting ready to welcome her husband home from the office. Three out of four of these young wives are themselves employed, almost as high a proportion as that of their husbands. Despite whatever trends there may be toward equal roles among young married couples these days, the man still appears to feel more burdened by the responsibilities of marriage than the woman. In our study, only 20 percent of the young wives said that they worry at least some of the time about paying the

The best of all possible worlds, for most Americans, is to be newly married and not have children.

household bills, but twice as many of their husbands (38 percent) do Eighteen percent of these wives describe their lives as "hard" rather than "easy"; 34 percent of the husbands see their lives as hard. These differences disappear, however, when the first child arrives and this phase of the life cycle ends.

The Stress of Parenthood. "Familiarity breeds contempt," wrote Mark Twain, "and children." Almost as soon as a couple has kids, their happy bubble bursts. For both men and women, reports of happiness and satisfaction drop to average, not to rise again significantly until their children are grown and about to leave the nest (age 18).

Couples with young children also report feeling more stress and pressure than any other group. The mothers, most of whom are between the ages of 25 and 34, carry the burden of childrearing, and the pressures are most acute for them. They are the most likely of any other group of wives or husbands to describe themselves as feeling tied down, to express doubts about their marriages and to wish occasionally to be free of the responsibilities of

parenthood. The husbands feel less satisfied with children too; but they don't show the great swing that their wives do, partly because they were less euphoric about marriage to begin with.

For most couples, the arrival of a child is a happy event, but one that puts unanticipated strains on the marriage. Part of the strain is economic, part is psychological; inevitably, husbands and wives have less time for each other after a baby is born, and adjusting to the loss of companionship can be difficult.

There is hope for the disgruntled or disappointed parent, however. Wait 17 years or so until you are alone with your spouse again. Your satisfaction with life and your all-around good mood will return to where it was before you had kids. Indeed, parents of older children were among the happiest groups in the study, and this was true for both sexes. Couples settled back in the "empty nest" reported feelings of companionship and mutual understanding even higher than they felt as newlyweds. Raising a family seems to be one of those tasks, like losing weight or waxing the car, that is less fun to be doing than to have done.

Children and marriage still go together and always will, but children are becoming less popular. The continuing, substantial decline in the birth rate in this country indicates that many people no longer regard having children as an inevitable process. The childfree marriage, once pitied or disparaged, is now increasingly recognized as a fulfilling lifestyle and many young couples simply admit, without embarrassment or apology, that they do not intend to have children. Sociologist Jessie Bernard marshalls evidence that they may have happier marriages as a result.

The decision not to have children does not doom a couple to loneliness, despair, and misery as the prochildren forces have assumed for years. Childless husbands over 30 reported the highest satisfaction with life, and they feel less pressure than most men. Altogether, the quality of their lives is higher than that of any other group of males, with the possible exception of fathers of children over 17 (which makes them childfree too, in a sense). Freedom from the economic worries that parents have is part of the reason. Childfree couples over 30 do not have particularly

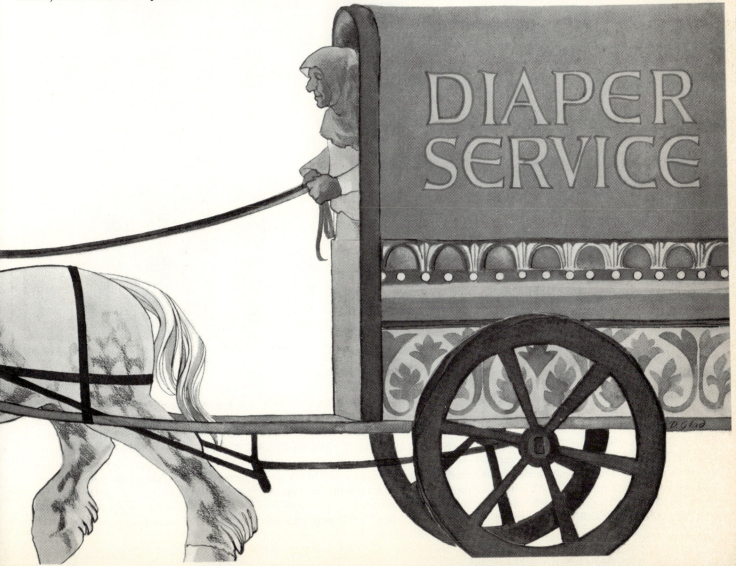

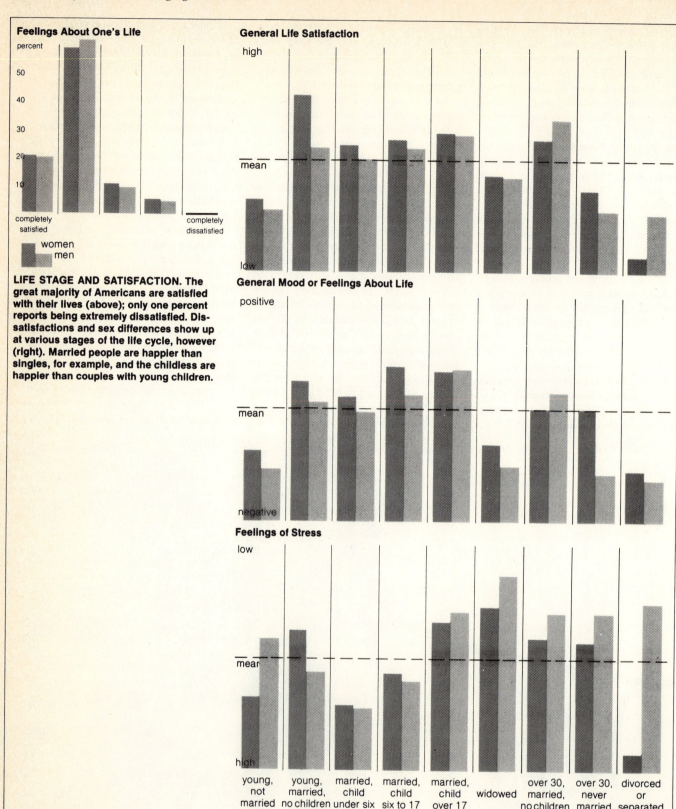

Feelings About One's Life

percent

completely satisfied

completely dissatisfied

women
men

LIFE STAGE AND SATISFACTION. The great majority of Americans are satisfied with their lives (above); only one percent reports being extremely dissatisfied. Dissatisfactions and sex differences show up at various stages of the life cycle, however (right). Married people are happier than singles, for example, and the childless are happier than couples with young children.

General Life Satisfaction

high

mean

low

General Mood or Feelings About Life

positive

mean

negative

Feelings of Stress

low

mean

high

young, not married | young, married, no children | married, child under six | married, child six to 17 | married, child over 17 | widowed | over 30, married, no children | over 30, never married | divorced or separated

high incomes, but they are the most likely group to be satisfied with their savings and the least likely to worry about bills.

Childless wives over 30 also describe their lives in generally positive terms. They aren't quite as rosy about life as their husbands, but they aren't *less* satisfied than women their age who do have children. Childlessness offers women a

different but not unsatisfying life—much less stress, somewhat fewer emotional rewards, but overall the same level of satisfaction. In view of the strong cultural pressures for women to have children, we were surprised that childfree wives find the grass on their own side of the fence green enough. Perhaps having children is no longer as essential to woman's role as it once was.

Possibly these couples will feel different about not having children when they are old, or when one spouse dies. When wife or husband is left alone, without the psychological support that the other provided, she or he may feel more keenly the absence of children. Still, grown children do not always pay much attention to their aging and sometimes lonely parents; perhaps a widowed person is better off with no expectations about children than with shattered ones.

Stress Dies With the Spouse. We tend to think that the quality of life for most widowed people is bleak, but this perception misses the mark. In terms of general life satisfaction, widows and widowers dip to slightly below average; even so, they are quite a bit more content than single or divorced people of any age. And they report the least amount of stress and pressure of any other group, even though their family incomes are the lowest. They don't, after all, have to worry about work—the great majority are of retirement age—or young children, and many feel free of the pressures to marry that the single and divorced experience. On the other hand, widows and widowers did describe the emotional quality of their lives in negative terms, about as negatively as single and divorced people. The difference between the two groups is that the widowed are more satisfied with their lives than singles are, which may simply reflect the willingness or resignation of older people to accept the conditions of their lives.

Divorce: Anxious Women, Carefree Men. In spite of all the cheerful books on creative divorce, no-fault divorce, and better living through divorce, people whose marriages fail are miserable. Most of them, men more than women, marry again, but while divorced they face problems that their single and married friends do not.

Divorce hits women hardest. Most of them have to work (71 percent) and care for children (84 percent), without moral, economic, or psychological support from a husband or partner. They earn less than single women their age, certainly less than divorced men, and less than married women who can rely on family incomes. Only four percent of all divorced women can afford to hire someone to help with the housework, so they have that to do too. And they lack the opportunities that

divorced men have to date and remarry. For all these reasons, divorced women feel the greatest pressure and stress of any group, report the greatest dissatisfaction with their lives, and describe the emotional quality of their lives in gloomy terms. Indeed, one fourth of these women admit to worrying that they might have a nervous breakdown, compared to only eight percent of the divorced men.

Divorced men aren't so happy with their lives either, but they feel less pressure than almost any other group of males. It is as if divorce was an instant relief; over half, 58 percent, say they never worry about meeting their bills, compared to 30 percent of the divorced women who report being that confident. Only 12 percent of the divorced men say they always feel rushed, but nearly three times as many divorced women (34 percent) see themselves as always rushed. Twenty-five percent of these men, but 42 percent of the women, describe their lives as difficult.

Then too, divorced men who find their new-found single status intolerable remarry more easily than their former wives, while those who enjoy the single life may choose to keep it. Divorced women have less freedom of choice, economically or socially, which contributes to their dissatisfactions. Of course, we do not know how the attitudes or feelings of divorced people change in the years after the marriage ends; we have only the sketch they paint as a group.

Life Stages and Satisfaction. When we compared all of the women in our study with all of the men, we found few differences. There were some reasons to expect, overall, that women would be more dissatisfied than men, but it turned out that it was necessary to specify *which* women and *which* men. There are some groups of women, such as those divorced, who describe their lives as more frustrating and less rewarding than men do. But there are also some groups of males who

are less happy than their female peers, such as unmarried men. To understand how people feel about their lives, it is less important to know whether a person is a woman than to know whether she is a young, childless wife or a single career woman or married with grown children. We can't assume that all men view their lives as rich and fulfilling, either; we must know first whether the man is an aging bachelor or an empty-nest father.

Several recent reviews of community-mental-health surveys found that women are in worse shape than men. Women consistently have higher rates of mental illness—both psychosis and neurosis, including depression, anxiety, suicidal tendencies—regardless of whether they come voluntarily for treatment, are committed, or take part in a random survey. Such symptoms of pathology would suggest that women's lives are less satisfying than men's, but women overall did not report this.

The reason may be that a person's evaluation of her life is based partly on the fit, or lack of it, between her objective circumstances, and her hopes and expectations. The black community in this country has raised its sights dramatically in the last 10 years, and women are beginning to do so also. The dissatisfactions reported by college-educated and divorced women in our study, for example, indicate that changes are occurring in the traditional values and roles for women. More women are going to college, working, and having fewer children. That's bound to make some changes eventually in the institution of marriage, which is currently the rock on which both sexes base much of their happiness and satisfaction with life. We can be sure that pressures for change will be met by resistance to change, and whether the irresistible force or the immovable object gives way, we'll be part of an interesting transition.

24

THE AMERICAN FAMILY: AN EMBATTLED INSTITUTION

Robert S. Pickett

. . . such are the nature and place of the family in the social order, as many and grave ills arise from its present legal and social conditions, and these matters are of such fundamental, universal, and urgent character . . . that "the family" is the most important question that has come before the American people since the war.

—Samuel W. Dike

It would be easy to imagine that the concern for "family break-down," to which Samuel Dike alluded, has emerged only in recent years, but such is not the case. The war to which Dike referred was the American Civil War, and he issued his statement in 1890.

Dike was neither the first nor the last to make such observations. While the meaning of "the family" has differed considerably over the years, there has never been an era in which someone did not mention that the family was either on the decline or already dead. Not long after the turn of the century, in the introduction to a monumental attempt to deal with the history of the family as an institution, G. E. Howard remarked that everywhere there was an expression of grave concern for the future of the family. Individualism had supplanted family loyalty, and marriage had become a mockery. The "bonds of paternal authority" had lessened, women's quest for equality had totally disrupted matters, and the state had intervened to rob the family of its powers. Thus, the family's decline was a notion that many accepted long before the development of family sociology.

In this brief introduction, I hope to describe some of the sources of our continuing dismay concerning the prospects of this fundamental social institution. I hope also to point out how the debate surrounding the family's functions may be viewed in entirely new ways. Through this group of articles, I hope to indicate current

and future prospects for what I call the "actualized family."

One of the more prominent and devastating of the recent attacks has been that by David Cooper, a radical English psychiatrist, whose book *The Death of the Family* has been widely published but inadequately reviewed. Many scholars in the field of family studies unfortunately have paid very little attention to this little tome of doom. Even though he purports to deal with the subject matter about which they write and from which they make their living, most family researchers and theorists have given Cooper's work only the most cursory inspection and have blithely gone about their business as if such pronouncements didn't exist. It would almost seem that scholars in the field either have come to expect such diatribes as standard fare or, in fact, believe Cooper's premises. At the risk of engaging in oversimplification, I am tempted to believe that the former is the case. Although a number of family specialists probably believe that the institution of the Western family has come upon parlous times, I would guess that most simply view it as an institution in a state of change. They tend to view the notion of family decline as the "straw man" that usually precedes a statement about the virtues of one's pet scheme for a better society. For example, Robert Rimmer's novel *Proposition 31* starts with a couple of muddled families, states some broad propositions about the sad state of many American marriages, and then goes on to provide a utopian alternative. Rimmer's critique of the family's situation is thus dismissed as being merely a buttress for his utopian schemes.

Such treatment, however, may be unwarranted in our current situation. Donald Ball has told us that the "classical stance of the family sociologists," many of whom wish to deny any fundamental changes in the family, has been founded on the continuity of demographic data. Statistics over the past twenty years have indicated a high degree of commitment to marriage and family life. The statistics, however, can no longer be viewed in an equivocal fashion. For the first time in sixteen years, the marriage rate has dropped. The rate of divorce, however, continues on its merry way. According to data compiled by the National Center for Health Statistics, 1974 was the twelfth consecutive year in which the divorce rate has increased.

Even if scholars and assorted liberals are not threatened by the fact that the overall marriage rate is declining and the divorce rate is rising, they might be concerned by the profound increase in divorce within the very sectors of society that have shown stability in the past, that is, the middle class. Remarks about the family's demise are not to be taken so lightly when matters come closer to home.

One of the problems inherent in assessing the magnitude of the current crisis is that we do not know whether we are looking at a modern phenomenon or whether we are witnessing something that has been with us from time immemorial. Our tendency to look at the past as somehow better than the present has blurred our vision of the family as a changing institution. This is particularly the case concerning our most recent historical past. It would seem necessary, however, to gain as much historical perspective as possible. However selective it might be, a brief historical analysis of past writings could shed considerable light on the current situation. As we look at the past, we may discover that the critique of the family is one of the most fascinating themes in Western history.

Historical Sources of Anti-Familism

The most obvious sources for insight into the failings of the family would seem to be those who have had a major impact upon our social and intellectual history. One of our earliest sources of anti-familism is Plato. Like most of the utopians who followed in his footsteps, Plato regarded family attachments as conflicting with loyalty to the ideal state. His writing about the family of Socrates provides us with an example of how Plato, as one of the founders of Western thought, viewed the family. In his *Dialogues*, Plato depicts the wife of Socrates as a harridan, who would snatch him away from important and momentous discussions. Loyalty to one's family was seen as more of an impediment than a virtue.

In spite of strong familistic sentiments expressed by the spokesmen for Christianity, much of the Christian tradition is frankly hostile to family life. Judaism's insistence upon marriage disappears in Christianity. Marriage and family life become at best a second-rate option—"It is better to marry than burn." St. Paul, of course, was busy preparing for the apocalypse when he uttered that statement, but its import was not lost on future generations. St. Augustine, whose life and preachings made him one of the more important enemies of womankind, furthered the cause of anti-familism in Christianity. While there was a minority within the early church who supported monogamy and family life as being at least on an equal footing with celibacy, their voices were eventually drowned out by Augustine and the later ecclesiastical figures who declared that the family's chief function was to deliver virgins to the church. The pronouncements of the early church fathers, taken together with the reflections of the Roman stoics and the cult of sensuality demonstrated by the aristocracy of the later period of the Roman Empire, present a composite picture in which the family unit has the lowest status.

Other historical accounts, of course, warn us that we should not take the writings of the ancient sages as indicative of the actual behavior of the majority of people during the period. In fact, we discover that the Greek *oîkos* and the Roman *familia* were strong and powerful units whose influence was not so easily avoided. Much larger units than our current nuclear family, these groups demanded and received the loyalty of their members even as they provided protection.

During the medieval period of European history, marriage and family life were held in exceedingly low esteem. Although most people probably lived and loved in the midst of their family, they left few traces of how they carried out their daily lives. The leisure classes were a different matter. Those who wrote and sang of love updated Ovid's *The Art of Love* with several new twists. While they reiterated the sentiment that it was better to long after someone else's spouse, they added the notion that such love should not be physical. There were many variations on this theme. For the devout Christian, an asexual adoration of the Virgin Mary was one possibility; the knight-errant declared his service to his "lady fair." One's spouse and family were mere matters of lowly economics; they insured the continuity of one's lineage. Beyond that, they counted for little.

With the rise of the bourgeoisie and the development of the New World, the trend of anti-familism declined somewhat. Intent upon populating the new land and developing a private life-style that depended upon the notion of the home as a sanctuary, people gave less support to expressions hostile to marriage and the family as an institution. According to Sidney Ditzion, the writing of Parson Weems, a popular polemicist of the period, reflected the predominant sentiment of the times. In his *Hymen's Recruiting Sergeant: or, the Maid's and Bachelor's Friend*, Weems admonished young men and women to marry early and have large families. This little pamphlet went through fourteen editions between the years 1799 and 1851. During this period, the United States produced a phenomenal increase in family size.

Despite the strength of this predominant theme, there were numerous examples of those who questioned marriage as an institution and of those who established alternative living arrangements. Prominent social thinkers, such as Thomas Paine and Robert Dale Owen, declared against traditional marriage. Frances Wright also stumped the country in her attacks on its sexist characteristics, thus anticipating the recent women's liberation movement by nearly one hundred fifty years. Intellectual groups such as the Associationists branded the "isolated home" as the spawning nest for unruly children and lecherous adults. The various communal groups, such as the celibate Shakers and the group-marriage advocates of the Oneida experiment, demonstrated successful alternatives to the traditional home.

During the nineteenth and twentieth centuries, anti-familism took many forms. In addition to utopian sects and religious groups, the leaders of political movements have often renounced the family as a reactionary force. The political zealot, on both the left and the right, has tended to demand total submission to the goals of the party. Other loyalties and identities apart from the party are simply not permitted. On a considerably larger scale, the totalitarian state exemplifies a similar tendency. If one hears a family member express sentiments hostile to the state, he must be "turned in."

The historical list of the enemies of "traditional marriage and family" has obviously been a long one. It is, in fact, so long that one wonders why a biographical dictionary has not been created from it. All sorts of flamboyant figures, as well as sober and pious souls, could embellish its pages. Even without such a dictionary, however, the point is abundantly clear. The nuclear-family form, originating from an exclusive, lifelong monogamous union, has been under substantial attack throughout much of recorded Western history. While awareness of this tradition of naysaying may not always be present in the intellectual community, its lack may go a long way toward tempering whatever alarm may have arisen from the prophets of doom.

The Defenders and Attackers

When it comes to discussing the family, a sober detachment has seldom existed in the community at large. There seems to be little question of the direction of things when one talks to "the man on the street." The only difference seems to be whether one is rejoicing at the fall of the family or whether one is mourning its passing. Although there are probably a number of people who think the family, as they understand it, is in rather good shape, most of those who express themselves seem divided into the expected camps of defenders and attackers.

Depending upon whether one regards oneself as an attacker or defender of the institution, the final death scene may be viewed in different terms. The attackers seem to see the family's death as being hastened by "natural causes"—that is, hardening of the institutional arteries or something akin to inability to make the evolutionary adjustment to a changed social and economic climate. In this latter view, something has caused the family, like some ancient dinosaur, to breathe its last. Some ardent defenders regard the family's demise as having been engineered by a devilish army of debauched sociologists, radical psychiatrists, "Commie perverts," bra-burning feminists, "knee-jerk liberals," and assorted libertines of predictable intent.

In the midst of the continual dispute about how the end of the family is coming or how it finally arrived, a number of relevant issues seem to have been largely obscured. It is far from clear, for example, what the answers would be if we were to ask both camps what they actually mean by the term *the family*. We might discover that there were even considerable differences *within* the two opposing forces relative to what was meant by the term. All that seems to be commonly shared are the convictions that the family is dead or dying and that one's own position is right and just and that one's opponents are essentially immoral or misguided.

Current Attempts To Clarify the Family's Situation

I doubt very much whether the pages ahead will go very far toward reducing the mordant character of the debate. I hope, however, that the positions taken by some of the authors will clarify several issues and that they will stand as reasonable articulations in the midst of much mystification. Also, I think that the reader will see that a number of current movements related to the family must be seen in their own terms and not as examples of a fiendish plot dedicated to undermining the family.

The authors reflect a wide range of backgrounds. Most of those who claim an academic specialty as their base of knowledge come from the fields of psychology and sociology. Several of them speak from long careers of public identification as practitioners of the arts involved in healing hurt families.

As the reader will discover, nearly all of the writers are partisans of the American family, but their understanding of what it is and where it is headed shows a considerable diversity of opinion. Some readers may wonder why more negatively oriented contributions have not been included. As the guest editor, I have decided that the naysayers were abundantly represented in various current publications. For several clear examples of positions counter to conventional marriage and family patterns, the reader is referred to

the March/April 1974 issue of THE HUMANIST. The article by Lawrence Casler and the interview with Robert Rimmer are particularly useful in stating the perspective that the predominant contemporary marriage and family patterns are often destructive to individual identity and to attempts at authentic relationships. Casler, for example, argues that "marriage and family life have been largely responsible . . . for today's prevailing neurotic climate." The reader might also wish to sample several of the more critical assessments pertaining to marriage in books such as the recently published reader entitled *Renovating Marriage*, edited by Roger W. Libby and Robert N. Whitehurst. A word of caution may be useful at this particular juncture. Criticisms of conventional monogamy and suggestions for alternative arrangements are not necessarily attacks upon the contemporary American family. This distinction is often overlooked, either by intention or oversight. Defenders of the conventional marriage and family system often choose to attack innovators on the grounds of willful destruction of the family. This overreaction may be genuine, in that the defenders see exclusive lifelong monogamy as the keystone to good family functioning, but it might also arise from a simple unwillingness to grant the validity of the attack.

> **"The internal vitality of family life calls for a renunciation of the family unit as a passive component that only reacts to external change. The family is a nurturing place for vital beings."**

Sometimes the reaction of the defenders of the family may be fully justified. In the case of someone like David Cooper, who is discussed briefly in John Crosby's article, and to some extent fellow travelers such as Casler, the ultimate goal is seen as a radical restructuring of society along different grounds. In his diatribe against the family as an idea and as a pervasive "system," Cooper remarks that it is "fatuous to speak of the death of God or the death of Man . . . until we can fully envisage *the death of the family*—that system which, as its social obligation, obscurely filters out most of our experience and then deprives our acts of any genuine and generous spontaneity."

If, however, one looks very closely at Cooper's approach, a rather familiar motif becomes apparent. Cooper's characterization of the modern family begins to look something like the constructions of the various social-contract theorists of seventeenth- and eighteenth-century Europe, who always felt duty-bound to initially posit a "Man in the State of Nature" early in their works. For Thomas Hobbes, the state of nature was a grim struggle for survival. The nature of man's existence was "nasty, mean, brutish and short." For John Locke, man's original state was less traumatic, but it was certainly "inconvenient." Jean Jacques Rousseau went one step further. His natural state was a gentle and glorious existence, which, in turn, had been turned into a nightmare by the civilization of man. Each philosopher, in his turn, went on to show how he viewed the emergence of society and the ways in which the social and political structure could be improved. Rousseau's notions, in fact, became the basis for much of the Romantic utopianism of communitarian reformers in the nineteenth century.

With the writings of David Cooper, we have a new variation on the older themes. Unfortunately, his writings are taken more as fact than as symbolic statement. When he launches an attack on the family as an idea and as a system of ideas and sounds the clarion call for truly autonomous individuals who can break through that system, his remarks are really directed less against the family and more against all primeval institutions that have nurtured and often suppressed human beings in their formative years. Like his mentor, R. D. Laing, Cooper feels that thousands of people struggling for their humanity are either blocked by their actual families or insidiously repressed by their own internalized concept of "the family." In the statements of Laing and Cooper, the latter force seems much more powerful in terms of its hold upon individuals. A person whose inner being is enslaved by a fantasy "family" cannot relate to himself or herself and is unable to interact with others and gain any perspective in terms of how they see the world. Family-bound persons tend to perceive others as opposing forces bent on destroying them.

Like Cooper and Laing, writers such as Rimmer also have a radical restructuring of society in mind, but their animosity to conventional family life is more in terms of its high failure rate. Rimmer's chief solutions, such as structured premarital education, communes, and cooperative families, seem far more related to broadening the selection of family structures than doing away with the conventional marriage and family. They seem to center on altering certain phases of one's interpersonal development in order that family life may be somehow enhanced. A critic of exclusive life-long monogamy as the single standard for everyone, Rimmer seems to want to alleviate some of the more confining and constraining aspects of marriage and family life, such as jealousy.

A careful scrutiny of many of the proposals that have scandalized the ardent and uncritical defenders of the status quo would most likely reveal that the majority of innovators are essentially supportive of family ties. The difference is that they wish to alter other facets of our contemporary life that appear to them as deleterious to human development, and their proposals often involve experimenting with marriage and family because it constitutes the "microcosm" of the larger society. Attempts to restructure this unit can be seen as leading to fundamental reorganization of the macrocosm. Rimmer, for example, sees America as an "age-segregated society." In his interview with Paul Kurtz that appeared in THE HUMANIST, he remarked that age segregation is dysfunctional in contemporary society and will be increasingly dysfunctional in the future. "In an age of limits of growth, our families and marriages must develop into interrelated communites of families. When this happens, we will integrate the old and the young into a total life involvement." Unlike David Cooper, Rimmer doesn't view the notion or the institution of the family as "the enemy" that we all must overcome in order to be more fully human. He seeks to make it a more flexible institution and focuses upon increased flexibility as a means of developing human beings who will possess greater capacities for loving and sharing. This, in turn, would seem to lead to a safer and more humane society.

In the following articles a clear perspective can be detected. The structure or form of the family is clearly less an issue than the *content* of family interaction. The old arguments about whether the family's functions have been lost to the state or to the school are no longer at issue. The internal *vitality* of family life, however, calls for a renunciation of the family unit as a passive component that only reacts to external change. The family is not seen only as a socialization factory that turns out whatever the larger society requests, but as a nurturing place for vital beings. It is in this context that I perceive the idea of the actualized family. The writers are concerned with fostering a warm and expressive tone in family life and suggest ways in which family members can help one another grow into fully developed human beings. If, indeed, their outlooks were to become part of the program in the majority of American homes and were to be carried from there into the various institutions in the larger society, we might well witness a renewal of faith in what Herbert Croly once called "The Promise of American Life."

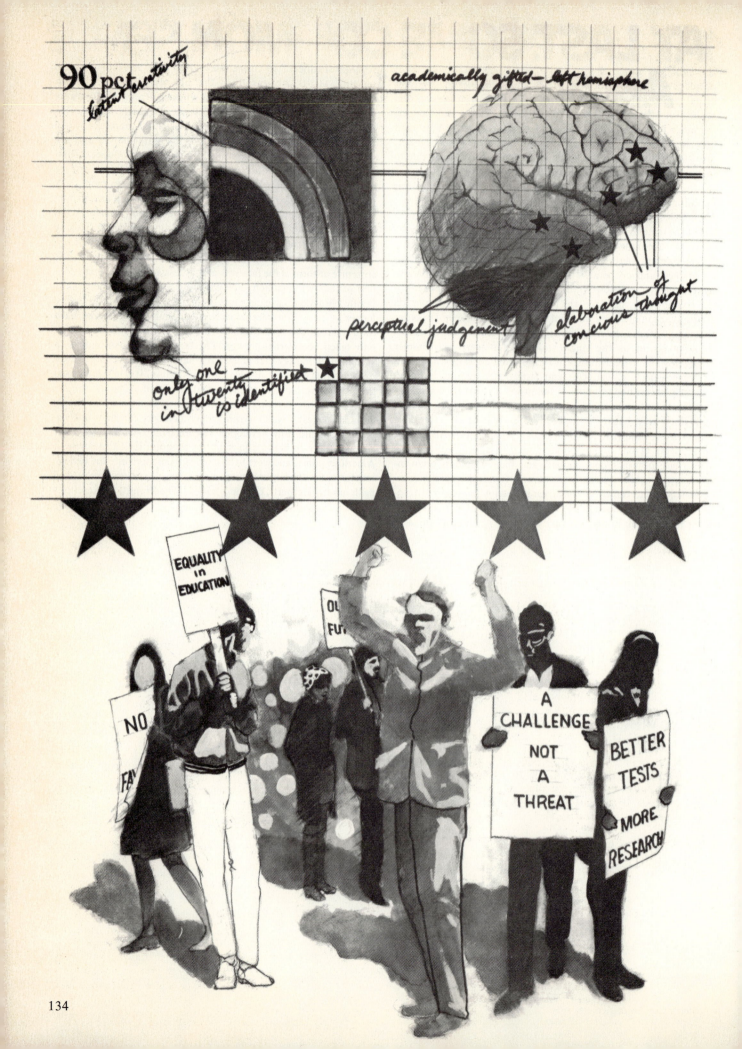

Depriving the Best and the Brightest

by JACK FINCHER

Bruce McDean 1976

A gifted child can be rich in mental resources but sorely deprived in our educational system. The loss to society may be more than we can afford.

Jack Fincher is a contributing editor to HUMAN BEHAVIOR. This article is adapted from a chapter of his book *Human Intelligence,* recently published by G. P. Putnam's Sons.

The scene is a peaceful oak-shaded elementary school in your neighborhood. The time is tomorrow. Arriving at his office, the principal is astonished to find it barricaded by a band of militant parents. As he blinks in the unaccustomed glare of television lights, they confront him with—can this be happening?—a list of nonnegotiable demands:

(1) The intelligence of *all* children must be individually tested and independently evaluated, regardless of teacher recommendations and classroom performance.

(2) Discrimination against the nonverbal gifted must be reversed.

(3) Better tests, more research into ways of determining special talents as well as general intelligence, must be developed.

(4) Above all, an imaginative and comprehensive program of full-time education designed for the gifted must be established with all possible speed, whatever the cost.

"Piecemeal tinkering, eclectic dabbling will no longer do," their prepared press release reads. "The latest ideas, information, techniques and materials must be massively employed. Even more essential, the program must be staffed by intensely committed teachers secure enough in their profession and safe enough in their jobs to see the gifted for what they are: a challenge, not a threat." Concludes the press release ominously, "At stake is nothing less than the future of this country."

Such demands, of course, are as inaccessible to instant satisfaction as they are nonnegotiable. The principal pleads for more time, other meetings. Whereupon the parents, fed up by what they see as a bureaucratic stall, join with older students (reform-minded achievers, vengeful dropouts) and volunteers from Mensa to throw a picket line around the school and invade the cafeteria for a teach-in. When they refuse to leave, police are reluctantly summoned, the pickets dispersed, the squatters arrested. The next day they are back, vowing not to allow classes to continue or to pay that part of their taxes destined for education "until the gross inequities victimizing the gifted child are remedied."

This time, however, they are not alone in their anger. Arrayed against them is an even larger and more indignant group of parents, brandishing such signs as Segregation Is Undemocratic, Testing—Private Discrimination at Public Expense and Equal Opportunity—Cornerstone of Our Republic. The playground has become a battleground for another bitter skirmish in one of the oldest unfinished wars ever to plague American social history, one with its roots plunged deep in our turbulent political past: the war between Jacksonian democracy, with its emphasis on the greatest good for the greatest number, and Jeffersonian democracy, with its concern for the unique needs of the individual. The last refuge of our dying innocence—a truly democratic but equal system of public education—has become the freshest arena for our clashing sensibilities.

As implausible as such a schoolhouse scenario sounds, it is anything but airily hypothetical. The fictive list of parent demands rests on a solid foundation of facts, feelings and attitudes. Teachers *are* notoriously biased in gauging public intellect. They tend to pick the clean, the polite, the orderly, the interested—and research indicates they are wrong more often than right. Schoolwork *is* a woefully inadequate index. The paralyzing sameness of the traditional curriculum panders to the lowest common denominator. It turns the brightest kids off or into chronic losers. Although some nonverbal children when carefully tested have proven gifted, being nonverbal *still* too often means a one-way ticket to trade school. Even when such children are detected, few schools know what to do with them or are equipped to do it if they did. Schools *do* continue to handle IQ scores as highly classified information or a bureaucratic embarrassment. Our frontier canons to the contrary, there is nothing sissified or shameful about exceptionally high intelligence; but the gifted child, assuming he is even recognized, is *still* shunted to the back rooms of academe legislatively and

"The traditional curriculum turns the brightest kids off or into chronic losers."

treated as an awkward stepbrother of the mentally handicapped. Finally, the best tests generally available provide only a narrow measure of human mental potential and practically no meaningful indication at all of latent creativity. They reflect, in fact, and only crudely, little more than those skills the schools are set up to teach, a mutually damning indictment. Little wonder, then, that parent law suits against schools for failing to do their job, unheard of just a few years ago, are sharply on the upswing.

In sum, these issues are very real and reflect an even deeper ecological issue that smolders just beneath the surface: if our children are, as we never tire of saying, our most precious resource, how shall we conserve and develop the best that is in them, for our sake as well as theirs?

There is sadly ample evidence that many of our creative and intelligent best are being wasted, as surely as our polluted lakes, oil-smeared beaches and smog-fouled air. In a 1970 report to Congress, the U.S. Commissioner of Education admitted that federal efforts to aid the gifted and talented were "all but nonexistent." Unfortunately, nothing much has happened since to mitigate against using the present tense in reciting the forlorn figures.

To wit: as a nation, we spend 43 times more on the underprivileged and 28 times more on the handicapped. Of an estimated four million gifted youngsters of all ages—a pool of potential talent with undreamed-of depths—fewer than *one in 20* is even being identified. Of those who are, *less than $10 a year* is being spent on each. State and local efforts are little better. Although 21 states have legislation, much of it goes scarcely beyond codified rhetoric. Only 10 states have at least one staff worker assigned more than half time. Only four—California, Illinois, Connecticut and Georgia—budget major moneys, and none comes close to realizing the full intent of its underlying philosophy. By no stretch of the bureaucratic imagination can any of their programs—a mixed bag of teacher training, limited curriculum enrichment and

special projects—be held up as shining models. Nor is the private sector much help. A dozen independent schools for the academically (left hemisphere) gifted are in operation, but their numbers of children are negligible, their impact slight. Where are the foundations, those flowing founts of scholastic innovation? Few if *any* dollars from the over $280 million granted annually to education—one-third of all foundation philanthropy—trickle down to the gifted.

Perhaps even worse, as nationwide hearings have made evident, there is scant public support for such programs beyond the parents of the designated gifted themselves. As it is, they represent only a fraction of the parents who might be interested if their children were identified—or, to be scrupulously fair, might not be. One in five parents, the Department of Health, Education and Welfare (HEW) found, either limit their gifted child's vision to high school or fail to communicate educational goals of any kind. Except for California, with its statewide platoon of volunteer organizations, advocates for the gifted compose at best a small and poorly organized lobby. Worse yet, the federal report indicates, their modest accomplishments and aspirations have met with "apathy and even hostility" among teachers, administrators, guidance counselors and school psychologists. As a consequence, the requisite identification process has been at most "piecemeal, sporadic and sometimes nonexistent."

Even where it exists, there are frustrations that undermine the most ambitious of efforts. Group intelligence testing, preferable because it is far cheaper for perennially strapped school districts (the best individual IQ tests cost $75 a child to administer and analyze), is no more reliable than teacher recommendations. And, unbelievably, over half the schools surveyed said they had no gifted students at all! How school attitudes and staffing result in such an Alice-In-Wonderland state of affairs can be seen in the results of an unpublished survey undertaken and filed away without fanfare by HEW during the Johnson administration. States with full-time consultants, the unreleased study shows, served 40 percent of the country's public school population and reported three-quarters of the designated gifted. Those having no consultants even part-time served a little less than a third of the population but uncovered only 1 *percent.* Says one of that survey's authors, Connecticut's Dr. William Vassar: "States without full-time programs just don't go out and discover the kids, much less do anything for them. It's like gardening. You can have good soil, but if you don't cultivate it, nothing much is going to grow."

Worst of all, notes the HEW report, the nation's approach to the gifted, limited as it is, is dogged by virtually every administrative and bureaucratic ill that can afflict government enterprise: lack of funds, lack of leadership, lack of trained personnel, lack of public understanding, lack of priority, lack of legislation, appallingly poor diagnosis of the very population it is supposed to serve, too much isolation, too little organization and a stubborn history of nonintervention and state autonomy in how federal funds should be used.

Concludes the commissioner's 1970 report with a candor astonishing in a government agency: "The educational system does not accept the right of an individual to be different from his peers. The general tendency is to pull the person [down] to the average. . . ."

Where, critics might well have asked had such a report ever been made public, is the evidence for such a damning

"The cream of our talent could rise in a supportive atmosphere missing in most schools."

indictment? If the grades of the gifted don't show it, how do we know they are superior in intelligence to others their age? Who says they can do much better than they are doing? What proves they are hurt by the lack of challenging outlets? If these children are so bright and creative, why can't they make it on their own? Doesn't the cream just naturally rise to the top?

Carefully and patiently, one by one, the commissioner's report sought to knock down each argument. In surveys of selected academic subjects, it pointed out, gifted kindergartners given free rein were found to be performing at the second-grade level; gifted fourth-graders, beyond the seventh; and gifted high school seniors, better than college seniors on tests employed for admission to graduate study. So not only were they superior, their superiority grew progressively as they got older. Another survey showed that over half the gifted consistently worked beneath their capability. So in a conventional atmosphere they were shortchanging themselves and society. Thousands of youth in the top intellectual bracket, moreover, were dropping out every year, taking with them into the menial (and increasingly limited) job market talents that would never be realized. That could not help but hurt society.

As for the cream rising, one official sourly noted that such a notion must stem from the assumption that human beings "are no more complex than a bottle of milk." The cream of our talent could rise in a warm, supportive atmosphere too often missing from our schools, he adds, but for now it appears "homogenized," if not "curdled."

The same year the Commissioner of Education made his gloomy report to Congress, I visited several California classes for the gifted in preparation for a national magazine article. What I saw, while encouraging, was hardly cause for unbridled optimism. And as with the commissioner's statistics, I suspect, little has improved since.

Eighteen miles south of San Francisco is a pleasant, modernistic structure of long, open galleries and polychrome plastic paneling. In one room, housing 17 fifth-through-eighth graders with tested IQs of 150 and above, there was a breezy bedlam of excited conversation, physical sprawl, incessant movement and awesome clutter. Teachers of the gifted spend little time on class control. Quipped one, "You just open the door in the morning and get out of their way." The walls were adorned with humorous collages. Punning headline: "He's Not Dead, Beatle Says Spiritedly." Aphorism: " 'Humor is nothing but grown-up play' —Max Eastman."

Few of them looked up as I walked in. They were either busy with their contracts—individual lesson plans mutually arrived at with their teacher—or absorbed in one of their two group projects: a book they were writing about their town, and an airline-sponsored competition among schools to see which class could create through the magic of advertising the most authentic-sounding airline. First prize: a flight to Europe. A quartet of boys and girls rehearsed the commercial they had written before running through it in front of their videotape camera, bought with state funds for the gifted.

"Did you know there's a partial eclipse of the sun next month?" a radiant little moonfaced 10-year-old named Janet asked me. "Don't miss it. There won't be another until the year 2017."

"These kids are great," one of their teachers told me when she could catch her breath. "But their *parents* sometimes need help. Janet's father drills her two hours a night." There was a commotion in the schoolyard. The teacher went out to investigate, then returned. "That was one of ours," she sighed. "Until Danny came in this class he thought he was the biggest brain in the world. His parents, I'm sorry to say, did nothing to discourage him. Now he can't stand to be crossed, even when he's wrong. Another boy just disagreed with him. Danny hit him and broke his glasses."

She nodded toward a handsome Chinese-American boy and moved slowly around the room with a friendly smile. "They'll drive themselves if you don't watch them. He's done a year's work in two months. Know what we've made his homework now? To play."

Across the bay and to the north, in Oakland's bleak lowland black belt, lies a low and grimy building of institutional red brick with a dreary outcropping of Quonset prefabs. Behind the windows of one, papered with festive drawings to keep out the slanting afternoon sun, is one of the city's special classes, this one for "high potential

IQs" among underprivileged sixth graders—minority kids from all over Oakland's underbelly, most of whose parents had never finished high school. They have every reason to be different but, except for the strident urgings of one gangly black girl that her girlfriend shadow-boxing a teasing boy "knock him out," they, too, were sky-high on learning. "What is a gall?" asked one pupil's poster, then defined it. "If I bring a snail," began another, part of a citywide natural science program, "do you think you could keep it alive one month?" The ghetto gifted class had kept it alive two.

Proudly, their teacher, a chunky, energetic redhead who was herself a onetime 15-year-old college freshman, ticked off their accomplishments: a letter-writing campaign to save the bay, an oceanographic cruise, class inquiries into piano tuning, lasers, bees, spinning, folk singing, Antarctica, the Soviet Union, urban crisis. "We talk a lot about core city problems," she told me. "They're quick to see the analogies to the underdeveloped everywhere. For instance, we screened a coffee company film about Brazil. It was sheer propaganda, and they knew it. They wanted to know where all the poor were."

Because ghetto young do not test as well as their suburban counterparts— whatever the reason—the district relies heavily on teacher recommendations. Out of the 22 pupils, says the teacher, "three don't belong here. But I refuse to let them be taken out." Contrary to what others might think, she says, their being there didn't hurt the rest and helped them. "I've taught the gifted several years, and it's fun," she admits, "but a few years ago another teacher with a low-IQ math group and I got together and taught them all. As a team. Both classes did fine. You couldn't tell one from the other." She watched several boys run the film strips they had drawn through a slide projector. "When they came in, a lot of these kids knew nothing about working on their own. One girl in art just sat there with a blank piece of paper. She was waiting for me to tell her what to draw. By midyear, though, I'd put these kids up against any gifted class in Oakland."

Forty miles down the peninsula and a day later, seven-year-old Kenneth exploded through the "magic door" to his classroom—a curtain of varicolored, floorlength paper streamers—and then remembered its significance: playtime was over, time to calm down. The previous year, Kenneth, son of a chemical engineer and a school teacher, had been trapped in a spiritual ghetto. In medical terms, he is hyperkinetic—for complex

"The teacher usually spends the first semester undoing what the regular school has done."

neurological reasons, feverishly overactive. While not crippling physically, his impairment is severe enough that he cannot master his movements sufficiently to ride a bicycle, handle a pencil or sit quietly in a chair for very long. One thing, however, he can do surpassingly well—he can think.

In the first grade, Kenneth wouldn't do arithmetic, and workbooks turned him off. He just daydreamed, "about things more important," he would later tell his teacher. In a class discussion one day about the meaning of Christmas, he blurted, "Christmas is the prism of life. That's when the love we keep to ourselves all year long is refracted out." The other children laughed; Kenneth developed a stammer. On the *Stanford-Binet,* he tested in the high 140s but wouldn't repeat any words less than five syllables or he might have done better. The first-grade teacher felt he was just lazy. Perhaps he was. But the district decided he belonged in their class for the underachieving gifted, taught by an imaginative young woman who was planning to return to Stanford for her Ph.D.

Number facts, she found, bored Kenneth. "Why do that?" he would ask. "We've got computers." He was ready for algebra and geometry, provided she would spare him repetitive exercises. Dick and Jane bored him, too. He had read a book on inorganic chemistry, taught himself braille and the manual alphabet and aspired to become a biochemist who would find a cure for blindness. Now, today, given his own choices, Kenneth reads at the junior high level. And when he talks in class, he doesn't stammer.

"These kids," his teacher says, "have tremendous capacity for self-direction and evaluation. But they're repelled by structure and drill. They're perfectionists. Sometimes they see their gifts as a threat. Their perceptions are so advanced, they feel overwhelmed. They think like 12-year-olds but function like seven-year-olds." For the first semester, she spends most of her time undoing what the regular school system has done the first year. She must build up their self-esteem. "When he first came

in"—she points out one boy—"he drew a sign on his desk: Dumb Sits Here." Their gifts, she agrees, can isolate them as effectively as a crippled arm or leg. They have little contact with children their own age at home and see the classroom as a haven. It is hard to get them outside; and when she does, they tend to congregate by themselves along the far fence. All stay for a creative workshop after the regular school hours have ended.

Her secret, if it can be called that, is simple. "It's respecting the child. It's listening to him, treating him as an individual. Put these kids back in a highly structured system—we did it once, experimentally—and their behavior reverts to chaos. That's our most serious problem, I think. How can I get them to accept the rigidity, the absurdity, of regular school when they leave here?"

She saw me through the magic door. "They won't line up, so I had to do *something* to cool them off when they came in. Six of them are hyperkinetics, and the rest have too much on their minds. It bugs the principal. They're not going to learn to stand in line, he says. Well, I don't think that's anything they're going to need—unless there's another depression."

Comparatively few case histories are even as happy as these scattered few in California—and for reasons that strike at the heart of the problem the gifted pose for American education: who is gifted and how? Today, high achievement in hundreds if not thousands of fields is not only possible but mandatory for the survival of modern society. Success depends not only on the traditionally recognized gifts of abstraction and symbol manipulation but on qualities of originality, fluency with ideas, intellectual curiosity, indepen-

dence of thought and flexibility in forging new concepts. What's more, giftedness of an equally distinctive character is clearly called for in such nonacademic but intellectually demanding disciplines as the creative and performing arts, human relations, group management, government and politics—in the spiritual leadership of Gandhi, the mechanical aptitude of Da Vinci, the psychomotor skills of Jack Nicklaus.

The question is further complicated by the perversely taxing and challenging nature of the child itself. How are we to winnow out the "Morning Glory," that precocious performer whose talents may mysteriously wax and wane before he is grown? How are we to recognize early the "Late Bloomer," whose abilities suddenly flower long after the school has assigned him to the back row of its awareness? How, finally, are we to spot either—by testing and, having tested, running the risk of freezing forever in the teacher's mind the upper limits of probable accomplishment for a child who may have had an off day (or because multiple-choice exams are anathema to his style of thinking, have an off day *every* day)? Or are we to risk trusting him to identify himself with his actions in an educational atmosphere often so pedestrian it causes him, in P. E. Vernon's haunting words, to "learn to be unintelligent"?

And what of the IQ numbers game with its habitual cutoff of 130 to 135, below which a child is not considered intellectually gifted? The distinction between 131 and 129 is at best arbitrary. There can be a difference of five points between tests on any two days, a difference that is entirely meaningless. Does that mean, then, that the cutoff should be lowered to 125? And having

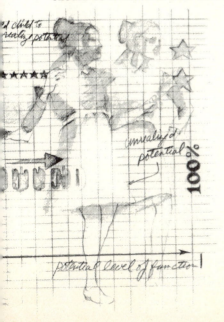

"Can the pursuit of excellence only be accomplished by a retreat from equality?"

lowered it, what about 120? Or 115? If you don't draw the line somewhere, many earnest and capable testing professionals squirm and confess, you don't draw it anywhere.

If there is an answer, what is it? It lies, perhaps, not in segregating the gifted but in offering, like the best of the alternative schools—like the best of *any* schools—individualized instruction, differentiated programs. If children, gifted or otherwise, can be trusted to work largely on their own, guided and occasionally helped by a competent teacher, then a true alliance of Jacksonian and Jeffersonian ideals is possible. Education can be both democratic and elite. The artificial distinction between 131 and 129—and 100—can be done away with. Certainly such an approach would take us far toward solving the problem of how to provide for the wide range of individual differences found in any school population.

That kind of education, manifestly, costs more than we as a nation have until now been willing to spend—for the gifted or any child—in faith and understanding as well as money and energy. Schools, after all, it can be legitimately argued, have enough trouble educating the great mass in the middle or raising up the disadvantaged at the bottom in the manner we have always employed. To divert a school's limited resources or further fragment a teacher's energies, especially to the heady requirements of those who by definition are already the most fortunate seems unthinkable to many. But ducking the issue is at best a cop-out, at worst a recipe for disaster. Ducking it leads to the Illinois high school senior who learned to read and write Russian on his own (although he had never heard it spoken) and buried himself so deeply in physics he failed the simpler math courses required for graduation. Ducking it leads to the Texas teenager who delighted in trigonometry but refused to do boringly simple fractions and was caught—horror of horrors—not smoking a joint or downing an upper but writing *her own math textbook* in study hall. Ducking it leads to her mother being told variously throughout 12

unhappy years of school that her daughter was retarded, brain damaged, abused, had emotional problems, had a defense mechanism, had a flawed personality because of some nameless mistake made by her parents. Ducking it leads at last to the principal telling them that the psychologist who had found her in the top half of the top bracket on the *Stanford-Binet* "did not know what he was talking about . . . that [she] was definitely from an unstable home life and would be treated and taught accordingly" because he, the principal, "was 'fed up.' "

Denying the gifted their fullest developmental opportunities, warns Columbia University educator A. Harry Passow, will not in itself upgrade the attainments of the less able. "Such misguided and meaningless egalitarianism," he says, "contributes to the development of no one in particular." Yet there looms always the danger that the pursuit of excellence can only be accomplished by a retreat from equality and vice versa, cautions Abraham Tannenbaum. The problem is as obvious as it is difficult. Whether it is insoluable only time will tell.

Meanwhile, the unsatisfied needs of the gifted are often subtle, their weakening effects hidden to all but the most discerning. For example, the staff of a Springfield, Virginia, elementary school held a seminar on the gifted and came up with some rather thoughtful questions and conclusions that suggest the deeper consequences of our neglect. The gifted child, they wrote, "may be a fluent reader, but does he skim difficult material and find he has learned little from it? He may be quick to abstract and generalize, but has he developed the habit of backing his conclusions with solid evidence? Is he learning to approach open-ended questions cautiously, identifying every possible position and its defenses?"

Their conclusions were equally incisive: in the crystalizing absence of a peer congregation, where instruction is aimed at the lowest common denominator, the gifted child is deprived of the chance to struggle for achievement, to triumph over obstacles, to toughen his mental muscles. He is deprived of the need to master his whims, rein in his attention, submit to discipline for the sake of future goals. He is deprived of a basis for realistic self-appraisal and a sensible humility in the presence of talents equal or superior to his own.

He is, in sum, the Springfield staff decided, in his own way, as deprived as the most bitterly impoverished child of the ghetto.

26

LET'S HEAR IT FOR AVIATION HIGH

By Peter A. Janssen

The school is flanked by a gas station and a men's clothing factory, across the street from the elevated subway tracks, in an industrial section of Long Island City. Next to the seven-story school building of glass and brick, some 16 airplanes, including a biplane, two helicopters, two twin-engine Beechcrafts and two reconnaissance drones left over from the Vietnam war, are scattered about a hangar and an apron. The whole, with its 2,700 students, is the Aviation High School, an exemplar of a flourishing new trend in career education.

In the past, most vocational schools had a well-deserved reputation as dumping grounds for blacks, Puerto Ricans and other minorities who were not regarded by most educators as college material. All too often, the vocational schools "trained" students for jobs that did not exist with equipment that was hopelessly outdated, or were used as a means of tracking students away from the more desirable high schools—and, as a consequence, into the least desirable jobs. A few years ago, however, many educators turned to "career education" as a means of effecting a reform in education generally. About 40 percent of all American high-school students were enrolled in a general curriculum which usually was a watered-down college-prep course that did not prepare students for either college or a job. Sidney P. Marland, then Commissioner of Education, called the prevailing general curriculum "an abomination," and quickly became the main spokesman for career training. The reformers promoted the idea that the institutional barriers between school and work should be broken down; that an end should be put to the secondary-school lockstep that was sending an ever-growing number of high-school graduates unquestioningly to college; and that high schools should train all students for a decent way to earn a living, whether they went on to college or not.

Today, the trend toward career education has received a boost from many educators—and parents—who are taking a second look at the merits of college. While four years at a public college now cost about $11,000, and more than $25,000 at a private college, the economic advantages of a college degree are shrinking. In 1969 men over 25 with a college degree earned 53 percent more than men with only a high-school diploma; by 1973, they earned only 40 percent more, and Harvard economist Richard B. Freeman predicts that by 1979 they will earn just 30 percent more.

Peter A. Janssen is education editor of Time magazine.

Vocational schools have had a reputation as dumping grounds. Now, in a sour economy, some of the schools—Aviation is a notable example—are turning away applicants.

With the end of the military draft, a smaller proportion of high-school graduates is going on to college or joining the armed forces. Increasingly, young people are leaving high school and going to work. Their presence on the job market gives extra impetus to upgrading the shopworn vocational and technical schools. And in the sour economy of the past few years, the trend toward career education has become a nation-wide boom.

New York has 23 technical and vocational high schools, currently with 305,486 students, or 14 percent of the city's high-school enrollment. Applications to these schools ran last year at double the number of openings, and those who get in seem to stay. Attendance, which often dips below 60 percent in the general high schools, runs about 75 percent in the vocational schools. The Board of Education claims that two-thirds of the vocational graduates get jobs in the fields they studied.

For all that, many of the vocational schools suffer from a lack of focus, offering vague courses in "office practices" or "career development"; many still struggle along with hopelessly outdated equipment—for instance, teaching television repair on black-and-white sets. The city's five "unit-trade" high schools, however, are a different story. Each of these concentrates on a single industry—aviation, automobile, fashion, printing, and art and design—and directs its training and technology towards a single goal. These specialized schools attract students with a particular desire to learn.

Aviation High School, one of half a dozen high schools in the country specializing in the aerospace industry, has a record that is far above the city average even for the vocational schools. Last year,

4,750 seventh- and eighth-grade students applied for Aviation's 850 places. Attendance was 96 percent, and Aviation principal Santo J. Frontario says he had more job offers (at $4.50 to $5.20 an hour) for last June's graduates than he had takers. The reason for Aviation's apparent success is that it offers both a highly technical job-training program—with plenty of cooperation and leadership from the aviation industry—and a solid college-bound curriculum. Students can take technical courses and graduate with both a diploma and a Federal Aviation Administration certificate of competency as air-frame or power-plant mechanics; or, in the senior year, they can take the "advanced placement" course with college-level physics labs, avionics (dealing with electronic instruments) and calculus, and earn the F.A.A. certificate, a diploma, and a leg up on college.

In addition, Aviation runs several dozen afternoon and evening courses for adults trying to land entry-level jobs. During the day, students from other schools come to use Aviation's unique shops and equipment; many students from Aviation and other high schools also sign up for after-school courses to get extra job training.

Eddie Luisl, an Aviation junior who is having only mild success in growing a mustache, stays two hours after school to take a paint-spraying course. This winter he will get a certificate of competency in paint spraying, and then he'll enroll in something else. "When I graduate, I'll have these things all piled up," he says. "I can work anywhere. I'll get a diploma and a license from the F.A.A.,

I'll have three or four of these certificates; I can go to college, the Air Force, work as a technician. Right now I don't know what I want to do, but I know I'll be ahead of a lot of other guys."

Perhaps because of the ever-present glamour of flying or the oft-mentioned $10-an-hour wage for airline mechanics with two years' experience, Aviation's students are uniformly enthusiastic about their school. Waiting for a bus outside the building one warm fall afternoon, Horacio Felgueiras, a sophomore, proudly and without any prompting declared, "It is the best school in New York City." A group of friends agreed, gleefully slapping Felgueiras's outstretched palm every time he mentioned anything remotely connected with the school. "For one thing," he said, "you get a job." Slap, slap. "JFK, La-Guardia." Slap, slap. "You know, $10 an hour." Slap, slap, slap.

Enthusiasm about Aviation is anything but a coincidence. Indeed, it is the result of a highly developed system of recruiting, admission and student motivation and control. The school is open to all city pupils graduating from the eighth and ninth grades. Every fall, Aviation's counseling office sends thousands of brochures and letters to public and private junior highs throughout the city. Frontario speaks at dozens of junior highs during the year, and he puts on at least one open house, so that parents, prospective students and counselors can see for themselves what Aviation is all about. "We work at recruiting," says Frontario. "We want to ensure that we get the largest possible pool of applicants." This fall, some 1,500 people turned out for a Friday evening open house; after visiting the shops and talking with teachers, they were shown a 28-minute, 16-mm. color film extolling the school's virtues.

The film was made in 1965; a new one has been shot and only awaits final editing. It is anything but subtle. The film opens with a DC-10 taking off, and cuts to the plane landing and taxiing toward a passenger terminal. The camera zooms in for a close-up of the co-pilot. "Hi, I'm George Wilson, first officer of American Airlines. I'm a graduate of Aviation High School, class of '62. My mechanical and technical training at Aviation High School provided me with a sense of direction and a foundation upon which to build my career." The highly professional film continues with more success

stories and interviews with old grads who are airline executives, pilots and mechanics.

To apply to Aviation, students fill out a standard Board of Education form, and take a written test at the school dealing with math, science and spatial relationships. They are then interviewed by Frontario, an assistant principal or a guidance counselor. "The interview is the most important part of the screening," says Antonio Pepenella, who has been a counselor for 16 years and is in charge of admissions. "That's how we tell about motivation." Aviation puts far more emphasis on a student's desire to learn and his ability to live by the rules than on his brilliance. "We don't take kids who are more than two years retarded in reading," says Pepenella. Frontario says, "We stress accuracy, workmanship, attendance, punctuality. We're vitally concerned about a boy's ability to assume responsibility for his actions."

Finally, all applications are spread out on two long wooden tables in a conference room, arranged in descending order of the test scores. A 12-member committee goes through the piles, with Pepenella and Frontario making the final decisions. Last year, 3,984 applicants took the written test, 1,600 were accepted and 850 were enrolled. "A lot of kids from parochial schools use us as insurance in case they don't get into their diocesan high school," Pepenella said. "But 90 percent of the kids we accepted from ninth grade in public schools actually came."

If, as occasionally happens, the screening process fails and a student does not fit in, he is invited to leave. (This works both ways; some students are astonished at Aviation's rules and regulations, and want out.) Each year, about 10 percent of the entering students are "transferred out."

Aviation does not seem to suffer from racial discrimination. About 38 percent of the students this term are Puerto Rican, 16 percent are black, 12 percent are Oriental and

34 percent are white. (Frontario has a Spanish-language cassette for his 15-minute slide and tape show when he recruits in heavily Puerto Rican schools.) However, another form of discrimination seems to be at work: The school does not have a single female student, although six are scheduled to come part-time for some shop courses in February. "A few girls passed the test and applied," says Frontario. "So I asked their parents in and showed them the shops and classes and all the boys, and then they said their daughters didn't want to come. Can't say as I blame them."

Starting with the 10th grade, an Aviation student spends half the day in shop courses and the other half in academic work. The school day, longer than in many New York high schools, runs from 8 A.M. to 2:56 P.M. and is divided into nine 45-minute periods. The only free period is lunch. There is no study hall or other free time.

The curriculum, of course, is dictated by Board of Education requirements. But two other agencies also control Aviation's technical courses: the F.A.A., which stipulates a specific curriculum for its certificate, and the Aeronautic Educational Advisory Commission, a group of 47 airline, union, management, military and other aviation-related men who meet at the school three or four times a year to review courses, discuss the job market and offer feedback on how graduates are performing. Commission members also make summer jobs available for Aviation teachers—keeping them up-to-date on industry demands and equipment—and donate supplies to the school.

In the 10th grade, students work in air-frame, sheet-metal and basic-electricity shops. In the 11th grade, they move on to airplane motor assembly and oxyacetylene and heliarc welding; in the 12th to jet engines, turbines and turbo-props, hydraulics and machine-tool controls. Wearing white coveralls with a flying letter A stitched on the back, students work on "live" engines in the hangar and test jet engines in two small labs behind huge soundproof doors.

Much of the training prepares students for jobs outside aviation. In the 11th-grade electrical shop, for example, Alvin Gorlick, who graduated from Aviation in 1963, teaches the fundamentals of wiring a circuit. Students strip a circuit board clean, and then rewire it. Gorlick has worked some summers as a mechanic for Allegheny, National and Mohawk airlines, "but I can do anything. Some summers I do air-conditioning or heating. These kids learn those same skills. If they can't get a job in aviation, they'll be able to get a job someplace."

For students who do want jobs in aviation, the school offers an "extended 12th year" program to the top 50 graduates. They can come back for six months and work in shops full-time. If they pass a qualifying test, they earn a second F.A.A. technician's license.

Not all the courses are oriented to shop and job. One elective English course for college-bound students is "Male-Female Relationships, or Sexuality Through Literature." Recently Martha Sussman, one of the few women teachers in the school, was perched on her desk discussing the previous night's assignment — a story about Mark, 19, a counselor at a summer camp, and Emily, 16, a young camper. At the end of the summer, Mark and Emily have an affair.

As Principal Frontario and Vice Principal Bob Grant quietly escort a visitor into the back of the room, Mrs. Sussman is explaining that "probably the worst thing you can do when you engage in sex is to want something to happen but you're too embarrassed to tell your partner." Frontario groans; Grant struggles with his jacket button; Mrs. Sussman flushes but gamely struggles on. "The worst thing in the world is to be naked with someone, exposing yourself in every way, but still to be afraid to ask them a question." The class, 33 teen-age boys, nods in agreement.

"What are your thoughts about women taking steps to avoid pregnancy?" Mrs. Sussman asks.

A Puerto Rican boy: "In my country, it's very hard for a girl to get a prescription for a pill or any help from a doctor."

Another boy, affecting a superreasonable tone of voice: "It's both their responsibility."

Mrs. Sussman guides the discussion from intercourse to other rites of passage, the class hanging on every word, until she is saved by the bell.

In addition to the standard Regents' requirements for academic courses, Aviation offers a dozen or so electives. The more popular: "The Adolescent in Literature," "Exploring the Film" and "Horrors, Witches and the Supernatural." Some 60 students are enrolled in the intense advanced placement program.

Aviation's teachers often use a blend of the Socratic method and practical examples. Frank Cordaro, who has taught at the school for 11 years (after 20 years in the Navy in aircraft maintenance), was leading 21 seniors through "The Theory of Lift" in a chemistry lab. Cordaro scrawled diagrams on the blackboard and gestured with a 2-foot-long wooden model airplane.

"Will the take-off run be longer at JFK or at Denver?"

"Denver," came the reply from several students.

"Why?" asked Cordaro, calling on a boy in the rear.

"Because the air has less density in Denver. High altitude—less lift."

Cordaro ran through the effects of weather on density: Air expands in heat, becoming less dense and offering less lift. "O.K. We're at Mexico City on a hot day. Are we going to have difficulty getting it off the ground?"

The class chorused "Yes," as Cordaro moved the model plane through a prolonged, low-level take-off.

After class, he explained: "I keep talking with the kids, asking them questions all the time to see if they're getting the stuff. It's also pretty effective to use a lot of visual aids like the model plane. The kids pick it up faster."

Paul Casella, who has been at Aviation for four years (after several years as an Army helicopter crew chief), was teaching a senior class in "Ground Operations." Eighteen boys perched on benches in the hangar, almost under the wing of a jet fighter. Casella ran a short movie showing how to service a private plane when it lands at a small airport; the proper hand signals to use in leading it to the service area; how to chock the wheels, fill the gas tank and check the tires. He then had the class practice hand signals.

"When you're on the ground walking a plane to the service area, why should you always look behind you?" he asked.

A sturdy boy, with "Mean Machine" written on the back of his coveralls, replied: "For Christ's sake, if you don't look where you're going, you'll walk into a propeller."

"Yeah, or you could trip on something, and before he noticed that you weren't there, the pilot could roll over you. It's happened." Casella said that later in the week the class would taxi a single-engine Cessna out of the hangar onto the apron and start up the motor—"and I want everybody to know exactly where they're going."

Throughout the school, Aviation has 172 certified teachers; 72 of them are certified F.A.A. air-frame and power-plant mechanics as well. One F.A.A. regulation that is causing some trouble requires that shop classes contain no more than 25 students. Frontario got a special extension last February permitting Aviation's shops to go up to 28 pupils, the maximum stipulated in the United Federation of Teachers contract. The U.F.T. maximum for high-school academic courses is 34; Aviation's classes usually are one or two below that.

Like the students, most of Aviation's teachers are uncommonly loyal to the school. Indeed, 35 are Aviation graduates. Aviation opened as the Manhattan High School of Aviation Trades in 1937, on Second Avenue and 63d Street. Frontario, who was born on the Lower East Side and graduated from P.S. 40 and Stuyvesant High School, joined it a year later. He helped plan the present building.

To a large degree, most schools are a reflection of their principals. Frontario, a licensed mechanic, pilot and F.A.A. examiner who "flies as often as I can," is polite, direct and businesslike. He was a colonel during the Second World War, flying B-17's in North Africa and Italy, and there is no doubt today about who runs the show at Aviation; almost everyone in the building defers to Frontario on any question of substance. Frontario works in "the industry" during the summer; this year he evaluated training programs for Pan Am.

The school's ability to produce graduates who land good jobs depends largely on the equipment in its shops. Frontario says Aviation's per-pupil spending is the same as in other vocational high schools. Aviation's operating budget is $3.1 million from the Board of Education this year. Frontario estimates that the budget has been cut about 15 or 20 percent lately. "They started cutting five years ago and I stopped counting," he says. "I can't even tell what the total cut is now."

The cuts that particularly hurt are in expendable supplies. In 1965, for example, the board allocated $47,000 for such supplies; this year the budget is $22,000. Teachers in after-school welding shops say they are now allotted one bottle of gas per class. "Now we show a film that's supposed to teach welding," says one bitterly.

Teachers say that most of the shop equipment is old, but good. "Most of the equipment I use comes from the 50's or early 60's, but it's still being used by the airlines," says Dominic Ciociari, who teaches advanced machine shop at Aviation and works during the summer as a pilot for Air Jamaica.

Frontario gets the most out of Aviation by motivating the students. Most, of course, already are motivated by the prospect of the F.A.A. certificate and a decent job. But Frontario uses other techniques to guarantee interest. At graduation, for example, each student with 100 percent attendance is given a gold lapel button in the shape of wings, plus a plaque. (Frontario always wears his wings.) Last spring 65 graduates won their wings. If a student attends four terms without missing a day he is given silver wings; last June, 165 boys, out of a graduating class of 515, got silver wings.

The wings ceremony has a mystique of its own. In a ritual not likely to be duplicated in many other American high schools, an Aviation senior leads the wings winners in reciting the Mechanics' Creed:

"I shall hold in sacred trust the rights and privileges conferred upon me as a wings recipient mechanic. In discharging this trust, I pledge myself never to undertake work or approve of work which I feel to be beyond the limits of my knowledge, nor shall I allow any noncertified superior to persuade me to approve aircraft or equipment as airworthy.

"I realize the grave responsibility which is mine to exercise my judgment on the airworthiness of aircraft and equipment. I therefore pledge unyielding adherence to these precepts for the advancement of aviation and for the dignity of my vocation."

On top of the motivation of the wings, students are required to start each day with 15 minutes in their home room while attendance is taken. The last five minutes of the day they report back for "checkout," while attendance is taken again. "This," says Frontario, "controls what other schools call 'selective attendance.'"

In many ways Aviation is like other high schools. It has the normal signs marking the Down Only and the Up Only stairs, and the P.A. system at the end of each period sounds like a submarine dive signal. But, in a scene more familiar to the 50's than the 70's, the school drill team, 60 strong, practices marching around the yard every afternoon. The drill team was very big this fall in the Columbus Day parade.

"These kids are some of the best in the city," says Vice Principal Grant. "They're good-natured, and that's unusual for high-school kids." Victoria Clark, an English teacher and adviser to Aviation Log, the student paper, agrees: "They're not particularly radical. They're really more or less ultraconservative. They're very pragmatic kids interested in getting jobs."

Whether Aviation graduates actually get the jobs they train for is open to some interpretation. Antonio Pepenella, the admissions director, who doubles as senior counselor, says, "The aviation industry does not have as many jobs as we would like. Also, if the kids want jobs in airlines they have to leave the New York area, and most of them don't want to do that. But things are picking up. We went through a worse period a few years ago."

When asked about jobs, Frontario pulls out a poll of last June's 515 graduates. Of the 258 who responded, 148 were enrolled in some kind of higher education for further technical training (most at City University under Open Admissions); 35 were studying liberal-arts courses; 16 were working full-time in nonaviation jobs; six were working full-time in aviation jobs; six were working part-time but looking for full-time jobs; 29 were unemployed and looking for jobs; 10 had joined the armed forces, and eight who answered the poll did not say what they were doing. There is no way to tell, of course, what happened to the 257 graduates who did not answer the poll.

Is Aviation worthwhile if only six out of 515 graduates are known to be working in aviation jobs? Frontario and many teachers claim that many more uncounted students are in the aviation industry, and that those who did not get aviation jobs immediately are well prepared to work in other fields. Frontario says he had 112 job offers in all parts of aviation last spring—"not as good as in the past, but I still had more jobs than I was able to fill." Many jobs involved working for subcontractors (where graduates would never see an airplane) or moving from New York. Frontario estimates that half of Aviation's graduates end up working in aviation, but he has no solid evidence to back this up.

Aviation graduates who do land jobs tend to perform quite well. Enrico Bello, general foreman for Trans World Airlines and himself an Aviation graduate, says, "They do a fine job. The school teaches fundamentals very well." Patrick Marinelli, maintenance director at Kennedy for Pan Am, and also an Aviation graduate, says, "Young guys get a lot of theory at Aviation; they know how to think, and we like that. We train them ourselves to our own way of doing things, but they already have good basics. We'd rather hire them than people who've been in the Air Force four or five years. The Air Force people have been doing it the wrong way all that time, and it's hard to retrain them." Anthony Vasko, general foreman for technical services for Eastern (yet another Aviation graduate), praises the school's products: "They are really a highly motivated bunch."

The *esprit* and enthusiasm that permeate the school are testimony to its success. Schools such as Aviation are not the entire answer to reforming the nation's high schools, but they certainly offer one alternative. If nothing else, Aviation can point to the pride of its students. Says Claude Laleau, a junior: "If you want to get something out of school, you can get it here." ■

27

Murder in Academe: The Demise of Education

Attacked from the right and the left, and abandoned by political moderates, education is in a decline that threatens the survival of American democracy.

by Fred M. Hechinger

America is in headlong retreat from its commitment to education. Political confusion and economic uncertainty have shaken the people's faith in education as the key to financial and social success. This retreat ought to be the most pertinent issue in any examination of the country's condition in its Bicentennial year. At stake is nothing less than the survival of American democracy.

Let us have no illusions about an American future with declining confidence in universal education and diminished access to higher learning. A slowdown in the escalator of upward mobility constitutes a break with the most fundamental American ideals. The consequence will be a stratified, classbound society ruled by a self-perpetuating power elite of economic and social privilege. It would be the end of the road that was opened by Thomas Jefferson when he called for a new aristocracy of talent to replace the old aristocracy of inherited power.

The threat of such a course is all the more serious because it is virtually universally ignored. None of those who are monitoring the nation's problems are paying attention to the far-reaching implications of the retreat from education. Few are even aware that such a retreat is actually in progress. Education's own leaders are so absorbed—understandably perhaps—in the battle for their institutions' short-term survival that they lack the energy, even if they had the vision, to warn about the greater danger ahead.

When President Ford outlined emergency plans for the possibility of New York City's fiscal default, he promised federal action to maintain "essential services," such as police and fire protection. Education was absent from such plans. Although New York's schools have suffered far more severe cutbacks than has any other municipal service, at no point has the public responded with the kind of angry protest that it raised

against similar reductions of other services. The curtailment of garbage collections was viewed as an unbearable threat to the city's life; the reduction of elementary-school instruction went unchallenged. Children saw as many as eight teachers pulled out from under them in one single term.

The New York experience is cited here only because it is the most visible example of a national trend. Education did not figure at all in President Ford's latest State of the Union address. In 1960 only 11 percent of all school bond issues were voted down; last year the negative votes rose to 54 percent, even though the recession had undoubtedly already reduced the number and size of bond issues submitted to the voters. The chancellor of one of the country's major state-university systems said recently: "A certain callousness has taken over. Unless we're really bleeding, the politicians don't even look up from their desks."

What makes the situation so serious is that education, caught in an unprecedented pincer attack, is under siege from two politically opposite directions. Conservatives who never really liked universal education and are particularly cool toward the massive expansion of college enrollments have been joined by the political left, which views education as an evil tool of capitalism.

In the past, when education had to ward off only the attacks from the reactionary right, the consequences were confined to occasional short-term setbacks. The expansive forward thrust was never deflected for long. Popular faith in each generation's capacity to do better than its predecessor was inseparably linked to education as, in Horace Mann's words, the "great equalizer" and society's "balance wheel." To be sure, there were recurrent complaints like those voiced in an editorial in *The National Gazette*, which, in 1830, opposed public financing of schools on the grounds that such expenditures would be resented by

affluent citizens who would be made to feel that "they had toiled for the benefit of other families than their own." Fortunately, such regressive views were out of touch with the main currents of American thought. The majority of Americans were in agreement with John Dewey's vision of America as an "intentionally progressive society," and they saw education as the key to progress.

During the ideological confusion of the Sixties, education first began to draw fire from the radical left. For the first time a new brand of intellectual revolutionaries looked on state-financed mass education as the major obstacle to their dreams of dismantling the political system. Revisionist ideologues, such as Edgar Z. Friedenberg and John Holt, lashed out against what they considered the coercive aspects of universal and compulsory schooling. They denounced the schools for Americanizing diverse ethnic groups and fitting them into an essentially middle-class socioeconomic pattern or, as they would put it, mold. Revisionist researchers, such as Christopher Jencks, measured the existing American society against their own ideals of the socialist state in which they expected all distinctions between affluence and poverty to vanish. Taking that blueprint as the yardstick, they proclaimed American education's failure in the war against poverty and economic inequality.

Infected with the heady spirit of the era, more moderate critics, who correctly identified and opposed the schools' real shortcomings, also allowed their rhetoric to drift toward sweeping condemnation, calling American schools joyless, autocratic, and oppressive. Many classrooms deserved these descriptions, but, by comparison with other schools throughout

---

Fred M. Hechinger is co-author, with his wife Grace, of the recently published book Growing Up in America, *a social history of the United States viewed through the perspective of education.*

the world, the all-inclusive image of a failed system was deceptive. It reinforced the destructive call for the "deschooling" of America, made popular by the neo-Marxist pamphleteering of Ivan Illich.

Had the decade of such revolutionary dilettantism been followed by a new era of prosperity and expansive optimism, the irrational interlude would have done little harm. But when the Seventies, after the disaster of Watergate, sank into the gloom of recession, unemployment, and little or no economic growth, the festering doubts about education as a force for social progress created an environment in which the anti-education and anti-intellectual virus flourished.

Hadn't some sociologists from such bastions as Harvard proclaimed education's failure to deliver the promised goods of economic equality and collective happiness? Hadn't respected think tanks, particularly those under contract to the Nixon administration, reported that all those strength-through-learning Great Society programs had come to naught? Hadn't Project Headstart, which not long ago was expected to wipe out the handicaps imposed on youngsters by decades of discrimination and neglect, fallen short of its promise? Never mind that none of these programs had been given either the funds or the time which their sponsors had always considered essential. With money suddenly even scarcer and the ax poised, all these doubts added up to a powerfully persuasive argument against the continuing support of education.

The immediately visible results of the recession did the rest. A college diploma and even a PhD no longer guaranteed a job, certainly not a position commensurate with the academic credentials. Only a few years ago, the industrial recruiters often outnumbered the graduating seniors on college campuses; during the turbulent Sixties, moreover, these very recruiters, viewed by dissident students as the handmaidens of the military-industrial complex, had been hooted off the campuses; now the recruiters have largely disappeared.

Gloomy forecasts predicted that by the decade's end hundreds of thousands of PhD recipients would have to take jobs considerably below their academic station, displacing equal numbers of those with only bachelors' degrees, who in turn would bump job-seeking high-school graduates. The 1975 starting salaries for male college graduates in industry dropped sharply. As a result, so did

the "return on the college investment" projected over a graduate's future working years—from an estimated 11 to 12 percent in 1969 to only 7 to 8 percent five years later. Between the class of 1958 and that of 1972, the proportion of new graduates holding non-professional, non-managerial jobs rose by 15 and 20 percent, respectively, for men and women, according to a study by Richard Freeman and Herbert Hollomon of the Center for Policy Alternatives at the Massachusetts Institute of Technology. At each level, then, education seemed no longer to be delivering the goods.

The educational image-builders were not without blame. Throughout the expansive years, they had indeed over-advertised the material rewards of college. Posters in buses and subways gave prospective students precise estimates of hard cash that would come their way. Dropping out was translated into nothing more than dollar losses. It is hardly surprising that such simplistic definitions of education's value invited an equally simplistic reaction: when the dollar value of education declined in a shaken job market, education itself took a nose dive in the public's esteem.

A question that today greets a speaker on any educational topic is almost invariably: "Aren't we sending too many people to college?" The unmistakable implication is that one should not waste the time and money when college can't deliver a lucrative job and a promising career.

Forgotten, amid such purely materialistic assessments, is the fact that young people have always gone to college for a variety of reasons, including getting a better perspective on themselves and the world, and doing so in the company of other post-adolescents. "Ten years after they leave college," says Harold Howe II, the Ford Foundation's vice-president for education and a former U.S. commissioner of education, "a very high proportion of them will find themselves doing a job they never prepared themselves for in high school or college.

"To suggest that such decisions might best be reached by telling youngsters and their parents that the return on the investment they make in a college education has declined from 11 percent in 1969 to 8 percent in 1974," Howe adds, "is at best a questionable practice. But if we are going to do it, we ought to tell them at the same time that the return from money spent on college is still much larger than if it were invested in

life insurance, savings banks, or the stock market."

Commissions headed by sociologists and other prestigious opinion-makers have recently been pounding away at the theme: how best to reduce the number of years of compulsory schooling. Ironically, less than a decade ago, and with the advice and consent of some of the same experts, the pressure was toward the extension of public education from 12 to 14 years, to include not only high school but also two years of college. Today, the wind is blowing in the opposite direction. The fashionable advice is to let youngsters cut short their formal education, to enter into the world of work at an earlier age, to make up their minds about their future careers sooner, and to become engaged in specialized, rather than general, education.

The Nixon administration's educational spokesmen began to push the newly reactivated concept of "career education." Children, from elementary school onward, were to be encouraged to view their school days with an eye on career choices. Books were published, guidelines were written, teacher workshops were held. Federal appropriations for the purpose rose from $9 million in 1971 to $61 million by 1974, at which time one-third of the nation's 17,000 school districts included career education in their operations.

Meanwhile, higher-education costs skyrocketed. At leading private colleges, the annual bill for tuition and board now exceeds $6,000. Stanford University recently warned future applicants that non-scholarship students for the four undergraduate years would be charged about $30,000. The State University of New York is expected to raise its tuition to nearly $1,000 some time this year.

Free tuition at New York's City University has come under heavy attack as a fiscally untenable concept. Politicians throughout the country, led by the President himself, have singled out the 128-year freedom from tuition, which had until recently been hailed as a shining example of sound social policy, as exhibit A in the case against New York's fiscal irresponsibility. All this despite the fact that the amount of money at issue is minuscule in an institution that serves mainly indigent students who would continue to be entitled to scholarships. What is at issue is the *new* principle— to make sure that nobody gets a free educational ride. This is the exact opposite of the principle that used to guide

American thinking: let the greatest possible number benefit from education.

If free tuition is only a minor skirmish on the sidelines, the impact of steadily rising tuition on what might be called the heartland of the population—the working and lower-middle class—is a matter for serious concern. It should be seen as a warning that the retreat from the educational commitment is turning into a rout.

When even low-cost public institutions require an annual investment for tuition, room, and board approaching $3,000 for one child in college, the family in the $10,000-to-$15,000 income bracket is on the point of being squeezed out. Attendance at the elite colleges will become virtually impossible for youths from such homes. Thus, only a select few from the poverty level and the very rich will find it possible to attend. Higher education, which has scored significant triumphs in assuring upward mobility and preventing the stratification of American society, is in danger of being forced to move in the opposite direction —to restratify America.

The issues can be easily identified, along with the political consequences that will have to be faced if the present regression is not halted. These are the major areas of concern:

UNIVERSALITY OF SCHOOLING. Under a variety of guises, pressure has been increasing to reduce the number of years of compulsory education. From the left the pressure has been generated primarily by claims that compulsory education is a form of oppression by the State, depriving children of their "right" not to go to school. (It is interesting to recall that a conservative Supreme Court in 1918 struck down a law prohibiting child labor on very similar grounds—the protection of the children's "right" to work.) From the right, and increasingly from the center as well, the pressure has been generated by a vague sense that the "work ethic" needs shoring up, and the trend has been helped along by educators who want to get rid of difficult students.

A strong case can be made for encouraging some students to combine school and work, in the hope that the two activities will reinforce each other. Rigid insistence on a fixed number of school years for all is neither good sense nor good pedagogy. Much can be said for California's new plan to let students leave school early, provided they are able to pass a proficiency examination.

What is disturbing is the growing advocacy by many divergent political, economic, and educational authorities of letting great numbers of youths opt out, without any effective academic controls. The consequence of such a breach in the dike of universal education is predictable. Those who will leave school—initially by being allowed to drop out and eventually by being surreptitiously pushed out—will not come from the mainstream of affluence. They will be the children of poverty and neglect. While such dropping out should not be expected to worry the political right, it is a remarkable testimony to either the naiveté or the callousness of those on the left who, in opposing compulsory schooling, ignore the historical evidence: the children of the rich have always been educated, with or without official compulsion; it is only for many children of the poor that the end of compulsory education will mean the end of educational opportunity.

THE NEW VOCATIONALISM. Strong currents of political and economic conservatism have raised questions about the value of general education. Although the proponents of specialization and career education insist that they want only what is best for each youngster, it is easy to foresee what the "new realism"—President Ford has already elevated the slogan to the position of his administration's ideology—may eventually mean in practice. The challenge of open horizons will be replaced by appeals to keep sights realistically low. The past era of rising expectations has had its pitfalls, but it was more in keeping with the American dream than was the impending era of modest aspirations.

It is one of the ironies of the new trend that vocationalism is particularly counterproductive in an uncertain economy, when jobs are both scarce and changeable. It makes slim indeed the chances of picking the right specialization years in advance of actual entry into the labor market. The writer of a recent article in *The New York Times Magazine* extravagantly extolling the virtues of New York's Aviation High School appeared unaware of its own ultimate contradiction: only 6 members of last June's 515-member graduating class reported that they had found jobs in the aviation industry. The primary reason for youth unemployment is not lack of training but lack of jobs.

EVEN SUCH specific objections are secondary to the more fundamental risk that conservatives will begin—openly or covertly—to sort out youngsters at an early age to be dispatched toward a preordained future on career-oriented tracks. This would be a sharp break with what in the liberal view has been American education's crowning achievement— keeping the options open by avoiding premature typecasting of children. Past experience shows that early focus on the children's prospects as adults reinforces the status quo of class and caste. America has probably progressed beyond the likelihood of a relapse to the days when Malcolm X, an honors student in a Midwestern high school, on informing his English teacher that he wanted to become a lawyer, was told: "A lawyer—that's not a realistic goal for a nigger." Yet, even in a society that has conquered such virulent racism, many educators still show a wide gap in their perceptions of what constitutes a "realistic goal" for the rich and for the poor.

Countries around the world, inspired by the success of America's open educational road, are abandoning their preselection. It would be an ironic tragedy if the United States were, at this very time, to retreat to a system which would aggravate, and freeze into a permanent mold, the differences in class and wealth.

RETREAT FROM HIGHER EDUCATION. As the argument against the benefits of higher education gathers force, the colleges will lose their capacity to infuse new blood into the nation's power structure. For nearly a century the campuses have increasingly fulfilled the function of elevating young people above their parents' station and of letting them infiltrate the executive suites, board rooms, and bastions of political influence.

Despite such democratization, the cards are still stacked in favor of the wellborn. Census figures for 1973 show that 53.7 percent of the college-age children of families with incomes of $15,000 and more were attending college. The proportion went downhill in direct relation to earnings until it reached a low of 12.7 percent for the same age group from poverty-level homes. In the past two years, moreover, the percentage of college attendance among youths from lower-middle-class families has declined sharply.

If this trend continues, young Americans from the old, established college "class" will increasingly dominate the campuses. Instead of helping to broaden the socioeconomic mix of the nation's leadership, higher education will then revert to its original restrictive function —to give children of inherited wealth an ever larger share of society's controlling positions.

Recognition of these developments without exposing and opposing them amounts to nothing less than complicity in democracy's slow strangulation. To avert such a catastrophe, ways must be found to change the present mood of political vacuity and public apathy. New and effective spokesmen must argue education's case, not in the present parochial singsong of those who simply bewail their own institutions' fiscal plight, but with a persuasive outline of future goals.

Without projecting a compelling, forward-looking agenda, education's leaders cannot hope to arouse the American people from the self-centered preoccupation with their own economic troubles. The public will not help to rescue the schools and colleges unless these institutions spell out once again what they can do for the American people.

But history has also shown that American education cannot change the nation's policies by getting too far ahead of those who wield political power. Alert political leaders, and eventually the government itself, must join with academic authorities, particularly but not exclusively those in the universities, in charting a future that harnesses education's capacities as a progressive social force. "The university cannot tell the people what it can do for them," said Ernest Boyer, chancellor of the State University of New York, "unless the government knows where it wants to go and what the university can do to help it get there."

Apathy is the fruit of interlocking aimlessness. Perhaps the demand for a new sense of purpose, based on the belief that beyond the recession lies an American future, will have to come from the people themselves. In the late Forties, when education was also in the doldrums after the hiatus of the Great Depression and World War II, a massive non-partisan campaign was mounted by the National Citizens Commission for the Public Schools. It managed to move public education onto the center of the nation's stage.

It may well be that a similar movement, this time to include the colleges and universities, may have to be launched to mount a coast-to-coast campaign for halting the retreat and going forward again. In this Bicentennial year no other objective seems more urgent than helping the American people regain their faith in education. The incentive to do so is elemental: to prevent the decline and fall of American democracy.

OLD-FASHIONED HERO OF THE NEW WORKING CLASS

OILCAN EDDIE SADLOWSKI
*'There's a fire in the steelworkers union,
and I'm not gonna piss on it.'*

By Joe Klein

The only logical place for this story to begin is in a bar:

Lombardi's, on the South Side of Chicago, a neighborhood joint where steelworkers hang out, drinking glasses of beer with shots of whiskey on the side. By day, it's a shadowy hole populated by older men who sit quietly pondering their hands—which often have several fingers missing, fingers they left behind in the mills. By night, the desperation turns boisterous. The room is suffused with a musty yellow light from behind the bar. A ballgame is on the tube. There are loud belches and guffaws and arguments over baseball, women, work . . . you name it.

Twenty-five years ago, when Ed Sadlowski would stop by Lombardi's with his shoeshine kit, they used to kick him out. He was a pain in the ass, a street kid bothering the patrons. Now, he's as close to a celebrity as they get in Lombardi's. At the relatively tender age of 37, he is the director of District 31, United Steelworkers of America. There are 130,000 men and women who work in the steel mills of Chicago and northern Indiana who are hoping that Ed Sadlowski will make their lives a little better. There are others who are watching him, too: The big shots in business and labor and government who suspect (and fear) that he may be this country's next great labor leader.

147

He sits down at the end of the bar at Lombardi's, surrounded by steelworkers, shooting the shit. He's well over six feet tall, 220 pounds (about 40 of which are a classic beer belly), with dark hair that often falls down in his eyes, dark eyes under dark eyebrows and a booming voice with a gravelly edge to it. They are talking union politics.

"Don't worry about these guys," he advises his colleagues. "I'm serious, we'll kick their ass."

"We'll get ax handles," jokes a steelworker with silvery hair. "Like that governor down South . . . Madigan."

"Yeah, like Maddox," Ed laughs. "Ax handles."

For the past several years, Ed Sadlowski and his pals have been waging a successful guerrilla war against the bilious autocrats who run big labor in this country. It is a rebellion that is pretty close to unique in the dreary world of labor politics since World War II—and probably as significant as the ouster of Tony Boyle and his thugs from the United Mine Workers Union after dissident leader Joseph Yablonski was murdered.

It began as a rebellion against Joe Germano, who had run District 31 (the largest of 22 steelworkers' districts in the country) with an iron fist since 1942. Germano was a tough guy, a pal of Mayor Daley's. He is best described by an old steelworker named Ray. "Joe started out okay. He was a real 'dese and dose' guy. But he changed over the years. He forgot about the guys in the mills. I guess he ate too many dinners at tables with tablecloths on them."

By the time Germano decided to retire in 1973, there were not many steelworkers who could say they'd even *seen* him. For his successor, Germano chose a bland functionary named Sam Evett, who had spent most of his life in the district office. Like many second-generation labor leaders, Evett seemed to have more in common with management than with the guys in the mills.

But Evett was the heavy favorite to succeed Germano. For one thing, he had the support of the "official family" of the United Steelworkers—the union staff from International President I.W. Abel down to the officers of the 288 locals that comprised District 31. In the past, such support had been enough not only to assure victory but also to discourage any competition. For another thing, when it came election time, Evett's people cheated.

Sadlowski, on the other hand, started working in the mills when he was 18 and was first elected to local union office when he was 22. His father had been a steelworker and so had his grandfather. "I didn't get involved because of any romantic reason like the boss punched me in the nose and I wanted to fight back, I just wanted to be part of the labor movement," Sadlowski says. He was a natural leader and rose quickly through the ranks.

"When we announced we were going to challenge Evett, people laughed," says Clem Balanoff, a friend who helped run the Sadlowski campaign. "I mean, no one ever did that, It was practically impossible to even get on the ballot: You had to get 18 of the 288 locals to nominate you and that was a lot tougher than it sounded. Evett's people would block us from meetings . . . hell, we didn't even know where half the locals in the district *were* and we couldn't find out because the district headquarters wouldn't give us the list."

Eventually Sadlowski got 40 locals to support his candidacy and the race was on. His slogan was: "It's time to fight back," and he campaigned at the plant gates, the union halls, the bars. His message was simple: "Times are tough and they're getting worse. High prices. Poor shop conditions. Not enough job security. Our union should be fighting back but we're falling farther and farther behind. . . ." It was like big government, didn't care about your basic populist appeal: Big labor, like big government, didn't care about the little guy—it was time to put

District 31 back in the hands of the rank and file.

Clem Balanoff remembers election night in February 1973: "We were winning by maybe three, four thousand votes. But then, about midnight, the results stopped coming in. . . . Now, in Chicago politics this can mean only one thing: It means they're stealing the election." Sure enough, when the returns started to come in again, Evett slipped ahead.

Sadlowski cried foul, hired the noted labor lawyer Joe Rauh (who'd also defended the dissident Mine Workers) and sued the union. The U.S. Department of Labor investigated and found massive fraud. Another election was held in November 1974, this time with federal supervision, and this time Sadlowski clobbered Evett, almost two to one. "When we won, everything was going crazy." Balanoff remembers. "They were shouting, 'It's over. It's finally over.' But I told them it wasn't over, it was just beginning. We had just taken on the most monumental task of our lives."

Bob is a steelworker in Joliet. He's in his mid-30s and wears a goatee and slicked back brown hair:

Why did I support Ed? I don't know. I read this story in the 'Sun-Times' about the election and how this young guy with a "ski" on the end of his name who used to work midnight shift in the machine shop was running against some hand picked flunky who never worked a day in a mill in his life. I work midnights and I know what

it's like: You watch a little 'Johnny Carson' and then you go to work. And then you get out in the morning when most normal people are starting their days. I figured a guy who worked midnights in the machine shop would know what that's all about, so I voted for him.

The biggest problem we have now is that most guys take everything for granted. They see vacations and holidays and time and a half and they figure that management just gives you that shit. They don't know that people had to fight for it . . . Hell, there ain't three or four guys in the shop who know ten people were killed by the cops at Republic Steel in 1937 . . . and the only reason I know is that Ed told me a couple of months ago. And that's what I think Ed is about. I think he wants to get us back to having the same kind of attitude guys had in those days.

"I want you to hear the greatest recording of the human voice ever made," Ed Sadlowski says. He puts on a 1906 version of the Irish tenor John McCormack singing the aria, "Il Mio Tesoro" from *Don Giovanni* by Mozart. Ed closes his eyes, his head sways slowly with the music. He opens his eyes, "Huh? What do you think of that? Great shit, huh?"

We are in Sadlowski's basement, which is a mess like the rest of his house. He's been trying to refinish the house for the last few years, with the help of his wife, Marlene, and their four children. But Ed has been busy with the union and Marlene has been busy with school (she recently got an associate degree in psychology), so the place has remained unfinished and in constant turmoil. It is a modest brick home in a neighborhood of modest brick homes sandwiched in among the steel mills on Chicago's Southeast Side. It is about a mile from the Republic Steel plant where the massacre occurred in 1937, the year before Ed was born.

His father told him about it when he was a kid—the strikers' peaceful Memorial Day picnic, the fiery speeches, the march on the factory, the shots, ten dead and many more wounded—and it remains a central fact of Ed Sadlowski's life. In a time when many labor leaders see themselves as "partners" of big business, he sees himself as an adversary. There is labor and there is management and woe to those who seek to smudge the line . . . like Steelworkers president I.W. Abel, who makes $75,000 per year and, Sadlowski says, "has begun to *think* that he makes $75,000 per year." But even so, even though Abel has become Sadlowski's prime target, "I would still take Abel

over the most liberal banker."

The Republic massacre lives on in Ed's basement, along with Homestead, Pullman and the other great labor struggles. There are stacks of books about labor history, copies of old union songs (Ed knows all the words), pictures and posters. His prize possession, though, is an old loose-leaf binder with copies of union documents from the Thirties. "Take a look at this," he says, "this is great stuff . . . I got a copy of the check John L. Lewis sent to help pay for the funerals of the guys who were killed at Republic. . . ."

And it *is* great stuff. Frantic telegrams from Chicago to Steelworkers headquarters in Pittsburgh, and back again. Rabble-rousing speeches. Reports of "gunmen hired by the company" threatening the workers. "Here, you see that signature?" Ed says, flipping a page. "George Patterson. He was the first president of local 65, my home local. He's still alive and one of my big supporters. We held this dinner for him and he got up to speak—it was about the time the police killed Fred Hampton here—and he says, 'I see the police killed two young black guys because they called themselves Panthers. I can remember when *we* were the Panthers.' After all those years, he still had the instincts. I mean, this was just a week after the shooting and the liberals were still trying to figure out what kind of position to take . . . and he *knew*."

"Ed," I say, "you're a romantic."

"Fuck you," he replies. "A romantic! A romantic could of never won that election."

In the old days, of course, labor leaders were a bunch of romantics (with the exception of an occasional stick-in-the-mud like Samuel Gompers) who rode the rails from town to town, speaking, organizing and not worrying about the details. Big Bill Haywood and Eugene Debs didn't spend much time bothering with pension funds, seniority squabbles or grievances. Ed Sadlowski has to do it every day.

Early one morning last summer, he drove across the state line to the District 31 office in East Chicago, Indiana. He drove past refineries and factories, through clouds of yellow smoke and godawful smells—the great corporations jammed up against each other on the shores of Lake Michigan. He was wearing a mint green short-sleeve shirt, dark green pants and large awkward black tie shoes. He had a Samsonite attaché case and was listening to some actors reciting Edgar Lee Masters's *Spoon River Anthology* on the radio.

The union headquarters was located

in a drab bank building and it resembled nothing so much as the principal's office in a high school. It was cold, metallic; lots of file cabinets and adding machines. Ed's office had a big desk and a conference table, several chairs for visitors, plywood paneling on the walls and the office equivalent of Astroturf on the floor. Also on the floor was a frammed photo of John L. Lewis which Ed had yet to hang.

There was a pile of telephone messages on his desk, a stack of mail and a pile of expense accounts to okay. He looked at the telephone messages one by one—complaints, grievances, health compensation, seniority. He began making calls, "Hello, Ed Sadlowski here . . . what can I do for you? . . . oh yeah? . . . what about your staff guy? . . . that figures . . . all right, I'll see what I can do." The conversation repeated itself about a half-dozen times during the next few hours. The key question was, "What about your staff guy?" The answer, invariably: "He doesn't do shit."

The union staff, which is supposed to handle the day-to-day problems, was never any great shakes to begin with. They were Germano's boys and they remain so, and there isn't all that much Sadlowski can do about it. I.W. Abel controls the budget, pays the salaries, and the staffers know that Abel would not be overly upset if Sadlowski's administration was made to look bad.

Later in the morning, five rather elderly black workers came into the office. They seemed even more uncomfortable than Sadlowski, sitting with their hats in their hands, not sure whether they should call him "Ed" or "Mr. Sadlowski." They described a very complex seniority problem; it was costing them a lot of money. Ed asked them if race had anything to do with it. They weren't sure but suspected so. "What about your staff guy?"

"He doesn't do shit."

"I'll see what I can do," Ed said. "If you don't hear from me by Thursday, give me a call. I mean it. Call me at home."

The men left and I said, "They seemed to be begging."

"Yeah," Ed said. "If we could ever get more guys to come in here and start demanding. . . ."

After another frustrating hour of phone calls, we left the office and drove to Gary where Ed was to do a radio show and then talk to some steelworkers. On the way, we talked about the staff problem. "You take a guy who's been working for the union 20 years in his shop. A good guy," Ed said. "And you give him a staff job because he's earned it. Now that pays $17,000 per year with a car and expenses. So one day this guy is going to work with a brown bag for lunch and the next day he's sitting across the table from management . . . and they're calling each other by their first names. They're pals . . . and that's the way it happens.

"The first time I ever rode on a jet plane, the union paid for it. They flew me to New York, and there I was at the Roosevelt eating New York strip steak, and the union was paying for it. . . ."

"So how come it didn't happen to you?" I asked. "How come you didn't turn out like the others?"

"I don't know. Maybe because I was younger, a different generation."

"You still could be bought, you know."

"Yeah, yeah . . . but I think I know their game," he said. "The biggest thing management has had going over the years in this game of divide and conquer—especially between blacks and whites. Like my pa·used to tell me about the sharecroppers down South. The black sharecropper would get a house that was just a little better than the white guy . . . but the white guy would get a dime more on a bale of cotton than the black. And so they'd always be jealous of each other about something and always fighting each other instead of the boss. Management's still doing that kind of thing.

"You can't be a union man and a racist. No way. You can't be a union man and be a redneck. I just can't handle that kind of shit. A guy will come up to me and say nigger this and nigger that and I'll just unload on him—you don't know me, I can be a mean sonofabitch. There's no way you can be a union man and a racist."

Jerry, age 28, is a steelworker in Gary. He has long blond hair and a moustache:

I'm laid off now but, I expect to go back soon. I'm next on the list to go back and I'm lookin' forward to it. The work ain't hard, the pay is pretty good —I make about $18,000 a year [the average steelworker makes about $14,-500 per year]*—I love the union and the guys I work with. I'm an electrician; there are about 50 guys on my crew and we stick together, you know? Something comes down and 42 of us'll back the guy who gets in trouble. And it pays off. For example, we wanted to have the company fix up the shanties where we take our breaks—put in air conditioning and picnic tables. Well, the company says no . . . and then things start happening in the plant.* [Laughs] *Things start breaking down. Wires get crossed. You know what I mean? Pretty soon the company fixes up the shanties.*

You ask me about politics. I don't know. None of those guys turn me on. I guess I'd vote for Kennedy if he ran but I don't think he's gonna. Wallace? I kinda like Wallace. He's against government gettin' out of hand the way it is, with 20 guys doin' a job one man can handle. He's against big business too, I think. He says things the average guy can understand. . . .

The radio show in Gary was rather bland. Ed Sadlowski doesn't get too specific when talking about politics these days. First, although he'd probably be loathe to admit it, he has to be careful. There's been a lot of red-baiting directed against him. Second, there isn't all that much you *can* say about politics these days without making a fool of yourself one way or another. National politics he dismisses brusquely: "Those guys are just sitting on their dicks. They should start calling each other bastards."

Local politicians fare not much bet-

'I don't have any strategy. I don't go for any of those 'isms.' It's really simple: People are hungry, you feed 'em.'

ter. Ed was one of the few Chicago labor leaders who refused to support Mayor Daley this year. And when Governor Dan Walker asked if he could speak at a steelworkers' dinner in March, Sadlowski refused. Walker *was* allowed, though, to buy a ticket and sit with rank and file union members.

Asf or discussions of larger, theoretical issues, Sadlowski will drop hints but steers clear of being pinned down. Driving to Gary, I asked him how he'd restructure big business if he could. "That's the ultimate question," he said. "That's the big one. Hell, if I had the answer to that . . ."

He was silent for a moment. Then, pointing to a row of suburban tract houses, "You see, *that's* what you got to contend with. The American Dream. You've got generations who've been brought up with that, had it drummed into their heads in the so-called institutions that are public schools. People believe in that bullshit."

And later, on the radio show: "I don't have any strategy. I don't go for any of those 'isms'—I think they're a trap. If I had to pick an 'ism,' I gues it would be humanism. It's really simply: People are hungry, you feed 'em."

There were several steelworkers waiting in the radio station's lobby and we immediately repaired to the nearest tavern to discuss union politics. The steelworkers were looking for advice: They were staging a miniature Sadlowski-style rebellion of their own, trying to overthrow the entrenched union leadership in their factory's local. "You've got to hit and hit and hit and hit," Ed told them, Knute Rockne style. "You have to keep going to their meetings. Keep plugging."

29

No Pride in This Dust

by Bennett Kremen

Young Workers in the Steel Mills

On a Greyhound speeding through a dark, icy night toward Chicago, I return to old memories of packing lunch bags and pulling on greasy overalls each morning before rushing desperately to beat the factory time clock—months and months of this drudgery my reward for temporarily dropping out of a Chicago high school during the mid-1950s. Now I head once more toward that muscular city on the lake, to struggle again with time clocks and lunch bags—this time driven not by necessity but curiosity.

Only seven others, mostly students picked up in a college town, share the heavy darkness inside the bus. And now, with recent memories of a tough month I've spent in Detroit futilely searching for work in the car plants, I can't help wondering about the boy nearby with the backpack, the long-haired one behind him, the shoeless girls in front of me. For though they're all dressed as insurgents in a rebellion against technology, they surely know little of the sooty bowels of industry, where millions their own age labor each day. Yet I quickly hear bitter voices behind me as we reach the flame-tinted skies over Gary:

"Wow—look at that mess!"

"Yeah, they're even burning up the clouds!"

"Why don't they just turn it all into a frisbee field?"

Laughter travels through the bus, and a flurry of conversation continues all the way into Chicago's Loop. And though I've heard similar exchanges countless times, I couldn't help being impressed again by such intense expressions of "alienation from the tools of production" by these fortunate people, even if it's only fashionable prattle. For they're the ones benefiting the most from industry and grunting the least in its service. What about those who grunt the most?

The sun isn't up yet and the "Hawk," Chicago's cruel wind, lashes down on the thousands of workers huddling at bus stops. Even in my heavy laborer's clothes, this frigid journey to the Southworks is an agony, for that mile-long mill owned by the United States Steel Corporation squats on the damp shore of Lake Michigan. But the final bitter reward for playing the early bird is having to queue up now in the frost outside the gate, waiting for the seven o'clock shift to start.

"That's when they open the employment office, isn't it?"

"Uh-huh."

The fellow I'm talking to has a huge, blond mustache and is wearing an army jacket with Vietnam markings on it; he seems as disgusted as I am.

"Been looking long?" I ask.

"Three months. But I think they're hiring here."

"They are," I assure him. "Maybe we'll get lucky."

"Lucky . . . ?" He shrugs and looks up at the rows of smoke stacks and blast furnaces, ". . . if you want to call it that."

When the gate finally opens, he rushes into the employment office like the rest of us and quickly fills out cards passed out by a guard. This haste, however, is only a wasted effort. The hours trickle away in this increasingly crowded room without a word said to most of us. All we can do is wait and stare.

All around me are young people, many fresh out of high school and the Army—or off the streets of the South Side. Most seem remarkably free of that classical, humble, hungry look of the job hunter. Throughout the morning they stream in like locusts. This isn't only the ordinary consequence of unemployment: crowded into this room are men who were conceived during the baby boom in the 1940s and '50s, now hitting industry as once the country's school systems. And this pounding on the doors can only intensify as the average age of workers in mills and factories continues to tumble dramatically year by year—as it has since 1968. By the end of the decade, 68 percent of the labor force will be below thirty-four, a sharp reversal of the age distributions during the '50s and early '60s. Already men in their twenties comprise a third of organized labor's entire membership.

As I look around, unpredictable things are confronting me. Where are the Polish kids who traditionally flock to this mill? For decades legend has always designated the Southworks, the huge mills next door in East Chicago, and the industrial wilds of Gary below it as a land flowing with *kolbassi* and boilermakers. Yet 70 percent of those here are black—yes, young, black, and beautiful. For they aren't wearing the overalls, that drab, humble uniform of the working stiff: their "vines," man, are their own—purple silk shirts with collars hanging halfway to their waists, fur coats, four-cornered velvet

151

hats, and bright, multicolored shoes that mock this somber environment where roughly 9.5 percent of all U.S. Steel's raw tonnage is poured. Watching these men filing one by one into the interviewing section, their loose ghetto walk declaring the assertiveness of the mean streets of the city, makes me wonder if the steel industry has provided a *confidential* document similar to the gloomy one put out in Detroit in 1969 by Malcolm Denise, Ford Motor Company's top labor-relations man.

"More than 35 percent of [Ford's 1968 work force] . . ." he confided at a company management conference "were nonwhite, compared to 15 percent in 1960." Then, after predicting unique labor troubles because of that anticipated flood of young workers into industry, he concluded with this warning: "Another feature of the landscape in which we will be operating [in the '70s] is our increasing dependence on blacks to get our work done. Whatever some may feel about the black issue in general, we are in fact dependent, and will continue to be, on black people to make this company go."

"Hey," I whisper to the fellow next to me with the big, blond mustache, "are there always so many spades looking for jobs around here?"

"Sure."

"What about in East Chicago?"

"Oh, those dudes are workin' all down the lake, even past Gary."

"What's happened to the Polish people who used to work these places?"

"They're still around—the older ones mostly. A lot of 'em moved away though and never want to come back around here anymore."

"Will working with all these black guys bother you?" I inquire suddenly. For a moment he eyes me warily before responding:

"Will it bother you, man?"

"No."

"Well, I don't give a damn, either."

We keep on talking, trying to beat the boredom of this incessant waiting. He tells me that even the local union president at the Southworks is a black man. Since this local is a large one in one of the largest steel-producing regions in the country, that's probably quite important, I tell him. Well, not only Local 65 but the whole region, he figures, will probably be mostly black in ten years.

"Then for the firse time, we'll see *black power* with real music behind it," I tell him. "And even if the blacks here don't really know it yet, that power probably already exists."

A sudden thoughtfulness—or is it distress—hovers in my young friend's eyes. And quickly I shift away from talk about race, even though he seems too indifferent to really care about it either way—and though that very indifference, if real, intrigues me. For such a sentiment would be a striking departure from the monolithic hatreds that flourished among the men I worked with in this city less than 15 years ago. These questions must remain hanging, for I'm being called for an interview.

Early the next morning, I'm in a room again with about 20 others—most of them young, many of them black—listening to a black personnel man in expensive tweeds playing the lay-it-on-the-line role:

"What I'm telling you now is the same for blacks and whites—there isn't no difference, because at least five of you, that's 25 percent," he says, "won't even last out the six-week probationary period—blacks or whites. But jobs are tight, so more of you might stick it out this year than last. Listen, I ain't going to lie to you—some of those foremen are nothin' but bigots, and I know that. But you don't settle things by hittin' 'em up side the head. And listen," he says with sudden urgency, "you just gotta come in every day; you just gotta come in on time!" And though he speaks now about not keeping valuables in our lockers 'cause dudes searching for marijuana or money will wrench them right open, he expresses far more concern in another plea for us "to get in here every day. If you can't make it, you gotta at least call in and let them know. Man, I don't know why guys don't even call in!"

Though this lecture is inappropriate for the beefy, red-headed fellow next to me droning on about fringe benefits and buying a house with a paneled basement, I'm sure that the man in front of us isn't simply wasting his breath on ominous predictions. And as we're being loaded now into a bus to be taken to our assigned locations, I'm almost convinced that what I'm about to experience might have little resemblance to my working days of—well—*long ago.*

Yet some things are ageless, like this ride through the teeming, fenced-in mill past flatcars loaded down with huge, glowing ingots of raw steel that cast their heat like giant radiators. We bump along past dozens of roads, ore docks, rail lines, and shops, some a block long and hissing and clanging with the sounds of hammers, alarm bells, and deadly molten metal that rears from the furnaces like harsh sunshine. Awe—and a touch of uneasiness—shows on the young faces of those sharing the bus with me, their feelings surely paralleling my own. For to the uninitiated, it seems impossible that all these steaming slag piles and ore boats, blast furnaces and cranes that travel on tracks far above us can be managed by 8,200 mere workers, though they labor around the clock in three swing shifts every day of the year.

"If they ain't got a lot of machines to do all this goddamn work," I announce in a fool-around tone, "we're all gonna have a sore back!"

"I'm hip—better they use a dynamo than Little Joe. They ain't got no spare parts for me, man!"

The laughter is heavy, though only the driver and a few new workers are left in the bus—Little Joe among them. And now, smack on the shore of the lake, where the wind hits like a razor, the driver calls out his last stop—our stop.

"This is #2 Electric Furnace—only a half-hour walking time to the gate."

He is smiling when he says it, but none of us stepping out into the damp cold share his amusement.

"You gotta be jivin' man—you mean from now on we gotta hoof it!"

"That's it, Little Joe—coming in and going out."

A low, angry grumbling at the thought of this cold, payless walk each day fades only gradually as we follow the driver through this noisy, dirty building to the foreman's office. When we enter, the grumbling is over, but a sullen silence remains.

"OK—each of you have a number on the card they gave you. Memorize it, because that's what you're going to be called around here."

31–445 then, is who I am to the pair of foremen in blue hard hats who've just given each of us a bright yellow helmet worn by production workers on labor gangs. For $3.19 an hour then, with a bit extra for late shifts and weekends, we now conclude these sterile preliminaries and don our hard hats, joining tens of thousands of other young workers thus initiated into the lowest ranks of the steel industry.

"Some of you young guys take too many days off! I just don't stand for that shit, or for you comin' in late either!" The sudden tough talk comes from Stanley, the smaller of the two foremen whose unpronouncible Polish last name is tagged to his helmet. The taller one, Mr. Lis, continues now, but in a gentler voice:

"Yeah fellows—you won't get ahead you know, if you do this AWOL stuff. And we want you to get ahead. So you try to watch those absences, huh?"

Neither this easy sell nor the shock tactics seem to ruffle the skepticism of my fellow workers, for they must have sensed, as I did, that Lis and Stanley were only going through a feeble ritual that neither of them really believed would prove effective. Behind Stanley's bluster and Lis's "sincerity" was a note almost of despair.

Had the foremen I'd once worked for displayed such helplessness, I would've been startled. But I'd already heard young workers in Detroit barrooms and bowling alleys groaning about having to face another day of tedium on the assembly line and boasting about how often they'd gone AWOL.

"Your generation hated that line too," a clever old workingman told me in a bar off Cadillac Square, "but you had a lot of guys proud to work for them big companies in those days. Remember that type? These kids have a different outlook on life. They've never been broke the way we were, and they've got a hell-of-a-lot more schoolin'. You want to know somethin'—*they don't even know how to take the crap we took!*"

Though he didn't speak of affluence and alienation, of levels of aspiration and the breakdown of traditional motivations, that old-timer summarized much of what I'd heard for almost a month from union officials, economists, and worried business executives all over Detroit: a mood of quiet despair descends in those executive offices when they lay out the statistics on their absenteeism problem and speculate on its long-range effects.

"From 1957 to '61" I was told at Ford, "we averaged 2.6 percent of our production workers off on a given day. Each year since then, the figure rose until it reached 5.8 percent in 1968. On Mondays and Fridays though, the figure often goes almost to 15 percent. And that really hurts inside those plants. Right now we're averaging 5.1 percent for the year."

"You mean you're still averaging that high even after three years of recession and inflation?"

"Yes."

"Then you're going to need chronic economic trouble to cut that figure—or a catastrophe."

"I guess so—but believe me, nobody's praying for it!"

At General Motors I was told by a major official that productivity and the quality of cars coming off the line are affected adversely by absenteeism—and that it enhances inflation. "This is a serious matter, and we certainly talked about it quite a bit with the union during the 1970 negotiations. These absences are occurring in every geographical area—and all races and types of people are involved." Though only 15 percent of the work force at GM generates most of the late arrivals and absences, he went on, most of these men are concentrated among the newer workers under 35. "They often take one or even two days off every week." When I asked him what he thought the outcome will be if this continues, I was given a brief lecture on the fall of Rome. Although this sort of instant Latin scholarship usually makes me impatient, I was impressed by his calm pessimism; for it was dramatic as perhaps only an immensely powerful man's pessimism can be when an element of habitual control is suddenly defying his grasp.

"It happened in the schools; it's happening in the Army—" Louie Streho, an old salt running the Detroit branch of the seamen's union, told me. "Why the hell did they ever think it wouldn't happen in the factories!"

In the mill now, as I lean leisurely on one of the brooms Stanley had thrust upon us, I begin to wonder about all this unexpected time I seem to have just to muse about things like Louie's bit of wisdom. I soon find out, from a few old mill hands, that these brooms we're pushing around often just keep us busy until enough men are AWOL—and we're really needed.

Yanagan, Charlie Chan, Scatterbrain, his brother Nobrain, Measles, Big John—almost everyone in the mills gets a nickname, including me after the second week:

"Out late last night, huh?" I hear while half asleep in the labor shack, a tiny room where the men warm up in this freezing, open building.

"Yeah," I tell Stash, one of the few older Polish guys still coming in here since the young blacks arrived.

"Chasin' whores, huh Ben . . . that's it—*Ben Whore!*" Everybody laughs except those still asleep, but they don't remain that way long:

"Get up—it's Biz!"

Four of my young friends leap up from their daze and dart out onto the floor away from the crotchety foreman: Stash heads upstairs where the electric furnace is blazing—and the big pay's made. I follow Yanagan, the burner, who lights up his torch and starts cutting up scrap, but only until Biz passes out of sight.

"Come on Ben Whore—let's get away from here!"

"Hey, that's some name Stash gave me."

"Yeah—he's all right."

"Why do most of those guys upstairs stay out of the labor shack, Yanni?"

"Why?—'cause they're jive-ass bigots!"

"Are the younger workers the same way?"

"Uh-uh—some of those white boys are all right—not all of 'em; but a lot are gettin' hip. We wrote a petition to get a new union man for this shop, and none of those lilly-asses upstairs would sign it, but those young dudes did."

"What about the union—you for it?"

"You gotta be—or this company'll fuck you up good! But none of us really gives a shit about the union, 'cause no kind of big shot is goin' to make it any different in here."

"How do you want it to be different, Yanni?"

"I don't know man—just different, *real* different."

Yanagan leads me through a dark corner of the shop now, his eyes cast cautiously at the overhead cranes scooping up scrap for the insatiable furnaces upstairs.

"Psssst!! Hey!"

Hissing at us from behind a half-filled gondola car is Tommy Thumbs, and huddled uncommonly close to him are Little Joe, two vets recently back from Vietnam, and the new Italian kid.

"It's a downer day, man—let's lift it up!" Tommy passes a joint to Yanagan who draws the smoke deep, then hands it to me. For a moment I hesitate till Little Joe pats me on the shoulder and says: "What you waiting for? When you're feeling bad, you take medicine, right? Well, this place makes you feel sick, and you got the medicine right in your hand!"

The smoke striking into my lungs sends my blood leaping. And soon the flying sparks, the hot steel, the raging, exploding furnaces above us seem like frivolities on a carnival night.

Not all the mills in the country are quite like this one, I'm told. But old hands insist they will be, as the older workers retire in the next five years.

"Maybe some big doses of economic trouble will shape these kids up," a toughminded company man told me in Pittsburgh. "But that's liable to murder us too. And I'd hate to see too many of this breed out on the streets without jobs. I just don't think it'd be healthy." Others both in Pittsburgh and Detroit reminded me that plenty of the younger workers—indeed many I've met—are diligently paying off mortgages and working hard for a second car, "and when that other type gets older and has a few kids, everything'll probably settle down." Yet when I asked what'll happen until then, I got only a shrug of the shoulders. A few clever economists, however, point out that the steel industry has invested more than $10 billion in capital expenditures since 1965, but that the expected soaring increases in productivity associated with such a huge investment hasn't materialized. The "productivity puzzle" is what this unprecedented mystery, found not only in the steel industry, is being called. And it's haunting the financial wizards of Wall Street and Washington. I recommend they spend a few days in a labor shack getting it all straight.

"Tommy—you've been out for two days. Don't you miss the bread?"

"I can get by. I rather have the time than the money."

"You know—if jobs stay tight, the company'll probably start cracking down hard."

A sudden, angry silence falls, and all the men in the shack are staring at me. But I keep on talking because after four weeks of digging choking lime from degasser pits, hooking scrap to cranes, and sweeping miles of dust and grime into neat little piles the way they do, I'm entitled to their trust. "What if they crack down, Yanni?"

"They don't own me, man! If I want a day off, I take a day off. Nothin's gonna stop that!"

"What if they fire you?"

"Then let 'em fire me. I ain't seen 'em do it yet."

"Why not?"

" 'Cause the next guy who comes along is going to do the same thing I am."

Everybody in the room is laughing—not at me or Yanagan but at the company, that slightly ridiculous Goliath they so easily can thumb their nose at. For just the other day when Biz, that old Yankee workhorse, caught Charlie Chan sleeping in the locker room, he rolled his cigar in his mouth and began barking:

"Get to work! You know you shouldn't be lying around in here—go on now!"

"Fuck you Jack!" Charlie hissed up at him.

"Get your coat mister!"

"Shut up, or I'll shove that cigar right down your throat!"

"You get the hell home!"

Charlie is laughing now as he tells us how mellow it was having the rest of the day off even though he lost the pay, and how he came in ten minutes late the next morning and not a word was said.

"Don't you care at all about getting the work done, Charlie?"

"They don't care about me—whether I'm livin' or dying! Why should I give a shit about them!"

Not all these young men are so bitter, and some even work hard—when they show up. But neither whites, blacks, skilled workers, laborers, militants nor conservatives—and there are conservatives—are thankful to the company for providing them with jobs.

"Oh—that's strictly Mickey Mouse," a young Polish millwright with hair flowing from under his hard hat said to me. "You find some guys upstairs talking that way—but not many my age. This company is using me to make money: I use them the same way. And that's all. . . ."

Another skilled worker, this one with short hair, who averages at least $5 an hour and who moonlights as a cop in the suburbs where he lives, told me: "The job's not bad, but this company stinks. You don't get anything from them without a fight."

"What about the union?"

"You got to keep on their ass too."

"Any niggers working in your unit?"

"A few."

"Don't they bother you?"

"No—why should they?"

"Plenty of older guys can't stand them."

"Some of the younger guys can't stand them either —but I don't think we're so steamed up about them. I'll tell you something, a lot of those black guys won't take any crap from the company. I don't mind working with them at all."

A few weeks later Ed Hojnachi, the treasurer at Local 65 of the Steelworkers union, my local, told me that he first realized things were profoundly changing when Bob Hatch, a black man, was elected president of 65. I answered that I wasn't at all surprised this had happened, "not after what I've been hearing in the mill. And you know Ed, a lot of locals in the Auto Workers have been taken by blacks too—with strong support from some young white workers."

"Well, it's about time. I guess they want a fighter these days—whoever he is."

"Yes—and maybe its' about time," I hear echoed from Ed Sadlowski, who nine years ago, in an era when local union power simply wasn't challenged, took the presidency of 65. He was only 23 then: today he's Bob Hatch's strongest supporter and, at 32, has his eye on the leadership of the entire Chicago–Gary–Milwaukee–Joliet district—a crucial one in the 1.2 million-man United Steelworkers of America.

"Of course there are changes coming," he says as he tours me now through the Bush, the neighborhood around the mill where the skies blaze every night and the barrooms are seldom empty. "In 1965—get this!—only a few hundred disciplines were issued to the guys in the Southworks. Guess how many the company gave out last year?" The number must have leaped, I was sure, but to hear just how much stuns me: ". . . that's right, 3,400 disciplines in 1970—for coming late, for not coming at all, for swearing, arguing, drinking. And the company guys are moaning. They'd love the union to play copper and get everyone in on time for 'em—sure!"

"What do you tell them?"

"No sir—that's not my job. 'Make life better in those mills!' That's what I tell them."

Eddie takes me for a shot and a beer to a bar with music from Durango or Huahuaca blaring from its juke box, an establishment run by a brother of his friend and colleague from Local 65, Johnny Chico; then through the black section of the Bush where exhausted frame houses hug the edge of the Southworks; and finally to Marti and Joe's at the mill gate where, this time, polkas from Cracow or Warsaw blast from the juke box.

Men fresh off the second shift with mill dust still in their throats eagerly belly up to the bar. Its blunt, plain mahogany and the heavy laughter of the men leaning against it would be home to John Garfield—except for the TV flashing images from outer space and the long-haired young worker next to us in the red-white-and-blue cleatless track shoes.

Soon Eddie begins talking to him and his drinking partner who works in the same shop. He asks why they don't come to union meetings, and they tell him that they're boring. He asks if they'd like to see things changing in the mill. They would. He asks if a lot of other young workers feel that way too. Many do. Then what can be done to make those changes come about? Their answer is a feeble shrug.

"Listen," he says, "you got to give more if you want more. I don't mean just wanting cash—I mean a better life. The union has to give more too. Sure, bread and butter's important—but maybe we spend too much time just thinking about money. Those companies (if they know what's good for them) and the unions too—everybody should be thinking, and soon, about giving people better lives."

Snow is blowing in through the open doors of the shop and steam rising from a slag pile by the lake turns suddenly eerie as the late-shift moon breaks through the clouds. The month is coming to an end, and so are my last hours in the mill. Despite the ceaseless clanging of metal echoing through the shop, the early morning brings a rare calm.

"Say José—did they really used to fire you after only three disciplines?" I'm talking to an intense, talkative old laborer who'd been in the mill more than 25 years.

"Sure they did. Now some of these young kids got six, seven, even eight of 'em and they're still around."

"How does that make you older workers feel?"

"We laugh."

"No kidding!"

"Sure—'cause those foremen used to be so tough. You'd stop shovelin' for a few minutes, and they'd say, 'What's the matter, you tired?' Now they catch these kids sleepin' on a bench and they don't even say nothin'. We're laughin' all right."

"But aren't you mad at the kids too?"

"Sometimes, especially when you gotta carry the load for 'em. But I'll tell you, they've made gentlemen out of a lot of those company guys—not the big shots, I mean the company guys right here in the plants."

"What's going to happen after you older fellows retire, and it's only younger workers in here?"

"I don't know—sometimes we wonder if there's gonna be a mill anymore. One thing's sure—it ain't gonna be the way it used to be!"

The sun is finally rising over the lake now, and tired men with dirt-streaked faces begin trudging into the locker room. After good-byes to José, I join the others at the huge wash basins and, imitating those around me, fiercely scrub the mill from my skin like a guilty man. How determined Yanagan, Tommy Thumbs, Charlie Chan, and even José are with that soap and water, for there's no pride in this dust, nor joy in the frigid walk along the lake to the gate where we hand in our cards to a guard and pass into the outside world.

"Hey," I say to Tommy Thumbs while we're standing in the street waiting for a bus, "should they turn this whole damn mill into a frisbee field?"

"Into what, man?"

"Forget it Tommy—it's just a stupid idea."

30

The White Collar on the Ex-Blue Collar is a Cool Collar

by Lewis Carliner

"Do I like my job—why shouldn't I?" The idea that he shouldn't like his job stops him for second. He flutters with his long collar points. "It's clean," he says, "just look." You look around, and it is clean, only a few people in the computer section. A tall, curving, thin man, white, is mopping, sweeping, and pushing a bucket, not simultaneously but in a methodical three-way pattern. The clock says 1:30, and the computers are rattling out paper, very like the sound of railroad wheels in another time. Reels of tape activating the takes, in spurts and stops, rock back and forth; small squares of light—red, yellow, green, blue—have their own character, some gleam, some brood, others flicker off and on. What the young man with long sideburns, long hair, and a wide, ornamented leather belt does not like is working on the third shift. He does not know anyone happier than he; he is independent, he has a sports car, a motor bike, and next year he is moving out of the apartment where he lives with his wife to a house he is going to buy, for which he has already saved up the down payment.

Twenty-four years old, computer operator on the third shift of the central computer installation of the largest company of its kind in the United States, which means the world. Salary $10,000 a year, married, his wife works, Italian, practicing Catholic, father was a truck driver and mother a cashier in a dress shop. He approves of the present Administration which is doing the best it can, he disapproves of the materialistic profit-oriented society, his candidate for president is Richard Nixon and he has no candidate for vice-president, thinks George Wallace is an effective politician but a bigot and wants no part of him. He has a natural preference for Italians, since he was brought up an Italian; but the people he admires most are Jews, because they have the ability to succeed. He thinks that the poverty subculture does not understand what the Jews understand, that it is possible to succeed.

The relaxed and happy ethnocentric Italian American (more American than Italian) is one of the computer operators on the second and third shifts, 4:30

in the afternoon to 12:30 at night to 8:30 in the morning, in two of the top 100 corporations in the U.S.—one of the largest corporations in its field and the other, a billion-dollar company among the top corporations in its market.

Altogether there were 14 workers in this category in the two companies, all, except three, former blue-collar workers. One of these was a woman; the other two were college graduates who refused to be interviewed—the one with the shining yellow tie, because he didn't want to have to do with anything that smelled of university research or foundations, and the other, who somehow kept hidden all night, his co-workers explained, was too shy to speak even to them, except in whispered monosyllables.

This report is part of a work in progress. When it is finished, it will describe interviews conducted with young blue-collar union workers, under thirty, interviews with blue-collar union workers in their middle age, and with blue-collar union workers who expect to retire within five years. They will be compared with nonunion factory workers in corresponding age groups.

Enough has been done to suggest that blue-collar workers under 30 have organzed their paranoic-tinted outlook on the world so that they see people, institutions, and events differently from middle-aged workers, largely because they are under a great deal more economic pressure. Middle-aged factory workers have responses of their own. They seem to respond with a faint defensive truculence politically and in part personally to events that threaten their economic well-being, which could be represented by a small money-bag in spite of the traditional union bugling that the average factory wage is less than it takes for a minimum standard of living for a family of four. (This is true but irrelevant, since about as many workers live on the average factory wage as angels on the head of a pin.) About the factory workers approaching retirement, just one impression—gentleness.

What makes it worth knowing these 11 former blue-collar workers who are now computer operators, in addition to their attractiveness, their intelligence, and their genuine interest in their neighbors in this world, is that they seem to represent something happening in American society.

Without exception they have working class parents, only one has a parent who went to college, and he is a black who is also the best educated of the 11 (he takes advantage of his night-shift employment to go to the university and will graduate in February 1972). Their fathers were laborer, electrician, garbage man, huckster, baker, truck driver, printer, factory worker, longshoreman, bus starter. One did not know what his father did because he deserted, leaving the mother to raise the abandoned children with the Aid to Dependent Children grant. The mothers were all housewives, or cooks, cashiers, or minimal white-collar workers. The black mother, a college graduate, was a domestic.

They are all ethnics, so-called, first-, second-, or third-generation immigrants—three Italians, one Cuban, one Dutch, one Norwegian, one Swede, one German, one Irish, one Czech, and the one black. (The Cuban-Spanish ethnic had a Puerto Rican mother, was married to a white Tennessee Protestant, had always been regarded as white. But recently he has decided that if he has any ethnicity, he is a black because blacks are more honest.) All except two of these former blue-collar workers are Catholic, the American black is Methodist, the Norwegian a Lutheran.

This is New Jersey, and it is notable that there are no Jews among these people, and no WASPS. There are both Jews and WASPS in the upper echelons of the companies, but none on this level. The computer operators do, or at least four of them do, admire Jews above all other ethnic groups in American society (only two other ethnic admirations were expressed; Italian, because, "that was the way I was brought up," and Polish, "they go to my church and they are good people"). They have this high regard for Jews because Jewish people know how to succeed, how to get educated, how to stick together.

Any meaningful definition of a working-class ethnic would have included these men until the day they got their computer-operator jobs. One completed grade school only, four went to high school and more or less finished, while six have gone to college, mostly community college for a year or so. They all quit school sometime between their 15th and 19th years. Most of the parents did not expect them to go to college. Only in three cases (one black) did the parents even hope that they might go to college. They wanted their sons to be bakers, own a business, but for the most part expected their kids would do well if they got a job. So they got jobs by going out and looking for them. In one case, there was something resembling a family exertion, a mother working in the office of a facory got her son his first job in the plant, which led in time to the computer job.

Now they are no longer blue-collar. They are white-collar, happy, conscious of progress. Seven of the eleven think they have made it up the social ladder past their parents; three said they were about at the same station in life, and one didn't know. They are middle-class, they say, at least seven described themselves this way, three say they are upper-working-class, and the Cuban-Spanish-Puerto Rican who has chosen black honesty insists he is working-class.

To understand what has happened to them, it is necessary to know something about their work. Computers in these two companies go around the clock, because the huge investment or rental demands that they be used almost continuously. The second and third shifts work in empty buildings at night. Since there is time left over on the computers after all the company demands are met, computer time is often sold to outsiders, in some cases computer operators who have worked up their own program to maintain payrolls or keep books for small businesses. And so in the two companies studied here, jobbers, brokers, time salesmen hang around the computer installation at night, living examples of free-dance entrepreneurs very like the computer operators, except that they have not only made it across the line from blue-collar but are also jousting for a chance to make it big. Some already have, and their legend echoes through the empty offices during the night shifts.

In these installations, there is a caste system. Keypunch operators, lowest grade, get salaries of $4,500 to about $5,000, mostly women, some black, but very few. In New Jersey women with blue-collar backgrounds, far from being bored punching cards and tape, are up-borne by the cleanliness, the air-conditioned cool, and the dignity. On the next rung are the computer operators, whose wages range from $7,500 to $10,000 in one of the two companies, and from $10,000 to $13,000 in the second. All except one of the computer operators walked off the street into the job. Three of them had gone to commercial computer schools which like most of such near-fraudulent operations promised jobs that were not delivered. The others picked up the skill, which is not a very high one, along the way.

Until about two years ago they might have gone from computer operator to computer programmer, which begins at about $13,000 and goes to about $17,000, but increasingly computer programmers and the higher level supervisors are now college-trained. Professionalization is setting in, lines are being drawn, and today the computer operators themselves recognize that they are locked in where they are unless they go to school. Above them are supervisors, some who made it up in the free-and-easy days, but chiefly men who were college-trained in accounting, engineering, or business administration, and who moved over. The field has opened up suddenly. In central New Jersey, the branch plants of all the big companies have on-site computers in addition to the central office systems. At Ford's Pinto plant, the manager gets a report each morning on the cost of every operation of the previous day. Independent companies of any size have them. Within a 30-mile radius of the two plants studied, there are 75 electronic data processing companies. White-collar jobs are opening up, and in New Jersey, at least, the people in the two companies apparently typify the people who are getting these jobs—white-skinned blue-collar ethnics, with an occasional black or woman.

They are young, average age 31, but three are less than 25, three are in the 25–30 bracket. Two are 35–40, 2 are over 40, the oldest is the black who is 46. The median age is 27. Most are married, eight out of the eleven—and the average family with children includes slightly less than five people, with a total of 19 children for the entire group, married and unmarried.

Whether they are affluent depends on what you consider affluence to be, but these ex-blue collars are almost euphoric when they talk about their economic situation. All except two of the eleven, like their parents, are buying their own homes, and unlike their blue-collar counterparts, buying a house and furnishing it does not exert pressure on them. Their mortgages with one exception are in the $10,000–$20,000 range, and one man's house is owned clear. Their debt outside the mortgage, even when the car is counted in, is no trouble; three have no debts at all, only one owes more than $1,000, the rest fall in the $100–$1,000 range.

What helps them enormously is a working wife, or a second job. Three moonlight, or rather daylight, since they go off their second- and third-shift jobs to other jobs in the daytime. Six are in families with more than one wage-earner. Working wives plus moonlighting mean that only three of the eleven men are completely responsible for breadwinning. In all, there was a substance in their talk about their finances. Moreover, they are also beneficiaries of family-life patterns that curiously are never reported by either Census or Bureau of Labor Statistics data. Inheritances have helped some buy houses, a settlement for an accident figured large in the financial history of another family, and support and gifts from families have helped. They have shared what might be called speculations or paying work prospects with their parents. Savings are important to them, they own mutual funds, one speculates in the market, (200 shares of Alpha Omega based on his admiration for James Ling), they buy government savings bonds, and they have savings accounts. One confessed that he had a thing about money.

Their sense of financial well-being is echoed in their attitude toward their jobs. They are where they were going, so for the most part they do not seriously intend to return to school for career advancement. Some say possibly. They intend to stay in computers, with two exceptions. The Cuban-Spanish black man is going to become an education administrator. The black without qualifications dreams of becoming a teacher. Seven of the eleven like their jobs without reservations, even the reservations of the others suggest that their attitudes are like those of a man critical of a wife who serves him well. The supervisors are overbearing, the pay is too low (this from the lowest-paid man), they don't like the night shift, too routine, too rushed, people don't associate with each other, and one said there was lack of opportunity. But even these criticisms washed out when they were asked to compare their jobs with the blue-collar jobs they once had held.

What they like about their jobs is that there is a future, jobs are interesting, indeed challenging, the pay is good, the workplace clean, and one, like the man who has a thing on money, has a thing on computers. He loves them.

Comparing these jobs with their former blue-collar jobs, only two claims were made for working in a factory, and these were not central to their opinions: there was less pressure on you in a factory, and there was the union in the plant that gave you the right to your own opinions. Otherwise there is no comparison.

As much as they are attached to their jobs, the ex-blues do not love the company, they are not starry-eyed about the administration, nor for that matter are they hostile to the company. They are alienated according to Marxist definition, but decidedly unalienated by psychological or sociological criteria. No one in the company, for example, in the judgment of six of the computer operators, is really admirable. Four, however, do have someone they respect—the same person, a night supervisor who made it up from computer operator and before that from assembly worker, and who went to college during the day while he worked at night, graduated, all the while taking superb care of his family and home. A fifth person had high respect for an accounting supervisor.

If they could change the operation so that it would meet with their approval rather more than it does now, all except two would make some changes, for the most part nonrevolutionary: greater fairness, two thought there should be an intensive on-the-job education program (there is a tuition refund benefit), two wanted more modern computers, 370s to replace the 360s, one wanted the management to be more honest, two wanted a friendlier shop with more cooperation.

What about the society they live in?

Articulate, intelligent, moderately well-informed, they hold opinions, relatively unstereotyped, on ethnic groups, on the nation, the administration, Richard Nixon, the candidates for president and vice-president, George Wallace, union leaders, government officials, and education.

All things considered, they are happy in their present situation. One, the black man, said not really, and one did not like his lack of freedom of movement, but he was also dissatisfied with his pay, didn't like his job because people did not associate with each other, and if he could, would require the company to live by a rule of fairness. As for the other workers, they are happy because they are doing what they want, are financially fulfilled; one has everything he wants, another is independent, one has a nice home and a wonderful child, one speaks of his joy with his wife and children, a man has a good family and a good living, and a man proudly asserts he has many of the things he wants for his children.

Their complaints about their present situation are strikingly few and these are moderate; one does not like shift work, one is not excited about the career ahead of him, one regrets his limited education and the necessity for his wife to work, one finds staying within his budget very hard (he has six children), one cannot really afford his house, and the black worker is uneasy because he is not doing more for youngsters, not his own, but youngsters in general.

In the society, in their personal lives, on radio or TV, in politics, or whatever, is there some person or institution, or collectivity they trust? Two could not think of anyone or any organization; four would trust priests and ministers if they were in some kind of crisis, three had faith in doctors in general, two would put their trust in police, two would seek out a well-known civil liberty or civil rights leader if they were in a jam (not the black, he would trust no one), one had faith in Ralph Nader, one believed in medical researchers, one trusted farmers in general, and one had total faith in his personal lawyer who unfortunately had died a month ago.

Among young blue-collar workers, by contrast, interviews and discussions were often barbed and bitter when the talk turned to their understanding of their experience. Blacks said whites got away with things that would have brought automatic discipline to them, and whites said they would rot in jail or be fired on the instant for the kinds of things blacks did.

Computer operators responded differently in their discussions, and perhaps one feature of their experience explains the difference: they have no immediate, continuing interchange with black people in the main, not on the job, which is white except for the demonstration black, and not in their neighborhoods, which are white also and outside of the urban centers. They consciously resist an impulse that might lead them to consider themselves bigots. One Irish father of six children bit his lips, gripped his hands until his knuckles whitened, and visibly seemed to be waging an inner contest with some evil within himself. He said he tried not to be a bigot—it was a mortal sin, he knew, to be a bigot—but he has a brother who is a policeman in New York and another brother who is a fireman, and try as hard as he can to see no color, blacks and Puerto Ricans have no respect for law and order and are unwilling to work their way. Of the eleven men, six disclaimed any ethnic preferences or animosities. When this question was approached in other ways—what kind of person would they want to live next door to? What kind would they want to marry into their family?—the assertion of nonbigotry held up, too. Perhaps they were hypocritical, but they did note without snickering that they had dated black women, Puerto Rican women, and had all kinds of friends. Whether they were speaking their mind or not, nothing like the hot resentment got into their manner which raised the voices of young blue-collar union workers on these subjects in earlier discussions.

With two exceptions, they like their homes and their neighborhoods. If they are troubled at all, anxiety seems to be a variation of an uneasiness that appeared also on their jobs, the neighbors could be more friendly. But all that considered, five of the eleven still would rather live in New Jersey than anywhere else in the world. The other six wanted to move to California or Florida, to Puerto Rico, or go back to Iowa in the case of the man who trusted farmers.

Looking out on the country they convey a sense of detached dismay, five think the country is in a pretty bad way, three insist things are really rather good in spite of what you hear, and one says things are okay. Two have comments on the world in general but they will not say good or bad. What is bad about the country is that it is screwed up; there is a cultural upheavel and the country is caught in a profit-taking, materialistic set of goals; it is regressing, Vietnam and the college upheavals have produced a situation where there is no respect for anything (a 42-year-old man); the country is money-oriented, drugs are a problem, there is an urgent need for money for pollution control and for the cities, there is graft and oppression, the war and high prices are worrisome, the country is polarized by factional politics and races, the nation is confused and divided, unemployment is high, wages drag, the democratic process is not working, there is no say for the masses. Vietnam recurs, but in all a quiet mutter of many things.

In a muted counterpoint against their quiet criticism, they insist there are good things about the country. Criticism of the society is mitigated by a strong belief that things are not really bad in spite of everything, there is progress, things are better than in the past, progress is slow but it's progress, young people's ideas give you hope, radical ideas are a reason to be optimistic, it is a good place to live, there is free enterprise, and freedom of speech.

President Nixon in their minds is a source of comfort. Tricky Dick is not an epithet they mouth. They were children when Nixon was a congressman, or senator, or a candidate for vice-president. To them President Nixon is not too unlike themselves, fair, sincere, doing the best he can, winding the war down. Five support him, he is the candidate of three for reelection, two are for him with reservations, while four do not favor him. The one person who calls him insincere is the oldest among them, the 48-year-old black man, and he holds Nixon accountable for his hypocrisy on civil rights and schools. The other objections to Nixon are that he is a liar, his price policy came along too late, he is not spending enough money on public projects.

However, if Nixon does not bother them, the government and government officials do. Only two men have anything good to say about government officials, one says they are representative of the country, the other believes they are doing what the majority want. As for the other nine, they simply do not like government officials because they are vague and crooked rich opportunists, many are bad locally but they are somewhat better nationally, they are too buyable, they are hot air, they could do more.

The hint of an antiestablishment commitment is carried forward in their reactions to George Wallace. One person had no views on the Alabama governor but eight reacted positively to him and only two rejected him—as a racist in one case, and in the second case, simply because he didn't like the man. The eight others, including the black worker, said he was open and frank; one man called him American, a radical but what he says makes good sense; even though he is a bigot he is a good politician; another agrees with Wallace's no-busing position, one agrees with reservations, and one says he is okay but farout.

The judgment of these ex-blue-collar workers on unions and union leaders have a similar quality. All except one of the eleven acknowledges the necessity for unions. There is an unvarying comment that unions should stick to bargaining, they are too powerful, they overreach, they are good for workers but still not satisfactory, they are not always positive, they are good but too strong, they are getting out of hand and, finally, they can be bought.

Union leaders are by no means the idols of these happy computers, but surprisingly there was no talk of goons, racketeers, or labor bosses. These words were as remote from their awareness as is the impression of President Nixon as a man you would not buy a used car from. Union leaders are seen as doing their job, in some cases quite well, although many are shifty and not too intelligent they do a good job, they represent the masses, but they are profiteers, pretty powerful, too self-important, or a cause for unemployment.

There is a final surprise in the attitudes of these new white collars, their attitude toward education. Ethnic, overwhelmingly Catholic, no college graduates among them, almost by specification they are the kind of people who are supposed to feel angry, betrayed, anti-Semitic, antiblack, antischool-system, and up in arms under the leadership of George Wallace against the school system. In fact, in a rather admirable way, they are not any of these and this is especially evident when they talk about schools. Seven of the eleven think the American schools are doing a pretty good job, the assimilated black man thinks they fail to motivate children (his own experience, except he had returned to college at the age of 27), the other black thinks they stink. Someone notes schools are outmoded, and another man, aged 42, remarks that kids are running the school system. Yet the convinced consensus is that the schools are good, the computer people themselves got good educations, and the schools are getting better.

The nighttime computers of two very large corporations are hardly the United States, or even an accurate sample of anything that could be described as broadly representative of anything in the nation, but that said, there are some clues in the attitudes of these people on new jobs in a new industry. They come out of the blue-collar, ethnic, working-class occupational trends which move workers toward bureaucratic white-collar employment. This does give these workers some color of importance as a possible clue to a measure of changes in attitude.

What emerges is that while there may not be affluence in these families with incomes in the middle ranges (they earn both more and less than blue-collar workers, more than most operatives, less than most skilled), there is still a sense of affluence, there is less anger and more patient patriotism and antiwar religious conviction than is assumed. Organizational loyalties are giving way to judgment of the personal qualities of leaders. Economic problems tend to be politicalized less in the minds of these workers than in the formulations of unions. The political language and currency of the 1930s, '40s, and '50s have ceased to circulate among these young workers. The new white collar with the long points is a cool collar.

Disenchantment and Reform
Politics Against Government

by Paul Starr

Few sentiments seem more characteristic of political life today than a widespread irritation with the works and scale of government. That irritation, abundantly evident in popular feeling and political rhetoric, and even in serious thought and research on the efficacy of government programs, has now been deepened by financial stringency. A peculiar conjunction of mood and necessity, of political culture and political economy, has encouraged the conviction among many in public life that there is no better politics today than a politics against government.

Unlike the antagonism toward "the system" that had its expression during the '60s, the current disaffection seems to be shared by both the left and the right, and by people with no clear political allegiance at all. The hostility is directed not at specific policies and decisions, but at the bureaucracies themselves. However, while the left and right seem equally dissatisfied with government, they tend to have different parts of it in mind. On one side the characteristic targets are the CIA and FBI; on the other, HEW and the regulatory agencies. The criticism is nearly the same: the bureaucracies are out of control, they're obedient only to their own internal urges. One voice warns that government is destructive of private interests; the other says it jeopardizes the interests of privacy. The left wants the government out of spying, infiltration, political machinations at home and abroad. The right wants it out of regulating business, busing children, redistributing income. Each has drawn its own lessons from the '60s, and now urges a particular kind of scaling down and pulling back. To this general disfavor of government, the fiscal crisis gives a further emphasis: retrenchment has become the prototypical political act.

Politics seems to be practiced today mainly in the negative mode. We debate which part of our past to find in error, what programs to set aside, whose interests to sacrifice in budgetary cutbacks. There is not a single major initiative on the horizon. All this lends a unique malaise to a political life that is both restless and motionless, hyperactive and sedentary, disenchanted and impassive.

How, in such a climate, can we find the capacity to deal forcefully with national and social needs? Is it possible to turn this irritation with government to good use? Are there alternatives, which can provide jobs and services to those who do poorly in a market economy, without at the same time expanding government bureaucracies and increasing the centralization of power?

First we must not take the current national temper, or distemper, at face value, disregarding its contradictions. The general sentiments of the country are thoroughly at odds with its specific desires. The more diffuse the reference to government, the greater the hostility. But whenever particular programs are threatened, voices cry out in anger and distress, and sympathy is stirred for those affected. The public, considered in its parts, simply does not have the same will as the public, considered as a whole. (Perhaps this is why we can elect an overwhelmingly Democratic Congress, favorable to particular programs, but at the same time send to Washington a conservative Republican administration generally suspicious of them.) In its various fragments, the society demands action here and approves of a new program there, but detached from particulars, it does not like the total of what it gets.

There is also a gap between expressed sentiments and objective conduct. Hostility to government, however widely felt, seems to have had little material impact. It has been under a Republican administration, after all, that the federal budget has gone from $220-to-$300 billion, and now is headed toward $400 billion. A Midwestern conservative President is now running deficits of 70 and 80 billion annually, which makes the mayors of New York seem parsimonious by comparison. Is the internal dynamic of expansion stronger than any President's will? Do the demands of the economy simply allow no choice? How much of our politics, let alone our budget, is discretionary?

The protests of concern about government may be signs, not of a determination to stop its growth, but of a faltering resistance to it. One reads that the protests against the "trusts" at the turn of the century were signs not of a determined opposition to growing corporate power, but of an uneasy accommodation. The rhetoric of hostility toward the rise of impersonal institutions may, in both instances, be no more than the consolation of a dying individualism. Political discourse often consists of imaginary solutions that disguise and invert the actual direction of historical change. So it may be today.

There is also a failure to recognize where government bureaucracy originates. It is hard to take seriously the frequent exclamations of dismay from private industry over the growth of the federal bureaucratic and regulatory structure. Much of the complexity and administrative burden is the result of attempts in Congress and the executive branch to placate private interests, in all their petty diversity. Responsibility for the intricacy and meddlesomeness of bureaucratic decisions rests, not so much with the agencies that carry them out, as with the private parties that succeed in getting their concerns written into the statutes and regulations. If Congress and the executive were less attentive to those interests, government could be greatly simplified and streamlined. But, were it ignored, the private sector would surely be more unhappy than ever.

The inefficiency of government is as proverbial as the meddlesomeness of its regulations, but here too one must be skeptical about assumptions. Government inefficiency is often the result, in part, of the fact that government takes on certain functions (such as services to the poor or the support of basic scientific research) because no private industry finds it profitable to perform them. The reason for their unprofitability is often related to the apparent inefficiency of the state: the tasks involve inherent difficulties and uncertainties; the products may be intangible and hard to measure or control. Frequently, through subsidies and incentives, government programs try to make these functions economically attractive to private interests, but this builds in extra costs and makes monitoring of the outcome even more difficult.

Moreover, because government services are public, we expect them to abide by standards other than efficiency. The wage structure of public employees, for example, seems to be more equal than that of the private sector, leading to losses of talent at the top and relatively greater costs at lower levels. Other considerations militate against observing strict notions of efficiency. If the mails were operated to keep costs down and make the postal service pay for itself, there would be no service to small towns, and most magazines and scholarly publications would go out of business. In many areas, government isn't efficient because nobody seriously wants it to be.

And yet, of course, the point still remains: there is inefficiency, there is cumbersomeness, there is unresponsiveness. There is good cause for disquiet because the bureaucracies are subject neither to the "discipline" of a market, nor to genuine public control. The state has acquired an existence of its own, over and against the rest of society.

So the quarrel between politics and government is entirely natural, and even useful. Men elected to public office in America are now judged in part on their capacity to control, to master, to restrain the established bureaucracies. Almost everywhere one looks today, elected officials and government employees are locked in struggle. The mayor or governor who can face down a threat to strike, or a strike itself, by a public-employees union almost assures his own popularity. Congressmen now find that they are increasingly called on to serve as intermediaries between their constituents and the federal bureaucracy. They have become not merely representatives to the legislature, but ombudsmen before the executive. Even the White House does not fully command the executive branch, but must at times deal with it as if it were another division of government. Nixon's janissaries correctly saw themselves as struggling to assert control over a fundamentally hostile federal bureaucracy. The Ford administration, on the other hand, seems to have made its peace with what might be called the standing government, and this may be partly responsible for the change in tone from the Nixon era.

But this standing government, independent of particular administrations, represents a powerful force of its own. With the proliferation of social services and state bureaucracies, it has become not merely a self-sustaining industry, but the source of new interests that coalesce around the benefits it disburses in contracts, jobs, subsidies and services. Groups and classes struggling against each other all see themselves as suffering the insensitivities and exactions of government. It becomes the object of displaced resentment—the target for groups that have lost political battles sometimes without having been aware of them. Government in America is sustained by a host of particular interests clamoring for satisfaction; it has little general support or enthusiasm. With no one in decisive control of the state, everyone feels, in one way or another, oppressed by it.

Historically there have been various responses, if not solutions, to the problem of the growth and autonomy of the state. Several continue to have some appeal, among them the Jeffersonian ideal of minimal government, the progressive ideal of professional government, the revolutionary conception of a dual party-state structure, and the decentralist model of direct and local control. For various reasons, none of these approaches has much relevance to the contemporary American situation.

The Jeffersonian ideal of minimal government had a radical content in early American society. In the colonial period, government had been an intimate participant in economic affairs, usually to the benefit of the privileged classes. At that point, to argue for less government meant arguing for less governmental action in favor of the privileged. But with the rise of corporations, the ideal of minimal government took on a different character: little state intervention meant a free hand for corporate power. The Jeffersonian ideal was already in eclipse by the time Jefferson died in 1826, and with Jackson it became clear, as Arthur Schlesinger, Jr. wrote some years ago, that Jeffersonian ends could only be accomplished through Hamiltonian means—in other words, the defense of the interests of less privileged groups had to be accomplished through an active state (less privileged including not only farmers and mechanics, but less dominant business interests as well). Since that time, liberals in America have been identified with the extension of government and conservatives with its restraint.

The progressive solution to the problem of the state, in the late 19th and early 20th centuries, was to encourage the development of professionalism. Through the civil service and city management, the progressives wanted to insulate government from politics and to instill in it the scientific spirit of efficiency. This was, in a sense, one removed from the Jeffersonian ideal—the minimization of political authority, if not the minimization of government itself. Its function, however, was to take power away from less privileged ethnic groups who gained influence through city machines. Today the ideal of neutral, technical authority has lost its hold on the imagination, and increasingly, the reforms the progressives promoted, such as the insulation of the civil service from political control, loom as some of the most stubborn obstacles to needed political change.

The revolutionary response to the problem of the state has been to strip it of final authority: a political party oversees governmental functions or directly assumes their operation. This is, in a sense, the antithesis of progressivism, in that it calls for the accentuation of politics, rather than its deemphasis. Used in some Communist and Fascist regimes, such a dual structure is clearly unimaginable in the United States, where political parties have never been more than electoral coalitions. The main objection, however, is that while lodging power in an ideological party may solve the problem of the state, it creates a new problem—the all-powerful party, which may be worse.

Decentralization has considerable appeal and much greater plausibility in the United States. Local government as Tocqueville observed, has been the school of democratic experience. On the right, one speaks of returning power to the states; on the left, of returning power to communities. Sometimes it is best to discuss these alternatives in the abstract, because when specific issues of great concern to either side are raised—say, civil liberties to the left or abortion to the right—neither really wants them left to local determination. Also, hardly anything inspires more warmth for the federal government than a good look at the way states

and municipalities are run. But more importantly, so long as the corporate economy is organized on a national and even multinational level, it is impossible for states and communities to deal with economic and social problems on their own. Only the federal government is in a position to act effectively. No doubt, some devolution of power is possible, and greater self-reliance could be achieved, both on a personal and local level, but this is not a realistic strategy for dealing with the most substantial national problems.

The modern economy consists, from one point of view, of three sectors: the domestic household, the market and the state (or "public household" as it is sometimes called). One line of contemporary thought holds that various functions that the state has historically taken over from the family and communal circle—education, provision for times of economic distress, the resolution of disputes, the care of the sick, the aged and the dependent—ought to be returned to the family or family-like institutions, such as communes or self-help groups. In this urge, traditionalists and radicals sometimes coincide. Another line of thought, more purely conservative, holds that functions the state has assumed ought to be turned over to the free operation of the market. The first of these positions I see as partially right and yet, like decentralization, of secondary importance; the second position, I believe, is wholly wrong and yet somehow closer to the point. For it is in the reconstruction of the market, and its relationship to the public household, that alternatives must be found.

Such an approach has actually been implicit in a great many ideas and reforms discussed in recent years. As I understand it, at least three elements are involved: 1) the creation of new participants in the market—that is, new institutions such as cooperatives and competitive public enterprises, 2) the establishment of new rules and conditions, governing such things as access to information and credit, and 3) the fostering, through such mechanisms as vouchers for health and education, of greater command over resources, among those who would otherwise do poorly in the market.

For historical reasons, the market economy has been associated with the exclusive dominance of private corporations, but the link is neither necessary nor inevitable. There are other alternatives: markets in which public enterprises and consumer and producer cooperatives play a large part. In the United States, "yardstick competition" has long been the justification for competitive public enterprises (CPEs). The Tennessee Valley Authority is the prototype. More recently, Sen. Adlai Stevenson III introduced legislation calling for the creation of a federal oil and gas corporation to exploit reserves on government-owned land.

State enterprises in America have generally been confined to industries where there are "natural monopolies." But as Peter Barnes and Derek Shearer have written ("Beyond Antitrust," *The New Republic,* July 6 and 13, 1974), there is no reason why, in industries where monopolistic conditions prevail because of the domination of a few firms, competitive public enterprises could not play a useful role. Barnes and Shearer, noting successful precedents in Canada and Europe, call for CPEs in a range of industries: auto, steel, aluminum, drugs, banking and insurance. Various levels of government, federal, state and local, could be involved. There might also be a variety of arrangements for shared control involving private investors, government and the firm's own employees.

CPEs would have three functions. The aim traditionally has been, first, to stir up competition to produce consumer savings and, second, to permit more adequate public regulation of private industry, by generating direct and independent information on costs and profits. But in addition to the traditional role as a "yardstick," CPEs might also generate revenues and thereby reduce the reliance of government upon taxation and borrowing. To do so, they would have to avoid being forced into "balanced-budget pricing" (*i.e.,* pricing just sufficient to cover costs). In some cases, municipally owned electric companies have served this purpose. In general, however, the enterprises taken over and operated by Western governments tend to be in failing industries, like railroads, that no longer serve private interests. The importance of going into the kind of markets mentioned by Barnes and Shearer is that they have high profit margins and could, therefore, serve as major sources of revenue.

While CPEs seem most useful in the oligopolistic sector of the economy, cooperatives have a role to play in the sphere of smaller, more local, more competitive enterprise. Cooperatives, as internally democratic institutions, are governed on a one member, one vote basis and probably work best on a local scale. In America, they have been successful almost exclusively in rural farming areas, but are now enjoying something of an urban renaissance. Cooperatives exist not only in retail distribution, food coops being especially popular these days, but also in housing and health care, where they seem to me potentially more promising. (The Group Health Cooperative of Puget Sound, in Seattle, has almost 200,000 members and its own hospital and clinics.) Yet cooperatives have always been short of capital; here again the state has a role. To avoid the expansion of its own bureaucratic structure, it has to advance the capital for nongovernmental, though not necessarily private activities. Perhaps more important, it has to create favorable legal and political conditions— the sort that private corporations have historically enjoyed.

Through revising the rules and conditions of the market, much can be accomplished, aside from institutional change. There are a whole range of policies that deal with information. Requirements for disclosure of

retail drug prices, comparative mortgage rates, and the fees of physicians, lawyers and other professionals have lately been acted on or at least been widely discussed. Such measures help reduce the "market power" of those, like druggists, bankers and doctors, who benefit from consumers' lack of readily available information on relative prices. The market power of professionals and other occupational groups can also be curtailed by eliminating artificial licensing requirements that block the entry of, say paraprofessionals in medical care and apprentice-trained practitioners in law. The regulatory boards that have been set up for each profession are now dominated by the professions themselves; they need to be opened up to public representatives.

In other areas, such as transportation, there is a need for substantial deregulation. Much of the regulatory system, despite the animadversion from private industry, was created at its behest and in its narrow interest: witness the recent squeals of trucking firms and Teamsters when the administration announced its plans to seek deregulation in their industry. There is, however, no way to disentangle the government from such areas of the economy completely. A great many sunken subsidies, like the enormous investment in highways, already favor particular interests over others. Wholesale deregulation, were it possible, would serve to leave past distortions of the public interest imprinted on the society.

Other reforms might involve the national chartering of corporations, and the elimination of some of the privileges and immunities enjoyed through the corporate structure. Ralph Nader, who has pressed these ideas, has also suggested watchdog groups within companies, funded by check-offs on consumer bills. The general principle is important: there is a need not only for information, but for people in positions to make sense and use of it.

Neither changes in organizational structure nor new rules and conditions, however, would be sufficient. The market responds only to effective demand, not to need—only to what people can afford, not to what may be necessary for them to live. This is, of course, the crucial matter. If the market is to be retained, the government must at least partially correct for the gap between need and demand by providing its citizens with the purchasing power necessary to survive in it. The distribution of vouchers or "drawing rights" for basic services like education and health care is one way to accomplish this objective, with the least central bureaucratic control. Such a system gives maximum power to consumers who can decide to use their vouchers as they see fit; unfortunately, for that very reason, it also tends to favor consumers who know how to use their resources wisely. Ultimately, income policy, which would include wage and tax reform as well as vouchers are adequate only when combined with changes in the structure and conditions of the market.

Clearly, no institutional form is without its limits and weaknesses. Neither cooperatives nor competitive public enterprises are immune from corruption. (One need only mention the role of the dairy cooperatives in Watergate.) A general tendency toward decay, or loss of commitment, may well prevail in all institutions. This is precisely the reason for retaining the market as well as cultivating democratic processes. In the language of the economist Albert Hirschman, there are two principal means of deterring "slack" in organizations: "exit" (the decision of a consumer to stop buying a product, of a member of an organization to drop out, or of an official to resign) and "voice" (voting, grumbling, protesting, resisting).

It would make things simple and straightforward if "exit" and "voice" could always be built into social institutions at the same time. But as Hirschman points out, one mechanism sometimes erodes the other. The availability of "exit" can lead to the atrophy of "voice": the people most likely to complain are often the first to leave. Thus the existence of alternatives may drain off the most quality-conscious and articulate customers or members, and actually lead to less pressure on organizations. Consequently, in some situations, it may be wise to create barriers to "exit" in order to strengthen "voice"—in other words, one may have to curb the market to improve democratic decision-making.

Considerations such as these complicate the picture.

Nonetheless, before trading off "exit" and "voice" as circumstances demand, it is important to recognize that both have intrinsic, not just instrumental, value. People ought to be able to leave organizations and states as they choose, and to participate in decision-making, not only for the good of the institutions and community, but as an exercise of their own freedom. Social policy should, therefore, have as its objective the design of institutions in which the avenues of "exit" and "voice" are both available and effective. (The problem of most people in the world, of course, is that they have recourse to neither.)

An approach along these lines would entail government action, in part because the market economy on its own tends to congeal through corporate concentration. Often the only way to preserve competition, and to make it serve social objectives, is by action of the state. The aim of government should be not to eliminate the market, but to use it, deliberately, through premeditated competition. In that way, perhaps, we can preserve diversity and inventiveness at the same time as we promote distributive justice and a democratic order.

This strategy entertains no illusions about the virtues of the unregulated market or of the unconstrained state. It seeks a third path between socialism and capitalism, as they have classically been conceived. Whether we explore it is a problem of politics, not of theory.

32

Bernard Rosenberg

CIA, DIA, FBI -and 50 More!

After reading the Rockefeller Commission report, Senator Frank Church declared, ''This is just the tip of an iceberg.'' A little later it looked like the tip of a glacier. From December 22, 1974, when Seymour Hersh's first dispatch on ''Massive Illegal CIA Operations'' appeared in the *New York Times*, we have been swamped with more ''classified'' information than anyone can assimilate. A media's worth of the stuff every day, plus weekly and monthly supplements, quarterly reactions, revelations, confessions; horror upon horror.

I. F. Stone's call for liquidation of the CIA surprised no one. Eyebrows were lifted, however, at least mine were, when Tom Braden took the same position. Braden, the conservative columnist? Newsworthy enough. But Braden, the long-time CIA agent who lately views his old organization as a threat to representative government? Much more interesting. Here's the same Braden who by April 1975 finally recounts a story about the time Allen Dulles bought an entire intelligence network ''for a lot of money'' and it somehow wound up with the KGB. Braden remembers when Dulles was obliged to appear about this matter before Senator Richard Russell's Armed Forces Committee, our first CIA Director announced to those around him, ''I guess I'll have to fudge the truth a little.'' That incident now seems paradigmatic to Braden. It implies power wedded to arrogance, secrecy and deception. This syndrome strikes one agent-turned-pundit as deadly to the democratic process.

The retrospective wisdom or sudden sensitivity of Braden and many men like him, who were immersed in the slime they could not then detect, is more than welcome. But what does it signify if all they have learned is that the Central Intelligence Agency should be abolished? For we have begun to see that the CIA is only one glacier in an Ice Age of covert operations. Since FDR created the OSS during World War II, a monstrously large American ''intelligence community'' has materialized. Its parts are dispersed like the limbs of Osiris. Seymour Hersh's colleague Nicholas Horrock has disclosed the existence of 10 regular federal agencies employing 200,000 persons who spend over $6 billion a year on intelligence activities. Concerning their machinations only the tiniest tip has so far surfaced.

Maybe Senator Church's Select Committee will discover something about the supersecret National Security Agency—compared to which the CIA is an open book. Horrock tells us that the NSA, with 20,000 employees, functions in a ''carefully guarded complex'' at Fort Meade, Md. One ''facet of its role'' is already under Senate investigation, namely, a program allegedly related to codebreaking and electronic spying that permits ''eavesdropping on literally thousands of long distance telephone calls'' in the United States. Calls outside the U.S. are more frequently monitored. Apparently it's not just Ma Bell who has us by the calls.

Among others, there's the Defense Intelligence Agency with its $100 million budget, a succubus that has been growing by cellular multiplication ever since Robert McNamara conjured it into being. The DIA is supposed to be a huge umbrella under which Army, Navy, and Air Force intelligence services cluster in separate but sometimes parallel or antagonistic action. When in the early '70s military intelligence was caught investigating such prominent politicians as Adlai Stevenson III and infiltrating various domestic groups, we were assured that these escapades would be halted and that the ''vast computerized information'' derived from them had been destroyed. ''Not likely'' is what most insiders think. How could such computers so readily disgorge those lovely dossiers?

If it is clear that the CIA overreached itself by encroaching on the domestic field of espionage, sabotage, and provocation, one should not forget that the FBI also greatly overstepped its bounds. Or that a genius in the IRS, not the CIA, dreamed up, say, Operation Leprechaun. In March, after a local exposé, Elizabeth J. Bettner called a press conference to explain that she was only one of 20 or 25 persons in the Miami area hired by Internal Revenue to pick up all the dirt she could on Florida politicians who from 1970 to 1973 annoyed Dick Nixon's gang. She vehemently denied having been ordered to sleep with any victim. If other operatives did that, her ''good work'' should not be tarnished by their immorality.

Although no past attorney general can ''recall'' it, CIA Director William E. Colby has testified to a 20-year agreement with the Justice Department not to prosecute CIA criminals. If so, Justice deserves no more exculpation than any other subdivision of the government.

Michael Harrington, the dedicated socialist—not

Michael Harrington, the liberal congressman who spilled too much about U.S. involvement in Chile—suspects that his syndicated column was dropped by a number of publishers under pressure from Naval Intelligence. He is suing that agency for deprivation of income. Congressman Harrington has been denied access to confidential data since June 1975. F. Edward Hébert. deposed chairman of the House Armed Services Committee, which practices oversight in the original sense of that word, resumed his old seat for the Harrington *auto-da-fé*, as Mary McGrory dubbed it.

The Socialist Workers party, the American Trotskyist—shall we say movement?—has been under continuous surveillance for at least *31* bloody years. By the CIA? No. By the FBI. Through its cunning counterintelligence arm, which is becoming familiar as Cointelpro, 3,138 pages of secret documentation on the SWP have now been made public. And what has all this expenditure of time and money led to? The Newark FBI, with only one forged letter of defamation, followed a scoutmaster whose wife attended party meetings and drove him from his job.

According to Jack Anderson, the Secret Service has a file number, CO 23970009205, on Groucho Marx for a wisecrack he made about President Nixon. The subversive comedian was 80 years old at the time and an obvious danger to the Republic. Look and you will find subtler dangers. The FBI is aware of them. Item: tipped off by H. R. Haldeman that Leonard Bernstein planned to sneak a peace message into his ''mass oritorium'' at the Kennedy Center, the FBI warned that this ''opera'' would follow ''an antiwar theme,'' that it would be sung in Latin and that if the President or other important government officials attended they might unwittingly applaud a message inimical to them. The FBI was right. Bernstein's *Mass* did contain one line, ''*Dona Nobis Pacem*,'' or ''Give Us Peace,'' that might have been disquieting to the Administration. Nixon stayed away. (Maybe he also acted out of a deeper conviction. ''Stay away from the arts . . . . They're Jews.'' is among his more notable aphorisms.) Further item: the after-hour passes of celebrated quarterback Joe Namath, his affair with an airline stewardess and additional proof of Namath's sexual prowess, are the subject of another FBI report. Take one more from the great miscellany currently in Senator Church's hands: a file on Gerald Ford presumably commencing on April 23, 1963, when the FBI bugged a conversation between two AVCO executives discussing how helpful Congressman Ford had been to them. TRIVIA? But who ever heard of a more devoted trivia-collector than the FBI? Billions of dollars for the Director's little hobby—in fact a rather sizable share of what's left over from the production and sale of instantly obsolete military hardware. Meanwhile, jobs, housing, education, health care, and freedom shrivel. A Secretary of HEW leaves with but one parting shot: *Beware of the welfare state* (which barely exists). Few officials warn about the

police state. If we are bemused as our cities rot, as pollution spreads through our waterways, as blight spreads across the countryside, it is a comfort to know that the beauty of Pennsylvania Ave. can always be enhanced. Consider the new block-size $126 million FBI building. TRB of the *New Republic* admonishes his readers to lower their voices when they pass ''Big Brother's home.'' ''He may have something on *you*.'' The new FBI citadel contains records of over 81 million Americans, with an annual flow of more than 7 million fingerprints pouring in from local and state police who more and more have their own secret squads. TRB makes it vivid:

> Suppose your name was in a telephone conversation monitored under court order by the FBI (or without court order under former Attorney General Mitchell); you may well have a red ''C'' card (cross-reference) in the index. The gray filing cabinets with six drawers bulge with three-by-five cards. There are some 58 million, with 1.3 million new ones coming in every year. There are 7,500 cabinets, growing at the rate of 300 a year. The electronic retrieval system is a marvel. Think of that huge building as a warehouse, wholesaling information on Americans.

We ought to do that. And we ought to think about the criteria by which names are assembled. Involvement in dissident politics is one. Here the overlap among agencies must be tremendous. Is that all? Not for the Secret Service, with its computerized ''watch list'' of people considered dangerous to the President—which once grew to 500,000 but has supposedly been trimmed down to a mere 47,000. The Secret Service acknowledges that much more than politics is involved. Thus Assistant Treasury Secretary David R. MacDonald recently told a House subcommittee that ''mental instability and failure in work and in personal relationships'' were also taken into account. By such criteria, which of us is immune?

If the psychologically and occupationally unstable but apolitical population is vulnerable, what of those who are not simply imperfect but political as well? A spokesman for the American Indian Movement said to a *Washington Post* reporter that the organization's former chief security officer was a paid FBI informant. Several clergymen who have mediated Indian/government disputes also claim that AIM has been infiltrated by FBI agents. ''The FBI would neither confirm nor deny the charges,'' and a Douglas Durham, ''the alleged informant,'' could not be reached for comment. Mr. Durham is accused, *inter alia*, of telling the Justice Department details of the legal defense prepared for Indians arrested at various demonstrations. Well, Indians are notoriously unstable. So are convicts. (Only Chileans and other foreigners need to be destabilized.) Hence, a front-page story in the *Times* begins:

> A 26-year old Buffalo woman said yesterday that she had infiltrated the Attica defense camp and reported back to the Federal Bureau of Investigation on legal

strategy surrounding the trials of former inmates under indictment for crimes stemming from the Attica revolt.

The woman, Mary Jo Cook, explained, "I have a big mouth—I said a lot," (to her "control agent") about "some Attica defendants" and the jury selection project on which their lawyers were working. Ten days later Miss Cook repeated her story under oath, adding that Gary Lash was her control agent. Mary Jo Cooper evidently does not subscribe to the general proposition that decency is an idea whose time has come and gone. Unlike the more exalted criminals in our midst, she was capable of this outburst:

> I took the FBI job on, thinking it was honorable. During the course of it, I realized it was not honorable. I committed a political crime. It was as if I was a TV monitor into people's lives. I can't believe I destroyed people's rights to privacy.

Hirelings sometimes feel that way. Only those at the top and the sycophants who surround them could lie their way nervelessly through a polygraph test. They are psychopaths in the strictest sense: men without a superego to check or a conscience to prick them.

Hear Clarence M. Kelley, celebrating the completion of his second year as FBI director, dilating on 30 years of national security break-ins and burglaries, known privately as blackjack jobs and publicly as "surreptitious entries" that, having been disclosed, are no longer "a viable procedure." Director Kelley finds that "in light of changing standards of law enforcement conduct," J. Edgar Hoover terminated certain "imprudent" counterintelligence practices. But the FBI still keeps tabs on the personal behavior of reporters and government officials, including members of Congress. "Some of this [material] might well be helpful in later investigations." Kelley refused to call continued collection "rank abuse." Anyway, less than rank abuse is for others. "I have not reviewed files to find out about reporters, Congressmen or other public figures," and "I do not subscribe to that type of thing." Director Kelley simply perpetuates it.

Why the scruple about not subscribing to that type of thing in which he finds "no gross abuse of authority," no "corruption of the trust that was placed in us?" Kelley insists that no *illegal* activities ever occurred in his bureau and that they have been discontinued. The Director's logic is as unassailable as his moral sense, which has been surpassed of late only by Jerry Ford. Our leader, upon careful study of the CIA report and the addendum on assassinations for his eyes only, asserted twice and thrice that he would make no judgment about it. Let the historians make a judgment, and let Congress use discretion.

This from Mr. Ford who if he had a clever Machiavellian on his staff would be best advised as follows: Jerry, stop chewing that gum for a minute, put a WIN cap or a helmet on your head, take a passel of journalists out to the Rose Garden and try to read this statement: "Upon due reflection, I have found it possible to make a judgment about the CIA, and ladies and gentlemen, that judgment is negative. The CIA has been compromised. Citizens are cynical about an intelligence organization that plotted, bugged, tapped, stole, killed, fought secret wars, overthrew democratic governments, installed dictators, blundered and lied. Accordingly, I hereby abolish the CIA."

Why not? With that heroic gesture, Mr. Ford, yet another amiable man of limited educability, might even clinch his first victory outside Grand Rapids. With that gesture, he would banish the doubt that has been overconcentrated on a single segment of the bureaucratic brontosaurus that envelops us.

WHO NEEDS the CIA? Voters are agitated about it. They can have the DIA. That would make the Pentagon happy. Military men who already manage an efficient spy-in-the-sky operation could bring it down to earth as a properly run war on restrictive mandates. And give the DIA the $86 million headquarters it wants. Congress has perversely balked at appropriating this paltry sum even though its members know that the DIA is housed in substandard facilities, and a former Air Force base is available for the new site.

If the DIA is too cumbersome, many another *apparat* is in place. Tom Wicker points out that more than 50 federal agencies have some law enforcement function that may involve the protection of "security" by spying, prying, and snooping. To remain ideologically pure, a measure of decentralization might be in order. The cities are already doing their job but still short of perfection. We have Dick Daley to show the way. His flacks proclaim that he makes Chicago work. And the voters agree. Before Daley's latest and biggest election victory, his city (or its press) was agog with scandal about the Chicago police who infiltrated the local Urban League chapter and similarly subversive community organizations along with the State's Attorney's office, while keeping Father Hesburgh of Notre Dame under surveillance and compiling dossiers on newspapermen and politicians like Richard Newhouse, a black who had the gall to run against Daley in the Democratic primary. The mayoral contest boiled down to Daley versus a reluctant Republican, John J. Hoellen who received less than a quarter of the vote. A *Chicago Sun-Times* staff writer noted that: "While Hoellen denounced 'Daley and his Gestapo' and called the mayor 'a paranoid old man peeping in keyholes'," Daley and Police Superintendent James Rochford defended police intelligence as a legitimate weapon against possible terrorist tactics. Rochford said that "the intelligence work would continue." It will. The point is to do better, not to botch the job and to cover up the coverup with more finesse.

Or make it so you don't have to cover up. Decriminalize semitotalitarian police action that strict constitutionalists have foolishly defined as unlawful. To this end Senator Birch Bayh, that paragon of liberals, and Senator James O. Eastland, never previously associated with progressive politics, have helped reintroduce Nixon's old bill to recodify the criminal law. The press has spotted but hardly highlighted two vital provisions of their law-and-order meat axe. One would empower the government to wiretap without a court order anyone the President may consider a "danger to the structure" of government, and the other would make it more difficult to prosecute a public official engaged in illegal conduct with the "express permission" of the President. You think that sounds too much like the Imperial Presidency? All right. Local officials can administer the new and better law.

But do let's rid ourselves of the CIA. Unfortunately, some of its valuable records have been shredded and dumped, producing an ecological mess. But let the rest be salvaged. Operation Chaos generated quite a yield. Its computer index contains 300,000 names, including all those associated with Grove Press, Inc., which once published a book by the British double agent Kim Philby. Punch a button and you can find reviews of the X-rated film *I Am Curious Yellow*, which Grove had a hand in distributing. And 7,200 "personality files" and a thousand dossiers on U.S. organizations should not go to waste.

Nor should we lose the knowledge scientifically gathered on LSD, or other drugs, in addition to certain unnamed "harassment substances," electroshock, and radiation. Who were the "unsuspecting volunteers" (Ay, how the language is enriched!), those unwittingly courageous CIA employees who, like the Army's 1,500 subjects and HEW's 2,500, contributed so freely to scientific advancement? So far we know only of one LSD subject's suicide. Ten years for sure, maybe 20 years after Frank R. Olson, his mind suitably altered, leaped out of a Manhattan hotel-room window, the LSD experiments still continued. Isn't it a pity to have lost all the records of that program? 152 separate files down the drain by order of Dr. Sidney Gottlieb, a biochemist "personally involved" in the fatal experiment. We are informed that this little obliteration, which showed our doctors to be so much less obliging than the Nazi MDs who at least left their records intact, was carried out shortly after Richard Helms "ordered other unspecified records to be destroyed."

Nevertheless, too many facts will out; some seem laughable at first sight (a file on Ford) but maybe they're not so laughable after all; most are grisly (like Operation Phoenix: can there have been *20,000* political assassinations in Vietnam?) Was there complicity or worse in the murder of heads of state like Allende, Trujillo, Lumumba, and Diem? Were the computers unable to predict that this kind of thing could only invite retaliation?

HOW did it all come to pass? A platitudinous but not therefore inaccurate answer is that it was a product of the Cold War. No doubt. In the long run, however, a search for historical origins leads us into an infinite regress. The Cold War had its precedent in President Wilson's Red Raids and, for that matter, in the Alien and Sedition Acts. And they had their European sources. None can have equaled President Nixon's if only because of advanced technology at his disposal. And with all that, as the tapes make monotonously clear, Nixon felt nothing but outrage at the intelligence community, which was never sufficiently responsive to his criminal needs, his extralegal and unconstitutional demands. And that community has been notably inept. With poorly planned mendacity, inadequate containment of informers, clumsiness, imbecilities piled on third-rate burglaries, we seem to have gone semi-Czarist, raising more of a goofed-up Okhrana than a KGB. No wonder Nixon, yearning for a little efficiency, wanted something more like the KGB.

"Leaders with eyes and no nose, with a nose and no eyes, with brains and no soul—but all of them with ambitions above their stature and their abilities." So wrote an Israeli, Michael Chilewich, of his government. And his government, besieged as it is, hardly deserves a fraction of the opprobrium that, looking back on the 'covert operations" of the last 20 years, we pour on ours. Still, that very opprobrium, the possibility of opposition, of alertness to abuse, of continuous crying out that fish stink, fish multiply and stink, is our great, remaining glory. Whoever despises it, constitutes a threat to our endangered species—whether by justifying the appalling record that has lightly been touched on here or by using that record for "leftist" or "rightist" contempt of democratic ways.

33

MULTINATIONALS AT BAY

Multinational corporations are today on the defensive: increasingly, they are being pilloried by consumer groups, unions, the media, Congress, and various international organizations. As Jacques Maisonrouge, chairman of IBM World Trade Corporation, recently put it, these attacks on multinationals have at times reached the level of "open political warfare." Are these attacks warranted? Or are multinationals, on balance, a force for good? This special section looks into the pros and cons of the multinational presence on the world scene.

Bruno Barbey: Magnum

The multinational presence in Nairobi—"On a collision course with the Third World."

The old law of physics that every action produces an equal and opposite reaction has lately seemed to apply with sardonic irony to multinational corporations. Last year that eloquent defender of the American position, Daniel P. Moynihan, now U. S. ambassador to the United Nations, singled out the multinational corporation as an example of the "enormous recent achievements" in international liberalism. "Combining modern management with liberal trade policies," he declared, "it is arguably the most creative international institution of the 20th century." That proposition once met with little argument. Five years ago multinationals, about half of them American, were expanding lustily across most non-Communist parts of the world, increasing their sales, profits, and penetration of foreign markets so rapidly that they already were producing about a sixth of the world's goods and services. Direct foreign investment, mainly and increasingly by multinationals, had already replaced trade as the most important ingredient of international economics. Some respectable authorities calculated that 300 giant companies might account for half the world's economic activity well before the end of the century.

Today the multinationals are bigger than ever but are under attack at home and abroad—their image tarnished, their prospects imperiled, their leaders dismayed. Consumer groups, the media, and academia are increasingly critical. Organized labor in the United States is demanding legislation to prevent the multinationals from "exporting jobs." Congress has taken away a few of their alleged tax advantages and may hit them with severe, even crippling, new restrictions. Many foreign governments are imposing tough new conditions on their operations, cutting into their profits and incentive to invest. The United Nations is moving on several fronts toward measures that may impede the future growth of multinationals. And the disclosures of bribery and political manipulations, which have seriously damaged their public reputation, are also fanning demands for "codes of conduct" that may impose onerous and perhaps unnecessary burdens.

Multinationals, it would appear, are unlikely to disappear from the scene any time soon, but considerable change is

Gurney Breckenfeld is a member of the board of editors at Fortune *magazine.*

clearly on the way. Lee L. Morgan, president of Caterpillar Tractor Company, an Illinois-based multinational with 11 plants in 9 foreign countries, recently predicted that the rest of the Seventies would bring "a rising tide of attempts at control and regulation" of multinationals. He added: "We have so far seen only the first small waves."

Foggy Statistics

For a perspective on the pros and cons of the intensifying debate about multinational enterprises, it helps to begin by looking at some economic fundamentals. U. S. investment in factories and similar facilities abroad, most of it by big multinational concerns, has now reached the impressive total of $110 billion, according to Treasury officials. That is nearly five times the foreign direct investment in the United States, and it brought the nation an equally impressive $17.6 billion income in 1974.

Until recently, U. S.-based multina-

reaching a crescendo as their expansion rate wanes.

Changing political and economic circumstances underlie the slowdown. In the Fifties U. S. companies pushed abroad to get around high tariffs and other barriers to American exports. In the Sixties they did so to cut production costs with cheaper labor. At the same time, an overvalued dollar made it cheap to buy assets abroad, the world economy was expanding at a brisk pace, prices were stable, and most foreign countries were quite receptive toward U. S. private companies. Not one of those conditions prevails today. Dollar devaluations have made our exports more competitive in world markets, lessening the need to produce overseas. Labor costs are rising faster abroad, especially in Europe, so that it is more attractive to expand factories at home.

These changes, in turn, have set others in motion. As U. S. exports boom, Japanese and European multinational com-

tionals had been expanding their overseas investment at the rate of about 10 percent a year. Investment abroad—$7.3 billion last year—is still rising, but the pace has slowed. Some bankers find the decline in American investment in Europe especially marked, and a study conducted last summer by the Department of Commerce provides supporting evidence. After surveying some 350 American companies and their 5,000 majority-owned foreign affiliates, the department reported that outlays for property, plant, and equipment abroad would increase by only 4 percent in 1975, a huge drop from the 25 percent rise the year before. In short (the second irony), the global row about global companies is

panies feel the effects in their own foreign sales. So multinationals from all three continents are shifting more and more production into the Third World, once chiefly a source of raw materials and domestic exports.

Though major trends are reasonably clear, some basic statistics are conspicuously murky. Odd though it may seem in a world overflowing with numerical data of every kind, no one can say for sure just how many multinational companies exist—even how many are U. S.-based. One reason, of course, is the lack of a single, standard definition of what a company must be and do in order to qualify for the label (see box, page 14). Nor do we know how big the sales and profits of multinationals are, in the aggregate. The Paris-based Organization for Economic Cooperation and Development estimates that four-fifths of the business done by the world's multinationals involves transactions among its 24 member nations, almost all of which are industrialized. In *Fortune*'s latest ranking of the world's largest industrial companies, all the top 15 are multinationals. Eleven are based in the United States, and eight are oil companies.

Beyond such shafts of light as these lies a dense fog of confusion, misunderstanding, and perhaps even outright lying with statistics. Figures appearing in scholarly works tend to be so out of date as to be misleading. And recent data are sometimes based on an estimate projected from a sample used to update a survey made years ago. As an example of the glop that passes for insight, consider some of the findings of a 1973 U. N. study. It reported, among many other things, that there were 7,300 multinational companies but instantly devalued that "fact" by noting that almost half of them had affiliates in only one country (a setup that might qualify them semantically to be called "bina-tional" but hardly multinational). The same report also asserted in a footnote that "almost all" of the world's 650 largest industrial companies were multinational. But that list, another footnote divulged, was based on *Fortune*'s domestic and foreign company lists for 1971.

How Things Fell Apart

With hindsight, it is now clear that the great turning point for the fortunes of the multinationals came in 1971, the year when the Organization of Petroleum-Exporting Countries (OPEC) first showed that it could impose its own

A Problem of Definition

At its simplest, a multinational corporation is one that owns or controls production or service facilities (for example, banks) in at least two countries outside the country where it is headquartered. Most authorities agree, however, that to qualify for the label, a company should operate in six or more countries and have sales of at least $100 million a year. It is the size and the power of the more than 200 multinational corporations with sales above $1 billion a year that have created popular concern over their activities. As a U.N. study ever so delicately suggested: "For most practical purposes, those [multinationals] with less than $100 million in sales can safely be ignored."

G. & C. Merriam, the publishers, in 1971 added the word *multinational* to their large dictionary; in 1973 it got into *Webster's New Collegiate Dictionary*—but only as an adjective. The 1975 edition also lists the word as a noun. Business semanticists insist that "international" is too broad a term, because it covers even small import-export firms, whereas a multinational company generally has a global strategy of investment, production, and distribution, in addition to its size.

The United Nations' Group of Eminent Persons, after a nine-month study of the multinationals, concluded that "multinational corporation" really isn't quite the right phrase to describe the phenomenon. The eminences argued that "transnational enterprises" would be a better label because the companies aren't all corporations but may be government entities, partnerships, or cooperatives. And "trans," of course, dodges the question of the number of countries involved. (After all, some 3,000 U. S. companies have direct investments abroad, but probably only a tenth as many have operations in six or more foreign lands.) The United Nations agreed in part, and last year it created a Commission on Transnational Corporations and an Information and Research Center on Transnational Corporations.

Definitional differences persist in several other areas. Some authorities classify any company as multinational if its foreign sales account for 25 percent or more of the total. Others insist that the dividing line should be whether direct investment in manufacturing facilities abroad amounts to at least 15 to 20 percent of a company's total investment. Even the term "direct investment"—as distinguished from stock or bond holdings—is subject to qualification. Most experts argue that at least a 25 percent equity ownership of a foreign enterprise must be involved—that is, a large enough share to provide operational control.

American firms expanded abroad as early as the 1850s, but only after World War I did U. S. overseas investment rise rapidly, especially in Mexico and Canada. After World War II, and especially after the Common Market was founded in 1958, the magnitude and the location of U. S. foreign investment changed sharply; Canada, Western European nations, and other industrial countries got the bulk of it.

In earlier times most U. S. investment abroad involved mining or raw materials, and by one recent estimate petroleum still accounts for about 30 percent of U. S. direct foreign investment. The post-war investment pattern has been quite different; perhaps 40 percent has been concentrated in such leading modern industries as electronics, chemicals, and autos. Yet despite the importance of underdeveloped countries as sources of new materials, 80 percent of international commodities trade (excluding oil) is still between industrialized countries.

The organizational pattern of big U. S. multinational corporations has tended to evolve by stages as the scope of foreign operations grew. Before 1950 a medium-rank export manager typically handled foreign sales. As demand for U. S. products increased, many firms created an international division to set up and run overseas subsidiaries. But further growth abroad often created difficulties, both in internal supervision and in coping with such ordinary but time-consuming activities as product design, pricing policy, quality control, and research. Some companies have responded by subdividing their international divisions into geographical sectors; others, by dismembering them and forming product divisions with global responsibilities.

With the resurgence of nationalistic fervor, especially in underdeveloped countries, multinationals in recent years have increasingly taken on foreign partners in their subsidiaries abroad. Though control has generally remained in home-country hands up to now, this pattern, too, is changing. Industry by industry, several Latin American countries are beginning to insist on majority control of foreign subsidiaries operating within their borders.   G. B.

terms for oil on industrialized Western nations of far greater economic and military strength. In the wake of that confrontation, which was followed by an extortionate price increase in 1973 and the outright nationalization of most Western oil company holdings in OPEC countries, other underdeveloped nations felt emboldened to impose tougher rules and higher taxes on foreign enterprises.

Another 1971 event, a book tellingly titled *Sovereignty at Bay* by Harvard Prof. Raymond Vernon, sounded a central theme, which critics of multinationals have been embellishing ever since. Vernon argued that "sovereign states are feeling naked." He contended that the great size, the financial strength, and the superior technology and organization of vast international enterprises set them beyond the effective control of individ-

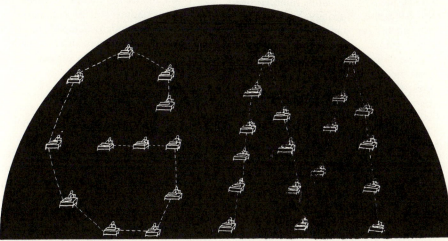

STUART LEEDS

ual nation-states, which needed their jobs and money too much to resist whatever came along in the bargain.

By now, a whole body of literature has appeared about multinational companies; some of it is factual, much of it a beguiling mixture of insight and fantasy. The American public is entitled to feel confused by the polemics, for many of the issues do not yield easily to simplification or sweeping generalization. In this cascade of words, the book with the mightiest impact is *Global Reach,* by political scientist Richard J. Barnet and economist Roland E. Müller. A readable best-seller, it has been serialized in *The New Yorker*, praised in the *New York Review of Books*, condemned by *Time* magazine ("a biased indictment"), and regularly cited by businessmen bemoaning "unfair" attacks.

The authors' thesis is that "the structural transformation of the world economy through the globalization of Big

Business is undermining the power of the nation-state to maintain economic and political stability within its territory." However plausible, that theory itself bestirs controversy. For it overlooks the powers that all governments possess. Idaho Democrat Frank Church, chairman of the Senate subcommittee that has been investigating multinational corporations, once put the matter in perspective. Noting that the spread of multinationals had helped to promote a "new nationalism" among the proliferating new nations of the post–World War II era, he remarked that a witness had likened the "developing confrontation" between the two groups to the dispute eight centuries ago between King Henry II and Thomas à Becket, archbishop of Canterbury—a contest that ended with murder in the cathedral. "It

is possible that murder could occur again," said Church, "this time the murder of the multinationals. For despite their enormous growth and wealth it is still an unequal contest. Armies march for governments, whether large or small, and each of these governments possesses, in its sovereign right, the power to tax, to restrict, to discriminate against, or to nationalize foreign-owned businesses, or indeed to confiscate their properties."

No armies have recently marched against a multinational company, but a recent U.N. study found that nationalizations by developing countries doubled from an average of 45 a year during the Sixties to 93 annually in the Seventies. And host countries, especially in Latin America, have become increasingly successful at extracting benefits for their economies from foreign investors. Mexico, for example, is forcing foreign-based automakers to export more of their Mexican output and will eventually

require them to sell as much abroad as in the local market. Colombia is placing branches of foreign banks under majority Colombian control. Iran is insisting that many foreign-based industrial companies sell 49 percent of their already limited equity to employees or to the general public.

Industrially advanced countries are also demanding a bigger share of profits, jobs, technology, and management in their dealings with multinationals. Several European nations, including even West Germany, which has had a particularly liberal attitude toward foreign investment, are starting to look closely at foreign investments for the national benefits involved. Last year Canada imposed a set of formal criteria on foreign-controlled companies, including a requirement that a majority of their boards of directors be composed of Canadians. The province of Saskatchewan decided to nationalize its huge potash-mining industry; of the 12 companies affected, 7 are American or American-controlled.

Five Issues, Pro and Con

In the debate about multinationals, at least five major questions deserve close scrutiny:

(1) *Are multinational companies exporting U. S. jobs?*

PRO: thousands of jobs in such industries as apparel, radios, and bicycles have been lost to American workers because U. S. companies have shifted manufacturing or the production of component parts to such places as Taiwan, Singapore, or Korea, where labor costs are far lower. Between 1966 and 1969, 500,-000 U. S. jobs were exported by such arrangements, says the AFL-CIO.

CON: the charges are correct in general but misrepresent the total situation. When companies moved production abroad, the usual alternative was to lose sales—perhaps even in the domestic market—to foreign competitors. Says Reginald Jones, the chairman of General Electric: "As the last company in the United States to give up the manufacture of radios, we know exactly how tough the foreign competition has been." Moreover, U. S. multinationals export so much to their overseas affiliates that the net effect is that more jobs are created than are lost (but not necessarily in the same occupations or cities). Robert S. Stobaugh, professor of business administration at Harvard Business School, found in a recent study "using every bit of information available" that on balance U. S. corporate operations abroad add 700,000 jobs to the domestic economy and add an income of $7 billion a year to the nation's balance of payments. Some other studies have put the figures much higher.

(2) *Do multinationals create "export platforms" abroad to ship back cheaply made goods to the United States?*

PRO: one need only consider where TV sets and radios are being made nowadays. Companies shift manufacturing overseas to exploit cheap labor, to circumvent anti-pollution laws, and to avoid taxes.

CON: again, the balance runs in the other direction. Less than 10 percent of the products manufactured by overseas affiliates of U. S. companies are imported into the United States. But nearly a third of all U. S.-manufactured exports go to foreign affiliates of American companies. The Department of Commerce, in its latest study of the matter, found that in 1972 majority-owned foreign affiliates of American companies sold 72 percent of their goods and services in the country where they were produced. Another 22 percent of their sales went to other foreign countries; only 7 percent was exported to the United States, an increase from 6 percent in 1966.

STUART LEEDS

(3) *Are multinationals the villains of currency crises?*

PRO: companies have shifted "hot money" out of weak currencies and into strong ones in such massive amounts that past efforts to stabilize the dollar were weakened. By so doing, it has been argued by Andrew Biemiller, the AFL-CIO's chief lobbyist, that "corporations and banks put profits ahead of patriotism." Sometimes they do so to protect their holdings against anticipated exchange-rate changes and sometimes to engage in outright speculation.

CON: since the major currencies have been "floating"—that is, allowed by governments to fluctuate in value day by day in the international money market—the complaint is partly moot. After a long study, the U.S. Tariff Commission concluded in 1973 that while multinationals do have the "capacity for disruptive movements" of funds, few of them use it. The commission found that "only a small fraction" of corporate treasurers and bank vice-presidents speculate in currencies. (When ITT tried to hedge against currency fluctuations in 1974, it miscalculated and lost more than $25 million.) The real cause of currency crises, as research economist Edward M. Bernstein told a U. N. inquiry, was the failure of governments to raise or lower the value of their currencies until long after it became clear to the world's financial experts that they must do so.

(4) *Do multinationals exploit the economies of underdeveloped countries?*

PRO: critics, mostly from academia, complain that even when multinational companies have accelerated economic development, as, for instance, in Brazil and (in the late Sixties) Pakistan, the poor remain as poor as ever. Sometimes the multinationals preempt scarce local resources. Barnet and Müller contend that between 1957 and 1965 U. S.–based companies financed more than four-fifths of their operations in Latin America with local capital or reinvested earnings.

CON: governments, not multinational corporations, set the policies that determine whether all classes in a given country will share in economic advances. The poor of most newly rich Arab oildoms have received little of much of their countries' larger slice of the petroleum pie. Peru has been busy expropriating U. S. subsidiaries in the name of control-

ling its own economy, but there has been no transformation of class structure or the power of the elite. It is probable that some siphoning off of local capital did occur, though host governments could have prevented it at the time. In any case, it is becoming much more difficult to do so.

(5) *Do multinationals evade taxes abroad by rigging prices?*

PRO: in buying or selling goods within the confines of a company, but across national borders, companies manipulate prices so that they can avoid taxable profits in high-tax countries and inflate profits in low-tax countries. According to a U. N. study, such intracorporate trade within multinational companies accounts for nearly a quarter of the world's foreign trade in goods. It is concentrated in a few industries, including chemicals and autos. Some studies contend that overpricing in underdeveloped countries has ranged from 30 percent to 8,000 percent; underpricing, from 40 percent to 60 percent.

CON: some of this activity undoubtedly does, or at least did, go on. But most big companies require "arm's length" pricing of sales between subsidiaries or divisions. In the United States and Europe, tax collectors are zealous about auditing corporate books to prevent such practices. Apparently few executives would object if governments reached an international agreement setting uniform rules for tax purposes on all transfer pricing.

Zeroing in on Bribery

The issue that may really cause trouble for U. S. companies, and not just for multinationals, is bribery and political manipulation. Companies can't condone the practice. Responsible executives are right to insist that it shouldn't happen. Many companies insist that they have strict rules prohibiting it. Oddly, Americans seem much more upset over such ethical problems than over the economic nitty-gritty that concerns rulers and power elites abroad.

Some businessmen argue that not as much corruption is going on as is widely suspected. But nearly four years of increasingly sensational disclosures add up to a lot of monkey business. For example, United Brands admitted that it had paid a $1,250,000 bribe to a Honduras official in an effort to win a reduction of that country's export tax on bananas. Gulf·Oil's chairman, Bob Dorsey, conceded that the company had made nearly $5 million in secret payments abroad for political purposes, including $50,000 to finance Arab propaganda in the United States. Exxon, the world's largest multinational, owned up to having made the biggest secret payment of all. Controller Archie L. Monroe told the Senate subcommittee on multinational corporations that an Italian affiliate had spent some $47 million between 1963 and 1971 to win tax favors. Monroe stressed that the payments were legal under Italian law but called them "a mistake."

The sequence of revelations dates all the way back to March 1972, when columnist Jack Anderson exposed U. S. government and corporate intervention by ITT in Chilean elections. Chile asked for a U. N. investigation, thus setting in motion the chain of events that has created wide demand at home, abroad, and in several international forums for stricter regulation of multinationals. The United Nations named a 20-member Group of Eminent Persons to make a far-reaching inquiry into the activities of multinational companies. Its report, rendered in June 1974, was largely critical. The only two Americans on the panel, Sen. Jacob Javits, a New York Republican, and J. Irwin Miller, chairman of Cummins Engine Company, filed dissenting opinions.

WITHOUT WAITING for that report, the U. N. General Assembly in April 1974 adopted its controversially one-sided proposal calling for a "new international economic order." Among many other things, it demanded "regulation and supervision of the activities of transnational corporations" but said nothing about whether such controls should be non-discriminatory or conform to the norms of international law. (The resolution also asserted all states' rights to nationalize economic activities without mentioning any duty to pay compensation.)

In December 1974 the United Nations went still farther in adopting, by a vote of 120 to 6 in the General Assembly, a Charter of Economic Rights and Duties of States. Article 2 provides that if a country expropriates a foreign-owned company, any disagreements about the compensation shall be settled "under domestic law of the nationalizing country" and "by its tribunals." Fortunately for the future of international investment, the charter is only a recommendatory resolution, lacking the force of law.

Otherwise, it might preclude an investor and a foreign state from effectively contracting in advance to submit disputes to international arbitration. And it certainly would prevent companies from suing in courts of another country, as Kennecott Copper and British Petroleum did in European courts after expropriations in Chile and Libya. State Department officials have labeled the charter "a step backward."

Considering the composition of the United Nations, dominated by an irresponsible majority of anti-Western Third World dictatorships, U. S. officials never had much chance of deflecting its attack. Anticipating that the United Nations would write just such an unfair, one-sided "code of conduct" as it seems about to do, the United States supported a similar effort by the Organization for Economic Cooperation and Development. Since the OECD's 24 member states are drawn largely from Europe, American strategists figured that the result would be more evenhanded and might even help sway the United Nations toward a more moderate stand. The tactic backfired. A draft code issued last fall by the OECD is "much worse than anything we contemplated," says one U. S. source close to the situation. The code proposed, among other things, that companies be required to divulge confidential financial data about their operations and taxes, country by country. The proposal would be, as one pained businessman puts it, "an open invitation to the world's tax collectors to raise taxes everywhere."

WORST OF ALL, although the proposed code would place tough restrictions on private multinational corporations, it is silent about government-owned enterprises and private national enterprises. With strong support from the business community, the United States is pressing for a parallel code of conduct for governments in dealing with multinational companies.

Remarkably, U. S. companies have so far been successful in staving off efforts in Congress to take away their right to defer paying income taxes on foreign profits until they are repatriated. Such a move would put U. S. companies at a disadvantage with multinationals based in other countries, none of which tax foreign earnings until remitted home. They have also dissuaded the tax-writing House Ways and Means Committee—so far—from voting to end their right to de-

duct foreign income taxes from their U. S. income taxes. If such a law were enacted, the loss of the foreign tax credit would mean double taxation, raising the effective tax rate on foreign earnings of U. S. companies from 48 percent to about 73 percent.

Sorting Out the Issues

In their fight to keep the United Nations and foreign countries from hamstringing multinational companies, U. S. businessmen have found an ally in Secretary of State Henry Kissinger. Addressing the U. N. General Assembly last fall, he praised multinational companies as "one of the most effective engines of development" and added that "the controversy over their role and conduct is itself an obstacle to development."

Somewhat similar views come from the Manhattan-based National Foreign Trade Council, a private, non-profit, non-partisan business association. "The major problem today," said the council in a policy declaration last November, "is not how to further restrict or leash the multinational enterprise but . . . how to encourage [it] to continue performing its essential international economic role."

A large element of socialist philosophy runs through the efforts to curb the multinational corporation. Jacques G. Maisonrouge, chairman of IBM World Trade Corporation, recently defined the struggle as "the latest manifestation of the long tug-of-war between the private and collective control of property." Many other businessmen would agree, but the conflict is not quite that simple.

THE FRAGILITY of the multinationals' arrangements for doing business abroad has legal underpinnings derived from the Napoleonic code, which holds that if changing circumstances make a contract impracticable for either party it should be revised. (In contrast, the U. S. Constitution explicitly prohibits states from passing any law "impairing the obligation of contracts.") The French doctrine has given rise to the notion that a sovereign state can override all commercial commitments. British economist Paul Frankel once observed that "this has downgraded international intercourse to the level of the jungle." In any case, the "new economic order" means that nowhere in the world is private foreign investment safe from the xenophobic pressures of nationalism. What began in oil is spreading throughout the world.

The recent surge of nationalistic fervor contains other seeds of evil. It is precisely because multinational companies can, and do, rise above the parochial interests of sovereign states that we ought to applaud their growth in the interests of world prosperity and, ultimately, abiding peace. Northcote Parkinson, the British historian, put the case well in his book *Big Business*:

If we are to save our civilization from tragedy, it will be through applying to politics the trained intelligence and methodical thought that we have already applied to science and technology. But even that will not be enough if we fail to apply the lessons of big business: the lessons of organization and control and, above all, of the international approach. . . . The whole idea of nationality rests upon divergent interests and mutual suspicion, sharply drawn frontiers, and ill-concealed fear. Set quite apart from the blood-stained arena of nationalism is the new world of big business, a world where the jealousies of the nation-states are actually forgotten. If we are to have a prosperous future, we shall owe it to men who have already learned how to cooperate and see the world as one.

The trouble with Professor Parkinson's vision of a world stripped of quarreling nation-states—many with selfish oligarchical elites and dictatorial rulers —is that nobody knows how to get from here to there. That is, to be sure, a depressing prospect. For nation-states and the fervid nationalism that they all too often inspire are surely one of the worst conceivable arrangements for the governance of a small planet. Yet, as Professor Vernon points out, the nation-state "is the only legitimate political process we've got, so the people of the world use it to do things for themselves. It's a terrible system, but everything else is worse." The practical probability is that both multinational corporations and nation-states are going to be around for quite a long time to come, and the frictions between the two will continue, if not increase.

MANY BUSINESSMEN insist that the great growth of multinational companies

is ending, if not already over. However, an upturn in global prosperity could give such predictions a short life span. It does seem likely that multinationals and governments will be able to compose their differences sooner in industrial countries than in the Third World, if only because nationhood is more important to the elite of underdeveloped countries than it is in industrial states. From today's perspective, multinational companies and the Third World are moving on a collision course that might, at the extreme, simply dry up much foreign investment. Still, as executive vice-president Wylie Robson of Eastman Kodak observes, "The more time that elapses, the more chance for cooling off." The economic interdependence of the world's 140 nations rises year by year. The great question is whether enough politicians and rulers will recognize the mutual benefits of cooperation before the increasingly global economy suffers serious damage.

V. Perspectives on Deviance and Social Control

The proliferation of the means for social control in America and other technological societies can be seen in the convergence of two emergent powers of the modern state: the police power from which grew the criminal justice system, and the power of *parens patriae* from which developed means of social control which Kittrie (1973) describes as the "therapeutic state." By the end of the nineteenth century the deterministic ideas of the positive school of criminology were introduced into America and "treatment," i.e., rehabilitation became one of the goals of the growing number of penitentiaries as well as the intent of the emerging mental hospitals (asylums). The lines between those incarcerated in prisons or mental hospitals were frequently blurred; both were stigmatized as "sick" and seen as equally dangerous.

The fact and fear of increasing crime has been a social problem of considerable concern in recent years. According to the FBI Uniform Crime Reports, crime increased eleven times faster than our population during the 1960s. However these statistics are based on crimes reported to the police, and we now know that the rate of crime is perhaps twice that reported. Fearful citizens ask, "Why don't we lock them up?" And recent societal reactions have been a hard line against criminals, for according to a report of a survey by *Corrections Magazine* (1976) we had 250,000 offenders locked up in our state and federal prisons as of January 1976. An equal number were locked up in our jails, half of whom were awaiting trial or sentence. Even with this increased reliance on punishment we still sentence only a small percentage of criminal offenders to jail or prison. However, many prisons are more overcrowded than ever, and one state prison system—Alabama—is under a federal court order not to accept any more prisoners until the prison population is reduced from 5100 to 2600 inmates (*Corrections Magazine* 1976:18).

In the lead article in Topic 12 Ernest Lendler focuses on some myths regarding the geographic distribution of crime rates. Scholars have been aware for some years of the doubtful validity and lack of reliability of crime statistics. And thoughtful newspaper readers have doubtless pondered at the press releases coming from the attorney general's office in the early 1970s to show the success of the "law and order" policies of the Nixon administration. We were told that the crime rate was increasing at a decreasing rate. A careful reading of the Crime Reports might suggest that our growing affluence is related to the growth of crime, for about half of all serious crimes reported in the Crime Index falls under the last two categories—auto theft and larceny. And it should be noted that "white-collar crimes" are not listed as such in the Crime Index.

White-collar "board-room" type criminals described by Fleetwood and Lubow are often overlooked as they do not fit the theory of the "sick" criminal. As the authors indicate, they often receive light sentences. Russell Baker's bit of irony should cause us to reflect on the damage done to our sense of justice by the discovery of crime in social strata as high up as the White House. He subtly reminds us that after the man behind the Watergate caper was pardoned, President Ford asked for $850,000 to ease his readjustment to civilian life, but the Congress appropriated "only" $200,000. By now we are aware that prisons do not solve the crime problem, yet they serve other intended and unintended functions, which are outlined by Reasons and Kaplan. The criminal deviant is a "collective representation" of evil and becomes a "servant" of the state.

The readings provided for in the topic Deviant Status and Victimless Crimes, as well as the remaining topics in this section, deal with behaviors that are seen as "bad" or "evil" because they are contrary to society's definition of "good" behavior. Sagarin describes the impulse to stereotype and stigmatize as a confusion of "doing" with "being." Thus deviance becomes a "master" status. Gilbert Geis presents an argument for limiting the overreach of the criminal law. Efforts to regulate private morality are expensive, he argues, and detract from dealing with the problem of crime.

The next topic includes readings which contrast the nonpunitive, yet stigmatizing approach to dealing with alcoholism, with the punitive policies *vis à vis* the drug problem. Beauchamp argues that the disease approach to alcoholism both adds to the burden of the individual and to the social costs of alcohol. Carr presents evidence that should convince most readers that the criminal law has failed to deter or decrease marijuana use. The question then becomes: What is the cost of maintaining a legal code that will collapse sooner or later? We have about 250,000 heroin addicts as compared to 9 million alcoholics. But the failure of the punitive approach is manifest not only in the continuation of the profitable drug traffic but in the spread of this addiction to middle-class youth. Kasindorf describes the difficulty of providing needed assistance to these youths.

Those who were seen as "insane" in the nineteenth century were commited to asylums. The number of these institutions increased as the idea of the therapeutic state developed. There are now nearly twice as many inmates in mental institutions as in prisons. The mentally ill person who is seen as potentially dangerous is described by Cocozza and Steadman; however it is impossible to predict dangerousness. Scheff's careful summary of research on the labeling theory regarding mental illness raises some crucial questions about the ambiguous criteria for mental illness. Szasz poses some insightful questions regarding the role of psychiatrists at the Patty Hearst trial. If brainwashing is "real," at what point can one be considered to be "brainwashed?"

References

1. Steve Gettinger. "U.S. Prison Population Hits All Time High," *Corrections Magazine*, Vol. 11, No. 3 (March 1976), pp. 9–20.
2. Nick Kittrie, *The Right to Be Different*, Baltimore, Penguin Books, 1973.

Crime in the sunshine

Top 25 crime centers
See box on the following page

By Ernest Lendler

The popular belief is that crime is an urban problem and that America's crime centers are the bleak, crowded, cold cities of the East and Midwest. But, according to the most reliable statistics available, that just isn't the case. The fact is, there is more crime in the sunny and warm states of the West and South than in any other part of the country. And the crime capital of America, according to these statistics, is not New York or Chicago or Washington, D.C.; it is Phoenix, Arizona.

The "Sunshine Crime Belt" is not new, nor has its existence been hidden away. But it has been easy to ignore. Early each year the FBI releases general statistics on crime (i.e., rape was up 9 percent nationally in 1974), in the nation's most populous cities, and that report generally makes a big splash in the press. But it is months before the Bureau issues a comprehensive area by area report on crime—its Crime Index—so those figures, though of greater significance, are rarely reported.

The information in the Crime Index is broken down into seven categories (murder, rape, robbery [use of threat of force in theft], aggravated assault [including attempted murder and rape], burglary [unlawful entry], auto theft and lar-

ceny-theft [theft without violence]), and it provides the single definitive evaluation of criminal activity in specific parts of the country.

One of the major criticisms of the Index is that it is compiled by Standard Metropolitan Statistical Area, usually one city and its surrounding county (the same areas on which all major government statistics are based) rather than simply by city. But to report by individual city, according to the FBI, would be "unfair" to the smaller cities and towns, since many would find themselves with extraor-

---

Ernie Lendler is a free-lance who lives in Brooklyn Heights.

179

dinarily high rates. In a city by city accounting, San Clemente, California, for example, would have higher robbery, larceny-theft and rape rates than New York City. Other small California cities would fare even worse: Inglewood has a crime rate of 10,100 incidences per 100,000 population; Lynwood, over 12,100; South Lake Tahoe, over 13,100; and Compton, over 16,100. New York's rate—6,100—is tame by comparison.

Within the "Sunshine Crime Belt,"

most police and elected officials initially deny that their areas have high crime rates and acknowledge the problem only after being confronted with the Crime Index. Even then, there are some who deny the validity of the statistics. Lt. Post of the West Palm Beach Police Department, for instance, insists that "there is no way we can compare to New York. Crime is worse in New York from what I read. There is no doubt in my mind about that."

However, once officials begin to list reasons for their high crime rates, three causative factors become apparent; the climate, social instability and an absence of fear of crime. Ray Marky, an assistant attorney general in Florida, has found that "weather has a lot to do with crime. In the heat of summer tempers flare, and I have read reports that crime increases with the temperature. I mean, who wants to go out to stalk a woman when it's zero degrees outside?" The

Top 50 crime centers

(Statistics are for metropolitan areas.
The figures in the right-hand column of all charts are the number
of crimes per 100,000, as reported by the FBI.)

1.	Phoenix, Arizona	8,165.2	18.	Bakersfield, California	6,560.7	37.	Jacksonville, Florida	5,861.8
2.	Daytona Beach, Florida	7,861.4	19.	Santa Cruz, California	6,489.1	38.	Lawton, Oklahoma	5,840.3
3.	Ann Arbor, Michigan	7,746.9	20.	Santa Rosa, California	6,464.3	39.	Lakeland—Winter Haven, Fla	5,785.6
4.	Las Vegas, Nevada	7,526.3	21.	Modesto, California	6,441.9			
5.	Fort Lauderdale—Hollywood, Fla.	7,519.8	22.	Kalamazoo-Portage, Mich.	6,432.3	40.	Melbourne—Titusville—Cocoa, Fla.	5,756.2
6.	San Francisco—Oakland, Calif.	7,277.8	23.	Orlando, Florida	6,404.3	41.	Little Rock—North Little Rock, Ark.	5,733.8
7.	Fresno, California	7,214.5	24.	Tucson, Arizona	6,391.5	42.	Spokane, Washington	5,714.5
8.	West Palm Beach—Boca Raton, Fla.	7,125.2	25.	Baton Rouge, La.	6,362.7	43.	Corpus Christi, Texas	5,705.1
9.	Reno, Nevada	7,000.8	26.	Riverside—San Bernardino—Ontario, Calif.	6,247.7	44.	St. Louis, Mo.—Ill.	5,675.1
10.	Albuquerque, New Mexico	6,966.4	27.	Eugene—Springfield, Ore.	6,232.2	45.	Austin, Texas	5,618.9
11.	Stockton, California	6,819.4	28.	Portland, Oregon	6,174.7	46.	Pensacola, Florida	5,613.1
12.	Miami, Florida	6,726.8	29.	San Jose, California	6,147.6	47.	Memphis, Tenn.—Ark.—Miss.	5,597.1
13.	Los Angeles—Long Beach, Calif.	6,628.5	30.	Sacramento, California	6,146.2	48.	El Paso, Texas	5,569.9
14.	Saginaw, Michigan	6,617.1	31.	Detroit, Michigan	6,098.3	49.	Baltimore, Maryland	5,545.6
15.	Denver-Boulder, Colorado	6,584.6	32.	Yakima, Washington	6,092.3	50.	Vallejo—Fairfield—Napa, Calif.	5,483.4
16.	Sarasota, Florida	6,584.1	33.	Tampa—St. Petersburg, Fla.	6,064.2			
17.	Gainesville, Florida	6,575.8	34.	Flint, Michigan	5,938.9			
			35.	Seattle—Everett, Wash.	5,924.9			
			36.	Anaheim—Santa Ana—Garden Grove, Calif.	5,889.4			

Burglary

1.	Las Vegas, Nevada	2,639.1	12.	Fort Lauderdale—Hollywood, Fla.	2,144.2
2.	Daytona Beach, Florida	2,634.1	13.	Santa Cruz, California	2,123.2
3.	Phoenix, Arizona	2,509.6	14.	Portland, Oregon	2,081.1
4.	Ann Arbor, Michigan	2,417.2	15.	Orlando, Fla.	2,051.4
5.	Sarasota, Florida	2,407.8	16.	Gainesville, Florida	2,050.4
6.	Fresno, California	2,383.8	17.	Stockton, California	2,031.4
7.	West Palm Beach, Florida	2,243.2	18.	Tampa—St. Petersburg, Fla.	2,024.2
8.	Albuquerque, New Mexico	2,231.0	19.	Santa Rosa, California	2,022.2
9.	San Francisco, California	2,205.6	20.	Baton Rouge, Louisiana	2,018.7
10.	Riverside—San Bernardino, Calif.	2,190.4	21.	Atlanta, Georgia	2,003.8
11.	Los Angeles—Long Beach, Calif.	2,187.6	22.	Denver—Boulder, Colorado	1,996.4
			23.	Sacramento, California	1,995.0
			24.	Anaheim—Santa Ana, Calif.	1,942.8
			25.	Saginaw, Michigan	1,936.1

Top 10 states

1.	Arizona	6,703.9
2.	Nevada	6,632.1
3.	California	6,304.9
4.	Florida	5,960.3
5.	Colorado	5,495.8
6.	Michigan	5,489.4
7.	Oregon	5,297.1
8.	Washington State	5,089.9
9.	Hawaii	4,958.8
10.	Alaska	4,943.3

Florida legislature has just finished a study of the state's crime and has concluded that the situation might require drastic measures. "We are going to have to do something," as Marky puts it, "or it's going to become a zoo around here."

According to Mike Sophy, a special assistant to the Arizona attorney general, the desert air attracts undesirables. "Even the criminals are deciding where they want to live," he says. "It's just as profitable to rob houses in Phoenix in the sun instead of someplace in the snow." He adds that high quality drugs are cheaper in the Southwest than in the East. Phoenix Assistant Police Chief Richard Porter is quick to point out that "our rate of increase is decreasing" and that, above all, it is Phoenix's property crime rate that is exceptionally high. There appears to be a reason for that, however; "It's so easy to steal around here," says one Phoenix cop, "that no one really has to use force to get what you own."

Most California officials refuse to publicly admit that their area has a high crime rate and evince surprise at the Crime Index figures showing California third in the nation in crime and in the top ten in every category except murder. One notable exception is Santa Cruz Police Chief Supervisor Charles Scherer, who states that "we are located in the most scenic place in the West Coast, the weather is real stable, don't get extra hot

Rape

1.	Memphis, Tennessee	64.6
2.	Tallahassee, Florida	63.6
3.	Las Vegas, Nevada	62.2
4.	Little Rock, Arkansas	57.7
5.	Albuquerque, New Mexico	57.0
6.	Los Angeles— Long Beach, Calif.	55.0
7.	Jacksonville, Florida	52.9
8.	Orlando, Florida	51.0
9.	Denver-Boulder, Colorado	48.8
10.	Santa Cruz, California	47.1
11.	Daytona Beach, Florida	46.8
12.	San Francisco, California	44.9
13.	Ann Arbor, Michigan	44.7
	Norfolk— Virginia Beach, Va.	44.7
15.	Fayetteville, North Carolina	43.3
16.	Detroit, Michigan	43.2
17.	Pueblo, Colorado	42.7
18.	Savannah, Georgia	42.5
19.	Atlanta, Georgia	42.4
20.	Charleston, South Carolina	41.4
21.	Riverside— San Bernardino, Calif.	41.2
22.	Gainesville, Florida	41.0
23.	Muskegon, Michigan	39.8
24.	Killeen—Temple, Texas	39.7
	Jackson, Michigan	39.7

Aggravated assault

1.	Columbia, South Carolina	552.3	14.	Flint, Michigan	409.4
2.	Miami, Florida	530.7	15.	Baltimore, Maryland	407.5
3.	Greensboro— Winston-Salem, N.C.	502.3	16.	Fayetteville, N.C.	406.4
4.	Lafayette, Louisiana	491.9	17.	Tallahassee, Florida	403.9
5.	Baton Rouge, Louisiana	469.0	18.	New York, New York	401.5
6.	Waco, Texas	452.5	19.	Los Angeles— Long Beach, Calif.	400.0
7.	Peoria, Illinois	442.3	20.	Charlotte, North Carolina	390.2
8.	Wilmington, N.C.	435.0	21.	Pueblo, Colorado	387.3
9.	Orlando, Florida	433.1	22.	Albuquerque, New Mexico	385.3
10.	Gainesville, Florida	428.2	23.	Corpus Christi, Texas	380.4
11.	Jackson, Michigan	426.4	24.	Ann Arbor, Michigan	365.2
12.	West Palm Beach, Fla.	417.8	25.	Little Rock, Arkansas	363.4
13.	Kalamazoo-Portage, Mich.	414.1			

Larceny-Theft

1.	Phoenix, Arizona	4,394.2	13.	Bakersfield, California	3,761.4
2.	Ann Arbor, Michigan	4,264.3	14.	Stockton, California	3,703.2
3.	Daytona Beach, Florida	4,130.6	15.	Yakima, Washington	3,696.8
4.	Fort Lauderdale— Hollywood, Fla.	4,120.3	16.	Santa Rosa, California	3,649.2
5.	Reno, Nevada	4,119.6	17.	San Francisco, California	3,643.0
6.	Modesto, California	3,977.9	18.	Champaign-Urbana, Ill.	3,631.9
7.	Tucson, Arizona	3,895.1	19.	Fresno, California	3,553.3
8.	West Palm Beach, Florida	3,838.8	20.	Santa Cruz, California	3,495.7
9.	Kalamazoo-Portage, Mich.	3,829.5	21.	Gainesville, Florida	3,477.2
10.	Eugene, Oregon	3,779.1	22.	Sarasota, Florida	3,475.2
11.	Saginaw, Michigan	3,778.8	23.	Albuquerque, New Mexico	3,468.7
12.	San Jose, California	3,772.2	24.	Melbourne-Titusville, Fla.	3,433.8
			25.	Spokane, Washington	3,433.2

Murder

1.	Atlanta, Georgia	21.8	10.	Detroit, Michigan	19.3	19.	Saginaw, Michigan	16.9
2.	New Orleans, Louisiana	21.6	11.	Fort Myers, Florida	18.8	20.	Gary—East Chicago, Indiana	16.8
	Waco, Texas	21.6	12.	Memphis, Tennessee	18.7	21.	Shreveport, Louisiana	16.7
4.	Jackson, Mississippi	20.8	13.	Macon, Georgia	18.2		Fort Lauderdale— Hollywood, Fla.	16.7
5.	Santa Cruz, California	20.3	14.	West Palm Beach, Florida	17.8	23.	San Antonio, Texas	16.6
6.	Savannah, Georgia	20.1		Atlantic City, New Jersey	17.8	24.	Stockton, California	16.3
7.	Jacksonville, Florida	19.8	16.	New York, New York	17.5	25.	Columbia, South Carolina	16.1
8.	Biloxi-Gulfport, Mississippi	19.7	17.	Gainesville, Florida	17.4			
9.	Lakeland—Winter Haven, Fla.	19.5	18.	Asheville, North Carolina	17.0			

or cold and attracts all sorts of people, and we were referred to a year or so ago as the crime capital of the world." Scherer confesses that there is ample reason for the designation; Santa Cruz has produced three mass murderers in the last two years. In late 1972-early 1973 one man killed five people, and in 1974 two men, acting independently, killed a total of 27. One of the '74 killers murdered 11 and the other killed 16 women. "He butchered the girls after killing them," says Scherer of the woman killer. "There was sexual assault after death in most cases, and he spread their remains all over the county." All three are now in jail, but, according to Scherer, the climate continues to attract "all sorts of people," with the current major problems being armed robbery and burglary.

Indeed, all of the "Sunshine Crime Belt" is a growth area, with thousands of new residents arriving daily. The resultant lack of social stability further contributes to the crime problem. Lt. Preston Hobbs of the Las Vegas Police Department notes that "people who live side by side for four years will not know each other, and when someone goes in and removes the TV or the whole house all they say is, 'I guess those people are moving.' "

But, in spite of the high crime rates, there is a general absence of fear of crime in the Belt, a fact which, in itself, makes citizens more susceptible to victimization. "In Phoenix," notes Mike Sophy of the attorney general's office, "there is not a noticeable fear of crime. People do not talk about crime as they do in the Northeast and, unlike the East, they are not afraid to go out of their homes after dark." In nearby Albuquerque, which was the nation's crime capital in 1971 and 1972, Bob Fenton, director of public information for the police department, finds "a more casual style of living and less a feeling among citizens that they are in the midst of crime. They feel that Albuquerque is a safe city." More and more "Sunshine Crime Belt" police departments are finding themselves in the position of having to try to actually create fear in an effort to bring the crime rate down.

Though the Northern urban centers certainly have their fair share of crime—New York leads in robberies, for example, and Boston in auto theft—the only cold weather area with as much crime as the Belt region is the Ann Arbor-Detroit-Saginaw area of Michigan. Ann Arbor Mayor Jim Stephenson is at a complete loss to explain his town's status, as are local police officials, though others variously blame the area's large student population, its seasonal auto industry, it's large unemployment rate or the large number of local gun owners.

But with that solitary exception, crime is most prevalent in more pleasant climes. The existence of the Belt hardly matches our beliefs about crime in this country, but it has been there for years, and there it will likely remain.

The only question that remains is which area within the Belt will be the crime capital when the next Crime Index is released late this year. Phoenix police, for their part, are sanguine about their city's prospects of retaining the title. "We'll probably lead the list again," says a public relations official for the Phoenix Police Department. "I can't see anyone beating us."

35

Pardon Me

OBSERVER

By Russell Baker

Wendell H. Howes
Chief of Police
Nantucket, Mass.
Dear Chief Howes:

I have your traffic ticket which was left on my automobile in August for a parking violation, said violation having occurred when I briefly left my car in a forbidden space while shopping for wine at Henry's package goods store near the Steamboat Wharf. Your ticket instructs me to remit a payment of $5 in punishment, and I would do so immediately were I not firmly persuaded that such punishment would constitute an injustice with which neither you nor the Town Selectmen wish to have your names forever linked in history.

I, therefore, request a full pardon from this $5 parking fine, in support of which proposal I cite the following precedents for pardon:

1. The "already suffered enough" precedent — Before being driven to commit the violation at Henry's, I had sought parking spaces in the vicinity, first, of Murray's Liquor Store, and second, of the Islander Liquor shop.

In each case I was waved out of illegal parking spaces by meter maids, who indicated their intention to ticket me if I persisted in parking. In both cases I gladly made the sacrifice out of my respect for law and order. By the time the illegal parking spot near Henry's was located, it was quite clear that I had already suffered enough in satisfying the law's harsh demands,

and so I parked the car.

At Henry's I purchased two half-gallon jugs of domestic red wine at $4.55 each for serving at a large dinner. An oafish dog later knocked one of these jugs off the kitchen table and smashed it, thus putting me out $4.55. Moreover, the guests criticized the remaining wine as inferior stuff and suggested that I had shown meanness of purse in serving it.

In the $4.55 financial loss caused by the dog and in the loss of face suffered before my guests, I contend that I have already suffered enough and, therefore, should not be asked to bear the additional burden of a $5 parking ticket.

2. The "hanging is enough, you don't have to draw-and-quarter-em" precedent — The paper shortage prevents me from listing all the money Nantucket extracted from me this summer, but even a summary must persuade you that I have already been hanged, financially speaking, if not drawn.

I mean, really now, $93 for water? And $62 a month for electricity. And $75 a month for oil? In a month when there was no heat running. And the ferry service. It costs more per mile to ride the ferry from Wood's Hole to Nantucket than it costs to travel to Europe first class on the France.

In view of the sums Nantucket has already exacted from my bank balance, I am certain you will agree with me that the insistence on yet another $5 check amounts to drawing and quartering the already hanged. As pardoned President Nixon once asked, do you want to pick the carcass?

3. The "American tragedy" precedent — I have never committed a mugging, cracked a safe, stuck up a gas

station or stolen fancy bicycles from children. In short, I am not a crook.

Is it not an American tragedy indeed when someone as eminently law-abiding as I finds himself caught parking in a forbidden space? When that space is in an area as crowded as the Steamboat Wharf, the tragedy is compounded, for his shame is flaunted before hundreds and hundreds of passers-by who inevitably see the parking ticket tied to the door handle of his humiliated car.

It is surely better for the country to put tragedy of this order behind it, and to grant its victim such poor mercy as is within temporal government's limited power.

I, therefore, urge the Town of Nantucket to rise above a too scrupulous passion for law enforcement and pardon me this $5 parking fine as a gesture of appreciation for the high quality of the tragedy with which my car and I have enriched Nantucket's otherwise humdrum summer season.

Assuming that the town will act favorably on my pardon, I will also take this opportunity to notify town authorities that I shall soon be requesting a substantial sum of money from the Nantucket treasury.

If I am to grant the town the boon of my residence there next summer, I shall require a considerable monetary allowance for office expenses, travel costs (that murderous ferry!) and miscellaneous, whatever that may be. A detailed estimate of these charges will be sent later. I mention them here only to give early notice that it may be necessary to increase parking fines in order to finance my continuing residence on the island.

In the meantime I await notice of my pardon.   Yours in law,

36

White-collar crime has reached epidemic proportions. Last year alone the cost to the nation was $40 billion. Yet the perpetrators continue to get off almost scot free

America's most coddled criminals

By Blake Fleetwood and Arthur Lubow

He had a businessman's suit and a businessman's tan, but Jack L. Clark no longer had a business. His nursing home construction company had collapsed in a gigantic stock fraud, leaving shareholders out $200 million and leaving Clark in a federal courthouse, awaiting sentence for stock manipulation. Ten million of the swindled dollars had allegedly gone for Clark's personal use, and prosecutors accused him of stashing away 4 million unrecovered dollars in a retirement nest egg. Out of an original indictment of 65 counts, Clark had pleaded guilty to one charge. He faced a maximum penalty of a $10,000 fine and five years in prison. But the judge, before passing sentence, remembered the "marked improvement" in care for the elderly that Clark's nursing homes had provided. He recalled Clark's "blameless life" as described by the defense attorney. He heard Clark's apology. He considered that Clark was a 46-year-old family man who coached little kids in baseball and football. Then he passed sentence. No fine. One year in prison. Eligible for parole after four months.

In another federal courtroom stood Matthew Corelli (not his real name), a 45-year-old, $125-a-week laborer who lived with his wife and kids in a $126-a-month apartment. Along with three other men, Corelli had been convicted of possessing $5,000 of stolen drugstore goods that government prosecutors identified as part of a $63,000 shipment. The judge considered Corelli's impoverished circumstances, his number of dependents, the nature of his crime,

and then passed sentence: four years in prison. Or, in other words, four times the punishment Clark received for a fraction of the crime.

An aberration? A mistake? Not at all. Former U.S. Attorney Whitney North Seymour, Jr., examined the federal sentences handed out four years ago, and discovered that only 22 percent of convicted embezzlers went to jail, and those who did received an average sentence of under two years. As for those guilty of security fraud, such as Clark, only 16 percent wound up behind bars, with an average sentence of less than one year. Judgments against "common criminals," on the other hand, were far higher: 71 percent of convicted auto thieves went to prison for an average sentence of three years, and 64 percent of those convicted of transporting stolen property, such as Corelli, were sent to jail with a typical sentence of four years.

In a moral climate like this, it is little wonder that we are currently in the midst of what Ralph Nader calls "a white-collar crime wave." Over the last six years, white-collar crime (defined by sociologist Edwin Sutherland 25 years ago as crime committed by a person of "respectability and high social status . . . in the course of his occupation") has risen 313 percent, while robberies have increased only 12 percent. The headlines tell the same story, but more eloquently. In the last two years, a stream of disclosures of high-level hijinks has poured through the original breach of Watergate. Executives of some of the nation's top companies—Exxon, Northrop, ITT, Lockheed—have admitted to bribing foreign officials with huge sums of money to

gain lower tariffs, higher profits and general privilege all around. An executive of United Brands, fearing disclosure of bribes made in Honduras, jumped to death from New York's Pan Am building last February—appropriately with his briefcase in hand. Dozens of other giant American companies—American Airlines, Ashland Petroleum, Gulf Oil, Braniff Airlines, Phillips Petroleum, to name a few—have admitted to siphoning off stockholders' money to make illegal political campaign contributions, often to both parties to ensure favoritism no matter who won. Stock swindles of enormous proportions, such as those by Equity Funding and Home-Stake Production, have bilked investors out of hundreds of millions of dollars. And on it goes: widespread payola in the music business, fraudulent grain inspections, massive expense-account padding, nursing home rip-offs, phony land deals . . . . It all adds up, according to the U.S. Chamber of Commerce, to a staggering $40 billion worth of white-collar crime per year. That's as much as the entire U.S. budget in 1950; or, to put it another way, 200 times the amount all the bank robbers in the country ran away with last year.

And that's a conservative guess. Adding up white-collar crimes is like counting stars: They're everywhere you look, and most of the big ones are invisible. A true estimate of the damage done to society by the thousands of crooks in

Blake Fleetwood last reported for New Times *on the shooting of 10-year-old Clifford Glover by a New York City policeman. Arthur Lubow is a free-lance living in New York.*

pinstripes and double knits is almost un-imaginable.

Less than ten years ago, this country felt smug in its own morality. Citizens of other countries cheated, bribed, swindled on a gross scale, but not us. Our Billy Sol Estes and Bobby Bakers were freaks, sideshows in the squeaky-clean circus of capitalism. It was possible then to even summon up outrage over the ways of others. In 1967, *Time* magazine ran an extraordinarily pious essay entitled "Corruption in Asia," in part to explain why American dollars were disappearing so fast with so little result. Conceding that "the evil of corruption, to be sure—is not peculiarly Oriental," the magazine suggested just how great the difference nevertheless was between East and West: "In the West, corruption takes ingenuity. In Asia, corruption is habitual and even traditional." As an example, *Time* cited the case of a friend of the mayor of Manila, who had given the mayor a loan of $7,700 without interest because he was the mayor's "compadre." The reader of today might wonder: What about Nelson Rockefeller's $1.75 million in interest-free loans or gifts to public officials over two decades? $625,000 to William J. Ronan, $50,000 to Henry Kissinger, $86,000 to L. Judson Morhouse, $176,000 to Edward J. Logue. Could it be that Rockefeller's accountant is Oriental?

Much of the piousness toward others has disappeared, but it has yet to be replaced with an outrage at ourselves. The breadth of corporate bribery, for instance, has left most of the nation's ethics experts temporizing. Asked by a *New York Times* reporter about the recent bribery disclosures, a professor of management and business at the University of California replied, "At a high level of abstraction, it's clear that American companies should not engage in wholesale bribery abroad, but I can't pass judgment until I get down to the operating details and ask when a bribe is a tip or a commission."

Such semantics seem to have become the order of the day, a Newspeak to cover Newcrime. Last month, during a Senate Banking Committee hearing on government loans to Lockheed, that company's chairman, Daniel J. Haughton, objected to the use of the word "bribes" to characterize $22 million the company had paid illegally to foreign officials and politicians. And how would Mr. Haughton describe such payments? Well, he said, his lawyer preferred the word "kick-backs." Later, when asked where the

For convicted businessmen, Watergate is only a memory

Not since the Kefauver hearings on the Mafia have so many wealthy criminals exploded so suddenly on the American consciousness. The list of illegal corporate contributors to the Republican 1972 campaign grew longer as the Watergate special prosecutor delved deeper. Now that the headline type has faded, most of us might assume that these convicts have suffered for their crimes. Right? Wrong. A recent *New York Times* survey of 21 business executives who admitted making illegal political contributions revealed that most had retained their jobs. The biggest executives of the biggest companies fared best. Harding L. Lawrence, chairman of Braniff, renewed his contract until 1980 at no less than $250,000 a year—an annual raise of $30,000. He will also, as in the past, be receiving $80,000 a year in Braniff consulting fees, and he can count on $85,000 a year in retirement benefits. Thomas V. Jones, although stripped of his title of chairman of Northrop, remains the corporation's chief executive officer, earning $286,000 a year. Harry Heltzer, who retired as chairman of the Minnesota Mining and Manufacturing Company, received $428,000 in compensation in 1974. His retirement benefits will total about $125,000 a year. Meanwhile, he is making an annual $100,000 doing special assignments for 3M. Another man who stepped down—William W. Keeler, former chairman and chief executive officer of Phillips Petroleum—will be taking home a pension of over $200,000 a year. His stock holdings in Phillips are estimated at today's prices to surpass $3.4 million.

Two of these men paid $1,000 fines. Jones paid $5,000 and Heltzer paid $500. For some, these would be prohibitive amounts; to these folks, obviously, it was pocket change. The exposure of their illegal activities gave corporate criminals some unpleasant publicity. For a few months, they were asked questions or heard comments about nothing else. But most of the questions were friendly, few of the comments were nasty and, now that the hubbub has hushed, they are back at their desks, making their fortunes.

money went, Haughton said he did not know. That is, he did not know where it ended up, only to whom it was first paid. So, asked Senator William Proxmire, how did he know the payments were effective? "If you get the contract," Haughton replied, "it's pretty good evidence. . . ."

As often as not, the reaction to our own recently perceived corruption is vague amusement. Take, for instance, the public response to the giant Home-Stake Production swindle, in which hundreds of people were bilked out of $100 million when they invested in oil wells that did not exist. Because of the people who were robbed—corporation presidents and show-business personalities such as Liza Minnelli, Walter Matthau, Andy Williams and Bob Dylan—the case drew mostly titters. The fact that Home-Stake Production President Robert Trippet and 12 other men from the firm were indicted by a federal grand jury seemed to cast almost no hint of probation on their characters. As one of Trippet's friends and Tulsa neighbors put it, "What he [Trippet] might or might not have done to Barbra Streisand or some G.E. executive isn't of much concern to us

here [in Tulsa]."

The real loss of Home-Stake was not that Dylan and Streisand and the other celebrities were swindled but that the story itself furthered the most popular and dangerous misconception about corporate crime: It either hurts people who are "somebody" or it hurts nobody at all. The truth is that most white-collar crimes victimize the American public far more than the more celebrated and feared street crimes. They seldom kill, but they inflict thousands of "little muggings" on the average citizen, driving up the cost of products and services and often obliterating jobs and life savings. Worst of all, white-collar crimes pollute the environment, sometimes literally but always psychically, tearing the social fabric of law and order and trust on which we all depend.

The press has never properly focused on white-collar crime because it is far easier to report off the police blotter, feeding the public a steady diet of rape, robbery and murder stories. City editors believe, no doubt rightly, that the bus rider wants a story with human drama and sympathetic victims. If the Bronfman kidnapping had not actually happened, the press might well have staged it, so well did it fill the traditional summer news hole. (Query: Would the grand-daddy of all political crimes, Watergate, ever have been reported or discovered at all had it not started out as a third-rate burglary?)

But occasionally some light breaks through and a newspaper or magazine will tackle the far harder assignment of stock manipulations, antitrust violations, grain inspection scandals, telephone rate fixing and bribery. After the giant Equity Funding scandal broke, in which a major life insurance company puffed up its stock value by manufacturing bogus insurance policies, *The Wall Street Journal* took a look at some of the losers. It found hundreds of middle-class workers who had invested all of their life savings in the company, only to wind up with no money and no recourse, their lives shattered far more than if they had been mugged and robbed by a stranger on a city street: a 74-year-old widow who had invested $7,000 and now, after 55 years of work, had $900 left in her bank account; a New Jersey man forced to keep working despite failing health, afraid to tell his family he had lost their savings of $25,000; a Nebraska couple who had borrowed on their assets to buy the stock,

---

Our pick

Ten bandits: what they did and what they got

This isn't the Chamber of Commerce list of brightest young businessmen, and it's not the ten best-dressed list. It's a list of ten very respectable criminals. Have any favorites you don't see here? Send them in.

Criminal	Crime	Sentence
Jack L. Clark	President and chairman of Four Seasons Nursing Centers, Clark finagled financial reports and earnings projections to inflate his stock artificially. Shareholders lost $200 million.	One year in prison.
John Peter Galanis	As portfolio manager of two mutual funds, Galanis bilked investors out of nearly $10 million.	Six months in prison and five years probation.
Virgil A. McGowen	As manager of the Bank of America branch in San Francisco, McGowen siphoned off $591,921 in clandestine loans to friends. Almost none of the money was recovered.	Six months in prison, five years probation and a $3,600 fine.
Valdemar H. Madis	A wealthy drug manufacturer, Madis diluted an antidote for poisoned children with a worthless, look-alike substance.	One year probation and a $10,000 fine.
John Morgan	President of Jet Craft Ltd, John Morgan illegally sold about $2 million in unregistered securities.	One year in prison and a $10,000 fine.
Irving Projansky	The former chairman of the First National Bank of Lincolnwood, Ill., Projansky raised stock prices artificially and then dumped the shares, costing the public an estimated $4 million.	One year in prison and two years probation.
David Ratliff	Ratliff spent his 21 years as a Texas state senator embezzling state funds.	Ten years probation.
Walter J. Rauscher	An executive vice-president of American Airlines, Rauscher accepted about $200,000 in kickbacks from businessmen bidding for contracts.	Six months in prison and two years probation.
Frank W. Sharp	The multimillion-dollar swindles of Sharp, a Houston banker, shook the Texas state government and forced the resignation of the head of the Criminal Division of the Justice Dept.	Three years probation and a $5,000 fine.
Seymour R. Thaler	Soon after his election to the New York State Supreme Court, Thaler was convicted of receiving and transporting $800,000 in stolen U.S. Treasury bills.	One year in prison and a fine of $10,000.

hoping the return would finance a needed operation for their son. "Where were the men who were supposed to watch out for us little people?" asked a retired man who had invested $21,000 in Equity. "They tell us it's all safe, all regulated, so they can get you to invest. Then you find out its still nothing but a big crapshoot, and you're marked for a loser."

Another candle in the dark and mysterious world of white-collar crime was lit recently by *Boston* magazine, which published a fascinating story on fraudulent warranty work charged by automobile dealers and paid by manufacturers. Investigating a Chevrolet dealership in Lowell, Mass., the magazine uncovered up to $20,000 a month in fraudulent claims, faked inspections, blackmail, manufacturer complicity—and one corpse (an inspector who would not play ball). Said one General Motors executive interviewed for the article, "Is warranty fraud endemic to the automotive industry?—that's absolutely true!" How much does it cost U.S. citizens? Every auto insurance policyholder pays approximately 20 extra dollars a year. And auto frauds form just the tip of the insurance iceberg. Fraud inspector James Ahern estimated on a recent NBC documentary that "ten percent of all insurance claims have some degree of fraudulent activity, and if that's the case, we're talking about an annual figure of one and a half billion dollars." Swindles in tax collection, automobile sales, construction work—in fact, in virtually every sector of economic life—suck a hidden tax of several hundred dollars from the average American's income.

The small investor is often the hardest hit in a stock swindle, since he has neither the sophistication to avoid fraud nor the assets to survive it. One classic stock shenanigan that has cheated the naive for 50 years is called a Ponzi scheme, after a Boston immigrant who in 1920 promised a 40 percent return in 90 days on every dollar invested. Before he was sent to prison for five years, Charles Ponzi collected $10 million. A Ponzi scheme requires money from new investors to pay the promised returns to the earlier subscribers. It builds and builds and builds . . . and then it bursts. Dr. Almeda Flores, an elderly general practitioner, lost her life savings of $150,000 to a Ponzi scheme engineered by Bennett Raffer, a 19-year-old, self-proclaimed "Boy Wonder of Wall Street" whom she was treating for gross obesity. Raffer said he'd turned his bar mitzvah gifts into $1 million through shrewd investments. His

lifestyle supported his claim. He had a fancy office, one Cadillac and two Mercedes limousines, and a Lear jet. But he had made no investments for Flores, or for anyone else. Instead, he had bilked a group of people ranging from his doctor to the doorman at the Drake Hotel out of a million and a half dollars. Although he and his father, a New Jersey accountant, were caught and sentenced to six and nine months in jail, respectively, none of the money was recovered. For the 65-year-old Dr. Flores, who had invested the earnings of 40 years of medical practice

Daniel Haughton, Lockheed chairman, prefers the word "kickback" to "bribe"

plus funds entrusted to her by South American relatives, the loss was shattering. "It was my whole life," she said. "How much longer can I go on working? I wish I was a girl of 25 again."

Related to the Ponzi scheme is the pyramid sales technique, a grandiose version of the old-fashioned chain letter. In pyramid sales, the investor buys a franchise to sell a highly touted but usually unmarketable product. His chance for big money lies in his ability to sell not the product but more franchises, on which he earns a hefty commission. The few who get in early come out rich. The base of

the pyramid consists of the hapless many who wind up with franchises and products they can't sell. The most flamboyant pyramid salesman, Glenn W. Turner of "Dare To Be Great" fame, is currently on trial in Florida on fraud charges.

Pyramid franchise sales, stock frauds and land-development schemes cheat investors who at least know they're risking their money. Many white-collar crimes, however, are committed by companies that swindle oblivious consumers and taxpayers. In the great electrical equipment price-fixing scandal of the early Sixties, executives of different companies met secretly before submitting their supposedly competitive contract bids to buyers of their machines. The collusion cost consumers an estimated billion dollars. Even in this case, where the proof of willful transgression was watertight, none of the convicted executives spent more than 30 days in jail.

Much of the electrical equipment was purchased by public agencies. That time the government officials were hoodwinked; but, as Vice-President Agnew's downfall dramatically illustrated, the cross-fertilization of government and business produces acres and acres of corruption. Much of this corruption, like much of white-collar crime, occurs on a small scale in small towns. The officials of one Pennsylvania town awarded a cable television franchise to a company that had paid them $15,000 in bribes. One administrator was convicted and sentenced to three years. Two others, including the mayor, pleaded guilty and received suspended sentences.

The only limits to fraud are the limits to man's ingenuity. Avarice is apparently limitless. One of the more un-

"How can we prosecute white-collar crime?" asked the prosecutor. "It appears that the Wall Street community is not anxious to get rid of its sharpies and thieves"

likely recent frauds involved frog's legs. The rural canals of India are teeming with frogs, and many of their legs find their way to this country. Unfortunately, the canals are also teeming with salmonella bacteria, a cause of food poisoning. Two years ago, the Food and Drug Administration cracked down, and the Customs rejection for frog's legs skyrocketed from 5 percent to 90 percent. Predictably, the policy created minor havoc in some culinary circles. But the frog's legs embargo had another, more surprising impact. Customs officials began to notice a year or so ago that many of the crates they had turned away were coming back for a surefire second rejection. Odd. Like so many odd occurrences, this one had a simple explanation: fraud. Since the frog's legs were insured against rejection, the shippers collected regardless of the FDA and Customs verdict. And since they were collecting once, why not collect two or three times? An insurance lawyer speculated that the fraud amounted to $10 million. The mammoth insurance companies make up their losses by raising their rates, and the costs are eventually paid by millions of people who will never taste a frog's leg.

There are other economic crimes whose costs cannot be measured in dollars. In 1970, a gas pipe exploded in a New York restaurant, killing 11 people. The pipe had been installed by an unlicensed plumbing firm. Two years earlier, in Richmond, Indiana, another leaky pipeline, which had earlier been identified as defective, blew up and killed 41. Since no federal or state law applied to the disaster, the Indiana Public Service Commission decided against a formal investigation. Last year a wealthy drug manufacturer admitted diluting a chemical that induces vomiting in poisoning victims. He was fined $10,000 and sentenced to one year's probation. In each case, criminals had recklessly endangered lives. In each case, they escaped serious punishment.

Just as hard to measure in terms of dollars are the jobs lost through white-collar crimes. Take the case of the Surety Bank and Trust Company in Wakesfield, Mass. Its president, Daniel Moore, not satisfied with his $40,000 salary, decided to augment his income by embezzling his own bank out of $8 million. When the theft was discovered in December 1972, the bank closed. The bank's depositors were compensated by the federal government, but the bank's 20 full-time workers were not so lucky: They were out of work, without warning and without anywhere to turn for help.

The cost of a ruined environment, like the price of lost lives and lost jobs, is difficult to quantify. But it's safe to assume that the damage has been ridiculously undervalued. A Long Island man was fined $500 last year after he admitted filling in a protected wetlands area to build a boat repair yard. American Cyanamid Company paid a fine of $1,000 for discharging chemical wastes into a Hudson River tributary. The city of Peekskill, N.Y., was fined $2,000 for dumping landfill illegally along the edge of Peekskill Bay. The penalties are a nuisance but hardly a deterrent.

At first it may seem natural that we overlook crime in the offices and focus instead on the more sensational

Over the last decade, white-collar crime in America has risen by 313 percent

streets. But this attitude is hardly universal. Most socialist countries, and especially the Soviet Union, inflict draconian punishments on white-collar criminals. Two Soviet businessmen who used stolen state goods to set up an underground lipstick factory were executed, and ten other Russians who parlayed a mental asylum and 460 tons of stolen wool into a fashionable sweater mill also received the death penalty. Last May a Soviet furniture manufacturer was sentenced to death for accepting bribes from a Western businessman. The payoffs, some only promised and not delivered, amounted to half a million dollars—small potatoes by American standards.

The difference in attitude is even more striking when we look at small primitive societies, in which a social sense develops naturally without imposition by a centralized state. Among the Zapetec Indians in southern Mexico, murder—a crime that usually involves only two quarreling individuals—evokes far less horror than the monstrous crime of polluting the river. Anthropologist Laura Nader at the University of California at Berkeley says that the preliterate societies she has studied lack white-collar criminals as well as white collars. About five years ago, she noted, floods ruined the Zapetec harvest and the Indians were forced to import corn. A wealthy villager brought in three truckloads. After he sold the first load at exorbitant prices, the mayor went out and met the next two trucks. He took them over with the approval of the community, and there was nothing the middleman could do. "American society is bizarre," Nader says, "in that it reserves its harshest punishment for crimes against individuals."

Recently, government agencies have begun to show more interest in white-collar crime. The proposed criminal code being thrashed out in the Senate would hold corporations or executives responsible for a list of new offenses. Attorney General Edward H. Levi is considering a recommendation by Ralph Nader and four congressmen to establish a division on corporate crime within the Justice Department. But these future possibilities are the only bright spots in a dismal picture. The Justice Department still devotes only 15 percent of its resources to eradicating white-collar crime, and prosecuting economic crimes is usually a long and expensive business. Preparing the case against Jack Clark, for example, took federal attorneys 18 months. A Florida state official investigating a land fraud that cheated investors of up to a billion dollars asked last May for an "emergency appropriation" of $250,000 because "the crooks are much better funded than the investigators." The shortness of money, the shortness of sentences, the shortness of attention spans—all signs suggest that in America, white-collar crime prevention gets short shrift.

If not for the lucky accident and the honest employee, most white-collar crimes would never be discovered. Roswell Steffen, an $11,000-a-year bank clerk, might still be betting $30,000 a day if police hadn't raided his bookie, checked the records and wondered where that money was coming from. For three years, Steffen pocketed cash deposits and, using the bank's computer, corrected each balance with funds drawn from dormant accounts. Like other computer crooks, Steffen benefited from the anonymity of modern technology. Computer records are difficult to audit, and to alter them you don't even need an eraser. One stylish young thief plugged his way into the Pacific Telephone and Telegraph computer and in two years stole close to a million dollars' worth of equipment. He was caught only because a disgruntled accomplice turned him in. After serving 40 days in jail, he went into business as a successful computer security adviser.

The Equity Funding Corporation would have had a much harder time fooling auditors if it had had to show them account books. Instead, it gave them computer tapes listing bogus insurance policies, policies made out to names drawn from the Chicago telephone book. A suspicious employee notified the authorities. If he hadn't, Equity Funding might still be flying high on Wall Street. Such whistleblowers deserve government protection because, at least on Wall Street, they are an endangered species. After two stockbrokers of the defunct K&M Securities Corp. were convicted of stealing $1 million in securities, the assistant state attorney general of New York, Sanford Pomerantz, had harsh words for two established brokerage firms. A Los Angeles company had fired Michael Claro, a former K&M clerk not involved in the theft, a few days after he testified at the trial. The other firm, whose securities had been stolen, "appeared to take the position that there had been an insurance settlement and that they had not sustained any loss," Pomerantz said, even though about $357,000 in securities was never recovered. "How can we prosecute white-collar crime if we cannot assure a prospective witness that his job is safe?" the prosecutor asked. "It appears that the Wall Street community is not anxious to get rid of its sharpies and thieves."

The way of life on Wall Street is far from straight and narrow. The smell of money hangs in the air, and the law encourages fraud. International banking secrecy laws, like Perseus' wallet, allow the criminal to act invisibly. The "holder in due course" defense permits securities buyers to ignore the provenance of their purchases; as long as they bought the notes in good faith, they're safe. The annual outside audit, required by law, can be circumvented through the use of diffuse computer records and the hiring of a different accounting firm for each company subsidiary. Insider trading—buying or selling shares on the basis of inside dope from the boardroom—is illegal, but the law has no teeth in it: No violator has ever been sent to prison. The Securities and Exchange Commission, the woefully understaffed federal regulatory agency, rules its wards like a cautious college president. A stockbroker who breaks a regulation is liable to be reprimanded or perhaps suspended for 90 days. He must

do something heinous to be exposed to criminal prosecution. One quaint bit of legal machinery, used by the SEC and other federal regulatory agencies, is the consent decree. The consent decree bears a surreal tinge of Freudian dreamlogic. A company that signs one makes no admission of past guilt but agrees not to do it again in the future.

There is something similarly perverse in the legal attitude toward accountants. Until recently, no member of a large CPA firm was ever sentenced to prison for his work, even though virtually every fraud has its accountant who, wittingly or unwittingly, overlooked it. The problem, of course, is in the "witting":

After the bank president's $8 million embezzlement was exposed, the bank closed and 20 employees lost their jobs

How do you prove that an accountant deliberately concealed facts and was not himself duped? Last November a government prosecutor proved just that to a New York jury. Two members of the nation's largest accounting firm, Peat, Marwick, Mitchell & Co., were convicted of fraud for their role in puffing up the proxy statement of the National Student Marketing Corp. One man was fined the maximum $10,000 and sentenced to a one-year prison term with all but 60 days suspended. The other received a $2,500 fine and a one-year term suspended to ten days. Not enormous penalties but, like a snow flurry in the Amazon, enough to attract a great deal of attention. Further indication that the climate may be changing came last May with the conviction in Los Angeles of three independent auditors of Equity Funding. After the trial, one juror told a reporter that although "there wasn't any direct evidence that they were involved" in fraud, the jurors felt that the defendants had signed unverifiable statements. Judging the actions of esoteric specialists, the jury had decided that negligence was tantamount to complicity.

That sort of aggressive attitude is required to pierce the shield of self-righteousness and professional detail that has protected white-collar criminals for years. After the Peat, Marwick convictions, a senior partner in the firm expressed "shock" and said he believed "the jury didn't understand the complicated accounting and disclosure questions in the case." More than a decade earlier, after the electrical equipment price-fixing affair, a G.E. vice-president had quit his job "madder than hell" when he learned the company wouldn't pay his salary for the month he spent in jail. The $135,000-a-year executive never considered himself a criminal. After sentencing, he expressed appreciation for "the letters and calls from people all over the country, the community, the shops, and the offices, expressing confidence and support."

People in the community, the shops and the offices still don't realize that white-collar crime is a critical problem. Even the experts in the universities look the other way. Harvard professor James Q. Wilson, who slurs over economic offenses in his recent book on crime, explains the omission of corporate thievery this way: "Unlike predatory street crime," he writes, white-collar crime doesn't make "difficult or impossible the maintenance of basic human communities." But the sort of community Wilson is talking about is hardly a community at all. It's simply a grid of streets that an individual can negotiate safely on his way to and from work and the supermarket. Are street thugs and stock manipulators separate problems? Or are they adaptations of the same blight to different environments? The Harris poll indicates that the population segment with confidence in business has dropped from 55 to 15 percent over the last decade. That old cynic, George Bernard Shaw, would find lots of support today for his observation: "We may take it then that the thief who is in prison is not necessarily more dishonest than his fellows at large. . . . He snatches a loaf from the baker's counter and is promptly run into gaol. Another man snatches a loaf from the tables of hundreds of widows and orphans and simple credulous souls who do not know the ways of company promoters; and, likely as not, he is run into Parliament."

Few people want to see white-collar crooks in Congress. But should they go to jail? With the air filled with cries for prison reform, many liberals are torn: They find the class bias in sentencing repugnant, yet they feel queasy about demanding that anyone short of Jack the Ripper be locked up. "We are really stuck between two modes of irrationality," muses Allen Dershowitz, professor of law at Harvard. "On the one hand, it makes no sense at all to imprison white-collar criminals, because they don't need walls around them. On the other hand, it's unthinkable to let them go free and simply subject them to fines as a license fee for criminality. Fines are not a stigmatizing event in our society." Dershowitz thinks that more imaginative punishments are needed. "Various methods which we might come up with are deemed uncivilized, although personally, I don't know whether I would regard it as more or less uncivilized to whip somebody or to confine them in prison."

For starters, Dershowitz suggests, steep fines should be proportional to a person's income. He mentions John Ehrlichman's request to work with the Southwest Indians as the right sort of punishment—one that would strip the white-collar criminal of his affluent trappings. But he concludes: "Under existing alternatives, it's essential that white-collar criminals go to jail." True, imprisoning economic offenders is "a symbolic punishment." But then—"It's precisely

the absurdity of it that serves as the form of punishment."

If the deterrent theory of punishment has any validity at all, it should apply best to white-collar criminals, who are usually motivated by greed rather than by need or passion. Nathan Lewin, the lawyer for recently indicted nursing-home owner Bernard Bergman, says that his personal experience with clients indicates that a jail sentence is a powerful deterrent for the affluent offender. Sociologist Edwin Schur agrees, noting that white-collar criminals, usually intelligent and well-educated, are best equipped to assess rationally the possible legal consequences of their crimes.

In the end, though, it all comes down to the judge. The judge has some idea of what the prisons are like. He's not dealing with sociological generalities, he's sentencing an individual. Is it really necessary to send this fellow to *jail*?

To the judge on his smooth oak bench, the stock manipulator is a fellow country club member and martini drinker who has been a bit too ruthless in his efforts to cop Boardwalk and Park Place, sweep around the board and pick up another few hundred dollars. Perhaps he should be fined. Perhaps he should go to jail and miss a couple of turns. But, unlike the mugger or burglar from the ghetto, he

is not an outsider who needs rehabilitation. The white-collar criminal has broken the rules, but at least he's playing the game. He's part of the community.

The vista looks quite different from the streets of Harlem. In the ghetto there are no computer terminals hooked up to a fast million. There are no investors to bilk, no expense accounts to fudge, no big taxes to evade. Instead, there are old ladies carrying shopping bags. The work is harder, the returns smaller, the risks greater—but mugging and burglary are the most lucrative careers available. And isn't making money what it's all about? The American Bar Association recently decided that all law students should take a class in ethics, and this year about 50 business schools are offering similar courses. But morality is not mathematics: It isn't learned in the classroom. You learn it from your parents or you pick it up on the street. How does a sense of moral community develop when everyone and his mother knows that the rich thief lives in a penthouse while the poor thief lives in the pen? If the Justice Department still believes in this country, it might try showing us that there really is a difference between capitalism and theft.

37

Tear Down the Walls?

Some Functions of Prisons*

CHARLES E. REASONS
Associate Professor, Department of Sociology, University of Calgary (Canada)

RUSSELL L. KAPLAN
Department of Sociology, University of Nebraska-Lincoln

Although prisons have been repeatedly exposed for their inherent degrading and dehumanizing effects, their survival suggests that they are fulfilling four important manifest *functions, in varying degrees: (1) reformation, (2) incapacitation, (3) retribution, and (4) deterrence. More significant are eleven* latent *functions serving various interests and needs: (1) maintenance of a crime school, (2) politicization, (3) self-enhancement, (4) provision of jobs, (5) satisfaction of authoritarian needs, (6) slave labor, (7) reduction of unemployment rates, (8) scientific research, (9) do-gooderism, (10) safety valve for racial tensions, and (11) birth control. These latent functions, largely unintended and generally unrecognized, suggest that abolition of the prison may not be as assured as some reformers suppose.*

FUNCTIONAL ANALYSIS has been employed in the study of many social problems.[1] The degree to which positive or negative functions are emphasized varies among academicians from problem to problem.

Why is it . . . that while we . . . [practicing sociologists] seem to be almost uniformly against poverty, mental illness, and racial discrimination, we are somewhat less than uniformly against war and . . . are for such things as divorce, adultery, prostitution, crime, delinquency, and interracial disorders.[2]

The researcher's analysis is shaped by his understanding and moral evaluation of, sympathy for, identification with, and belief in the negative societal impact of various phenomena and people identified as problematic. Thus, in large part, the researcher is "taking sides" *vis-à-vis* a social problem.[3]

Criminology and Functionalism

Within the divisions of criminology—(1) sociology of law (formulation, enforcement, and administration of law), (2) etiology of criminal behavior, and (3) penology (prevention and correction)[4]—some investigators have taken an appreciationist, or empathic,

* Adapted from a paper presented at the American Sociological Association annual meeting, Criminology Section, Montreal, August 1974.

perspective of criminality and the criminal rather than a correctional perspective.[5] Nonetheless, a major portion of criminology remains focused on "correcting" the crime problem. American criminology was born in an era of reformism and rapidly gained a reputable status envied by criminologists in other societies.[6] The reformist bent produced "applied criminology"; it concentrated attention on the criminal, who was to be rehabilitated.[7] One trained in criminology is expected to be well equipped to solve the crime problem in our escalating "war on crime." As the traditional conservative perspective on corrective criminology has changed to a more liberal-cynical perspective,[8] it has been recognized that crime is a function of the values and institutions of a society—i.e., societies get the criminals they deserve.[9] This functional approach tends to demythologize the "bad guy" view, in which crime is seen as some sort of disease; as observed by Durkheim, "the pathological is normal." This perspective has led many criminologists to analyze the legal and criminal justice system as a causal element in the creation and maintenance of crime. While belief in the ability to win the war on crime has deteriorated to a cynical acceptance of crime in society, many criminologists still feel that analysis of the legal and criminal justice system will help alleviate some of the problem.

We have focused long enough on the offender and his weaknesses. It is time we look to ourselves—to this chaotic, decaying, degrading system and indict it for its failures.[10]

On Correcting Correction

Of the three major divisions of criminology previously noted, penology has understandably been the most imbued with a correctionist perspective. Although correction is probably the part of the criminal justice system that the public sees least of and knows least about, recent events—uprisings at Soledad, the Tombs, Attica, McAlester, Michigan City, Joliet—have alerted the public to the need for pe-

nal reform.[11] Such reform should be based on knowledge of the historical antecedents of contemporary correctional philosophies and practices as well as on sound empirical knowledge of the social reality of institutional life. Nonetheless, the history of penal reform has been based mainly on humanitarian ideology rather than scientific research.

Decency, empathy, the ability to feel at least to a degree the lash on another's back, the removal occasionally of our customary blinders to human suffering, a respect for each individual springing from religious or humanitarian beliefs— these have been the motive forces of penal reform, not any validated knowledge concerning the better prevention of crime or recidivism.[12]

Since prisons have failed to solve the crime problem, some professionals and concerned citizens are calling for the end of prison construction and eventual abolition of most, if not all, penitentiaries.[13] Report after report and study after study have fully exposed the horrors of correctional institutions and their actual contribution to the crime problem. The following analysis by the Boston Prison Discipline Society in an 1829 report has contemporary relevance:

Our favorite scheme of substituting a state prison for the gallows is a prolific mother of crime. . . . Our state prisons, as at present constituted, are grand demoralizers of our people.[14]

Community-based correction has been heralded as the "new penology" that will help bring an end to the crime problem. The President's Commission on Law Enforcement and Administration of Justice (1967) and the President's Commission on Violence (1970) point out the valuable aspects of community involvement in habilitation.[15] The *ad populum* appeals of habilitation and economic savings through the increase of such programs as work-training release, furloughs, probation subsidy, and community-based facilities have brought about a multiplicity of activities and much high hope among those concerned with correction. Somewhat paradoxically, a great deal of pessimism concerning the problems of crime in our society in general and of prisons in particular accompanies an ever increasing faith in the wisdom of community-based correction and in reforming the policies and practices of correctional institutions. In a penetrating historical analysis, Rothman describes the birth of the penitentiary in the mid-nineteenth century, an era of profound pessimism about the multitude of temptations ever present in society and incredible optimism about the potential of the penitentiary as a change agent:

The prison would train the most notable victims of social disorder to discipline, teaching them to resist corruptions. And success in this particular task would inspire a general reformation of manners and habits. The institution would become a laboratory for social improvement. By demonstrating how regularity and discipline transformed the most corrupt persons, it would reawaken the public to these virtues. The penitentiary would promote a new respect for order and authority.[16]

Today's antiprison bent is cogently presented by Martinson:

The long history of prison reform is over. On the whole the prisons have played out their allocated role. They cannot be reformed and must be gradually torn down. But let us give up the comforting myth that the remaining facilities (and they will be prisons) can be changed into hospitals. Prisons will be small and humane; anything less is treason to the human spirit.[17]

Though we agree that flexible alternatives in correction are needed,[18] we maintain that the prison as an institution has a viability of its own. While we are ideologically and professionally committed to the "tear down the walls" movement, our understanding of institutions suggests that the prison serves functions generally unrecognized, overlooked, or minimized by many advocates of that movement.[19]

The following discussion will delimit fifteen functions of prisons. It is assumed that the prison continues to survive because it is functional for certain segments of society that may be either not served or ill-served by alternatives to the prison. Although we have tried to make these functions all-embracing, the task is not easily performed. Probably some functions that prisons serve have gone unrecognized in this analysis. Furthermore, the unevenness in the amount of discussion and the evidence cited for each function does not necessarily indicate a proportional variation in its significance. The functions of the penitentiary are categorized according to the extent to which they are manifest or latent.[20]

Manifest Functions

Functions of a social phenomenon are classified as "manifest" when they are intended and generally recognized. The major agreed-upon manifest functions of prisons are reformation, incapacitation, retribution, and deterrence.[21]

1. REFORMATION

Reformation usually comprehends change, rehabilitation, treatment, etc. While efforts to treat and rehabilitate inmates within the prison are increasing (although reformation has always been an important manifest goal of correction), some penal authorities are abandoning correctional treatment.[22]

Early proponents of the penitentiary saw it as "a grand theatre, for the trial of all new plans in hygiene and education, in physical and moral reform."[23] The Reverend James B. Finley, chaplain at the Ohio Penitentiary, stated in his memoirs in 1851: "Could we all be put on prison fare, for the space of two or three generations, the world would ultimately be the better for it. Indeed, should society change places with the prisoners, so far as habits are concerned, taking to itself the regularity, the temperance, and sobriety of a good prison," the goals of peace, right, and Christianity would be advanced. "As it is, taking this world and the next together . . ., the prisoner has the advantage."[24]

Although the viability of the whole prison system was doubted by even its most dedicated supporters in the early nineteenth century, it managed to survive and thrive.

2. INCAPACITATION

The low rate of successful escapes attests to the general effectiveness of isolating the prisoner from society. Although the convicted felon is kept "on ice," he is not isolated for a very long period, the average being twenty to thirty months; nonetheless, he is not physically able to perpetrate further crime in the larger society during this period, and thus the manifest function of incapacitation is served.

3. RETRIBUTION

The "pains of imprisonment"[25] include lack of freedom, routinization, sexual deprivation, rigid control, and dehumanization. Corporal punishment was significant in the early history of prisons. Ohio's warden in 1852 emphasized the need for strictness, "For whenever the Penitentiary becomes a pleasant place of residence, whenever a relaxation of discipline . . . converts it into something like an Asylum for the wicked, then it loses all its influence for good upon the minds of men disposed to do evil."[26] The most recent revelations regarding the Arkansas penal system, among others, suggests that severe corporal punishment still survives.[27] Finally, most outside observers of penitentiaries are struck by the oppressive, rigid, demeaning routine of life within "the walls."

4. DETERRENCE

Sentences imposed for deterrence are intended to reduce crime by the convicted and to serve as a warning to others.

In regard to the first function, studies vary in their findings of effectiveness: some report a recidivism rate as low as 30 per cent; others, a rate as high as 70 per cent. A high recidivism rate (over 60 per cent) is generally cited to support the need for alternatives to imprisonment but is regarded skeptically by others as the "two-thirds myth."[28] Since about two-thirds of most prison populations have been in prison before, it is easy to conclude that the failure rate is therefore 60-70 per cent. However, the prison is a dumping ground for its own failures. Studies based upon institutional populations at any given time will find 50+ per cent recidivism because repeat offenders receive longer sentences and are less likely to be paroled. Thus, they accumulate in prison and are disproportionately represented in any inmate population. Longitudinal follow-up studies, which provide a better indication of recommitment rates, suggest that about two-thirds of those released make it in spite of the prison and do not return. According to Glaser and others, the "two-thirds myth" is produced by faulty methodology.

The physical structure of prisons serves to solidify the "collective conscience" of law-abiding citizens, to reinforce their value system, and to demonstrate the fate of those who contemplate and perpetrate illegal acts. It supports the notion that crime doesn't pay.[29] The prison helps to define and maintain boundaries[30] and defines the "enemy" for the purposes of solidarity.[31] While the deterrent effect upon the general public needs further investigation, findings thus far suggest it operates under certain conditions.[32]

Latent Functions

While manifest functions are intended and generally recognized, latent functions are unintended and not generally recognized. The following list, though not exhaustive, suggests several functions that are not usually intended or entirely recognized as important outcomes of imprisonment.

1. Maintenance of a Crime School

The prison system establishes an atmosphere in which values supportive of criminal behavior are reinforced and additional criminal behavior is learned. By serving as a training ground for criminals it helps to provide a supply of criminals sufficient to maintain the criminal justice system.

The criminal produces not only crime but also the criminal law; he produces the professor who delivers lectures on this criminal law, and even the inevitable textbook in which the professor presents his lectures as a commodity for sale in the market. ... Furthermore, the criminal produces the whole apparatus of the police and criminal justice, detectives, judges, executioners, juries, etc. ... The criminal, therefore, appears as one of those "equilibrating forces" which establish a just balance and open up a whole perspective of useful occupations.[33]

2. Politicization

Prison provides the opportunity for politicization of the "dangerous classes." Given time for reflection and contemplation, prisoners, especially blacks, have recently become conscious of themselves as a collective, evidenced by inmate councils, prisoner unions, the emergence of Black Muslims and Black Panthers as a political force, Eldridge Cleaver's *Soul on Ice,* etc. The prison, says Malcolm X, is where he formulated many of his ideas.[34]

Youth, nonwhites, the poor, and other previously powerless groups, now politically sensitized to a greater degree than ever before, are the prime "recruits" for correctional institutions.

One way to understand the development of political protest in prisons is to view protest activity as a political resource that is used by disadvantaged groups to gain political power and influence when more traditional sorts of political activity are unavailable or unsuccessful.[35]

This politicization can be understood only within the context of attempts to make major social institutions more democratic. Attacks by the Civil Rights Movement, the Anti-War Movement, the Poor People's Movement, and the Welfare Rights Movement on the distribution of power in our society include changes in inmates' concepts of the causes of criminal behavior. Says Angela Davis:

Prisoners—especially Blacks, Chicanos, and Puerto Ricans—are increasingly advancing the proposition that they are political prisoners. They contend that they are political prisoners in the sense that they are largely victims of an oppressive politico-economic order, swiftly becoming conscious of the causes underlying their victimization.[36]

This perspective is being espoused not only by prisoners[37] but by some criminologists.[38]

Inmates have taken legal action against the prison administration and are pursuing unionization and other techniques to bring about institutional change. Furthermore, the demands made by inmates in recent disturbances transcend the traditional prison riot demands for better conditions; they call for larger social changes signifying political concerns.[39]

3. Self-Enhancement

The larger society and the criminal justice system often strip men of their dignity and identity, and the prison epitomizes the final step in the dehumanization process. But this process is countered by the formation of an inmate social system, which provides the prisoner with status, self-esteem, identity, a positive image, and self-enhancement.[40] While there is some question about how the inmate social system arises,[41] most authorities recognize the importance of this system and attest to its impact on the institution and individuals. Thus, indirectly and unintentionally, the prison enhances the inmate's self-esteem and prestige.

4. Provision of Jobs

The prisons give employment to over 70,000 persons, many of whom would have difficulty procuring positions elsewhere. This is especially true of the custody staff, given their relatively low educational attainment and lack of skilled training. Many members of the treatment staff—counselors, sociologists, psychologists, and teachers—have no more than a bachelor's degree in subject matter, which, in today's job market, is a surplus commodity. At the administrative level, many of the positions are obtained through political patronage as a reward for political loyalty, an element of no relevance in the nongovernmental job market.[42]

The penitentiary also gives employment to the paraprofessional whose skills are not well enough developed to be marketable in private employment.

5. Satisfaction of Authoritarian Needs

The prison offers psychic satisfaction for authoritarian employees in need of rigidity and domination. Within such a "total" institution, custody and treatment staff have nearly complete control over their wards, a degree of power they could not achieve in most other occupations for which they qualify. A significant fact of the large turnover among guards is that those with the most marked authoritarian traits are the ones most likely to remain in this occupation.

6. Slave Labor

Because it controls a relatively large group of idle men, the prison is a source of cheap labor for the state and for private industry.[43] Generally, all inmates who do not suffer a major disability are assigned specific jobs after their initial orientation period. Their duties cover maintenance of the institution—laundry, food preparation and service, janitorial work, etc.—for a nominal fee (e.g., 35¢ a day). Furthermore, inmates have provided labor for state use in furniture manufacture, license plate making, automobile repairs, land improvement, agriculture, etc. In the absence of penitentiary slave labor, the state would be forced to turn to the open market and hire labor at prevailing wages. It is, therefore, understandable that attempts to institute minimum wage laws in prisons are not looked upon kindly by state officials and prison administrators.

The prison system also benefits private enterprise. Usually an important requirement for obtaining parole is that the inmate must have a job waiting for him. Just as the penitentiary permits the state to avoid paying competitive wages for institutional maintenance, the parole system helps private business to subvert the open labor market. The inmate eligible for parole must choose between increasing his chances of parole by accepting a job at a low wage and hurting his chances for parole by not accepting that job. Some private businesses would have to be more competitive if there were not an inmate population from which they could draw employees. The classic form of this feudal economy was the lease system, under which prisoners were virtually sold into servitude to private employers. It enabled some states to boast that their penal system was self-supporting.

7. Reduction of Unemployment Rates

In a depressed economy prisons keep low-income individuals out of the job market. Inmates are generally unskilled; if they were out in free society, they would be competing with other unskilled individuals for a steadily shrinking supply of jobs. Imprisonment reduces the competition. Removing 200,000 unskilled persons from the labor market makes the economy look better: if they were not institutionalized, the unemployment rate would be higher. Thus, the prison keeps the unemployment rate lower than it would be otherwise.

8. Scientific Research

Inmates perform an important role as guinea pigs for various groups that need human subjects. Among such groups are the drug companies that use inmates to test new drugs. If it were not for prisons these companies, like the state and private businesses mentioned above, would be forced to rely on the open market. "If the prisons closed down tomorrow, the pharmaceutical companies would be in one hell of a bind."[44] Federal Drug Administration standards necessitate a three-phase testing of new products on human beings. Prisons furnish virtually all the subjects for Phase I testing.[45] In this phase, the new compound is tried out for effectiveness and possible toxic properties on a relatively small group of normal and healthy persons. If they survive without serious side effects and the drug seems promising, further testing ensues. Medical concerns also hire convict labor—technicians, nurses, paramedical and clerical personnel—for wages ranging from $5 to $8 a month, about one-hundredth of what free personnel would command in their position. Such savings are great incentives to private medical entrepreneurs and large drug concerns.

In the realm of legal training, the prison system provides valuable experience for law students and young lawyers to develop their legal skills. This captive population also provides a rich source of data for criminological analysis, psychological and sociological testing, and research. Furthermore, criminologists have gained financially from consulting, research grants, and similar endeavors.

9. Do-Gooderism

Prisons give volunteers and civic organizations an opportunity to discharge their humanitarian impulses at little economic cost. At many institutions there are several of these organizations, some set up mainly to provide furloughs for the inmates and to put people on inmates' visiting and mailing lists. Other organizations —e.g., the Jaycees—regularly hold meetings within the walls. The prison is a convenient theater of operations for volunteerism: it has a large number of subjects in a small area—literally a captive audience.

10. Safety Valve for Racial Tensions

Economic and political power tips the scale of justice[46] against nonwhites. Although explicit manifestations of racism have been removed from the law[47] in the last few decades, a defendant who is nonwhite and penniless bears a double burden before the law. Cultural bias operating in law enforcement and the courts produces a prison population that is largely nonwhite and poor.[48]

The disproportionate number of blacks, Chicanos, and American Indians in correctional institutions reflects differences in opportunity structures and, ultimately, power.

Nationally, 58 per cent of the inmates in federal and state correctional institutions in 1970 were white, compared with 41 per cent black and 1 per cent American Indian.[49] The disproportionate incarceration rate of nonwhites is greater in state institutions than in federal institutions.[50] The above ratios remain essentially the same for local jails and workhouses in 1970.

Wright notes that, on any day in 1960, one out of every twenty-six black men twenty-five to thirty-four years old was in jail or prison, compared with one of 163 whites.[51] On any one day in California in 1970, one of eight black men between twenty and twenty-four years of age was in prison, in jail, or on probation, compared with one of thirty whites. Extrapolation suggests that, during a year, one of four black men in his early twenties spends some time in prison or jail or on probation or parole, compared with one of fifteen whites.

In analyzing racism at San Quentin, Wright noted that (1) the vast majority of the guards and officials are white,[52] (2) blacks and Chicanos are disproportionately represented in "the hole," (3) the perception that prison officials are more lenient with whites is expressed not only by black prisoners but also by many white prisoners, and (4) black prisoners frequently serve longer terms before parole than white prisoners convicted of the same offense and having the same prior record.

The actual prison population is an index of what the society really views as crimes. Any study of prison populations in the U.S. indicates the determining factors in incarceration are always racial and social and economic.[53]

As one correctional authority has observed:

If we stop to analyze Attica and all other prison eruptions we find that the underlying cause in each case was racism—plain and simple white racism aimed at blacks. Racism is more intense, more vicious, and thus more inhumane in correctional institutions than anywhere else. What is happening in these prisons is essentially what is happening throughout the country outside prison walls: Black people and other minorities are becoming more vocal and militant in demanding basic rights that are still being denied them. But whereas on the outside the system has given in to the pressure and made some changes, such as dropping of certain racial barriers in the South, practically nothing has changed inside correctional institutions.[54]

The problem of racism in prisons suggests larger structural problems in subordinate/superordinate relationships between racial/ethnic groups.[55] While racial/ethnic tensions may be reduced through recruitment of minority personnel, establishment of racial/ethnic identity groups, cultural centers, human relations training, and other techniques, the imprisonment of a disproportionate number of racial/ethnic group members will continue to work as a safety valve for larger social-economic-political problems in the United States.[56]

11. Birth Control

Approximately 200,000 men and women are serving time in prisons in the United States. Their separation from the opposite sex reduces the birth rate. Given the fact that prisoners are generally drawn from the poor, whose birth rate is higher than the middle class's, imprisonment serves to lower the number of "undesirables" in the general population.

Taken together, these eleven latent functions, largely unintended and generally unrecognized, suggest that abolition of the prison may not be as certain as some reformers suppose. Assuming the eventual disappearance of prisons as we know them today, what would its consequences be for these functions? What can correctional reformers offer as functional alternatives? Are functional alternatives necessary?

1. Robert K. Merton and Robert Nisbet, *Contemporary Social Problems*, 3rd ed. (New York: Harcourt Brace Jovanovich, 1971); Robert A. Dentler and Kai T. Erikson, "The Functions of Deviance in Groups," *Social Problems*, Fall 1971, pp. 99-107; Lewis A. Coser, *The Functions of Social Conflict* (New York: Free Press, 1956); Kai T. Erikson, *Wayward Puritans* (New York: Wiley, 1966); Herbert J. Gans, "The Positive Functions of Poverty," *American Journal of Sociology*, Fall 1972, pp. 275-89.

2. Melvin Tumin, "The Functionalist Approach to Social Problems," *Social Problems*, Spring 1965, p. 383.

3. Howard S. Becker, "Whose Side Are We On?" *Social Problems*, Winter 1967, pp. 239-47.

4. See Edwin H. Sutherland and Donald R. Cressey, *Criminology*, 9th ed. (Philadelphia: Lippincott, 1974), p. 3.

5. See David Matza, *Becoming Deviant* (Englewood Cliffs, N.J.: Prentice-Hall, 1969).

6. According to Leon Radzinowicz, *In Search of Criminology* (Cambridge, Mass.: Harvard University Press, 1962), ch. 7, the dominance of the United States in criminological research is explained by (1) the prominence of social sciences, (2) the separation of criminology from faculties of law and their juristic view, (3) the prevalence of and public attention given to crime, and (4) the availability of funds for research and study.

7. Denis Szabo, Marc Le Blanc, and André Normandeau, "Applied Criminology and Government Policy: Future Perspectives and Conditions of Collaboration," *Issues in Criminology*, Winter 1971, pp. 55-83.

8. Don Gibbons and Peter Garabedian, "Conservative, Liberal, and Radical Criminology: Some Trends and Observations," *The Criminologist: Crime and the Criminal*, C. E. Reasons, ed. (Pacific Palisades, Calif.: Goodyear, 1974), pp. 51-65.

9. For an indictment of certain societal values and institutions, see Edwin M. Schur, *Our*

Criminal Society: The Social and Legal Sources of Crime in America (Englewood Cliffs, N.J.: Prentice-Hall, 1969).

10. Marvin E. Wolfgang, "Making the Criminal Justice System Accountable," *Crime and Delinquency,* January 1972, p. 22.

11. Angela Y. Davis, ed., *If They Come in the Morning* (New York: New American Library, 1971); Burton M. Atkins and Henry Glick, eds., *Prisons, Protest, and Politics* (Englewood Cliffs, N.J.: Prentice-Hall 1972); Vernon Fox, "Why Prisoners Riot," *Federal Probation,* March 1971, pp. 9-14; Robert Martinson, "Collective Behavior at Attica," *Federal Probation,* September 1972, pp. 3-7; John Pallas and Bob Barber, "From Riot to Revolution," *Issues in Criminology,* Fall 1972, pp. 1-19; *Attica: The Official Report of the New York State Special Commission on Attica* (New York: Bantam, 1972).

12. Norval Morris and Gordon Hawkins, *The Honest Politician's Guide to Crime Control* (Chicago: University of Chicago Press, 1970), p. 246.

13. Board of Trustees, National Council on Crime and Delinquency, "Institutional Construction," *Crime and Delinquency,* October 1972; "The Nondangerous Offender Should Not Be Imprisoned," *Crime and Delinquency,* October 1973; Sol Rubin, "Developments in Correctional Law," *Crime and Delinquency,* April 1973, pp. 251-52.

14. David J. Rothman, *The Discovery of the Asylum* (Boston: Little, Brown, 1971), p. 93.

15. In light of basic criminological research findings, "habilitation" seems more appropriate than "rehabilitation." To habilitate means "to make suitable or clothe, equip, or outfit"; re prisoners, to *resocialize.* Rehabilitate means "to restore a dependent, defective, or criminal to a state of physical, mental, or moral health through treatment and training." Its bases are the religious concept of "falling out of grace," which fails to recognize the social and cultural pluralism of our society, and the irrelevant "medical model" of deviance. A convict's assessment of rehabilitation: "Ain't no way I want to return to the former state of my life." See John Irwin, *The Felon* (Englewood Cliffs, N.J.: Prentice-Hall, 1970); Elmer H. Johnson, "A Basic Error: Dealing with Inmates as though They Were Abnormal," *Federal Probation,* March 1971, pp. 39-44; Charles W. Thomas, "The Correctional Institution as an Enemy of Corrections," *Federal Probation,* March 1973, pp. 8-13.

16. Rothman, *op. cit. supra* note 14, p. 107.

17. Robert Martinson, "Planning for Public Safety," *New Republic,* April 29, 1972, p. 23.

18. See "Turn 'em Loose: Toward a Flexible Corrections System," *Southern California Law Review,* Spring 1969, pp. 682-700.

19. Both of us have had experience in prisons through research and occupation and have, like others, ingested a significant portion of the voluminous literature on prisons. While this analysis does not negate our involvement in penal reform, it has forced us to look at many aspects of the prison from a different perspective and it makes us increasingly aware of the limitations of our efforts.

20. The difference between "manifest" and "latent" *functions* is not the same sort that distinguishes manifest from latent *social problems.* See Merton and Nisbet, *op. cit. supra* note 1, pp. 806-10. While prisons are manifestly a social problem to many, they serve a number of latent and manifest functions. Furthermore, we have purposely avoided use of the terms "positive" and "negative" in referring to functions because of their evaluative denotations. Obviously some functions are "positive" for certain groups and "negative" for others.

21. Sutherland and Cressey, *op. cit. supra* note 4, p. 497.

22. M. Cordon, "Volunteer and Academic Education for Rehabilitation of Prisoners," *Adult Leadership,* July 1971, pp. 48-50; J. M. McKee, "Contingency Management in a Correctional Institution: Draper Correctional Center, Elmore, Alabama," *Educational Technology,* April 1971, pp. 51-54; J. P. McWilliams, "Rehabilitation versus Recidivism: Correctional Education in Texas," *Junior College Journal,* March 1971, p. 88; Albert R. Roberts, "Developmental Perspective of Correctional Education," *American Journal of Correction,* May-June 1969, pp. 14-17. One observer has suggested that prisons can escape the onus of failure only by abandoning the goal of rehabilitation: Charles R. Tittle, "Prisons and Rehabilitation: The Inevitability of Disfavor," *Social Problems,* Vol. 21, No. 3, 1974, pp. 385-95. For a critique of the coercive and repressive functions of rehabilitation, see Alberto Mares' letter on "A Program to Cripple Federal Prisons," *New York Review of Books,* March 7, 1974, p. 23; and Roy G. Spece, Jr., "Conditioning and Other Technologies Used to 'Treat?' 'Rehabilitate?' 'Demolish?' Prisoners and Mental Patients," *Southern California Law Review,* Spring 1972, pp. 616-81.

23. See Rothman, *op. cit. supra* note 14, p. 84.

24. *Id.,* pp. 84-85.

25. Gresham M. Sykes, *The Society of Captives* (New York: Atheneum, 1958).

26. See Rothman, *op. cit. supra* note 14, p. 102.

27. For a comprehensive discussion of "horrors of correction," see National Commission on the Causes and Prevention of Violence, *Law and Order Reconsidered* (Washington, D.C.: U.S. Government Printing Office, 1969), ch. 24, esp. pp. 576-85.

28. Daniel Glaser, *The Effectiveness of a Prison and Parole System* (Indianapolis: Bobbs-Merrill, 1964). For other longitudinal assessments which support the two-thirds "success" rate see Gene Kassebaum, David Ward, and Daniel Wilner, *Prison Treatment and Parole Survival: An Empirical Assessment* (New York: Wiley, 1971) and Tittle, *supra* note 22.

29. Gary T. Jensen, "Crime Doesn't Pay: Correlates of a Shared Misunderstanding," *Social Problems,* Fall 1969, pp. 189-201.

30. Erikson, *op. cit. supra* note 1.

31. Coser, *op. cit. supra* note 1.

32. Charles R. Tittle and Charles H. Logan, "Sanctions and Deviance: Evidence and Remaining Questions," *Law and Society,* Spring 1973.

33. Karl Marx, quoted in T. B. Bottomore, *Karl Marx: Selected Writings in Sociology and Social Philosophy* (New York: McGraw-Hill, 1956), pp. 229-30.

34. Malcolm X, *The Autobiography of Malcolm X* (New York: Grove Press, 1964).

35. Atkins and Glick, *op. cit. supra* note 11, p. 3. For a critical analysis of the political prisoner from the correctional perspective, see Stuart A. Brody, "The Political Prisoner Syndrome," *Crime and Delinquency*, April 1974, pp. 97-106.

36. Davis, *op. cit. supra* note 11, p. 37.

37. See George Jackson, *Soledad Brother* (New York: Coward-McCann, 1970), *Blood in My Eye* (New York: Bantam, 1972); Virginia Engquist and Frances Coles, " 'Political' Criminals in America," *Issues in Criminology*, Summer 1970, pp. 209-20; Howard Levy and David Miller, *The Political Prisoners* (New York: Grove Press, 1971); Huey Newton, "My Days in Solitary," *Ramparts*, May 1973.

38. Schur, *op. cit. supra* note 9; Richard Quinney, "The Ideology of Law: Notes for a Radical Alternative to Legal Oppression," *Issues in Criminology*, Winter 1973, pp. 1-35; Charles E. Reasons, "The Politicizing of Crime, the Criminal and the Criminologist," *Journal of Criminal Law and Criminology*, December 1973, pp. 471-77; Richard Quinney, *Critique of the Legal Order: Crime Control in Capitalist Society* (Boston: Little, Brown, 1974); Reasons, *op. cit. supra* note 8. For a recent overview, see Stephen Schafer, *The Political Criminal: The Problem of Morality Crime* (New York: Free Press, 1974).

39. Pallas and Barber, *supra* note 11. For an overview of legal assaults upon correction, see David Gilman, "Developments in Correctional Law," *Crime and Delinquency*, April 1974, pp. 169-83; Ronald Goldfarb and Linda Singer, "Redressing Prisoners' Grievances," *George Washington Law Review*, December 1970, pp. 175-320; "Selected Materials on Prisoners' Rights," *Record*, March 1972, pp. 188-95; National Advisory Commission on Criminal Justice Standards and Goals, *Corrections* (Washington, D.C.: U.S. Government Printing Office, 1973).

40. Sutherland and Cressey, *op. cit. supra* note 4, pp. 530-50.

41. Charles W. Thomas and Samuel C. Foster, "The Importation Model Perspective on Inmate Social Roles: An Empirical Test," *Sociological Quarterly*, Spring 1973, pp. 226-34.

42. Joint Commission on Correctional Manpower and Training, *A Time to Act* (Washington D.C.: JCCMT, 1969).

43. This does not mean that prisons exist today mainly to provide cheap labor but that, given the existence of such manpower pools, their economic exploitation is easily justified (as punishment as well as rehabilitation) because of their status. For an overview of the historical significance of this latent function, see Martin B. Miller, "At Hard Labor: Rediscovering the 19th Century Prison," *Issues in Criminology*, Spring 1974, pp. 91-114.

44. Jessica Mitford, "Experiments behind Bars," *Atlantic Monthly*, January 1973, p. 68.

45. *Ibid.*

46. Loren Miller, *The Petitioners: The Story of the Supreme Court of the United States and the Negro* (Cleveland: World Publishing, 1966); C. Vann Woodward, "Our Racist History," *New York Review of Books*, Feb. 27, 1969, pp. 5-11; Kenneth M. Stamp, *The Civil Rights Record: Black Americans and the Law* (New York: Crowell, 1970); Warren H. Cohen and Phillip I. Mause, "The Indian: the Forgotten American," *Harvard Law Review*, June 1968, pp. 1818-58; Sidney M. Willhelm, "Black Man, Red Man, and White American: the Constitutional Approach to Genocide," *Catalyst*, Spring 1969, pp. 1-62; A. Leon Higginbotham, Jr., "Racism and the Early American Legal Process, 1619-1896," *Annals of the American Academy of Political and Social Science*, May 1973, pp. 1-17.

47. William H. Hostie, "Toward an Egalitarian Legal Order: 1930-1950," *Annals of the American Academy of Political and Social Science*, May 1973, pp. 18-31; George W. Crockett, Jr., "Racism in the Law," *Science and Society*, Spring 1969, pp. 223-30.

48. Daniel Swett, "Cultural Bias in the American Legal System," *Law and Social Review*, August 1969, pp. 79-110; Charles E. Reasons and Jack L. Kuykendall, *Race, Crime and Justice* (Pacific Palisades, Calif.: Goodyear, 1972); Marvin E. Wolfgang and Bernard Cohen, *Crime and Race: Conceptions and Misconceptions* (New York: Institute of Human Relations Press, 1970); David M. Rafky, "Police Race Attitudes and Labeling," *Journal of Police Science and Administration*, March 1973, pp. 65-86; Terrence P. Thornberry, "Race Socioeconomic Status and Sentencing in the Juvenile System," *Journal of Criminal Law and Criminology*, March 1973, pp. 90-98; "Blacks and the Law," special issue of *Annals of the American Academy of Political and Social Science*, May 1973; "Proceedings: Founding Convention of the Judicial Council of the National Bar Association," *Journal of Public Law*, 1971; Herbert O. Reid, Sr., "The Administration of Justice in the Minority Communities," *Howard Law Journal*, June 1972, pp. 266-325; Robert L. Zangrando and Joanna Schneider, "Law, the American Value System and the Black Community," *Rutgers Camden Law Journal*, Spring 1971, pp. 32-44; David H. Bayley and Harold Mendelsohn, *Minorities and the Police: Confrontation in America* (New York: Free Press, 1969); Jerome H. Skolnick, *The Police and the Urban Ghetto* (Chicago: American Bar Foundation, 1968); United States Commission on Civil Rights, *Mexican Americans and the Administration of Justice in the Southwest* (Washington, D.C.: U.S. Government Printing Office, 1970); *Report of the National Advisory Commission on Civil Disorders* (Washington, D.C.: U.S. Government Printing Office, 1968).

49. If you classify people of Spanish origin as an ethnic/racial group (which we do), then only 51 per cent of the incarcerated population are white and 7 per cent are of Spanish origin (Mexican, Puerto Rican, Cuban, other). For these racial/ethnic groups the ratio of their representation in prisons compared to their representation in the total U.S. population is

whites, .6; blacks, 3.7; American Indians, 3.4; Spanish origin, 1.8.

50. These national data have been compiled from the following sources: Bureau of the Census, *The American Almanac: The U.S. Book of Statistics and Information* (Washington, D.C.: U.S. Government Printing Office, 1972), *Persons in Institutions and Other Group Quarters,* 1970 (Washington, D.C.: U.S. Government Printing Office, 1973); Bureau of Prisons, *Statistical Report, Fiscal Years 1971 and 1972* (Washington, D.C.: U.S. Government Printing Office, 1973); *The 1973 World Almanac and Book of Facts* (New York: Newspaper Enterprise Association).

51. Eric Olin Wright, *The Politics of Punishment: A Critical Analysis of Prisons in America* (New York: Harper and Row, 1973).

52. Though it has been suggested in recent years that recruitment of minority personnel in prisons is needed, their representation, as in other sections of criminal justice, remains low. Black judges constitute 1.3 per cent of the nation's judiciary. In numbers of policemen, minorities are greatly underrepresented. While blacks constitute over 40 per cent of the prison population, they make up only 12 per cent of the correctional work force and only 3 per cent of all top- and middle-level administrators. See "The Black Judge in America: a Statistical Profile," *Judicature,* June-July 1973, pp. 18-21, 24-25; Louis Knowles and Kenneth Prewitt, *Institutional Racism in America* (Englewood Cliffs, N.J.: Prentice-Hall, 1969); Joint Commission, *op. cit. supra* note 42.

53. Howard Moore, Jr., and Jane Bond Moore, "Some Reflections: on the Criminal Justice System, Prisons, and Repressions," *Howard Law Journal,* No. 4, 1973, pp. 831-43.

54. Winston E. Moore, "My Cure for Prison Riots: End Prison Racism," *Ebony,* December 1971, pp. 84-95.

55. For a similar problem in Canada, see Yvon Dandurand, "Ethnic Group Members and the Correctional System: A Question of Human Rights," *Canadian Journal of Criminology and Corrections,* January 1974, pp. 35-52. For a supportive statement of ethnic identity groups by a correctional administrator, see Milton Burdman, "Ethnic Self-Help Groups in Prison and on Parole, *Crime and Delinquency,* April 1974, pp. 107-18.

56. Charles E. Reasons, "Racism, Prisons, and Prisoners' Rights," *Issues in Criminology,* Fall 1974, pp. 3-20.

38

Deviance as a Method of Coping*

ALEXANDER B. SMITH
Professor of Sociology, John Jay College of Criminal Justice,
City University of New York

HARRIET POLLACK
Professor of Government, John Jay College of Criminal Justice,
City University of New York

A deviant person is one who does something we would not do. Thus defined, deviance is subjective. But not all deviant conduct is culturally relative. Acts malum in se *such as rape, murder, and assault are almost universally considered to be crimes. Noncriminal deviance, however, frequently exists more in the eye of the beholder than in the real world.*

Deviant conduct may be divided into three categories: crime, sin, and poor taste. Crime refers to those acts which are objectively and measurably harmful to the community and which cannot be tolerated by any society that wishes to continue as a stable organism. Violent crimes against the person and serious property crimes fall into this category. Sin refers to those actions which were originally prohibited by the dominant religion or religions of the community and which at various times may have been incorporated into secular law. Prostitution, gambling, drug use, alcohol consumption, and obscenity are examples of conduct that does no measurable damage to an unwilling victim; when such conduct breaks the law, it is frequently referred to as victimless crime. Poor taste refers to a whole host of social practices which are unpleasant and abrasive and which may or may not be symbolic of conduct that society may wish to prohibit. Overt public sexual practices, peculiar methods of dress, and the wearing of unpopular political symbols all fall into this category.

Most deviants recognize that their conduct is personally destructive and may be socially harmful as well. Yet they continue to deviate from the socially prescribed norms because this conduct enables them to cope with the stresses that a highly organized society imposes on their personalities. Many forms of deviant conduct are tension relievers. Some create a short-lived euphoria, and some are acts of rebellion against socially prescribed norms impossible to reach.

In coping with deviance society must first look at what the deviant is attempting to tell us through his conduct. If other ways of relieving stress can be provided for him, he can be persuaded to conform. If he cannot conform and his conduct is violent, we must physically restrain him; if he is nonconforming and nonviolent, we should let him alone.

SUPERFICIALLY, IT IS VERY EASY to define deviance. A deviant person is one who does something we wouldn't do. In the words of Howard Becker, he is an outsider, one who is outside the consensus of what constitutes proper conduct. The problem is that from someone's point of view we are all outsiders in one respect or another. Discussions of deviance, therefore, really turn on searches for universals, for modes of conduct that all human societies consider unacceptable.

In the classroom, anthropology professors like to upset their students by pointing out that there are no such universally disapproved modes of conduct. Even a killing that we would consider murder is acceptable in some societies: infanticide was common in Sparta, as was deliberate starvation of old people by Eskimos. In actuality, however, assaultive acts against the person or someone else's property, such as murder, assault, rape, and robbery, are considered taboo in almost all human societies, and people who perform such acts are clearly deviant. These acts, however, constitute only a tiny fraction of all the modes of conduct that our own and other societies have from time to time labeled as wrong.

If today we were to ask a middle-class, middle-aged, white American what kinds of acts (outside of assaultive crime) he considered deviant, he might respond as follows:

Being a homosexual; reading dirty books or seeing pornographic movies; going to prostitutes; engaging in sex outside of marriage; having illegitimate children (especially if the children wind up on welfare).

Using drugs—not prescription drugs or over-the-counter items like Alka Seltzer or Geritol or Vitamin E—but heroin, LSD, and pep pills.

Drinking too much; eating enough to make you fat; smoking cigarettes (maybe); smoking marijuana (positively).

Not taking care of your obligations; being lazy or shiftless; losing money at gambling; swearing and using bad language publicly.

If we accept this list as typical, it is as interesting for the conduct it omits as for that which it includes. Many acts which once were or now are attacked as highly immoral are not even mentioned: for example, contraception, abortion, and sexual and racial discrimination. Our Everyman also seems unconcerned about profiteering, sharp dealing, tax evasion, consumer fraud, and other kinds of white-collar crime. To be sure, if questioned specifically about these unmentioned acts, he would disapprove of all of them (except possibly for contraception), but the term "deviant conduct" would not bring them immediately to mind.

---

*Adapted from a paper originally presented at a symposium on Justice and Victimless Crimes, conducted at the University of Akron, April 1973.

The reason for our Everyman's perceiving deviance selectively lies in our description of Everyman: middle-class, middle-aged, and white. From where he stands, some acts affect his world adversely, others have little effect, and some are simply irrelevant. He doesn't care especially about racial or sexual discrimination because he is neither black nor female. He believes in sexual regularity because he is a family man and his world is stabilized by the nuclear families of his friends and neighbors. Furthermore, illegitimacy (as he sees it) is a direct and undeserved burden on taxpayers like him because of its effect on the welfare rolls. On the other hand, contraception doesn't seem wrong to him since his middle-class status probably depends on his success in limiting the size of his family. Even abortion has much to be said for it, since anyone can get into trouble and anyway maybe abortion will keep some of those babies off welfare. He doesn't worry too much about tax evasion because he is not aware of the activities of large-scale tax evaders, such as giant corporations and wealthy individuals whose accountants and tax lawyers have created tax shelters for them; and small-scale tax evasion is probably a fairly common and socially acceptable activity in his milieu. Sharp dealings (such as exploitative landlord-tenant or seller-consumer transactions) are likewise a middle-class way of making a living; and in any case, most middle-class persons are able to cope with dishonest landlords or tradesmen. On the other hand, persons who take or sell drugs are enormously threatening, both because drug use frequently leads to assaultive or dangerous criminal conduct and because drug addicts threaten the stability of the social system by their aberrant attitudes toward work and other social obligations. In fact, if there is one thread that runs through the fabric of Everyman's scheme of desirable social conduct, it is the desire to maintain stability, to preserve the status quo. As a member of the middle class, he has made it, and he recognizes that life is as good for him as it is ever likely to be. He doesn't want to lose what he has. Change is threatening and makes him very uncomfortable.

The laundry list of unacceptable conduct varies with the age and status of the person compiling it. Inner city blacks, for example, might list racial discrimination first and not list gambling at all. Marijuana smoking might be quite acceptable to middle-class university students, but tax evasion, sharp dealing, and profiteering would be high on their list of forbidden conduct. In the Bible Belt of the Deep South, blasphemy, secularism, and atheism are still heinous offenses, yet relatively free use of firearms, moonshining, and blatant racial discrimination are regarded with considerable tolerance.

Obviously, deviance is to some extent in the eye of the beholder—but only to some extent. All classes and status groups reject violent assaultive crime.[1] They differ, however, in respect to other types of unacceptable conduct, some of which in our system are illegal, some of which are immoral, and some of which are merely displays of poor taste. In considering these widely varying perceptions of what constitutes deviant conduct, we must ask not who is right and who is wrong but what kinds of conduct society can tolerate and still exist as a viable society and what kinds it cannot accept. Part of the answer to this basic question must lie in one's perception of a desirable society. For purposes of this discussion we are assuming an ideal closely akin to the traditional Jeffersonian model: an open society predicated on a belief in equality of opportunity and equality before the law, with a reasonable level of material comfort and economic security for all. In such a society, what kinds of behavior are necessarily beyond the pale? In this connection, we propose to discuss three categories of conduct: crime, sin, and actions that are in poor taste.

Deviance: Crime

Clearly, heading the list are murder, rape, arson, assault, robbery, burglary, and larceny, acts which are totally unacceptable and which can be condoned, if at all, only under very special circumstances.[2] We label these acts *crimes,* meaning that their violation of the public order is so severe that they must be handled punitively and coercively by the police, courts, and prisons. Even those who commit them agree that this type of conduct is wrong. A housebreaker does not want his own house to be burglarized and, except in Robin Hood legends, robbers do not argue that what they do is legitimate. This type of conduct is taboo because if it is tolerated a viable society is not possible. The control of such conduct, indeed, is one of the central problems faced throughout history by philosophers who have attempted to construct model societies. Whatever their point of view and whatever type of Utopia they have created, they all agree at least that this type of act must be forbidden. While Hobbes and Locke, for example, differed radically in their perceptions of the fundamental nature of man and in their prescriptions for social control of human conduct, they agreed that the principal difficulty in human society is the governance of violent assault by one individual against another.

However, assaultive conduct is only one category of crime. So-called "white collar crime," while nonviolent, is basically an attack on legitimate property arrangements in society. Acts such as tax fraud, stock manipulations, commercial bribery, misrepresentation in advertising and salesmanship, short weighting and misgrading of commodities, embezzlement, etc., are all methods of obtaining money or other property illegitimately. Since the function of an economic system is to prescribe how one may properly obtain property, white-collar criminals are subversive of accepted economic relationships.

---

1. An exception might be black revolutionaries such as George Jackson, who, while imprisoned in San Quentin for armed robbery, wrote extensively on the place of blacks in white society. Jackson felt that because "Amerika" was a "society above society" in which blacks were "captive," they were under no obligation to obey the laws. All crime, therefore, was an act of rebellion. Even Jackson concedes however, that noneconomic crime—e.g., "the rape of a Black woman by a Black man"—is an expression of racial violence turned inward. It is "autodestructive" and hence presumably wrong even if understandable. Tad Szulc, "George Jackson Radicalizes the Brothers in Soledad and San Quentin," *New York Times Magazine,* Aug. 1, 1971, p. 10.

2. We are referring here, of course, to random acts by individuals or small groups such as gangs and are omitting discussion of governmentally organized and sponsored violence such as that practiced during the Hitler period in Germany, the Spanish Inquisition, or any war. Whether this kind of organized violence is ever justifiable depends on one's politics, religion, nationality, and time in history.

As such, like their more violent criminal counterparts, they are a threat to a viable society and it is reasonable that their acts be included in the penal codes.[3] Although the prescribed penalties for white-collar crimes may sometimes be as severe as those for burglary or larceny, these acts do not carry the stigma or the punishment of violent crimes.

Basically our law is ambivalent. Property crimes are crimes, but they are not really heinous if they are not violent or potentially violent. Far less ambivalence in regard to so-called "economic crimes" is exhibited in the Soviet Union, where some offenses of this type, such as currency manipulation, are punishable by death sentences whereas certain kinds of homicide are treated relatively leniently. This probably reflects the orientation of the legal system toward preservation of the Soviet economic and social order rather than, as in this country, protection of individual rights. From this point of view, the inconsistency of the American system, which punishes personal crimes more severely than property crimes, is understandable. Whatever our ambivalence, however, it is clear that nonviolent crimes of property must be handled punitively, at least to the extent necessary to maintain the legitimacy of both our property arrangements and our system of law. The latent admiration of Americans for Robber Baron types may never disappear from the culture. Nevertheless, if business dealings are to be conducted in an orderly way and if prohibitions on assaultive crimes are to be taken seriously, there must be reasonable enforcement of the law relating to white-collar offenses. As the public conscience grows in sensitivity, moreover, the criminal sanction will be extended to dealings which are now considered unsavory but not illegal. The basic push in the developing field of poverty law is to extend the criminal law to cover some actions of landlords against tenants and of merchants against customers that were not considered illegal before. For example, may a landlord be paid rent by his tenants if he has failed to provide the agreed-upon level of services? May a merchant misrepresent the quality of the merchandise he is selling and demand continued performance of a time-payment contract if the goods in question have already deteriorated? These practices are probably permissible at present. The trend, however, is toward making such actions illegal—probably an indication of our feeling that even nonassaultive crimes of property are a threat to the viability of our society.

Our penal law, thus, contains prohibitions against both assaultive crimes against persons and property and nonassaultive crimes against property. Assaultive crimes offend our notions of natural justice; nonassaultive property crimes undermine the economic arrangements that are basic to the stability of society. The penal code contains, however, strictures against a number of modes of conduct which are included because of a relatively parochial cultural determination that they are immoral: drinking, gambling, homosexuality, doing business on Sunday, prostitution, drug addiction, abortion, etc. While at the time these prohibitions were enacted, the particular legislative majority which enacted them doubtless felt they were preventing subversion of the legitimate social system, many societies quite similar to ours do, in fact, tolerate such prohibited conduct quite well or, in any case, handle it nonpunitively. Many of these regulations are, moreover, both inconsistent and incomplete in their regulatory schemes. Prostitutes are punished but not their customers; heroin is forbidden but not amphetamines; it is permissible to bet on a race but not on a football game, etc.

Deviance: Sin

Many of these modes of conduct were originally thought of as sin and were *religiously* prohibited. Our use of secular law to regulate them is a relic of the time when the authority of the state was used to enforce the rules of an established church. That era is past, but we can see our cultural heritage most clearly perhaps in the laws we inherited from the Puritan theocracy in New England. We have (or have had in the recent past) laws against blasphemy, obscenity, contraception, Sabbath breaking, extramarital sexual relations, lewdness, homosexuality, gambling, and drunkenness. We also have inherited a distrust of self-indulgence and hedonism: even a rich man is expected to be constructively, if not gainfully, employed.

This heritage reflects a culture in which religion once was dominant. As our culture has changed, as religion has waned in importance, as our economic system has developed, as scientific discoveries have occurred, and as improved communications and the development of the mass media have reduced both social and cultural isolation, our feelings about what constitutes sin have undergone a marked change. Some behavior once regarded as sinful has become virtually acceptable today—for example, blasphemy; some, like heroin use, is still taboo. About other forms of conduct such as gambling, drinking, homosexuality, and abortion, we have ambivalent feelings. Some of this conduct is still subject to criminal sanction; some is not. If we remove the religious component, the criterion for whether the conduct in question should be forbidden should rest on whether there is *any demonstrable, objectively measurable social harm resulting from it*. To determine this, we must separately consider and evaluate each mode of conduct. In a totally rational world we would expect to find a correlation between the prohibition of conduct and its objective harmfulness. But this is not a rational world and the correlation does not exist.

Of all the modes of conduct in this culturally determined category, drinking is probably the most harmful and also the most widely accepted. Alcohol is involved in at least half of all fatal automobile accidents, a majority of private airline crashes, thousands of industrial accidents, millions of lost man-days annually, etc. We have in this country approximately 9,000,000 alcoholics who are unable to support their families, do their jobs, or function normally in the community. Alcohol use is involved in 55 per cent of the arrests made by police. From a medical point of view, furthermore, even moderate drinking puts a strain on the liver and complicates many maladies.

Yet alcohol consumption is widely accepted today in the United States, where nondrinkers constitute only a

---

3. While many political theorists have attacked the American economic system and consequent property arrangements as illegitimate—as violations of "natural justice"—none has seriously suggested that the types of fraud usually encompassed by the term "white-collar crime" are justified as an attempt to remedy economic inequity. The embezzlers and stock manipulators have not yet produced their George Jackson.

small minority of the population. Historically, the temperance movement waxed and waned in strength for over a century before it culminated in the "noble experiment" of Prohibition in 1920. However, within a few years after enactment of the Eighteenth Amendment, it became apparent that Prohibition was a disaster and, since the repeal in 1933, the temperance movement appears to be all but moribund. Thus, drinking has been handled both coercively and noncoercively, and while our current noncoercive approach has fewer adverse effects in the form of enforcement difficulties and police corruption, alcohol abuse still presents a problem—a problem not reflected in public attitudes.

Even more permissive than our attitudes toward drinking are our feelings about cigarette smoking and overeating. The medical evidence against both smoking and obesity is overwhelming but to forbid them by law would be ludicrous, a civil liberty horror. Even attempts to regulate cigarette advertising have met with great resistance. Though smoking and overeating are seriously harmful, medically and sociologically speaking, and though there is considerable consensus that people should not smoke or get fat, Americans who do not smoke and who are not overweight probably constitute a minority.

In contrast to drinking, smoking, and overeating, there is no medical evidence that moderate use of marijuana is harmful and no medical evidence of physiological harm from reasonable heroin consumption. That many heroin or marijuana users exhibit undesirable psychological symptoms is undoubtedly true. It is not clear, however, whether these symptoms are a result of drug use or whether both drug use and behavioral dysfunction result from a prior existing pathological, psychological, or sociological condition. Most of the other adverse sociological effects of drug use, such as crime and prostitution, result from our present coercive handling of the drug problem rather than from drug use per se. Yet few modes of conduct are looked upon with more social disapproval than heroin use and only recently has a similar attitude toward marijuana been softening. Moreover, in certain respects our method of handling drug use has been precisely opposite from

our handling of alcohol: alcohol, formerly handled punitively, is now handled nonpunitively; opiates and marijuana, formerly handled nonpunitively, are now handled punitively. Neither punitive handling nor extreme social disapproval has resulted in a decline (or even a stabilization) of the number of marijuana and heroin users in the United States. In 1967 there were in the United States about 100,000 addicts, of whom 50,000 were in New York City; five years later the estimates had precisely tripled: 300,000 addicts in the United States, with 150,000 in New York City.

In contrast to our attitude toward alcohol and drug use, which has fluctuated between acceptance and rejection, our attitude toward deviant sexual conduct has become consistently more permissive. During the eighteenth and nineteenth centuries in this country, man-woman relationships reflected a society that placed high value on premarital chastity and monogamy. Divorce was frowned upon, and premarital dalliance (except possibly for young men who were sowing their "wild oats") was strictly taboo. Prostitution, at least from the middle-class point of view, was considered degrading and abhorrent, and the fallen woman became a stock figure in literature. In the same period, homosexuality was considered so dreadful that there was no public discussion of the subject and, except for some very guarded indirect references, no literary mention of the problem. Today we are permissive in regard to premarital sex, we permit divorce, we have ambivalent attitudes toward prostitution, and we are slowly coming to a grudging acceptance of homosexual conduct. Some of these attitudinal changes have been reflected in changes in either the criminal law or its application; others have not. Nevertheless, few people would dispute the proposition that our attitudes toward sexual conduct have changed substantially even if the conduct in question has not.

To understand this phenomenon one must appreciate that the older rules for sexual conduct were drawn up in a society which had vastly different needs: until the twentieth century the need was for more population rather than less; venereal disease was an uncontrollable plague; and

production of goods and services was directly dependent on the family in a way that no longer exists. Twentieth century advances in public health and medical knowledge have changed all this.

Medical knowledge and technology have turned the older rationale for monogamous units upside down. One hundred years ago, a couple might have to produce ten or twelve children to be certain that five or six would survive them; today the parents of two can reasonably expect to raise both to adulthood. Formerly children represented a source of income and social security for one's old age; today children are economic liabilities at least until they reach adulthood, and sometimes thereafter.

In the face of these substantial changes, it is understandable that many of the older rules of sexual conduct are anachronistic. This is not to say that our commitment to monogamous union as the basis of family structure has diminished. Nor does it mean that actual sexual practices (as opposed to the accepted social standards for what those practices should be) have changed very much. What it means is that deviation from these sexual norms is accepted more readily and less fearfully than before. We are not so hysterically defensive about our rules of sexual conduct because we no longer regard deviations from them as subversive of the entire social order. We no longer need a strict sexual code to provide for population maintenance or growth, industrial or agricultural production, or prophylaxis against rampant venereal disease. We adhere to our family structure—and hence our sexual code—not so much to meet societal needs as to fulfill our own, the achievement of personal happiness and an optimal setting in which to raise children. Under these circumstances the desire of some individuals to find personal happiness through premarital sex, homosexuality, prostitution, etc., becomes less terrifying and is, if not acceptable, at least understandable.

Gambling, however, is a mode of conduct which probably has come closest of all to shedding the stigma of immorality inherited from the past. American attitudes toward gambling have always been ambivalent. Even in Puritan times we find mention of gaming and lotteries at the same time the churches were exhorting against such wordly pleasures. Gradually, however, our attitudes have softened, probably because of the general relaxation of the personal standards of behavior and possibly because of the possibilities of relief for the hard-pressed taxpayer through state-sponsored lotteries. In, any case, at the present time, not only does Nevada have legalized gambling and New York the OTB (a public corporation to conduct off-track betting) but increasingly the criminal justice system is refusing to use its resources to enforce antigambling laws. The police protest openly at the futility of picking up small-time gamblers who are doing no more than the OTB employees, and such gamblers as are prosecuted are handled by the courts perfunctorily and with minimal penalties. The change in public opinion, the negative attitudes of police and prosecutors toward gambling law enforcement, and general awareness that illegal gambling is a major source of income for organized crime have combined to hasten the repeal of many—perhaps all—gambling statutes. There is virtually no effective interest group in the United States that espouses the retention of gambling laws. Apparently, legislative repeal is retarded only by public apathy and the fear of criticism by zealots.

Deviance: Poor Taste

In contrast to acts which are crimes or sins are actions which are matters of taste and which, even when disapproved, are rarely regulated by law. Manners and style fall within this category. Pants on women were once an object of scandal; girls' bobbed hair in the 1920's was viewed as dubiously as boys' long hair in the 1960's. In Puritan New England it was a misdemeanor for a man and a woman to kiss in public even if they were married; we think nothing of more overt expressions of affection although we become increasingly offended as the conduct becomes more explicitly sexual. Adults smile benignly at little Boy Scouts and Girl Scouts in their uniforms, but glare at black-jacketed Hell's Angels and similarly dressed members of black and Puerto Rican youth gangs. Frenchmen may kiss each other heartily; American men may not. It is all right to wear a cross or a mezuzah, but a swastika arm-band, a hooded sheet, and a clenched fist salute are perceived with considerable hostility and, under certain circumstances, are forbidden by the authorities.

To the visitor from Mars all of this can be very confusing. Why, for example, is it all right for an adult to appear in public wearing a skimpy bathing suit but not his underwear? To us, however, it is not confusing at all, although few people when pressed could rationalize all the idiosyncrasies of manners and style that go to make up taste. It is clear that to a great extent these modes of conduct are cultural accidents. Pants are no more ordained by nature for men than skirts are for women, and in some tribal societies men do wear skirts and women pants. There is nothing in the shape of a cross that necessarily suggests Christianity and nothing in the shape of the swastika that necessarily equals fascism. As a method of greeting, handshaking is neither more nor less rational than a kiss on the cheek or a deep curtsy. But while the conduct in question may be irrational, the inferences drawn from it may be highly rational. The wearing of the swastika by American fascists is a reliable indicator of a belief in racial inequality, a totalitarian system of government, etc. A man who appears in public in a woman's dress probably is sexually deviant. What we object to in these modes of conduct, therefore, is that they suggest or anticipate other actions to which we take exception. They are in a sense symbolic conduct, symbolic of some type of overt action to which there is or may be a rational objection. Thus, the objection to the swastika is an objection to fascism; and the more we object to fascism as a mode of conduct, the more we will object to the swastika. Many modes of dress are objectionable because they appear to anticipate undesirable sexual conduct: slacks and bikinis on women, long hair and feminine looking clothing on men. Interpersonal conduct—modes of greeting and communicating with other people— are evaluated by our interpretation of the hidden messages those modes send out. When attempts are made to change matters of manner and style, objection is frequently vigorous simply because such changes are viewed as a precedent to change in more serious forms of nonsymbolic conduct.

Opposition fades away when the symbolic conduct loses its symbolism. In Victorian times a woman who showed her ankles freely was considered "fast," aggressively inviting promiscuous conduct. When enough women wore short skirts without the occurrence of the undesirable sexual conduct that had been anticipated, short skirts became acceptable. The first men wearing long hair in the current style were considered to be homosexually inclined. When the majority of adolescent youths and young men adopted the fashion, long hair as a symbol of homosexuality faded.

Thus the problem in regard to matters of taste is to recognize, first of all, that they are cultural accidents and may be intrinsically quite irrational. We must also recognize, however, that such conduct is symbolic conduct and may be the surface manifestation of far more meaningful attitudes and actions. In regulating such matters of taste, then, we must know when the surface conduct is truly symbolic and when it has lost its symbolism. If the symbolism is extant and the conduct to which it refers is truly harmful, it is possible that even symbolic action may need to be regulated socially.

If deviance then, is not entirely in the eye of the beholder, what is it? Albert K. Cohen defines it as "behavior which violates institutionalized expectations . . . which are shared and recognized as legitimate within a social system."[4] This is an admirable definition, though for practical use its difficulties lie in determining precisely what the institutionalized expectations are and how legitimate they may be. Nevertheless, in many situations there is widespread agreement, even by the actor himself, that a particular mode of conduct is deviant. The burglar knows he is doing wrong, the cigarette smoker knows he is ruining his health, the alcoholic knows he is bringing grief to himself and his family, the fat person knows he is shortening his life, and the drug user knows that his euphoria is false and that addiction is really an unsatisfactory way of coping with life. Why,

4. Albert K. Cohen, "The Study of Social Disorganization and Deviant Behavior," in Robert K. Merton, Leonard Broome, and Leonard S. Cottrell, Jr., eds., *Sociology Today: Problems and Prospects* (New York: Basic Books, 1959), p. 462.

then, does anyone rob, smoke, drink, overeat, or take drugs? If he himself recognizes the legitimacy of society's institutionalized expectations, why does he engage in modes of conduct that violate those expectations? He deviates because society places great stresses on every individual; when those stresses become too great, he makes adjustments in his conduct, adjustments which may, from a medical, psychological, or sociological standpoint, be highly unsatisfactory but which may nevertheless be the best he can achieve at that particular point. *Deviance is, in short, an attempt to cope. From this point of view, almost everyone is deviant in some respect.* Almost everyone smokes or overeats or drives too fast or drinks too much or does something else that is personally or socially destructive.

Deviant conduct is not necessarily related to personality abnormality. If everyone who is deviant were considered abnormal, the definition of abnormality would be so broad as to be virtually meaningless. For the purposes of the discussion here, without becoming involved in the controversy over what constitutes personality abnormality, let us define a psychotic as a person who is out of touch with reality with respect to time, place, or circumstance. All others—i.e., all those who are in touch with reality—are nonpsychotic. Within this nonpsychotic group are many neurotics—i.e., persons who can cope with reality but at some psychic cost. Some neurotics develop facial tics; some develop stomach ulcers; others indulge in various forms of deviant behavior. It is difficult to determine in any group who is neurotic and who is not, partly because neurotic and normal behavior are not clearly separated from each other but in fact form a continuum. The kinds of deviant behavior we have been discussing here can be found widely dispersed among all groups—psychotic, neurotic, and normal—and the degree of social destructiveness exhibited by various kinds of deviant behavior is not necessarily related to the degree of personality disorganization of those performing such behavior. The Puerto Rican boy in the *barrio* who conforms to the drug-taking habits of his peers may be far less "neurotic" than the successful businessman who is thirty pounds overweight and smokes three packs of cigarettes a day.

The wellsprings of deviant behavior, thus, lie not so much in personality as in society. It is the interaction of society's stresses with a given individual's personality that is the determinant of behavior, whether deviant or otherwise. This is not to say, however, that deviance is mechanically foreordained by the individual's place in society. While there is probably a causal relationship between poverty and crime, for example, not every poor person becomes a criminal, and middle-class children with every advantage sometimes go wrong. No person, no matter how pressing the claims that society makes upon him, ever entirely escapes some degree of personal responsibility for his behavior. Avoidance of socially disapproved or socially destructive conduct may be very difficult but if behavior were determined entirely mechanistically, many persons simply could not endure the adverse circumstances and crushing pressures of their lives. The assumption that there is some area in which free will operates is absolutely basic to any type of free society. If man is a robot, then Big Brother must be the robot-master. It is the continuing belief that individuals still count and can affect their personal destinies at least to some degree that makes the democratic faith possible.

If deviant behavior is an attempt to cope, the form that deviance takes depends on the total circumstances of the person plus the opportunities that his culture offers him. Ninety-eight pound weaklings do not become second-story men because it takes physical strength, coordination, and stamina to be a competent burglar. Adolescents with problems in isolated rural communities may burn down barns but do not become drug addicts because drugs are not available in such communities and barns are. Jews seldom become alcoholics but have a strong tendency to overindulge in food; food rather than drink will normally be chosen as their vehicle for deviance simply because it is a more acceptable form of deviance in Jewish culture. On the other hand, deviants who wish to shock by their behavior will choose a mode of conduct that is as abrasive or unacceptable as possible. Thus, rebellious adolescents in our culture will smoke hashish; in a Moslem society they will drink whiskey. Before tobacco was discovered and distillation was learned there were no smokers and no whiskey drinkers. In the nineteenth century Jesse James held up railroads and stage coaches; today we have airplane hijackers. Our social culture provides the means for deviance as well as the pressures that lead toward it. The individual's personality, physical make-up, and environment determine what form his deviant conduct will assume or whether indeed he will become deviant at all. Aggressive tendencies in the ghetto may be translated into rape or assault; in a middle-class community they may be transmuted into the ambition that leads to a professional accomplishment and advancement; in a wartime army they may produce a winner of the Congressional Medal of Honor.

While insight into the nature of deviant conduct and its causes is interesting intellectually, practically it is useful primarily in answering the most important question of all: What do we do about deviant behavior in society? This question is essentially similar to the new mother's inquiry about what to do with her crying baby. What one does about a crying baby depends upon why the baby is crying; what society does about deviant conduct depends on what kind of adaptation the deviant is attempting to make by his deviance.

Conclusion

By and large, efforts to control deviant conduct by reforming the person fail. They fail because the roots of deviance lie in his effort to cope with social and psychological pressures that he cannot handle in any other way. If these pressures cannot be relieved, he will not stop his deviant conduct merely because well-meaning therapists and social workers exhort him to stop it. To recognize the limitations of exhortation, however, does not mean that we can or should cease our attempts to structure rational policy for the handling of deviance. If the foregoing analysis is correct, certain conclusions seem implicit:

1. The most serious form of deviant conduct is crime. In the handling of criminals we must recognize that physical punishment, such as imprisonment, serves almost one function exclusively: restraint. Put-

ting a man in prison effectively keeps him away from the rest of the community, an entirely appropriate policy for all offenders whose conduct is violent or potentially violent. No viable community can exist if this type of offender is permitted to remain at large. We must recognize, however, that imprisonment is simply a holding action, it does little or nothing toward reforming the criminal himself. Imprisonment, on the whole, tends to embitter the prisoner and teach him new and better ways of committing crime. Again, this does not mean that we should tear down our prisons or abandon incarceration as punishment for crime. It simply means that we must understand we are keeping wild animals in the zoo but not taming them.

It follows then that, except for the purpose of protecting the community from the offender, imprisonment is utterly pointless. To put gamblers, pornography peddlers, nonviolent drug users, alcoholics, and homosexuals in prison is farcical at best and sadistic at worst.

2. To reform the deviant as opposed to simply restraining him, some sort of nonphysical coercive pressure must be applied. This pressure may take many forms: for example, for criminals, probation or parole counseling, educational or vocational rehabilitation, or psychiatric therapy; for alcoholics, Alcoholics Anonymous, individual or group counseling or chemotherapy; for drug addicts, drug-free communities such as Synanon, heroin or methadone maintenance programs, psychotherapy, etc. The degree of success that these programs are likely to have depends, at least in part, on how successful the therapist is in teaching the offender to cope with his problems in ways other than the conduct that we find objectionable. Unfortunately, the reality of the deviant's situation may frequently be the strongest impediment to reform of his conduct. Probation and parole workers are frequently unable to convince the incompetent burglar that he would be better off as an honest man, because the truth of the matter is that (especially if he is semiliterate, poor, and black), he may *not* be better off if he were an honest man. It is hard to convince such a person that he shouldn't desire material affluence when the entire society around him is structured on praise of material affluence. Under those cir-

cumstances, we must recognize that, unless we give up our materially oriented society (which is highly unlikely) or reduce the disparity of status and opportunity between the favored of our population and the poor (which at this moment seems only a little less unlikely), we shall not have too much success with probation and parole.

The same principles apply in the handling of drug addicts and alcoholics. If we cannot relieve sociological and psychological pressures that force such people to take refuge in the surcease provided by consciousness-altering chemicals, alcoholics and heroin users will continue to remain addicted. The roots of their conduct frequently lie in the well-known evils of poverty, racism, broken homes, etc. Long-range social efforts to control such conditions are necessary if we expect to correct this type of conduct.

3. The amount of pressure, coercive or noncoercive, that society should apply to a deviant depends on how harmful his conduct is to the entire community. This harm must be real and demonstrably measurable. Violent criminals must be restrained. In regard to others, the extent of pressure would vary, from intensive efforts in behalf of alcoholics and drug addicts, whose conduct brings intense pain and suffering to their families as well as to themselves, to relatively mild pressures on overeaters or smokers. While it is true that overeating and smoking are physically harmful, it is also true that, in the absence of a Utopian society, the pressures on every individual must have some outlet, and to choke off an outlet like smoking or overeating may simply force the individual into some other tension-releasing syndrome that may be even more harmful or deviant. A certain amount of tolerance for and acceptance of mildly deviant conduct is probably essential in a society as complex and imperfect as our own.

4. In the light of the above, it is clear that we should resort to the criminal process sparingly and as a last resort in the handling of deviant conduct. Punishment, after all, is only a stopgap measure. We keep the offender off the streets to give the community a rest, or in the hope that he will grow physically or emotionally tired as he matures and will lack the energy to continue his antisocial conduct. We cannot handle all deviants

that way. To do so not only would be an enormous waste of social resources and the human talents possessed by these deviants but would be destructive of the basic ideal of an open, free, pluralistic society. If we are not going to imprison, there is far less impetus for the use of the criminal process. Drug addicts and alcoholics can be handled medically at least as effectively. Gamblers and homosexuals probably should not be handled at all, except insofar as they seek help, since their conduct is only minimally harmful to the community at large.

To sum up, deviant conduct is ubiquitous in a society such as ours. While deviance lies, to some extent, in the eye of the beholder, certain forms of it that are objectively and measurably harmful to the community or that violate rational institutionalized expectations are always deviant. The roots of deviance lie in sociological and psychological pressures generated within the individual by social forces frequently beyond his control. Since, however, the very notion of a free society is based on the responsibility of each individual for his own conduct, the responsibility for the control of deviant conduct lies with both the individual and the community at large. Deviance is an attempt by the person to cope with the pressures that beset him and he can be neither punished nor persuaded out of or away from his unacceptable conduct unless other methods of coping are available and feasible for him. Physically coercive punishment must be used only as a last resort and for the protection of the community, for it has almost no rehabilitative effect and serves only to keep the offender away from the community. For this reason the criminal process should be reserved almost exclusively for persons who must be restrained at all costs or who are so seriously disruptive of the peace and good order of the community (e.g., swindlers and embezzlers who commit nonviolent property crimes) that rehabilitative counseling should be carried on in a semicoercive setting such as probation. For all others, either we should attempt education and persuasion by appropriate therapists or, in regard to those whose conduct really harms no one but themselves, *we should let them alone*, recognizing that to some extent we are all deviants.

39

Thieves, Homosexuals and Other Deviants

The High Personal Cost Of Wearing A Label

To "come out of the closet"—publicly accepting
a label of deviance—is self-limiting and wrong.
We are what we do, not what we say we are.

by Edward Sagarin

The little verb "to be" has caused a great deal of pain. I want to alleviate some of that pain by clearing up a terrible confusion.

When we speak about a person who behaves in eccentric ways—who does eccentric things and commits eccentric acts—we tend to say that he "is" an eccentric. This usage is perfectly harmless because eccentricity doesn't raise many passions these days. It's the same when we say that a person "is" a thief, a cheat, a philanthropist or a jaywalker. "Being" any of these things may mean that the actions are committed once, sporadically, or commonly. But they are still actions, and we wouldn't necessarily say that they concerned a person's identity.

The problems crop up when we start talking about other types of deviant behavior. We say of a person who drinks too much that he "is" an alcoholic, and we say of people who think bizarre thoughts that they "are" schizophrenic. This person is a drug addict and that person is a homosexual. Others are sadomasochists, pedophiliacs, juvenile delinquents. The English language is constructed in such a way that we speak of people *being* certain things when all we know is that they *do* certain things.

The result is an imputed identity, or rather a special kind of mistaken identity. Since a person's sense of his identity can have immense consequences, mistaken identity can be tragic. The tragedy has been particularly acute among people thought "to be" homosexual, and the confusion increases with today's demand by the Gay Liberation movement that thousands of men come out of the closet and identify themselves as homosexuals.

Let me make my point about the verb "to be" as plain as possible. The word's meaning varies depending on its context. "He is a prisoner," for example, need not imply that a person is permanently a prisoner, or that prison is essential to his being. "He is male," on the other hand, does imply a more or less permanent identity. In other cases ("the chicken is a two-legged animal") *is* refers to certain traits or characteristics; and in still other cases *is* refers to a certain kind of behavior, deviant or average. Behavior, however, is not necessarily identity. Behavior can change, but identity cannot change.

Good-Boy Delinquents. Perhaps the confusion started with Freud and the concept of latency, the imagined quality of people who had an identity that had not yet manifested itself. Some years ago, August Aichhorn, Freud's chief disciple in the field of juvenile delinquency, suggested that there were two types of juvenile delinquents: those who committed what he classified as "dissocial" acts, and those who did not. One would think that the two together make up the entire youthful population, but not Aichhorn. For him, there were good-boy delinquents, youths with unresolved internal psychological problems of which they were unaware. One might call them potential delinquents, although that terminology is shunned by many who insist that it can become a self-fulfilling prophecy. For Aichhorn, the term "delinquent" was an identity, existing in an individual regardless of his behavior, desire, knowledge of self, or self-description. Some persons, he said, did not realize that they were delinquents. In the language of homosexuality, they had not yet "come out."

The idea of "coming out" implies that a condition existed before its recognition, that it is there to be discovered, that it will remain even if repudiated. It would be scientifically more accurate, and offer infinitely greater freedom of choice to individuals in their development, if our language implied change, or at least changeability, rather than permanence and immutability. Note, for example, what Wardell Pomeroy, close collaborator of Kinsey, wrote about the early work at the Institute for Sex Research. "In Kinsey's files were the records (as early as 1940) of more than 80 cases of men who had made a satisfactory heterosexual adjustment which either accompanied or largely replaced earlier homosexual experience." People do change, and Kinsey knew it. He had seen enough people who had changed, Pomeroy writes, "to convince him that the psychologists were making matters worse by starting with the assumption

The idea of "latent" homosexuality is scientifically unsound, conceptually useless, and socially pernicious.

that homosexuality was an inherited abnormality which could not be cured simply because it was inherent." The "inherited-abnormality" idea has been long abandoned but in its place there has appeared something equally resistant to change—the idea of identity. This idea presumes that one realizes what one is, that one discovers an identity rather than becoming it through behavior.

Deviants as Victims. That kind of identity is a myth. Admittedly, if a person believes the myth, the chances rise that he will assume the appropriate, narrowly defined role. Believing that one is an addict, an alcoholic, a schizophrenic, or a homosexual can result in relinquishing the search for change and becoming imprisoned in the role.

Social scientists, unfortunately, have contributed to such real-life prisons through their work on labeling theory. Labeling theory reached its academic zenith during the 1960s, a period of great social change, and it did a mighty job of turning the world of social respectability upside down. Labeling theorists sympathized with deviants of various sorts; they questioned the norms, labels and stereotypes of middle-class society, and they found it useful to look at deviants more as victims than as victimizers.

Labeling theorists have outlined clearly the stages by which a label becomes a reality. A person takes his first hesitant steps toward deviance; he learns the roles and social expectations; he learns how to navigate within his own role, and so on, until he becomes entrenched in it. A deviant identity emerges. And after being treated by society as if he actually were what he was supposed to be, he eventually becomes just that. But—some writers contend —maybe the person was just that all along. He did not realize it, because the behavior had not yet come to the fore; in other words, it was a matter of latency.

The concept of latency, used in this manner, is scientifically unsound, conceptually useless, and socially perni-

cious. It is unsound because a potential for developing in a heterosexual or homosexual, sober or alcoholic direction is nothing more than being human. In that sense everyone has latent tendencies. The concept is useless, since it fails to distinguish between those who might more easily or less easily develop in a given direction. And it is pernicious because it supports the belief that one can somehow "be" whatever is under consideration, even though one does not behave in the manner called for by the role, or even have conscious desires or interests. This deviant identity is a sort of presumed being, a little gremlin within the individual.

It is true, of course, that all forms of behavior are preceded by certain developments of character and personality. But this is as true of pre-heterosexuals as it is of pre- or proto- or latent homosexuals. If the idea of latency has any validity, then it should be used for all kinds of behavior. Moreover, it should only be used with full knowledge that a mere potential is quite different from an all-but-born reality. It *can* come to the fore, but it can also be channeled elsewhere. In fact, no behavioral, characterological, or personality type that is not yet in existence within the individual is inevitable.

This distinction can mean the difference between success and failure to anyone looking for therapy, since a belief in the possibility of change, both by therapist and patient, is crucial to the therapeutic process. I suspect that this belief can be created, particularly in the patient, by emphasizing that schizophrenia, depression, alcoholism and homosexuality refer to what a person does rather than to what he is. Unfortunately, the commoner belief is that a person either is or is not a schizophrenic, alcoholic, or homosexual, and this belief carries with it a sense of destiny.

In general, the language we use when we talk about such matters tends to become flesh and blood and behavior. It can reinforce an identity and imprison someone in a role. As C. Wright Mills once put it, "Men discern situations with particular vocabularies," and of course these vocabularies have particular consequences. Thus sociologists and other behavioral scientists, although intending just the opposite, have helped create a trap for deviants. The liberal-minded labeling theorists are the ones who have insisted on the importance of identity, being, discovering, realizing what one is—in a phrase, "coming out."

Part of the problem here may lie in the positive associations of the word "identity." People are urged from all quarters to know who they are and to accept themselves. Erik Erikson, for example, who has written extensively on this theme but who has avoided a definition, uses the expression "ego identity" to describe "a persistent sameness within oneself and a persistent sharing of some kind of essential character with others." But no matter *how* persistent it is, a characteristic of personality or behavior need not be permanent unless it has biological, chemical, or physiological referents—and even then the characteristic would not necessarily be permanent. Moreover, "the sharing of some kind of essential character with others" tends to be self-perpetuating, especially when a person internalizes the notion of identity and says to himself, "That is what I am." He would be freer if he said, "That is what I do." There are choices inherent in doing, in action; the future is open. There is a relative lack of choice in being.

To "come out" and accept any identity is not freedom but a renunciation of freedom. The ultimate freedom of a human being is to become what he chooses and wishes to become, restrained only by forces that are genuinely beyond his control. There is no alcoholic, heterosexual, or homosexual identity. There are only people who behave in a given manner, at various times of their lives, in some cases over an entire lifetime. The behavior is real, but the identity is an invention. It is an invention believed in so thoroughly by some people that they have become what they were improperly tagged as being.

40

The Criminal Justice System Without Victimless Crimes

by Gilbert Geis

The temptation, hardly resistible to polemicists such as myself—persons who ardently favor decriminalizing acts such as consensual homosexuality, gambling, prostitution, drug use, and other so-called "victimless crimes"—is to put forth a catalogue of the consequences of such "rational" political action that would make it appear as if we would finally be coming up to Dr. Pangloss' vision of the best of all possible worlds—at least as far as the administration of criminal justice is concerned.

Things such as the following could be said to happen when victimless crimes are excised from the law books. Blackmail, certainly one of the ugliest of crimes, would decrease significantly as homosexuals lost their fear of the police and the courts, and their terror of possible jail sentences (Karpman, 1954; Simon & Gagnon, 1969). Vice squad officers, now tempting and teasing with prostitutes, would be freed to set forth and capture the "real" criminals, the perpetrators of violence and predatory white-collar and property crimes (Caughey, 1974; Women Endorsing Decriminalization, 1975). Judges, their working days now almost hopelessly cluttered by parades of drunks, hustlers, number players, pot smokers, and homosexuals, no longer would need to participate in the farcical morality play that pretends either to rehabilitate those persons or to deter them or others inclined to imitate them (Boruchowitz, 1973). "Congestion is strangling the courts in big cities throughout the country and is turning justice into a commodity that Americans regularly find elusive, capricious and uncertain," a nationwide newspaper survey noted. The survey quoted an angry and frustrated judge, after a particularly questionable drug case, shouting at some policemen in the courtroom: "There are wolves out there, and you keep sending me chipmunks and squirrels!" Summarizing conditions in Philadelphia as typical of those throughout the nation, the survey noted:

> When officials talk about the basic quality of cases coming into the system and the various elements that contribute to overloading the courts, sooner or later most of them cite enforcement of the drug laws.
>
> More people in Philadelphia came before the Court of Common Pleas for drug offenses than for any other cause last year. The judges handled 2,848 of these cases but only 2,613 burglaries, 1,330 robberies and 452 murders (Rugaber, 1971).

Attempts to cope with long delays in court processes include the suggestion, the same report notes, "that cases designed to uphold the community's moral standards have no business in court, no matter how carefully prepared and ironclad the evidence seems." It is said that if necessary such cases could better be handled by social agencies (see also Price, 1974):

> The idea is discussed fairly widely and openly, but the suggested pruning is far too rigorous for many. No one wants to think of promoting, say, legalized smut in his state legislature. And the "social agencies" already are admittedly inadequate to the task.
>
> A number of judges seem to be asking instead for law enforcement that is a little more discreet. The police could concentrate informally, for example, on cases most important to the community—more wolves, fewer chipmunks and squirrels (Rugaber, 1971).

In addition to its impact on the courts, decriminalization of victimless crimes might undercut the lure of the behaviors, their delicious sense of difference and danger. Homosexuality, Oscar Wilde (1923, p. 93) once said, was particularly exciting because it was as daring as "feasting with panthers." With decriminalization, perhaps some of the victimless behaviors, hopefully those which seem to produce more than usual amounts of unhappiness and unhealthiness in their practititioners, would diminish.

This list of boons from decriminalization is highly expansible. It can also include, in shorthand form, the saving of money and human lives, the enhancement of values such as decency, fairness, and compassion, and the promotion of a justice less biased by racial and sexual discrimination; in short, the achievement of numerous things contributing toward making the criminal justice system function more as I believe it should in a democracy, where the majority will not be allowed to tyrannize over or otherwise unreasonably hurt a minority without first meeting severely stringent standards of proof that to do so is essential to the protection of nonconsenting victims. These are, of course, difficult terms to operationalize. Herbert Packer (1968, p. 151) has indicated with some elegance, and at great length, the conditions he believed necessary for an act to be defined as criminal in a society aiming toward democracy: the foregoing is my paraphrase of what I consider the essential element of such conditions.

There are other persons, however, who hold other views. Their temptation, rarely resisted, is to set forth a series of consequences of decriminalization of acts without complaining witnesses that make Kafka's nightmares seem by comparison like Eden. Moral decay, Communist takeover, unbridled aggression, staggering escalation of the rates of indulgence in the now-outlawed behaviors, peripheral effects impinging remorselessly upon the young and the innocent, and out-of-control welfare costs—these matters, obviously rather caricatured here, are but a few of the sequelae vividly portrayed by opponents of decriminalization of victimless offenses. That persons holding such views tend to believe that most of us—or of them—only await the repeal of the restrictive laws before succumbing to the magnetic appeal of homosexuality and/or heroin is in itself an interesting matter. That they cannot see the blatant class biases in current practices is also a little surprising. Perhaps they simply do not ponder why there is legal Off-Track-Betting at a booth in Grand Central Station for suburban commuters, while gambling on numbers remains illegal in Harlem, or they do not wonder why, after all those earlier years when Blacks and others in declassé positions were the almost exclusive users, marijuana smoking now, suddenly, as the middle-class youth begins to use the drug, has been found to be severely overpunished by the law (cf. Geis, 1973).

These, then, are the polar positions regarding victimless crimes. For the present discussion, we will hypothesize that everything and everyone would react only in a "commonsense" manner following decriminalization of victimless crimes, though we know otherwise. We will presume, for instance, that removing victimless crimes from the criminal justice system will see more time and energy devoted to activities with more important priorities (on my list), and will free up funds for what seem to be more desirable things, and will not effect social arrangements in subtly periperhal ways, ways beyond the obvious ones. Thus, decriminalizing heroin use can readily be seen to reduce the economic incentive for syndicated crime to push the drug, and also to reduce the need for property and occasionally personol crimes to be committed by addicts. We will not speculate, however, regarding what else the freed-up syndicate criminals might do, or how otherwise the state- or medically maintained addicts might behave, and how other persons and institutions might alter their behavior and policies under these circumstances—much less what the consequences might be for opium growers in Turkey.

It should be evident by now that final adjudication of the matter of decriminalization of victimless crimes cannot rely fundamentally upon social science; the matter is basically one of values. It would be pretentious of social science, for one thing, to suppose that it could delineate adequately the eddying ramifications of any change of such far-reaching consequence as decriminalization; for another thing, social science cannot determine a reasonable price that a society ought to pay to achieve a stipulated end; it can only suggest what some aspects of that price might be. Nobody knows or can discover empirically whether it is politically worthwhile to have fewer guilt-ridden and fearful homosexuals or a greater number of happy and arrest-proof homosexuals—or vice versa, or any combination thereof.

As a final, overall stricture, I would emphasize that timeworn and time-proven cliché: the road to hell is paved with good intentions. It can be decent and essential to press for the removal of victimless crimes from the statute books because the result would seem to enhance human and political philosophies that deserve support. But it is self-righteous and self-deceptive to maintain categorically that decriminalization will inevitably produce either short-run or especially long-run social arrangements which on balance tip in favor of desired values. It may happen—but it may not. The Swiss historian Jacob Burkhardt put the matter well: "The essence of tyranny," he wrote, "is the denial of complexity."

These introductory observations have perhaps been overlong, but it seems extremely important to me to establish a context in which discussion of decriminalization as it bears upon the criminal justice system can proceed. In the following sections, I want to concentrate first on the financial costs of continuing criminalization and, then, for illustrative purposes, I will focus on the likely impact of decriminalization on one of the major components of the criminal justice system—the police.

Financial Costs

Perhaps more than their moral concerns, opponents of decriminalization concentrate on the fiscal unfairness of their having to support the sinful in their self-indulgent ways. Their argument suggests that allowing legalized gambling, for instance, will ensnare marginal earners and welfare clients, and that these persons will lose what little money they have on reckless wagering, thus forcing hard-working taxpayers to render up even greater portions of their wages to support them and their impoverished families. Similarly, legalizing marijuana, it is said, will induce large numbers of potential contributors to social well-being to opt for drug-induced nirvanas, and thereafter these dropouts too will have to be supported by escalated food stamp subsidies and welfare doles.

Perhaps so—perhaps not. But we do have some information regarding the present cost of processing victimless crimes within the criminal justice system, one of the foremost considerations that would have to be entered into the ledger before striking a fiscal balance.

The Public Safety Systems research group in Santa Barbara, California (Poole, 1973), calculated the costs involved in the prevention, detection/apprehension, adjudication, and correction of four categories of offenders in Ventura County, California. Detection and apprehension costs, for instance, involved expenses for the police dispatchers, patrol officers, detectives, and laboratory services. Corrections included costs associated with probation investigations, adult and juvenile supervision, and operation of the county jail, juvenile hall, honor farm, juvenile camps, and ward placement program.

Offense categories include crimes against persons (7 percent of the County's reported crimes) and crimes against property (60 percent), non-victim crimes (24 percent), and miscellaneous crimes (9 percent). Non-victim crimes were primarily drug offenses, gambling, consensual sex offenses, public drunkenness, and delinquent-tendencies adjudications. Miscellaneous crimes included offenses such as drunk driving and illegal possession of weapons.

The two major cost findings of the study were these:

(1) Non-victim crimes accounted for the greatest expenditure of funds among the different offense categories. Some 33 percent of the total of $19 million spent annually in the County on its criminal justice system went for such offenses. Crimes against persons accounted for 15 percent, against property for 28 percent, and miscellaneous crimes for 24 percent of the expenditures.

(2) Non-victim crimes were particularly expensive to deal with in the areas of detection/apprehension and corrections. The cost of victimless crimes to the criminal justice system broke down as follows: prevention (8 percent); detection/apprehension (36 percent); adjudication (20 percent); and corrections (36 percent). The corresponding figures for all offense categories taken together were: prevention (12 percent); detection/apprehension (34 percent); adjudication (24 percent); and corrections (30 percent).

It should be noted that Ventura County's per capita crime rate is not too different from that of other metropolitan areas. For homicide, robbery, aggravated assault, grand theft, and auto theft, the reported crime rates are somewhat below the national average, while they are slightly higher than that average for burglaries and forcible rape. Since Ventura County (1970 census figures) contains 376,430 persons, the cost per person per year of criminal justice concerns with victimless crimes comes to $16.63. If this figure is extrapolated to the national scene, the cost for the United States amounts to $3.4 billion. Obviously, rural conditions might deflate this figure, while megalopolitan considerations might raise it, and other things—such as salary levels—might alter it somewhat. More obviously, the costs will not disappear totally with decriminalization. Nonetheless, it seems worth putting on record an approximation of the financial costs within the criminal justice system of the enforcement of laws against crimes without victims in the United States today.

The Police

Speculation regarding the possible impact of decriminalization of some or all victimless crimes upon police performance is easy enough to generate. Hard facts, however, are virtually non-existent, and satisfactory experimental designs which could tap the variety of apparently significant issues involved are difficult to establish. A review of a small portion of writing on the subject should provide an indication of the complexity of the issues.

A Watergate analogy can be used to make one point. It has often been argued, for instance, that the saving of time and energy and money by the police, if they are no longer charged with enforcing laws against victimless crimes, will allow them to turn these spared resources to ends more in keeping with the safety and security of the society. It is possible, however, that additional available resources may be used for even more nefarious undertakings than campaigns against perpetrators of victimless crimes. Thus, the formation of the Plumber's group, the attempted theft of the Ellsberg medical records and the infiltration of the organizations of political opponents sprang from, among other things, a sudden large surplus of funds, which were then defined as requiring expenditure that would make their possessors more secure and self-perpetuating.

A rather typical outline of the consequences for law enforcement of decriminalization is that of John Kaplan (1973), who uses gambling as a prototypical victimless offense. Kaplan notes the following kinds of consequences for the police because of continuing outlawing of gambling: (1) demoralization of law enforcement officers because gamblers tend to be given light sentences, in part because of overcrowded jail facilities and absence of great public and judicial indignation regarding gambling activity; (2) the emergence of appellate court decisions in the area of search and seizure which unduly inhibit success in regard to more serious crimes. The court decisions, Kaplan observes, stem from the fact that the police almost inevitably tend to push too hard against constitutional restraints when they have to deal with behaviors that are by their nature private matters; and (3) the corruption of the police by bribes from gambling figures who calculate such costs as part of their business overhead.

Very much the same line of reasoning is expressed by Norval Morris (1973) in his inventory of the implications of victimless crime statutes for law enforcement work, though Morris offers a significantly different interpretation regarding the impact of victimless crimes on the character of search and seizure law:

> Police work is almost by definition more difficult in cases of victimless crime; the best evidence is lacking, no injured citizen complains to the police and serves as a witness. The police must therefore "develop" cases with unreliable informers, undercover work, tapping and bugging entrapment and decoy methods, swift seizure of evidence and forceful interrogation. Drug cases account for most of our constitutional difficulties with search and seizure. Organized crime and gambling account for most instances of wiretapping and other invasions of privacy. Attempting to balance, in these tilted scales, constitutional concerns for privacy and due process with a concern for police effectiveness has lessened for the rest of us the protection of our constitutional rights. In the long run, this enervation of the power of the Constitution may not be the least of the harms flowing from the overreach of the criminal law (p. 58).

The stress on police practices in regard to victimless crimes by Kaplan and Morris, both law professors with strong social science interests, is complemented by statements which add other considerations, as well as repeat earlier ones. A New York Appellate Court judge has noted, for instance:

> [W]e ought to legalize gambling. The existence of gambling crimes are a gross hypocrisy. They congest the courts, they encourage corruption, they are a primary source of income for organized crime, they lead to disrespect for the law, and they deny the state an important source of legitimate revenue (Wachtler, 1973, p. 360).

In regard to illegal drugs, former Chief Justice Earl Warren observed in 1970 that "The Narcotics traffic of today . . . could never be as pervasive and open as it is unless there was connivance between authorities and criminals," a view echoed a year later by the New York State Commission of Investigation which reported "significant corruption" in the area of narcotics law enforcement in New York City (Knapp Commission Report, 1973).

Finally, we can add to the record the remarks of former New York Police Commissioner Patrick Murphy:

> The policeman would be more effective in his crime prevention duties and he would be held in higher public esteem if he were not required to enforce so many regulations which attempt to control morals —the so-called victimless crimes.
>
> By charging our police with the responsibility to enforce the unenforceable we subject them to disrespect and corrupting influences. And we provide the organized crime syndicate with illicit industries on which they thrive (Johnson, 1971).

Murphy is said to have reached this opinion largely because of his belief that it was impossible otherwise to limit the corruption of policemen by gamblers. In 1971 in New York, fifty of the 450 plainclothesmen in the Police Department's 17 divisions who were charged with enforcing the gambling laws had been transferred out of their units on suspicion of misconduct. Police officials were considering having officers with ten years or more in the Department, rather than younger men, assigned to gambling, on the presumption that veterans would stand to lose more by accepting bribes; to cut the opportunity for temptation they were also planning to reduce tours of duty in gambling enforcement from four to two years (Gage, 1971).

Conclusion

The foregoing observations regarding the consequences for police work of the existence of victimless crimes may appear to have been marshalled to demonstrate that the evidence is very strong, indeed almost incontrovertible, regarding the malevolent outcomes of continued criminalization of such acts. Decriminalization, the preceding materials seem to be saying, will produce a better world, at least in regard to the matters under review, things such as civil liberties, corruption, police morale, and citizen protection from real danger.

I prefer to conclude, however, by emphasizing a somewhat more oblique theme. I believe that it can be argued with some persuasiveness that elimination of victimless crimes (with questions of reasonable regulatory controls thereafter remaining negotiable in regard to each of the acts involved) will probably reduce certain specific kinds of undesirable consequences directly associated with the current existence and enforcement of the laws. But I find the arguments much less persuasive when they pretend to possess convincing evidence, either in fact or in logic, that decriminalization will decrease in the aggregate either the undesired outcomes or will not bring about other results which by the same standards can be deemed meretricious. I would emphasize here that I believe this latter point largely irrelevant to meaningful review and considered judgment regarding victimless crimes, either in jurisprudential or in practical terms. I think discussion of victimless crimes has tended overmuch to concentrate on derivative effects of criminalization and for understandable, but largely spurious, reasons. For one thing, it is important to have evidence that is responsive to things that an antagonist defines as important, to be able to say, as some do in another criminal justice area, that, no, it is more expensive to have the death penalty than to eliminate it, or, in this area, that it costs the citizen more money to see the victimless crime laws enforced than it would cost him if they were repealed. Information on derivative effects may become particularly important as source material for debate when/if empirical work of adequate quality is available that allows better adjudication of basic issues. Tactically, it always seems more civilized somehow to be able to cite "evidence" for a position—no, capital punishment does not deter homicide, the studies indicate—than to stand firmly, or perhaps, lamely, on a categoric moral position—capital punishment is immoral and uncivilized, and that is that.

I think, though, that it is especially important to stress, again, the derivative consequences ought to be dealt with on their own terms, and not turned back against positions which are irresistibly rooted in concepts of fairness and justice.

Thus, for instance, it was argued in 1971 that the OTB approach to gambling in New York City should not be imported into California because it seemed likely, according to the California Attorney General, that a major scandal was likely to eventuate in such a program where political appointees were involved and so many different persons handled money. The Attorney General believed that law enforcement would have more rather than fewer headaches with legal gambling such as OTB (Younger, 1971). Two years later, the California Attorney General could have felt somewhat smug if he had read in the *New York Times* that "nine alleged bookmakers were arrested yesterday and charged with using offices of the Offtrack Betting Corporation to take illegal bets on horses and sports from OTB customers" (Perlmutter, 1973).

But the point is that, accurate or not, the view that legalized gambling will lead to more problems than it solves should not be regarded as probative evidence against legalized gambling, but as warning regarding the need to deal constructively and fairly, with those elements of the new approach which seem to be causing difficulty. Indeed, I have been told by analysts of the police scene that corruption is functional to a more satisfactory police performance; at least, the hypothesis is that the police in New York City are more sympathetic to the needs of citizens because the police are corrupt, thus more human, than are the "automatons" who make up the ranks of the Los Angeles Police Department. Perhaps so—but the answer is not to victimize victimless "criminals" in order to continue corruption, but to find a satisfactory concatenation of ingredients that will make better policemen.

Parallels to paradoxical outcomes in the victimless crime area can be found throughout the literature and lore on criminal justice. Provision of constitutional safeguards (such as the right to legal representation) for parolees faced with revocation, for instance, was be-

lieved to have led some parole boards to restrict more severely their original granting of parole—thus undercutting a basic aim of the reform, that of making people freer from arbitrary deprivation of liberty. The response is not to retreat from advocacy of due process in revocation proceedings, but to move forward in demanding now that due process be employed in parole hearings, that, for example, parole boards be required to defend their denials at hearings conducted with due process scrupulousness.

In conclusion, then, this presentation has tried to convey the idea that visions of the criminal justice system without victimless crimes probably represent as often as not inventories of filtered outcomes, with the process of filtering mediated by the ideological preferences of the commentator. Even in the best of such inventories, there exists no satisfactory manner of delineating satisfactorily the full range of consequences that bear on the values whose enhancement is being sought. This, of course, is hardly a novel dilemma when social science attempts to bring its insights and information to bear on policy issues.

My theme is that, such conditions notwithstanding, social science reasonably can seek to discover and diagnose possible consequences of decriminalization across a broad range of issues. But, more important, it should recognize that even if decriminalization were to be "shown" to create more problems and more malaise than it relieves, these derivative problems must be dealt with on their own terms, and they cannot be employed as part of a sophistical exercise whose aim is to deprive persons indecently and undemocratically of their liberty or their pursuit of happiness when such persons do not in any direct or serious way injure the legitimate interests of others.

References

Boruchowitz, Robert C. 1973. "Victimless Crimes—A Proposal to Free the Courts." *Judicature* 57 (August–September):69–78.

Burckhardt, Jakob. 1921. *The Civilization of the Renaissance in Italy* (1885). Trans. by S. G. C. Middlemore. 8th ed. London: Allen, 1921.

Caughey, Madeline S. 1974. "The Principle of Harms and Its Application to Laws Criminalizing Prostitution." *Denver Law Journal* 51:235–262.

Gage, Nicholas. 1971. "Legal Gambling Proposed by Murphy to Curb Police Graft." *New York Times,* September 13.

Geis, Gilbert. 1973. "Abortion and Prostitution: A Matter of Respectability." *The Nation* 217 (September 3): 179–180.

Johnson, Thomas J. 1971. "Numbers Called Harlem's Balm." *New York Times,* March 1.

Kaplan, John. 1973. *Criminal Justice: Introductory Cases and Material.* Mineola, N.Y.: Foundation Press.

Karpman, Benjamin. 1954. *The Sexual Offender and His Offenses*. New York: Julian Press.

Knapp Commission Report on Police Corruption. 1973. New York: George Braziller.

Morris, Norval. 1973. "Crimes without Victims: The Law is a Busybody." *New York Times Magazine* (April 1): 10–11, 58–61.

Packer, Herbert L. 1968. *The Limits of Criminal Sanction*. Stanford, Ca.: Stanford University Press.

Perlmutter, Emanuel. 1971. "OTB Indictments Handed Down," *New York Times,* October 2.

Poole, Robert W. 1973. *Criminal Justice Resource Allocation*. Santa Barbara, Ca.: Public Safety Systems.

Price, Ray R. 1974. "Victimless Crime." *Social Work* (July):406–411.

Rugaber, Walter. 1971. "Justice is Slow and Unsure in Nation's Busy Courts." *New York Times,* August 8.

Simon, William and John C. Gagnon. 1969. "Homosexuality: The Formulation of a Sociological Perspective." In Ralph W. Weltge (ed.) *The Same Sex: An Appraisal of Homosexuality*. Philadelphia: Pilgrim Press, pp. 13–23.

Wachtler, Sol. 1973. "The High Cost of Victimless Crimes." *Record of the Bar Association of the City of New York* 28 (May):357–363.

Wilde, Oscar. 1923. *De Profundis* (1905). In *Complete Works*. Garden City, N.Y.: Doubleday & Page, Vol. XI.

Women Endorsing Decriminalization. 1973. "Prostitution: A Non-Victim Crime." *Issues in Criminology* 8 (Fall):137–162.

Younger, Eville J. 1971. *Task Force Report on Legalized Gambling*. Sacramento, Co.: Attorney General's Office.

41

The Alcohol Alibi: Blaming Alcoholics

by Dan E. Beauchamp

Alcohol problems cost American society a staggering $25 billion annually in illness, family disruptions, arrests, property destruction, loss of productivity and death. There is no doubt that alcohol is the nation's number one drug problem. Yet, alcohol is definitely not the nation's number one drug issue. Despite the creation of the National Institute on Alcohol Abuse and Alcoholism (NIAAA) in the Department of Health, Education and Welfare in 1970, and despite several decades of promoting the concept of alcoholism as a major community problem, lesser drug problems such as heroin use receive far more attention from the media, public officials and the public.

It is not widely recognized that the concept of alcoholism is itself a major reason for this public inattention to alcohol problems. Our idea—or our myth—of alcoholism is the major obstacle to recognizing alcohol as the leading drug issue. It is no myth that there are at least nine million persons in the United States who are, because of the amount of alcohol they drink, at serious risk of physical, psychological or social damage. The myth is the false idea that these people have some inner condition—called alcoholism—which explains their drinking problems.

The function of the myth is to achieve a particular apportionment of responsibility for the huge social costs of the substance of alcohol. With this myth, we have convinced ourselves that the nation's alcohol problems are caused by a small minority of drinkers, who are unable to use alcohol properly. This misdefinition of the problem obscures the fact that alcohol problems are a function of existing inadequate public and private controls over availability and use of alcohol. The alcohol industry and all those who drink must bear the costs of preventing problems through more stringent safeguards. By holding the alcoholic responsible for the social costs of alcohol, we add to the stigma of those who suffer alcohol damage. Finally, by avoiding reference to alcohol when considering alcohol problems, we have managed to make the latter less visible to the public.

Alcoholism Idiom

The myth of alcoholism is based on a very simple, and in some contexts, quite legitimate notion: people possess powers, abilities, skills or capacities that account for their success or failure in performing actions involving difficulties or hazards. Further, people differ in their abilities or capacities.

These ideas are valid—when used in the right context. Flying an airplane, skiing on a steep slope, swimming a dangerous river or performing difficult surgery involve skills and capacities and the risk of failure.

The trouble begins when we use the notion of abilities or capacities incorrectly. Smokers who do not develop lung cancer do not avoid this particular fate because of their skills or abilities, nor do those who do not commit suicide, become juvenile delinquents or commit murder possess special capacities which account for their "success."

In the case of alcohol, however, we continue to talk about alcohol problems in the language of individuals and their successes and failures. Countless definitions consider alcoholism to be an individual inability to control drinking or individual loss of control over alcohol.

Thinking about alcohol problems this way seems natural because of the simple but misleading fact that most individual drinkers do not experience problems with alcohol. In light of this, we assume that the "nonproblem" majority of drinkers avoid difficulties with alcohol because they each have the "ability" to control their drinking. Those individuals in the minority who experience problems lack this ability. The fallacy is that most individuals do not have an inner capacity to control their drinking.

Although it may be perplexing to state that those individuals who escape alcohol problems do not necessarily have some ability or capacity to control their drinking, the confusion arises from trying to explain community or societal phenomena, such as alcoholism, in an inappropriate idiom of individual power, capacity or ability. Thus, the myth of alcoholism arises precisely from the way we talk about alcohol problems, discussing these collective phenomena as if they arise because individual members of that collectivity fortuitously possess the power to properly control the substance of alcohol.

Myths and Ideology

Myths begin with false analogies but their goal or function is ideological; they subtly distort reality in order to protect key values of the larger society. Myth is the alibi that serves as the "cover story" for the rest of society in face of problematic social conditions. This is because the myth defines the origins of these problems in a way that diverts suspicion from favored practices and powerful interests when the question of collective action arises.

William Ryan, in *Blaming the Victim,* unmasked the myth of attributing economic and social inequality for blacks and the poor to behavioral factors within these individuals, such as an inability to achieve, cope, plan or manage. Instead, as Ryan shows, these problems are primarily the result of systematic social inequality and racism. Discussing these problems in terms of individual successes and failures and individual abilities or capacities diverts attention from the origins of these problems in powerful systematic forces and instead looks at the problem in terms of behavioral failures rooted in specific individuals and caused by remote and distant events. Explaining alcohol problems in terms of the individual protects a powerful alcohol industry and the drinking public from the threat of more stringent public controls over availability of alcohol, and also from the frank realization that we need stronger private (cultural, social and ethical) norms which support limiting the availability and use of alcohol.

Above all else, the myth of alcoholism provides a perfect alibi for a $27 billion alcohol industry with annual advertising expenditures approaching $250 million. People view this giant industry, which manufactures, distributes, advertises and retails the nation's number one drug, as simply providing another "commodity," which the vast majority of drinkers "are able" to use without serious problems. This benign view of the alcohol industry stands in sharp contrast to the treatment increasingly accorded other industries perceived as producing not only goods and services, but also social costs such as pollution or defective or excessively marketed products.

However, there has been a constant and steady increase in the industry's sales in the past several decades and a corresponding increase in the per capita consumption of alcohol. This is despite the fact that the number of abstainers has remained relatively constant. Since 1960, for example, per capita consumption of alcohol has risen by one-third. There are signs of sharp increases in the consumption of alcohol by those under 21, a trend not unrelated to the lowering of the drinking age to 18 in many states. Also, the United States now rivals France for the lead in the per capita consumption of distilled beverages, a statistic which many experts believe to be related to the rather light taxes placed on this form of alcohol as compared to other countries.

Climb in Consumption

The continuing climb in the per capita consumption of alcohol has ominous implications for the rates of alcohol problems, a connection which the myth of alcoholism helps to conceal. It is largely because of this myth that these statistics are ignored, even by alcoholism experts. As a result, the alcohol industry is not widely viewed (outside of the small temperance camp) as an industrial or social "polluter," and not significantly responsible for these statistics. Thus, the myth of alcoholism provides a powerful alibi for this influential industry which opposes more stringent controls over availability of alcohol as a means of reducing alcohol problems, controls which would jeopardize industry sales and profits.

For nearly a century, alcohol and alcohol controls were one of the most salient issues in America. Two constitutional amendments dealt with the subject of alcohol. After the failure and collapse of Prohibition, all of this changed. Suddenly, the entire issue of any responsible controls over availability of alcohol to help contain alcohol problems vanished from the national scene. While the alcohol industry is still regulated, these regulations function mainly to bring order to the industry, rather than to reduce or contain alcohol problems. In some areas of the country, the subject of controls still arises, but these are usually regarded as marginal issues, raised by militant temperance minorities and not related to the problem of alcoholism.

Because of the myth of alcoholism, alcohol problems do not appear to be directly related to inadequate social, cultural or ethical norms supporting limits to the availability of alcohol or to inadequate public controls over the availability of alcohol, such as taxation, physical accessibility or age restrictions. Instead of focusing on the availability of alcohol as a central public issue and instead of calling for responsible public controls, we spend our time and research trying to find out what causes a minority of drinkers to suffer from a disease which makes them "unable" to control their drinking.

Unfortunately, this myth makes the entire drinking public unwitting allies of the alcohol industry by encouraging them to see themselves as successful in "controlling" their use of alcohol and hence not implicated in society's problems with alcohol. The majority is encouraged to view alcohol problems as originating with that minority of drinkers who have failed to control their drinking. This minority suffers from the "disease" of alcoholism. For the majority, the correct public policy is to treat the disease of alcoholism and to search for its etiology, not to penalize the vast majority of drinkers who "know how" to drink.

Referring to alcoholism as a disease (and many alcoholism experts persist in this mislabeling) does not suggest a condition which anyone might experience if exposed to the same infectious agent or some similar hazard. Rather, the disease in this case suggests an inner deficiency or a missing capacity, much as does the "disease" of mental illness. This defect stigmatizes and differentiates alcoholics from others who drink, further encouraging the idea that the entire drinking public should not be penalized and forced to bear some of the costs of preventing alcohol problems.

Even leading experts encourage this view that alcoholics and nonalcoholics are drastically different. Morris Chafetz, director of the NIAAA, said that a wide chasm separates alcoholics and most others who drink. Selden Bacon, another leading expert on alcoholism, wrote that alcoholics do not drink—at least not for the normal and customary motives surrounding the custom of social drinking. According to Bacon, alcoholics only ingest alcohol, using this drug for entirely asocial motives. This kind of sophistry portrays the alcoholic as categorically different, differing from other drinkers in kind, rather than in degree, and further supports the position that public policy to reduce these problems must be aimed primarily at the alcoholic and not at the social drinker.

To say that alcoholics suffer from a disease does not explain what causes deviant drinking. This notion only labels "loss of control" over alcohol as being an illness. Nor does explaining deviant drinking as "alcoholism" offer a causal explanation of this deviant behavior. Thus, we are faced with a circular assertion: drinking behavior which shows loss of control is alcoholism, a term which mainly means loss of control.

Chafetz, who is a psychiatrist, is an unabashed spokesman for the alcoholism point of view. In *Liquor: Servant of Man*, Chafetz argued that alcohol is not the issue. He asserted that alcohol's positive contributions to civilization far outweigh its costs. Problems which arise with alcohol lie with man's misuse of the substance, not with the substance itself. The problem is alcoholism, not alcohol, and for alcoholism the fault lies within men themselves.

The alcoholism movement, originally consisting of Alcoholics Anonymous (A.A.), the Yale (now Rutgers) School of Alcohol Studies and the National Council on Alcoholism, arose after Prohibition. This special way of viewing alcohol problems may have been devised in part as a defense against the charge of neoprohibitionism and also to generate public support. There has also been a long tradition in this country of explaining social problems in behavioral terms as a way of avoiding the necessity of painful collective action. This tendency is still with us as William Ryan has brilliantly demonstrated.

To its credit, the alcoholism movement was dedicated to developing a scientific approach to the study of alcoholism which would help lift the stigma associated with the "condition" and would encourage community sympathy and treatment, rather than rejection and often imprisonment. However, the concept of alcoholism has only added to the burden of those with alcohol problems.

Double Jeopardy

The idea of alcoholism and the role of the alcoholic places those with alcohol problems, and especially those ex-drinkers who have experienced alcohol problems, in an excruciating dilemma. On the one hand, these individuals are encouraged to accept the role of alcoholic to symbolize the fact that alcohol is or has been a source of serious damage to their lives. On the other hand, if these individuals accept the role of the alcoholic, they also are forced to accept the label of "drinking failures." They are thereby coerced into falsely witnessing that they are the source of society's alcohol problems and that alcohol and its availability in society are not at issue. This label of drinking failure taints them with stigma and separation, suggesting that they are deficient in a widely shared ability to perform a morally approved social custom.

Thus, those who accept the label of alcoholic are like double agents. In accepting the label of alcoholic, they attempt to work for themselves by acknowledging their problems with alcohol. However, this acceptance compels them to work as society's agent by forcing them to accept a definition of themselves that exonerates the issue of alcohol.

The basic function of the alcohol alibi is to make the social costs of alcohol invisible by blaming the alcoholic. The irony is that the alibi not only makes alcohol invisible, but also makes alcoholics invisible as well. The alcoholism experts have coined a name for this phenomenon: the hidden alcoholic. This term means that the alcoholic is hidden within our midst, but refuses to identify himself because of stigma and shame.

But there is another, more subtle reason why alcoholics are invisible to the public. The very words "alcoholic" and "alcoholism" have become special cues which shape our perceptions of alcohol problems in terms of personal failure instead of hazardous substances. The subtle code of double meaning surrounding the word "alcoholism" permits reference to alcohol problems without in any way indicting, implicating or indicating the substance of alcohol as a public issue.

In this stylized way of discussing alcohol problems, the word "alcoholism" does double duty. The manifest message is that the alcoholic and alcoholism are our chief alcohol problem. The hidden message is that alcohol is not the problem. Each time we use the word "alcoholism," we simultaneously indicate that alcohol, the alcohol industry and all nonalcoholic drinkers do not constitute the problem.

This is the essential genius of the myth of alcoholism. Every time we raise the issue of alcoholism, we suppress the issue of alcohol. We pay a painful price for the triumph of the myth. Those who wish to call the public's attention to problems with alcohol have no way of publicly indicating or representing these problems. The rules of the myth do not permit referring to alcohol in any direct way when discussing alcohol problems. There are no visible and easily recognized conditions, widely perceived as affecting large segments of the population (such as the rising per capita consumption of alcohol), which can serve as the public sign for alcohol problems, as smog serves as the public sign for air pollution. There is literally no way of indicating, pointing to or signifying the cause of alcohol problems in visible, recognizable terms since this would inevitably introduce the issue of alcohol.

Instead, the special language of alcoholism demands that society's alcohol problems be attributed to some hidden and invisible condition causing individual drinking failure, experienced by a minority of drinkers and with little relevance or implication for alcohol and the larger public. It is difficult, if not impossible, to mobilize attention for a public problem if its basic causes are invisible, hidden and obscure.

The A.A. Underground

This potency of the myth of alcoholism in concealing both the issue of alcohol and the alcoholic is nowhere more striking than with A.A. and its policy of anonymity, which means organizational anonymity within the community as well as individual anonymity. A.A. bears a striking resemblance to underground organizations in that both are radically nonpublic organizations.

Members of A.A. are not permitted, as a matter of policy, to reveal their public identity to the media. One of the founders of A.A., Bill Wilson, refused a cover story in *Time*, even though the magazine offered to photograph only the rear view of his head. Also, A.A. does not publicly recruit its members, nor does the organization call attention to the magnitude of alcohol problems or to the social costs of alcohol.

There are other similarities to the underground. A.A. has no formal leadership, no visible hierarchy, virtually no permanent facilities and no membership lists. Unlike the underground, however, A.A. did not adopt this nonpublic posture because of a hostile and threatening environment. Its policy of anonymity and withdrawal from the public issues surrounding alcohol and alcohol problems derives from acceptance of the myth that these problems are not public ones. A.A. sincerely believes that alcohol problems are problems of individual drinking failure, and that its mission is only to help the individual suffering alcoholic. Thus, A.A.'s policy of anonymity is essentially political and meant to participate in the depoliticization of the issue of alcohol. The policy of anonymity is simply another expression of and evidence for the myth of alcoholism.

Each time an A.A. member observes the prohibition against revealing his identity, the message is communicated that alcohol problems are problems of individuals who have failed in performing a widely practiced social custom. Each time A.A. as an organization refuses to enter the public debate on alcohol problems, it endorses the view that alcohol and its availability in society is not the issue. With its radical nonpublic stance, A.A. denies to the community public witness of the magnitude and scope of alcohol damage in our society.

Shattering the Alibi

The most difficult task is to appreciate that the myth of alcoholism is based on what philosophers call a category mistake. We have mistakenly classified avoidance of alcohol problems as an individual ability or a skill, and consequently have tried to account for the numbers of alcoholics in a community or society by finding out why some individuals are unable to control their drinking. From the start, we make the mistake of assuming that avoiding alcohol problems is mainly due to an individual capacity which most drinkers possess.

In some cases, this is explicit. Chafetz compares avoiding alcohol problems to a skill or an ability like hitting a hard target or driving an automobile. This has led to his suggestion that we ought to train young people in school "how to drink" as a way of reducing alcohol problems, much as we train young people how to drive as a way of reducing highway accidents.

More often than not, we treat avoidance of alcohol problems as an ability or skill indirectly by making a seemingly legitimate comparison. We notice that the great majority of drinkers drink without problems and that only a few drinkers experience problems. Then we unthinkingly assume that this "majority" must possess some inner power, something inside them (such as their capacity for self-control) that enables them to avoid problems.

Considering alcohol problems in an inaccurate idiom of individual abilities is misleading for several reasons. Most

adults whom we call "drinkers" actually drink very little. According to survey research, 60 percent of all people called drinkers are less than "moderate" drinkers. A total of 20 percent of all those called drinkers imbibe less than once a month. It is strange that in the case of alcohol we attribute ability or skill to people who have such a minimal exposure to the hazard in question. Usually, we attribute a skill or ability to a person or a group when it is clear that they have been exposed to actual hazards and avoided them because of their ability, such as when a driver is able to skillfully maneuver his automobile around a hazard that suddenly appears in the road. However, here we use the word "ability" in a much different and highly questionable sense by seeing drinkers as possessing an ability to *not* place themselves in a dangerous position.

Obviously, it is not possible to be exposed to enough alcohol over time to risk problems and then escape them by ability. Fate, not ability, controls the occurrence of problems here. When we use the term ability in connection with alcohol problems, we must mean an ability to *not* drink excessively or to avoid alcohol problems, which is a misleading way of using the concept of ability or skill. How is it possible to believe that all people who do not attempt dangerous acts—such as not jumping off a bridge or not using a harmful drug—have some ability to control themselves so that they do not do these things?

Saying that individuals who do not fall into a certain category have the ability to avoid falling into that category often leads to logical confusion. This would be like holding a contest where the winners are all those who do *not* shoot at the target. There is no criterion for establishing that all those who do not shoot at the target had to overcome some difficulty or hazard in performing this action. Abilities and skills are attributes assigned to tasks that are "hard" or "easy." For the most part, drinking relates to categories classified as "safe" and "unsafe." When we mix these two categories up and start treating members of the safe group ("social drinkers") as if they had done something hard or difficult and vice versa, the confusion is compounded.

The Alcohol Connection

Recently, impressive, new empirical evidence has emerged to support the thesis that the availability of alcohol in a society, rather than individual factors, plays the major role in determining rates of alcohol problems. A group of researchers at the Addiction Research Foundation in Canada have, over the past several years, gathered evidence that the most important factor associated with rates of alcohol-related cirrhosis in a society is the overall per capita consumption of alcohol. Data amassed from nearly all of the industrialized nations shows this clear and unmistakable relationship: in countries where the average consumption of alcohol is high, alcohol-related cirrhosis rates are high. In countries where the average consumption is lower, the rates of alcohol-related cirrhosis are lower. As the average rates of alcohol consumption increase, so do the rates of heavy or damaging drinking. Jan deLint and Wolfgang Schmidt, the senior members of the Canadian research group, have drawn upon earlier work by a French expert, Sully Ledermann, who was among the first to notice that rates of alcohol damage were systematically related to the overall consumption of alcohol throughout society.

The Canadian researchers have found that in nearly every society where alcohol is widely used, the largest groups of drinkers use alcohol infrequently. Another and much smaller group uses alcohol fairly frequently, but still not heavily. Finally, there is a much smaller group that is exposed to damaging levels of alcohol. As the overall or general level of consumption of alcohol in a society goes up, the number of persons who drink infrequently decreases and the number of those who drink at moderate and ''alcoholic'' rates tends to increase. The overall pattern of distribution of alcohol in society suggests a gradual and smooth shift from the infrequent categories to moderate categories and finally to the heavier damaging category. Thus, separating drinkers into distinctive groups is ultimately arbitrary.

The most plausible interpretation of these findings is that the general or per capita consumption of alcohol is an index of the adequacy of existing public and private controls over alcohol. These controls or limits over the substance of alcohol, especially as they encourage high rates of minimal or infrequent exposure to alcohol, are the crucial policy variables that produce low rates of exposure to damaging or unsafe levels of alcohol. When these limits or controls are weakened and the general level of consumption increases,

rates of exposure to damaging levels of alcohol tend to increase.

The implications of the Canadians' findings for the myth of alcoholism are devastating; it is simply not possible to argue—without refuting this evidence—that the goal of controlling the rates of heavy or unsafe drinking is not connected in some way to the overall availability of alcohol in society. To the contrary, if we seriously intend to reduce the rates of unsafe drinking, we must create more adequate public and private controls over the availability of alcohol in society. These more stringent controls will necessarily impact upon the alcohol industry and all drinkers, since their primary purpose is to encourage high rates of infrequent or minimal use of alcohol. More stringent controls over the availability of alcohol necessarily entail a lowering of the overall or general level of consumption. As a start, an overall goal of public policy for alcohol might be zero growth of the per capita consumption of alcohol.

Although we may never eliminate alcohol problems or even reduce them significantly, we can at least try to contain them. Alcohol problems are predictable and inevitable consequences of the widespread availability of alcohol in our society. By banishing the myth of alcoholism from our midst, we may be able to help alcoholics everywhere by sharing with them some of the responsibility for their plight.

42

THE POT VOTE

by ROBERT R. CARR

No doubt there are a few old-timers who still sit around and argue about Prohibition. In the not-too-distant future they may be sitting around talking about today's marijuana laws.

Robert R. Carr is senior program officer of the Drug Abuse Council in Washington, D.C.

For a nation that does so much important business in smoke-filled rooms, we have failed to appreciate the importance of what is really going on in the Great Marijuana Debate. The various special commissions labor on. Legislatures pick their way through possible bills. The police still arrest smokers by the paddy wagon. Lab rats by the thousands smoke grass by the hundred weight. But the end of the controversy is in sight. The marijuana users are bound to win.

Within a generation, the United States will probably accept legally what it has learned to accept illegally. Decriminalization of marijuana will come about through the same process that solved the problems of Civil War veterans and what to do with all the horses that used to pull milk wagons. The old generation that doesn't use grass very much will be replaced by the younger generation that does. The demographics are irresistible.

The truth is that policymakers at all levels will continue to be replaced by younger men and women who most likely have either tried marijuana themselves or are at least much more tolerant of those who have. When leaders from the younger generations take control with the support of the majority of their peers, the marijuana debate will be over.

If younger adults maintain the attitudes they now have as they grow older, and if marijuana use continues to remain at its present level or increases in subsequent "younger adult" groups, we can expect an ever-increasing acceptance of marijuana in the years ahead and an increasing pressure to remove criminal sanctions for its use and possession.

The reasons are clear. In spite of massive law-enforcement efforts in the last decade to suppress its sale and use, marijuana is gradually taking its place with alcohol as the recreational drug of choice for millions of Americans. Marijuana is readily available to all who seek it, and the indications are that its use will continue to rise with each succeeding generation.

"It is now much too late to debate the issue: marijuana versus no marijuana," a Consumers Union report correctly observed as early as 1972. "Marijuana is here to stay. No conceivable law-enforcement program can curb its availability."

The most recent national surveys confirm that 1972 forecast. The National Commission on Marihuana and Drug Abuse reported to the public that, as of October 1971, 24 million Americans had tried marijuana, with eight million of them using it regularly—all illegally. A national survey commissioned by the Drug Abuse Council in October 1974 indicated that 29 million Americans had tried marijuana, with over 12 million of them using it regularly.

Indeed, if you look at marijuana as a consumer product, the demographics are enough to light up the heart of any marketing expert. Those who have tried the product are, most of all, young. While marijuana use cuts across all demographic lines, age is the single sharpest dividing line. Almost one-half of those between the ages of 18 and 25 report having tried marijuana at least once, while only 3 percent of those over 50 say that they have ever tried it.

Smokers also tend to live in big cities, easing the problems of distribution and advertising. Marijuana use varies significantly according to city size and region of the country. If you live in a city of one million or more, the chances are that one of every four adults you meet has at least tried marijuana. If you live in a city of less than 500,000, the chances of your meeting an adult who has tried marijuana are reduced to one in 10.

The highly lucrative western-states market has the highest percentage of users: 27 percent of adults say that they have ever used marijuana, with the northeastern states running a close second at 22 percent. A little more than one-half as many adults in the north central and southern states say they have tried marijuana.

The marijuana users of today are thus concentrated in urban centers and are particularly strong in the country's two largest markets. And because of their age, the marijuana smokers of today are likely to be tomorrow's majority. At the high school level, almost one-half of all students surveyed said they had tried marijuana. At the college level, that figure jumps to over two-thirds.

"Marijuana is here to stay.
No conceivable law-enforcement program
can curb its availability."

223

"The old generation that doesn't use grass will be replaced by the younger generation that does."

Illustrations by Abe Gurvin

224

A recent follow-up study of a nation-wide sample of high school boys first studied in 1966 reflects usage trends in a young adult male population, as reported to the U.S. Congress by the secretary of health, education and welfare. In 1969, when this group turned high school seniors, 20 percent had tried marijuana. By 1974, five years later, over three times as many (62 percent) had done so.

Professionals rank among the highest of all adult occupational groups in at least experimenting with marijuana. In the years to come, the legal and medical professions will be dominated by those who have sampled marijuana, if not by those who use it regularly—at least insofar as surveys of students at law and medical schools can be taken as barometers.

By any standard, marijuana is plainly a growth market right up there with quadraphonic stereos and digital watches. It is also a nonpartisan favorite. Of those adults declaring a political affiliation, a significantly greater percentage of independents have used and continue to use marijuana than either Democrats or Republicans. Democrats, however, use pot more often than Republicans—a fact that will probably not come as a surprise to either group.

We are witnessing the gradual acceptance of a new recreational drug into our society despite efforts at repression and medical warnings. Law-enforcement efforts are apparently having the same effect as they did during alcohol prohibition—large numbers of individuals are ignoring the law and rendering it ineffective.

But the law has hardly been ludicrous to those ensnared by it. Since 1965, almost two million arrests have been made by state and local authorities alone for marijuana violations. During that same period, law-enforcement officials have contined to assure us that marijuana law enforcement is a low priority, especially for personal possession and use. Yet in 1974 alone, marijuana arrests numbered 450,000, compared with only 19,000 in 1965. The overwhelming number of those arrests were for possession, not for sale.

Obviously, punitive criminal sanctions have failed to deter millions of people from using marijuana, and it remains readily available in every part of the nation. High school and college students report that "marijuana is easy to get." They are offered marijuana by friends, and it is often at parties they attend. Among adults who choose not to use marijuana, the reason usually has very little to do with their ability to obtain it.

California's experience with severe criminal penalties for marijuana possession illustrates the law's minimal impact on either use or availability. California had until recently one of the harshest antipot laws in the nation, with a maximum penalty of up to 10 years in jail for possession of any amount. Yet a Drug Abuse Council-sponsored survey in February 1975, when this tough law was still on the books, revealed that almost three out of 10 California adults had tried marijuana at least once, perhaps the highest experimentation rate among adults in any state.

The survey also revealed that of those Californians who were not currently using marijuana, the possibility of legal prosecution or the unavailability of marijuana ranked at the bottom of those reasons chosen for abstaining. Instead, over 90 percent of nonusers cited a lack of interest or perceived health dangers as their reasons for not trying grass.

In his appearances before local lawmakers, John Finlator, retired deputy director of the former Bureau of Narcotics and Dangerous Drugs, underscores the ineffectiveness of the criminal law as a deterrence to marijuana use. "Our criminal laws are a failure," he told a Vermont legislative committee. "We are simply fighting a ghost."

Policymakers are beginning to respond to the reality that the marijuana laws have not only failed in their purpose, but that draconian punishments do not fit the offense. As early as 1972, the National Commission on Marihuana and Drug Abuse, authorized by the Congress and created by ex-President Nixon, issued its first report, aptly titled *Marihuana: A Signal of Mis-*

understanding. The commission recommended that possession of marijuana for personal use no longer be treated as a criminal offense and that distribution of small amounts of marijuana not involving profit be treated the same. The president ignored the report, but others were listening.

Within 18 months after the report was made public, the state of Oregon abolished criminal sanctions for possession of one ounce or less of marijuana and replaced them with a civil fine of $100 or less, similar to a traffic citation. The Oregon model is similar to that recommended by the commission—an official policy of discouragement of use by the imposition of a civil sanction and the elimination of criminal penalties. Criminal sanctions are retained, however, for possession of over one ounce, for selling and for cultivation.

What would be the results of the abolition of criminal penalties for possession of marijuana, and would the public accept that change? Evidence on this question comes from Oregon, where the Drug Abuse Council sponsored two identical surveys to assess the impact of their decriminalization law—the first survey was conducted one year after the new law went into effect, and the second was conducted one year after the first.

The fears of many that marijuana use would dramatically increase if criminal penalties were removed are not borne out by the Oregon experience. The first survey found that the number of individuals using marijuana had not significantly increased among Oregon adults during the year following removal of criminal penalties for simple possession of one ounce or less. Indeed, through a series of interviews with 802 respondents—a cross section of Oregon residents aged 18 or over—we found that only 72 adults (9 percent) reported being current marijuana users. Only four of the 802 respondents (0.5 percent) reported that they had started using it in the year following decriminalization.

Surprisingly, of those adults using marijuana at the time of the survey, four of every 10 reported an actual de-

"Professionals rank among the highest of all adult occupational groups in at least experimenting with marijuana."

marijuana. Several other states are presently considering such an approach. The Alaskan Supreme Court has gone even farther by declaring criminal penalties for marijuana possession to be unconstitutional invasions of privacy.

Yet criminal penalties remain in effect in 44 states, and the arrests continue. According to the latest federal statistics, state and local enforcement agencies spend some $600 million per year enforcing their marijuana laws.

Public attitudes are divided on what should be the proper legal response to marijuana use, but they seem to be moving toward more lenient approaches. Survey results compiled by the National Institute on Drug Abuse (NIDA), the federal drug-abuse treatment and research arm, indicate that 86 percent of adults are against sending marijuana smokers to jail for first conviction of possession, but they prefer other alternatives ranging from no penalty to probation and mandatory treatment.

The Drug Abuse Council's own national survey points to a sharp division of opinion toward legal alternatives to possession of small amounts of marijuana between those who have used it and those who have never tried it. Eight of every 10 adults who have ever used favor reducing or eliminating criminal penalties, compared with three of 10 of those who have never used.

The public's attitude toward the various legal alternatives varies from region to region, paralleling those in patterns of use. Of adults in the western states where use is the highest, 51 percent favor outright elimination of all criminal penalties for the possession of even small amounts of marijuana; that percentage drops precipitously to 31 percent in the southern states, where use is among the lowest.

Similar sharp variations in attitude are evident among age groupings, with younger adults by far the most lenient in outlook and older adults opting for the law as it now is or for stiffer penalties. Again, however, it should be noted that attitudes among these age groups generally follow patterns of use. Even more lenient attitudes toward mari-

crease in the amount they smoked during that year, while only one of 20 reported an increase. More than one-half (52 percent) of current users reported no change in consumption.

MARIJUANA USE IN OREGON

	Adults who have ever used	Adults who currently use
Oct. '74	19%	9%
Oct. '75	20%	8%

The follow-up survey found no significant difference among adults who said either that they had ever used or currently use marijuana. And, among those currently using, a similar de-

crease in consumption was reported. It would appear that marijuana use has stabilized among Oregon adults during the two years following the removal of criminal penalties.

The Oregon surveys also indicate that once the law has been changed to remove criminal sanctions, the public will accept that change. In both surveys, almost six of 10 adults favored the elimination of criminal penalties for the possession of small amounts of marijuana—the majority favored either the new law as is or even more lenient legal alternatives.

Within the last year, California, Maine, Alaska, Colorado and Ohio have substituted fines for jail sentences for possession of small amounts of

"Marijuana is plainly a growth market right up there with quadraphonic stereos and digital watches."

juana laws are seen among the youth who will be reaching voting age in the next few years.

Decriminalization of marijuana is thus a matter of time. But meanwhile we are bombarded with a vociferous, if not acrimonious, rearguard action. Some of the summary language used, for example, to preface the marijuana hearings before the U.S. Senate Subcommittee on Internal Security in 1974 was reminiscent of the national hysteria of the 1950s. The subcommittee saw the marijuana euphoria as a danger to democracy with "subversive groups" playing a "significant role in the spread of the epidemic." It saw the nation being "saddled with a large population of semizombies." If the "epidemic is not rolled back," the subcommittee summary warns, "our society may be largely taken over by a marijuana culture."

The more serious debate about the possible health consequences of marijuana use has been flawed by a series of research reports, some of which resemble propaganda more nearly than scientific research. Science itself has become a weapon in a battle between conflicting values and lifestyles, and many of the scientists have taken off their hats to become protagonists or antagonists.

Without considering the detailed research findings, it is useful nonetheless to put them in the general context of the questions scientists themselves are asking about their purposes and methodologies. In early 1975, the Drug Abuse Council sponsored a conference in Washington, D.C., designed to comprehensively review the major marijuana studies reported since the commission issued its final report in March 1973. The participants were 19 distinguished scientists from the fields of immunology, genetics, endocrinology, pharmacology, psychiatry, psychology, internal medicine and neurology—those areas where the more serious allegations of potential health harm have been raised.

There was general agreement among the participants that "there are no new reasons to be especially disturbed by the use of marijuana." The scientists cautioned against acceptance of most of the recent findings prior to the com-

pletion of corroborating research. They called for large-scale epidemiological investigations to identify potential health consequences of chronic marijuana use, rather than the isolated animal research and retrospective studies that have dominated the area.

The National Institute on Drug Abuse, charged with the yearly responsibility of reporting to the U.S. Congress on research related to marijuana and health, says that "none of the results of marijuana research are conclusive." The institute itself spends over $5 million a year on marijuana-related studies. Yet, in five consecutive annual reports, it has never concluded that marijuana use poses a significant health danger, although it does point to possible negative consequences such as genetic changes and interference with driving skills. Everyone seems to agree that it is wise to abstain from marijuana if pregnant or when driving a motor vehicle or flying an airplane.

Few responsible scientists, however, would question that marijuana can be harmful, especially when taken in high dosages over an extended period of time. This is true of almost any drug, licit and illicit, with alcohol and tobacco ranking at the top of almost anyone's list of potential health hazards. But in pursuing a policy of discouraging use of alcohol and tobacco, especially at harmful levels, we have not framed our laws to make criminals of users.

The discouragement approach for marijuana is attracting increasing support among high-level policymakers. At a February 1976 news conference called to discuss the government's fifth annual report to Congress on marijuana and health, NIDA director Robert L. DuPont, M.D., endorsed the view that civil penalties should be substituted for criminal prosecution of possession of small amounts of marijuana. DuPont, who had previously avoided drawing comparisons among the three most widely used recreational drugs, declared alcohol and cigarettes to be far more dangerous to the health of the user than grass.

Legislation to remove criminal penalties for simple possession of marijuana has been introduced in Congress

by Sen. Jacob Javits (R.-N.Y.) and Rep. Edward Koch (D.-N.Y.).

President Ford's Domestic Council Task Force on Drug Abuse released yet another major review of the nation's drug problems in its white paper to the president in December 1975. While not going so far as endorsing decriminalization of the Oregon variety, it did recommend that the marijuana laws go virtually unenforced.

The task force ranked drug-abuse priorities among the major classes of drugs according to dependence liability, severity of personal and social consequences and size of core problem. Marijuana was not only declared to be the least serious of the various problems associated with a variety of drugs, but it ranked "low" on each of the measurement scales.

There are signs that President Ford, unlike his predecessor, is listening to the advice of his domestic council that "public policy should be most concerned with those drugs which have the highest social cost." Ford has offered a general endorsement of the report and promises to put its recommendations into effect. It is too early to know whether the president will recognize the desirability of going beyond unenforced laws to repeal of those laws. He would attract considerable public suport if he did, and the experience with marijuana decriminalization, at least in Oregon where it has had a good chance to be tested, tells us that he ought to forge ahead.

The evidence to date should convince all but the most obstinate that the criminal law is not the answer and has failed to deter or decrease marijuana use. The attitudes those laws embody have gone up in smoke. A substantial number of Americans have voted with their lungs for their repeal.

The relative youth of today's marijuana users, their wide geographic spread and their heavy representation in the ranks from which the power structure of the future will be drawn makes the decriminalization of their drug of recreation inevitable. The major remaining question is the final cost of maintaining an archaic legal code that is bound to collapse sooner or later.

"The evidence should convince all but the most obstinate that criminal law has failed to deter or decrease use."

43

By the time it gets to Phoenix

There's an alarming market
for Mexican heroin in the prosperous—and
seemingly stable—middle class.

By Martin Kasindorf

PHOENIX, Ariz.—On a typical 111-degree Saturday afternoon in August, a slim, rich 23-year-old heroin user named Gary kept an appointment at a dimly lit steakhouse on North Central Avenue, the main drag here. He wore a white crepe see-through shirt and a necklace of white puka shells and chain-smoked as he discussed his five-year habit. Gary lives on the affluent North Side, where tall palms nod over the red tile roofs and swimming pools of $150,000 Southwestern architectural gems. It is also "where the newer Anglo addicts hang out," a research team from the Drug Abuse Council, Inc., of Washington, D. C, recently informed the municipal government.

"I started on heroin out of boredom, too much money and pressure to take over my father's businesses," Gary explained to me without embarrassment. "I could use an account my parents set up for me when I was a child. A couple of my friends told them about my habit, but they kept demanding proof. One day my mom finally had proof. She came home and saw me sitting on the john in the main bath with a needle in my arm. My blood had coagulated. I needed her help, and she tied me off. My parents started supporting my habit for me. They were afraid of getting their name smeared all over the papers. I would tell them that I needed $300 or $600, and my mom would lay an envelope with the money beside the kitchen cupboard. We've never talked it out. Sometimes I've been sick and my mother has picked up an envelope from my connection, a Mexican-American guy named Indio, in the Glendale housing projects. She's never opened the envelope."

Although heroin addiction is still considered shameful in conservative, predominantly middle-class Phoenix, use of the opiate is increasing faster among Anglo whites (80 per cent of the city's 783,000 residents) than among the blacks (only 3.4 per cent of the population) and the Mexican Americans, who live in the barrios of South Phoenix across the Southern Pacific tracks. An estimated 8,400 addicts live here (proportionately about as many as there are in Washington, D. C., where the population is predominantly black and poor) and almost half appear to be the sun-bronzed offspring of families in at least average circumstances. Such, at least, are the conclusions to be drawn from the records of Terros, a respected street-level organiza-

Martin Kasindorf is Newsweek's deputy bureau chief in Los Angeles.

tion which operates detoxification programs and emergency ambulances for overdose cases, and from interviews conducted at The New Arizona Family (known simply as The Arizona Family before a change in leadership). This is a communal residence for persons trying to kick the drug habit, where three-quarters of the clientele is drawn from the middle class. The average addict in Phoenix is 25 years old, but on one night each week a furtive enfilade of middle-aged white men and women can be seen leaving their late-model cars and entering the Valle del Sol methadone-maintenance center.

From Sun City, the retirement enclave on the northwest, to Mesa, the pious Mormon town to the east, Phoenix is an undisputably "nice" community, and its experience is a convincing demonstration that the heroin problem in the United States is far from moribund. Nationally, a high incidence in the use of smack is no longer confined to the inner cities of large metropolitan centers in the East, where addiction reached its peak between 1969 and 1971. Now, such an unlikely place as Jackson, Miss., a city of 154,000, is suffering what

Brown heroin is tested in the Phoenix police lab.

is described as a "current epidemic," particularly "a rapidly growing problem in the white community." Such is the assessment of the recently disbanded White House Special Action Office on Drug Abuse Prevention. The same study found a "growing problem" in Eugene, Ore.; a "micro-epidemic" among young Omaha (Neb.) whites, and a "dramatic current increase in heroin incidence among white males" in Des Moines, Iowa. A "ripple theory"—that a heroin problem increases in ever-smaller cities as it peaks and declines in larger ones—is being validated, the researchers concluded.

Only two years ago, Federal officials were talking optimistically of having turned the corner in the fight against heroin. The army of Eastern junkies was going through a severe supply shortage. The U. S. Drug Enforcement Administration guessed happily that as much as two-thirds of the so-called French Connection heroin had been cut off. It was assumed that Turkey's 1971 ban on the growing of opium poppies, undertaken at the prodding of the Nixon Administration, had severely restricted the traffic between Turkey and Marseilles' illicit laboratories.

Then came the Mexican Connection. Crude brown heroin, made in the city of Culiacán from poppies cultivated in the state of Sinaloa, began filling the demand—and creating vast new markets in the process. Since the nineteen-forties, Chicano barrios in Southwestern U. S. border cities had been having their troubles with heroin imported by tight little family organizations. Quickly, small organizations of Anglos moved into the business alongside the old-timers. "Mexican brown" accounted for only 20 per cent of the heroin seizures across the country in 1972. Now policemen find it in 70 per cent of their cases in both slum and suburban neighborhoods throughout the U. S.

Customs and Drug Enforcement Administration officials estimate that, at most, only 10 per cent of the shipments in the new Mexican pipelines are intercepted. The drug's ready availability has encouraged new types of customers to try it. In the words of Dr. Robert L. DuPont, former director of the President's Special Action Office and now head of the Health, Education and Welfare Department's National Institute for Drug Abuse, "heroin used to be an East Coast problem, and there was a lot of truth to the saying that half of all American addicts were in New York. This is no longer the case. The fastest-growing use of intravenous drugs has been among suburban and nonminority groups —although there is still a higher rate of use among minorities and the poor."

The new trends are more observable in Phoenix than almost anywhere else. (Tentative findings in

1974 by the Special Action Office suggested that a similar situation may exist in San Diego, a city of comparable size.) Since a car or a smuggler's cantaloupe truck traveling on the freeway can make it from the border to the city in three hours, Phoenix has become a busy terminal for the Mexican Connection. An estimated 25 per cent of this heroin (at least half a ton passes through the city annually) remains in Phoenix, where it is making striking social inroads.

Thomas Bryant, a physician and president of the Drug Abuse Council, says there are more heroin addicts in Phoenix than he would have predicted on the basis of comparisons with other cities similar in size, geopolitical and socioeconomic make-up—places like Atlanta, Denver and Seattle. "Estimates of the number of addicts in Denver are 3,000 to 4,000 tops," he says. "There are now substantial numbers of heroin dependents in every city over 100,000, and in city after city you can identify heroin in the suburbs. But Phoenix sort of stands out. I don't like the word 'epidemic,' but Phoenix certainly has a serious problem—a rapidly increasing one. In large measure, it is due to the proximity of the Mexican border, the high availability of heroin and the relative unavailability of treatment."

In a study of the city's ability to cope with its addiction problem, the Drug Abuse Council's nine-member research team found that publicly funded treatment of any kind was available for only 649 cases; of these, only 251 could be accommodated in methadone programs. (Proportionately, New York

'There are now substantial numbers of heroin addicts in every U.S. city with a population over 100,000.'

City offers eight times as much help to junkies wishing to kick the habit.) Phoenix's meager treatment facilities are financed almost entirely by Federal grants, with little money from the community.

Phoenix is dominated by a small-town, paternalistic system; the nominally nonpartisan Charter Government group has been in power since 1950, when the city's 100,000 residents were outnumbered by the lizards and saguaro cacti. (Senator Barry Goldwater got his political start as a Charter city councilman.) An oligarchy of entrenched businessmen influences city and county policies with a frontiersman's wary eye toward anything suggesting welfare. At the same time, the Phoenix area has been adding 60,000 new residents every year. Most of the population is young—the median age is 25—and frequently bored.

For young people, there is little to do but cruise between the high-rises and shopping centers of North Central in hot rods on weekend nights

in a scene straight out of "American Graffiti," or brave the machine-made "ocean" waves on surf-boards at an amusement park called Big Surf. Voters regularly turn down proposed bond issues for parks, community youth centers and mountain hiking trails. At only $10 a fix for heroin of 9 to 15 per cent purity (compared to 3 or 4 per cent in Harlem), smack is only the latest compensatory thrill for middle-class youths who, in their time, have taken up every other California fad, from LSD to amphetamines to downer pills.

Although the city's conservative newspapers, The Phoenix Gazette and The Arizona Republic, raise at least as much fuss about marijuana as they do about heroin, their headlines about hard drugs have appeared often enough to provide residents with proof of heroin's breakout from the shanties of the South Side. Law-and-order Phoenix is listed by the F.B.I. as having the third worst record in the nation (after St. Louis and Boston, in that order) for rates of the addicted-related crimes of robbery, burglary and auto theft. Police narcotics sergeant Manuel Quiñonez says unhappily, "We're just catching up with the rest of the world."

During his 1973 election campaign, Mayor Timothy Barrow, 41, freely admitted the addiction problems of his 39-year-old sister, Sinda. She has now been "clean" for more than a year. "I'm proud of her," Mayor Barrow says. A few months ago, Mayor Albert Seledon of suburban Tolleson, a jovial insurance agent who coached Little League baseball, was sentenced to 10 years in Federal prison. He

had been arrested in a parking lot near the Smuggler's Inn restaurant, of all places, while delivering nearly a pound of Mexican brown to an undercover agent. Timothy LaPrade, 20, son of a county judge and grandson of a late chief justice of the Arizona Supreme Court, died accidentally last December after combining heroin and alcohol. Guy Stillman, chairman of the U.S. Naval Academy board of governors and former Democratic national committeeman from the state, was grief-stricken last year when his son, Chris, was arrested on smuggling charges (involving cocaine).

There are plenty of well-heeled people the newspapers haven't mentioned. While wintering here, the 20-year-old daughter of a top executive in the automobile industry went through a cold-turkey "detox" program at a discreet private hospital without much success. She has spent $300,000 on heroin, a friend says, and has smashed up a Ferrari, a Maserati and a Jaguar in the process. "The debutante scene here is not exactly Grosse Pointe or New York," the friend explains. The son of an influential Episcopalian priest has been a resident at The New Arizona Family in the onion fields 10

miles west of town. U. S. District Judge Carl A. Muecke reports sadly, "Both children of a lawyer I know became addicts, and one is now dead of an overdose." A recent Phoenix Gazette survey of 1,000 high-school students indicated that one in every 12 seniors had used heroin, morphine or cocaine. Teachers and lawyers have personal files at Terros, where many file cards indicate incomes from $12,000 to $50,000 a year.

One sultry afternoon recently, two well-mannered, college-age men in sport shirts and blue jeans walked hesitantly into the funky old converted mansion Terros occupies a few blocks west of North Central. They wanted help in hauling a stricken friend from their car. Three staff members—Don Peyton, a tall young man with long hair, and two young woman paramedics — strained to lift onto an emergency - room table a strapping youth who was retching and thrashing. "He's cyanotic," one of the women remarked, noting the youth's bluish skin, and she quickly injected a narcotic antagonist into his arm. She smiled when she saw the pupils of the victim's eyes flutter.

"Fresh tracks," said Peyton after a quick glance at the youth's right arm. A stretcher was readied for an ambulance run to Maricopa County Hospital three miles away.

"How long has he been like this?" Peyton asked one of the youth's friends.

"Since last night."

"Does he fix much?" asked Peyton.

"Not lately," the friend said quickly and then amended. "Well, he's been fixing for three or four months."

One of the woman paramedics climbed behind the wheel of one of Terros's two blue and white ambulances, and as its siren screamed through the heat eddies on the streets, Peyton sat in back with the other paramedic, using a suction apparatus to clear mucus from the youth's throat. At the hospital, the doctors took over.

Terros sees a lot worse among the 40 overdose calls its ambulances make every month. Phoenix has recorded a sharp rise in overdose deaths—from eight in 1973 to 30 last year to 33 so far this year—four in one grim weekend. The high and fluctuating quality of the Mexican heroin is responsible—along with the ignorance of the victims.

"The majority of overdose

victims are not junkies," reports Terros executive Mark Scharfman. "They are chippers — experimenters, fumblers—who don't know the quality or quantity of what they're taking. Heroin in Phoenix is of a higher purity than in other cities."

Called *chiva* (nanny goat) or *carga* (load) in Mexican slang borrowed by its Anglo users, the brown heroin in Phoenix is of higher purity because it hasn't traveled enough distance and consequently passed through the hands of enough middlemen to be diluted to any great extent with the dental painkiller procaine, a process that extends the profits.

According to Vic Pollack of the Do It Now Foundation, another private-aid group, "Most overdoses happen in the middle-class areas of town. People in the South Phoenix ghettos and barrios know better than kids in Paradise Valley how the stuff tends to vary. They are more cautious." But neither the death figures nor a stiff new state law, mandating a two-year prison term for a first offender possessing at least $250 worth of heroin, has stopped the experimenting.

Since it has a higher pro-

portion of middle-class heroin users than most cities, Phoenix is witnessing an unusual variation in the addiction problem. Though the growing crime rate may provide evidence that many local addicts must turn to theft to support their habit, a significant minority manages to do so without turning to street crime. These are the local users who remain either "weekend chippers" or stay on their jobs and support an average-sized habit (at Phoenix's bargain rate of $200 to $280 a week).

Nobody starts into heroin with the intention of becoming hooked. The self-delusional "I can handle it" is as prevalent in Phoenix as anywhere else. The user is most often introduced to the narcotic by a well-meaning friend at a party—not by a pusher. The friend may be a needle-using weekend "mainliner" who evangelizes about the painless pleasures of heroin. It is only those mainliners who realize they are getting "strung out," or hooked—usually after a year of proselytizing—who stop promoting their habit.

In the darkened North Side restaurant, Gary reminisces: "When you start out as a weekender, you do one balloon ($25 worth of heroin, enough for three or four fixes)

Friday night, one Saturday and one Sunday. That feels so good that the next weekend you'll do two balloons, then three. More commonly, you'll do dope on Sunday but not on Monday. But on Tuesday a balloon pops up in front of you and you don't turn it down."

There is a minority of weekend chippers — perhaps 20 per cent, say Terros workers—who really can handle heroin without getting addicted, in addition to thrill-seeking "snorters" and the "skin-poppers" who inject the heroin solution subcutaneously, not into a vein. (They obtain heroin's euphoria but miss the crashing "rush" which gave rise to the name "smack".) "Heroin definitely has a recreational use," reports Vic Pollack. "We find people using it on weekends for eight and 10 years who never become addicts. This is leading us to believe that a whole revision of the image is possible."

Among those addicts who manage to feed their monkeys without resorting to crime, some are spoiled "trust funders" like Gary. The rest, incredibly enough, are highly paid men and women who have kept their habits on a budget—for the time being, at any rate—and who work hard and honestly for the cash to pay their connections until they lose control, if they ever do.

One prominent lawyer, traumatized by his divorce, conducted himself blamelessly in court during a year of addiction, a judge reports, before he entered a private California institution to cure himself. In Scottsdale, one of the poshest enclaves in the metropolitan area, there is a $60,000-a-year general practitioner who has handled his heroin usage so well for five years, he says, that "no patient has ever noticed."

Such motivation is not confined to professionals with comfortable savings accounts. A 25-year-old carpet layer who makes up to $1,500 a month and spends 90 per cent of it on dope finds working in an opiatic euphoria positively invigorating. "When I'm loaded at work," he says, "I don't sit there and nod off. When I do heroin, it stimulates me like speed would. I fly through a job. When I nick my finger on the tack strip, I don't feel it. My only problem is cotton mouth. You don't have any saliva. When you drink water, you throw up. So I put nails in my mouth to start the saliva, and I shut up." (However, in spite

of the advantages he has found in working while high, he has decided he has had enough and is about to check into a methadone program.)

Dr. DuPont of the National Institute for Drug Abuse sees nothing odd in such accounts. "That's quite common," Dr. DuPont says. "Between 20 and 30 per cent of the people entering treatment centers have jobs when they come in." Clayton Price, who runs The New Arizona Family center, says, "People in the middle class can function better on a dope habit than working-class people, even on their jobs. We've had some people function for 20 years in the community without being detected."

This phenomenon, raised by the relatively prosperous nature of Phoenix, also raises a troubling question. Is narcotic addiction itself debilitating, or are only the poor debilitated by what they have to go through to pay for it?

There is evidence pointing each way. Methadone maintenance is a form of narcotic addiction, if a widely approved one, which enables some motivated users to live productive lives. (Tino de Anda, director of the Valle del Sol methadone maintenance center, has put the "cure" rate there at only 12 per cent. Methadone is no panacea.) Most of the American GI's who got themselves hooked on cheap heroin in Vietnam have stayed completely off the drug back home and have suffered no ill effects, judging from preliminary results of a study conducted by researcher Lee Robins of the Washington University School of Medicine in St. Louis. And even long-time junkies are able to scheme for money. "How debilitating can heroin be if a junkie can pull a burglary and run down an alley with a color TV?" asks Don Peyton, who was an addict in Vietnam.

Physiologically, of course, the vast majority of addicts find themselves unable to hold their heroin intake at any given level. Some put themselves through the agonies of periodic lonely withdrawals to lower their needs; others have eventually miscalculated their bodies' ever-building tolerance and have taken fatal overdoses. In any event, heroin's effects on most people make addiction incompatible with normal job-holding. "The addict has to take the stuff five or six times a day," says Dr. DuPont, "and is constantly going back and forth between

withdrawal and a nodding-out kind of euphoria. It can't be easy for anybody."

For those who do turn to serious crime, Mexico's proximity can make crime pay. In Sonoran border towns like Nogales and San Luis, cars and guns stolen in Phoenix are often traded for dope. Hot items these days are automatic weapons and four-wheel-drive vehicles, which find their way to dissident guerrilla bands in the Mexican interior. The price of an ounce of heroin 60 to 80 per cent pure is $500 in the Mexican streets, $1,000 just across the border and $1,200 up the road in Phoenix. Each succeeding

---

'A recent Phoenix survey of 1,000 high-school students indicated that one in every 12 seniors had used heroin, morphine or cocaine.'

---

buyer cuts, or dilutes, the heroin to increase his profits on the resale. Phoenix law-enforcement efforts are frustrated by the ease with which small-time users cut off from their normal supply by the arrest of a dealer can get single fixes in the "shooting galleries" of nearby Mexican towns, or pool their cash with friends and pick up a 25 per cent pure ounce of heroin in the towns' grubby *cantinas*. Back home, they may cut it once or twice and become small-scale sellers themselves.

How available is heroin on the streets of Phoenix? Police have identified 22 "retail outlets," popular connection places that include bowling alleys and package stores in the colossal, antiseptic shopping centers that embody Phoenix's shiny character. Junkies learning of the ease with which *chiva* can be had are moving into town from other states, habits and all. "I moved from West Phoenix to Sunnyslope to South Phoenix to Tempe, fooling myself that I was going to quit," says a 22-year-old college dropout from Iowa. "Every time, I

'A $60,000-a-year general practitioner has handled his heroin usage so well for five years, he says, that ''no patient has ever noticed.'' '

had a next-door neighbor who was doing dope, too."

It is the wholesale traffic, however, which most marks Phoenix's place in the post-1972 patterns of international heroin trafficking. According to Philip Jordan, 32, the beefy Chicano ex-football player in charge of the 15 agents in the local district office of the U.S. Drug Enforcement Administration, "The Mexican Connection means anybody capable of coming across a 1,933-mile border with one, two or three pounds of heroin." Arizona has 400 of the international border's loneliest desert miles. Phoenix, with a population big enough to offer a smuggler the shelter of anonymity, is an obvious distribution point. It has excellent transit facilities and

a large user population to soak up the leftovers. An unknown but certainly large amount of contraband is overlooked at Sky Harbor International Airport, where no single city, county or Federal agency has broken through a jurisdictional maze to organize a search-and-seizure program. A few airline baggage handlers voluntarily feel around for drugs whenever they have the time. "We got a lucky half pound of heroin on that basis in 1974," says Phoenix police detective Samuel Gonzales. The underfunded police are now applying for Federal money to buy a drug-sniffing dog.

Fundamentally, most respectable Phoenix citizens are still unwilling to face the bizarre reality in their midst. "Heroin is such a scary thought here," says Robert Arthur, head of the Scottsdale police narcotics unit, "that people don't believe you even when you show them the crime statistics." The Phoenix police have been shortchanged on money to make undercover narcotics buys. "This is a town of low police pressure, low political pressure and low public awareness," says the Do It Now Foundation's Vic Pollack.

Brown heroin may soon have competition in view of Turkey's decision to let her farmers cultivate the opium poppy once more. The first fresh 150-ton poppy crop since 1972 came to harvest

all across Anatolia in June. The white Turkish heroin is due for a comeback on the streets of Eastern cities. But Dr. DuPont thinks the new brown heroin from the Southwest will manage to coexist in most of the new markets it has gained "There is still a substantial unmet demand,' he says, "and there will be consumers for both products. It could be quite ominous."

On a hot Friday afternoon after a wearying week in Phoenix's Federal courthouse, the chief assistant United States Attorney, Thomas Crowe, leaned back in an office chair, put his arms behind his head and, only half in jest, proposed a solution not unlike Britain's controversial policy. Old-line, proven British addicts are allowed heroin by National Health Service prescription, although all new cases—80 per cent of British junkies—are placed on methadone maintenance. The optimistic idea of cutting the social costs of heroin by legalizing it retains a clean kind of appeal in this country among those who despair of any other possible answer.

"For 10 per cent of what we spend now," said Crowe, "on property losses, detox programs and police efforts, we could have banks of fix machines, like a row of bank-teller windows. The addict sticks his arm in, the machine goes 'Ding! Ding!' and it's all over very quickly."

44

The Labelling Theory of Mental Illness*

T. J. SCHEFF

University of California
Santa Barbara

*The first part of this paper is a response to several recent critiques of labelling theory.
The second part assesses the state of the evidence on the labelling theory of mental
illness. The majority of the studies reviewed support the theory.*

This paper will present an evaluation of the
labelling theory of mental illness. To this
date, there have been three critiques of
labelling theory, those by Gove (1970a),
Gibbs (1972), and Davis (1972). Gibbs and
Davis, for the most part, evaluate formal
aspects of the theory; Gove evaluates its
substance. Gibbs suggests that the labelling
approach is not really a scientific theory, in
that it is not sufficiently explicit and unambiguous. Davis proposes that there are
ideological biases in the labelling approach,
and points to other approaches as alternatives.[1]

Although the papers by Gibbs and by Davis
raise important questions, neither considers at
length the most fundamental question that
can be asked about a theory: how well is it
supported by empirical studies? Gove considers this question in his critique, and the
present paper is devoted to it. In the first
section of this paper, I will respond to Gove's
evaluation, and in the second, present my
own.

First, however, I wish to comment on
Gibbs' paper, since it raises a methodological
question relevant to assessing evidence to be
presented here. In his analysis of labelling
theory, Gibbs demonstrates that the concepts
used in the theory are ambiguous, since they
are not defined denotatively, i.e., in a way

which allows for only a single meaning for
each concept. He argues that this ambiguity
leaves open many alternative meanings and
implications. For this reason, he concludes
that the theory in its present state is of little
value.

I will make two observations about Gibbs'
argument. First, virtually every other sociological theory lacks denotative definition. Indeed, Gibbs observes that the concept of
social norm, an important element in labelling
theory, has never been denotatively defined.
Since this concept is perhaps the most basic
sociological idea, Gibbs' critique is less an
evaluation of labelling theory per se than the
state of social science.

Note that Gibbs' critique is equally applicable to psychiatric theories. At this writing, I
know of no psychiatric theory of functional
mental illness which is based on denotatively
defined concepts. The four basic components
of the medical model, cause, lesion, symptoms, and outcome, as applied to mental
illness, are not denotatively defined (Scheff,
1966:180). Nor are such specific concepts as
depression, schizophrenia, phobia, and neurosis. Gibbs' critique of labelling illness, therefore, applies equally well to all of its competitors in the field of mental illness.

My second observation is that Gibbs' critique implies that there is only one kind of
science, a positivistic one modeled on natural
science. He appears to be saying that a theory
has no value unless it can be unambiguously
stated. It has been argued, however, that
concepts and theories can have a sensitizing
function quite distinct from their literal truth
value (Blumer, 1954). Theories based on
nominal (connotative) definitions can direct

---

*I wish to acknowledge the helpful advice re-
ceived from Norman Denzin, James Greenley, C.
Allen Haney, Arnold Linsky, and William Rushing,
who read an earlier draft of this article.

[1] For a considered response to the question of
bias in labelling theory, see Becker (1973).

attention toward new data, or to new ways of perceiving old data, which challenge taken-for-granted assumptions, and shatter "the attitude of everyday life" (Bruyn, 1966; Schutz, 1962). In such a view, the very ambiguousness of nominal concepts is of value, since they have a rich evocativeness which denotative concepts lack (Bronowski, 1965).

Science may be viewed as a problem solving activity, with two distinct phases (Bronowski, 1956). In the first phase, the problem is to somehow transcend the traditional classifications and models which imprison thought. In the second, the problem is to test a new idea meticulously. Sensitizing theories are relevant to the first phase of scientific problem solving. They are attempts to jostle the imagination, to create a crisis of consciousness which will lead to new visions of reality. Sensitizing theories are as valuable as denotative theories; they simply attempt to solve a different problem.

The need for new research directions in the study of mental illness has long been apparent. Although thousands of studies have been based on the medical model, real progress toward scientific understanding, or even a fruitful formulation of the problem, is lacking (Scheff, 1966:7-9). The sensitizing function of the labelling theory of mental illness derives precisely from its attempt to contradict the major tenets of the medical model; it is less an attempt to displace that model than to clear the air, as I indicated in *Being Mentally Ill:*

> It should be clear at this point that the purpose of this theory is *not* to reject psychiatric and psychological formulations in their totality. It is obvious that such formulations have served, and will continue to serve, useful functions in theory and practice concerning mental illness. The . . . purpose, rather, is to develop a model which will complement the individual system models by providing a complete and explicit contrast . . . .By allowing for explicit consideration of these antithetical models, the way may be cleared for a synthesis . . . (Scheff, 1966, 25-27).

It seems to me that none of the three critiques discussed here appreciate the point that a sensitizing theory may be ambiguous, ideologically biased, not literally true, and still be useful and even necessary for scientific progress.

While the labelling theory of mental illness is a sensitizing theory, it can still be used to evaluate evidence, in a provisional way. The proper question to ask is not, as Gove asks, whether labelling theory is literally true, but whether the relevant studies are more consistent with labelling theory than with its com-petitor, the medical model. I will now turn to this question.

In his critique, Gove reaches the following conclusion: "The available evidence . . . indicates that the societal reaction formulation of how a person becomes mentally ill is substantially incorrect" (1970a: 881). My own reading of the evidence is contrary to that of Gove. First, Gove's interpretation of most studies he cites seems at least questionable and, in some cases, inaccurate. I wish first then to state my objections to several of Gove's interpretations. Secondly, since Gove's articles were published, several new studies have appeared which have bearing on the controversy. Also, several relevant articles which Gove failed to mention were published earlier than his article. Later in the paper, I will review all of these articles.

Gove concluded that the majority of the evidence failed to support labelling theory through two kinds of distortion: first, by overstating the implications of those studies he thought refuted labelling theory and, second, by misrepresenting those studies he thought supported labelling theory. I will not try to refute all of Gove's interpretations, since to do so would be to restate labelling theory. I will simply indicate some representative errors that he makes.

Apropos of Gove's overstatement, let us examine how he interprets the study by Yarrow et al. (1955). To study the processes through which the next-of-kin come to define a person as mentally ill, Yarrow et al. interviewed wives of men who had been hospitalized for mental illness. Gove summarizes that study as follows: "Only when the husband's behavior became impossible to deal with would the wife take action to have the husband hospitalized." Gove's interpretation is questionable for two reasons. First, Yarrow et al. studied only those cases of deviance which resulted in hospitalization. They did not study all cases of the same type of deviant behavior which led to hospitalization, in the entire population. The Yarrow study thus covers only a clinical population and is entirely ex post facto. Gove's interpretation repeats the classic fallacy of the medical model, which is to assume that hospitalization was inevitable, even though no observations have been made on the incidence and outcome of similar cases in the unhospitalized population. The history of physical medicine has many analogous cases. For example, it has been found that until the late 1940's, histoplasmosis was thought to be a rare tropical disease with a uniformly fatal outcome (Schwartz and Baum, 1957). Field investigations discovered, however, that the syndrome is widely prevalent and that death or impairment is highly unusual. Analogically, it is possible that the symptoms reported by the wives in the

Yarrow et al. study, even if accurately reported, might terminate without medical intervention.

The question of the accuracy of the wives' report raises the second problem in Gove's interpretation. Yarrow et al.'s descriptions of the husbands' behavior are based entirely on the wives' uncorroborated account. Yarrow et al. recognize this difficulty, warn the reader about it, and are unassuming about the implications of their findings:

> Ideally to study this problem, one might like to interview the wives as they struggle with the developing illness. This is precluded, however, by the fact that the problem "is not visible" until psychiatric help is sought. The data, therefore, are the wives' reconstructions of their earlier experiences .... It is recognized that recollections of the prehospital period may well include systematic biases such as distortions, omissions, and increased organization and clarity (p. 60).

Although Yarrow et al. clearly recognize the limitations of their study, Gove does not. He reports the wives' account of the husbands' behavior as if it were the thing itself. Judging from Gove, Laing and Esterson's (1964) detailed study of the way in which the next-of-kin sometime falsifies his account and colludes against the pre-patient may as well have never been written. Laing and Esterson spent an average of twenty-four hours interviewing members of each of the eleven families in their study, with a range of sixteen to fifty hours per family. They found considerable evidence which supported the patient's story rather than the next-of-kin's. For example, in one of their cases the psychiatrist indicated that the patient Maya had "ideas of reference," which supported one of the complaints against her. By interviewing the patient, the mother and the father together, however, Laing and Esterson put this "delusion" in quite a different light:

> An idea of reference that she had was that something she could not fathom was going on between her parents, seemingly about her. Indeed there was. When they were interviewed together, her mother and father kept exchanging with each other a constant series of nods, winks, gestures, and knowing smiles so obvious to the observer that he commented on them after 20 minutes of the first such interview. They continued, however, unabated and denied (Laing and Esterson, p. 24).

Laing and Esterson found many such items of misrepresentation by the next-of-kin in all their cases. Their study suggests that the uncorroborated account of the next-of-kin is riddled with error.

This is not to say that Laing and Esterson's interpretation is correct and that Gove's is not. I am saying that Yarrow et al.'s study and the other studies that Gove cites in this context were not only not organized to test labelling theory, but were innocent of any of the possible interpretations (such as that of Laing and Esterson) which labelling theory suggests. Until such time as systematic studies are conducted which investigate both clinical and non-clinical populations, and which do not rest entirely on the uncorroborated testimony of one or the other interested parties, interpretations of the kind that Gove makes are dubious.

Another example of how Gove distorts the evidence, seeking to discredit studies which support labelling theory, is his analysis of my article, "The Societal Reaction to Deviance: Ascriptive Elements in the Psychiatric Screening of Mental Patients in a Midwestern State" (Scheff, 1964). The study reported in this article consists of two phases. In the first, preliminary phase, I had hospital psychiatrists rate a sample of incoming patients according to the legal criteria for commitment, dangerousness, and degree of mental impairment. In the second phase, we observed, in a sample of cases, the procedures actually used in committing patients, particularly the psychiatric examination and the formal commitment hearing. The purpose of the psychiatric ratings was to provide a foundation for our observations in the second phase; they were used to determine the extent to which there was any legal uncertainty about the patients' committability. The second phase of the study described how the judges and psychiatrists reacted to uncertainty. The article stated clearly that the study was divided into two parts:

> The purpose of the description that follows is to determine the extent of uncertainty that exists concerning new patients' qualifications for involuntary confinement in a mental hospital, and the reactions of the courts to this type of uncertainty (p. 402).

In the first phase of the study, the psychiatrists' ratings of the sample of incoming patients were as follows:

Dangerousness

How Likely Patient Would Harm Self or Others		Degree of Mental Impairment	
Very likely	5%	Severe	17%
Likely	4%	Moderate	42%
Somewhat likely	14%	Mild	25%
Somewhat unlikely	20%	Minimal	12%
Unlikely	37%	None	2%
Very Unlikely	18%		

These findings, it is argued, are relevant to the question of the legal uncertainty concerning the patients' committability. The legal rulings on the presumption of health are stringent. The courts "have repeatedly held that there should be a presumption of sanity. The burden of proof should be on the petitioners (i.e., the next-of-kin). There must be a preponderance of evidence and the evidence should be of a clear and unexceptional nature" (Scheff, 1964: 403). Given these rulings, it seems reasonable to argue, as the article did, that the committability of all patients except those rated at the extremes of dangerousness or impairment was uncertain. The ratings, it was argued, suggested uncertainty about the committability of 63% of the patients in the sample, i.e., those patients rated as neither dangerous nor severely impaired.

In the second phase of the study, when we observed the actual commitment procedures, we sought to find out how the psychiatric examiners and judges reacted to uncertainty. To summarize our observations, we found that *all* of the psychiatric examinations and judicial hearings that we witnessed were perfunctory. Furthermore, virtually every hearing resulted in a recommendation for commitment or continued hospitalization. The conclusion of the article is based not on the first phase only, but on both phases of the study. Since the first phase suggests uncertainty with respect to the committability of some of the patients, and the second phase suggests that the commitment procedures were perfunctory for the entire sample, and yet resulted in continued hospitalization rather than release, in virtually every case, the study appears to demonstrate the presumption of illness.

Gove's treatment of this article is somewhat irresponsible. By ignoring the second phase of the study, he takes the first phase out of context. Ignoring my argument concerning uncertainty, Gove suggests that had I placed the cutting point on the psychiatrists' ratings differently, by including as committable patients rated as moderately impaired and/or somewhat likely to harm themselves, my data "would have shown instead that the vast majority of committed mental patients were mentally ill" (Gove, 1970b). He implies, therefore, that the results of the study rest entirely on my arbitrary choice of a cutting point.[2] In light of all the evidence presented in the article, where the cutting point in the psychiatrists' ratings is placed has little signif-

icance. Gove disregarded the problem that the study posed, which was whether or not patients were being committed illegally. He misrepresents my conclusion by imputing to me the conclusion that most of the patients are not mentally ill. The study did not make this point, since I regard the criteria for mental illness as even more ambiguous than the legal standards for commitment.

Gove's other criticism of the study concerns the questionnaire given the psychiatrists to obtain ratings of dangerousness and mental impairment. He suggests that I should have provided the psychiatrists with descriptions of the behavior that the scales refer to. This criticism begs the question, however, since it seems to assume that there are precise psychiatric or legal criteria of committable behavior. In fact, the legal statutes, though they vary in language from state to state, are all vague, general, and ambiguous. They state simply that persons who are dangerous or unable to care for themselves may be committed if a strong case can be made. No statutes or psychiatric statements set forth behavioral criteria. My study sought not to help psychiatrists and judges interpret these vague laws, but to describe how they reacted to the law's ambiguity.

Some of Gove's criticism seems based on a misunderstanding of labelling theory. He seems to think that showing that the commitment rates reported in various studies are considerably less than 100%, somehow refutes labelling theory (Gove, 1970a: 877-9). The argument made by labelling theorists that official agents of the societal reaction usually presume illness does not imply that commitment will always occur, any more than presuming innocence in criminal courts implies that acquittal will always occur. The master question which labelling theory raises with respect to commitment rates is more complex than Gove implies. At what point and under what conditions does the process of denial stop and labelling begin? Gove apparently acknowledges that labelling occurs, but only in the last stages of the commitment funnel, i.e., in the formal commitment procedure itself. I suspect that his formulation is much too simple, and that labelling occurs under some conditions much earlier in the process, even in the family or neighborhood; and, conversely, under some conditions, denial may occur late in the process, as some of my studies showed (Scheff, 1966: 135).

The crucial question we have raised vis-a-vis the medical model concerns contingencies which lead to labelling that lie outside the patient and his behavior. Greenley, for example, established that, independent of a patient's psychiatric condition, the family's desire to bring him home seems to be the most powerful determinant of his length of

---

[2] Gove's criticism of the cutting point applies more to an early report of some of the initial results of the study, a brief note in the *American Journal of Psychiatry* (Scheff, 1963). That report acknowledged that setting the cutting point on the psychiatrists' ratings was problematic (p. 268).

hospitalization (Greenley, 1972). Labelling theory proposes that the patient's condition is only one of a number of contingencies affecting the societal reaction and, therefore, the patient's fate. Further contingencies are suggested in *Being Mentally Ill* (pp. 96-7). Gove's interpretation of labelling theory is simplistic and incorrect.

SUMMARIZING THE EVIDENCE

Since most studies of "mental illness" were not designed to test labelling theory, seemingly plausible interpretations of most of them can be constructed either for or against labelling theory. Furthermore, since the conflict between labelling theory and the medical model engenders such furious partisanship, we should also exclude studies based on casual or unsystematic observations, in which the observers' bias are more likely to influence the results he reports. I have surveyed the research literature, therefore, for studies that meet two criteria. First, they must relate to labelling theory explicitly; and, second, the research methods must be systematic. At this writing I have located eighteen studies of this type. Of these eighteen only five, those by Gove (1973, 1974), Karmel (1969, 1970) and Robins (1966), are inconsistent with labelling theory; the remainder, those of Denzin (1968), Denzin and Spitzer (1966), Greenley (1972), Haney and Michielutte (1968), Haney, Miller and Michielutte (1969), Linsky (1970a, b), Rosenhan (1973), Rushing (1971), Scheff (1964), Temerlin (1968), Wilde (1968), and Wenger and Fletcher (1969) are consistent with labelling theory.

These eighteen studies vary widely in the reliability of the inferences that we can make from them. Four studies among those consistent with labelling theory use zero-order correlations—those of Denzin and Spitzer; Denzin; Haney and Michielutte, and Haney, Miller and Michielutte. For example, Haney reports the correlation between the decision to commit and social characteristics of the patients and petitioners. He finds positive correlations between commitment rates and these social characteristics. For example, he reports a higher rate of commitment for non-whites than whites. Although his findings are consistent with labelling theory, they provide only very weak support since he has not controlled for the patient's condition. We are left with the question that occurs so often in social epidemiology: Are non-whites committed more often because of the societal reaction to their social status, or because this particular social status is itself correlated with mental illness? That is to say, are non-whites committed more often than whites because of their powerlessness, or because there is more mental illness among them? Haney's studies do not

answer such questions, nor do those of Denzin and Spitzer, Denzin.

Similar criticism can be made of the two studies by Karmel which fail to support labelling theory. Based on interviews with patients after their hospitalization, her data fail to show any evidence of the acceptance of a deviant role predicted by labelling theory. These are simple correlation studies with no controls (Bohr, 1970). Gove (1973) studied the amount and effects of stigma on a sample of ex-mental patients. His data indicate that the amount and effects of stigma were not very large, and therefore fail to support labelling theory. His data are somewhat ambiguous, however, since there is no control group of similar persons who were not hospitalized.

A series of much stronger studies, whose findings support labelling theory, are those of Greenley, Rushing, Linsky, Scheff (1964), Wenger and Fletcher and Wilde. My study has already been discussed. Greenley, as indicated above, studied the relationship between length of hospitalization and several social and psychiatric variables. He found that even when the patient's psychiatric condition is controlled, there is a strong relationship between the family desire for the patient's release and the length of hospitalization.

Rushing and Linsky each did studies on the relationship between psychiatric commitment and social class and other social characteristics. Since they indicated that their data only partly overlap, I will cite both studies (Linsky, 1972; Rushing, 1972). Both used the same technique, which I believe controls for the patient's condition. If they had merely used commitment rates as their dependent variable, we would be left with the perplexing question: are commitment rates higher in the lowest social class because there is more mental illness in that class or for other reasons? (See the New Haven studies by Hollingshead and Redlich [1958].) However, both Rushing and Linsky used an index made up of the ratio of involuntary to voluntary hospital admissions, as a measure of societal reaction. I believe that such a ratio will control for gross variations in rates of mental illness. What the index provides, hopefully, is a measure of the most severe societal reaction, i.e., involuntary confinement, but with the phenomenon of mental illness at least partly controlled, assuming that the voluntary commitments are equally "mentally ill." Perhaps this assumption should also be investigated. Both studies show a strong relationship between powerlessness and commitment rates. In the study by Wenger and Fletcher, the presence of a lawyer representing the patient in admission hearings decreased the likelihood of hospitalization. This relationship held within three degrees of manifest "mental illness."

Finally, Wilde's study (1968) concerns the relationship between the recommendations for commitment made by mental health examiners and various social characteristics of the pre-patients, with controls for the patient's psychiatric condition. In all five of these studies strong relationships are reported between such social characteristics as class, and commitment rates, with psychiatric conditions controlled for. These five studies support labelling theory since they indicate that social characteristics of the patients help determine the severity of the societal reaction, independent of psychiatric condition.

The controlled studies by Robins (1966) and by Gove (1974) provide data which fail to support labelling theory. Robins used psychiatric diagnoses of adults who had been diagnosed as children as part of an evaluation of child guidance clinics. Robins noted that some of the children diagnosed were treated and some were not. She argues that this data can be used to evaluate the effects of "the severity of societal response to the behavior problems of the children." She found that, of the adults who had psychiatric treatment as children, 16% were diagnosed as having sociopathic personalities as adults. Of the persons who did not receive psychiatric treatment as children, 24% were diagnosed as having sociopathic personalities as adults. Since the difference between the two percentages is not statistically significant, the hypothesis that psychiatric treatment was beneficial is not supported, but by the same token, neither is the labelling hypothesis that psychiatric treatment, particularly when involuntary, may stabilize behavior that would otherwise be transient. This finding is somewhat equivocal, however, because of the sampling problems of the original Cambridge-Somerville study.

With a sample of hospitalized mental patients, Gove (1974) has studied the relationship between the patient's psychiatric record and his economic and social resources. His data suggest that individual resources facilitate treatment, rather than allow the individual to avoid the societal reaction, and therefore support the medical model rather than labelling theory. Some caution is necessary in interpreting these findings, however, since patient characteristics were based on hospital data. For example, he finds that more of the records of patients with low resources present the patient as "never psychiatrically normal," than patients with higher resources. Does this mean that low resource patients have been "mentally ill" longer, or that the hospital tends to construct their case histories in this way, retroactively (Goffman, 1961, p. 145)? In any case, Gove's interpretation of his data contradicts the conclusions of Linsky and of Rushing. Since the studies do not use the same indices, it is not possible to compare them directly.

The final two studies to be discussed provide still stronger support for labelling theory. The first, Temerlin's (1968), is a test of the influence of suggestion on psychiatric diagnosis. Temerlin finds that psychiatrists and clinical psychologists are extremely suggestible when it comes to diagnosing mental illness. Four different groups diagnosed the patient in the same recorded interview under different conditions. One control group diagnosed with no prior suggestion, one group was given a suggestion that the interviewee was sane, and a third group was told that they were selecting scientists to work in research. In the experimental group, it was suggested that the interviewees were mentally ill. The diagnoses of the control and experimental groups differed greatly. In the control groups the great majority made diagnoses of mental health; whereas in the experimental group, not a single psychiatrist out of twenty-five, and only three out of twenty-five psychologists, diagnosed mental health. One weakness of this study is that it takes place in an artificial setting, with an enacted interview; but it strongly supports the unreliability of psychiatric diagnosis and the presumption of illness.

The study by Rosehan (1973) took place in real settings—twelve mental hospitals. For this study, eight sane persons gained secret admittance to the different hospitals. They all followed the same plan. In his initial admission interview, each pseudo-patient simulated several psychotic symptoms. Immediately upon admission to the ward, the pseudo-patients stopped simulating any symptoms of abnormality. In all twelve cases the pseudo-patients had enormous difficulty establishing that they were sane. The length of hospitalization ranged from seven to fifty-two days with an average of nineteen days. The study's major finding is as follows:

> Despite their public show of sanity, the pseudo-patients were never detected. Admitted except in one case with a diagnosis of schizophrenia, each was discharged with a diagnosis of schizophrenia in remission. The label "in remission" should in no way be dismissed as a formality for at no time during any hospitalization had any question been raised about any pseudo-patient's simulation . . . the evidence is strong that once labelled schizophrenic the pseudo-patient was stuck with the label (p. 252).

Rosehan also collected a wide variety of subsidiary data dealing with the amount and quality of contact between the pseudo-patients and the hospital staff, showing a strong tendency for the staff to treat the pseudo-patients as non-persons.

This study, like Temerlin's, strongly supports labelling theory. Both provide good models for future studies of labelling theory, the Rosehan study with its use of actual hospital locations, and the Temerlin study with its experimental design.

We can now provisionally summarize the state of evidence concerning labelling theory. If we restrict ourselves to systematic studies explicitly related to labelling theory, eighteen are available. Of these, thirteen support labelling theory, and five fail to. Although the studies vary in reliability and precision, the balance of evidence seems to support labelling theory.

REFERENCES

Becker, Howard
1973   ''Labelling theory reconsidered.'' Pp. 177-208 in Outsiders. New York: Free Press.
Blumer, Herbert
1954   ''What is wrong with social theory?'' American Journal of Sociology 19 (February): 3-10.
Bohr, Ronald H.
1970   Letter to the Editor. Journal of Health and Social Behavior 11 (June): 52.
Bronowski, J.
1956   Science and Human Values. New York: Harper and Row.
1965   The Identity of Man. Garden City, N.Y.: Natural History Press.
Bruyn, Severyn T.
1966   The Human Perspective in Sociology. Englewood Cliffs, N.J.: Prentice-Hall.
Davis, Nanette J.
1972   ''Labelling theory in deviance research: a critique and reconsideration.'' Sociological Quartery 13 (Autumn): 447-74.
Denzin, Norman K.
1968   ''The self-fulfilling prophecy and patient therapist interaction.'' Pp. 349-58 in Stephan P. Spitzer and Norman K. Denzin (eds.), The Mental Patient. New York: McGraw-Hill.
Denzin, Norman K. and Stephan P. Spitzer
1966   ''Paths to the mental hospital and staff predictions of patient role behavior.'' Journal of Health and Human Behavior 7 (Winter): 265-71.
Gibbs, Jack
1972   ''Issues in defining deviant behavior.'' Pp. 39-68 in Robert A Scott. and Jack D. Douglas (eds.), Theoretical Perspectives on Deviance. New York: Basic Books.
Goffman, Erving.
1961   Asylums. Garden City, N.Y.: Doubleday Anchor.
Gove, Walter
1970a   ''Societal reaction as an explanation of mental illness: an evaluation.'' American Sociological Review 35 (October): 873-84.
1970b   ''Who is hospitalized: a critical review of some sociological studies of mental illness.'' Journal of Health and Human Behavior 11 (December): 294-304.
1973   ''The stigma of mental hospitalization.'' Archives of General Psychiatry 28 (April): 494-500.
1974   ''Individual resources and mental hospitalization: a comparison and evaluation of

the societal reaction and psychiatric perspectives.'' American Sociological Review 39 (February): 86-100.
Greenley, James R.
1972   ''The psychiatric patient's family and length of hospitalization.'' Journal of Health and Social Behavior 13 (March): 25-37.
Haney, C. Allen and Robert Michielutte
1968   ''Selective factors operating in the adjudication of incompetency.'' Journal of Health and Social Behavior 9 (September): 233-42.
Haney, C. Allen, Kent S. Miller, and Robert Michielutte
1969   ''The interaction of petitioner and deviant social characteristics in the adjudication of incompetency.'' Sociometry 32 (June): 182-93.
Hollingshead, August B. and Frederick C. Redlich
1958   Social Class and Mental Illness. New York: John Wiley.
Karmel, Madeline.
1969   ''Total institution and self-mortification.'' Journal of Health and Social Behavior 10 (June): 134-41.
1970   ''The internalization of social roles in institutionalized chronic mental patients.'' Journal of Health and Social Behavior 11 (September): 231-5.
Laing, Ronald and Aaron Esterson
1964   Sanity, Madness, and the Family. London: Tavistock.
Linsky, Arnold S.
1970a   ''Community homogeneity and exclusion of the mentally ill: rejection vs. consensus about deviance. Journal of Health and Social Behavior 11 (December): 304-11.
1970b   ''Who shall be excluded: the influence of personal attributes in community reaction to the mentally ill.'' Social Psychiatry 5 (July): 166-71.
1972   Letter. American Journal of Sociology 78 (November): 684-6.
Robins, Lee
1966   Deviant Children Grown Up. Baltimore: Williams and Wilkins.
Rosehan, David L.
1973   ''On being sane in insane places.'' Science 179 (January): 250-8.
Rushing, William A.
1971   ''Individual resources, societal reaction, and hospital commitment.'' American Journal of Sociology 77 (November): 511-26.
1972   Letter. American Journal of Sociology 78 (November): 686-8.
Scheff, Thomas J.
1963   ''Legitimate, transitional, and illegitimate mental patients in a midwestern state.'' American Journal of Psychiatry 120 (September): 267-9.
1964   ''The societal reaction to deviance: ascriptive elements in the psychiatric screening of mental patients in a midwestern state.'' Social Problems 11 (Spring): 401-13.
1966   Being Mentally Ill: A Sociological Theory. Chicago: Aldine.
Schultz, Alfred
1962   The Problem of Social Reality: Collected Papers I. The Hague: Martinus Nijhoff.
Schwartz, J. and G. L. Baum
1957   ''The history of histoplasmosis.'' New England Journal of Medicine 256 (February): 253-8.
Temerlin, Maurice K.
1968   ''Suggestion effects in psychiatric diag-

nosis." Journal of Nervous and Mental Disease 147 (4): 349-53.

Wilde, William A.
1968   "Decision-making in a psychiatric screening agency." Journal of Health and Social Behavior 9 (September): 215-21.

Wenger, Dennis L. and C. Ritchard Fletcher
1969   "The effect of legal counsel on admissions to a state mental hospital: a confrontation of professions." Journal of Health and Social Behavior 10 (June): 66-72.

Yarrow, Marian Radke, Charlotte Green Schwartz, Harriet S. Murphy, and Leila Calhoun Deasy
1955   "The psychological meaning of mental illness in the family." Journal of Social Issues 11 (4): 12-24.

45

Patty Hearst's Conversion

Some Call it Brainwashing

by Thomas Szasz

Like all persons accused of a dramatic crime, Patty Hearst has managed, for however brief a period, to make people pay attention to her. Although the play in which she now appears is likely to have a short run, she is its undisputed star—the victim of mind-rape. Truly, life imitates art. We have had *The Manchurian Candidate* and *A Clockwork Orange*. Now we have *The Brainwashed Heiress*.

Gone are the days when people asked: "Did she or didn't she?" Who cares any more what people do—legally or sexually? What people now want to know is what's in other people's brains. So they ask: "Was she or wasn't she brainwashed?" Having asked it they demand an answer with the same impatience with which a spoiled child demands an ice cream cone. And the experts on brainwashing will give them an answer as eagerly as doting parents give ice cream cones to their whining children. In fact, although people are asking for only one answer, they shall inevitably get two: yes, she was brainwashed; no, she was not.

But the question is meaningless. Asking it is an intellectual and moral copout; answering it is psychiatric prostitution; and believing the answer is self-deception.

Nietzsche was right when he said that "a criminal is frequently not equal to his deed: he makes it smaller and slanders it." Patty Hearst, the victorious SLA soldier, with gun slung snappily over her shoulder, seemed proud and self-assured. Her lawyers claim that she was then "brainwashed." Patty Hearst, the victim of kidnapping, with a decorous dress draped over her slender frame, seems shrunken and bewildered. Is this what Nietzsche had in mind when he remarked that "lawyers defending a criminal are rarely artists enough to turn the beautiful terrible mess of the criminal's deed to his advantage"?

Has there been any significant change in Patty Hearst's behavior? Before her arrest, she demeaned and denounced those who "helped" her as a child; now,

---

Thomas Szasz is professor of psychiatry at the State University of New York, Syracuse.

240

she demeans and denounces those who "helped" her as a fugitive. For whatever reason, she seems to be inclined to make her life exciting at the expense of the dignity, liberty and property of others.

The basic facts in the Hearst trial are simple and uncontested. The defendant engaged in numerous acts which, unless legally excusable, and excused, constitute serious crimes. What legal excuses mitigate or negate "criminal responsibility" for such acts? There are only a few. One is actual, physical duress. If a person forces another to commit an illegal act—say, literally at gunpoint—then the coerced actor is not legally responsible for his act. Another excuse is insanity. The illegal act, according to this claim, is not something that the defendant has done; it is something that has happened to him. The defendant is therefore no more responsible for his illegal act than a patient with myocardial insufficiency is responsible for his abnormal electrocardiogram. Patty Hearst does not claim this defense.

What excuse is left? Only what used to be called "temporary insanity," a concept that has become as unfashionable in forensic psychiatry as narrow ties have in menswear; hence, "temporary insanity" has been refashioned into "brainwashing." The defendant, according to this claim, was not "really" himself when he committed the illegal acts; he was "really" someone else, that is, his "brainwashed" self; hence his "un-brainwashed" self cannot be held responsible for these acts. This is Patty Hearst's defense.

The crucial question thus becomes: What is "brainwashing"? Are there, as the term implies, two kinds of brains: washed and unwashed? How do we know which is which?

Actually, it's all quite simple. Like many dramatic terms, "brainwashing" is a metaphor. A person can no more wash another's brain with coercion or conversation than he can make him bleed with a cutting remark.

If there is no such thing as brainwashing, what does this metaphor stand for? It stands for one of the most universal human experiences and events, namely for one person influencing another. However, we do not call all types of personal or psychological influences "brainwashing." We reserve this term for influences of which we disapprove.

In other words, "brainwashing" is like "perversion": as the latter term refers only to those sexual activities that one disdains, so the former refers only to those educational or psychological influences one abhors. While she was with the SLA, Patty Hearst was no doubt influenced by her captors and associates; Hearst, Bailey, the press and nearly everyone else calls this "brainwashing." Between the time of her arrest, when she identified herself as an "urban guerrilla," and her appearance in court as a demure and dutiful daughter, Patty Hearst was no doubt influenced by her new captors and associates: no one calls this "brainwashing."

In short, trying to ascertain whether Patty Hearst has been brainwashed by having her examined by psychiatrists—is like trying to ascertain whether holy water is holy by having it examined by priests. Terms like "brainwashing" and "holy water" (and others like them) are invented and deployed strategically by these very "experts" for their own purposes. If we really want to understand what holy water is, we must examine priests, not water; if we really want to understand what brainwashing is, we must examine psychiatrists, not brains (or criminal defendants).

What, then, are the psychiatrists doing in the Hearst trial? They are "testifying" for whoever pays them. More than 300 years ago, an English aristocrat defined an ambassador as an honest man sent abroad to lie for his country. I would define a forensic psychiatrist as an honest doctor sent into court to lie for his masters.

We have done away with canon law and no longer look to priests to tell us about the purity or pollution of the soul. But we have substituted for it mental hygiene law and look to psychiatrists to tell us about the purity or pollution of the brain.

46

Dangerousness and the Social Control of the Mentally Ill

by Joseph J. Cocozza and Henry J. Steadman

From survey data gathered in the late sixties, Rubin (1972) estimates that there are 50,000 mentally ill persons a year in the United States who are preventively detained through psychiatric predictions of dangerousness. In addition, 30,000 to 60,000 criminal defendants are evaluated annually for dangerousness to determine correctional versus mental health institutionalization, while another 10,000 individuals are designated as mentally ill offenders whose type of treatment depends on estimation of dangerousness. The use of the dangerousness criterion has reached these dimensions in the absence of adequate definition, without predictive criteria and while awaiting empirical documentation that such a standard can be justifiably applied either for the individual being confined or for the protection of society.

In many ways the use of dangerousness as a standard for involuntary commitment or differential treatment has become more evident as a result of the mental health civil liberties movement of the late 1960s and early 1970s. Its use has grown through attempts to limit involuntary commitment criteria to observable behaviors that would reduce judicial reliance on purely intrapsychic phenomena reported by psychiatrists. This approach to involuntary hospitalization of the mentally ill as described by Stone is "premised on the moral and constitutional argument that the only legitimate justification for civil commitment of any kind should be a proven likelihood of dangerous acts" (1975:25). Stone goes on to suggest that the emergence of dangerousness as "the paramount consideration in the law-mental health system" and the accompanying rejection of the medical model and treatment rationale can be understood as an attempt to "transcend all of the ideological disputes which currently confound the law-mental health system" (1975:25).

As frequently occurs, a bit of historical perspective indicates that what is seemingly a new approach has very old roots. In fact, as Deutsch (1949) points out, the earliest laws referring to those we now label mentally ill allowed for the arrest and confinement only of individuals who were "furiously insane" or deemed too

"dangerous to be permitted to be at large." These insane persons, namely the violent and dangerous were confined for the duration of the period of dangerousness on the basis of the police power of the state.

The detention of the insane during this period was in whatever type of facility was available or could be constructed with local resources. Construction was often necessary because jails had yet to replace the gallows and no penal facilities were available in which to detain those insane people who were dangerous. Deutsch notes that the first known provision in this regard in Pennsylvania was reported in the 1676 records of the Upland Court:

> Jan Corelissen, of Amesland, Complayning to ye Court that his son Erik is bereft of his natural Senses and is turned guyt madd and yt, he being a poore man in not able to maintain him; Ordered: yt three or four persons bee hired to build a little block-house at Amesland for to put in the said madman. (1949:42)

These facilities were only for detention and public protection. They were in no way expected to benefit the individual confined there.

The first actual hospital for the insane was the Pennsylvania Hospital opened in 1756. The early record of this facility reflects little that differed from the prisons from which the insane were supposedly being removed. Strict discipline, chains, and cells were the standard features. What seems most significant about Pennsylvania Hospital is that although its practice differentiated it little from prisons, it established the principle of attempting to treat the mentally ill rather than simply detaining them as malfactors. An example of early U.S. legislation in these regards was the 1788 New York State provision which was copied practically word for word from a 1744 English law:

> Whereas, There are sometimes persons who by lunacy or otherwise are furiously mad, or are so far disordered in their senses that they may be dangerous to be permitted to go abroad; therefore,
> Be it enacted, That it shall and may be lawful for any two or more justices of the peace to cause such

person to be apprehended and kept safely locked up in some secure place, and, if such justices shall find it necessary, to be there chained. (Deutsch, 1949:420)

Thus, for as long as there have been any laws permitting the involuntary confinement of the mentally ill in the United States, dangerousness has been a primary reason for their detention.

Between the late 18th century and the mid 20th century, state legislators did enact commitment laws formalizing procedures which gave additional protection to involuntary patients. However, while these laws consistently incorporated dangerousness as a reason for commitment, until the late 1960s little specificity was added as to what constituted dangerousness, how it related to mental illness, and what was required judicially to document its presence. What was affirmed during these years was the role of the psychiatrist as the primary predictor of dangerousness of the mentally ill. This ascendance developed from the general responsibilities psychiatry staked out for the care of the mentally ill. As the experts of mental illness they were assumed to also be skilled in the diagnosis of dangerousness.

The psychiatrist became the major predictor of dangerousness in the United States not because of any documented skills at such predictions, but because this standard has always been a primary one for the control of individuals seen as mentally ill and psychiatry gradually came to dominate the care of the mentally ill and the institutions to which they were committed. Whereas penal facilities have always overtly involved punishment for defined past behaviors, mental hospitals and predictions of dangerousness have developed into mechanisms which detain individuals who, because of some diagnosed mental illness, are expected to behave in certain dangerous ways in the future. The psychiatrist has become a seer of social control through the commitment practices in U.S. civil and correctional mental hospitals.

Since the time of Colonial America, many changes have occurred with regard to the conception of the mentally ill, the development of hospitals with formal goals of treatment and care, the development of medical technology, and so forth. However, the criterion of dangerousness for commitment under the police power of the state has remained. Therefore, its current use is more correctly seen as a redirecting of emphasis back to the concept of dangerousness and the social control functions of the state than as a new approach. Given that psychiatrists have ascended to this position of accepted predictors of future dangerous behavior, it is enlightening to examine what research data exist which examine their performance in these areas. How accurately have they predicted? How effective has been their protection of society? How appropriate is the use of the dangerousness standard in the mental health system?

Addressing Psychiatric Accuracy in Predicting Dangerousness

There is actually very little research which directly addresses the ability of psychiatrists to predict dangerousness. Yet all the available research evidence, whether indirect or direct suggests the same conclusion —psychiatrists cannot accurately predict dangerousness. Much of the evidence typically offered to demonstrate the inaccuracy of psychiatric predictions is indirect. This includes discussions of the vagueness and imprecision of the concept of dangerousness as defined in mental health statutes and in the professional literature, examples of unsuccessful attempts to predict violence among non-mentally ill groups, and studies of the arrest rates of ex-mental patients usually in comparison to the general population. These bodies of work suggest: (1) that predictions of dangerousness are hampered by the imprecision of the concept which has been defined as many things ranging from only violent criminal acts through any criminal act and has also been taken to include violent thoughts and crimes such as writing a bad check (Katz and Goldstein, 1960; von Hirsh, 1972; and Steadman, 1973); (2) that even using sophisticated statistical analysis for identifying potentially violent individuals the best that can be attained is a ratio of eight wrong predictions of dangerousness for every one correct prediction (Wenk, et al., 1972); and (3) that even in those studies where mental patients are found to be arrested more often than the general population for certain crimes, the absolute rate of dangerous behavior is extremely low and as an infrequent event, attempts to predict dangerousness share with attempts to predict other low base rate behavior serious methodological problems (Steadman and Cocozza, 1975).

Although all of this evidence relates to the use of dangerousness in the social control of the mentally ill, it does not deal directly with the accuracy of psychiatric predictions of dangerousness. The crucial research on this question is that which directly examines psychiatric predictions of dangerousness on specific groups of patients and in which the level of accuracy is determined through a systematic follow-up of the patients. There are three such studies.

The first of these three is our previous research on a group of patients referred to as the Baxstrom patients (Steadman and Cocozza, 1974). These patients were so named because they were generated by the U.S. Supreme Court ruling in the 1966 *Baxstrom* v. *Herold* case (383 U.S. 107). The ruling held that Johnnie K. Baxstrom could not be held in a maximum-security hospital for the criminally insane beyond his maximum sentence without proper judicial review. This decision ultimately resulted in the transfer of 967 patients *against* psychiatric advice from New York's two hospitals for the criminally insane to regular civil hospitals.

These patients were considered to be among the most dangerous in the New York facilities. As such, the civil hospitals reacted with much anxiety to the point of requesting additional pay and judo training for their staff. Furthermore, it was estimated that at least a fourth, or approximately 250, of the patients would prove to be so dangerous that they would have to be returned to the more secure hospitals for the criminally insane. Our 4-year follow-up revealed that only 26 of these 967 patients acted violently enough in the civil hospitals to justify their return as dangerous to hospitals for the criminally insane. Furthermore, in a sample of 98 released patients selected for intensive study we found only 2 felony convictions resulting from 20 arrests. This and other data led us to conclude that few of the Baxstrom patients were dangerous and provided striking evidence of the inability of psychiatrists to predict dangerousness accurately. As Ennis and Litwack have written:

> In statistical terms, Operation Baxstrom tells us that psychiatric predictions are incredibly inaccurate. In human terms, it tells us that but for a Supreme Court decision, nearly 1,000 human beings would have lived much of their lives behind bars, without grounds privileges, without home visits, without even the limited amenities available to civil patients, all because a few psychiatrists, in their considered opinion, thought they were dangerous and no one asked for proof. (1974:713)

The second major work is that of Kozol et al. (1972). This research involved a 10-year study of a group of 592 male convicted offenders, most of whom were sex offenders. On the basis of intensive interdisciplinary diagnostic methods, the dangerousness of the offenders was judged. The authors conclude that dangerousness as measured by recidivism rates can be reliably diagnosed and treated. During the 5-year follow-up period it was found that 8% of those predicted to be not-dangerous committed serious assaultive acts following their release while 35% of those they evaluated as dangerous, but who were released by the court against psychiatric advice, recidivated.

The study's findings and conclusions, however, are questionable on two grounds. First, the authors, failed to take into consideration the length of time at risk in the community for the various groups. It was possible for the patients diagnosed as dangerous but released by the court against their advice to have been at risk in the community for as much as four years longer than the treated group released as non-dangerous. Such a difference in the length of time at risk in the community would certainly account for a large part of the reported differences. in recidivism rates for the dangerous not-dangerous groups and casts serious doubts on the validity of their conclusions.

The second major problem with the Kozol et al. study is one of interpretation. If we ignore for the moment the serious methodological flaw just discussed, we find that most of those predicted to be dangerous were not. While 35% of those predicted to be dangerous violently recidivated, 65% did not. Despite the extensive examinations conducted by psychiatrists, psychologists, and social workers, despite the use of batteries of psychological tests, and despite the meticulous reconstruction of the patients' life histories, they were still wrong in 2 out of every 3 predictions of dangerousness.

The third and most recent study directly assessing psychiatric accuracy in predicting dangerousness resulted from a revision in the New York State Criminal Procedure Law (Cocozza and Steadman, 1977). New York State's Criminal Procedure Law (CPL) became

effective on September 1, 1971. One section of the statute mandated a determination of dangerousness for all indicted felony defendants found incompetent to stand trial.

Between September 1, 1971 and August 31, 1972, there were 257 indicted felony defendants found incompetent to stand trial in New York State. These individuals were predominantly non-white, from the New York City area, and averaged 31 years of age. Of these, 154 (60%) were evaluated as dangerous and 103 (40%) evaluated as not-dangerous by the psychiatrists. Were the defendants the psychiatrists determined to be dangerous more dangerous than those they judged to be not-dangerous? This is the crucial question and this research, we feel, represents a crucial test since an explicit and specific determination of dangerousness was made for each defendant and the defendants represent a clinically relevant cohort. Also the period at risk during the follow-up is similar for both groups.

In order to determine the accuracy of the psychiatric predictions of dangerousness we obtained data on the defendants' assaultiveness from five sources: (1) the maximum security hospitals to which both groups were initially sent; (2) civil hospitals to which some members of both groups were transferred immediately after the maximum security facilities; (3) hospital readmission records; (4) inpatient records of all subsequent hospitalization; and (5) subsequent arrest records. All of the indicators of dangerous behavior revealed only slight differences between the two groups. None of the differences were statistically significant and, therefore, all could be explained on the basis of chance alone.

On the inpatient indicators, the psychiatrically predicted dangerous group experienced slightly higher rates. Forty-two percent of them as compared to 36% of the not-dangerous group were assaultive during their initial incompetency hospitalization; 8% as compared to 0% were assaultive in the civil hospital of transfer; and 29% as compared to 19% were assaultive in the hospitals to which they were readmitted. None of these differences are statistically significant.

Conversely, the indicators on the dangerousness of the two groups once in the community reveal the not-dangerous groups to be more assaultive but again only slightly more so than the group predicted to be dangerous by the court psychiatrists. The gross measure of community behavior we utilized was the percentage of those released to the community at some time who were rearrested for a crime. It was found that 40% of the released dangerous group and 54% of the released not-dangerous group were rearrested.

Perhaps the single most important indicator of the success of the psychiatric predictions is the number of these patients subsequently arrested for violent crimes. Yet even here only a slight difference is revealed by the data. Of those who had been evaluated as dangerous, 14% (13 of 96) of those released to the community were subsequently arrested for a violent crime. Of those who had been evaluated as not-dangerous, 16% (11 of 70) of those released to the community were arrested for a violent crime.

How accurate, then, were the psychiatric predictions of dangerousness? On the basis of all of these indicators, the answer would be that they were not accurate at all. There were no significant differences between the two groups on any of the measures of assaultiveness examined. Those defendants evaluated by the psychiatrists as dangerous were not any more dangerous than those they felt were not-dangerous.

Mental Illness and Violence

In 1969 a psychiatrist, S. Halleck, concluded that:

> Research in the area of dangerous behavior (other than generalizations from case materials) is practically non-existent. Predictive studies which have examined the probability of recidivism have not focused on the issue of dangerousness. If the psychiatrist or any other behavioral scientists were asked to show proof of his predictive skills, objective data could not be offered. (1969:11)

Objective data do now exist in the form of the three studies just discussed. Each has collected empirical data with which to evaluate the accuracy of psychiatric predictions of dangerousness and in each case the data have shown psychiatrists to be rather inaccurate predictors of future dangerous behavior.

Perhaps as important as this finding is another implication to emerge from these studies—psychiatrists consistently err in the direction of overpredicting dangerousness. The medical ideology and practice of avoiding false negatives (releasing sick people) at the cost of an indefinite number of false positive errors (hospitalizing sick people) pointed out by others (Scheff, 1966) appears to carry over to the field of psychiatry and the prediction of dangerousness. As we have seen, all three studies indicate that the overwhelming majority of the patients deprived of their liberty, placed in maximum-security settings, and differentially treated because of a prediction of dangerousness did not, in fact, subsequently commit a dangerous act.

Clearly, it is easier to establish the occurrence of a past act than it is to accurately predict the occurrence of a future event. Yet the standards actually employed appear to assume the opposite. In criminal court proceedings the evidentiary standard used to establish a criminal act in the past is very high as suggested by the statement "better 10 guilty men go free than one innocent man be confined." In establishing the "fact" that a mentally ill individual will commit a violent criminal act in the future, the position appears to be "better 10 non-dangerous men be confined than one dangerous man go free."

There are many reasons that have been offered to explain why psychiatrists cannot accurately predict and why there is a strong tendency for them to overpredict dangerousness (Monahan, 1975). More important than the explanations, however, are the empirical findings that, in fact, psychiatrists are rather inaccurate predictors and that their conservative bias results in the confinement of many individuals as dangerous who are not. Such data, one would reasonably expect, would lead to the removal or at least deemphasis on the criterion of dangerousness in civil and criminal mental health statutes. Yet these data not withstanding, legislation mandating wider uses of the dangerousness standard and psychiatric predictions of it continue to proliferate.

To a large extent this trend becomes understandable given the generally perceived association between mental illness and violence. Mental illness and violence are frequently seen as two sides of the same coin. Whether one examines the history of the treatment of mentally ill summarized briefly above or reviews the literature on public attitudes toward the mentally ill (Crocetti et al., 1971; Rabkin, 1972), one finds a constant perceived associated between mental illness and dangerousness. The assumptions usually made are that most individuals who commit a violent act are mentally ill and that most mentally ill individuals are dangerous. Nunnally in his classic study of popular conceptions of the mentally ill, for example, concludes that "as is commonly suspected, the mentally ill are regarded with fear, distrust and dislike by the general public." (1961: 46) This conclusion has been found to hold for various populations and over time (Olmsted and Durham, 1976) despite research findings which show that very few of the mentally ill and even of the criminally insane do commit violent acts.

While it is the psychiatrists who have made the predictions; it is the legislators who have written the laws mandating such predictions, it is the mass media who have reinforced the need and importance of such laws; it is the court and legal community who have accepted their supposed expert testimony; and it is the public who have supported the entire enterprise because of their belief in the dangerousness of the mentally ill. This is not to attempt to fix blame but to suggest that the inappropriate and unworkable use of the dangerousness criterion to deprive the mentally ill of their freedom cannot simply be laid on the doorstep of psychiatry.

So, it is clear from the available literature that there currently exists no set of experts nor any statistical, psychiatric, or psychological method for accurately determining who will be dangerous. Any such attempts result in the misclassification of many individuals who will not be dangerous due to statistical (absence of empirically sound predictive criteria); ideological (conservative medical diagnostic ideology), and political (loss of professional esteem and media criticism) factors. As Wenk and colleagues have reflected, "Confidence in the ability to predict violence serves to legitimate intrusive types of social control" (1972:402). For those labeled or being labeled mentally ill this problem is particularly acute and despite a growing body of research on the inability of psychiatry to accurately predict dangerousness this standard promises to continue as a dominant standard for social control in the United States as long as the perceived association between mental illness and violence and the belief in psychiatric predictive expertise persist.

References

Cocozza, Joseph J. and Steadman, Henry J.
1977 "The failure of psychiatric predictions of dangerousness: Clear and convincing evidences." *Rutgers Law Review*.

Crocetti, Guido, Spiro, Herzl R. and Siassi, Iradj
1971 "Are the ranks closed? Attitudinal social distance and mental illness." *The American Journal of Psychiatry 127*:1121–1127.

Deutsch, Albert
1949 *The Mentally Ill in America*. (Second Edition) New York: Columbia University Press.

Ennis, B. J. and Litwack, T. R.
1974 "Psychiatry and the presumption of expertise: Flipping coins in the courtroom." *California Law Review 62*:693–752.

Halleck, A.
1969 *Psychiatry and the Dilemmas of Crime: A Study of Causes, Punishment and Treatment*. New York: Harper & Row.

Katz, J. and Goldstein, J.
1960 "Dangerousness and mental illness." *Journal of Nervous and Mental Disorders 131*:404–413.

Kozol, H., Boucher, R., and Garofalo, R.
1972 "The diagnosis and treatment of dangerousness." *Crime and Delinquency 18*:371–392.

Monahan, J.
1975 "The prevention of violence," in J. Monahan (Ed.), *Community Mental Health and the Criminal Justice System*. New York: Pergamon Press.

Nunnally, J. D., Jr.
1961 *Popular Conceptions of Mental Health*. New York: Holt, Rinehart, and Winston.

Olmsted, Donald W. and Durham, Katherine
1976 "Stability of mental health attitudes: A semantic differential study." *Journal of Health and Social Behavior 17*:35–44.

Rabkin, Judith G.
1972 "Opinions about mental illness: A review of the literature." *Psychological Bulletin 77*:153–171.

Rubin, B.
1972 "Prediction of dangerousness in mentally ill criminals." *Archives of General Psychiatry 27*: 397–407.

Scheff, T.
1966 *Being Mentally Ill: A Sociological Theory*. Chicago: Aldine Publishing Co.

Steadman, H. J.
1973 "Some evidence on the inadequacy of the concept and determination of dangerousness in law and psychiatry." *Journal of Psychiatry and Law 1*:409–426.

Steadman, H. J. and Cocozza, J. J.
1974 *Careers of the Criminally Insane: Excessive Social Control of Deviance*. Lexington, Mass.: D. C. Heath
1975 "Violence, mental illness, and preventive detention: We can't predict who is dangerous." *Psychology Today 8*:32–25, 84 .

Stone, Alan A.
1975 *Mental Health and Law: A System in Transition*. Rockville, Maryland: National Institute of Mental Health.

von Hirsh, A.
1972 "Prediction of criminal conduct and preventive confinement of convicted persons." *Buffalo Law Review 21*:717–758.

Wenk, E., Robinson, J. and Smith, G.
1972 "Can violence be predicted?" *Crime and Delinquency 18*:393–402.

VI. Perspectives on Social Policy

To the extent that the more than forty articles in the preceding sections of this book have provided us with alternatives for analyzing and considering courses of action regarding the issues presented, the various authors were involving us in an aspect of the policy of social issues. Indeed, in the words of C. Wright Mills, had they not made demands for such alternatives they would have been indulging in "the pretentious triviality that passes for social science" (Mills, 1959:184). However, the topics which follow focus on social policy—courses of action or programs in existence—as the social issues. The selections provided within these topic areas suggest some competing, and even contradictory, policies to present policies relative to problems of the life cycle, health and medical care, and planning for the future.

Social scientists have come to view problems of the life cycle as interrelated. That is, an emphasis on the life cycle in the development of the individual enables us to relate "personal troubles" of that process to structural forces in the social environment. Child abuse is merely one "trouble" which occurs in the life cycle of the young in our society. Although it affects only a minority of the young, it raises questions about the extent to which we are a "child-centered society." A significant percentage of the victims are the very young, and many of those responsible for child abuse are young parents who were abused or neglected themselves. Although in recent years the public has become increasingly aware of this problem, we remain without adequate legislation making intervention possible. In fact, early efforts to intervene on behalf of abused or maltreated children were based on laws prohibiting the cruel treatment of animals. Within the past decade, however, every state has enacted laws to deal with the problem. These empower Child Protection workers to remove the child from the natural family and substitute foster care. Yet studies indicate that a majority of children placed in such foster homes become wards of the state, and fail to develop a continuing relationship with one family. Consequently, intervention does not mean that the child will be provided with "normal" conditions for development, and all too often careers of delinquency and crime may be related to such backgrounds. As Besharov points out, we need more than administrative solutions. He argues for a community commitment to foster the emotional well being of the family and the individual. Aging is a life-cycle problem difficult to define due to its diverse socioeconomic implications. With nearly 10 percent of our population over 65 we are developing a "senior citizen" subculture. Herein lies one of the basic flaws of our response to aging, "age segregation." Only about 10 percent of those over 65 reside in the nursing homes scandalized in the press for the manner in which some of them have "ripped-off" their clients. What about the other 18 million aged? Marge Casady's article points out that not only is a diversity of social and interpersonal life styles possible but it is also necessary.

Policies and programs that do not involve the aging in the planning are too often insensitive to the diversity in this growing segment of our population. An alternative to present policies may be to develop ways in which the life styles of our elderly citizens are characterized by "dignity." The American approach to death may typify the "ultimate in dignity" against the human spirit. For death and dying has long been a "taboo" issue. The dialogue between two playwrights in "A Right to Die" raises several alternatives relative to the "death with dignity," who will "pull the plug?" and should we be allowed to "pull the plug?" issues.

Alternative structures for health care are much discussed. Congressional committees hold hearings and health care plans are outlined by individual politicians and study groups. Yet the United States remains the only western nation without a national health care plan. Health care costs have risen at a record rate—to the extent that the average American family now spends about 10 percent of its income for such services. Despite the fact that Americans spend over $100 billion for medical care, we rank near the bottom of western nations in the prevention of infant mortality—eighteenth in 1970. Levine's article proposes an alternative to our present health delivery system which would be designed to promote health, not merely treat illness. Both articles included under this topic argue that we must move beyond a reliance on an outmoded, costly "fee for service" basis, to a humanized, preventive emphasis in health care. Rodgers contends that it is possible to develop a system of health care in which there will be no "second class" citizens.

Social planning will doubtless be relied upon in the public sector as it is in the private sector. The questions raised by Heilbroner in the penultimate article are pertinent: what gets planned and who makes the plan? Whose interests will be served? The final reading was selected from among the growing body of literature in the futurist genre. Carolyn Symonds contends that we must control technology and utilize it to promote a "world-wide utopia or face oblivion."

Reference

C. Wright Mills, *The Sociological Imagination,* New York: Oxford University Press, 1959.

Building A Community Response to Child Abuse and Maltreatment

by Douglas J. Besharov

Child abuse is a hurt to all communities. Children from all racial, religious, social and economic groups are its victims. Abuse and maltreatment are symptoms of a society in trouble—a society in which the individual is dehumanized and the family is disintegrating.

News stories daily remind us of the horrors of child abuse and maltreatment. Nationwide, public agencies receive over 300,000 reports of suspected child abuse or maltreatment every year, and each year 2,000 children die in circumstances in which abuse or maltreatment is suspected. But no one knows for sure how many more children suffer harsh and terrible childhoods without their plight being detected and reported to the authorities.

Everyone pays the price of a young child's suffering. From the most practical as well as the most humanitarian points of view, it is less expensive and more humane to protect and nurture these children within a rehabilitated family environment than it is to endure the social costs of their continued abuse and maltreatment.

Unless we take compassionate yet firm steps to improve their plight, we consign these children to a life of continuing deprivation and peril. And we consign our communities to a future of aggression, drug abuse and violence.

Douglas J. Besharov, J.D., Ll.M., is director, National Center on Child Abuse and Neglect, Children's Bureau, OCD. His article is based on a speech delivered at the Louisville Child Abuse Colloquium in May 1975. It was prepared with the assistance of Nancy Fisher and José Alfaro.

Abused children often grow up to be socially destructive—to vent on others, particularly their children, the violence and aggression their parents visited upon them. As New York City Family Court Judge Nanette Dembitz rightly said: "The root of crime in the streets is neglect of children."

As a society, we have provided a combination of laws and procedures through which professionals and private citizens who come in contact with endangered children can, and in some situations *must,* take protective action. Laws have established reporting procedures, authorized the taking of children into protective custody and assigned child protective responsibilities to social agencies and the police. Laws have also created juvenile and criminal court jurisdictions and fostered treatment programs—all to protect vulnerable children and families.

But in almost every community in the nation, there are inadequacies, breakdowns and gaps in the child protective process. Detection and reporting are haphazard and incomplete; protective investigations are often poorly performed; and suitable treatment programs exist more in grant applications than in practice.

For far too many endangered children, the existing child protection system is inadequate to the life-saving tasks assigned it. Too many children and families are processed through the system with a paper promise of help. For example, as many as three-quarters of those children who die in circumstances in which abuse or maltreatment is suspected were known to the authorities before their deaths.

More fundamentally, prevention is an easily touted though little understood and unevenly pursued goal. Existing child protective procedures treat child abuse and maltreatment only after the fact, not on a primary preventive level. As was pointed out ten years ago, "Preventing neglect and battering depends in the long run on preventing transmission of the kind of social deprivation which takes children's lives, damages their physical health, and retards their minds, and which contributes through those who survive to a rising population of next generation parents who will not be able to nurture children."[1]

The challenge we face is not so much to discover what works; to a great extent we know what works. We must now discover how to develop the cooperative community structures necessary to provide needed services efficiently, effectively and compassionately.

According to conventional wisdom, the failure of our child protective institutions is caused by a dreadful lack of facilities, protective workers, social workers, judges, shelters and probation workers, and of all sorts of rehabilitative, social and psychiatric services. Undoubtedly, if we poured more millions of dollars into existing programs, the picture would be less bleak. But existing facilities and services, if properly utilized, could go a long way toward fulfilling the need to protect children.

Rehabilitative services are delivered by a social service system that is fragmented, overlapping and uncoordinated. If such diversity and competition created better services for children and their families, the lack of focus and unity in the system would not be of great concern. But the result of such fragmentation has been blurred responsibility, diluted resources and uncoordinated planning, all of which severely limit the effectiveness of the overall approach. Local child protective agencies, police, juvenile courts, hospitals and a variety of other public and private agencies share, divide and duplicate scarce resources. The waste in manpower, expertise, record keeping, administration and policy planning caused by the existing fragmentation of services was never justified. It cannot now be tolerated in this period of severe budgetary constraint.

The patchwork complex of agencies and laws with divergent philosophies and procedures that makes up the average community's child protection system has been widely criticized.[2] Responsibility is frequently passed from one agency or individual to another. Anywhere from three to eight agencies can be involved in a particular case. This means that three to eight separate individuals must become acquainted with the case, three to eight separate sets of forms must be filled out, three to eight separate filing systems are maintained with possibly inconsistent information recorded and three to eight referrals are made—all offering the possibility of administrative or bureaucratic fumbling.

The result is a system that limits the involvement of individuals and makes them powerless. As Dr. Ray Helfer has complained, often no one person is responsible and no one person is accountable. Additional consequences of fragmentation are frequent losses of information—situations in which one agency has critical information concerning a child's care or condition which is not communicated to the "appropriate" agency. Compounding this fragmentation and lack of involvement is a general absence of follow-up of referrals among agencies. One can well appreciate the frightful reality of endangered children "falling between the cracks."

While present efforts to prevent and treat child abuse and maltreatment are of limited effectiveness, the potential for helping families meet their child care responsibilities is great.

Children can be protected and their well-being fostered by helping parents to "parent." There are programs in all parts of the nation helping parents cope with the stresses of family life in our modern society. Social casework, psychological and psychiatric services, child abuse teams, lay therapists, parent surrogates, day care, Parents Anonymous groups, homemaker services, education for parenthood, and a whole range of other concrete services and programs can and do make a difference in the level of family functioning.[3] Unfortunately, these successful programs often are not seen as part of the child protection process in most communities. Either they are not available to protective services or they are not used. To fail to involve these family building programs in the protective process is to ignore an approach that can and does make an improvement in the level of family functioning.

Treatment is a community process. Without the use or, when necessary, the development of diverse, indigenous and, therefore, responsive programs, we consign the child protective process to the abusive removal of children from their homes, the overuse of foster care and the futility of treatment during brief bimonthly home visits.

Prevention, too, is a community process. It is necessary to incorporate into our individual, family and community life a greater understanding of family hygiene. A renewed sense of respect for the human growth of all individuals within the context of the family would do more to lower violence and aggression against the young than any number of social agencies which can become involved only after the process of family breakdown has progressed almost past the point of irremediable damage.

Public Support

Though the efforts of concerned professionals are indispensable to the coordination and improvement of services, the key to real progress is an informed and aware citizenry. Child abuse and maltreatment are not new problems but, traditionally, the moving force for the development of treatment and preventive programs has existed largely in the professional community. Broad based public support—crucial for the funding of programs and the breaking of bureaucratic logjams—has been missing. Although sympathetic citizens have been enraged and shocked by the inherent sensationalism of individual child abuse and maltreatment cases, until very recently overall public awareness, understanding and support have been sporadic and unfocused.

When exposed to an abused child, the first reactions of most people are utter disbelief, denial and avoidance. Finding the cruel and tragic condition of the child beyond their capacity to understand, they deny that the injury was deliberately inflicted or that a parent could be responsible. They deny the horror of a child's home environment and the probability that the child and his siblings had been battered previously. Even more painfully, people meeting such children evade their own responsibility, explaining "I don't want to get involved"; "It's not my job"; "I don't want to come between the child and his parents"; or "Don't ask me to report a parent to the authorities—that would be interfering with the privacy and rights of the family."

Because of the tremendous publicity generated by numerous sensational cases in communities across the nation, we are reaching a time when the public can no longer refuse to see the evidence for what it is—that children do suffer almost unbelievable harm at the hands of their parents.

Now, there is a danger that denial will turn to outrage and overreaction. Upon confronting child abuse, citizens as well as some professionals sometimes act as if they have discovered absolute evil.

The reality of child abuse is so awful that a harsh, condemnatory response is understandable. But such reactions must be tempered if any progress is to be made. If we permit feelings of rage towards the abusers of children to blind us to the needs of the parents as well as of the children, these suffering and unfortunate families will be repelled and not helped. Only with the application of objective and enlightened policies can treatment, research, prevention and education be successfully performed.

Hitherto, the publicity attached to spectacular cases has served to educate the public and professions to the existence and nature of the problem. Henceforth, the burden will be on concerned members of society to devise procedures for the protection of these unfortunate youngsters through the rehabilitation and strengthening of their families. There must now be a reversal in the attitude of the public toward parents who have been seen as cruel perpetrators. In the words of Dr. Vincent J. Fontana, "We must come to realize that there are *two* victims of child abuse—the child *and the parent.*"

Mounting public awareness now needs to be sharpened and developed into a constructive, effective force for far-reaching reform. An intensive national public service campaign on child abuse and maltreatment can meet prejudices, emotionalism and misunderstanding head on. Sympathy for abused and maltreated children must be channeled into constructive help in their behalf.

All citizens must recognize the critical need to strengthen the family so that it can better cope with periods of stress. The public must come to understand that in certain circumstances almost any family can have difficulty coping and that, at such times, the family members must be able to seek and find help. Only if this level of understanding is reached can public concern be channeled into true community action.

Child abuse laws provide only the legal and institutional framework for action. A law lives in the way it is used. Child abuse and child maltreatment are family and community problems. If we are to prevent and treat them, we must have a community commitment to fostering the emotional and behavioral hygiene of the individual, the family and the community.

Child abuse must be understood as a function of uncontrolled or uncontrollable personal, familial and social stress. Despite popular misconceptions, most abusing parents are not sadists, criminals or mentally retarded persons. Abusing parents are capable of loving the children they harm and they often experience great guilt and remorse about their abusive behavior. In many ways, they are like all parents. But when they experience moments of anger and frustration, they are likely to take it out on their children. Sometimes they confuse discipline with the expression of their own inner fury.

All parents and parents-to-be can benefit from family-life education and a knowledge of child development. Parenting is not instinctive, and experts have learned a great deal about child-rearing that needs to be communicated to parents. As a first step, parents must be taught that when they are under stress their children can be in danger.

The abusing or imminently abusing parent must be reached. Parents who have problems in rearing their children are acutely sensitive to being labeled sick, sadistic or degenerate. They also fear punishment and jail. If these parents sense this attitude in treatment programs, they will pull away, further endangering their children, or forcing a protective agency to remove a child from his home. A truly rehabilitatively oriented social system must create an understanding atmosphere, even though further abuse or maltreatment cannot be condoned.

Often these parents are the most difficult to reach, for they are usually isolated people, fearful of the possible community response to their behavior. But they must be reached and told that help is available—help that can enable them to better meet their parenting responsibilities, keep the family together and protect the child within the family home. Parents need to be told where they can seek help, including help from family service agencies, child protective agencies, self-help groups, doctors, visiting nurses, day care programs, clergy, neighbors, friends and family. They need to be assured that someone cares, that someone is willing to help them when they need help. But if we expect troubled families to come forth, the help offered them must be real.

Prevention and treatment are a community responsibility. We know that there are many current programs which have demonstrated that they can successfully help parents care for their children and maintain family life. Every community must take inventory to see whether it has the basic ingredients for a comprehensive, indigenous and responsive program to meet local needs for the prevention and treatment of child abuse and maltreatment and to aid parents in stress.

Over 100 years ago, Emerson wrote: "If a man can write a better book, preach a better sermon, make a better mousetrap . . . the world will make a beaten path to his door." So too, if we build community resources that better help families function, families in need will beat a path to their doors.

[1] Morris, Marian G., Gould, Robert W., and Matthews, Patricia J.,"Toward Prevention of Child Abuse," CHILDREN, Mar.-Apr. 1964.

[2] See, e.g., DeFrancis, Vincent, *Child Protective Services: A National Survey* (1967) and New York State Assembly Select Committee on Child Abuse, *Report* (April 1972).

[3] See the special series of articles on child abuse and neglect in the May-June 1975 issue of CHILDREN TODAY.

48

Senior Syndromes

by MARGIE CASADY

If life for senior citizens isn't a downhill ride, then what is it? After a lot of study, it appears difficult to say, except that it isn't what we thought it was.
Margie Casady reports on the behavioral sciences from Del Mar, California.

No matter what you call them, old people, old folks or senior citizens, most labels conjure up images of senility, poor health, loneliness and misery. Emerson spoke of the aged as "rags and relics," and Shakespeare was no more complimentary when he said the twilight years usher in "a second childishness and mere oblivion. Sans teeth, sans eyes, sans taste, sans everything." What Simone de Beauvoir calls the "inescapable decline" is not a pretty sight, and most of us dread our own impending deterioration. Researchers, however, are finding that most of our fears are based on outdated beliefs that are more fiction than fact.

Over the past decade, gerontology, the study of aging, has received the attention of social scientists who are studying large, representative groups of older persons. Their work provides the first real insight into the aging process. Bernice L. Neugarten, a psychologist and former chairperson of the Committee on Human Development at the University of Chicago, says, "These studies go far toward exploding some of our outmoded images. For example, old persons do not become isolated and neglected by their families, are not dumped into mental hospitals by cruel or indifferent children, are not necessarily lonely or desolate if they live alone. Few of them ever show overt signs of mental deterioration or senility, and only a small proportion ever become mentally ill." Even retirement does not deserve its bad name. According to Neugarten, more and more older people are choosing to retire early. She points out that in one recent national study, three out of four of the older persons were satisfied or very satisfied with their lives since retirement.

Two other psychologists, Paul Baltes of Pennsylvania State University and K. Warner Schaie of the University of Southern California, are also skeptical about mental decline in old age. They tested the intelligence of 500 persons ranging in age from 21 to 70, then retested them seven years later. When they compared the average scores of different age groups at a given point in time, their findings supported the stereotype: the older the group, the lower the performance. But when they looked at any given age group's performance on the first and second tests, they found a systematic increase in scores for verbal comprehension, numerical skills, inductive reasoning and in the ability to organize and process visual materials. Even people in their 70s improved from first to second testing. This study, and later ones confirming it, convinced Baltes and Schaie that "intellectual decline is largely a myth." (They speculated that the differences between age groups may indicate that the measured intelligence of our population is increasing as the substance and length of U.S. education improves.)

William Masters and Virginia Johnson, the researchers who studied physiological responses during sexual intercourse, were probably the first to tell us that sex at 70 is not only possible, it's good for us. Other studies report that many older couples have an active sex life and that sexual desires continue far into old age.

Gerontologist Victor Kassel stresses the mental and physical benefits of sex for older persons and insists that society must change its rigid thinking on the subject. According to Kassel, some nursing-home operators, aware of the anxiety-reducing capacity of sexual intercourse, turn their backs on their patients' sexual liaisons. He says that an enlightened few even encourage it!

The evidence is clear; life for senior citizens is not a downhill ride. But then what is it? Henry Maas and Joseph Kuypers of the Institute of Human Development at the University of California in Berkeley found that we can't really say. It's as difficult to buttonhole lifestyles and personalities of older persons as to guess at those of younger individuals.

The two psychologists came to this conclusion after analyzing data from a longitudinal study initiated in the '30s when their Bay Area subjects were young parents, and continued into the late '60s when they were in their early 70s. Their most consistent finding was diversity.

In their book *From Thirty to Seventy*, the researchers describe the wide variety of interests, capacities, needs, lifestyles and personalities of these California septogenarians. Among their 142 subjects, they found at least 10 different lifestyles and seven personality types. The men fell into four lifestyle groups; the women, into six.

Almost half of the men were homebodies whose lives revolved around wives, children and grandchildren. Other men also busied themselves at home, but in solitary pursuits such as carpentry. The socially active grandfathers were also politically active and concerned about social issues. Eight ailing older men withdrew from life.

The primary life focus of one-fourth of the grandmothers was their husbands, while others, mostly widows who had few interests of their own, became involved in their adult children's activities. A third group occupied themselves by visiting a large network of friends and relatives. Twelve women who were still employed put work first; 11 were active in community groups; a dozen were sickly, emotionally distraught individuals who, like their male counterparts, withdrew from life. "The diversity of the 10 different lifestyles seems limited only by the size and nature of our panel," report the two psychologists.

Further, they found no relationship between personality type and lifestyle. A woman who centered her life around her husband was as apt to be dependent as independent, aggressive as passive, person-oriented as socially retiring. And a conventional, conservative man might center his life around his hobbies, his family or his job. "If anything," says Kuypers, "we become more diverse as we age."

These findings have important implications for social planning. Kuypers insists that basic policy must provide different alternatives for different types of old people. Choices about retiring or tapering off from work are essential. He believes a variety of living arrangements should be

Photograph by Jean-Claude Lejeune

available to older citizens. Interestingly, not one of the individuals in the study chose to live in a high-rise apartment complex or other age-segregated community, the type of housing most often provided and built by government and private industry.

The most pertinent influence on life in old age appeared to be lifestyle in early adulthood. Maas and Kuypers found that our lives at 70 have a lot more to do with our lives at 30 than with the onset of old age. "We don't lose our connection to the past and suddenly become something or somebody else," says Kuypers. Women who were depressed, fearful and unsure of themselves at 70 were similarly afflicted at 30. Those who were outgoing, busy and cheerful in early adulthood were happy, active septogenarians. And sickly older persons also had ailments when they were younger.

Moreover, there was a strong relationship found between poor physical health and emotional problems. In every case where an old person withdrew from society, the researchers found that he or she also had physical infirmities. "Being in good health was crucial to allowing old people to lead the type of life they wanted," says Kuypers, adding, "early adult health care may pay multiple dividends for old age—not only for health status, but also for aging personality dispositions and aging lifestyles."

Although the Berkeley study showed some consistency over the life-span, it also uncovered differences between the sexes on what most influenced their lifestyles. The personal and physical environments of the women as mothers had the most impact on their lives, while experiences in early adulthood were the best predictors of later lifestyles for men.

Specifically, marital status, age, economics, social networks and geography had the most effect on women. Those who centered their lives around their husbands were younger than the others, healthier and lived in remote suburbs or in the country. The most sociable women were church members and highly energetic women who lived near family and friends. The least well-adjusted women who had few interests and rarely socialized were older, widowed, in poor health and somewhat economically deprived.

Women who had centered their lives around their families had the most difficult time as old persons. Those who had maintained outside careers and interests were best off after their husbands' deaths. "The evidence in the study," say the two researchers,

"quite unexpectedly gives support to the idea that wives and mothers should expand their interests and involvements beyond the circle of the family if their later years are not to become problematic ones." Although this may have been difficult for these women, born at the turn of the century when society frowned upon working mothers and when husbands encouraged their wives to stay at home, now women have options. They can broaden their horizons so that losing their husbands will be less traumatic.

Because the family arena was so influential in determining women's lifestyles, Maas and Kuypers expected that "work" would be an equally potent force for men. Not so. The older men's lifestyles were untouched by whether or not they continued to work. Equal proportions of fathers who worked and fathers who were retired were family-centered, hobbyists, social activists or men who withdrew from society. The researchers hypothesize that because these men always had been involved in several arenas—work, family, friendships, hobbies—that the loss of one of them was not catastrophic. The balanced lives that men lead, say Maas and Kuypers, would benefit women as well.

As previously mentioned, the best predictor of an elderly man's lifestyle was his lifestyle as a young man. While changes in environment, usually made to accommodate the husband's needs, sometimes led to radical changes in lifestyle for women, men's lifestyles remained fairly constant.

Those who centered their lives around hobbies in old age had been dissatisfied with their lack of free time as young men. For these men, marriage had never been central in their lives. Still relatively uninvolved in their marriages as oldsters, and now retired, they finally had the free time to pursue new activities—alone and with vigor.

The central feature in the lives of older men whom Maas and Kuypers called "unwell disengaged" was their poor health and social withdrawal. At 30, they tended to be irritable men who fought with their wives over religion and leisure activities. They were tense, nervous and explosive. And they were sickly. They were much the same at 70.

The most successful young men, who were satisfied with their social status, finances and jobs, were relaxed, controlled, removed, interpersonally cool and the most affluent of the lot. As older adults, they maintained their self-satisfaction and aloofness. Although they always had a large network of friends, they had few intimate relationships. In their old age, they continued to spend little time with their wives. But there was no indication that these couples were unhappy with their "separate" lives.

Older men who centered their lives around their families were an enigma. There was little in their early adulthood to predict their later family orientation. They were rich and not so rich, of high social status and low, energetic or lazy, continued to work or had retired early. The only traits that related to their lifestyle in old age were personal ones. Since early adulthood, these men had been more affectionate and demonstrative than the others. They were less likely to withdraw from marital conflict, and their marriages were more important to them than to the other men.

The idea that old age brings with it massive physical and psychological decline and drastic changes in lifestyle simply doesn't square with the facts. A majority of old people continue to lead rewarding, interesting lives. Continuity, however, is not synonymous with sameness. As men and women move from the work world into retirement, as their children leave the nest to start their own families and careers, older adults have the opportunity to travel, to pursue new interests and hobbies. As Maas and Kuypers conclude, "Old age can provide a second and better chance at life." On life's merry-go-round, the brass ring may take a long time coming around. When it does, grab it.

49

A RIGHT TO DIE? TWO VIEWS

1. The case for euthanasia by a man who has known mortal pain

BEVERLEY NICHOLS

Since the 1920s Beverley Nichols has been one of Britain's most distinguished and prolific novelists and playwrights. His article is reprinted from the conservative weekly "The Spectator" of London.

•

In March, 1974, out of the blue, I had a hemmorrhage and was rushed to the hospital for an exploratory operation. This revealed a deepseated cancer, and two days later there was a further operation, lasting six hours, in which the growth was removed. There followed several weeks in which I hovered between life and death, for, in spite of devoted nursing, there were "complications." But these would make painful reading, so that is all you will wish to be told about my operation, and probably more.

The reason for this article—the first that I have been able to write for nearly a year—is that during these long months of physical torture I have had more than adequate opportunity to check some of my most deeply held convictions concerning the values of life and the values of death, and to reassess them in the light of this experience. Such an examination, if it is honestly conducted, inevitably compels the quester to face the ultimate problem of suicide. This obliges him to make up his mind about voluntary euthanasia—the legalized inducement of death.

And please do not console yourself with the idea that this is an academic problem in which you have no concern. Some 10 per cent of the readers of this article will be obliged to face up to it before they die, either on their own behalf or on behalf of some relation or friend. Why not do so *now*, before pain has deprived them of the power of logical thought?

I imagine that if there were to be a national poll on the pros and cons of suicide it would produce a result in which the "don't knows" greatly outnumbered all the rest. If the poll were international the confusion would be even greater. In Japan, in certain circumstances, it is a proof of honor and courage; in India it can be greeted as a pious duty; throughout the realms which obey the doctrines of the Roman Catholic Church, it is a mortal sin. The Protestant churches, apparently, are not so sure. Such a confusion argues an equal confusion of understanding.

Which side are you on? And why?

To me the whole problem begins and ends with physical pain, and I often suspect that those who are most vehement in their denunciation of voluntary euthanasia have never really experienced pain at all. Not pain with a capital "P." They may have had broken arms or fractured wrists, various abscesses, hernias, migraines, shingles, fistulas, kidney stones, etc., etc.—to mention a few of the physical bothers of which I have personal experience—but to describe these as 'pain' is ridiculous. Compared with the pain of certain cancers they are minor annoyances.

I have actually *seen* pain, very clearly indeed, at close quarters. You may be interested to learn what it looks like. Pain, pictorially, is a cluster of serpents in various shades of color that are essentially evil—virulent green, arsenic pink, muddy crimson and slimy black. When they first flash across the vision they are huddled together, at some distance from the body, in a loathsome cluster, palpitating, watching, waiting. Then as the crisis mounts, they begin to detach themselves, and to slide closer and closer, slowly, relentlessly, with a soft, gloating hiss. And now they are upon their victim, beginning to enter his body, one by one, gliding up his limbs, flooding him with scalding poison through their forked tongues, higher and higher, till they reach the brain. This is the moment when, if one is lucky, one loses consciousness—the moment when one drifts into a temporary limbo of hell or—if one is very lucky indeed—into the permanent liberty of death.

But one is not always that lucky. For the serpents of pain are very cunning creatures—schooled by Nature, the arch-sadist, in every trick of the torturer's trade. They know precisely when to stop. So they begin to retreat, slithering downwards, flickering their poisoned tongues, detaching themselves, withdrawing to the distance, regrouping, waiting, watching.

And there is a sharp prick in the arm, the sickly reek of ether, and the nurse gives another injection. Till the next time. That is Pain.

This picture that I have painted is not an airy fantasy; still less is it a horror comic. It is a factual description by a practiced reporter of an ordeal to which thousands of men and women are subjected, often for months and sometimes for years, because those who framed our laws are too blind, ignorant, or prejudiced to face the facts.

If it is a crime to kill a man, is it not a greater crime to sentence him to a living death? We did not wish to come into this world, so why should any man dictate to us how or when we decide to leave it? These are questions that have never been satisfactorily answered, least of all by the church.

Sometimes, during the crises of the past year, I have received religious consolation at the bedside, and it was indeed consolation of a sort. There is a blessing in the holy sacrament even when you are too weak to lift the cup that holds the sacred wine. But it does not dispel the serpents. They lie there coiled, watching, ready to strike again. When the priest had gone, leaving me alone to await their assaults, I have wished that he might have stayed a little longer, not only to comfort me by his presence but to answer the fundamental questions which all Christians should try to answer, but seldom do. For example. . . .

If suicide is to be regarded by the church as a mortal sin, why did Christ never even bother to mention it? Why was it left to the church to assume, with no authority whatsoever, that He *would* have condemned it if anybody had asked Him? The ecclesiastical argument, conveniently ignoring the teaching of the Master—or rather His lack of teaching—is to the effect that it is a mortal sin because it is an affront to God—a rejection of the "gift of life."

The "gift of life"! I have small patience with that phrase. The value of a gift is to be measured by the happiness which it brings to the recipient. I wonder if any of my readers chanced to see a photograph recently reproduced by a scientific journal in America—of a pair of Siamese twins? They were both girls, about two years old, and no operation could be devised to separate them. One of them had been born with a high intelligence but she was gradually losing it because her sister, remorselessly attached to her by chains of flesh, had been born mad. By what possible concept of religion can it be argued that these children should be compelled to endure their tortures to the bitter end?

Here is a very personal confession with a direct bearing on the subject. It was inevitable during the past year that I should contemplate suicide, and through the long nights when the serpents would permit I lay awake devising schemes which would involve the least difficulty for myself and the least distress for my friends. Some of these schemes had an element of farce. There was one, in particular, which involved going down to Cornwall and driving out to Land's End in the middle of the night. Having arrived I would get out of the car, swallow a handful of pills washed down with a bottle of spirits, and struggle into a heavily weighted overcoat. Thus equipped, I would stagger down the cliffs, and tot-

ter off a rock into the icy waters.

The trouble was that I did not know what sort of spirits to swallow nor what sort of tablets to take. Then, as though to confirm my resolution, the papers reported the death of Desmond Donnelly, the former MP for Pembroke. He killed himself in a hotel near Heathrow. By his bed was an empty bottle of vodka and an empty bottle of barbiturates. He had taken twenty 200-milligram tablets of . . . we will call it "X". I had a full bottle of this powerful drug in my medicine cupboard at home. So that was that. I knew what had to be done.

But I did not do it, for two reasons. The first was another operation, which left me too weak to make any plans at all. The second was a visit from a very dear friend. We will call him Derek. I had known him for twenty years; we had no secrets from one another; and I told him that I had lost the will to live and wanted out. He took the news quite calmly. He certainly was not shocked, for he was suffering from an incurable

---

"Those who framed our laws are too blind . . . or prejudiced to face facts . . ."

---

disease of the bones. "But if you are thinking of suicide," he said, "forget it." Then he told me that a month ago he had tried to kill himself, using precisely the same methods as Donnelly. But something went wrong. He had taken either too much or too little, and after three days his body dragged him back to life. Six months later he died after the amputation of his right leg.

I shall always remember his last words when he left me alone to grapple with the serpents. "In a civilized society," he said, "it would be as easy to buy the ingredients of a suicide, with precise directions, as to buy a first aid kit."

"But if that were possible," cry the opponents of euthanasia, "people would be committing suicide for the most trivial reasons—a headache, a row with the wife, a warning letter from the inspector of taxes." I very much doubt it. The will to live is the most potent force in the heart of man. Only in the absolute extremities of pain is it likely to be surrendered. Voluntary euthanasia is for those extremities.

For what they are worth, which is

very little, let us consider the moral and practical objections.

The anti-euthanasiasts draw horrifying pictures of the legal abuses which, they claim, would inevitably follow any act empowering the medical profession to ease the last days of the dying. They present us with the prospect of wicked nephews gathering around the bedside of the nearly departed, doing terrible things with last wills and testaments, aided and abetted by evil nurses and unscrupulous doctors. Such fears are ridiculous. The safeguards suggested in the charter of the Voluntary Euthanasia Society, which would almost certainly form the basis of any future legislation, are so comprehensive and so stringent that even the wickedest of nephews would find it impossible to get away with any dirty work. He would be checked at every stage.

Perhaps the most illusory argument against legalized euthanasia is the one which claims that it is no longer necessary because of the discovery of so many hypnotics, sedatives, analgesics, and tranquilizers, which keep pain within "tolerable" limits. This is simply not true. How can any narcotic, however potent, make life "tolerable" for a man who is suffering from an inoperable cancer of the throat, which gradually make it impossible for him to swallow and after a few weeks makes it almost impossible for him to breathe? And why, since there are so few hospitals for terminal illnesses, should he be condemned to breathe his last in the full publicity of a public ward, which is almost certainly understaffed?

When all other arguments are exposed as false the opponents of legalized euthanasia usually invoke some form of moral code, claiming that it would be against the will of God. It would transgress the sixth commandment; it would violate the principle that "suffering is God's gift for the good of our souls that we may grow in grace." The best answer to this pious nonsense was made by the late Dean Inge of St. Paul's. "I cannot believe," he said, "that God wills the prolongation of torture for the benefit of the sufferer's soul."

There is one—and in my opinion only one—valid argument against the immediate legalization of voluntary euthanasia with the patient's consent. This is that it might be the means of deterring some patients suffering "terminal" disease from receiving the benefits of spirit healing. In spite of the massive body of evidence in its favor, the attitude of the majority of doctors towards spirit healing is that it "can't do any harm," and the majority of patients turn to it as a last resort. The very fact that it *is* so often a "last resort," the final effort to escape an "incurable" condition, when all else has failed, gives added weight to the miracles which the healers have accomplished. I use the word "miracle" advisedly, for it is the word which has constantly been used by doctors, nurses, and hospital matrons when confronted by the otherwise inexplicable cures for which the healers have been responsible.

This article could go on for ever, and I need hardly say that I would willingly have forgone the year of torture which has given me the material to write it. But I would like to think that one man's agony and his reactions to it may help, in however small a measure, to bring comfort to many. As I said before, this is not an academic matter. The serpents of pain are no respecters of persons.

(Feb. 8)

THE INALIENABLE RIGHT TO LIVE

2. To authorize killing under any circumstance is inhuman.

EUGENE IONESCO

Rumanian-born author Eugene Ionesco lives in France and is a Chevalier of the Legion of Honor. His many plays, written in French, have been translated and performed in twenty-seven languages. His article, which first appeared in the independent weekly "Deutsche Zeitung" of Stuttgart, is adapted from a pamphlet he wrote against euthanasia.

•

The head doctor of a Zurich clinic who withheld medication and nourishment from incurably ill patients who might have lived another month, a year, or two, has been released from jail. He still has to answer to a court of law but, although fired from his position, is again free to treat his private patients. The Swiss Medical Association is defending him. Numerous petitions have been submitted on his behalf. We have the right, say the undersigned, to demand that we be permitted to die when we want. That is one point of view. However, requesting death to cut short suffering can be likened to suicide, which is condemned by religions. Do we have the right to commit suicide?

Worse yet, scientists and doctors are assuming the right to make this decision for others. That is the same as murder. The doctor in question assumed this right when he refused to prolong the life of patients who had not specifically asked to be allowed to die. Hospitals and the medical profession are asking us to take this step from suicide to authorized murder. A sign of the times.

After the liberation of France an SS "hero" was put up against the wall. He begged, he pleaded on his knees, he defended himself desperately before he was executed. This soldier, a murderer to be sure but nevertheless brave in battle, was, when faced with his own death, turned into a blubbering wretch.

Each evening a priest visits the cells of condemned men to give comfort. Their lives hang on the hope of a reprieve. The priest avoids the cell when he learns that a plea for clemency has been denied. At the last moment the condemned prisoner knows—fifteen minutes before his execution—that his plea for mercy has failed. He is instantly turned into an agitated, collapsing bundle of humanity that has to be propped up and forcibly dragged to the place of execution. And when a condemned man is notified that his sentence has been commuted to life at hard labor his joy knows no bounds.

Famous authors, humanitarian organizations, legal, medical, and academic societies, and all manner of well-intentioned souls have lobbied for years to outlaw the death penalty. And most countries have done away with capital punishment.

Why the present turnabout? What is the point of letting the murderer live when the innocent patient is executed? A sentence of death is the ultimate penalty. In the seventeenth century a tragedy that did not end with the death or murder of the main character was merely a tragicomedy. In many novels we read of condemned men who—when the early morning hour for execution has passed—are gripped with unspeakable joy because they have been granted at least another twenty-four hours of life.

There are cases of doctors incurably ill, often with a disease in their area of specialization, who nevertheless allow themselves to be lulled like innocent children by considerate colleagues who offer impossible hopes for recovery. I also know the case of a gravely ill woman who for years bravely bore her suffering. Finally the surgeon brought her up short: "You have survived your ailment seven years. What more do you want?" The woman wanted nothing more—her will to carry on left her. She returned home and died within a few days. I wonder what this brutally frank doctor would have done were he struck down by the same disease.

We have often heard of doctors who are emotionally drained by the death of their patients. Poor doctors! Perhaps they should eliminate their patients more quickly to be relieved of this trauma. Then they could devote their full efforts to helping the sick die expeditiously. Doctors will then be like the executioners of old who did not give the condemned "another minute."

To look death in the eye you have to be either a Christian or a Stoic. Even then the Mother Superior of Bernanos dies a terrible death, wracked by fear despite her strong faith. Something else must be added. There are too many sick people in hospitals—too much bother for doctors and nurses; their burden must be made lighter. We know what goes on in hospitals. Sue me if you will but we know what goes on: indifference, irregular doctors' hours in the overcrowded wards, negligence, and, again, indifference.

One of my colleagues of the Academie Française recently wrote in a newspaper that one has to talk to the sick about death, that one has to help them in dying. What idiocy! Who in these understaffed hospitals has time for that? Can you call a priest to each patient's bed? There are no longer enough priests. The few who remain have all they can do converting jazz and pop singers to the Church.

And can you imagine how a doctor or a nurse would go about preparing a dying patient for death? Go ahead, ask them. They'd laugh in your face. There's too much to do as it is. What more do you want? It's much easier to stop the treatment or to administer a shot. All of these incurably ill take up entirely too much space and too much time in dying.

One should let any person live who can still take comfort in the rays of the sun, the occasional visit of a child or a relative. Let live the one who is still warmed by memories and how the windows of the room light up at dawn. Who knows of the dreams of an unconscious patient? What does it mean to take the life of a terminally ill patient? Who is incurable?

We are born incurable. Even Christ on the cross complained that God had forsaken him. Joan of Arc recanted and was burned as a redeemed heretic.

Only yesterday we did our best to keep up the spirits of a terminally ill patient. But today a new approach is taking shape: We cannot evade the issue of dying, but it should be death with dignity. How considerate! The en-

Ionesco—"The poor, the moderately well off, the rich all cling to life."

tire propaganda, the whole temper of our times, is based on lies and deceit; every truth gets twisted around, nothing is cast in its true light, we are living a lie. Lies are our daily bread, and instant communication spreads them around the world. The political process is in the main the learning of lies; the end justifies the means and the means are lies.

But now the white lies that kept hope alive in terminally ill patients are considered inexcusable. And all this in the name of "human dignity," which at other times we mock and spit upon.

A number of facts tell a different story. The life of a dying hospital patient must be terminated because the bed is needed for others. That fits the pattern—legalized abortion, euthanasia, the killing of infants born deformed. Recently a British doctor urged publicly that newborn babies not be recorded officially until several days after their birth so that a determination as to their viability could be made. Does that not have the eerie ring of the Hitlerian death camps—only those still able to work are preserved a bit longer?

50

Expanding the Scope of Health Care

by Sol Levine

There is no longer any need to justify the judicious use of paraprofessionals to extend the capacity of the health delivery system. Even if there were no important new developments in the organization of health care, there would be obvious need to expand significantly the employment of public service workers in the health sector. However, in any deliberations about the future deployment of public service workers in the health delivery system, we can be much more informed in our thinking and more pertinent in our recommendations if we develop a clear image of the kind of health system which is evolving. What kind of health delivery system can we envision in the next few years? What will be the main goals and objectives and what types of services will be provided by the emerging health delivery system? If we can answer these questions, we can specify more appropriately the roles new public service workers will perform in the health system.

In this article I will focus on specific goals and functions which, in my judgment, must be encompassed by the delivery system if it is designed to *promote health* and not merely to treat illness. Our legitimate aspirations regarding the scope and functions of a health system have been so frustrated by our present mode of organizing, financing, and delivering health services that we have become embarrassed to delineate and project simple basic goals for the system lest we sound hortatory or platitudinous. Even some of the most sophisticated critics of the present health system have been mentally imbued and affected by the assumptions and criteria of the present system. When we speak of improving health services, who among us does not conjure in his/her mind the building of new hospitals, additional coronary care units, cobalt machines, dialysis, and other impressive forms of medical technology? They are important components of our medical armamentarium, to be sure, but how far do

these take us in promoting health and preventing illness?

This is not to deny that we do, in fact, possess an impressive medical technology which can often spell the difference between health and sickness, even life and death. Moreover, the American people, for the most part, cherish and seek the technical care they can obtain. Indeed, one major task in the next few years will be to find ways of making the health technology we already possess readily available to the American population, particularly low-income people and minority groups in inner cities and in rural communities. While relatively few people complain about the technical level of care they receive from the health delivery system, harsh criticism and even indignation is often expressed about other aspects of the health system: the high cost of care, the unavailability of neighborhood physicians, the amount of time required to obtain care and the frustration involved, and dehumanization which patients and families experience as they try to cope with the inadequacy, complexity, and segmentalization of the health system. Dramatic testimony to the unsatisfactory state of our present mode of organizing health care is provided by the specter of tired and sometimes desperate patients pushing their way into crowded and overtaxed emergency rooms in an effort to obtain care which otherwise is not available.

Clearly, then, our elaborate technology should be made available to patients in a more humanized manner. This will require, among other things, that we move away from a delivery system which is hospital-centered, geared to the needs and practices of medical specialists, and organized to provide services for episodic illness. We should try to move toward a health delivery system which uses the hospital as a significant resource but which is mainly concerned with providing primary care on an ambulatory basis in neighborhoods and communities. It would seem that new public service workers could play a much more significant role in a health delivery system which emphasizes community-based primary care

SOL LEVINE is professor of sociology and community medicine at Boston University.

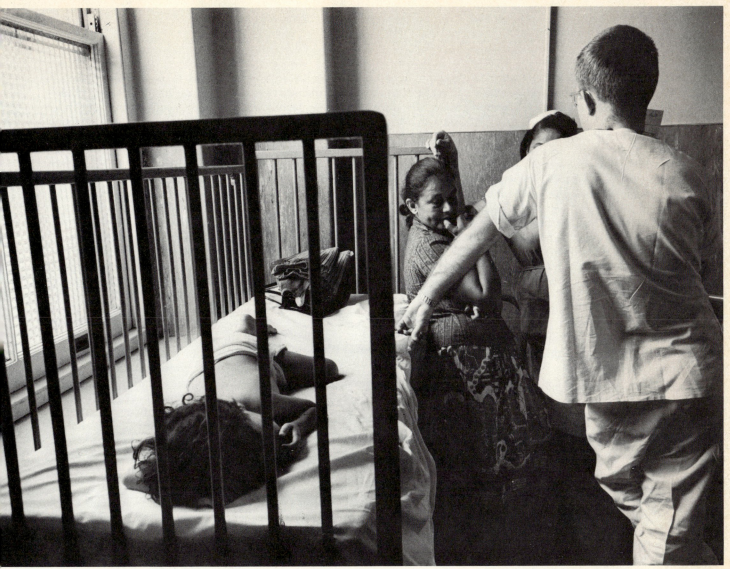

to recipients.

1. *The goals of the delivery system of the future should include to a much greater extent the promotion of health and the prevention of disease.*

Public service workers will be able to contribute even more significantly if the goals and functions of the health delivery system are changed. We must move away from a "medical repair system" which focuses upon episodic illness, and, in large part, reflects the failures of our present system, to a health delivery system whose primary goals are the promotion of health and the prevention of disease. This would represent a most serious shift in our focus and emphasis. And if we are serious and deliberate in changing the goals and

functions of our health system, there will be enormous opportunities for usefully employing new public service workers.

It will be necessary for us to develop and to use a definition of health which encompasses significant social components. Health will not be viewed as the mere absence of disease but as the ability of the individual to control her/his life and to perform crucial social roles such as worker, parent, spouse, and citizen. The health delivery system will then be assessed largely in terms of the degree to which it contributes to the ability of people to perform their social roles maximally and to control their lives to the fullest possible extent. The health goals would vary for each individual with

the objective of having each person achieve the fullest level of health possible. What is to be emphasized is that each person could achieve a maximal level of health for him or herself, depending on age, physical condition, life circumstances, etc. A specific example can be used to illustrate the general principle. If, with the appropriate social supports and health care, an aged person has the capacity to participate in the community and to follow a pattern of living which she or he found enjoyable, it would violate the health goals we are espousing to place him or her in a nursing home. A health system which, in fact, placed such people in nursing homes where they could not fulfill their health potential—where they could not perform their social roles and control their lives—would be regarded as failing in its essential purpose.

2. *As the health-care delivery system shifts from one which is primarily a hospital-based "repair system" to one with great emphasis on providing primary care and promoting health, an additional major function may be assumed by the health system: intensive and comprehensive health education.*

Studies by epidemiologists, economists, medical sociologists, and other health investigators have demonstrated that the health status of a people is determined less by the traditional patient-care services which are dispensed to them than by social conditions in which they live and the health practices they follow—in short, by their style of life. There is little doubt that the things we eat, how much we smoke and drink, how we manage our automobiles, and the way we live—all of these play a tremendous role in affecting our health. The distinguished public health physician George James once remarked that if we encouraged people to give up cigarettes we could do more to improve the health of our people than all the skills and technology presently in the domain of medicine. The health system must include intensive and comprehensive health education as basic and essential functions. To do this adequately, it will be necessary to make use of the skills of the new public service workers.

We can expect some resistance to these new health goals and functions from a number of health professionals who regard themselves as specially trained people using complex and sophisticated skills to manage illness and pathology, not to interfere with people's personal habits or way of living. Some will argue that personal health habits are so deeply embedded in people's history and culture that they are very difficult, if not impossible, to modify. Others will contend that we have no right to tamper with people's way of life.

We believe that humanistic values, concerns about costs, as well as our

changing definition of health will cause health professionals and others involved in forging a new health system to address themselves finally to personal health styles. Many physicians, nurses, and other health professionals already take into account the personal and cultural life-styles of their patients. When interpreting pain and symptoms and in prescribing appropriate health regimens, health professionals have found it necessary to consider the personal characteristics, life-styles, and cultural backgrounds of their patients. It will be necessary for health personnel to expand their knowledge, skills, and understanding

---

Many of the people who come to the health system because of disability and dependence require social care and supports more than they require traditional medical service ... we will have to train public service employees to provide necessary social services and social supports to meet these problems.

---

regarding psychological, social, and cultural factors as they begin to achieve the new goals of the health system: promoting health and fostering preventive care.

One prototype of the new form of health delivery may be found in the present Multiple Risk Factor Intervention Trial Centers (MRFIT) which attempt to prevent heart disease among patients who have a high risk of developing heart disease: adult males who are overweight, have high cholestrol levels, high hypertension, and who smoke are clearly very likely candidates for heart disease. The program attempts to use a wide range

of methods to modify the behavior and style of life of these people. Accordingly, counseling is sometimes provided as well as various forms of group discussion or group therapy. In attempting to modify the health habits and life-styles of these adult males, physicians have found it necessary to enlist the aid of other personnel such as counselors, clinical psychologists, and social workers.

If programs like MRFIT were expanded on a much broader basis, it would clearly be necessary to make use of many new public service employees in the health delivery system. It would be desirable to develop new kinds of personnel who know a good deal about appropriate health habits, who can assess the kinds of problems people from different ethnic cultures, communities, and social-class backgrounds will encounter in modifying their health behavior and styles of life. Public service employees working in this field will not only have to know much about health care but a great deal about sociology, psychology, and health education. In addition, they will have to possess a range of specialized interpersonal skills, and they will have to be equipped to work with different kinds of groups in varying settings. Clearly new employees will have to acquire not only cognitive knowledge of social science disciplines but they will also have to possess interpersonal, clinical, and group work skills. Some of them may work in physicians' offices, others in clinics or health centers, and others may serve as outreach workers who visit the homes of patients and families.

It is important to add a clarifying note here. Some people may recoil from the idea of an aggressive health system dictating tastes and habits to people in matters of physical and mental health. While it is preferable to have individuals make their own choices, so long as their behavior is not harmful to others, it would be the responsibility of a health system to make a serious and sustained effort to inform the public: not merely to transmit information casually or mechanically but to get people's attention, to reach them psychologically, to provide them with realistic alternatives, and, when indicated, to help them implement their decision to change their health practices. Public health service workers and other health personnel will have to relate to recipients on a face-to-face basis and to consider their cultural values and preferences in order to find the most appropriate ways of informing them and helping them to change their practices. If an individual elects to pursue a mode of living which departs from the ideal prescriptions of the health workers, the latter, at least, have fulfilled their responsibility in having informed the patient.

3. *The emerging health delivery system will also have to pay attention to various kinds of social services and social supports which people need so that they may be able to perform their social roles and control their lives.*

A considerable start has already been made in this direction in some health delivery systems. Various social services are provided and there is awareness that the patient is a whole person who performs different social roles and is part of the social network which impinges upon her/his health status. Thus health professionals have learned to rely upon social workers to ascertain whether the social resources of a patient recovering from surgery are sufficient and appropriate to permit her/him to return home, or whether the job setting to which a cardiac patient is returning may be too stressful, or whether there is need to redesign family goals and responsibilities so that the physical recovery of a cardiac patient is not obstructed. In such cases, social services have been used as an instrument to achieve medical care of therapy objectives.

Unfortunately, the role of the social worker in medical settings has often been narrowly defined and his or her skills have often not come to the fore unless a patient is referred to social services by a physician. There have been a host of social needs which patients and families have had in managing illness which have been ignored or which have received little attention from the health delivery system. It is hoped that as the health delivery system develops new goals, these social dimensions will receive much more attention. For example, we have not given sufficient attention to the dying patient or to the problems of his or her spouse or kin or to the mother of a child with a newly diagnosed genetic illness or to the family of a patient who has undergone a serious surgical procedure. A dying patient may frequently be capable of performing fuller social roles for an appreciable and treasured piece of time if the health system were

Studies by epidemiologists, economists, medical sociologists, and other health investigators have demonstrated that the health status of a people is determined less by the traditional patient-care services which are dispensed to them than by social conditions in which they live and the health practices they follow—in short, by their style of life.

properly oriented and capable of providing appropriate services. But even more, the families of sick and dying patients are not capable of performing their own roles and living their lives to the fullest or maintaining a state of social health because of the disruptions which they encounter and the failure of the health system to provide appropriate social services and supports to them.

Navarro has argued that many patients come to the health delivery system for care rather than cure. This is understandable when we consider that health problems are increasingly chronic in nature and are amenable to palliation but not cure. Many of the people who come to the health system because of disability and dependence require social care and supports more than they require traditional medical service. How adequate are the available services for a blind person whose physical condition is not amenable to medical intervention or for a child with a serious physical or emotional handicap? The health delivery system has not done much for people who come to it with problems of living such as drinking, boredom, loneliness, or the lack of capability to function well at daily living or to utilize the existing sources of society. As the health delivery system assumes the goal of fostering health and helping people to perform their social roles, it will no longer be able to ignore these concerns, for these are the main business of a health system.

We will have to train public service employees to provide necessary social services and social supports to meet these problems. Many of the skills which will be necessary for the public service employees to obtain will resemble some of the skills which social workers presently possess. They will include making an inventory of patients, families, and community resources, counseling, life rearrangement, discussions and deliberations with employers as well as other diagnostic and interpersonal services.

To achieve the new goals of the health system it would also be necessary to expand various social support services which go beyond individual or group counseling or social services to sick patients on a one-to-one basis. The health system will have to develop and make use of a number of social support services such as child- and day-care services, foster homes, homemaker services, transportation services, income maintenance, etc. Clearly, an expanding number of positions will have to be filled by public service employees as we try to achieve health goals which have been articulated here.

However, it is necessary to realize that the new functions which will be assumed by the health delivery system and additional health workers may not automatically have impact or be effective in modifying the status and behavior of recipients. Our experience with health education efforts to date does not give cause for easy confidence. We have learned that health education methods may fail for all kinds of reasons. If the message which is conveyed by health personnal conflicts with existing values, beliefs, attitudes, or health practices of recipients, considerable resistance may be encountered. In these cases, recipients may fail to hear or attend to the message or they may forget or reinterpret it so that the objectives of health educators are frustrated.

On the other hand, we have learned a good deal about ways of overcoming various types of resistance. In addition, we have developed greater knowledge about what kinds of psychological conditions must obtain in order for health education methods to be effective. We have learned about the limits of mass media and the relative potential of face-to-face methods in varying contexts and settings. We have also learned how the characteristics of the educator, the message, and the recipients may all influence the success of the health education venture. What becomes readily apparent is that the new functions which the public health service workers will be asked to assume are in many ways much more complex and difficult to learn than some of the other skills which paraprofessionals have assumed in the health delivery system. They are qualitatively different from serving as a dental aide or an orthopedic assistant or a medical librarian assistant or even a mental health worker. The new skills which will be necessary for public health service workers to learn involve a combination of basic scientific knowledge such as psychology and sociology, clinical skills such as interviewing group work, and health education and various kinds of interpersonal and intergroup skills. Indeed, unlike many other tasks for which paraprofessionals have been trained in the past, the new roles assumed by the public health service workers may

require specific personality characteristics which may be an important basis for recruitment and selection. It would appear that the task of developing appropriate selection criteria and training requirements will be much more difficult.

It will be necessary to develop very specific job descriptions of the roles the new public service workers will assume, the functions they will perform, and the services they will provide. Even today the actual roles and job requirements of the professional social worker and health educator, who to some extent will

Unless the specific tasks assumed by the new public service workers are explicated, legitimated, and covered by emerging health insurance legislation, our projection of a delivery system which will incorporate new functions and be staffed by public health service workers will be little more than a rationalistic exercise.

serve as models for the new public health service workers, though with some important modifications and refinements, are only vaguely appreciated or recognized by many other health workers such as physicians, nurses, and administrators. As a prior condition for the effective use of the new public service workers, it will be necessary to explicate and legitimate the services provided by the social worker and health educator and provide for their services under the new health insurance legislation. Furthermore, unless the specific tasks assumed by the new public service workers are explicated, legit-

imated, and covered by emerging health insurance legislation, our projection of a delivery sytem which will incorporate new functions and be staffed by public health service workers will be little more than a rationalistic exercise. One crucial question which must be addressed is how the new functions and activities outlined here will be related to and integrated with other parts of the health delivery system. How, for example, will these new functions be grafted onto an ongoing neighborhood health center or a health maintenance organization? If we are to incorporate a new definition of health with all of its social implications and to deal with the health styles and practices of recipients, should we consider new ways of organizing personnel and assigning responsibilities? Should we consider, for example, assigning the role of captain of the team to someone other than the physician since medical care will be but one, though an important component, in the promotion of health? Whatever changes we contemplate in the mode of organizing and deploying personnel, it is crucial that we give considerable forethought, planning, and evaluation to how the new functions are and will be incorporated into the existing health organization structures. If we do not plan carefully, there is good reason to believe that we may be creating new sources of confusion and frustration within the health delivery system.

51

DAVID LEIGH RODGERS

THE MORAL PROVIDER

A reply to Thomas Szasz's "The Moral Physician" in THE CENTER MAGAZINE, *March/April, 1975*

In 1967, the National Advisory Commission on Health Manpower reported that "medical care in the United States is more a collection of bits and pieces than an integrated system in which need and efforts are closely related." Today, despite seven years of Medicare and Medicaid, the bits and pieces remain.

As a result, within the next twelve to eighteen months the federal government will be fully prepared to take over the management of American health care. The executive summary of the Department of Health, Education and Welfare publication, *Forward Plan for Health for Fiscal Year 1976-1980,* states, "The major health industry problem . . . will not yield to less than a well-planned, concerted set of interventions by the federal government."

So, government medicine will come, as surely as night follows day; the spottiness of the delivery of care demands it. But as we refine the logistics of the delivery of care, we should keep in mind Tom Paine's observation that "government, like dress, is the badge of lost innocence." Government characteristically deals with large numbers, very large numbers, while the care of human beings ultimately comes down to a very small number — specifically, one. That "one" must not get lost, nor must his identity, his individuality, or his hard-to-measure human needs. The vast system which is made expressly for him in mass must somehow keep him as its focal point — its end in view. Can the system do it?

(Mrs. Sarah Murphy is eighty years old. She lives alone in an apartment and takes care of herself. She fell and fractured her right upper arm. After it was set and tied down to her chest she could not even feed herself with her left hand. She needs to be sent to an extended-care facility. However, she cannot be transferred into extended care because the law says that only fractures of legs — the lower *extremity — can qualify for extended care.)*

(Mrs. Florence Lamb is eighty-eight years old. She is dying of cancer of the liver. She has two, maybe four, weeks left. She has no pain and it would be absurd to extend her situation with intravenous feedings. She cannot be discharged from the hospital to a skilled-nursing facility — the only care facility available — because she does not need injections, and the law says if there are no injections no skilled-nursing facility can be used.)

Maybe the system is too big to do the job. Maybe bureaucracy cannot come down to the "one." However, a transition which can focus on the individual and his special needs may be possible.

In 1971, there were 345,000 physicians in the United States, 287,000 of whom were engaged in direct patient care. Most physicians who are engaged in patient care are in private practice, which, like sweaters knitted in Galway, is termed a "cottage industry." For all its faults, our medical cottage industry has provided individual attention for those who could gain access to the system.

We must appreciate certain virtues of the old traditional medical care ethic — even as applied to the current transitional system — to understand what has kept it alive so long, and so that we may determine how we can transfer its virtues into a new system.

(Mrs. Murphy has been in my care for twenty years and I could not in any conscience let her be thrown back into her apartment alone with her useless arm where she was certain to fall again and break something else. Therefore I "discovered" an anemia which required three weeks' more hospitalization to investigate. Of course, this pursuit cost Medicare considerably more than extended care would have, but I'll have to let Medicare take care of itself. My job is to take care of Mrs. Murphy.)

(Mrs. Lamb has been in my care for twenty-five years and I could not possibly let her out of the hospital to go home to die neglected and alone. It was no difficult solution to order unneeded shots — that weren't given — so she could legally qualify for the skilled-nursing facility to ease her brief period of dying.)

Traditional medical practice, with its ethic of individual care and concern, was well-established at the time of the birth of this nation, a time when people were imbued with the idea of the social value of the individual citizen. That a physician should be committed to, responsible for, and loyal to his particular patient seemed only proper in the natural order of things. Although there have been lapses (during the plague, physicians were afraid to enter plague victims' houses), this ideal has ancient roots, even stated in second millennium Egyptian papyri. The Hippocratic Oath — considered a cornerstone for the way a physician ought to behave — makes clear the physician's responsibility to his patient. It is no wonder, therefore, that the cottage-industry ideal has persisted largely unchanged, despite gaps in the availability of medical care.

The physician's single-minded responsibility to his patient and his dependence upon his patient for his livelihood are solid virtues — even though his reluctance and that of his representative organization (the American Medical Association and its satellites) to extend care to all is anything but virtuous. However, the private practitioner *is* his patient's ombudsman; he offers a secure interface between his patient and the social stresses of this complicated society.

(James Jordan, age forty-six, is married and has a happy home life. Fifteen years ago he attended a convention, went out with "the boys," visited a prostitute, and contracted gonorrhea. He received adequate treatment (duly recorded in my chart) before he could infect his wife. Recently he was in an auto accident in which his car was struck from behind and he sustained neck injuries. The case is coming to trial and, as part of the pretrial discovery process, my records and chart on Mr. Jordan are subpoenaed — all of them. I must swear that the record is complete. I do, but I neglect to mention I removed the page about the gonorrhea. I'll leave questions of what is perjury and what is a violation of personal privacy to future legal philosophers. The discovery law intends well — it is to speed up trials so justice can be done — but it can no more recognize Mr. Jordan's individual situation than it can serve Mrs. Murphy and her broken arm.)

As Congress and H.E.W. seek to improve health, they must show more concern for the software and imponderables of human care than they have to date. H.E.W. states: "Significant new progress in advancing the health status of the American people is dependent upon the development of new knowledge, knowledge of everything from basic physiological processes to the consequences of changing a formula for reimbursing health care providers." The 1976-1980 H.E.W. summary is jammed with statistics about every conceivable economic aspect of health care. But there is not a single word in it about the individual, nor any hint of the four thousand years of knowledge we have acquired about how to deal with him in a respectful, considerate, personal way.

The official attention to health care and its monumental problems obliterates considerations about other urgent social issues which must be attended to if national medical care is to be salutary. Peter Isacson says in a *New Republic* article: "Malnutrition, air pollution, poor education, more frequent pregnancies, higher rates of venereal and other diseases, inadequate housing, inadequate sanitation, inadequate rodent control, and inadequate clothing" are causes of disease which afflict the poverty-stricken. Social improvement must come from many sources, and improvements in the delivery of health care are bound to be disappointing unless supported by other social advances as well.

The imminence of a federally managed health care system does not spring fully mature from solo-practice medicine. Rather, over the past many decades numerous adjustments in solo practice have been made, some, like the Kaiser system, highly successful.

On balance, group practice has been considered a more effective way to provide medical care than is solo practice. Even now, the Robert Wood Johnson Foundation is making available thirty million dollars to develop primary group practice in sixty selected hospitals. The purpose of these grants is to find a better way than now exists for patients to gain access to the medical care system. With such substantial, no-strings-attached funding, there is good reason to hope progress will be made. To date, however, all we know for sure is that group practice tends to make a better way of life for the doctor: he has more regular hours; he has group insurance benefits; he is relieved of administrative tasks; and he even gets paid vacations. Richard M. Bailey reported in *Medical Economics* that "the solo practitioner, though he works harder, may be more efficient than the group."

Multi-specialty group practices are predicated on the assumption that total care is more effective than care in less closely knit associations. Multi-specialty groups have the singular disadvantage that patients are always referred to other physicians within the group, even when better talent may be available in the community at large. The patient and the income from his care are thus locked into the multi-specialty group. The same result among solo practitioners amounts to the long-abhorred practice of kickbacks, where one doctor profits from hidden shared fees for the care given by his hand-picked colleague.

Prepaid multi-specialty group practice (Kaiser is the prime example of this system of medical care delivery) is a quantum jump from solo practice and even from fee-for-service group practice. The pre-pay system collects a certain sum of money and it guarantees medical care for a predetermined amount. If the system is to work, everyone in it must cooperate to deliver the care promised and also to keep costs down. Kaiser has succeeded in doing just this over the past four decades.

The Health Maintenance Organization (H.M.O.) is the federal government's bid to provide pre-pay

medical care similar to that of Kaiser. In contrast to Kaiser, the H.M.O. has been a dismal failure, even though funded by Congress with hundreds of millions of dollars. In California, accusations of waste, piracy, and fraud have attended its abortive initial efforts.

One reason for the H.M.O.'s failure is that its guidelines include the care of people with psychiatric and drug problems — two types of illness Kaiser has always recognized as hard to insure and basically economically unsound and therefore has included only with additional fee requirements. Another reason is that Kaiser has had forty years' experience, and even though it is a large organization it is not the crystallized bureaucracy characteristic of government.

The very name, "Health Maintenance Organization," implies an ability to maintain health or prevent disease. There is considerable doubt if this purpose can be accomplished. The H.E.W. *Forward Plan . . . 1976-1980* states: "The importance of preventive activities is nearly equaled . . . by our ignorance of effective ways to accomplish prevention."

Even Kaiser has made a notable about-face on the practicality of prevention of illness. Dr. Sidney Garfield, for a generation the director and guiding light of the Kaiser-Permanente medical system, said in 1970: "The clear definition of a health care service, made possible by health testing, is a basic first step toward a positive program for keeping people well." Few in the medical field or among the millions of Kaiser members are unaware of the "multiphasic" testing used so widely and so often in pursuit of Dr. Garfield's goal. However, a few years after his hopeful statement, the Kaiser organization's bulletin, *Planning for Health,* went on record as discouraging "routine annual physical examinations except for women of childbearing age and persons fifty years of age and older."

When it comes down to what we really know about "health maintenance" or "keeping people well" we can sum up the present state of the art very simply: keep the water clean and you will have done the most of what you can do!

❦

So far, the H.M.O. has yet to prove itself. The Kaiser system has proved it can give medical care more efficiently and less expensively than the cottage industry can. There is more to the secret of Kaiser's success than just the surcharge for psychiatric and drug problems. It is worth restating that everyone — not just the managers and administrators, but the physicians as well — is committed in the Kaiser system to keeping costs down. Instead of spending money on his patient's care the Kaiser group physician has a real stake in not spending money on his patient's care. There is, after all, only so much money to go around, and although basic needs are met, the soft, time-consuming, humanistic fringes of the human care of human beings — which often are expensive in physician time — must be rationed or abandoned.

It would be libelous and untrue to state that Kaiser does a poor job of meeting its commitment to set broken legs or treat heart failure, or to imply that Kaiser-associated doctors are unconcerned with doing a good job. However, the fact is irrefutable that Kaiser-associated physicians have a dual commitment: one is to the patient and the other is to the organization, their partners, and the economic vitality of the company with which they work.

The manner in which the system is legally constructed, with both a medical partnership and a health business organization, avoids any charge of conflict of interest. If you were of a mind to sue the American Telephone & Telegraph Company, however, you might feel a bit disconcerted to find that your attorney was a member of the law firm which represents A.T.&T.

The secret of Kaiser-Permanente success goes further. Dr. Garfield has been able to determine categories of health: the well, the worried well, the early sick, and the sick. His view of the care of the well: "Most doctors these days have more work than they can handle, and begrudge the time they must spend on well people." His view of the care of the worried well: "It is wasteful of the doctor's time and boring and frustrating for him." Also, "since the well and the worried well people are a considerable portion of our entry mix, the usurping of available doctors' time by healthy people actually interferes with the care of the sick."

What worries me are those worried well. They are the ones with the symptoms: the headache, the backache, the sprained rib they think may be a heart attack, the cold they think is pneumonia, or the diarrhea they fear may be cancer. Their numbers make up fifty per cent or more of the ordinary office practice, and I believe they truly need help — because, if for no other reason, they are you and me.

Those patients require me to use my "doctor" definition (teacher) while I practice my "physician" definition (healer). I can teach the worried well how to use their bifocals properly and relax their necks

to relieve their headaches, how their ribs can sprain at the cartilage to cause their chest pain, and how the change in bulk in their diets is a better explanation than cancer for the change in their bowel movement. Relieving their worry makes them well again — and that is the proper use of my physician definition.

And who are those well? No pediatrician would dream of not observing a child during his growth so that a bad direction could be detected early. What is different about adults? They may no longer be growing bigger bones, but they are getting into situations in their work and home life which will lead to hypertension or rosy noses. With proper advice, some of these pathological pathways may lend themselves to redirection.

Of course, these categories to limit care are the main secrets of success for the prepaid multi-specialty group. Advice by a physician to the well to keep

> *Efficiency and cost control are hard masters. The "person" part of the care must be eliminated.*

them well, or care of the worried well (which all of us are at one time or another) waste the Kaiser doctor's valuable time. Since the physician's time is the most expensive item in the system, following Dr. Garfield's definitions and applying care accordingly will make the system work.

I have sought a definition which might distinguish the H.M.O. and Kaiser systems from the cottage industry, and one seems to describe it all: the former practice earthquake medicine. That is, they take care of the necessities as would be the case in a general catastrophe. The niceties, individual needs, attention to the person who is attached to the fracture or the burn, must wait until the disaster is over. Traditional cottage-industry medicine, geared to a more civilized, stable society, must take a back seat when the emphasis is on bare necessity.

Kaiser has had to perform in a world of competition, so in some manner it has been able to meet more than bare animal needs, at least often enough to stay alive. Government programs will have no competition when they follow Kaiser's lead. The National Health Planning and Resources Development Act of 1974 empowers the secretary of H.E.W. to "(1) permit those delivering health care services to *keep extra funds* they save through effective management and cost control; (2) *create incentives* for health care deliverers to be as economical as possible" (emphasis mine).

Imagine what attention the worried well will get in that system! There isn't a physician practicing today who cannot conduct a thirty-minute patient interview in five minutes if he sets his mind to it. This is "left-ear medicine." If the patient complains about his left ear the doctor looks at his left ear, prescribes for the left ear, and goes on to the next patient. The "person" part of care must be eliminated, and when it is, the system will work. Efficiency and cost control are hard masters, but there is nothing in a physician's training which unfits him to practice left-ear, earthquake medicine.

The concern here is not that we are going to make a system efficient by asking a surgeon to remove two gall bladders at once. And even though he has ten fingers, we will not expect the family physician to do ten rectal examinations at the same time. However, to make the system efficient all indications are that we will require the physician to attend only to basic animal needs and to deny the patient the time and latitude they both must have to provide care that is humanistic.

The purpose of a government-managed national health care system is a worthy one: to make access to medical care available to all persons and thus improve the health of all the citizens in our land. This will be done at the risk that persons will become numbers in the system, much as they have become in so many other areas of our society. A mere number at a checkout counter, or in a traffic jam, or in a computerized billing or junk mail system is hard to tolerate — but it is tolerable. But a mere number when our health or self is at stake is of a different order of magnitude. Medical care affects us to the core, and if we lose our individuality in that area we will reach 1984 sooner than we like; but it will not be our 1984, it will be George Orwell's.

Merely knowing that the medical practitioner in the cottage industry is able to deal with his patients as persons will not be enough to avoid the transition to namelessness. Positive efforts must be made to preserve the physician-patient bond within a government system.

This bond is easier to feel than to describe. Call it friendship. It is very real and important in patient care. It permits the patient a comfort with his physician, a feeling of safety; it lets him be unguarded, secure in the knowledge that the physician means well by him. The bond does not develop overnight, and it cannot exist in a system which prohibits recurrent physician-patient interchange — that is, where different doctors see the patient every time he calls.

Because assembly lines do things more cheaply than individual efforts, economists conclude that mass activities are more economical. In medical care this conclusion, more often than not, is false. A physician and patient who know and trust each other can often dispense with the diagnostic procedures and therapies that strangers must engage in. Thus, the cost of preserving personal values may be less in the long run.

⟡

Most of us, since childhood, have thought of physicians as powerful people. We therefore expect that any system of medical care will be something the physicians have determined will be right for all. We may fail to realize that a system of medical care will be made by politicians, economics technicians, other nonmedical advisers, and by a few selected physicians who have little association with actual patient care. Therefore, it is worthwhile to understand the characteristics and limitations of practicing physicians, to appreciate how passive they can be when they are designated as "providers" by insurers of government, to visualize how easily they can be co-opted by third-party economic influences, and to recognize how readily they can abdicate a leadership role. Rather than a powerful leader in a quasi-fascist state, such as was philosophized by Plato in his *Republic,* the physician is far more prone to be a pawn in whatever socio-economic construction is thrown up around him.

The private practitioner has already succumbed to forces beyond his control in the insurance industry, as anyone can testify who has ever had to use his Blue Cross, Blue Shield, or other medical insurance. Even though a person's insurance is paid up and in force he cannot simply submit bills for services and a declaration of what ailed him in order to receive payment from his insurance company. He must submit an affidavit from his doctor! In effect, his insurance company considers him fraudulent and will not pay up without the doctor's sworn report of diagnosis, periods of disability, and numerous other data the patient is fully able to supply himself. It is, after all, the patient's insurance; he paid the premium; it was he who was sick; and it is he who has insurance claim money coming to him. The doctor has no involvement in this transaction whatever. Yet he and the insurance companies persist in their claims coziness, as they have for decades.

The physician did not have to be a party to his patient's insurance coverage or to enter the arrangement between the patient and his insurer. He could have let the insurance company honor its bills to its client, or sue for fraud, or let the client sue for breach of contract. But the physician has chosen to cooperate and appease the insurance companies. So now the stage is set for more cooperation and more appeasement — all of which locks him in tighter with the economics rather than the services of health care. With this background it is fearsome to contemplate the extent to which the physician may enter transactions with the government.

Physicians' culpability does not even end there. They have cooperated with Blue Cross-Blue Shield when these insurers have made out benefit checks to their beneficiaries with the doctor's name also on the check. That is, until the doctor signs the check (which by no stretch of the imagination is his check — he has no part of the contract) the patient cannot cash it. This is a patently illegal activity, but doctors have refused to require Blue Cross-Blue Shield to change it.

If physicians have been co-opted by the insurance industry, they are dominated when they become involved with government. Medicaid (MediCal in California) is a system of incredible control of the physician's freedom to care for his patient. Sadly, most physicians have readily cooperated with this program. As is always the case, the purpose of the program is worthy — it is to permit the disadvantaged an entry into the mainstream of medical care. With Medicaid there should be no second-class citizens, medically speaking; everyone, regardless of his means, can see the private physician of his choice.

With this noble purpose (newly cost-accounted) in mind, the MediCal laws have resolutely thrown roadblocks in the way of medical care for these patients, and many physicians refuse to take care of them. Physicians would rather see patients free, as they used to, than get involved in the endless paperwork and obscure requirements set out by the program. MediCal determines what laboratory procedures may be ordered, how often a patient may be

seen, and whether a patient may or may not be hospitalized. MediCal even determines in a teaching hospital who stands on which side of the operating table and so who is in charge of the patient's care.

Thus, the average American physician (and the incomparably reactionary organization — the A.M.A. — which is made up of tens of thousands of his kind) has amply demonstrated his inability to withstand the pressures of the socio-economic system in the care of patients. He cooperates in the belief there is no other option and that his patient will suffer if he takes a different course of action. Generally, physicians take what appears a safer course because they are very conservative; it is hard to be otherwise when one is dealing with problems as difficult to contend with as nature gone wrong. Radical therapy is seldom good therapy; conservative solutions are usually successful solutions.

Physicians have thus permitted themselves to be termed "providers" and their patients "recipients," as they have cooperated with insurance companies which at the moment of payoff consider their customers fraudulent, with inadequate government programs which tell them what they can and cannot do for their patients, and with prepayment schemes which honor the economics of the delivery system above the humanistic needs of the individual person.

So, even though the physician's day-to-day commitment is to the individual (a commitment running through the political fabric of this nation), any expectation that physicians will serve as more than pawns in the brave new medical care world will leave only a disappointing vacuum. The physicians' track record demonstrates they will be no help in maintaining their patient's individuality unless some significant adjustments are made in the mechanistic, cost-oriented, regulation-dominated latticework of health delivery.

All is not lost, however. Even as pawns in a gargantuan governmental health care system, physicians can serve as ombudsmen. They can promote the individuality of citizens, so basic to our historic ideal of democratic institutions. If they have to they can play the system — as for Mrs. Murphy, Mrs. Lamb, and Mr. Jordan — or they can support and work for a better system.

❦

First, we should seek to understand what and who the physician really is. Efforts to penetrate the mystique of the physician are often so off target or out of focus that the picture we receive is one of simple bias — "My doctor is wonderful, but doctors are bums." If we do succeed in understanding the physician, we can see that his participation in even the most bureaucratic, cost-determined system will benefit the individual citizen.

John Stuart Mill observed that "men are men before they are lawyers or physicians . . . and if you make them capable and sensible men they will make themselves capable and sensible lawyers and physicians." In Mill's day, after a genteel education in college, a physician's training consisted of one year of anatomy and some time spent as an apprentice. What the man was to start with and what he became suited Mill's description very well.

Today, however, the physician-to-be spends most of his college time preparing for medical school. He then spends four years in medical school itself, and another three, four, or more, years in post-medical-

> *The ordinary physician is hard-working, independent, responsible, compassionate, paternalistic, and makes a good living*

school training. Most of the development of his capability and sensibility, therefore, is done in the physician template — from age eighteen, when he starts, to age thirty-or-so, when he finishes. His mind, spirit, attitudes, and performance become fully formed in the mold of a physician by the end of this long process.

During this time he decides if he has the stomach for the emotionally exposed pursuit of direct patient care, or whether he would rather use his M.D. degree as he would a Ph.D. and enter the often more intellectual and cloistered world of research. Of course, he has other options which can also take him away from the patient-care definition of physician: administration, public health, industrial management, insurance evaluation.

When the conditioning process has had its effect, physicians share a number of characteristics. First, they had to learn to work hard. Even the person with

superior tools has had to work hard and long to survive. Sir William Osler said the secret of becoming a good physician could be summed up in one word — "work."

Second, physicians have had to develop the talent of thinking independently about medical matters. The amount of conflicting data which applies to every medical case, the uniqueness of every person, and the manner in which a given disease afflicts one person differently from another require this independence of thought about every single diagnostic and therapeutic challenge.

Third, physicians must develop a high degree of responsibility. Although proctors in hospitals (and nowadays in courts) are remotely present, day-to-day performance is largely in the physician's own hands.

Fourth, if they haven't it to start with, physicians must develop a strong sense of humanism. I have rarely seen even the most technically oriented physician fail to respond to human needs.

Fifth, physicians develop a strong sense of personal independence, are often spoiled by the trust they are given, are used to some degree of affluence which they consider their due, and express paternalistic behavior.

This, then, is the physician: a hard-working, independent, responsible, compassionate, paternalistic person who makes a good living in the course of applying his knowledge of science to the practical art of healing. If we are to take good things, eliminate bad things, and move toward a better world in medicine we must understand that the creature we have to work with has been formed in the manner described. He serves a well-defined and limited function, and he would be the first to agree that the politician who makes good legislation, or the public health engineer who keeps the water clean, or the scientist who invents a new antibiotic does more social good than he ever will.

I have described the ordinary, hard-working, patient-oriented physician — the one who will be expected to deliver individual health care in our future "healthy" national medical system. This is not the ideal physician as described in 1968 in the *Journal of the American Medical Association* by Dr. M. O. Rouse, a former president of the A.M.A. Dr. Rouse's ideal physician belongs to service clubs, the A.M.A., the church; and with these and other activities, he comes across as a medical Mr. Babbitt.

Nor is the physician we have looked at the moral physician described by Dr. Thomas Szasz in the March/April, 1975, issue of THE CENTER MAGAZINE.

That physician does not know the moral mandate of medicine (which is to give medical care), or whom he should serve (the patient); he is the same as the biologist (when in reality they are as different as night and day — the one at the laboratory bench and the other at the bedside). Further, Dr. Szasz's physician has an active role of ugly leadership in Plato's oligarchical society. Szasz's moral physician also frets about eugenics, abortion, experimentation when our real problems right now are to bail out the boat, to reinsert individualism in medical care systems. We will be better off if the physician becomes a moral provider. We can worry about navigation later.

Dr. Irvine H. Page, in his complaint in *Modern Medicine* (April 1, 1975) about the facelessness of institutional medicine, concludes that "expertise in the science of medicine . . . must be coupled with warmth, politeness, and kindness, qualities that private practitioners usually have." Here is a voice which is attending to the present and to the values which will be in jeopardy when the institution is enlarged from a university hospital (where his complaint was lodged) to a federal medical health delivery system. Now *there* will be an institution to contend with!

The past twenty years or so have seen us move gradually away from the physician as the focus of his patient's needs. Dr. Dwight L. Wilbur described the fractionation of medical care in an article in *California Medicine* in April, 1970: "More than 250 categories of workers play a specific role in health care, and, as members of the health industry, take part in association with physicians in the diagnosis, treatment, and prevention of disease, and in rehabilitation. At the beginning of this century there was one allied health worker for each physician; today there are approximately thirteen. Projections for the future indicate there may be seventeen to twenty or even more such workers for each physician by 1985 or 1990." Proliferation of persons associated with the health industry has "led to increasing institutionalization and organization in delivery of health care. The hospital and medical center have become increasingly important; the individual less important, be he the physician, nurse, therapist, technician, *or patient*" (emphasis mine).

As though attempting to follow Dr. Wilbur's prediction, a report in *Healing Arts* from Stanford University Medical Center states with some pride:

"Health care and education at Stanford Medical Center go beyond physical problems to the emotional needs that also must be met. While a medical team of ten to fifteen people focuses on keeping a patient alive, the social worker may be the only person who has the time to talk to a patient and the family as human beings."

Whether it be pre-pay medical systems, alteration of the cottage industry, the use of allied health professionals, or whatever — the key to the promotion and protection of individualism is to have enough physicians. Cost-saving techniques, rules and regulations, the use of non-physicians, the exclusion of the well and worried well are all means of spreading out the deficient number of physicians to cover the vast health needs of the society. Where medical programs are extended, the present deficit of physicians will be magnified — and attention to the individual and his humanistic needs will be further curtailed, not just to control cost, but because of inadequate numbers of physicians.

Incredibly deans of medical schools are telling each other and the public there will be too many physicians by 1985. Actually, the reverse is true. There is a deficit of fifty thousand physicians in the United States today and, as a result of the current malpractice insurance crisis, the deficit could rise to one hundred thousand. With the advent of national health insurance the relative deficit will become even greater. And in the absence of adequate numbers of physicians no system of health care — cottage type, pre-pay, or government — can attend to the human needs of the persons receiving care. It will always be earthquake and left-ear medicine until we get more physicians.

To give patients the benefit of individual attention, we will have to produce at least double, probably triple, the number of physicians we are currently educating and training.

At the time of the Flexner Report in 1910, there were three hundred medical schools, most of them third-rate. As a result of Flexner's work, the number of medical schools was pared to about seventy first-rate schools. Since then the number of schools has gradually increased (at one hundred million dollars, or more, apiece), so now there are slightly more than one hundred which graduate approximately 12,800 doctors of medicine each year. Death, retirement, careers in research and administration, extended training, specialty practice, attention to paper work, and other absorbents of physicians' time actually decrease the number of physicians proportionate to the growing number of people in the United States.

New medical schools are far too expensive to be created in adequate numbers. But new medical schools are unnecessary. The number of physician graduates could be doubled at relatively minor cost if administrative lines from existing medical schools were extended to the thousands of existing colleges and universities and to the thousands of first-rate community hospitals which already exist and function daily to provide patient care.

The pool of pre-physician student talent is already in abundance: only half of qualified college graduates ever have a chance to attend medical school.

The expansion of the physician pool can be started in the facilities in undergraduate institutions which already exist. The traditional first two years of medical school can be taught as the last two years of college. It has long been thought that a student should come to medical school fully educated in the humanities with a good grounding in science. But that is seldom realized today; the student usually arrives at medical school barely educated in the humanities and glad that that part of his education is behind him. (Eighteen- to twenty-year-olds are better suited to science studies in which memory exercises and basic logic are all that are required of them than they are to history, philosophy, and social science. The latter are more valuable to the older student when confronted with the issues of life, disease, and death — the concerns of clinical medicine.)

Tradition can be reversed. Students during their last two years of college can learn anatomy, physiology, bacteriology, and even pathology. Then during their clinical years they can learn non-science courses (subjects which will suit them better as advice-giving physicians) when their clinical medical training is also being learned in the community hospital setting under the aegis of medical school educators.

A particular advantage of this simple reversal of traditional education is that the student may choose to enter research after his college years and thus not go on to become a physician. He may still choose to become expert in a clinical subspecialty such as hematology (blood diseases) where, in conjunction with a physician, he can apply his specialized knowledge to the treatment, for example, of leukemia.

Part of today's physician drain is the result of the physician having to attend to many single specialty problems — problems which could be better attacked with one physician guided by scientist specialists in particular disease areas. Also, specialty referral can be greatly reduced when physicians' offices are equipped with specialty-information computer-bank sources. Instead of requiring a consultation, the primary physician in such offices can obtain the information he needs from the computer.

In San Francisco there is a freeway which goes nowhere. It is a towering concrete structure which extends about a mile along the central waterfront. Then, suddenly the freeway ends. This imposing structure, halted because of public outcry, is reminiscent of the mighty, sand-covered statue of Ozymandias. The freeway was mighty in conception and imposing in construction, but it bears silent testimony to the highway engineers who asked the question, Could they build it? before they asked, Should they build it?

A new freeway to national medical care is now being constructed by medical care engineers. We do not want it to end nowhere or to be so ugly it should be torn down.

It will not be if we attend to a few basic necessities. The medical care system must be applied in such a manner that individual human needs are not neglected or suppressed. American citizens should not have to choose between being sick in a free society or well in a controlled society. They can be well in a free society if the system is constructed with that end in view.

Medical care planners must recognize that, through education and commitment, the physician is ideally fitted to serve in a properly constructed system. They must also realize that the physician's talent is not directed to leadership in medical social planning. He can serve the system, but he cannot make it. Finally, the planners must realize that no creditable system will be possible unless there are adequate numbers of physicians.

When we have achieved nationwide health insurance and when medical care of all citizens can be given with the personal concern and dignity they deserve, we will be able to look with confidence at our nation and enjoy the truth of Plato's apothegm, "What is honored in a country is cultivated there."

Dr. Rodgers is Associate Clinical Professor of Medicine at the University of California, San Francisco; Associate in Medicine at the Stanford University Medical School, Stanford; and Chief of Staff of Presbyterian Hospital in San Francisco.

52

The American plan

National economic planning will arrive when businessmen demand it —
and demand it they will, to save the capitalist system.

By Robert L. Heilbroner

America is drifting into economic planning. One may deplore the fact—Herbert Stein, chairman of the Council of Economic Advisers under President Nixon, tells us that planning will make the economy "more inflationary,, less free, and less efficient." One may denounce it—Thomas Murphy, chairman of General Motors, predicts that national planning will be a "prescription for national chaos, or, at best, national stagnation." One may dread it—Walter Wriston, chairman of First National City Bank, warns us that planning will destroy our personal liberties.

But I do not think one can any longer deny it. Senators Hubert Humphrey and Jacob Javits have joined forces to introduce a bill (called by Humphrey his "single most important piece of legislation") establishing a national planning agency. A roster of eminent economists led by John Kenneth Galbraith and Nobel Prize winner Wassily Leontief have endorsed the bill. So have many labor leaders, following the lead of Leonard Woodcock of the United Automobile Workers. Most surprising of all, a small but growing number of influential businessmen, such as Felix Rohatyn of Lazard Frères and Henry Ford, have spoken out for the establishment of some form of national economic planning.

Robert L. Heilbroner is Norman Thomas Professor of Economics at the New School for Social Research.

Thus, for better or worse, whether we welcome it or not, under the Humphrey-Javits bill or another, I expect that within five years, perhaps much sooner, we will be officially embarked on something called National Economic Planning.

What will that planning be like? What changes would it bring to the American economy? In what follows I shall try to give plausible and realistic answers to some of the main questions that planning will force us to confront.

WHO GETS PLANNED IN A PLANNED ECONOMY?

Quite properly, the first question that people ask is how national economic planning will affect their lives.

This is not an easy question to answer, because the impact of planning may be large or small, depending on what our planning effort is trying to achieve. National planning may mean an attempt to reach ambitious but narrowly defined goals—for example, converting the economy entirely to solar energy in, say, 20 years. Such a plan would have an immense impact on a limited number of people. It would do away with jobs in oil refining or coal mining. It might bring bankruptcy to innumerable businesses hitched to coal or oil and unable to find another berth. On the other side, of course, it would mean a bonanza for everyone connected with the development of solar energy. So far as the majority of households is concerned, however, it would probably mean

little, until it came time to change over from gasoline-powered to electric-powered automobiles or from home furnaces to heat pumps.

But not all national planning will be narrowly targeted, and the wider and more general its goals, the larger the number of individuals who will be affected. Planning to limit inflation, for example, is likely to exert its impact on nearly everyone—perhaps only mildly, if the anti-inflation plan is limited to taxes; probably much more sharply if it includes controls over wages and salaries and profits and prices. So, too, planning to avoid dangerous economic growth might brush lightly over our lives if it required no more than slight curtailments in our use of energy (smaller cars, or higher electricity charges), or it might interfere with life very significantly if a plan sought to bring industrial growth to a virtual halt because of the actions of a world-wide cartel such as OPEC or because of a very serious danger of atmospheric pollution.

Thus, one cannot give bland assurances that planning will be painless, any more than one is warranted in issuing pronouncements that it will be traumatic. What determines the extent of planning is the need for it, but that selfsame need may diminish the psychological impact of planning. For example, we are not likely to impose wage, price and profit controls unless inflation continues its ravages, in which case we are apt to welcome intrusive planning, not object to it. We will certainly not plan for a low rate of economic growth unless considerations of national survival are involved. In that case, too, planning will more likely be felt as a form of collective guidance than as an invasion of our freedom.

WHAT GETS PLANNED IN A PLANNED ECONOMY?

It must already be clear that there is no preordained size or shape to the activity we call "national planning." It is possible to plan for very clearly defined objectives. But we can also plan on a much broader scale. A national economic plan will probably be a coordinated set of *general* economic targets; say;

a 50 percent reduction in unemployment, plus a reduction of the rate of inflation to 5 percent, plus an expansion of economic growth to 6 percent. Needless to say, these economic targets are not picked at random. In fact, one of the main purposes of planning is to discover what combinations of such general goals are compatible.

It follows that planning is by no means a wholly foreign kind of economic activity. Every deliberate effort to bring about an outcome of the economic process different from that which would emerge spontaneously from the market system is a form of planning. Unemployment compensation, Social Security and Medicare are forms of planning just as much as wage and price controls. The anti-inflationary actions of the Federal Reserve Board are efforts to plan the outcome of the economic process just

as much as the designation of a national target of, say 4 percent growth. What we mean by national economic planning, in its broadest sense, is thus an effort to coordinate existing plans, quite as much as an effort to extend the reach of our control over the economy.

HOW IS THE PLANNING DONE?

This brings us to a consideration of the planning mechanism itself Here a basic misconception must first be put down. It is the idea that planning means the creation of an enormous blueprint of production, specifying the size and number and quality of buttons on every shirt.

There have been efforts at such total planning, notably

in the Soviet Union, and they have been largely adjudged as failures. Useful for mobilizing an economy on a war basis (and the early Soviet planning efforts were a kind of war mobilization for economic growth), they have proved cumbersome and harmful once an economy has attained the complexity of a fully industrial system.

Only the advent of another conventional war or an environmental threat of warlike proportions would cause national economic planning in the United States to assume this kind of exacting specification. Rather, planning would almost certainly take the form of a series of steps of a very different nature.

The initial step in planning would necessarily be an effort to expand the amount and accuracy of the economic information at our disposal. Although we possess the largest and probably the best statistical service in the world, we are still woefully ignorant of many of the essential facts about our economy. When the Arab oil embargo struck, for example, we did not possess information about the size of our stocks of gasoline. Although we pretend that we have 8 percent unemployment, it is common knowledge that the unemployment "count" is extremely inaccurate, especially for the black and Puerto Rican minorities, and to this very day we do not possess an inventory of the numbers or kinds of job openings in the economy. Our estimates for many important economic magnitudes — our stock of money, our balance of payments, our Gross National Product—are all much too unreliable.

The first step in national planning must, therefore, be an expansion and improvement of our fund of economic information. The next step is to use this information to create a bigger and better flow-chart for the economy. We call such a flow-chart an input-output matrix. An input-output matrix is a kind of recipe book for production. Developed by Wassily Leontief, it enables us to ascertain (albeit only very roughly) how much steel, rubber, copper, cloth, etc., it takes to "cook" an automobile, a steel girder, or a billion dollars' worth of G.N.P. of a given kind. This is a much more complicated calculation than it might at first appear, because the ingredients for a given menu of output are larger in number and more diverse in kind than one could divine by looking at the final products. Input-output may

show us that an attractive-looking menu of output cannot be produced without expanding our facilities for production, or it may reveal an unexpected bottleneck that would abort a seemingly feasible plan for expansion.

Nevertheless, input-output, indispensable though it may be, is not planning itself. The act of planning consists of the selection and realization of goals for the economy. These may be narrow, specific "micro" targets, such as an energy program, or broad "macro" goals, such as a reduction of unemployment, or both. (Needless to say, this brings up the question of who selects our goals, but I will defer this problem momentarily.)

Goal-setting, as it is envisaged in the Humphrey-Javits bill or in any variant of this bill that is likely to become law, does not consist of the designation by a planning agency of one set of targets known as "the national plan." Rather, the procedure in goal-setting is to work up a number of alternative planning possibilities. These may be a series of specific microprograms—housing, urban rehabilitation, mass transit—any one of which could be undertaken singly, but all of which could not be mounted simultaneously because of the strain on our labor or material capacities. Or the alternative plans might consist of different combinations of macrotargets. Plan A might suggest 5 percent inflation and 6 percent unemployment. Plan B might suggest 8 percent inflation and only 4 percent unemployment. Plan C might offer 4 percent inflation and 3 percent unemployment—a more attractive combination, but one that would require much stiffer controls than Plans A and B.

The job of the planning agency, working with its statistical information and input-output "recipes," is to concoct a number of such feasible alternative plans or scenarios. But a number of feasible plans having been hatched, the full-fledged public debate now begins. This debate may be limited to Congress, or might possibly be extended to the public, especially if Plan A were endorsed by one party and Plan C by another. Eventually one or another set of plans is decided on—housing is given preference to mass transit, or vice versa; Plan D is arrived at by a process of compromise. The final plans are given the approval of Congress and the

President and become the official economic goals of the nation.

How are the various goals to be reached? Written into each plan is a series of stimuli and sanctions designed to bring the objective into actuality. These may be nothing more than an appropriation of funds, comparable to the plans that once built the Union Pacific Railway or the Panama Canal. Or the necessary measures may be of a broader kind, such as a general injunction to use "all monetary and fiscal means" to achieve such and such a level of inflation and employment. It is also entirely possible that a given plan will include tax changes as part of its means-ends machinery: tax incentives for industries to invest in ways that are congenial to the plan; tax penalties for industries that do not; tax inducements for consumers to use their purchasing power in consonance with the objective of speeding up economic expansion, or slowing it down, or changing the composition of output.

If the plan is of the highest importance for national survival, it will surely contain coercive measures of various kinds. Materials may have to be allocated to industries deemed to be of the highest priority; crash programs of investment may have to be mounted, perhaps by the creation of a Government effort such as the Manhattan Project; very stringent controls or prohibitions might have to be imposed on industry and household alike if we had to execute an abrupt aboutface in our economic direction as a consequence of a very serious external threat.

WHO MAKES THE PLANS IN A PLANNED ECONOMY?

A vast amount of alarm and confusion surrounds the problem of decision-making. Conservatives warn us of faceless experts who will substitute their judgment for the "democracy" of the market. Business fears a paralyzing bureaucracy. The left is suspicious of a corporate take-over of the planning apparatus.

None of these warnings are to be lightly disregarded, and I shall return to them. But I think it is best to begin with a more positive approach. I envisage the planning process as closely resembling the legislative process. This means that at every stage of planning—informa-

tion gathering (what information?), input-output model-building (under what assumptions?), alternative planning goals (for what ends?) —there will be a struggle to insinuate many views. Corporate élites, charismatic individuals, powerful politicians, labor unions, regional and other lobbies, public groups of many sorts will be writing letters, taking people out to lunch or trying to pull strings to get some portion of the plan to represent their interests or points of view.

Hence I suspect that the goals presented for debate and deliberation will already reflect the untidy, adversary, influence-peddling ways by which a democratic system runs. I also suspect the final plans will be as good and as bad, as outrageous and as sensible, as reactionary or as radical as the mass of legislation that today emerges in roughly the same way. In a word, if one has faith that a democracy can govern itself, there is no reason to believe that it cannot plan for itself.

Of course, it is possible to harbor severe doubts about the self-governing abilities of a democracy; and for the same reason it is possible to harbor serious doubts about planning. There is a danger that the planning options may be usurped by faceless experts who will try to apply to the national economy the same masterminding that they applied to the conduct of the Vietnam War. It is certainly possible that the planning agency will become bureaucratic.

And I would assuredly not dismiss the fears of the left that planning may become an instrument of corporate capitalism. Indeed, it seems very plain that the main purpose of planning will be to shore up and underpin, not to weaken or undo, the business system. Nevertheless I do not think that business interests must dominate planning even though the business interest is served by it. Labor and consumer groups will probably have more power and influence under a planning arrangement than they have today.

HOW MUCH MARKET WILL BE LEFT IN A PLANNED ECONOMY?

The great hue and cry of those who oppose planning is that it will replace the market—that vast, flexible, democratic instrument by which a "free" economy makes its collective decisions

about the kinds of goods it will produce.

I have no desire to deprecate the usefulness of the market, whose capabilities have been reluctantly recognized even within the Soviet bloc. But it is necessary to view the market with the same degree of skeptical criticism that we apply to planning. First, we should recognize that what we call "the market" is not a single great current of economic activity against which no institution can assert its independent will. This may be true for the individual farmer, retailer, or small businessman, but it is emphatically not the case with large companies that dominate their fields and that can assert their wills to a very considerable extent. As American Telephone and Telegraph states in a series of recent advertisements, "The telephone system didn't just happen. It was planned, right from the start."

In fact, the big corporations in all industrial areas act like private planning agencies, a point eloquently expounded by Galbraith. To a very great degree, the big companies hold the market at bay, raising or lowering prices when they want to, not when an oceanic flood of competition forces them to. So, too, they expand (or contract) their enterprises according to long-range forecasts that ignore the immediate press of business conditions.

Second, we must realize that the market is far from the democratic institution that is popularly projected. The market is a kind of continually recurring economic election, in which households vote with their dollars for the kinds of goods they want. That would be democratic indeed, if all households had equal votes. But of course they do not. The top 20 percent of households own 40 percent of the economic "voting" power; the bottom 20 percent only 5 percent of the purchasing power. A family like the Rockefellers casts as many votes as ten thousand families at the poverty line. Is this democracy?

Last, the market surely serves very well to express the collective, albeit lopsided, appetites of its constituency for commodities, but it has no means of giving voice to objectives that are not themselves given the status of commodities. For example, the market brings forth an assemblage of cars—big cars for big pocketbooks, small cars for small pocketbooks.

Even if we accept this distribution of output as "right," we must not forget that in addition to automobiles, the market process has also brought forth traffic congestion, pollution, risk to life and limb. But the market place is blind to these "externalities"—that is, to these side-effects of production.

Perhaps the planning-market controversy can best be summed up by saying that the market is a poor goal-setting mechanism. The "goals" it establishes reflect the buying power of the rich far more than that of the poor, are distorted by powerful aggregates of massed corporate wealth, and are without recognition of any end-result of economic activity that bears no price tag. Planning is an effort to remedy this distorted or missing goal-setting ability along the messy but workable ways we have described.

On the other hand, the market is a remarkable administrative mechanism, even in those areas where private power is most evident. Far better than any corps of planning inspectors, it oversees the quick adaptation of new techniques; it provides factories and stores with opportunities to deal with efficient suppliers; and it offers customers the ultimate weapon of choice. Planning does all these things badly, if at all. Therefore, any national economic plan, save one designed to implement a crash program of vital importance, would lean heavily on the market system. The flow of goods from plant to plant or from plant to customer, the entry of labor and capital into industries or their exit from those industries; the organization of production, will all be largely entrusted to the profit-seeking, competitive ways of the accustomed market mechanism. Planning may have to intervene in nonmarket ways, such as by control over prices and wages or by direct materials allocations, but only if milder techniques for influencing inflation or output are ineffective. The preferred ways of making a plan work will be by techniques that work through the market, rather than against it.

IS THERE NO ALTERNATIVE TO PLANNING?

I began by saying that America was drifting into planning. But is this drift inevitable? Is it not possible to go on as we are, or even to dismantle some of the planning that is already embedded in our system?

Whether they say it explicitly or not, the opponents of planning maintain that things *can* go on as they are. This is not an irresponsible position. Social inertia is always a powerful force. Inertia may hold together cities that have lost their fiscal soundness. It may permit 10 percent unemployment and 10 percent inflation to persist for years with little more than grumbling.

I might myself incline to the view that we could go on without national planning —even though I think that planning could greatly improve economic conditions— were it not for the fact that there are forces at work that will probably make things worse. To begin with the mildest of these, our population is still increasing, bringing strains that are particularly felt in the underfinanced cities: the pressure in the ghetto is building. Meanwhile, technology is relentlessly invading the social order with products whose destructive potential continues to take us by surprise and to fill us with alarm: nuclear wastes, chemical wastes, thermal wastes all press on the life-carrying capacity of the environment, and threaten to overwhelm it in the foreseeable future. At the same time, the process of economic growth continues its ravenous progress, reaching further and further into the earth's crust for the materials essential for its continuance. Many of the easily reached pockets of resources will be exhausted within a generation or so, requiring much larger applications of energy to maintain the snowball of mounting production. And the underdeveloped areas, now coming into possession of nuclear arms, and hence in a better position to make their views count, no longer regard the export of their mineral wealth to the rich industrial nations with the indifference or unalloyed pleasure that was once the case. The clear necessity, in a word, is for an ever more vigilant monitoring of the pace and pattern of economic growth—a monitoring that cannot be attained without economic planning.

And, not least, there is the change in the scale of private enterprise. The reach of business enterprise continues to grow. Big corporations now extend their operations around the world. As the scope of enterprise grows, business becomes ever more enmeshed in social problems. The cry for regulation grows, as much engendered by the increasing prominence of big business as by the growing acuity of the problems themselves.

Thus I doubt very much that things can go on as they are. The present situation is unstable, and the forces of technology, environment, and sheer growth in size and complexity make a return to a simpler—or at any rate, less planned—economy impossible. When we are told by Thomas Murphy of General Motors, and by others, that "the solution is not for more government direction, but less," we are hearing a prescription for a world that does not exist. That is why there is no capitalist economy in the world today that does not have a growing core of economic planning. In some countries, such as our own, that planning is piecemeal, cross-purposed, inadequate. In others it is institutionally elaborate. France, for example, has a Planning Commission that regularly draws up national plans of roughly five years' duration specifying many objectives for the French economy. The plans are drawn only after lengthy consultations with industry, and the guiding idea behind the scheme is that the consultative process itself will bring about a voluntary adoption by industry of the very actions needed to make the national plan come true.

This "indicative planning" effort leans heavily on the French organization of industry and its long tradition of *dirigiste* policies. But every nation's planning mechanism adapts to prevailing traditions. Japan has a high-level, largely "unofficial" coordination of national and private

policies that has been popularly dubbed Japan, Inc. Norway and the Netherlands have small planning apparatuses that put to good use the traditions of consensus prominent in both countries. Sweden works through its employers and union federations; Germany through its banks.

Probably none of these techniques of planning could be imported directly into this country. We are larger and more diversified than our European or Japanese counterparts; perhaps more important, we are less accustomed to authority, less respectful of government. Planning in America will have to make its peace with regional differences, political realities, national temperament. Thus the Humphrey-Javits bill, the most likely measure to be passed, is careful to include provisions for regional consultation and for Congressional involvement, and tactfully omits any mention of enforcement mechanisms.

The Humphrey-Javits bill proposes a number of institutional departures. It would establish a small Economic Planning Board in the Executive Office of the President. The board would be charged with a number of technical functions, including the preparation of a proposed "economic-growth plan." This proposed plan would then be reviewed by a Council on Economic Planning comprised of the Cabinet and other chief economic officials, and also by an Advisory Committee made up of representatives of business, labor and the public, appointed in part by the President and in part by Congress. The plan that emerged from the executive branch would then be referred to the Joint Economic Committee of Congress. Here, futher hearings would be held, and the plan would be revised or amended as Congress wished. Ultimately, the plan would be passed by a concurrent resolution of the Congress and sent back to the President.

Of course the actual advent of planning will depend on political events. If the Democrats win the next election, some form of national economic planning is likely to become a reality in the next President's first term. If the Republicans win, planning will be postponed. But only postponed, not permanently shelved. As Leontief has said, planning will come not when the radicals want it, but when businessmen demand it. And demand it they will, for without more planning it is difficult to believe that capitalism can last out the century.

WILL PLANNING SAVE U.S. CAPITALISM?

It may not. We do not know if the best-drawn plans can iron out the sheerly economic problems of a business system—its tendencies to instability, inflation, economic waste. We do not know if planning can overcome political and social rigidities that have locked us into a tradition of malign neglect of minorities, or if it can reverse a corrosive commercialization of life. Not least, we do not know if planning can be made to work effectively. We cannot plan better than we can govern. Planning will force us to discover how well that is.

Certainly, then, planning is no panacea. It is an option, an alternative, an opportunity —the only opportunity, I think, to arrest the course of slow self-destruction on which we now seem to be embarked. It would be foolish to deny that planning carries great risks, including that of a grave constriction of freedom as the consequence of a reckless proliferation of controls. But it would be even more foolish to ignore the risks associated with a refusal to move into national planning, including the danger of a rush to political extremism as a consequence of economic frustration or failure.

In the end, I believe that planning offers hope. In part it is the hope that a restored economic society can regenerate a high sense of social and political morale. In still greater part it is the hope that we can once again experience a sense of mastery over events. We will need such an assertion of purpose to prepare for a future full of disquieting portents.

53

Technology and Utopia

by Carolyn Symonds

The question frequently arises as to whether or not Utopia, by definition, requires a retreat to the past. Many of the communes, and groups of people who gather together or retreat by themselves, whether indicating a religious or secular philosophy, feel that the evils of the world have come about because of industrialization. They attempt to retreat into a past that seems more Utopian than the present or the foreseeable future. Would it not instead be possible to build a Utopia utilizing the technological advantages brought about by industrialization?

Webster's definition of Utopia is an imaginary country with ideal laws and social conditions 1: a place (as a region, island, country, or locality) that is imaginary and indefinitely remote; 2: *often caps:* a place, state, or condition of ideal perfection, esp. in laws, government, and social conditions.[1]

There is nothing in this definition that implies a step into the past. People view life in the past as more Utopian than the present and mechanization is seen as the villain to be rejected. However, I would like to propose a society built on the utilization of technology.

My response to the question has been greatly influenced by R. Buckminister Fuller[2] and his discussion of the direction of technological change and the ultimate capabilities of modern technology. He brings out two points that are very important and need to be mentioned.

The first is the concept of more-with-lessing. In effect, the greatest technological impact on society is the application of the principle of doing more with less. He says that no new mining would have to be accomplished to support the entire world population if reclamation was made of previously worked materials, if the more-with-less concept was consciously developed.

The other point he makes is that our present war technology (where most technological development occurs) is such that humanity will be in the bind of having to secure world-wide Utopia, or face oblivion. This is an aside. The big issue is that there is, with the concept of more-with-lessing, potential abundance for all. Technology developed to its present conceivable ultimate would be capable of furnishing all of humanity not only with a comfortable life style, but with luxurious living. Competition is only necessary where there are scarcities, and in a highly technological world there is plenty for all and no scarcities, thus undermining the concept of survival of the fittest.

We will look at a theoretical society that is attainable with current trends in technology. The fact that it hasn't happened doesn't mean that it couldn't, nor that it won't. Technology develops at such a fast rate that what appears to be the science fiction of yesterday is the reality of today.

Economy

Energy is supplied to each housing complex or center where people congregate, in a small nuclear package. It perhaps occasionally needs replacing or modification, but it is reliable and supplies all the power needed for one or more complexes, depending on size.

Materials and styles for housing and buildings have been so developed that full use may be made of natural resources, with malleable and easily handled units.

New food sources and food supplements have been developed so that cultivation of the land to grow food products is not necessary. Gourmet tastes may be satisfied with carefully cultivated food from a private garden, but this is engaged in as a hobby, rather than a necessity.

Water is attained either by private wells that are powered by the energy unit, or piped to different parts of each country from the salt water processing stations located in coastal regions throughout the world.

The division of labor is great, among those who labor. A new concept of work and leisure time is developed because nobody is in need of an income. There

---

[1] *Webster's Third New International Dictionary, Unabridged.* G. & C. Merriam Co., Mass., 1961. This is the current and popularized definition of "utopia." The original root meaning is no (u) place (topia) from the Latin. Just as all great religious thoughts have been bastardized by their followers so has "utopia" by its. People like to put things outside themselves but the "ideal state" is not an institution but within the self. There can never be "ideal laws and social conditions . . . a place of ideal perfection." That's a contradiction in terms and contrary to everything we experience in life (the laws of nature —ugh). We can *improve* laws, institutions, social conditions, but make them perfect *for everyone?* While utopia is not-a-place, nowhere—now here—we as individuals, can get much closer to it. Even shit is a part of utopia—sanitation regulations are not essential. And, yes, pain, too, can be a part of utopia. The perfect state is not that of a contented cow chewing on her cud.— Ed. [Richard Fairfield]

[2] R. Buckminister Fuller, *Utopia or Oblivion: The Prospects for Humanity,* Chapter 9. Bantam Books, N.Y., 1969.

are plenty of material goods for all, and it is only those who desire to do so and/or who possess a much needed aptitude that are part of the labor force. There are many scientists following the concept of more-for-less in every conceivable area. These people have laboratories in their housing complex, maintain close-televised communication with each other and meet in groups for massive pooling of information.

Information and knowledge is stored in gigantic computers to which there is access at every local level that would require it. There is some need for computer maintenance although most of it is done by other than human resources.

Factories for production of consumer goods are strategically located throughout each country. When a household needs a specific item, a request is made (by computer) and the item is either manufactured or removed from storage (all done mechanically). It is then shipped to the requestor by whatever transportation system is currently in use, considering the distance. Portions of the transportation system are mechanized so that a person can request an item that arrives the following day and has no contact with humans.

Communication is immediate and reliable,. Voice or visual projection are available to all individuals anywhere. Access to numerous taped programs of almost limitless variety is available at all times, as well as live output from information centers.

Health is an area that has had a great deal of study. Lifelong immunizations are made shortly after birth against the most destructive diseases. There are medical doctors in the society, but frequently the households are large enough to each contain one of their own. If a medium sized household is lacking an M.D., attempts will be made to socialize one of the young into gaining an education in that area.

Transportation is advanced. Each housing complex has as many private airborne vehicles as they desire, but the desire is not great. Most travel is to far away places and massive space or airliners are efficient in getting people to their destination. Resorts for visitors are located throughout the world, but communication is such that most people have made personal contact with individuals worldwide and visit in private housing complexes. There is a trend toward a universal language.

There are a few central air and space control centers. They develop and disseminate the special instructions concerning use of the atmosphere for transportation purposes. They keep constant tabs on what is going on and where, and dissipate potential air jams and emergencies of various sorts. Even the smallest air machine maintains communication with the air and space centers.

Socialization of the young has been a crucial element in the transition of the industrial society to this post-post-industrial society. The concept and value of competition and laissez faire have been replaced with values and new concepts of leisure and cooperation. The positions that human beings fill in factories, computer centers, and other centers, for instance hospitals, are highly regarded and individuals must possess certain aptitudes to be accepted to fill them. Most of the educa-

tion necessary to fill these roles is available in each housing complex. If accepted for a position, there are a variety of ways of handling it. Some people like to go to work every day. Others like to do most of it at home. Some people will work at their center for several days and then return home for several days of leisure. There is variation, depending on the individual and the type of work.

Socialization of differences between male and female diminishes. The female is as apt to become the medical doctor or the scientist or the air-space control technician as the male. The male is as apt to tend the children and take pride in gourmet cooking and gardening. This is more dependent upon aptitude than upon anything else.

With plenty of everything for all, a monetary system is not necessary as in the industrial competitive society. Collections might be made of rare items for a hobby, and occasional exchanges made between individuals, but this is an individual matter.

Family

With no necessity for mobility, and rapid transportation when mobility is desired and required, there is general evolution from the small conjugal family to an extended family. The extended family is not necessarily a kinship group. It may consist entirely of non-blood relationships because of other bonds. Since housing facilities are simple and available, a housing complex may be as large or as small as desired. The smaller ones will rely on more outside institutions than the larger ones. The larger ones may be internally self-sufficient. Some couples may be attracted exclusively to each other for varying periods of time. A couple thus attracted might move from both of their respective housing complexities into a third complex where they are welcomed and where they feel comfortable. Or they may desire to begin their own private complex. . . .

Education

With the economy decentralized, all goods available to everyone, a division of labor that concerns only a small portion of the population, and large family units, the institution of education diminishes and most education and socialization is conducted in the housing complex. Learning machines are available, and it is only when someone's specialty and aptitude [are] quite unique that the learner goes outside of the housing complex for his education. . . .

Summary

A lot of things have not been considered here. For instance, deviance. How will disruptive deviant behavior in a society of this kind be handled? Or will there be unacceptable behavior? Are there enough behavioral paths permitted that the concept of deviant behavior, especially in a negative sense, is no longer applicable? Another area, probably fitting under the heading of deviance, is mental health. The definitions of neurotic and psychotic will change as the value system changes.

One of the big problems any society like ours, with a competitive and monetary system has is the difficulty of accepting the notion that there is plenty for all, and that we can eliminate the excessively wealthy as well as those who now live in poverty. Another concept which would have to disappear is that everybody, to have self-fulfillment, needs to have an occupation. At this point the middle class and working class are at a disadvantage. Those at each end, with inherited wealth, and those living off of welfare or who can't get employment, are already more accepting of this philosophy and would have less difficulty accepting the technological Utopia, that is they would have less trouble socializing their children with the values of the new system, because it probably wouldn't come about overnight.

Perhaps this is an unrealistic approach to the search for Utopia, but it is any less realistic than turning one's back to the mechanization of the modern world and trying to dig a good life from the land by more primitive means? Would it not be more practical to begin seeking means to utilize the technology in order to achieve a more meaningful life? Some of the current uses will have to be rejected, but to reject technology because of the manner in which it is used seems a waste of knowledge. Nuclear energy can be used for purposes other than for bombs and destruction.

It is hard with our socialization and values (even though we frequently don't approve of them) to visualize a society such as the one postulated here. Our current trends would lead us to believe that the novel *1984* by George Orwell would more nearly represent our future. The novel *Island* by Aldous Huxley presents a lovely Utopia, but it realistically ends up being destroyed by other war-like people of the world. With the impact and strength of modern technology and weapons, it would appear that Fuller is right, it will be world-wide Utopia or oblivion.

54 Epilog: Social Problems Awareness Test by Peter M. Wickman

Social Problems Awareness Test

(Post-Test Form)

This is a different form of the SPAT which you took at the beginning of the book. Indicate the correct answer in the appropriate space.

1 Medicare programs provide complete health care for the aged.

_____Completely Agree _____Tend to Agree
_____Tend to Disagree _____Completely Disagree

2 The family's child rearing function has been largely replaced by alternative public and private agencies.

_____Completely Agree _____Tend to Agree
_____Tend to Disagree _____Completely Disagree

3 Our free public education system provides an equal "ladder" of opportunity and success for all youths.

_____Completely Agree _____Tend to Agree
_____Tend to Disagree _____Completely Disagree

4 There is more crime in the sunny and warm states of the West and South than in any other part of the country.

_____Completely Agree _____Tend to Agree
_____Tend to Disagree _____Completely Disagree

5 There is conclusive evidence that marijuana use leads to the use of heroin and other "hard" drugs.

_____Completely Agree _____Tend to Agree
_____Tend to Disagree _____Completely Disagree

6 White collar criminals are underrepresented in terms of arrests and severity of prison sentences compared to other types of criminals.

_____Completely Agree _____Tend to Agree
_____Tend to Disagree _____Completely Disagree

7 Since homosexual acts between consenting adults are no longer illegal in some states homosexuals are seldom stigmatized.

_____Completely Agree _____Tend to Agree
_____Tend to Disagree _____Completely Disagree

8 The direct and indirect cost of alcoholism and alcoholics is much greater than that of drug addiction.

_____Completely Agree _____Tend to Agree
_____Tend to Disagree _____Completely Disagree

9 Psychiatrists now know how to identify and treat potentially dangerous and aggressive individuals.

_____Completely Agree _____Tend to Agree
_____Tend to Disagree _____Completely Disagree

10 Since untreated mental patients have nearly the same rate of recovery as those committed to mental hospitals, it is questionable that institutionalization of the mentally ill is effective.

_____Completely Agree _____Tend to Agree
_____Tend to Disagree _____Completely Disagree

11 The social consequences of death and dying fall with equal severity on all socioeconomic groups in society.

_____Completely Agree _____Tend to Agree
_____Tend to Disagree _____Completely Disagree

12 If gambling and other victimless crimes were decriminalized, our criminal justice system would operate more effectively.

_____Completely Agree _____Tend to Agree
_____Tend to Disagree _____Completely Disagree

13 In general there is an inverse correlation between socioeconomic status and involvement in voluntary oragnizations and political involvement.

_____Completely Agree _____Tend to Agree
_____Tend to Disagree _____Completely Disagree

14 The higher the occupational status of the worker, the higher will be his/her job satisfaction.

_____Completely Agree _____Tend to Agree
_____Tend to Disagree _____Completely Disagree

15 Native Americans (American Indians) in our society have not borne the brunt of institutional racism to the extent that Blacks and Chicanos have.

_____Completely Agree   _____Tend to Agree
_____Tend to Disagree   _____Completely Disagree

16 Although there are differences in I.Q. scores between races, these are not as great as the differences in I.Q. scores found within given racial groupings.

_____Completely Agree   _____Tend to Agree
_____Tend to Disagree   _____Completely Disagree

17 The "multi-problem" poor suffer from the impoverishment of the "culture of poverty" and a "deviant" value system; thus, they unwittingly cause their own troubles.

_____Completely Agree   _____Tend to Agree
_____Tend to Disagree   _____Completely Disagree

18 Large corporations, with their emphasis on profits, require irrational practices such as planned obsolescence and wasteful consumption.

_____Completely Agree   _____Tend to Agree
_____Tend to Disagree   _____Completely Disagree

19 Some surveys indicate that heavy TV viewers are more apt than others to be politically active and vote more frequently.

_____Completely Agree   _____Tend to Agree
_____Tend to Disagree   _____Completely Disagree

20 Although the "Green Revolution" increased food production in developing countries it did not provide a long term solution to the international food problem.

_____Completely Agree   _____Tend to Agree
_____Tend to Disagree   _____Completely Disagree

21 Through a national urban policy which provides public housing for lower income groups, it now appears that urban decay will disappear by the end of the decade.

_____Completely Agree   _____Tend to Agree
_____Tend to Disagree   _____Completely Disagree

22 During the first sixteen years of his or her life, the typical child now spends at least as much time watching television as in school.

_____Completely Agree   _____Tend to Agree
_____Tend to Disagree   _____Completely Disagree

23 Since the United States occupies a continent rich in natural resources we have no population problem of any significance.

_____Completely Agree   _____Tend to Agree
_____Tend to Disagree   _____Completely Disagree

24 Fornication, adultery, cohabitation, as well as homosexual relations between consenting adult partners are all violations of the criminal codes in most of our states.

_____Completely Agree   _____Tend to Agree
_____Tend to Disagree   _____Completely Disagree

25 The existence of a given social problem and its resolution can be decided upon objectively, i.e., without reference to the values and interests of the various groups concerned.

_____Completely Agree   _____Tend to Agree
_____Tend to Disagree   _____Completely Disagree

We need your advice

Because this book will be revised every two years, we would like to know what you think of it. Please fill in the brief questionnaire on the reverse of this card and mail it to us.

Business Reply Mail

No postage stamp necessary if mailed in the United States

First Class
Permit No. 247
New York, N.Y.

Postage will be paid by

Dale Tharp
Editor
Harper & Row Publishers Inc.
College Dept.
10 East 53rd St.
New York, NY 10022

Social Problems

SOCIAL PROBLEMS: CONTEMPORARY PERSPECTIVES

I am a ____ student ____ instructor

Term used _____ 19____

Name_____ School_____

Address_____

_____

City_____ State_____ Zip_____

How do you rate this book?

1. Please list (by number) the articles you liked best.

_____ _____ _____ _____ _____

Why? _____

_____

2. Please list (by number) the articles you liked least.

_____ _____ _____ _____ _____

Why? _____

_____

3. Please evaluate the following:

	Excell.	Good	Fair	Poor	Comments
Organization of the book	_____	_____	_____	_____	_____
Section introductions	_____	_____	_____	_____	_____
Overall Evaluation	_____	_____	_____	_____	_____

4. Do you have any suggestions for improving the next edition?

_____

_____

_____

5. Can you suggest any new articles to include in the next edition?

_____

_____

_____

_____

_____

_____

_____

_____

Thank you very much

NOTE: You must fill in the name of the person (or department) to whom the form should be sent.

Business Reply Mail

No postage stamp necessary if mailed in the United States

Postage will be paid by

Harper & Row Publishers Inc.

Attention: _____

10 East 53rd St.

New York, NY 10022

ATTENTION

Now you may order individual copies of the books in the CONTEMPORARY PERSPECTIVES READER SERIES directly from the publisher.

The following titles are now available:

Readings in ABNORMAL PSYCHOLOGY, Edited by Lawrence R. Allman and Dennis T. Jaffe (Note: fill in SBN here)

Readings in ADOLESCENT PSYCHOLOGY, Edited by Thomas J. Cottle (SBN)

Readings in ADULT PSYCHOLOGY, Edited by Lawrence A. Allman and Dennis T. Jaffe (SBN)

Readings in AGING AND DEATH, Edited by Steven H. Zarit (SBN)

Readings in ECOLOGY, ENERGY AND HUMAN SOCIETY, Edited by William R. Burch, Jr. (SBN)

Readings in EDUCATIONAL PSYCHOLOGY, Edited by Robert A. Dentler and Bernard J. Shapiro (SBN)

Readings in HUMAN DEVELOPMENT, Edited by David Elkind and Donna C. Hetzel (SBN)

Readings in HUMAN SEXUALITY, Edited by Chad Gordon and Gayle Johnson (SBN)

Readings in SOCIAL PROBLEMS, Edited by Peter M. Wickman (SBN)

Readings in SOCIAL PSYCHOLOGY, Edited by Dennis Krebs (SBN)

Readings in SOCIOLOGY, Edited by Ian Robertson (SBN)

$5.95   Paperback

Order your copies of any of the above titles by filling in the coupon below.

Please send me:

_____ copies of _____ (SBN)

_____ copies of _____ (SBN)

_____ copies of _____ (SBN)

_____ copies of _____ (SBN)

at $5.95 each. My check or money order in the amount of $_____ is enclosed. (Harper & Row will pay the postage and handling.)

_____
Name

_____
Address

_____
City

_____
State   Zip

46586

Wickman

Readings in social problems: contemporary perspectives

DATE DUE			
MAY 12 '82			
GAYLORD			PRINTED IN U.S.A.

77 78 79 80 9 8 7 6 5 4 3 2 1